CULT
MOVIES 3

Also by Danny Peary

Guide for the Film Fanatic

Close-Ups: The Movie Star Book, editor

The American Animated Cartoon, coeditor with Gerald Peary

Cult Movies

Cult Movies 2

Omni's ScreenFlights/ScreenFantasies, editor

CULT MOVIES 3

50 More of the Classics, the Sleepers, the Weird, and the Wonderful

DANNY PEARY

SIDGWICK & JACKSON
LONDON

First published in Great Britain in 1989
by Sidgwick & Jackson Limited

Originally published in the United States of America
by Fireside Books.

ISBN 0-283-99806-7

Designed by Kathy Kikkert

Printed by Butler & Tanner Limited, Frome, Somerset
for Sidgwick & Jackson Limited
1 Tavistock Chambers, Bloomsbury Way
London WC1A 2SG

Acknowledgments

I am pleased that Fireside-Simon & Schuster has decided to resume my *Cult Movies* book series, which was initiated by Dell in 1981 and continued in 1983. I especially want to thank my editor and late friend Tim McGinnis, who initiated this project and made it fun to write. He is missed. I am also indebted to Fireside's Liz Cunningham, Steve Messina, Sol Skolnick, Sydny Weinberg-Miner, George Wen, Laura Yorke, and my designer, Kathy Kikkert. Deep gratitude also goes to my agent, Chris Tomasino, and to Cathy Hemming, who made this project possible.

I also appreciate the contributions of my researcher, Kathy Wilson, and Henry Blinder, who, for the third time, was my lone guest contributor.

I also thank Bob Fitzpatrick, Cynthia Vartan, Mary Corliss, Bob Nowacki, Paula Klaw, Ira Kramer, Deborah Fersh, Ben Barenholtz, Rosane McCarron, Karen Schiff, Yuri Neyman, Richard P. Rubenstein, John Landis, Jenny Agutter, Griffin Dunne, Rick Baker, George Miller, Ridley Scott, Richard Crenna, Jerry Stahl, John Randolph, Lewis John Carlino, Jerry Goldsmith, and Edward Lewis.

Photo credits go to the following: Universal, United Artists, United Artists Classics, the Ladd Company, the De Laurentiis Entertainment Group, Caribbean Films, Island Alive, Columbia, Hammer-Seven Arts, 20th Century-Fox, Cinevista, Laurel Entertainment, Allied Artists, Warner Bros., Tepeyac, Paramount, Orion, Republic, MGM, RKO, Movie Star News, Jerry Ohlinger's, and the Museum of Modern Art Film Still Collection.

And I thank my wife, Suzanne, and daughter, Zoë, for keeping my mind on even better things than movies.

*To Suzanne and Zoë
and Laura and Joe
and in memory of Bea.*

*This book is also dedicated
to the memory of
Tim McGinnis,
who made it possible.*

Contents

Foreword

It has been five years since I wrote *Cult Movies 2.* Since then there have been cult movie festivals all over the country, on college campuses and in museums. Not only have "cult movies" been almost legitimized, but also it has become increasingly important for films to achieve a degree of "cult" status if they are to survive after their initial theatrical releases. There are now fewer repertory theaters, fewer college film societies that show movies that are more than a couple of years old, fewer films that are released in 16mm, and fewer television stations that show movies. And competition is fierce in the video market. Cult status is desired by filmmakers of unusual films that flop at the box office because they can still turn a profit in video. In fact, the producers of those wildly titled low-budget horror pictures that only have brief theater life try to create instant cult movies in anticipation of their video releases.

While there has been increased interest in cult movies, their definition hasn't really changed. As I wrote in the foreword to *Cult Movies 2:* "Not so long ago 'cult movies' were considered to be only those obscure pictures that were admired by a small, sad coterie of film 'experts' and other social outcasts. (It's still mighty hard to get a middle-of-the-week date to an Edgar G. Ulmer double feature.) The phenomenal success of midnight movies, particularly *The Rocky Horror Picture Show,* resulted in 'cult movies' becoming those pictures that are seen countless times by large, somewhat fanatical communal groups who turn every screening into an audience-participation party. I choose to define 'cult movies' quite broadly. I consider them those special films that elicit a fiery passion in moviegoers long after their initial releases; that have been taken to heart as if they were abandoned orphans in a hostile world, cherished, protected, and enthusiastically championed by segments of the movie audience; that are integral parts of people's lives. These are pictures that people will not miss whether they are playing on the *Late Late Late Show,* at a grindhouse in the most dangerous part of town, or at a drive-in in the next county; pictures that people will brave blizzards, skip their weddings, ignore their most solemn religious holidays, and even

date their least-appealing cousins to see for what may be their tenth, twentieth, or one hundredth time."

And as I wrote in the foreword to *Cult Movies:* "When you speak of cult movies, you speak in extremes. Hard-core cultists, ranging from polite to lunatic, insist that their favorite films are the most intriguing, unusual, outrageous, mysterious, absurd, daring, entertaining, erotic, exotic, and/or best films of all time. Also they point out that cult movies differ radically from standard Hollywood films in that they characteristically feature atypical heroes and heroines; offbeat dialogue; surprising plot resolutions; highly original story lines; brave themes, often of a sexual or political nature; 'definitive' performances by stars who have cult status; the novel handling of popular but stale genres. Outstanding special effects, spectacular camerawork, and a willingness by the filmmakers to experiment distinguish many cult movies. . . .

"The typical Hollywood product has little potential for becoming a cult favorite because it is perceived by *everyone* in basically the same way. Almost everyone agrees on the quality of these films, on what the directors are trying to say, and on the correct way to interpret the films' messages. On the other hand, cult films are born in controversy, in arguments over quality, themes, talent, and other matters. Cultists believe they are among the blessed few who have discovered something in particular films that the average moviegoer and critic have missed—the something that makes the pictures extraordinary. They grasp the elusive points of their favorite films, the filmmakers' most personal visions, the cult stars' real selves coming through; and they find glory in that they are among the few on the same wavelength as the people involved in making these films. While word of mouth certainly plays a large part in the growth of cults for individual films, what is fascinating is that *in the beginning* pockets of people will embrace a film they have heard nothing about while clear across the country others independently will react identically to the same picture. There is nothing more exciting than discovering you are not the only person obsessed with a picture critics hate, the public stays away from en masse, and film texts ignore."

As in the first two volumes, I have attempted to present a strong cross section of cult films, from classics to sleepers to fiascos. I have included critics' favorites, personal favorites, video favorites, and films that readers of the earlier books have suggested I write about. Some of these films were smash hits when initially released, eventually faded away, and later reemerged as objects of cult adoration; others have never emerged from obscurity. As before, I have limited the number of horror and science fiction films because I realize every one ever made has at least a minor cult. Also, in order to include films from all eras, I am forced to limit the number of recent movies that have quickly become cult movies; for instance, *Blood Simple* and *Brother from Another Planet,* movies I like very much, will have to wait for future volumes. Once again, I have been selective about the inclusion of midnight movies since it's apparent that not all movies that play midnights have achieved cult status. Although the three *Star Wars* movies, *Gone with the Wind,* and *E.T.* have fanatical followings, I have not included them because they are still distributed with the intention of attracting the mass audience. Only when they are released primarily for their hardcore fans will they be classified as legitimate cult movies.

CULT MOVIES

MOVIES

3

An American Werewolf in London

1981   Color   Universal release of a PolyGram picture
Director: John Landis
Producer: George Folsey, Jr.
Executive Producers: Peter Guber and Jon Peters
Screenplay: John Landis
Cinematography: Robert Paynter
Special Effects Makeup: Rick Baker
Original Music: Elmer Bernstein
Editor: Malcolm Campbell
Running Time: 97 minutes

Cast: David Naughton (David Kessler), Jenny Agutter (Alex Price), Griffin Dunne (Jack Goodman), John Woodvine (Doctor Hirsch), Brian Glover (chess player), David Schofield (dart player), Lila Kaye (Gladys, the barmaid), Frank Oz (Mr. Collins), Don McKillop (Inspector Villiers), Paul Kember (Sergeant McManus), Anne-Marie Davies (Nurse Gallagher), Michael Carter (Gerald Bringsley), Landis (car-crash-victim cameo).

Synopsis: American students David Kessler and Jack Goodman are backpacking in Northern England. Seeking refuge from the cold, rain, and darkness, they enter The Slaughtered Lamb, a pub in tiny East Proctor. When Jack becomes too inquisitive about burning candles and a pentagram on the wall, the hostile and secretive dart and chess players force them to leave, despite the barmaid's concern for their safety.

Although the moon is full, David and Jack wander off the road and get lost in the moors. They hear loud growls. They joke around but are terrified by what lurks in the dark. A huge wolflike beast lunges on Jack and rips him to pieces. It then attacks David. Shots ring out. Before he loses consciousness, David sees a naked stranger lying dead beside him and the armed men from the pub standing above him.

Three weeks later, David awakens in a London hospital. Nurse Alex Price and her supervisor Doctor Hirsch inform him of Jack's death. Heartbroken, David refutes police inspectors who claim they were attacked by an escaped lunatic. He insists that an animal caused the bites and bruises on his body.

David has terrible nightmares. So when dead Jack, whose blood-drenched face and body are decaying, appears in the hospital room, David assumes he's just dreaming. Between wisecracks, Jack says they were attacked by a werewolf and that David will become a werewolf when the moon is full. Jack tells David to kill himself before he murders innocent people and they too become miserable, walking corpses. Jack can be freed from his limbo state only when David, the last of a line of werewolves, is dead.

Alex asks David to move in with her. They make love, they fall in love. But Jack, who has further decayed, pays another visit. David worries he is going crazy. That's also the concern of Hirsch, who thinks David may start to act like a werewolf.

David is alone in Alex's apartment when the next full moon rises. He undergoes an agonizing metamorphosis and becomes a wolf. That night, a couple on the way to a party, three bums, and a gentleman in an underground station are savagely killed by a wolf. David wakes up naked in the wolf cage at the zoo. He doesn't remember what happened, but is full of energy. He wants to have sex with Alex but she takes him by cab to see Hirsch. However, when David learns of the deaths, he jumps out. He tries to get arrested. When this proves unsuccessful, he tells Alex that he loves her and runs off, not wanting to put her in danger.

In the back of a porno house in Piccadilly Circus, David meets Jack, whose face has rotted away completely, and the bloody and scarred victims of his murder spree, now of the undead. They insist that David commit suicide.

The full moon rises while David is in the theater. He becomes a werewolf. He kills a patron and an usher, then charges outside into the crowd that has gathered. He bites off an inspector's head and breaks loose. There is panic. Cars crash and people are killed and injured. The werewolf runs into an alley. Sharpshooters take aim. Alex arrives and runs into their path. She moves toward the wolf, saying she loves David and wants to help. The wolf growls viciously. Rifles are fired. Alex cries as she sees the human David lying dead.

David (second from right) and Jack seek refuge in The Slaughtered Lamb. Only Gladys the barmaid makes the strangers feel welcome.

John Landis wrote the first draft for his strange "pet" project in 1969, before he had turned 19 and two years before he'd direct and write (and star in) his first picture, the mini-budgeted *Schlock!* (1971), another cult favorite. It took Landis 12 years, half a dozen lapsed options, numerous dialogue (but not plot) rewrites, and three "monster" hits—comedies *Kentucky Fried Movie* (1977), *National Lampoon's Animal House* (1978), and *The Blues Brothers* (1980)—before he had enough muscle to secure $10 million financing for a picture most moneymen believed was too frightening to be a comedy and too funny to be a horror film.

Schlock!, which spoofs the silly Joan Crawford missing-link horror film *Trog!* (1970), was meant to be a comedy. This time Landis took his subject seriously—he made a *horror* film. His work may contain outrageous humor, but the horror isn't undermined by the wisecracks exchanged by David Naughton's David and his pal, Griffin Dunne's Jack (even after Jack has become a walking corpse); the quirky major and minor characters (several were hired from Rent-a-Punk); the offbeat use of rock music (Bobby Vinton, Sam Cooke, and the Marcels sing their versions of "Blue Moon," Van Morrison sings "Moondance," and Creedence Clearwater Revival sings "Bad Moon Rising"); and the consistently weird situations. To the contrary. I think the off-the-wall humor keeps viewers so off-balance that it heightens their nervousness; similarly, it's the very absurdity of backpackers David and Jack's plight in the opening sequence—they must enter a pub called The Slaughtered Lamb; the men inside treat them like lepers; they soon find themselves lost in the moors at night while

Alex brings David home to recuperate. They quickly become lovers.

a wild, growling beast circles them—that causes *their* terror to increase. The jittery pair continues to make wisecracks (Dunne is extremely funny) in an attempt to cover their fear, but for them, as well as the audience, the humor doesn't dissipate the horror. The high doses of humor are never at the expense of the genre; Landis adheres to horror movie conventions rather than mocking them and, as a result, has made a respectful, *traditional*—thematically, if not in approach—werewolf movie. So it's fitting this PolyGram production was released by Universal, the studio that produced the seminal werewolf films, *The Werewolf of London* (1935) and the underappreciated horror masterpiece *The Wolf Man* (1941), in which Lon Chaney, Jr., introduced the "definitive" movie werewolf, Lawrence Talbot.

Surely Universal didn't participate in the project in order to revive its werewolf-film tradition, but to show its gratitude to Landis for making the studio so much money with his past comedies and to compete with Avco-Embassy and Warners, which were busy preparing horror movies with wolf themes. Indeed, for horror movie fans, 1981 became the long-anticipated Year of the Wolf. In addition to Landis's film, Joe Dante directed Terence H. Winkless and John Sayles's tongue-in-cheek adaptation of Gary Brandner's novel *The Howling*, in which newscaster Dee Wallace happens upon a colony of California werewolves. Also, Michael Wadleigh—who made *Woodstock* (1970) but not the TV movie *The Werewolf of Woodstock* (1974)—directed and scripted (with David Eyre) an adaptation of Whitley Streiber's allegorical *Wolfen*, in which New York detective Albert Finney hunts a murderous pack of supernatural wolves. Not surprisingly, the three films were often compared to each other, with *The Howling* (also destined for cult status) edging *American Werewolf*, my preference, as the favorite among moviegoers and critics.

I was struck by this quote from a *Village Voice* review by Carrie Rickey (a critic I admire): "Unlike *The Howling*'s insinuation that werewolfery is an expression of sexual liberation or *Wolfen*'s suggestion that the animal state is superior to human civilization, *AW* doesn't deal with the metamorphosis angle at all, which is the heart of the matter. Why do werewolves do what they do? . . . [Landis] assumes good and evil, doesn't illustrate them." I don't agree.

Certainly Landis does rightly touch on—subtly at times, I admit—the sexual aspects of lycanthropy. It's no coincidence that both Jenny Agutter's nurse Alex Price and Nurse Gallagher, who admits peeking at David's genitals, find their patient sexually attractive. Alex, who is confused by her own strong feelings for this stranger she invites into her bedroom, tells him, "I find you very attractive" and, later, "terribly attractive." Landis might have had David confess women were never much attracted to him in the past, but his point is clear: Once the blood of a wild beast flows in David's veins, he gives off an irresistible sexual scent. Just as David's new state "liberates" the sexual feelings of Alex, who has had few past lovers, his own sexual feelings increase considerably. For instance, on the morning after his first night on the prowl as a wolf, during which he murders and half-eats six people, what the newly energized David desires most is a "quickie" with Alex.

When David and Alex do have sex, it is a far cry from the antiseptic lovemaking in the hilarious porno film David and Jack will watch, *See You Next Wednesday*. It is tender, but it's also deeply passionate and definitely *animalistic*—in the shower, Alex (since 1970's *Walkabout*, an Agutter role typically requires her to be nude in water) licks and kisses away the drops on David's shoulder; in bed, David moves his tongue down Alex's body. Throughout the film, Landis draws a strong correlation between one's hunger for food, one's sexual appetite, and one's bloodlust (composed of the hunt, attack and kill, and the devouring of the prey). Landis cleverly includes several scenes in which characters are unable to satisfy their hunger for food; because *eating food = sex = bloodlust* in this film, there is an increase in our anticipation/anxiety for sexual and violent release. Subconsciously we become nervous as David and Jack are denied food at The Slaughtered Lamb; David refuses to eat hospital food until Alex, using food for seduction, feeds him (even so, because we see David eat only a trifle we don't sense his nourishment); David's breakfast is interrupted by Jack's corpse; Alex and David shop for groceries but we never see them eat what they buy; John Woodvine's Doctor Hirsch is also denied food at The Slaughtered Lamb; prior to turning into a werewolf, David twice opens the refrigerator but takes nothing out (his hunger for food is replaced by this thirst for, as he recites, "the blood of an Englishman"); a couple is attacked on the way to a dinner party; an underground passenger barely gets a candy into his mouth—he has no time to chew it—before he must run for his life.

Wolfen's "suggestion that the animal state is superior to human civilization" is neither original nor stimulating, so I don't think Landis would want to make a horror film with that as its major theme. But he has his human characters share their world with animals—lambs, deer, wolves, lions, dogs, a cat, and gorillas, which are revered by Landis and FX expert Rick Baker (who both *played* them in past films). And, in this film in which man and beast share one body, Landis twice *equates* man with beast: David and Jack first appear sitting on a truck amidst lambs, coming across as "human lambs" on their way to The Slaughtered Lamb and then to their own slaughter by a werewolf; in the funniest scene, caged simians watch David, running nude through the zoo, make a "monkey of himself."

Rickey contends that Landis assumes good and evil are at war in his tale but doesn't bother to draw the battlelines. I think the good-versus-evil confrontation is implicit in traditional werewolf movies, in which the lead character, be he Naughton's David Kessler or Chaney's Lawrence Talbot, is a good person who through no fault of his own becomes a werewolf. (*The Howling* would be *traditional* if Dee Wallace became a werewolf earlier in the picture.) The battle is for the soul, and because the man himself is never corrupted (he remains pure in heart) he may return to his human form (a state of grace) after being killed while in his werewolf state. Of course, the monstrous appearance the man assumes when the moon is full and his subsequent monstrous acts represent the evil that flows through his bloodstream since being bitten (defiled and cursed) by another werewolf. All horror fans know that the "beast" within this pure man, which emerges when the moon is full, is as much the embodiment of evil as the vampire. Nevertheless, Landis makes it clear to the novice that the werewolf represents evil, even in a religious sense. David and Jack may be Jewish but their first action is fitting for a Christian parable: They are "lambs" foolishly leaving the flock. The last name of Jack, the first werewolf victim, is Goodman as in *good man*. Equally significant is that when people confront a werewolf, they speak to the heavens: "Mary, Mother of God"; "Good Lord!"; and "Jesus Christ!"—even when undergoing his own metamorphosis from man to wolf, David cries "Jesus Christ!" and "God!" Furthermore, I believe that David, in the tradition of past movie werewolves, can't bring himself to commit suicide because this act would betray God.

It is not of central importance in traditional—the type

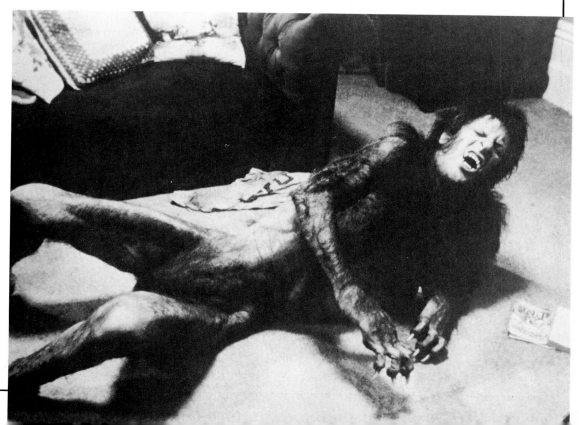

In a truly remarkable special effects sequence, David becomes a werewolf before our eyes. Unlike werewolves in past horror movies, such as Lon Chaney, Jr.'s Lawrence Talbot, David takes on the shape and exact appearance of a wolf. Whereas men in past horror films seemed to be in a semi-trance while their face, hands, and feet changed, David's lengthy transformation process is extremely painful.

In a scene quite similar to one in 1980's Altered States, *although they were conceived independently, David awakens from his first night as a werewolf and finds himself naked at the zoo. His trip through London back to Alex's apartment is the picture's comedic highlight.*

I prefer—werewolf movies *why* werewolves do what they do. Because we fans of the subgenre already know the reason. *American Werewolf* and its predecessors, all bona-fide tragedies, instead deal with the hopeless, lonely struggle of the good, decent protagonist once he realizes he has become a werewolf, must murder innocent people, and is a threat to the ones he loves. Not only does a battle rage within David between good and evil (the modern age of reason and the dark ages, science/sense and superstition, angels and demons), but also the body itself is in revolt (a man's worst fear according to the horror director David Cronenberg), growing hair, fangs, and long nails, and twisting, contracting, and elongating until the human form has given way to the form of a large, four-legged wolf. In the amazing, convincing three-minute metamorphosis sequence (as Sam Cooke's calm "Blue Moon" plays), which helped win Baker the first Oscar ever given in the special effects makeup category, David suffers both tremendous terror and pain as changes take place in his body and face (a wolf snout bursts out of David's nose and mouth!). It's different in *The Howling*, where evil men and women will their own, painless transformations from humans to two-legged wolves. The celebrated transformations in Dante's picture, orchestrated by Baker-protégé Rob Bottin after Baker left the project to work with Landis (they'd first discussed *AW* while collaborating on *Schlock!*), are visually stunning. However, they happen so frequently within a brief time span that they slow down the climax and,

more annoying, are there mostly for effect on viewers. On the other hand, Baker emphasizes how the transformation affects the *character*, David. This is the first werewolf movie in which our sympathy for the character increases all the way through the transformation. (Baker told me: "Being a makeup artist is like being a dentist or doctor. The guy in the chair associates you with discomfort. As a rule, I don't like actors and they don't like me. But David was the most cooperative actor I ever worked with. For one week, I spent ten hours a day putting on his makeup. He didn't like the discomfort, but he enjoyed being in the makeup."*)

Other than meeting Alex, nothing pleasant happens to David Kessler. And we feel extra sympathy for him because he's played by the instantly likable Naughton, previously Dr. Pepper's vested pied piper in a series of popular television commercials. David can't even die the "romantic" death he envisioned, being killed with silver bullets by someone who loves him, which is how Lawrence Talbot

• •

*Griffin Dunne was less enthusiastic about the many hours he had to spend in his decaying-cadaver makeup. He told me: "The makeup was incredibly uncomfortable—it was boiling under the makeup, there were clumps on the back of my neck, and I got rashes. It made me depressed. I had nightmares about being dead and watching my own funeral. Once I was made up, no one wanted to look at me. They'd say, 'Hello, Pizza Face.' I ate alone."

Rick Baker applies grisly makeup to the face of an uncomfortable Griffin Dunne. As the movie progresses and Jack's walking corpse further decays, the makeup becomes heavier and more gruesome.

dies in *House of Frankenstein* (1944). He truly fits in with the tragic figures of werewolf-movie lore: Henry Hull in *The Werewolf of London*; Chaney in *The Wolf Man*, which critics should add to the list of fatalistic *noir* films of the forties—*Frankenstein Meets the Wolf Man* (1943), *House of Frankenstein*, and *Abbott and Costello Meet Frankenstein* (1948), perhaps the best horror-comedy ever made; Michael Landon in the underrated *I Was a Teenage Werewolf* (1957); Oliver Reed in the overrated *Curse of the Werewolf* (1961); as well as Simone Simon in Val Lewton's *Cat People* (1942), a werewolf-theme variation with blatant sexual overtones.

Because this picture contains ferocious, bloody violence it has never been compared to the works of Lewton. Yet there is much that reminds me of the forties producer who made an art of "suggestive," offscreen horror—including the argument that there is as much reason to believe in the supernatural as in Christian teachings or science. The opening sequence certainly has Lewton elements: familiar characters in unfamiliar, hostile surroundings (the Black Mountains in Wales); a setting, East Proctor, that has remained unchanged through the centuries (filming took place in Crickadarn, a Welsh village with six cottages, one farm, and two churches with graveyards); strange, secretive, superstitious characters (played by members of the Royal Shakespeare Company's cast for *Nicholas Nickleby*); a mysterious, forbidding statue (Landis contributed the Angel of Death statue); endangered characters walking at night. The scene on the moors (until we actually *see* the werewolf attack Jack) and the scene (although brightly lit) in which the commuter is chased through the deserted Tottenham Court Road underground station recall classic sequences in *Cat People* and *The Leopard Man* (1943) in which Lewton characters are threatened by wild beasts. They are genuinely terrifying. Oddly, the scene in which the three homeless men are approached by the werewolf would have worked better if it hadn't been as reserved as Lewton—the scene is too short to not have included either a more suspenseful buildup to the attack, or the attack itself. Landis filmed the men being mauled but later cut the footage, despite preview-audience approval. As

he later told *Fangoria*: "I made a change that, I think, hurt my picture commercially."

I'd have liked more screen time for Jenny Agutter, a personal favorite, including moments when her character is in danger; I wish more would have come out of Dr. Hirsch's investigation of the attack on the moors; and I'd have liked David to have looked into the mirror a second time just before his transformation and scared himself and us by really growling this time (he pretended to growl earlier). But other than the attack on the homeless men, the only scenes that don't work come at the end. I dislike the long scene in the porno theater (although I love the appropriate identity-confusion humor in *See You Next Wednesday*), in which David is confronted by the skeletal Jack (here Baker created a "puppet" to replace Dunne, who still provided the voice) and his six victims, who urge him to kill himself. It is silly, takes away our feeling that their deaths were tragic (because we see them talking and, in some cases, in good humor), and leads nowhere because David doesn't even try to commit suicide afterward. It would have worked if Landis included a subsequent scene in which a bystander prevents David from committing suicide and is killed for his trouble when, as they struggle for David's knife or gun, David turns into a werewolf.

I'm also bothered by the elaborate car-crash sequence in Piccadilly Circus (for the film, Landis also ambitiously and sneakily filmed in Trafalgar Square and Windsor Castle, the Queen's country residence). Landis's inspiration was a real-life incident in which a dog ran onto the San Diego Freeway and caused many deaths. However, I don't think such a scene works during the climax of a monster movie. Perhaps, we could have just *heard* the crashes and screams while the camera stayed on the werewolf as he headed toward the alley. The ending in the alley is too abbreviated—I'd like to have seen the wolf leap into the air toward Alex—but from a story point it's satisfying. At the very least, Landis deserves credit for not having the open ending that mars almost every horror film nowadays. It's somewhat ironic that one of the best horror films of recent years is one of the few that didn't leave room for a sequel.

Annie Hall

1977   Color   United Artists
Director: Woody Allen
Producer: Charles H. Joffe
Screenplay: Woody Allen
   and Marshall Brickman

Cinematography: Gordon Willis
Editor: Ralph Rosenblum
Running Time: 94 minutes

Cast: Allen (Alvy Singer), Diane Keaton (Annie Hall), Tony Roberts (Rob), Carol Kane (Allison Portchnik), Paul Simon (Tony Lacey), Colleen Dewhurst (Mom Hall), Shelley Duvall (Pam), Janet Margolin (Robin), Christopher Walken (Duane Hall), Donald Symington (Dad Hall), Helen Ludlam (Grammy Hall), Marshall McLuhan (himself), Jonathan Munk (Alvy, age 9), Mordecai Lawner (Alvy's dad), Joan Newman (Alvy's mom), Christine Jones (Dorrie), Russell Horton (man in movie line), John Glover (Annie's actor boyfriend), Lauri Bird (Tony's girlfriend), Paula Trueman (elderly street stranger), Shelley Hack (shallow street stranger), Jeff Goldblum (party guest), Sigourney Weaver (Alvy's date), Beverly D'Angelo (TV actress), Tracey Walter (TV actor), Dick Cavett (himself).

Synopsis: Comedian Alvy Singer tells us that life is "full of loneliness, and misery and suffering, and unhappiness; and it's all over much too quickly." He also tells us that he finds it difficult to desire a woman who would desire him.

Alvy thinks back to the circumstances leading to his breakup with Annie Hall. He grew up in a house beneath the Coney Island roller coaster. His father, who ran the bumper car ride, and mother always argued. Even as a youngster Alvy thought only about sex and the sorry state of the world. When he became an adult he still thought constantly about sex and death. He also worried about the rise of anti-Semitism. Nothing gave him pleasure, except movies like *The Sorrow and the Pity* and sex. Alvy and Annie argued constantly, even in movie lines. Each thought the other hostile. She thought him so egocentric that when she missed therapy, he thought of it in terms of how it affected him. She told him that her not wanting sex with him was just a phase, that he had been hot for his first wife, Allison, but that too cooled off.

Alvy met Allison at an Adlai Stevenson rally at which he was performing. She was smart, beautiful, and always eager to make love. But Alvy pushed her away, not desiring a woman who would desire him. His second wife, Robin, always rejected Alvy's sexual advances, claiming he used sex to express hostility.

Alvy met Annie, an aspiring singer, when he and his best friend Rob went to a tennis club. Later she shyly and awkwardly invited Alvy to her apartment. There was a mutual attraction between him, an intellectual New York Jew, and her, a naive WASP from Wisconsin. They fell in love. But Alvy wouldn't let her move in with him because he feared another commitment. She thought he didn't take her seriously because she was ignorant. He gave her books to read, encouraged her to take adult education courses, and got her to see a therapist. But he began to realize that as she improved her mind, she drifted away from him. He resented that she would only have sex with him if she smoked grass first. He resented that she made more progress with her therapist in one session than he had made with his in 15 years. He resented her teachers. She resented his jealousy, conservatism, possessiveness, and consistently bad mood. They split up. But they missed each other and reunited.

Alvy and Annie visited L.A., where Rob had moved, so Alvy could pick up an award. He hated L.A. and couldn't wait to leave. But Annie enjoyed it, especially spending time with mellow Tony Lacey, who wanted to produce a record with her.

Alvy and Annie broke up again. Annie moved in with Tony. Alvy got a girlfriend, but she hadn't Annie's humor. He missed Annie terribly and went back to L.A. to try to convince her to marry him. But their meeting went badly. She felt grateful toward Alvy, but didn't think she loved him anymore. Much later, Alvy and Annie ran into each other again. Annie had moved back to New York and was dragging her date to see *The Sorrow and the Pity*. They spent a happy day together and parted. Alvy realizes she is a terrific person and that it was great knowing her. He tells us that relationships are "irrational, crazy, and absurd" but they're worth any suffering they cause. Annie was worth it.

It's safe to say that every Woody Allen film has a cult following. But only *Annie Hall* is loved—loved *is* the correct word—by *every* Allen fan, as well as those obstinate moviegoers who still won't concede Allen is a *great* filmmaker. It's actually hard to find anyone who hasn't seen this irresistible movie several times, who doesn't have a tender spot for it—how many now-married couples saw it together when they dated!—who wouldn't make it *the* Woody Allen film they'd like to have if stranded on a desert island. I am among those who believe *Manhattan* (1979) is Allen's best and most mature film, and many other Allen admirers think *Hannah and Her Sisters* (1986) is his masterpiece, but none of us would argue with someone who remains loyal to *Annie Hall*. I think it is the film that generates the most warmth among Allen fans, for it was the pivotal film of his career. It marked Allen's gigantic step up to a new, much higher artistic level, much as the *Rubber Soul* album quickly took the Beatles to a new plane and on the path to *Sgt. Pepper's Lonely Hearts Club Band*, and proved he was capable of truly extraordinary work we hadn't thought possible before. We recognize that without *Annie Hall*, there would be no *Manhattan* and *Hannah and Her Sisters*.

Annie Hall marked Allen's transition from a functional and slapdash, though instinctively funny, filmmaker to one who is technically innovative, thematically sophisticated, intent on capturing the beauty of the women and the city (New York) he loves, eager to explore his characters, and passionate about using this storytelling medium to its fullest. For the first time, he seemed fully secure as a director, for he was willing to tone down his humor and give up easy laughs by cutting back on the outrageous sight gags and ridiculous one-liners that ran uninterrupted from start to finish in his earlier films. Now, instead of making us laugh with preposterous characters and completely absurd situations, he attempted to make us laugh by showing us real people who act in preposterous ways (relationships make anyone act irrationally, he tells us) and the absurdities of real life (in which everyone, he tells us, suffers, is lonely, and is unhappy, but gripes because life is too short). And he no longer wanted to present us with a "reel" Woody Allen—a bumbling, sex-crazed, neurotic comic figure—to be laughed at, but an "almost-real" Woody Allen—a not-so-bumbling (except when driving or sneezing $2000 worth of cocaine across the room), sex-crazed, neurotic, comical but sensitive and serious-minded person, who does laughable things but elicits our empathy.

There are traces of Allen in his earlier films, but with *Annie Hall*, Allen became the most personal of filmmakers, abandoning the parody of *What's Up, Tiger Lily?* (1966), *Take the Money and Run* (1969), *Bananas* (1971), *Everything You Always Wanted to Know About Sex (But*

The most familiar shot from the picture: The uniquely dressed Annie Hall and new acquaintance Alvy Singer—destined to become one of the cinema's most beloved romantic couples—return from playing tennis and awkwardly figure out how to prolong their time together. She invites him to her apartment and he accepts.

Were Afraid to Ask) (1972), *Sleeper* (1973), and *Love and Death* (1975) for semi-autobiographical material.* Allen fans can appreciate *Annie Hall* more than his other films because they sense Alvy Singer is the Allen character most like the real Allen; that Allen's views on life, death, relationships, women, art, health food (in California he orders mashed yeast), drugs (a stoned fool delivers that all-too-familiar refrain, "Hey, that's a great film if you're high!"), pretentious intellectuals, sex, therapy, New York culture, and Los Angeles "culture" are accurately conveyed; that the failed relationship between Alvy and Annie Hall reflects the failed romance between Allen and Diane Keaton (whose real name is Diane Hall, and whose nickname was Annie) in 1969, when they were living together while costarring in Allen's hit Broadway play, *Play It Again, Sam.*

Also, taking *Annie Hall* as Allen's breakthrough to developing-artist status, we can watch it in relation to his later films to gauge how much he has developed as an artist since 1977. For instance, in *Annie Hall*, for the first

---

*In this list, I include Allen's first film, *What's Up, Tiger Lily?*, although Allen appears only briefly to explain that he has taken a silly Japanese spy movie and added his own soundtrack. I have not included *Play It Again, Sam* (1972), which Allen starred in and scripted, because it was directed by Herbert Ross, or *The Front* (1976), in which he starred, because it was directed by Martin Ritt. However, the Allen characters in those two films are the most similar to Alvy Singer. And I suggest that his participation in *The Front* helped convince him to inject more serious material into *Annie Hall* than he'd had in his previous films.

time, he was willing to let other actors, especially Keaton, *act*, and be funny on their own, as opposed to just following his direction and spouting his (and Marshall Brickman's) words. This was a significant, extremely positive development, because it had become uncomfortable watching his actresses suppress their talents and instincts and come across as shallow male-written women—Keaton had been funny in both *Sleeper* and *Love and Death*, but you never felt, as you do in *Annie Hall*, that the humor was coming from her and not Allen. In future films, especially his next effort, the ultra-serious and much underrated *Interiors* (1978), and *Hannah and Her Sisters*, Allen would both experiment with ensemble *acting* and, like idol Ingmar Bergman, attempt to give insight (with, significantly, the help of his actresses) into the nature of women. (Allen has said it was Keaton who taught him to be more sensitive toward women.)

It's noteworthy that Allen was amenable to being Keaton's straight man in several scenes of *Annie Hall* (when Annie clumsily asks Alvy if he wants a ride home from the tennis club; when she tells her wacky and morbid story about her narcoleptic relative). But it's apparent that Allen still didn't trust another player to carry a significant portion of his film. *Annie Hall* may be a film taken from Alvy's point of view, but only when Annie sings in the nightclub and dances in obnoxiously "mellow" style with Paul Simon's obnoxiously mellow Tony Lacey is Alvy offscreen. Even when Annie is alone with her psychiatrist, Allen uses a split screen so that we simultaneously see Alvy with his therapist. But at the end, Allen came through: it was a truly generous gesture to name the film *Annie Hall* and not "Alvy Singer" or even "Alvy and Annie," two titles that were considered. This was a sign of things to come. With *Interiors*, Allen decided it was unnecessary to be in every film he made; with *Hannah and Her Sisters*, he wrote a part for himself that was secondary to that of three

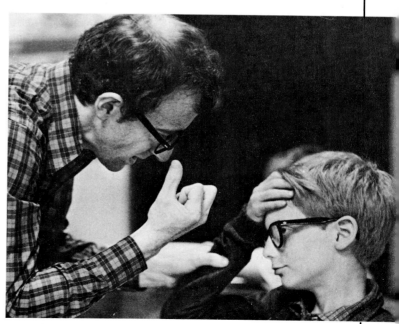

Alvy enters his own flashback to give special instructions to the boy playing him as a child.

female characters. His films reflect his growing maturity: In *Annie Hall*, he dared play a man who is so pessimistic and exasperating a character that we can't blame Annie for leaving him rather than being caught in his unhealthy syndrome; in *Manhattan*, he took a bigger chance, getting rid of his pathetic, victim-of-females image and playing a man who not only has no trouble getting women, but is actually *mean* to one (sweet young Mariel Hemingway). At the end of *Hannah*, Allen, who seemed to be enjoying life more himself, finally cast aside the death phobia Alvy and other Allen characters exhibited and played a character (Mickey) who, despite being told by doctors that he can't produce children, becomes such a life force that he impregnates Dianne Wiest's character. (This wasn't long before Mia Farrow became pregnant with Allen's child.) Whereas nothing gives Alvy pleasure—the reason Allen originally intended to call his picture *Anhedonia*—Allen's character in *Manhattan* would derive pleasure from everything available in New York City (museums, walks in Central Park, wonderful views of the Brooklyn Bridge, Marx Brothers revivals) and his taped litany of favorite things that make life worth living (including Hemingway's face). And Allen's character in *Hannah* would derive pleasure from life itself. The pessimistic filmmaker of *Annie Hall* eventually gave way to a truly positive, progressive filmmaker.

Annie Hall hasn't the visual beauty of *Manhattan*, *Interiors*, and *Hannah and Her Sisters*, or the technical invention of, say, *Zelig* (1983) or *The Purple Rose of Cairo* (1985), but it shows that Allen was finally attempting to use *film* creatively. As Mel Gussow pointed out in the *New York Times*, Allen, working with cinematographer Gordon Willis, employed "a deliberate three-color scheme. The New York scenes, Annie and Alvy's love story, were filmed only on gray, overcast days or at sundown, the most romantic light. Alvy's past, at home and in school, is very yellow and golden, the hue of nostalgia. California, which Alvy–Woody hates, is shot, Woody tells me, 'right into the sun. Everybody is so white that they seem to vapor-

ize.'" Through some dramatic alienation devices, we are constantly reminded that we're not watching exactly what happened to Alvy and Annie but only Alvy's story (did Annie really sing "Seems Like Old Times" or is that what the nostalgic Alvy wants her to have sung?); that is, Alvy's story as filmed by Allen.

It's Alvy, Allen's surrogate, who talks directly to us; speaks to strangers on the street about Annie and the secrets to the strangers' happiness ("We use a large vibrating egg"; a young woman says, "I'm very shallow and empty and I have no ideas and nothing interesting to say," and her boyfriend adds, "And I'm exactly the same way"); takes physical excursions into his and Annie's pasts; gives instructions to the young actor playing him as a 9-year-old; pulls out—this idea was Keaton's—Marshall McLuhan from behind a poster to tell the blowhard professor who speaks pretentious drivel about McLuhan in a movie line that "You know nothing about my work" (Alvy shrugs, "If life were only like this"); converses with Annie's spirit that withdraws from her body when they have sex. But it's Allen who lets us know that when Grammy Hall looks at Alvy at the dinner table she sees a Hassidic Jew, with a long black beard, curls, black hat, and black frock coat. And, in the film's funniest scene, it's Allen who lets us see, through the use of subtitles, what Annie and Alvy are really thinking while they try to fake a serious conversation about photography (she: "He probably thinks I'm a yo-yo"; he: "I wonder what she looks like naked"). And it's Allen who uses that split screen effect so we can simultaneously eavesdrop on Annie and Alvy's therapy sessions: When their respective psychiatrists ask how often they have sex, and Alvy moans, "Hardly ever, maybe three times a week," and Annie sighs, "Constantly, I'd say three times a week," it's like when one teenager on *American Bandstand* says a new record has a great beat and is great to dance to and a second teenager says the opposite and then they both rate it an 80.

Perhaps Allen's alienation devices were derived from his earlier works—Allen speaking to the imaginary Bogart

In a flashback, ex-wife Robin finds Alvy watching the Knicks on TV rather than entertaining at their party; as usual, she rejects him when he suggests making love. Janet Margolin, who played Robin, was the female lead in Allen's Take the Money and Run.

Annie and Alvy discuss their deteriorating relationship with their respective therapists, giving completely opposite impressions of the same situation. Although the use of a split screen for this sequence is quite original, it underlines the fact that Allen originally intended his film to be about Alvy and didn't want Annie to have the screen to herself.

in the Herbert Ross–directed *Play It Again, Sam* (1972), Howard Cosell broadcasting an Allen sexual encounter in *Bananas*—but I think he was aiming more for the surrealism of Fellini's autobiographical *8½* (1963). In fact, the film was intended to be much like *8½*, with an artist evaluating his work and his past and current life (including his romances). His decision to use childhood scenes was partly inspired, I believe, by Fellini's *Amarcord* (1974). However, when it came time to edit the film, Allen shelved the *8½* concept—he would return to it for *Stardust Memories* (1980). Allen maintained some of his childhood material but saved the rest for his *Amarcord*-like *Radio Days* (1986). It was important to keep some scenes of his youth because a man obsessed with death would be obsessed with a bygone era, and we can see Alvy got both his argumentative nature and his fear of marriage from being around his constantly bickering parents. I'm also glad Allen decided to keep flashback scenes of Alvy with his two former wives—Janet Margolin's Robin (who can't understand why he'd rather have sex or watch the Knicks than mingle with her important and pretentious party guests) and Carol Kane's Allison (who rightly believes Alvy can't stop talking about the "second-gun" theory because he doesn't want to have sex with her)—and with a date—

Shelley Duvall's humorless Pam (who, after taking a very long time to have an orgasm, tells the sore-jawed Alvy that "Sex with you is a Kafkaesque experience. . . . I mean that as a compliment"). Not only are these three fine, offbeat actresses memorable in their small roles (Kane has never been more controlled or seductive) but it is through Alvy's relationships with their characters that we understand what he expects from women at the time he falls in love with Annie.

Initially, as editor Ralph Rosenblum and Robert Karen documented in *When the Shooting Starts*, Allen conceived a film (*Anhedonia*) centering on Alvy Singer, his weird past and his sorry present. They quote Brickman: "The first draft was a story of a guy who lived in New York and was 40 years old and was examining his life. His life consisted of several strands. One was a relationship with a young woman, another was concern with the banality of the life that we all live, and a third was an obsession with proving himself and testing himself to find out what kind of character he had." According to Rosenblum and Karen:

The first cut of what has come to be known as *Annie Hall* was two hours and twenty minutes long. . . . Far from being the story of a love affair . . . it was the surrealistic and abstract adventures of a neurotic Jewish comedian who was reliving his highly flawed life and in the process satirizing much of our culture. [Annie Hall] makes a brief appearance after [Alvy's] reference to her in the opening monologue, and disappears for ten or fifteen minutes thereafter. The movie was like a visual monologue, a more sophisticated and philosophical version of *Take the Money and Run*. Its stream-of-consciousness continuity, rambling commentary, and bizarre gags completely obscured the skeletal plot. "The thing was supposed to take place in my mind," says Woody. "Something that would happen would remind me of a quick childhood flash, and that would remind me of a surrealistic image. . . . None of that worked."

The original cut included fantasies set in Nazi headquarters; L.A., where Rob tries to replace them with pod people; the Garden of Eden; and the seven layers of Hell (where there are criminals, fascist dictators, people who don't appreciate oral sex, and Richard Nixon). There was also a scene in which Annie's mom, played by Colleen Dewhurst, asked Alvy to interpret a dream she had, and he scandalizes the whole family by calling it "A phallic dream . . . it represents an unconscious impulse toward castration." But this cut didn't work. Rosenblum writes: "It was clear to Woody and me that the film started moving whenever present-tense material with [Alvy] and [Annie] dominated the screen, so we began cutting in the direction of that relationship. We were still, as far as we knew, working on the same film about a comic who can feel no joy and about his jaded view of the world. But we sensed immediately where the life was, and Woody, with his sure commercial sense, had no hesitation about trimming away much of the first twenty minutes in order to establish Annie more quickly." Rosenblum quotes Allen: " 'There was a lot of material taken out of the picture that I thought was wonderfully funny. I was sorry to lose just about all that surrealistic stuff. It was what I intended to do. I mean the whole concept of the picture changed as we were cutting it. It was originally a picture about me, exclusively, not about a relationship.' "

We can feel fortunate that *Annie Hall* was cut so that it became a film about a relationship, for there are few films about relationships that are as perceptive. Relationships, according to Allen, have wonderful moments of romance (it's so sweet when Alvy and Annie kiss for the first time), laughter (Alvy and Annie, her camera clicking, make a big production of getting live lobsters off the floor and into a pot), compliment exchanges (Alvy's attempts to build Annie's confidence are sometimes warmly accepted, other times rebuked), insanity (as when Annie asks Alvy to kill a spider "that is as big as a Buick" in her tub), emotional reconciliations, and bizarre family gatherings (I love Alvy's terrified expression when Annie's weird brother Duane, who admitted to him earlier that he is tempted to have a head-on collision, drives them to the airport). But relationships are poisoned by sexual hang-ups, misunderstandings, disappointments, jealousy, possessiveness, irrational behavior, and warm people turning off their emotions. We laugh throughout, but are aware of the magnitude of the problems Annie and Alvy have. We take their relationship seriously and are greatly saddened when it doesn't work out.

If *Annie Hall* recalls *The Way We Were* (1973), it is no wonder. As I wrote earlier, Allen gave up parody with *Annie Hall*, but in *Annie Hall* he applies his own story, perhaps unconsciously, to *The Way We Were* just as he did to *Casablanca* (1942) in *Play It Again, Sam*. Both *The Way We Were* and *Annie Hall* are about failed romances between quirky-looking, neurotic, strident, antisocial, intellectual Brooklyn Jews (Barbra Streisand's Katie Morosky and Alvy) and gorgeous WASPs (Robert Redford's Hubbell Gardner and Annie). Katie and Alvy constantly encourage their lovers to reach their potential in their respective arts: Hubbell is a writer, Annie is a singer. Hubbell and Annie truly appreciate the encouragement, but they know they can never live up to the high standards demanded of them. This pressure to be perfect, plus the fact that Katie and Alvy refuse to relax and be happy because they find the world a sorry place in which to live, takes its toll. Both Hubbell and Annie are seduced by Los Angeles's mellow life and are driven by ambition to stay there (Hubbell writes a commercial movie, Annie is offered a record deal). Their romance over, Katie and Alvy return to New York. The two couples reunite in New York (Annie has come to her senses, Hubbell has come to write television shows). Their time together is brief but warm. Katie and Hubbell part just a five-minute taxi ride from where Alvy and Annie part. We cry both times. We know that Katie and Hubbell and Alvy and Annie still love each other and know just how wonderful their former partners are, but we realize, as they do, that they are mismatched—even if Annie's profession is the same as Alvy's last name.

It's touching when Alvy pays tribute to Annie at the end, saying what a "terrific person" she is and making it clear that knowing her was great fun and well worth the pain he had during the relationship and after its collapse. Refreshingly, Allen and Arthur Laurents, who wrote the novel and screenplay of *The Way We Were*, refused to make the females the villains of their romances. Hubbell's decision to sell out his principles is the ultimate reason his marriage to Katie dissolves. Alvy's refusal to change himself (to lighten up, to become less demanding) while trying to change Annie is his crime. Like Keaton, who, Allen told Frank Rich, "had not a trace of intellectualism when I first met her, but could always cut right to the heart of the matter," Annie is nearly perfect in her innocence when Alvy meets her. Yet he insists she *improve* herself by reading books on death, going to movies (about death), taking adult education courses, and seeing a therapist five times a week. Yet he doesn't attempt to improve himself. As do many intellectual males, Alvy takes on the role of mentor to Annie's naive pupil, all the time making her insecure about her lack of knowledge (she thinks he won't take her seriously because she's ignorant). Naturally when pupil Annie learns enough, she is wise enough to want out of such a destructive relationship. Allen realized that it was despicable of Alvy to force Annie into such a humbling, subservient role. His anger toward such people—including himself in his younger days—comes to light in

Hannah and Her Sisters when he cast the imposing, Nosferatu-like Max von Sydow as Barbara Hershey's possessive, soon-to-be-dumped mentor.

Allen thinks Annie is blameless for what goes wrong with the relationship. He isn't interested in criticizing her, but instead wants to make us understand why Alvy would love her so much—and, surely, why he thought any man would fall in love with Diane Keaton. Keaton's Annie Hall, who, of course, is patterned on the Keaton who once captured Allen's heart, is one of the most endearing of screen heroines. She may be naive, but she's funny and smart, hasn't a mean bone in her body, has no prejudices, doesn't choose men because of looks, has no idea about the "proper" way to eat (she orders pastrami on white bread with mayonnaise) or dress. Her mismatched men's clothing—a polka-dot tie, shirt, vest, pants, and hat—reflects her independence, her flakiness, and, if we stretch it, her willingness to enter mismatched relationships and to have her identity defined by men. There was a reason for the loose-fitting, mismatched "Annie Hall" look that became the fashion trend in America. As costume designer Ruth Morley, who helped Keaton assemble Annie's wardrobe, said: "Diane plays a very creative character, but an unformed one at the beginning, and that was the aim of [our costume choices]." Keaton not only looks great, but she expresses herself to Alvy in such a zany manner that you may get the urge to hug her: She looks to the heavens and the floor, babbling to herself about her inability to communicate, throwing in "God!" and "Yeah!" and "Oh, dear" and Grammy's "La-dee-dah," placing a fist on her hip and keeping her arms akimbo, laughing until the very end of her story about her relative's horrible death. Just as Jack Fisk knew how to present his wife, Sissy Spacek, at her most beautiful and lovable, revealing those idiosyncrasies and expressions he adored, in *Raggedy Man* (1981), Allen shares what he found most appealing about Keaton's mannerisms and personality. He would later do the same with Mia Farrow.

Keaton deservedly won the Best Actress Academy Award for her portrayal, Allen won as Best Director, Allen and Brickman won for Best Original Screenplay, and *Annie Hall* became the rare comedy to win Best Picture. Voting Academy members apparently temporarily forgot their anti-Allen, anti–New York-filmmaker bias because Allen did include several scenes that were shot in Hollywood. Never mind that they were completely unflattering to the city!

Alvy, Annie, and Rob return from their journey through seven layers of Hell, a fantasy sequence that was deleted from the picture.

The Black Cat

also known as *House of Doom* and *The Vanishing Body*

1934 B&W Universal
Director: Edgar G. Ulmer
Producer: Carl Laemmle, Jr.
Screenplay: Peter Ruric
Screen story: Edgar G. Ulmer and Peter Ruric
Suggested by the story by Edgar Allan Poe
Cinematography: John Mescall
Music: Heinz Roemfield
Editor: Ray Curtis
Running Time: 65 minutes

Cast: Boris Karloff (Hjalmar Poelzig), Bela Lugosi (Dr. Vitus Werdegast), David Manners (Peter Alison), Jacqueline Wells [later Julie Bishop] (Joan Alison), Lucille Lund (Karen Werdegast Poelzig), Egon Brecher (the majordomo), Harry Cording (Thamal), Anna Duncan (maid), Henry Armetta (sergeant), Albert Conti (lieutenant), John Peter Richmond [later John Carradine], Herman Bing.

Synopsis: American novelist Peter Alison and his wife, Joan, are honeymooning in Hungary, and are on their way to Gömbös. They must share their train compartment with a strange man, Dr. Vitus Werdegast. Once a prominent psychiatrist, Werdegast is coming home after 18 years—3 years at war, and 15 years in the Kulgaar prison. He believes his wife, Karen, and baby died. Werdegast is going to see his "old friend," architect Hjalmar Poelzig, who betrayed him and thousands of other Hungarians to the Russians. The Alisons, Werdegast, and Werdegast's large, mute servant, Thamal, travel by bus through a driving rainstorm. The driver informs them that Poelzig has built a mansion on the site of Fort Marmaros, above a bloody battlefield, "the greatest graveyard in the world."

The bus crashes and the driver is killed. The four passengers walk through the storm to Poelzig's modernist mansion. They are greeted by a mute servant and maid. Werdegast tends to Joan's injured shoulder and gives her a knockout drug. Poelzig is awakened by his young, blonde wife. He comes to see his guests. There is tremendous tension between Poelzig and Werdegast. Werdegast wants to kill his longtime acquaintance. These two men know each other well. Poelzig is not surprised when Werdegast kills his black cat with a knife—he tells the Alisons that Werdegast has "an all-consuming fear of cats."

Poelzig takes Werdegast down long winding stairs that lead into what was the old fort. Werdegast is horrified to see his dead wife suspended in the air. Poelzig embalmed her after her death, two years after the war. He had married her. He says Werdegast's daughter died. Werdegast attempts to shoot Poelzig, but he almost collapses when a black cat appears. Later, Werdegast tells Thamal to pretend to be Poelzig's servant. They must be patient about killing Poelzig because the house is rigged with dynamite.

Poelzig invites Werdegast to a Black Mass he'll be performing the next night. Werdegast realizes Poelzig plans to sacrifice Joan as part of the ritual. The two men play chess to determine Joan's fate. Poelzig wins. Joan is locked in her room. Peter is locked in a chamber below. The young blonde woman visits Joan. She says she is Karen, Poelzig's wife and Werdegast's daughter. Joan reveals her father is alive! Poelzig overhears the conversation. Soon Joan hears Karen's screams.

The satanic cult arrives. Poelzig presides. One cultist screams when Poelzig is about to sacrifice Joan. Poelzig is distracted. Werdegast and Thamal sneak Joan downstairs. Meanwhile Peter has escaped. He fights the majordomo but is knocked out. Thamal kills the majordomo, but only after being shot. Joan tells Werdegast his daughter is in the mansion, but Werdegast's joy is short-lived—he finds her corpse on an operating table. Poelzig suddenly appears. He and Werdegast fight. Thamal helps Werdegast secure Poelzig to the embalming rack. Thamal drops dead.

Poelzig is skinned alive by the delirious Werdegast. Meanwhile Joan and Peter come to. Joan tries to get a key out of Thamal's fist. Werdegast tries to help. Peter thinks he is harming her, so he shoots him. Werdegast tells the young couple to flee. When they are safely outside, he blows up the mansion.

Early in the picture, Werdegast visits Joan in her room in Poelzig's bizarre castle. Her door slides open and he enters. About 20 seconds of *screen* time later, Poelzig enters the same door. Apparently his entrance was filmed later, after everyone forgot about the sliding door . . . because Poelzig *pushes* the door open. Also there is now what looks to be a light switch next to the door, although there wasn't one when Werdegast entered. For the rest of the film, this door is next to the switch and must be pushed open. In another film, this might seem like a blatant gaffe, but in *The Black Cat* it almost seems logical, as if it were all part of a weird vision. After all, director Edgar G. Ulmer, who worked in Germany's film industry for 10 years, admitted his influence was *The Cabinet of Dr. Caligari* (1919). If Robert Wiene's silent classic can be interpreted (incorrectly) as the deranged vision of an insane character, then it can be argued that *The Black Cat* is the irrational vision of two insane characters, architect Poelzig, who—I'm speaking theoretically—conceived the film's outlandish set design, and psychiatrist Werdegast, who was responsible for the film's psychological perversity.

If the story we are watching unfold is indeed meant to be the weird manifestation of the postwar delirium shared by Poelzig and Werdegast, then Ulmer can get away with any inconsistency, any break in continuity. Joan's door can, logically, slide open one moment yet need to be pushed open the next. (It's most believable in a house that has a revolving room.) Peter can be wearing a perfectly fine jacket, yet walk through a door (and into another camera setup) and be wearing a jacket with a ripped shoulder. Joan can be wearing a long white gown as she races up the circular steps of the fort, yet when she enters the mansion proper be improperly dressed in a thin white nightgown, which is hiked above her knees, and a black cape. It's also acceptable that the revolving room in which Peter is imprisoned—it turns until the door space faces a brick wall—actually contains the controls that spin the room . . . therefore it takes him all of 10 seconds to escape. Somehow it makes sense that the previously calm Werdegast so overreacts to seeing Poelzig's first black cat that he automatically throws a knife through it, and that Poelzig has no emotional reaction to either the execution of his pet or his guest's unruly behavior. And it's okay that nothing comes of Werdegast's cat phobia. It even makes sense that Werdegast would threaten to shoot Poelzig—until he falls through a wall upon seeing a second black cat—yet in his next scene order Thamal to put away his knife and be discreet about their plan to kill their host. When Werdegast explains to his servant that they have to be careful because the house is rigged with dynamite, it doesn't bother us that there's no way Werdegast knows about the house being rigged with explosives and no reason Poelzig would rig his own house to be blown up in the first place. Likewise it's acceptable that Poelzig be nonplussed the entire film, yet panic at the conclusion and race alone into the cellar and engage Werdegast in hand-

Released from a Russian prison, Dr. Vitus Werdegast asks newlyweds Peter and Joan if he can share their train compartment.

to-throat combat. And we do not lose our "suspension of disbelief" just because Poelzig truthfully tells his young bride that she is "the very core and meaning of my life" and then kills her for no reason soon after. We don't question his hasty act, even though he might have held off a few minutes and sacrificed her at the Black Mass, rather than Joan. Since this was a low-budget picture, we wouldn't expect Ulmer and his writer, Peter Ruric, to have included a transition scene that informs us of the practicality of Poelzig murdering Karen—although perhaps this was one of the scenes Universal excised despite Ulmer's protests. And we wouldn't expect Ulmer to bring Karloff back to dub one of Poelzig's offscreen lines when someone else could do it quicker, or to reshoot scenes in which Lugosi, whose English was far from perfect, blew lines: Forgetting the verb, his Werdegast queries Poelzig about his embalmed wife, "Why she, why she like this?"; unable to decide between "flay" and "tear," his crazed Werdegast tells Poelzig he's going to "fayr [sic] the skin from your body."

Everyone in the film but Karloff seems to have pronunciation problems. Other than Budapest and Vienna, no town is pronounced the same way twice. "Marmaros" comes across as "Mamorish," "Kulgaar" as "Kurogarde." Until Peter and Joan joke that Poelzig's name sounds like "Pigslaw," you might think his name is Persik or Perlzig. It's hard to figure out the spelling of "Werdegast"

from hearing Lugosi say it—and, though it's spelled Werdegast in the titles, if you look at the studio's publicity material, you'll find it spelled Verdegast. In the titles, Lucille Lund's young bride is Karen; in the film, Werdegast refers to his wife (after whom his daughter was named) as Karin, Lund introduces herself to Joan as Karine (or Kareen), and Joan—Jacqueline Wells certainly has no ear—immediately refers to her as Karen. You know there's going to be trouble with names in the first scene, when Lugosi introduces himself as Dr. Vitus Werdegast and neither Peter nor Joan even raise their eyebrows. We don't find out Joan's name until several scenes later because Peter's introduction is "I'm Peter Alison and this is my wife." It reminds me of when that symbol of the original, hapless New York Mets, tight-lipped "Choo Choo" Coleman, who didn't know the derivation of his own nickname, was asked his wife's name and responded, "Mrs. Coleman." (To "What's she like?" he answered, "She likes me, bub.")

The Black Cat is only a couple of whiskers away from the movie loony bin, inhabited by those cuckoo films that we admiringly call "the worst films ever made." If Dwain Esper had directed Peter Ruric's script and hired the identical crew and cast of nontalents he used in the same year's Poverty Row atrocity, *Maniac*, then I'd bet that film would rival *Maniac* as the worst film of the era (and beyond). After all, they both contain characters who are off their

Hjalmar Poelzig conducts a Black Mass in his house. Joan is to be sacrificed.

rockers, Edgar Allan Poe elements (in *Maniac*, one crazed character gouges out and swallows a cat's eye, another imagines himself the orangutan in *Murders of the Rue Morgue*), knock-down fights in basements, characters making perverse use of corpses, characters in trances, and outlandish story lines. As it is, even with horror icons Karloff and Lugosi, and a decent supporting cast, and obvious talent behind the camera, *The Black Cat* could be regarded as a travesty on *Maniac*'s low level, *if* it were dissected. But while *Maniac* has so many obvious moments of awfulness that it is considered entertaining, *The Black Cat* is so entertaining that everyone overlooks its many awful moments. (Strangely, it isn't even regarded as campy.) In truth, as William K. Everson points out in his book

Classics of the Horror Film (1974), "the weakness of the script, decidedly vague and contradictory actions and motivations, while probably accidental, adds to the perversity of the film."

Few films that have taken Poe titles for their own have even remotely followed the plots of their sources, and *The Black Cat*—like Karloff and Lugosi's intriguing follow-up, *The Raven* (1935)—is no exception. Yet it is not alien to Poe. Everson writes: "It is slow and stately, an aura underlined by its deliberate use of classical music in place of original scoring, the macabre story of devil worship imbued with a sense of decay, furthered by some extremely literate . . . dialogue. It may be considered one of the most successful attempts to transfer Poe to the screen, even though it transfers only a mood and not a plot." Bill Krohn, in an article on Ulmer for *Film Comment* (August 1983), concurred:

> Ulmer was faithful to the letter to Poe, to his symbols, which he manipulates with such sensitivity that Marie Bonaparte's analysis of [Poe's] *Tales* could serve as a commentary of the film as well: Lugosi's cat phobia, the subterranean crypt, the upright posture of the embalmed woman, even the uncanny whiteness of the castle walls à la Roderick Usher's painting of a vault the walls of which emit "an inappropriate and ghastly splendor," and the especially morbid connotations of which are unravelled at the end of Bonaparte's reading of "The Narrative of A. Gordon Pym."

The Black Cat's genesis was a screen treatment by Universal writers Stanley Bergerman and Jack Cunningham. Although the studio hadn't done well with Lugosi's *Murders of the Rue Morgue* (1932), Bergerman and Cunningham still believed that Poe could provide good source material as well as attract viewers. So they came up with a story titled "The Brain Never Dies" that combined two Poe tales, "The Fall of the House of Usher" and "The Black Cat." It dealt with two New England recluses, Roderick and Madeline Usher, and their mad physician who plans a series of brain transplants. At the end, the transplants are prevented and the physician's black cat, whose brain is half human, pushes its master to his death in the collapsing house. This story was junked, but Universal was intrigued by the black cat angle and came up with a second story. In his book *The Count: The Life and Films of Bela "Dracula" Lugosi* (1974), Arthur Lenning writes:

> This time Universal followed Poe's story more closely and planned to star Boris Karloff as Edgar Doe, a man who, through too much drinking, becomes a sadistic brute who tortures both wife and cat. One night he gouges out the cat's eyes, strangles the animal, and ultimately picks up another cat. Finally he kills his wife and buries her in a wall. When the police come to investigate, Doe shows off the new wall in the cellar. The cry of a cat is heard, the wall torn down, and the body of the wife discovered with the cat perched on it.

This story was fairly faithful to Poe's tale, yet when Ulmer wrote his own treatment, he jettisoned everything in it, except the title and the presence of two black cats. In fact, he used more elements from the Bergerman-Cunningham story, including the doomed Usher-like recluses, the mad doctor, and the crumbling house. Ulmer named his evil architect Poelzig after Hans Poelzig, the scenic designer on the German horror classic *The Golem* (1920), the first film on which Ulmer worked (as a silhouette cutter). And he based him on British satanist Aleister Crowley, who would later also serve as Charles Gray's model in *The Devil's Bride* (1968) and, perhaps, Christopher Lee's Lord Summerisle in *The Wicker Man* (1973). As Lenning writes, Crowley called himself the "Beast of the Apocalypse" and tried to build a reputation as a symbol of evil. In the early twenties, he and his followers established the Abbey of Thelema in a Sicilian farmhouse, and from time to time newspapers carried sensational reports of their devil-worship practices. In 1933, when Ulmer was writing his screen treatment, Crowley made headlines by initiating a suit against artist Nina Hammett, who described his activities in her autobiography. Crowley took the stand during the trial and his shocking testimony caused the press to refer to him as "the wickedest man in the world"—Karloff's Poelzig would match this description.

What made *The Black Cat* more significant than most horror films of the era is that it had thematic relevance. Ulmer infused his story with a postwar anguish that was peculiar to Europeans, because they continued to live on soil where their loved ones were buried in mass graves. Poelzig has built his mansion overlooking, as the bus driver boasts, "one of the greatest battlefields of the war—tens of thousands of men died here." His modernist mansion stands, in fact, directly on top of Fort Marmaros, "the greatest graveyard in the world." Death presides. In such a morbid setting, neither Poelzig nor Werdegast can forget their common past; for them there is no future, just overdue death. Poelzig is actually touching when he discusses this truth with Werdegast:

> You say your soul was killed and that you have been dead all these years. And what of me? Did we not both die here in Marmaros fifteen years ago? Are we any less victims of war than those whose bodies were torn asunder? Are we not both the living dead?

In a 1970 interview printed in *Film Culture* and reprinted in the book *Kings of the B's* (1975), Ulmer spoke of this theme. When Peter Bogdanovich asked him where he got the idea of a castle being built on a graveyard, Ulmer responded:

> "That came out many years before. I met at that time Gustav Meyrinck, the man who wrote *Golem* as a novel. Meyrinck was one of these strange Prague Jews, like Kafka, who was very much tied up in the mystic Talmudic background. We had a lot of discussions, and Meyrinck at that time was contemplating a play based upon Doumont, which was a French fortress the Germans shelled to pieces during the First World War. There were some survivors who didn't come out for years. And the commander was a strange Euripides figure who went crazy three years later when he was brought back to Paris, because he had walked on that mountain of bodies. And I thought it was a subject that was quite important. And that feeling was in the air in the twenties. . . . I wanted to write a novel really, because I did not believe the literature after the war and during the war, on both sides. In Germany and in England, [war] was very much the heroic thing. . . . I couldn't believe that. Therefore I took two men who knew each other and who fought their private war during the time that capitalism flourished. I thought it was quite a story stylistically. I had a wonderful cameraman [John Mescall], and [producer Carl Laemmle] Junior let me do the sets and everything at the same time. . . . It was very much out of my Bauhaus period."

In Germany, Ulmer had designed and helped build mammoth expressionistic sets for theater director Max Reinhardt, and had worked at UFA as production designer ("which meant the designing of every angle [because] our sets were built in perspective with rising and sloping floors") for such camera-conscious film directors as Fritz Lang and F. W. Murnau. He came to the United States in the mid-twenties and was employed as art designer and set and model builder for Carl Laemmle, Sr., at Universal. Ulmer again worked with Murnau, when Murnau came to America, William Wyler, Erich von Stroheim, and Cecil B. De Mille, among others. He was also given a chance to direct, beginning with silent Westerns and graduating to sound features, *Mr. Broadway* (1933), starring Ed Sullivan, and an anti-syphilis film, *Damaged Lives* (1933).

His next film, *The Black Cat*, was the first of his works as director that allowed him to make proper use of his set design experience. He collaborated with Universal's resident art director, Charles D. Hall, and came up with Poelzig's Bauhaus mansion, with shining white floors, walls, and ceilings, white furniture and curtains—a far cry from Hall's gloomy, Gothic interiors in Universal's other horror films like *Frankenstein* (1931) and *The Old Dark House* (1932). One could imagine Astaire and Rogers dancing through Poelzig's Art Deco living room area and up those fancy stairs. It's a house that is out of tune with the dark fort below and the figure of evil who resides in it, who wears black robes, black pajamas (he dresses as rarely as Hugh Hefner), black slippers, and black lipstick—Poelzig has black cats, performs a Black Mass, for which he provides his guests with black robes, reads a book with a black cover; and when he goes out on his balcony, the trees and sky are nightmarishly black. (We know what his favorite color is.) I like Ulmer and Hall's long, winding staircase that leads to the fort area—although I'm sure actors hated doing more than one take of climbing scenes—and the revolving room concept. But the fort area doesn't compare to the modernistic house. It's quite bare. Poelzig explains to Werdegast that the guns are gone, but military charts still hang on the wall. Wouldn't it have been more interesting if the charts were gone (how useless they are) and the guns remained?

The Black Cat is one of the most visually interesting horror films of the period. Credit goes both to Ulmer, who used tricks from his silent days, and to John Mescall, who would do the exceptional cinematography for *Bride of Frankenstein* (1935). There are some eerie close-ups of Karloff (what a hairstyle!) and Lugosi, alone and together; and erotic close-ups of misty-eyed Poelzig as he lies over the entranced Karen and looks down into her face, and of Peter lying on top of Joan, kissing her injured shoulder. There is an effective use of shadows—the flaying is conveyed by shadows on the wall. And there are three extremely haunting silent passages: Poelzig rising in his veiled bed, as if he were a vampire sitting up in his coffin, upon the arrival of the guests; the satanists' arrival, the Poelzig-led procession, and their donning of robes (an image that recalls German horror classics); Ulmer and Mescall's use of a subjective camera and dissolves to convey Poelzig and Werdegast's "deathwalk" through the fort.

The subjective camera scene is the most artistic moment in the film, the specific moment that reveals how vast is the talent (director, cameraman, set designer) behind the camera, the moment that injects class into the preposterous proceedings. Other scenes specifically designed to give the film class are truly silly: Poelzig playing classical music on the organ, Poelzig and Werdegast engaging in the most famous cinema chess game prior to *The Seventh Seal* (1956)—more interesting is how Poelzig (is Karloff improvising?) twice cuts off Peter's protests by insisting the game must continue—Poelzig delivering his Black Mass in Latin. But such scenes don't detract from the film—they contribute to the charm. They also greatly enhance the intended overly dramatic nature of the film. Remember this is a film where the pretty heroine screams and faints, and faints and screams, and the bland hero (Manners is well cast) spends most of his time knocked unconscious and manages only one aggressive act—he fatally shoots Werdegast, the one person trying to help (no wonder Werdegast calls him "fool"). It's a film with *two* mute servants. And it's a film where a man marries, murders, and embalms his friend's wife, then marries his stepdaughter and kills her, too, and then is skinned alive by his father-in-law.

Of course, the greatest delight for viewers is watching Karloff (*Boris* is not used in the titles) and Lugosi in their first film together. It was Ulmer's idea to bring the stars of *Frankenstein* and *Dracula* (1931) together; the presence of Lugosi caused him to pad the Werdegast role and to switch the locale from Italy to Hungary. Ulmer told Bogdanovich:

> "[Karloff] was very charming . . . my biggest job was to keep him in the part, because he laughed at himself. Not the Hungarian, of course. You had to cut away from Lugosi continuously, to cut him down. . . . One of the nicest scenes, I had with [Karloff], he lies in bed next to the daughter of Lugosi, and the young couple rings down at the door, and he gets up and you see him the first time in costume, in that modernistic set. I explained the scene to him and he said, 'Aren't you ashamed to do a thing like that—that has nothing to do with acting?' So I told him to be nice and do it, and he never took himself seriously—he got into bed, we got ready to shoot, and he got up, he turned to the camera, after he put his shoes on, and said 'Boo!' Everytime I had him come in by a door, he would open the door and say, 'Here comes the heavy . . .' He was a very, very lovely man."

Karloff's deadpan, tongue-in-cheek performance is perfectly balanced by Lugosi, whose early dignified manner soon gives way to his singular brand of histrionics. It's a joy listening to conversations between two actors with such different accents and speech patterns. As Everson writes: "Dialogue in the film is relatively sparse, but the lines conceived for Karloff and Lugosi, quite apart from theatrical bravura, seem almost to have been story-boarded to take advantage of their accents, and to extract the maximum from those lines via skillful cutting." Karloff is the superior actor and he mesmerizes us with his stare and his philosophical discourse. But here, as in *The Raven*, when *he* assumes the villain role, Lugosi holds his own. For who but Lugosi could get away with "It's after all better to be frightened than to be crushed" or the picture's most famous line, "Superstitious, perhaps—*baloney*, perhaps not!"

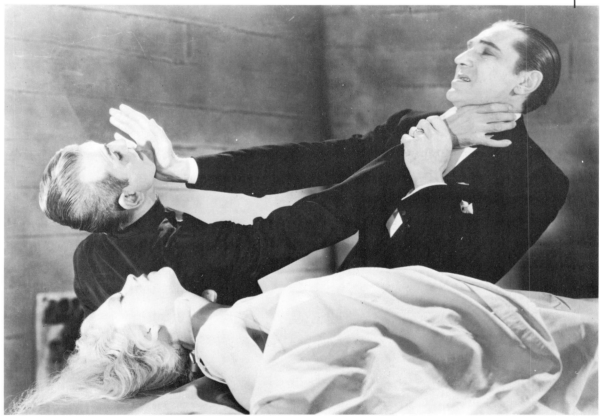

The escalating battle between Werdegast and Poelzig, played by the horror cinema's two greatest stars, Bela Lugosi and Boris Karloff. Top: In the most famous cinema chess game prior to The Seventh Seal, *they play for Joan's life.* Middle: *They fight next to the body of Karen, whom Poelzig has murdered.* Bottom: *Werdegast informs the skinny Poelzig that he is about to be skinned alive.*

Blade Runner

1982 Color Ladd Company in association with Sir Run Run Shaw

Director: Ridley Scott
Producer: Michael Deeley
Screenplay: Hampton Fancher and David Peoples
From the novel *Do Androids Dream of Electric Sheep?* by Philip K. Dick
Cinematography: Jordan Cronenweth

Special Visual Effects: Douglas Trumbull, with Richard Yuricich and David Dryer
Production Designer: Lawrence G. Paull
Visual Futurist: Syd Mead
Music: Vangelis
Editor: Terry Rawlings
Running Time: 118/122 minutes

Cast: Harrison Ford (Rick Deckard), Rutger Hauer (Roy Batty), Sean Young (Rachael), Edward James Olmos (Gaff), M. Emmet Walsh (Harry Bryant), Daryl Hannah (Pris), William Sanderson (J. F. Sebastian), Brion James (Leon), Joe Turkel (Tyrell), Joanna Cassidy (Zhora), James Hong (Chew), Morgan Paull (Holden), Hy Pyke (Taffey Lewis).

Synopsis: The sun doesn't shine on the overcrowded, rubble-strewn, neon-lit streets of cold Los Angeles in 2019. It is blocked out by the heavy (acid?) rain and huge, grimy buildings. There are few public works; crime is rampant. Tyrell, head of the city's replicant-producing Tyrell Corporation, is one of the few rich people who haven't vacated unhealthy earth for an off-world colony. Through genetic engineering, he produces replicants to serve as slaves in off-world exploration and colonization. He intends his replicants to be "more human than human."

Four supersophisticated Nexus 6 replicants have come back to Earth, where they are illegal and hunted by human detectives called blade runners. Roy Batty, Pris, Leon, and Zhora massacred 23 humans and stole a shuttle in outer space. Since such replicants may in time develop human emotions, they are designed to die in four years. Their time is almost up. One replicant, Leon, has infiltrated the Tyrell Corporation as a worker. Blade runner Holden gives him a Voight-Kampff test, with questions designed to indicate his level of empathy. The machine reveals he has none, indicating he is a replicant. Leon shoots Holden. So heavy-drinking, depressed ex–blade runner Rick Deckard is ordered by police captain Bryant to return to work and track down the replicants. He hates this assignment—it's why he quit in the first place.

Tyrell asks Deckard to use the machine on a young female worker, Rachael. Deckard is very attracted to her and is upset to discover she is a replicant. Because she has been implanted with memories and given fake photos of a nonexistent past, she only now learns she is a replicant. Replicants aren't supposed to be emotional, but she is heartbroken. Once Deckard felt prejudice toward replicants, but killing them now depresses him. And he finds himself falling in love with Rachael. Deckard tracks down Zhora, who works as a snake dancer. She is strong and almost kills him. She flees. He shoots her in the back. Leon, who demands to know how much longer he'll live, almost beats Deckard to death. Rachael kills Leon. Deckard and Rachael make love.

Pris flirts her way into the apartment of simple Sebastian, who works for Tyrell as a genetic engineer. Sebastian takes Batty, her lover, to Tyrell's luxurious apartment. Batty demands Tyrell extend the replicant life span, because he feels he is dying. Tyrell can do nothing. Batty squashes his head. He then kills Sebastian.

Deckard enters Sebastian's apartment. Pris flies through the air and almost crushes him with her powerful thighs. He shoots her, and she dies in agony. Batty arrives. He is grieved by Pris's death. He chases the terrified Deckard all over the building. He breaks Deckard's knuckles. Deckard leaps to another building. He holds on by his fingers. Batty says, "Quite an experience to live in fear, isn't it? That's what it's like to be a slave." Batty pulls him to safety. Deckard watches Batty die. He thinks Batty saved him because he loved *life*, anybody's life.

Policeman Gaff, who wants Deckard's job, reminds Deckard he must kill Rachael. Yet Deckard discovers that Gaff didn't kill her when he had the chance; after all she had only a short time to live anyway. Deckard and Rachael flee to the uninhabited country. Tyrell had told Deckard that she has no fixed termination date.

Ridley Scott's ambitious, $15 million adaptation of Philip K. Dick's *Do Androids Dream of Electric Sheep?* flopped with critics and was a box-office bust when first released, but it has since emerged as a cult favorite, midnight movie staple, and perhaps the first "thinking person's science fiction film" since *2001: A Space Odyssey* (1968). Too often we hear people claim that a particular film improves on second viewing, but it's definitely true with *Blade Runner*. On second viewing, the awesome visuals no longer overwhelm the story and themes, as critics had complained. Now we can understand that the visuals (particularly those that depict the city in the year 2019) help tell the story and advance the themes. While the slow pacing and Deckard's *noir*-style narration were initially off-putting, we now realize they are essential for helping create the picture's somber, melancholy, memories-lost ambience and, because Deckard sounds cheerier than his brooding character in his story (remember this is his flashback), for confirming Deckard has undergone a positive change since the action we witness took place. (His rosier attitude is the result of the action we witness.) And on second viewing we can take delight in the marvelous cast—what faces and bodies!—and their fascinating characters. Harrison Ford's narration is weakly delivered, but he has strong screen presence; Sean Young will steal your heart; Rutger Hauer, Daryl Hannah, and Joanna Cassidy are the cleverest, best-looking, and deadliest "bad guy" gang in recent memory.

In Dick's novel, Deckard is an active android bounty hunter in San Francisco, after a nuclear war. He is (unhappily) married, not divorced, and his wife lays a guilt trip on him for his line of work. Like everyone else, Rick adheres to Mercerism, a quasi-religion that I make out as a celebration of being human; constantly watches TV comedian Buster Friendly; takes artificial brain stimulation to alter moods; and dreams of owning one of the few remaining real animals on earth (fake animals are the next best thing). The androids he tracks down are without the sympathetic qualities of their film counterparts. They have no feelings for each other or other living things. They represent pure evil. The book's Rachael is more sympathetic than the rogue androids, yet she too is cold—she spitefully kills Deckard's prize goat (to compensate for his murdering her comrades?). Rachael looks exactly like Pris, as they are the same android model. That's why Deckard worries that he won't be able to shoot Pris. There is no subplot having to do with androids trying to convince their maker (Rosen, rather than Tyrell) to increase their life span. Mercerism proves to be a sham; Buster Friendly turns out to be an android; Deckard discovers a parallel police department run by androids and senses that he—and everyone else—may be an android, because there is no longer a clear distinction between man and android.

The origin of the novel was Dick's research of Nazis for his book *The Man in the High Castle*. In the late forties he had come across prime Nazi documents, including the

Blade runner Deckard chases a replicant through the mazelike L.A. of 2019, on streets that are overcrowded, unhealthy, and surrounded by huge buildings that are covered with electrical advertising.

diary of an S.S. man stationed in Warsaw. In an interview published in *Starlog* (February 1982), he told James Van Hise:

> "I still remember the one line he had in there: 'We are kept awake at night by the cries of starving children.' . . . [T]hat influenced me. I thought, there is amongst us something that is a bipedal humanoid, morphologically identical to the human being but which is not human. It is not human to complain that starving children are keeping you awake. And there . . . was born my idea that within our species is a bifurcation, a dichotomy between the truly human and that which mimics the truly human."

Herb Jaffe optioned the book and Robert Jaffe wrote a screenplay in 1973 that Dick claimed "turned it into a comedy—a spoof, along the lines of *Get Smart*. Everybody was a clown and it was full of smart ass remarks." Dick was relieved when Jaffe's option lapsed. In December 1980, Hampton Fancher wrote the first script for what would turn out to be the Ridley Scott movie and Dick was as dissatisfied with it as he'd been with Jaffe's. Terming it "Philip Marlowe meets *The Stepford Wives*," he wrote an angry essay for *SelecTV Guide*, criticizing SF films like Ridley Scott's *Alien* (1980) for using special effects instead of

a story, and insinuating *Blade Runner* would fall into the same category, a simplistic shoot-'em-up with fantastic Douglas Trumbull special effects. He wasn't pleased that Scott had told an interviewer that he had found the book too difficult to finish. Dick's attitude toward the project changed drastically when he read David Peoples's February 1981 rewrite. Peoples maintained his draft had been inspired by Fancher's, but Dick insisted it was faithful to the book and—he was correct—"in some ways Peoples improved over the book. . . . Each reinforces the other. If you start out with the book, the screenplay adds material to that, and if you start out with the screenplay, the book adds material to that, so they're beautifully symmetrical." Dick believed Peoples's shooting script contained his two major themes. In *Starlog*:

> "The first is what constitutes the essential human being and how do we distinguish and define the essential human being from that which only masquerades as human. . . . And the second theme is the tragic theme that if you fight evil, you will wind up becoming evil, and that's the condition of life. . . . Deckard, to kill the replicants . . . is brutalized and dehumanized. . . . You have Deckard becoming more and more dehumanized and the replicants becoming more and more human, and at the end they

 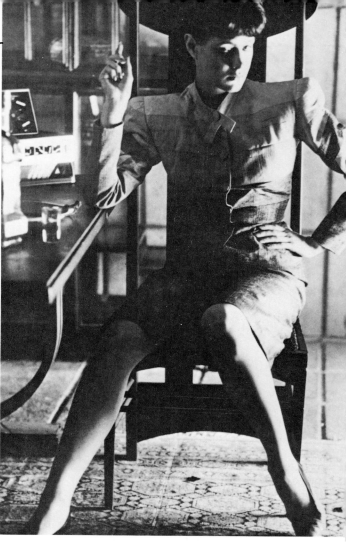

In the novel, replicants Rachael and Pris are the same model and look exactly alike. In the film, they are played by two upcoming actresses, the brunette Sean Young (right) *and the blond Daryl Hannah. It's interesting that such sensual actresses were cast as androids.*

meet and the distinction is gone. But this fusion of Deckard and the replicants is a *tragedy.* This is not a victory where the replicants become humanized and there is some victory by humanity over inhumanity. This is horrifying because he is now as they are. So the theme of the novel is completely and essentially retained."

I only disagree with the last statement because the film replicants turn out to be sympathetic, not pure evil.

Because Dick died suddenly before the release of the film, it's difficult to guess how he would have approved of the final result. Disastrous screenings in Denver and Dallas—the audiences expected a Harrison Ford film along the lines of *Star Wars* (1977) and *Raiders of the Lost Ark* (1981)—caused Scott to make changes and, in some cases, revert back to Fancher's script. The controversial narration and an upbeat ending were added. At the very least, Dick would have approved of the look of the film. When I interviewed Ridley Scott for *Omni's ScreenFlights/ ScreenFantasies* (1984), he said Dick once visited the set and looked at Trumbull's just-completed special effects work:

"Dick was more than delighted—I think he was stunned by the look of our environment. He said it was exactly how he had envisioned the world with which we were dealing. *Blade Runner* was a difficult project to conceive because it is set only about thirty-five years from now, in a 'tangible' future rather than the obscure future of *Alien.* . . . I think that the mistake a lot of futuristic films make when they attempt short leaps forward in time is that they devastate whole cities and erect hokey-looking utopias. Things wouldn't work that way. . . . As we move farther and farther into the future, the probability is that the construction of new buildings will diminish . . . and the constant repairing, shoring up, and modernization of older architecture will begin to take on a rather retrofitted look. Our vision was really of a clogged world, where you get the sense of a city on overload, where things may stop at any time. . . . Everything is old or badly serviced, and the bureaucratic system running the city is totally disorganized. One of the few things in fine order is advertising. I expect by this time that billboards and electric signs will be everywhere."

Raymond Durgnant wrote in the May 1983 issue of *American Film*:

Highly painterly is the only way to describe the look of *Blade Runner*, which sets out to give its fantastic world an intricate texture of Hi-Gloss and Technosleaze, of glitter and haze, rain and neon, crumbling stonework and torn body stockings. Director Ridley Scott has described the care taken to push the cityscape beyond mere correctness, and to achieve a kind of visual charge, which reminded me of the astonishing paintings of Richard Estes. Indeed, the film is so dominated by painted mattes and detail animations—by multiple opticals, model miniatures, and invented shapes—of cars, toys, megastructures, and a weirdly bloated sun (painted) that it is very largely just a painted-and-sculpted construction.

No picture since Fritz Lang's *Metropolis* (1927) has presented such a compelling, forbidding vision of the future. Conceptual artist Syd Mead and production designer Lawrence G. Paull created an overly crowded, hazy city, where (acid?) rain falls constantly, electric advertising—for Atari, Coca-Cola, TDK, RCA, Bulova, Schlitz, Budweiser, Kinney shoes, etc.—covers tenement windows and walls, factory chimneys spew flames and fumes into the air, and police spinners and blimps—with aural advertisements for off-world travel—fly about. Mammoth, pyramid-shaped buildings dominate the skyline. Industrial tubing and pipe fixtures are in plain sight. Water covers landings in buildings as well as the streets. Bright strobe lights repeatedly shine through open windows. A mass of humanity—Asians comprise a large percentage of the population—marches impersonally through the always-dark streets; there is much activity in the Red Light district and the animoid black market. Faceless bike riders whiz by; bands of scavengers emerge from the shadows. Rich people live far above in the high rises, with security systems fit for fortresses. There are violent magazines (*KILL*) on newsstands, pay videophones, extravagantly priced parking meters. Everything is impersonal, old, and unhealthy. As Mead told critic/screenwriter Ed Naha, present-day New York served as the model, just as it had inspired Lang in the 1920s: "We drew a profile of a city taking the two World Trade Towers as the norm. We figured that, as you went up higher, the street level as we know it today would become some sort of massive service alley sequestered beneath these enormous megastructures that would, in turn, give the streets a sort of subterranean sewer look." (So those people who walk on the foul streets are literally of the "low-life" variety.)

In an article Mead wrote for *Omni's ScreenFlights/ ScreenFantasies*, he explained the thinking that went behind his design work for the film:

The city of 2019 was getting progressively dense. Buildings were over three thousand feet high, with older buildings of ten or twenty stories being used as bases for the entire superstructure. Cables and tubes, delivering air and removing waste, would climb along the outsides of old buildings. The street level would be a service alley to these towering megastructures. Street level fixtures such as fire hydrants, parking meters, and the noodle bar where Deckard eats, were, again, all conceived using the social theory of *retrofitted utilization*. Ridley Scott, Ivor Powell (the associate producer), Lawrence G. Paull, and I

Joanna Cassidy as Zhora, in her exotic snake-dance outfit. I asked Scott if he cast the beautiful Cassidy, Young, and Hannah as his female replicants so that men in his audience would be attracted to their characters and the distinction between human and android would be diminished. His simple reply: "If you're going to make female replicants [in the future], why make them ugly?"

developed the concept. Because in 2019 there was so much energy being devoted to off-world activity, for which the replicants were made, the consumer base wasn't getting much attention. This meant that the population was very actively collecting bits and pieces of add-on layers to make their original articles work. Today in many Third World countries you'll find . . . retrofitted machine constructions that bear superficial resemblances to the original articles, but they've been overlaid by so many add-ons that they've taken on a style of their own. We labeled that style, which influenced the look of the film, "retro-deco."

Indeed, what's so frightening about what we see in the picture—the environment, the technology, the clothes and makeup, genetically produced human and animal duplicates—is that it seems to be a logical future for us. (Only the off-colony exodus seems rushed.) In this cautionary tale, we are presented with much from our own present and past to remind us that what we see is the end result of our unfortunate progression. The colossal, sloping high-rise buildings are patterned after Egyptian pyramids or, suggests SF writer Robert Silverberg, "Aztec temples or Babylonian ziggurats"; the columns at the Tyrell Corporation are more suitable for a Greek or Roman palace; Trumbull designed Tyrell's bedroom as if it were the pope's in the Vatican. The setting used for Deckard's cluttered, claustrophobic, low-ceilinged apartment is a Frank Lloyd Wright house built in the 1920s in the Los Feliz hills; the police department is located in what is L.A.'s 45+-year-old Union Station—a set Scott liked because of "the art deco and neo-Fascist architecture." Deckard's favorite noodle bar was designed by Paull, who wanted it to be an outdoor version of the White Castle hamburger joints he loved as a kid in the forties. Characters dress in outfits that mix future, present, and past. Policemen wear uniforms that combine the style of the forties with projections of the future. Pedestrians look like they come from countless eras, from every possible country. There are even Hare Krishnas, as well as young men with New Wave hairstyles and dark glasses. Deckard and Sebastian dress in what appear to be, in the year 2019, functional clothes that are long out of style—those clothes that are in fashion are either too expensive or, judging from the department store mannequins, kinky. Zhora looks ready for an S&M party. Pris looks like a cross between a New Wave punk and a hooker on New York's 8th Avenue. Rachael's stunning black suit, with each stripe consisting of a separate piece of silk, and with the wide shoulders and trim waist, is appropriate for heroines of forties *film noir*. With her hair tied back, dark brows and eyeshadow, watery eyes, red lips, perfect skin, and swirling cigarette smoke serving as a veil, beautiful Sean Young's Rachael is supposed to be like those mysterious movie heroines who, the heroes had to decide, were either completely honest and loyal or

Roy Batty (left) *and Pris act friendly toward Sebastian so that he'll take Batty to see Tyrell.*

"inhuman," with blood that ran ice cold. As much as the wet, dark, neon-lit streets and claustrophobic imagery (hypnotically filmed by Jordan Cronenweth), Rachael is a visual reminder that we are watching classic *film noir* transported to the future. Deckard may have a futuristic job—blade runner—but he is the classic disillusioned, morally ambivalent detective hero, complete with hard-boiled narration. Scott told me:

> "When we first meet Deckard, he is already thinking of [permanently] giving up his job as professional exterminator. The job was in fact getting to him, as it did to, say, Philip Marlowe. His attitude toward his profession had already discolored his vision of the world and affected his attitude toward himself. As in classic detective stories, his background is suggested by innuendo rather than fact; but what I wanted to do at the beginning was show a man who wanted to change his whole way of life and was in a way trying to find some kind of absolution or, maybe, a conscience."

The reviews of *Blade Runner* that most annoyed me when it was released were those that claimed the film had no theme and had such poorly drawn characters that it appeared the replicants were more human than Deckard. Somehow there were *many* critics who failed to comprehend that it was by intention that the replicants came across as more human than Deckard and that, in fact, *this* was the missing theme they were looking for. Remember how critics who reviewed *2001* thought they were making a clever observation when they asserted the HAL 9000 computer seemed more human than the human characters? Of course, this was Stanley Kubrick's intention. Keir Dullea's Bowman doesn't regain his humanity and display human emotions until he battles and defeats the machine, reestablishing man's supremacy over machine (thereby qualifying to meet his gods). At the beginning of *Blade Runner*, Deckard has withdrawn into the wave of impersonal humanity on the L.A. streets. He is, as his ex-wife complained, a "cold fish." He suppresses his (human) feelings with alcohol and a heavy dose of guilt for having killed replicants. It's through his interaction with the supersophisticated, lifelike replicants during the course of the film that he regains his emotions—if a replicant can have emotions, then so can a blade runner—and establishes himself as the earth's one *male* human being: His ability to love is rekindled by Rachael—Ford and Young didn't get along but their seduction scene is incredibly erotic—and he learns to appreciate life because of Batty's generous decision to let him live. (Having been taught to love by Deckard, and having learned from him that she has a finite but indeterminate life span, Rachael, though a replicant, evolves into the one *female* human being.) It is fortunate for Deckard that the replicants he engages have been endowed with human qualities that humans no longer have in these inhuman times—it is only through interaction with them that he becomes as human as they are. In Dick's book the replicants are evil, so when Deckard becomes like them, he becomes evil—but in the film, through sincere, sensitive Rachael and Batty's gracious final act, we realize that if Deckard becomes like these replicants it is a positive

Deckard's human life is in the hands of angry replicant Roy Batty.

step. Indeed, Deckard may be a replicant, as Scott believes, but he at least qualifies to carry humanity's torch.

Blade Runner deals with the arrogance of the rich, who would literally trash their home world, turn it into a barely habitable ghetto, and simply fly away to the off-colony suburbs and leave their mess for the poor. And like those who settled earth's New World in the seventeenth century, they expect slave labor. That gap is filled by replicants, "niggers" of the future who are considered less valuable than animals, have no legal rights, and, like the light bulb to which insensitive Tyrell equates Batty, are not built to last so that new ones can be sold. Man is so arrogant that he would create these genetically human androids, give them more intelligence and athletic proficiency than humans and the ability to develop the exact emotions of man, yet still consider himself superior to them. He is so arrogant that he assumes such creations would be satisfied being slaves to man. And he is so insensitive that he doesn't bother to provide the replicants with a life span that compares to that of human beings, much less the reasonable life span man has been denied by God. Smug Tyrell actually thinks Batty should be grateful for his four years of

existence. (Of course, we wouldn't be happy being born into our prime of life knowing we had only four years left.) He is like a slave owner who, because he hasn't killed his slave as the law permits, doesn't understand why the slave wants to kill him; he is like a Frankenstein who doesn't understand why his monster has returned to kill his maker, the person who provided him with a hellish life. On the other hand, Deckard is like a man hired to track down runaway slaves in pre–Civil War America who becomes enlightened. He comes to realize that replicants are not only equal to humans, but are everything humans should be. So are they human? When Rachael flees his apartment, he tells her, "I've had *people* walk out on me before"; when he kills Zhora he refers to her as a *woman*. Disposing of Batty, Zhora, Leon, and Pris becomes for Deckard like killing four human murderers—if they hadn't committed heinous crimes, he surely couldn't do it and live with himself. (He could never harm Rachael.) Their crimes aren't forgivable but are understandable considering their fears and impossible situation. So trying to kill them is more traumatic—surely it helps to know they would die soon anyway—and painful than Bowman's dismantling of the human-like HAL in *2001*.

Scott intended his film to be "a heavy metal comic strip." But the best scenes in *Blade Runner* are real and strike emotional chords. My favorite moments are slow and overwhelmingly sad: In Deckard's apartment, teary-eyed Rachael, having learned her own photos are counterfeit, looks at Deckard's collection and wonders if they're real (Scott doubts they are); she sees if she can really play the piano ("You play beautifully," Deckard assures her) or if she previously played only in false memories. These scenes create instant nostalgia, like walking into an elderly person's parlor and seeing an entire life on display around you. How important are memories (even fake ones) and how vacant are lives without them. Even bad memories are essential; as Batty eloquently laments, "I've seen things you people wouldn't believe. . . . All those moments will be lost in time, like tears and rain." Like Deckard, we learn to respect life, and we are sad when the lives of the replicants are snuffed out . . . along with their (fake and real) memories. Scott properly treats their deaths with respect and gives them dignity. It is thrilling watching Deckard battle Joanna Cassidy's lovely yet lethal, funny but fierce Zhora (in this case, sex and violence do mix), Pris (Daryl Hannah almost steals the film with her gymnastic fighting), and terrifying Batty—he doesn't seem competent against such foes—but again, one can better appreciate the sorrowful moments after battle, when we contemplate the unfair lives to which Tyrell sentenced the replicants. No humans on this earth would do it for their own, but Batty kisses the dead Pris on the lips and uses his tongue to push hers back into her mouth so her beauty is restored. Then he almost kills Deckard, but rescues him instead. It's a wonderful, touching moment, complete with a flying white dove of peace and powerful, haunting music by Vangelis (who composed a brilliant score). This is the ultimate peaceful gesture in the science fiction cinema between man and machine. Along with Rachael's decision to go away with Deckard, it gives us hope that we can live in harmony.

Blue Velvet

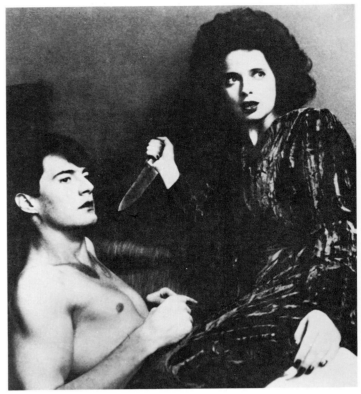

A knock on the door only temporarily interrupts the bizarre relationship of Jeffrey and Dorothy.

1986 Color   De Laurentiis Entertainment Group, Inc.
Director: David Lynch
Producer: Fred Caruso
Screenplay: David Lynch
Cinematography: Frederick Elmes
Music: Angelo Badalamenti
Editor: Duwayne Dunham
Running Time: 120 minutes

Cast: Kyle MacLachlan (Jeffrey Beaumont), Isabella Rossellini (Dorothy Vallens), Dennis Hopper (Frank Booth), Laura Dern (Sandy Williams), George Dickerson (Detective Williams), Hope Lange (Mrs. Williams), Dean Stockwell (Ben), Priscilla Pointer (Mrs. Beaumont), Frances Bay (Aunt Barbara), Jack Harvey (Mr. Beaumont), Brad Dourif, Jack Nance.

Synopsis: When his father suffers a debilitating stroke, college student Jeffrey Beaumont returns to Lumberton. He stays in his nice house with his mother and Aunt Barbara and works in his father's hardware store. While in the fields, he discovers a human ear. He takes it to Detective Williams, who is secretive about the case this severed ear figures in. Williams's pretty teenage daughter, Sandy, tells the curious Jeffrey she overheard her father speaking about a singer named Dorothy Vallens. Sandy has a boyfriend, Mike, but is attracted to Jeffrey. And he thinks she's neat, too. She agrees to help him investigate.

Dorothy lets Jeffrey into her apartment when he says he's an exterminator. While she talks with a man in a yellow jacket, Jeffrey steals an extra set of keys. That night, Jeffrey and Sandy watch Dorothy sing "Blue Velvet" at the Slow Club. They return to her building. Jeffrey snoops inside her apartment. Still in his car, Sandy beeps when Dorothy returns. But Jeffrey doesn't hear her signal. When Dorothy walks in, he hides in the closet. He watches her undress. She catches him and threatens him with a knife. She forces him to strip and fondles him. When there is a knock, she hides him in the closet. Jeffrey sees Frank Booth enter. He is an angry man who curses continuously, and inhales gas from a plastic mask. They have brutal sex. She enjoys when he slaps her, but she is obviously frightened of him. When Frank leaves, Dorothy, who insists she's not crazy, wants Jeffrey to make love to her and hit her. He wants to help her, not hurt her. She is depressed. Jeffrey deduces that Frank has kidnapped her husband, Don, and little son, Donnie, and is forcing her to do his bidding so they won't be killed.

Jeffrey follows Frank and three cohorts to his apartment building. He takes photos of Frank and the man in the yellow jacket and, later, the man in the yellow jacket and a well-dressed, mustachioed man with a briefcase—not far from where a drug dealer was just murdered.

Jeffrey returns to Dorothy. They make love. She convinces him to hit her. This upsets him afterward. Frank and his men arrive as Jeffrey is leaving. They take him to the apartment of effeminate Ben, who is involved with Frank's drug dealings. Then they drive to a deserted area of town. Frank puts on lipstick and kisses Jeffrey. Then he savagely beats him up. Jeffrey gives his photos to Detective Williams and promises to stay off the case. He learns that the man in the yellow jacket, Gordon, is Williams's detective partner. Jeffrey and Sandy go to a party. When they return the nude, beaten, and crazed Dorothy stands on his porch. Sandy is heartbroken to learn that Jeffrey has been sleeping with her. But she forgives him. After accompanying Dorothy to the hospital, Jeffrey goes to her apartment. He's on his own because Williams is off leading a raid on Frank's building. Jeffrey discovers the bodies of Gordon and Dorothy's husband in the apartment. The mustachioed man enters. He is Frank. Jeffrey takes Gordon's gun and hides in the closet. When Frank opens the door to kill him, Jeffrey shoots him between the eyes.

On a bright, sunny day, Jeffrey and Sandy have lunch with their parents and Aunt Barbara. They marvel at the returning robins, symbols of love. In a park, Dorothy hugs her son.

"It's a strange world, isn't it?"

Easily the most controversial film of the decade, *Blue Velvet* has stirred heated debates and polarized critics like no film since *A Clockwork Orange* (1971) and *Last Tango in Paris* (1973), other works that drew a disturbing correlation between sex, power, and violence. Like Kubrick and Bertolucci, screenwriter-director David Lynch was applauded for his astonishing artistry and unflinching determination to get across a bold, unsanitized personal vision in an era of safe assembly-line films (he accepted a salary cut from Dino De Laurentiis in exchange for total control), yet was attacked by many viewers who felt his personal vision was so dark and disgusting that it should have been kept to himself. They had trouble respecting a film that came into being because, as Lynch told *Cineaste* (March 1987), he "always wanted to sneak into a girl's room and watch her into the night and that, maybe at one point or another, I would see something that would be a clue to a murder mystery." Because *Blue Velvet* is both *so* uncompromisingly weird and *so* well made, it was destined for cult status on the level of Lynch's *Eraserhead* (1977), the bizarre independent venture he made before going commercial with *The Elephant Man* (1980) and *Dune* (1984). But unlike *Eraserhead*, it became a box-office hit before it played midnights, after it was unexpectedly embraced by those mainstream newspaper/TV/radio critics who usually feign outrage against any film they fear might offend their readers/viewers/listeners. It was voted Best Film by the National Society of Critics; Woody Allen regarded it his favorite film of the year, over his own *Hannah and Her Sisters*. It received so many friendly notices—even its detractors admitted it was a one-of-a-kind film, with remarkable wide-screen imagery—that many unsuspecting viewers who detest screen sex (particularly the kinky kind), graphic violence, and vulgarity, went to theaters expecting a Hitchcock-like thriller and left in a nauseous daze. (I warned my parents just in time!) One shudders to think of some viewers being subjected to the repellent acts and language of Dennis Hopper's demented Frank Booth. I don't find *Blue Velvet* mean-spirited, like many contemporary films—I don't think Lynch gets a kick out of Frank being so vile—but at times it is terribly unpleasant. The ugliness heightens the film's impact but it also tends to cut down on one's enjoyment. I agree with critic David Denby, of *New York*: "*Blue Velvet* is a work of art, but it's not an exhilarating experience."

As *everyone* agreed, the picture has a brilliant opening, with Lynch presenting a red (roses), white (picket fence), and blue (skies) America that is so spookily real that it is unreal. Just as one would expect in Middle America, mother is in her lovely house drinking coffee and watching television, father is leisurely watering his beautifully manicured green lawn, a crossing guard is directing schoolchildren, and a red fire engine, with a waving fireman and a dalmatian you just know is named Sparky, rolls by in ghostly slow motion, as if it has been stuck in space and time since the forties. We are in Lumberton, a self-contained, out-of-synch, dream-logic town that exists only in an alternate America, along the lines of the too-real Americas found in *Blood Simple* (1984), *Gremlins* (1984), *Trouble in Mind* (1985), *True Stories* (1986), and *Little Shop of Horrors* (1986). Everything is so perfect on the surface, that you can sense evil brewing underground; you can feel the approaching explosion, the American dream about to burst. Mr. Beaumont's hose becomes tangled—a snake is loose in the Garden of Eden—and he has a seizure. As he lies on his back clutching the hose, the neighbor dog props itself on his belly and snaps at the water shooting skyward, and a diapered toddler walks about alone, like a silly figure you discover in the corner of a *Mad* magazine frame. What a shot! Perverted Norman Rockwell! While things are topsy-turvy above ground, Frederick Elmes's camera dives into the grass and, at the roots, finds a swarm of ravenous black bugs. It is another startling image, illustrating one of Lynch's two main themes: If you search beneath the surface of idyllic, tree-lined Norman Rockwell America you'll find a terrifying, violent, soulless world. Lynch's scientist father researched disease in trees, and now we sense disease is infesting Lumberton. This unsettling image of scary black bugs is our introduction to the insect motif that is so important to the picture. It is Lynch's intention to present his villains, Frank and the other criminals of Lumberton, as the "less-than-animal" human equivalents of insects (*ugly* insects—not ladybugs or butterflies, etc.). Just as bugs emerge at night and run rampant, depraved criminals rule Lumberton once the sun goes down.

With his father in the hospital, capable of making only inhuman (insect?) noises, Jeffrey Beaumont (a fine off-center performance by Kyle MacLachlan, star of *Dune*) returns home from college (although I doubt there's a real

world outside Lumberton and that Jeffrey doesn't just disappear when he goes away). As it is for Kevin McCarthy's Miles Binnell when his nurse calls him back to Santa Mira in *Invasion of the Body Snatchers* (1955), Jeffrey finds his town has changed in his absence, that evil has surfaced, that there is a sense of paranoia in the air, that *everyone* is secretive. Only in Jeffrey's case, the sinister world he now discovers was probably there before he left. He'd just been too young and innocent to recognize it or want to explore it. While walking through the fields, he discovers a severed ear. It is covered by ants—once we equate insects with gangsters, we'll realize these ants are a clue that the ear was severed by Lumberton gangsters. There is a penetrating close-up of the ear, accompanied by sound effects (by Alan Splet) of what may be brain waves or the roar of the ocean one hears when listening to a seashell. The curious Jeffrey retrieves the ear, his open-ended conduit into a world as perplexing as the brain or the ocean, the perverse nightmare world inhabited by the criminals of Lumberton. It will serve as his (rite of) passageway from young innocent to far-from-innocent adult. Jeffrey will be Lynch's link between the normal and abnormal worlds that coexist in Lumberton . . . and everywhere else in our America. Through Jeffrey, Lynch reveals his other important theme—that beneath the surface of "normal" people you'll find people with "abnormal" desires. Like most adult males in America, Jeffrey (who crosses the line from child to adult) will struggle to control his baser instincts. Like the paragons of society who leave their suburban homes and sneak into the seedy sections of town, perhaps in search of prostitutes, Jeffrey will move back and forth between the normal square world and an "abnormal" secret world of sex, violence, and madness. He'll prove himself as capable of debauchery as those corrupt people who are shunned by society.

Jeffrey goes to police headquarters and, in office 221—Lynch's movie puzzle includes many numbers and signs—

Young sleuths Jeffrey and Sandy fall in love as the mystery intensifies.

Watching from the closet, Jeffrey sees Frank excite Dorothy by tormenting her during kinky sex. Who knows what Frank inhales!

gives the ear to Detective Williams. But he's too curious to step aside from what he knows is a strange case. He wants to taste adult excitement, adult sin. That night, he opens his bedroom door, becoming a shadowy figure above dark stairs—an image out of *Invasion of the Body Snatchers*—and descends. In Lynch's paranoia film, everyone, including our hero, is mysterious. No one in this film will fully understand who anyone else is, nor will we fully understand anyone, including Jeffrey. The suspense music comes from the television Mrs. Beaumont and Aunt Barbara watch. Earlier a hand holding a gun filled the screen and now we see legs climbing stairs—Lynch is telling us that in mysteries, including this one, you never get the full picture. To satisfy his curiosity, Jeffrey takes a nocturnal stroll to Detective Williams's house. He is greeted by Mrs. Williams. That she looks like Mrs. Beaumont indicates that suburban housewives tend to become replicas of one another. They exist only within the house. Being a policeman, Detective Williams has rare insight into the wicked criminal world. He keeps his knowledge to himself so that his wife, teenage daughter, Sandy (the extremely appealing Laura Dern), and law-abiding Lumberton citizens can sleep well at night without realizing that crime and corruption teem around them. Perhaps he is part of the corruption. He won't tell Jeffrey about the case he is working on. He is the first person in the film to keep a secret from another character. We may think he's just being protective, but we don't trust him—we won't change our minds.

It is Sandy who provides Jeffrey with the vital information—Dorothy Vallens's name and address—that leads to his becoming personally involved in the case. We consider this lovely blonde to be an all-American girl, honest as the day is long, and someone to be trusted with your darkest secret. Yet, while she is completely open with Jeffrey, she immediately goes behind her father's back and reveals his secret to Jeffrey and goes behind her boyfriend's back to pursue a relationship with Jeffrey. Furthermore, she and Jeffrey will not tell Detective Williams, or their mothers, that they are investigating the case on their own. On one level, a square hometown-boy-falls-for-

the-girl-down-the-block level, Jeffrey and Sandy are attracted to each other because they find each other "neat." But there are less wholesome reasons for their mutual attraction. For starters, they find each other mysterious (Jeffrey admits he loves mysteries), the same reason Jeffrey will be drawn to Isabella Rossellini's Dorothy Vallens. They are also intrigued by each other's daring and willingness to commit crimes (theft, breaking and entering) during their sleuthing. To Jeffrey, Sandy, as sweet as she is, actually represents a forbidden love, being a mere teenager, having a football player boyfriend, and having a strict policeman father (who, if Lynch is suggesting that in America there is abnormal behavior by normal people, may harbor incestuous designs on his daughter). To Sandy, Jeffrey is the much-coveted "older man," who leads her down a path almost as dangerous as the path the older, married Dorothy will lead Jeffrey. Their relationship isn't as innocent as it seems. They aren't whom they seem; as Jeffrey points out when Sandy questions their snooping in Dorothy's apartment: "No one will suspect us because no one would think two people like us would be crazy enough to do something like this." As in Hitchcock films, predictable people eventually do something completely off-the-wall.

After climbing her building's winding, outdoor stairwell (a truly creepy visual), Jeffrey meets Dorothy, a woman completely outside his experience (it makes sense she is played by a foreigner). *Her* secret is that her husband and son have been kidnapped by Frank, and that to ensure their survival, she must be Frank's sexual slave. Significantly, Jeffrey gets her to let him enter her apartment by posing as an exterminator. He kills bugs now, he will go after human insects later. A heavyset man visits Dorothy. He's the first villain we see and since he's in a yellow jacket (think of the wasp)—Jeffrey will call him the Yellow Man—and Jeffrey is spraying, we make our first real connection between bugs and criminals. When he turns out to be a cop—the Yellow Man's secret—we understand how extensive is the corruption in Lumberton.

That night when Dorothy returns home before he is

finished snooping in her apartment, Jeffrey fulfills almost every adolescent's dream—he hides in a woman's closet and watches her undress. But he is caught, every adolescent's worst fear. Then the older woman forces him at knife point to have sex, every kinky adolescent's dream. At this point Jeffrey still hasn't done anything that we'd find perverse. It's back into the closet again, when Frank enters. Through the louver doors, Jeffrey watches Frank and Dorothy engage in sadomasochistic sex. As Frank calls Dorothy "Mommy"—she immediately falls into the victim role—and she calls aggressive Frank "Daddy," Jeffrey plays out the fascinating yet traumatic experience of every child who spies on parents while they have sex, doing all kinds of filthy things he or she doesn't understand. It's a dramatic and traumatic moment in the growing-up process. Dressed in black and with a plastic inhaler over his contorted face, Frank actually resembles an insect. Frank is meant to be the human counterpart of those hideous black bugs we saw in the opening—that's why it is necessary for him to have *no* human qualities, not even an ounce of sensitivity to make him more palatable. His foul language reflects how the bugs would speak if they could. His brutal sexual manner, consisting of groping, clutching, slapping, and mounting—while spewing vulgar threats—seems patterned on a bug's violent reproductive act. This sequence is regarded as the most shocking in the film, but I think it's too badly staged, too ridiculous, with Frank's constant cursing and repeated use of the inhaler (who knows what he's breathing?), and too phony, complete with zipper-up intercourse, to be effective. Since we don't yet know anything about Frank, when he enters we don't think "There's Frank" but "There's Dennis Hopper"—so our suspension of disbelief dissolves and we think "It's only a scene in a movie" . . . a scene with some truly offensive language. It takes a while for the film to draw us back in.

Jeffrey still has done nothing more shocking than James Stewart in *Rear Window* (1954). But after Frank leaves, he no longer is just a voyeur. This time when he holds Dorothy, he isn't passive but a willing participant. However, he's still not quite ready to step across the line into *adult* perversity. The next time Sandy wonders if he's "a detective or pervert," he wants to assure her he's just a detective. So when Dorothy tells him to hit her during lovemaking, he balks, saying he wants to help her, not hurt her. Although his blood is pumping, he tries to deny her assumption that men desire control during lovemaking and their female lovers to be victims. He'd also like to think he's not the type to take advantage of an emotionally unstable woman.

While trying to figure out Jeffrey's motives it's really not important for us to know why Dorothy enjoys being slapped during sex—although her low self-esteem seems to be a pretty obvious reason. It's enough to know that there are masochistic women out there like Dorothy who, for diverse reasons, are willing to be sexual slaves and quench (perhaps for money) the most wicked desires of America's men. Dark-haired Dorothy represents temptation to Jeffrey, a woman who offers gratification far beyond what he can expect with blonde Sandy if they have sex. The reasons that he doesn't want to have sex with Dorothy—she is older, she is married, she is a mother,

she is a masochist who wants him to hit her, she is a nymphomaniac, she is crazed and doesn't know what she's doing, she is willing to be his sexual slave and do *anything* he desires, he will be betraying Sandy's trust, he'll be getting in over his head—are the very reasons he wants to have sex with her! Lynch has, as David Denby points out, "suffused his thriller plot with a Catholic schoolboy's sense of sexual dread—sex as overwhelming pleasure and overwhelming danger." Jeffrey's sense of morality forces him to leave Dorothy that first night. But he keeps thinking of her in his arms and her request to be hit. He also thinks of nice girl Sandy. While they are parked in front of a church, and Lynch puts organ music on the sound track, Sandy delivers a sermon about robins returning to Earth and replacing the darkness with sunshine and love. I wish Lynch didn't play this scene in a manner to flatter his audience for being hip enough to recognize it's all tongue-in-cheek cliché, but it's an important scene (well played by Dern) because it indicates the film is a mock parable about good (Sandy's dream world) and evil (Dorothy's nightmare world), sin and salvation.

Although Jeffrey's attraction to good-girl Sandy increases, he can't stay away from bad-girl Dorothy. Welcome to the adult world. He returns to her apartment and becomes her lover. He tells Sandy that he photographed Frank and the Yellow Man making a drug transaction during the *day*, when gangsters and insects are most vulnerable. But he doesn't tell Sandy about Dorothy, his darkest secret. Eventually he succumbs to their mutual desire that he hit Dorothy during sex. He now has made the transition from detective to pervert. For his sin, he deserves to go straight to hell, and the devil himself, Frank, escorts him into the bowels of the Earth. He and his men take Jeffrey (and Dorothy) to the gangster den—which reminds me of an insect hive—inhabited by overfed females (another insect image) and the effeminate Ben (Dean Stockwell will give you chills), *queen* of the gangster insects. After some mild degeneracy—pill popping, drug money changing hands, Jeffrey being slugged—they head to a deserted area of town. Here, in a truly terrifying and offensive scene, Frank threatens Jeffrey with a knife, uses his inhaler, curses ad nauseam, smears lipstick on his own lips and kisses Jeffrey, tells Jeffrey that they're alike, and beats Jeffrey to a pulp. When Jeffrey wakes in the morning sun, his descent into hell is over. He decides to step off the immoral path that would make him another less-than-human Frank. He delivers the incriminating photos to Detective Williams and, though he lies to him about Sandy's involvement, decides to walk the straight-and-narrow. His romantic date with Sandy, during which they kiss passionately and hold hands, is excitement enough for him. Jeffrey has learned, as Pauline Kael believes, "through flabbergasting and violent expression to appreciate a relatively safe and manageable sex life." He has learned his lesson. He's humiliated when the hysterical Dorothy tells Sandy that Jeffrey made love to her, but it gives him a chance to come clean. Although hurt, Sandy, who, by learning the world is strange, has evolved to Jeffrey's age level while he has evolved to Dorothy's, forgives the man she loves (it's the American way for the woman to welcome home her wandering lover/husband). Now that Jeffrey is

Frank and the heavily made-up Ben make a business transaction.

a moral man, with an angel by his side, he can rescue Dorothy and her child and triumph over Frank.

I can't really figure out what's going on in the last couple of scenes. Why does Jeffrey *rush* to Dorothy's apartment? I assume Frank killed the Yellow Man and Dorothy's husband (who, earless, resembles an insect) but why did he do it? What happened? And why did he leave them there? Why does Frank return to Dorothy's apartment, especially if he already left the corpses there? And why is he in disguise, especially a disguise the cops must be familiar with? At least the cat-and-mouse game he and Jeffrey play is exciting. When Frank opens the closet door in anticipation of killing Jeffrey, only to be shot between the eyes, you realize what would have happened if Janet Leigh had taken a gun into the shower in *Psycho* (1960).

The finale, with Sandy and Jeffrey welcoming the return of the robins (a mechanical one has a black bug—symbol of Frank—in its beak), is amusing. It signals the reestablishment of idyllic America and the burial of the insect-gangsters. But I don't understand why Jeffrey, after all he's been through, retreats to such an innocent state. When we see Dorothy hug her little boy (in an insect-like propeller hat) in the park, she too seems to have risen from the mire. Are Jeffrey and Dorothy really so cleansed . . . or are they anticipating a secret rendezvous?

I know Lynch doesn't want viewers to completely figure out his film. He wants it to be, like *Eraserhead*, a puzzle with too few or too many pieces, a dream-nightmare that will be interpreted differently by everyone who sees it. But, while I am satisfied with the ambiguity in *Eraserhead*, I feel shortchanged here because this time Lynch is dealing with a world we can relate to. John Powers wrote in *American Film* (March 1987):

> [His film] makes for an assault on cherished American myths, yet its most radical implications would probably be rejected by Lynch, a social conservative

who insists his work has "nothing to do with politics." His radicalism is more aesthetic, and psychological, than social; he cares more about expressing what excites him than analyzing what his excitement means. There's nothing wrong with such an intuitive approach to art (think of Kafka), but it marks a limitation of Lynch's work. More important, it hints at a problematic feature in [recent American Gothic] films. They're interesting because they subvert the "feel good" ethos of most American movies, but at the same time they display a film-school callousness. . . . Their style too often runs away with their meaning—their chic gets in the way of their bleak. Indeed these films suggest how the formal gifts and ambitions of today's filmmakers can get in the way of their most serious themes.

Despite all the violence in the film, *Blue Velvet* will also be remembered for its sensual visuals (i.e., Rossellini lying in Jeffrey's arms), thematic use of colors, deadpan humor (Jeffrey is startled when he discovers the photo of Dorothy's missing family *because* the boy is wearing a funny hat), Diane Arbus–like background characters, weird tableaux, creative use of sound effects, eclectic background music, and erotic renditions of pop songs: Dorothy crooning a soulful version of Bobby Vinton's "Blue Velvet" (Vinton's version plays on the soundtrack at other times); Ben lip-synching Roy Orbison's "In Dreams" (the strangest moment in the film); and Jeffrey and Sandy kissing and dancing to "Mysteries of Love." No one will ever forget Hopper in this film—he may be the most evil villain in film history. But I prefer the more subdued performances by MacLachlan and Dern. Rossellini seems miscast—but you've got to admire her for taking such a potentially embarrassing role. And you've got to admire Lynch for daring such a chancy project on the heels of his *Dune* debacle. I only worry what Bobby Vinton will do for a title when it comes time to write his long-awaited autobiography.

Body Heat

1981   Color   Ladd Company, released through Warner Bros.
Director: Lawrence Kasdan
Producer: Fred T. Gallo
Screenplay: Lawrence Kasdan
Cinematography: Richard H. Kline
Music: John Barry
Song: ''Feel Like a Number'' performed by Bob Seger
Editor: Carol Littleton
Running Time: 113 minutes

Cast: William Hurt (Ned Racine), Kathleen Turner (Matty Walker), Richard Crenna (Edmund Walker), Ted Danson (Peter Lowenstein), J. A. Preston (Oscar Grace), Mickey Rourke (Teddy Lewis), Kim Zimmer (Mary Ann Simpson), Jane Hallaren (Stella), Lanna Saunders (Roz Kraft), Carola McGuinness (Heather Kraft), Michael Ryan (Miles Hardin), Larry Marko (Judge Costanza), Meg Kasdan (nurse).

Synopsis: There is a heat wave in Miranda Beach, Florida. Third-rate lawyer Ned Racine is bored with his job, his sexual partners, his life. At a band concert, he tries to pick up Matty Walker, a beautiful, sexy, married woman from Pinehaven. She walks away, but only after exciting him with some suggestive language. On another night, he finds her at a Pinehaven bar. Her husband, Edmund Walker, is away, so he follows her home. To the sound of her wind chimes, they have wild sex. They become lovers, having sex whenever Walker is away on business. Twice, Ned almost reveals the affair: He makes a lewd remark to a woman he thinks is Matty, only to discover it is her visiting lifelong friend, Mary Ann Simpson; he sneaks into Matty's house for quick sex, and they are caught in the act by Matty's young visiting niece, Heather. And he inadvertently meets Walker, a nasty man who became rich through ruthless methods and underworld ties. Matty swears she loves Ned and confesses she wishes Walker were dead. Ned devises a murder plan. Matty suggests he alter Walker's will so she doesn't have to split the inheritance with Heather. He says they can't chance raising suspicions. She agrees, saying the money doesn't matter—only he does.

Ned acquires an explosive device from his former client Teddy Lewis. He checks into a Miami motel, but sneaks back to Pinehaven. Walker hears Ned break into his house and eagerly goes after him with a gun. Walker is killed in a struggle. Ned plants the body in the Breakers, one of Walker's properties. He blows it up.

Ned is unhappy to discover that Matty independently altered the will, forging his signature. The witness was Mary Ann Simpson, who can't vouch for its validity since she has supposedly gone to Europe. Because of errors (attributed to Ned's usual incompetence), the will is declared invalid—so, because of Florida law, the wife gets all the money.

Ned learns from friends, assistant D.A. Peter Lowenstein and policeman Oscar Grace, that Matty is suspected of murder and that he should stay away from her. But Ned says he will *begin* to pursue her. Soon Oscar realizes Ned was her secret lover—the one whose face Heather doesn't remember. He learns Ned wasn't in Miami that night because someone—Ned suspects Matty—called the motel and insisted they check the room. Ned is shocked to discover that Matty sought him out initially, after learning he had once written an invalid will. Teddy tells Ned that Matty just came to him for more explosives.

Matty gets the inheritance money. She tells Ned to retrieve Walker's missing glasses, which the blackmailing housekeeper placed in the boat house. Ned sees explosives attached to the door. When Matty returns from Miami, he confronts her. She swears she loves him and walks through the dark to the boat house. There is an explosion. Dental records reveal that the dead woman found inside is Matty Tyler Walker.

Imprisoned, Ned looks through Matty's high school yearbook. As he figured, Matty Tyler, the dead woman, was actually Mary Ann Simpson. And Mary Ann Simpson was the woman he knew as Matty Walker—she had changed names to keep her lurid past from Walker. Her ambition, as stated in the yearbook, was ''To be rich and live in an exotic land.'' At this moment, this rich woman lies on a beach in an exotic land.

The May 1984 issue of *American Film* revealed the existence of a unique *Body Heat* fan club in Washington. While most members were bankers, librarians, and trade association types, its president, Royelen Boykie, was the administrative assistant of the National Conference of State Legislatures. Two hundred people received the club newsletter. Those who attended meetings not only saw the movie but also were invited to bid on satin sheets and wind chimes (important props in the film) that were raffled off. Some members took tap lessons specifically to emulate Ted Danson's dancing attorney. It makes sense that a cult, much larger than this club's membership, developed for *Body Heat*: It has steamy sex (including nudity), violence, atmosphere (director-writer Lawrence Kasdan uses sweat the way goremeister Herschell Gordon Lewis uses blood), hip dialogue, a clever plot, offbeat touches (like Danson's tap dance on the pier), and striking performances by attractive leads William Hurt (his third picture) and Kathleen Turner (her debut) and supporting players Richard Crenna, Mickey Rourke, and Danson. What's surprising, however, is that despite its many commercial elements (including the reintroduction of the femme fatale, a prototype that disappeared with the ''dumb blonde'' in light of the women's movement), it disappointed at the box office. I believe critics underestimated it and chased away the mass audience.

True movie lovers feel protective of classic movies. We detest cut television prints, abhor colorization, resent needless remakes, and are annoyed by spoofs made by filmmakers who neither understand nor admire the genre they're parodying. We also distrust neophyte directors who claim that their pictures, which contain much familiar material, are homages to masterpieces—we're inclined to suspect they are lazy rip-offs. I'm sure that if *Body Heat* were released today, now that we recognize writer-director Kasdan's knowledge of and sincere appreciation for past movies and particular genres, it would get a better critical reception than it did in 1981. But then, as a first-time director—never mind he had received script credit for *three* major films, *The Empire Strikes Back* (1980), *Raiders of the Lost Ark* (1981), and *Continental Divide* (1981)— he was an easy target for critics who sensed the picture was merely *film-noir*-by-the-numbers.

For instance, David Denby began his review in *New York*: ''I suspect that even people who have never seen *Double Indemnity* [1944], *The Big Sleep* [1946], the original *The Postman Always Rings Twice* [1946], or any of the other forties *film noir* classics will sense there's something tinny and derivative about *Body Heat*, the first film directed by Lawrence Kasdan. [It is] a self-conscious imitation of those deliriously paranoid forties pictures about a sexually overpowering woman who inflames a decent but weak man, turning him into a remorseless killer.'' And, in the *New Yorker*, Pauline Kael called *Body Heat* a ''40s pastiche that verges on camp but takes itself straight. [Kasdan] has devised a style that is a catalogue of *noir* clichés.'' According to Kael, Kasdan's catalogue included: ''Deco

Matty keeps Ned aroused so that she can manipulate him into doing her bidding.

titles, flames and a heat wave, ceiling fans, tinkling wind chimes, old tunes, chicanery in muted voices, a weak man and a femme fatale dressed in white [Turner even dons shorts to remind viewers of Lana Turner in *Postman*], and an insinuating, hotted up dialogue." Add to her list such *noir* essentials as the dark frame, with the blackness representing a growing evil—as embodied by Matty—that is primed to engulf and destroy all those weak or overconfident characters who pass through; white props and flickering lights—symbols of the last gasps of decency in the universe; the seductive jazz score (effectively arranged by John Barry); the liquor; the smoking cigarettes; the tainted characters; the story involving adultery, lust, greed, money, murder, and double cross. At times it does seem that Kasdan lucked upon footage from a *noir* classic that, for some reason, was missing actors—so all he had to do was use a script that utilized the sets of the classic, photograph his own cast, and mix the new footage with the old. That's how much his film resembles—visually and thematically— *Double Indemnity* and other *noir* classics. But I don't think he was merely being an imitator. I'm impressed by what I believe is a film lover's attempt to re-create the *noir* style so he could thoroughly explore the elements that made those films so fascinating—just as he'd utilize the Western format for *Silverado* (1985). In that film, he remained faithful to the Western, but expanded the parameters of the genre by presenting a whole slew of novel but believable characters—a black cowboy, a woman bartender, an English lawman, etc.—and making them (even the villains) more chatty and witty than Western prototypes. With *Body Heat*, Kasdan remained faithful to *film noir* yet similarly expanded the parameters of the genre.

For example, Matty Walker, who knows the difference between right and wrong (instead of watching without emotion, she turns away when Ned kills her husband), is probably the genre's first femme fatale who is bad not because she is controlled by her evil impulses (she lies when she tells Ned she is *weak*) but because she *chooses* to be evil. She realizes she must be ruthless to fulfill her lofty ambitions ("To be rich and live in an exotic land").

Kasdan incorporates the fatalism that is prevalent in *noir* classics, but he gives it a twist. *Both* adulterers are not doomed the moment they seal their conspiracy with a kiss; only Ned, the weaker *male*, will fall. When talking about whether they will get her murdered husband's huge inheritance, Matty convinces Ned, "There's nothing we can do about it, now. We'll either have the money or we won't. It's out of our hands." She may sound like she's leaving everything to chance, but this smart schemer is coaxing Ned into passivity while aggressively carrying out a secret plan to secure the money for herself. She determines her own destiny, which is why she is the cinema's lone femme fatale to get away scot-free. On the other hand, Ned, in the *noir* tradition, does let the chips fall where they may. Even when he realizes he has fallen into Matty's web and then her trap, he passively plays out the game, her game, to the end, curiously watching how the sly vamp he loves choreographs his destruction. Because he doesn't fight Fate, he becomes its victim, like Fred MacMurray in *Double Indemnity*, Tom Neal in *Detour* (1945), John Garfield in *The Postman Always Rings Twice*, and Robert Mitchum in *Out of the Past* (1947). Like these *noir* prototypes, Ned has a masochistic streak that takes over once the woman has destroyed his once-great male ego by revealing she doesn't need him or love him after all: When he realizes he has been the sap (something Sam Spade refused to be), he shrugs and accepts his punishment, like a married man who rationalizes he had it coming when a hooker runs off with his wallet. An important difference between Ned and his *noir* predecessors is that he doesn't even get the satisfaction of knowing that the woman will go down with him.

Ned pretty much fits the profile for *noir* "heroes." He drinks and smokes constantly, is cynical and bored, thinks any woman would fall for him and that he is better than the man she is with now, tries to impress the femme fatale by devising and carrying out an intricate crime (while she says things like, "You're right, darling"), and assumes Fate is too strong for him. But he differs from most in that he's not particularly sympathetic (Hurt grew a mustache and dyed his hair to a darker shade of blond to give Ned a seedy look). Ned (can you root for someone named Ned?) doesn't have any good qualities. He isn't even good at his profession. (Even Neal, a real loser in *Detour*, is a talented pianist.) Playing the role of Super-WASP, he's more interested in sexual conquests and bragging about them to his best friends, Jewish Peter Lowenstein and black Oscar Grace, than in honing his meager skills as a lawyer. After Ned unsuccessfully defends a client who tried to defraud the county in a "toilet caper," the annoyed judge suggests he come up with either a "better defense or a better class of client." In fact, Matty becomes interested in Ned because he isn't very intelligent ("You're not too smart are you? . . . I like that in a man")—it's the rare William Hurt character who is a lazy thinker—and because he is an incompetent lawyer, the type who would draw up an invalid will. We can't really worry about Ned because he doesn't have much to lose when he enters the relationship with Matty. He hasn't accomplished anything. When he watches a restaurant he ate in as a child burn down, we believe his conclusion: "My history is burning up out there." Matty will just come along and wipe out his future as well—no one will miss him because he didn't leave his mark; it's as if he never existed. In interviews in the *New York Post* (with Ed Naha) and *American Film*, Kasdan (who seemed to be talking about characters from his upcoming 1983 film, *The Big Chill*) spoke about the basis for Ned's character:

> "A lot of us felt that we could change the world, do anything we wanted to and get away with it. When we entered the real world we found out how rough it was. . . . For some people, the frustration of no longer having their own way turned into this casting about for quick solutions to their own happiness. Suddenly they're looking around for that great business deal or that great scam that's going to make them a mint and buy their freedom. Ned is one of those people. He has an ease and charm that probably served him well in high school and college and he made it through law school. He sort of floated through and he didn't have to be terribly good at anything. Now he finds himself doing work that is totally unsatisfying, there is no focus to his life, and those things he desires are constantly out of reach. Morals get turned around. Corruption sets in."

This character Kasdan describes is a disappointment in

Kathleen Turner became an instant star as Matty Walker, a throwback to the screen vamps of the forties. Her Matty looks aggressive, dresses sexily, and uses her smoking cigarette as an instrument of seduction.

scene one—there's no reason to believe he will wise up or change for the better during the course of the film.

Kasdan also breaks convention with the third major character, Edmund Walker, in what is essentially a Greek tragedy (an ambitious woman manipulates her lover, an insignificant man, into murdering his better, the rich and powerful head of the House; a man succumbs to Fate; the wind chimes are like the sexual Sirens that tempted Jason and Odysseus; Lowenstein and Grace serve as a chorus, filling in plot points). In *film noir*, the husband whom the lovers try to kill typically is an absolute victim, unaware

Ned's friends Oscar Grace (standing), *a police detective, and Peter Lowenstein, an assistant D.A., try to keep him out of trouble, but Matty's influence is too strong.*

that there is a plot against him and too weak to put up a defense if he did know. Not so with Richard Crenna's creepily played Walker; anything but an unaggressive patsy, he has reached his position of wealth and power by stepping on weaklings and exhibiting a callous disrespect for the law. He gets a kick out of a situation in which his wife and lover are trying to do him in. As Richard Crenna told me: "I'm sure that if Matty and Ned hadn't gotten him first, he'd have loved playing the whole thing out. He has such a feeling of being in control, such an ego. He would have loved to have manipulated Ned right into the sewer as a way of impressing Matty." The despicable Walker, rather than Ned, is the ideal mate for Matty.

The biggest difference between *Body Heat* and the forties' classics is in the presentation of sex. Like Bob Rafelson's Jack Nicholson–Jessica Lange remake of *The Postman Always Rings Twice* (1981), it brings to the forefront the sex in James M. Cain's novels that was only hinted at in the forties' film adaptations. The initial dialogue between Matty and Ned is almost lewd (she says brazen lines she knows will impress him), and their sex scenes are extremely explicit for an R-rated film. Whereas forties' femme fatales used their sex appeal to lure unsuspecting men into their webs and to keep them willing prisoners, Matty uses the sex *act* to keep Ned in line. Other women may promise sex in the future (or *off*screen), but Matty holds nothing back: She makes mad, passionate, sweaty love to him over and over; she lies on the floor and pulls Ned on top of her, pleading "Do it!"; she licks

sweat off his chest; she drops to her knees and unzips his fly—although her young niece is in a nearby room; she takes ice baths with him; she keeps him greedy with such come-ons as "I need you so badly!" and "I want you right now more than I ever have!" She makes sure Ned can think of nothing but sex by keeping him aroused at *all* times. "I'm red; I'm sore," he whines, but she doesn't let him have a spare moment to think and figure out her motives. She wakes him by fondling him beneath the covers. She pulls him across the frame with a hand that, beneath the frame, clutches his penis (a significant image that defines their relationship). She believes "most men are little boys"; and Ned has the sexual maturity of the teenagers in *Porky's* (1981)—he thinks with his penis. As Lowenstein warns him: "Your dick is going to lead you into a very big hassle." Watch how Matty, for Ned's benefit, treats her cigarette as a phallic symbol—when she comes on to Ned at the beginning, she places it firmly between her lips and makes sure it always faces directly out or slightly upward (while Ned's cigarette dangles from his mouth); she inhales deeply, almost swallowing the smoke before blowing it high into the air. But when she's through with that cigarette and Ned's not really paying attention, watch how she crushes it beneath her feet—we know that Ned is in deep trouble.

Of course, just because I believe *Body Heat* stretches the parameters of *film noir* doesn't mean I think it's on the same level as the classics of the genre. I don't. It lacks a plot twist or two, a sense that these characters existed before the film began, and moral conflict, which we don't have because of the type of person Ned is: He tells Matty matter-of-factly: "A man is going to die for no reason but we want him dead. He doesn't deserve it—let's not ever say that . . ." (His words should have been left for movie reviewers to supply.) However, Kasdan's film is a worthy, legitimate, most enjoyable entry to the genre. I really like the cinematography—the prowling camera, the interesting light patterns—of Richard Kline, and how adeptly John Barry's bluesy score complements the visuals and helps establish the proper sense of nightmare. Kasdan himself adds to the *dream* ambience by keeping his daytime transition scenes very brief; tension builds because it seems Matty and Ned, who meet each night, are rarely out of each other's arms. Tension also results from the amusing dialogue scenes between the various paranoid characters, including the sexual-innuendo–laced chats between Ned and Matty and the sparring male-ego-on-the-line dinner conversation between Ned and Walker. (Kasdan said he wanted to make the rare contemporary film moviegoers had to *listen* to.) What's apparent is that everyone is, with good reason, suspicious of the people they are talking to.

Best of all is Kathleen Turner, fresh from a year and a half on the TV soap *The Doctors*. She's at her most svelte here (when she got the part she also was going to audition for Robert Aldrich's 1981 women's wrestling comedy . . . *All the Marbles*), and proudly displays her long legs and daringly does nudity, revealing what her *The Man with Two Brains* (1983) costar Steve Martin would rate "a behind you'd like to eat lunch off." Turner's Matty is extremely sexy, not just because of the way she looks ("You shouldn't wear that body!" Ned raves) and her

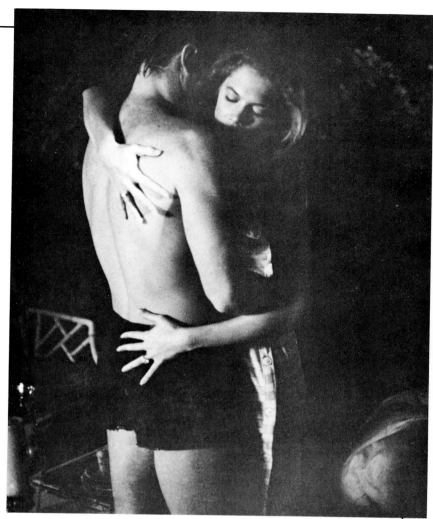

What promises to be one of the more passionate scenes in the film, although neither character is nude, is about to be interrupted by a surprise visitor.

Edmund Walker is delighted that he may have the chance to shoot a prowler.

uninhibited nature in bed, but equally because of her energy and eagerness (she always thrusts her face forward, keeps her chin slightly upward, and keeps her flirting eyes wide open and interested), her confidence, her strength, her ambition, her perseverance, and her intelligence: As the awed Ned comes to realize, it was kind of an honor to be duped by such a woman. Turner's performance as the tough-as-nails femme fatale is truly memorable, yet no one really knew how good it was until she revealed her

versatility with an equally convincing portrayal as the soft, vulnerable, sweet heroine in *Romancing the Stone* (1981). While Meryl Streep searches for interesting *parts* to play and has the talent to do them justice, the more daring Turner (along with Jane Fonda and Sissy Spacek) searches for *women* to play (sometimes in mediocre films like 1984's *Crimes of Passion*) that she feels she can make interesting. Beginning with Matty Walker, she has had remarkable success.

The Cabinet of Dr. Caligari

1919   B&W   German   Decla Film
Director: Robert Wiene
Producer: Erich Pommer
Screenplay: Carl Mayer and Hans Janowitz
Cinematography: Willy Hameister
Art Direction: Hermann Warm, Walter Röhrig, and Walter Reimann
Running Time: 69 minutes

Cast: Werner Krauss (Dr. Caligari), Conrad Veidt (Cesare), Lil Dagover (Jane), Freidrich Feher (Francis), Hans van Twardowski (Alan), Rudolf Lettinger (Dr. Olsen), Rudolf Klein-Rogge (criminal).

Synopsis: Francis sits on a garden bench with a frightened older man, who insists there are spirits everywhere. A beautiful young woman in white walks by as if in a trance. Francis says she is his fiancée, Jane. He tells about the horrible experience they had.

A traveling fair arrived in Holstenwall, where Francis always lived. Dr. Caligari went to the town clerk to apply for a permit to show his exhibit at the fair: Cesare, a somnambulist, who, while in a 23-year sleep, could predict the future. Caligari was upset at the rude treatment he received. That night, the town clerk was stabbed to death.

Alan, his best friend and fellow student, dragged Francis to the fair. Francis and Alan entered Caligari's tent. Caligari opened a coffin-like cabinet, revealing the frightening Cesare, a tall, slender man who appeared to be in a trance while doing Caligari's bidding. Alan asked how long he had to live. Cesare told him he'd die at dawn. Alan failed to contain his fears.

Francis and Alan walked Jane home. They both loved her and agreed to remain friends, no matter whom she married. At dawn, Alan was stabbed to death. Francis and Jane were heartbroken. Francis suspected Cesare of the crime. He and Jane's father, Dr. Olsen, got a permit to examine Cesare. Caligari was upset when they came to his caravan. But before they examined Cesare, news came that the murderer had been caught.

Francis and Dr. Olsen returned to the police station. The suspect admitted he killed an old woman, hoping that the murderer of Alan and the town clerk would be blamed. He insisted he was innocent of those two murders. Jane went to Caligari's caravan in search of Francis and her father. When Caligari presented Cesare, she became terrified and fled.

That night, Francis spied on the sleeping Caligari and Cesare, who slept in his cabinet. At this exact time, Cesare crept into Jane's bedroom. He couldn't bring himself to stab her. When she awoke and screamed he dragged her off, over rooftops and along a country road. The townspeople gave chase. He dropped Jane. He died of exhaustion.

Francis and the police discovered that it wasn't Cesare in the cabinet, but a dummy. Caligari fled. Francis tracked him to a mental asylum. He went to the director to learn if Caligari was one of the patients. He was horrified to discover that Caligari was the director! While the director slept, Francis and several doctors looked through his books and diary. The director had read about Caligari, an eleventh-century (seventeenth-century in some prints) mountebank, who used magic to induce a somnambulist named Cesare to murder for him. The director wanted to be Caligari. He got his chance when a somnambulist arrived at the asylum.

Francis and the doctors confronted Caligari. When he was presented with Cesare's corpse, he became a raving maniac. He had to be restrained. He was put in a cell, forever.

Francis goes to the asylum courtyard. He joins the other patients—including Cesare and Jane! Francis asks Jane when they'll marry. She says that being of royal blood she can't follow her heart's wishes. Francis becomes crazed when he sees the asylum director, whom he insists is the Caligari of *his* story. The benevolent director says that he can cure Francis now that he is aware of this delusion.

This masterpiece—museum piece?—of the silent cinema was the first *horror* film of real, lasting quality and the first motion picture to fully incorporate the German expressionism that was pervasive in postwar art and theater. It also qualified as the first "cult movie." According to *Midnight Movies* (1983) by J. Hoberman and Jonathan Rosenbaum, it played in one Paris theater for seven consecutive years, a record that lasted until *Emmanuelle* (1974). And throughout the twenties, in Europe and America (Sam Goldwyn imported it in 1921), it was a cause célèbre among the arising avant garde and intelligentsia, who were either excited or angered by its filmmakers' bold attempt to eradicate the distinction between cinema and art. "More than any other film," wrote Arthur Knight in *Rogue* (August 1962),

> . . . it convinced artists, critics, and audiences that the movie was a medium for artistic expression. With its weird spatial distortions and pre-Freudian psychology, it set the pattern for art houses—decades before there were any art houses. It triggered a cycle of movies that continues today. . . . New levels of reality had been penetrated by the camera; an illusory world, a world that existed solely in the mind, had been made palpable and real. The motion picture, hitherto concerned primarily with externals, was demonstrably able to plunge beneath the surface and externalize dreams, fantasies, and the workings of the subconscious.
>
> Inevitably the film had an enormous effect. Post-World War I Europe was swarming with artists who wanted to break out of the conventional modes of art, who fought with bare fangs against the bourgeois culture and bourgeois standards they had inherited. . . . They argued for a *cinéma pur*, a type of movie that did away with plots and happy endings.

The Cabinet of Dr. Caligari was conceived by Hans Janowitz and Carl Mayer, two artistically inclined young pacifists who met in Berlin after the war. They saw film as a revolutionary form of artistic expression—visual storytelling that necessitated collaboration between writers (novelists, poets, playwrights) and painters, cameramen, actors, directors. New itself, film was the ideal medium through which to both call attention to the emerging pacifism in postwar Germany and exhibit the radical anti-bourgeois art. Although neither writer had connections to any Berlin film company, they decided to concoct a scenario. As both were enthusiastic about Paul Wegener's works, they chose to write a horror film. They drew on past experiences. Janowitz still had disturbing memories of a night in 1913, in Hamburg: After leaving a fair he had walked into a park bordering the Holstenwall (the name of the town in the film) and glimpsed a bourgeois stranger as he disappeared into the shadows after having mysteriously emerged from the bushes . . . where a young

Caligari presents Cesare to the terrified Jane. Later he will send Cesare to her bedroom.

woman's ravaged body was found the next morning. And Mayer still was embittered about his sessions during the war with an autocratic, highly ranked, military psychiatrist. At night, like Francis and Alan in the film, Janowitz and Mayer would often go to a nearby fair. One evening, they saw a sideshow titled "Man and Machine," in which a man did feats of strength and forecast the future while supposedly in a hypnotic trance. Inspired by this, Janowitz and Mayer devised their story that night and wrote it in the following six weeks. The derivation of the name Caligari? At the time, Mayer happened to be reading *Unknown Letters of Stendhal*, in which an officer named Caligari was mentioned.

Erich Pommer tried to get rid of the two young men who burst into his office at his small Decla studio. But Janowitz and Mayer insisted on telling him their fantastic film story, and the future head of UFA was so impressed by "The Cabinet of Dr. Caligari" that he bought it on the spot. He even agreed that it should be made in expressionistic style, partly as a concession to his studio only having a limited quota of power and light. Pommer, in his essay "Carl Mayer's Debut," which can be found in Paul

Rotha and Richard Griffith's *Film Till Now* (1949), recalled:

> The artist whose style they wanted followed was Alfred Kubin, the hero of Prague's radical artists. While Mayer and Janowitz talked about art, I was thinking of rather a different aspect of the script. The mystery and macabre atmosphere of the Grand Guignol was currently in vogue in German films, and this story fitted perfectly. They saw an "experiment" in the script—I saw a comparatively inexpensive production.

While Mayer and Janowitz were off courting Kubin, Pommer put *Caligari* in the hands of designer Hermann Warm and painters Walter Reimann (Pommer writes of "Herlth" instead of Reimann) and Walter Röhrig, "whom I'd met as a soldier painting sets for a German military theatre in Braila, Rumania." All were of the *Sturm* group (taken from the name of a magazine), which promoted expressionism in every field of art. When Pommer began to have second thoughts about how the film should be designed, they had to convince him that it made sense to *paint* lights and shadows directly on set walls and floors

Cesare passes through one of the film's strange, expressionistic sets.

and background canvases, and to place "fantastic, unreal, flat sets behind real, solid people." Director Robert Wiene, who replaced first choice Fritz Lang after Lang withdrew to finish his serial *The Spiders*, did a test scene to demonstrate the artists' theories. It was so impressive that Pommer gave his artists free rein, and his writers decided there was no further need to pursue Kubin. In fact, Janowitz and Mayer would write their next film for Pommer, *Genuine* (1921), with the new method in mind. It would be a disaster. (In future years, Mayer would become known as the silent screen's most skilled poet, writing the visually oriented scripts for F. W. Murnau's *The Last Laugh*, in 1924, and *Sunrise*, in 1927.)

No film is more bizarrely designed than *Caligari*—in fact, the design is so startling that you tend to overlook Mayer and Janowitz's truly intriguing story. The characters walk about in sparsely furnished yet tiny, claustrophobic sets. They move in and out of the inevitable shadowed areas of the frames. The few props (the high chairs, the beds) are oddly constructed, or are conspicuous by their absence (as in the jail cell). The backgrounds are obviously painted—as if done by a 6-year-old with his off hand—and there are even markings on the floors. The costumes and makeup are also exaggerated and sloppy, as if put on by someone without taste: Conrad Veidt's somnambulist Cesare wears black tights, a polo sweater, and white pancake makeup. The high, weirdly shaped hats and walking canes that jut out from the men's hands (even gloves have lines on them) are at odds with everything on the streets of Holstenwall: Most odd is that *everything*, including the numerous scribbled straight lines on windows, walls, and floors, zigzags at odd angles so that there is an exaggerated perspective to everything we see and the frame looks out of whack. For instance, Caligari's caravan is crooked, has a door that is even more slanted than that, and a window that is even more slanted. The only thing that stands straight and tall is Cesare; yet when he dies, his body starts to crumble and he raises his arms so that they form angles similar to the twisted tree branches near him.

Future filmmakers, in and out of the horror-fantasy genre, would come to understand from watching *Caligari* that one can express the emotional or mental states of characters through the design of sets they walk through. This is ironic because it wasn't the intention of the men who made *Caligari* to use the decor to express what the characters were thinking or feeling. It's easy to fall into the trap of assuming that the film was bizarrely designed because what we are seeing is a story being told by a madman. Indeed Siegfried Kracauer in his seminal book on the German cinema, *From Caligari to Hitler* (1947), quoted one of the many early "self-assured" critics who thought this was what the film implied: "The idea of rendering the notions of sick brains . . . through expressionist pictures is not only well conceived but also well realized. Here this style has a right to exist, proves an outcome of solid logic." But for us to equate the expressionism with the cerebral world of the madman, Francis, we must either ignore that the final scene at the asylum, which takes place *after* Francis has completed his bizarre story, also has the wild designs we saw during his story or figure that director Wiene badly blundered and simply forgot that the set in the finale should be realistic. Even so, common sense tells us that men who wanted to promote expressionism wouldn't represent it as the visualization of madmen—that would only mock the art form. Obviously the expressionistic design is meant to represent the visualization of the creative, quite sane minds of the men who are telling a 69-minute story in which Francis tells a briefer story. The expressionism is meant to add dramatic force to the filmmakers' horror story and to help remove it from reality (but not from sanity), as do the impossible time lapses (i.e., the scene in which Caligari asks the rude town clerk for a permit and the scene in which police discover the town clerk's body would logically take place the day and night before

Francis and Alan attend the fair, but these scenes are placed between the time Francis and Alan leave for the fair and arrive a few minutes later).

Having seen the opening, in which Francis informs his companion that he will tell a story of the horrible events that befell him and Jane, and the twist ending, we naturally assume that what comes in between is Francis's story. Yet we don't have to believe a story in which his romantic rival, Alan, is conveniently killed off, and he heroically traps the criminal mastermind, Caligari. We only wonder why in his tall tale Francis doesn't also rescue Jane from Cesare and win her heart forever. I think that if you remove the opening and finale from *Caligari* you would still recognize what remains as Francis's wishful tale, in which he wins the lady he loves and simultaneously prevents his homeland from being taken over by a dictator and his human killing machine. It would still fall into the category of "psychological" horror film.

It's certainly appropriate to conjecture how the removal of the framing scenes would alter the picture because they weren't included in the original scenario. They were added, depending on your source, by Lang, Pommer, or Wiene. Mayer and Janowitz bitterly objected to the framing scenes because they—or at least the ending—completely alter the meaning of the film. The twist ending is a lot of fun, and certainly has a great deal to do with the success of the film, but Mayer and Janowitz had reason to complain. It not only led critics astray by providing them with, they wrongly believed, the explanation for the expressionism, but also it reversed the political messages the writers were trying to get across. The writers, who detested authority figures, sensed that Prussian authorities were turning the German population into zombie-like creatures like Cesare, who'd blindly follow all orders. They worried that the time was ripe for a mad Caligari figure, a mountebank and demagogue, to rise from obscurity (small-time power) and, while the ineffectual police and government officials sit on high chairs and do as little as they do in the film, hoodwink the sleeping, defeated masses of postwar Germany into following his evil ways. "According to the pacifist-minded Janowitz," Kracauer wrote, "they had created Cesare with the dim design of portraying the common man who, under the pressure of compulsion of military service, is drilled to kill and be killed." In their scenario, Mayer and Janowitz had clearly anticipated the rise of Hitler and Nazi Germany. However, by including the final sequence and making the director at the asylum a benevolent man who wants to help the insane Francis, those in power at Decla (who didn't listen to hirelings Mayer and Janowitz) actually showed a high regard for authority figures, who, judging by the director, have understanding and consideration for those under their supervision. This wasn't what the writers had in mind. They may have had some solace in knowing that after seeing Werner Krauss as the villainous Caligari the entire picture, it's difficult for us to trust Krauss's asylum director at the end. We still suspect he is Caligari and wonder how he's certain he can cure Francis just because he realizes Francis thinks he's Caligari. What will the *cure* be? (You wouldn't want to be in Francis's straitjacket.)

No one has ever tried to duplicate *Caligari*—except for

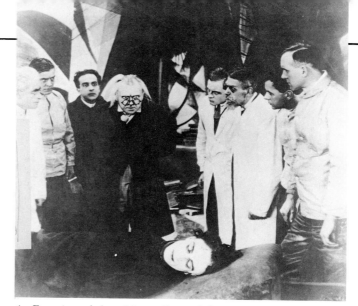

As Francis and the white-uniformed doctors look on, the head of the asylum is upset at the sight of the dead Cesare. It's now clear that he is the mad Caligari, as Francis asserted.

Mayer and Janowitz, who flopped with *Genuine*—but its impact and influence have been immeasurable. For instance, it showed future horror filmmakers how to blend shocks, suggested horror (we see Alan's murder in shadows) and psychological horror. It was the first of the genre to prove that what happens offscreen or in the mind can be as terrifying as physical shocks. It's easy to understand why this film frightened audiences in 1919 (it was actually released in February 1920) and for years after. There are specific scenes that would be repeated in future films. Cesare's coming to life while in his crypt anticipated numerous vampire movies; the nocturnal strolls of the "woman in white" in *Dracula* (1931) wouldn't be much different from Jane's ghostly walk through the asylum garden; the spooky scene in which Cesare sneaks into Jane's bedroom was copied in later horror classics like Murnau's *Nosferatu* (1922) and James Whale's *Frankenstein* (1931); and Cesare's walk through the expressionistic forest prefigured a similar scene with the monster in *Frankenstein*. The marvelous scene in which Cesare carries Jane over the weirdly designed rooftops and along the country road has certainly been repeated in many horror films, especially those in which townspeople chase after the monster, but as he walks into the fantasy-world horizon, I wonder if this scene also inspired the winding Yellow Brick Road in *The Wizard of Oz* (1939).

If you have seen *The Cabinet of Dr. Caligari* only on videocassette or in an Introduction to Film course—I fell asleep watching a musicless, shaky 16-mm print in college—or in cut form (there are several versions, with different subtitles and running times), give it another try. Under the right circumstances, with loud music and a pristine print, it suddenly doesn't seem so slow, the camerawork doesn't seem so static, and the acting comes across as powerful rather than silly—I particularly enjoy Lil Dagover, whose anguished reactions upon learning of Alan's death and meeting Cesare are worthy of Nazimova. After all these years, it is still an astonishing film.

Cafe Flesh

also known as *Café Flesh*

1982 Color Caribbean Films
Director: Rinse Dream
Producers: Rinse Dream and F. X. Pope
Screenplay: Herbert W. Day and Rinse Dream
Cinematography: F. X. Pope
Music: Mitchell Froom
Editor: Sidney Katz
Running Time: 80 minutes

Cast: Andrew Nichols (Max Melodramatic), Paul McGibboney (Nick), Pia Snow (Lana), Marie Sharp (Angel), Darcy Nichols (Moms), Dondi Bastone (Spike), Kevin Jay (Johnny Rico), Pez D. Spencer (Mr. Joy), Robert Dennis (the Enforcer), Joey Lennon, Neil Podorecki, Ken Starbuck.

Synopsis: Following a nuclear war, 99% of the population becomes violently ill if they even try to have sex. These Sex Negatives remember how wonderful sex was before the Nuclear Kiss and they still crave sex. Their frustration increases when, for their nightly entertainment, they go to clubs to see performances by those Sex Positives that have been rounded up by government enforcers. One of the most famous clubs on the sexual circuit is Cafe Flesh. It is owned by Moms, a former beautician. Its emcee is Max Melodramatic, a two-bit Borscht Belt comic before World War III—he viciously mocks the pathetic audience. The male and female stars perform without emotion, in explicit, theatrical sexual vignettes. The viewers are simultaneously turned on and tortured by what they see. They can't turn away.

Two regulars are Nick and his girlfriend, Lana. Nick hates going to the Cafe Flesh because it makes him want to have sex with Lana. But they are both Sex Negatives and get sick if they try. Max always ridicules Nick for coming to the club when it makes him so miserable. This night, sex-performer agent Silky brings Angel, a new girl from Wyoming, to watch the show. She's thrilled to be at the club she's heard so much about. There is excitement in the club when it's rumored that sex legend Johnny Rico has been signed to appear soon.

After a couple of acts, Nick insists that he and Lana go home and attempt to have sex. He immediately becomes ill. Lana pretends to be sick also. She is not a Sex Negative, after all. She hides that she is a Sex Positive because if this were known she'd be forced to leave Nick and perform on the sex circuit. When she thinks she's alone in the club, Lana masturbates. Max sees her. He knows her secret.

A government enforcer discovers that Angel is a Sex Positive. She had kept this a secret because she is a virgin. Angel is forced to perform. She tells Lana she had a wonderful time.

When Moms catches Max harassing Nick, whom she adores, she makes Max get on his knees and recite a humbling poem: He reveals he lost his penis in the war. Max tries to coax Lana into revealing herself, knowing how this will destroy Nick.

Johnny Rico comes to the club. As Nick notices, Lana becomes aroused just seeing him. Johnny and Angel perform. Lana has trouble controlling herself. Max urges her to join the couple on the stage. Nick tries to hold Lana back, but she's almost in a trance. As the audience goes wild, Lana climbs onto the stage. While Johnny stands casually to the side, she and Angel perform in a bed. They enjoy themselves. Max laughs at Nick. Johnny pulls Angel off Lana, and now he and Lana perform. Nick is terribly upset. Max laughs at him, until Nick's friend Spike knocks him unconscious. . . . Spike drags Nick from the club, and Johnny and Lana continue to have sex.

I think that most movie fans, especially those under 30, welcomed the sudden emergence of hardcore-sex features, circa 1970. It was a weird and oddly exciting experience being allowed (by law) to see the types of films that had thrilled bachelors in smoky back rooms for years. Now we could watch 16-mm and 35-mm porno features (as opposed to loops) in theaters, without fear that storm troopers would barge in. It was a kick seeing Clint Eastwood's *Play Misty for Me* (1971) in one theater on San Francisco's Market Street and then walking a few steps to the theater next door to see *Mona* (1970), the first hardcore porno feature. And it felt satisfyingly decadent going to the plush Four Star Theater on Wilshire Boulevard in L.A. to see former Ivory Snow girl Marilyn Chambers in the Mitchell Brothers' *Behind the Green Door* (1972) and *The Resurrection of Eve* (1973). But it almost felt too proper, too hip, to join all those middle-class couples at New York theaters playing Gerard Damiano's stupid but groundbreaking *Deep Throat* (1972), which made Linda Lovelace porno's first superstar. Much better was Damiano's more arty *The Devil in Miss Jones* (1972), featuring an erotic and skilled (!) performance by Georgina Spelvin. When I was at the University of Wisconsin, we male and female

The openings of two stylized stage performances. The scenes will become weirder and much more sexually graphic.

students would go in bunches—some would even hitch from Madison to Chicago—to satisfy our curiosity about the nature of the sex and the well-publicized, singular sexual talents of Lovelace, Chambers, Spelvin et al. We also were curious to find out if these films would excite, inspire, or embarrass us. Afterward, we'd argue about their merits and, naturally, whether they were sexist, and whether we should be ashamed for not walking out.

We appreciated porno films because they were a powerful affront to conservative America and a by-product of the free speech movement; they successfully challenged antiquated obscenity laws, and during the protest era we had so few victories out in the streets that we were happy with victories in the theaters, even if the real victors turned out to be the apolitical slimeballs who were making fortunes producing and exhibiting these films. We also welcomed the birth of what we recognized as a daring new movie "genre"—we believed the sex film both reflected and was a natural outgrowth of the sexual revolution—and immediately predicted porno (which I distinguish from pornography) would be a viable alternative to mainstream Hollywood films. We expected the low-budget porno film would attract many aspiring filmmakers who were shut out of Hollywood. We hoped these unknown, underground talents would pioneer a more honest type of film, which

would deal, at least in part, with those sexual themes Hollywood was scared of, contain the explicit sex we always wanted to see, and have acceptable acting, writing, direction, production values, stories, and characters. We even thought some Hollywood filmmakers would make an occasional XXX-rated film. Of course it was a lot of fun to go to porno films for no reason other than to see pretty, uninhibited young women do bizarre things on screen—I still have fond memories of the stars of *School Girl* (1971) and *Teenage Cheerleader* (1974)—but we expected something better and more creative to evolve, perhaps "art" films with hardcore sex, like *I Am Curious (Yellow)* (1967) or *In the Realm of the Senses* (1975). While its existence certainly caused Hollywood films to become more explicit, the porno film never improved on the early works of Damiano, the Mitchell Brothers, and Alex De Renzy, and those were no better than feeble attempts to make artistic adult films. Although the female stars became prettier, and some (Samantha Fox, Kelly Nichols, Veronica Hart) showed they could act and have sex at the same time, the plots and, worse, the sex became repetitive. It stopped being chic to go to a porno film—it became a waste of time. That's why the theatrical porno film was given back to the raincoat crowd.

There may be something to the theory that porno films

are meant for private home viewing (so viewers can be more than voyeurs?) because they turned out to be in the vanguard of the video revolution. In turn, the dramatic change in viewing habits caused by VCRs signaled the demise of theatrical porno films. Soon porno producers began making their product directly for the new market, on videotape rather than on film. Ironically, just when the heavy-breathing theatrical porno film began its last gasps, two of the best XXX-rated films ever made were released, *Blonde Ambition* (1981) and *Cafe Flesh*. These were adult films of the kind we had hoped for a decade before, with appeal to a crossover audience. Both became midnight movie hits. *Blonde Ambition*, sparked by a delightful comic performance by Suzy Mandell (once a Benny Hill regular), successfully mixed erotic sex with offbeat humor. *Cafe Flesh* successfully mixed sex, satire, and avant-garde theater.

Cafe Flesh is "the thinking person's porno film," an adult film that works on an intellectual as well as a sexual level. It is the rare XXX-rated film where graphic sex is not gratuitous, but necessary to the plot. There had been thousands of assembly-line adult films before this, yet director Rinse Dream (my favorite porno alias since Abe Snake) and his cinematographer F. X. Pope managed to come up with an imaginative way to stage and photograph the sex scenes. This is a sex film in which everyone in the cast is not required to have sex on screen. The result is that there is good acting, particularly by Andrew Nichols

as Max Melodramatic, the malevolent Joel Grey–inspired emcee at the nightclub. Credit "Dream" and co-screenwriter Herbert W. Day—actually journalist Jerry Stahl—for creating several intriguing, recognizable characters and for injecting the morbid proceedings with witty dialogue, including references to Roger Maris, Jack Lord, June Taylor, Tab Hunter, Fabian, Frank Sinatra and Dean Martin at Caesar's, and Dagwood and Blondie.

Cafe Flesh is certainly provocative because it's a post-nuclear film with a sexual twist. But even more unusual is the treatment of the relationship between Nick (Paul McGibboney) and Lana (Pia Snow). We usually think of women faking sexual arousal to please their men, but in this film Lana pretends *not* to be sexually aroused so she can be Nick's "equal" and not damage his fragile ego—and not be forced to leave him for the government-run sex circuit. We admire Lana for opting for love rather than sex. However, Lana eventually gives in to her lust and leaves impotent, war-casualty Nick to seek sexual fulfillment (just as "Ruby" ignored singer Kenny Rogers's pleas and took her love to town!). Her act of betrayal will surely convince men in the audience that if they want to keep their women, there had better be no Third World War.

If *Cafe Flesh* doesn't seem like your typical porno film, it is because "Dream" and Stahl didn't intend to make a porno film. ("This film was *Cabaret*-goes-New Wave," contends Stahl, "an irradiated *Ship of Fools*.") Their sneaky

As if in a trance, Lana passes a line of Sex Negatives who urge her to join the performers on the Cafe Flesh stage.

plan, as laid down by Stahl in the October 1983 issue of *The Movies* and in *Omni's ScreenFlights/ScreenFantasies* (1984), was to film their picture with two separate arenas of action, offstage and onstage at Cafe Flesh, and to make those offstage scenes with the Sex Negatives so impressive that the gold-chained moneymen (whom he calls Dino, Desi, and Billy) would be willing to eliminate the more graphic onstage action by the Sex Positives. "Dream" and Stahl hoped that the picture would ultimately get an R rating. It never did, but when it played midnights all but one of the male orgasms were eventually eliminated, at their suggestion. (However, the video version includes the "wet shots.")

Watching *Cafe Flesh* today, it's hard to believe it wasn't made to comment on AIDS: In its version of near-future America, almost everyone has given up sex because it brings on illness, although they still crave it and envy those who somehow avoided getting the sexual illness. (It remains to be seen if we'll become a country of frustrated voyeurs.) But *Cafe Flesh* was made before anyone knew about a sexually transmitted disease that would affect our population in the exact way the Nuclear Kiss has affected this film's population: killing them, contaminating them, making them paranoid (with good reason) about having sex, making their existence hellish. One might question the film's contention that people who can't have sex would flock to sex shows even though this will increase their frustration. ("In *Cafe Flesh*," writes Stahl, "each soul arrives wrapped in [his or her] own poisoned mortality, denatured, as the scorched earth he, she, or it inhabits, yet driven to come and slaver over sin they can no longer commit.") But as masochistic Nick knows, people who have nothing, who have lost everything but their lives, like to torture themselves ("Torture is the one thing left I can feel"). I don't disagree. Why else would we passively sit and watch other people win prizes and trips to Hawaii and so much money on TV game shows? Are we really happy for lottery winners? Or do we relish our own failure and suffering? This is what the film suggests. It's an angry attack on those people who don't worry about nuclear devastation, who anticipate it being the ultimate high, the ultimate climax. To some, death is the ultimate *sexual* climax. Stahl, in *Omni's ScreenFlights/ScreenFantasies*:

> Wasted youth of every age peg the Flesh-ites as themselves in a few years: high-style mutants hanging out in an underground bar, fed up to their mohawks with the Nowhere they've grown up to inherit. Nuclear War, when it finally hits, will prove that all those postadolescent nihilists were right all along.
>
> Sex, clearly, is not the issue here. Apocalypse itself is what titillates. For the jaded throng who view their own future as a function of a World Gone Rotten, *Cafe Flesh* is a logical destination. . . . There are a million dirtier movies in the cosmos. But for an alarmingly large segment of our little world, obliteration seems the sexiest ticket around.
>
> *Cafe*'s concerns are terminal: the mechanics of lust *après* mega-death; the impotent salacity of the living doomed; the fetish for fiery climax that gives some folks a secret frisson at the prospect of the Holocaust to come, so that survival itself hinges on continued repression.

It is obviously chancy for a film to mock the audience that comes to see it. Paul Bartel's *Death Race 2000* (1975) managed to attack people who enjoyed violent sports, yet made a lot of money because these very people flocked to his film to see the violence. *Cafe Flesh* is not kind to the sex-film audience; as Max taunts, "Hey, not too pathetic that the biggest night of your life is watching some strange palooka getting his hog washed by some bimbo you don't even know." Max is deriding the Cafe Flesh regulars, but he is actually putting *us* down for sitting through the film's bizarre sexual vignettes ("Class act," Nick says sarcastically, after watching sex between a housewife and a man wearing a rat snout and tail) instead of doing something more constructive with our lives. (The filmmakers are hitting us below the belt—it's not fair to attack people for watching a sex film *while* they are watching it.) It makes us theater viewers uncomfortable to be equated with those pathetic voyeurs at the nightclub. Stahl writes:

> They groan; they drool. They weep and panic and scratch their eyes . . . but they never turn away. That audience, in a sense, stands out as the most telling element of the film, most evocative of a future well on its way from nightmare to real-life *Walpurgisnacht*.
>
> The audience within Cafe Flesh exists as more than a symbol for the one outside. The onscreen voyeurs emerge as our shadow selves: post-bomb doppelgangers, just plain folks adapting to an option that's never more than a shudder away. . . . Their itch for a vicarious fix is the same as the one that brought the paying public in off the streets. . . . They're aroused by the image of their own debasement. They seem to need it.

"Dream" and Stahl didn't want us to be excited by their sexual vignettes because they were afraid they'd be accused of pandering to the hardcore sex-film audience. Stahl asserts, "The last thing we had wanted were *erotic* erotic scenes." That's why there is no passion in the sexual vignettes and why all the performers seem uninterested and mechanical—even Sex Positives have been *dehumanized* by the nuclear war. But that doesn't stop the sex in *Cafe Flesh* from being *very* erotic. After all, anybody who has seen porno films knows that almost every sex scene is performed without emotion by actors just going through the motions. At least in *Cafe Flesh* the men and women having sex don't try to hide that they are *performing*. We don't have to put up with those awfully awkward dramatic breaks in which unskilled, improvising actors try to provide motivation for stripping ("It sure is hot in here!") and getting into bed together ("I sure could use a back rub!"). Seeing the sexual participants in weird masks, sailor hats, skimpy underwear, crotchless pants—none is totally nude—makes the vignettes more interesting than the sex scenes we're used to. A couple of things are a bit repellent (the rat tail for instance), but for the most part, the apparel, which doesn't hide anything vital, adds to the eroticism. The sexual tension is further heightened by the stylized sets and choreography; the eerie, pounding music; the background characters who serve as part of the decor; and the dramatic, extremely graphic photography: Stahl writes,

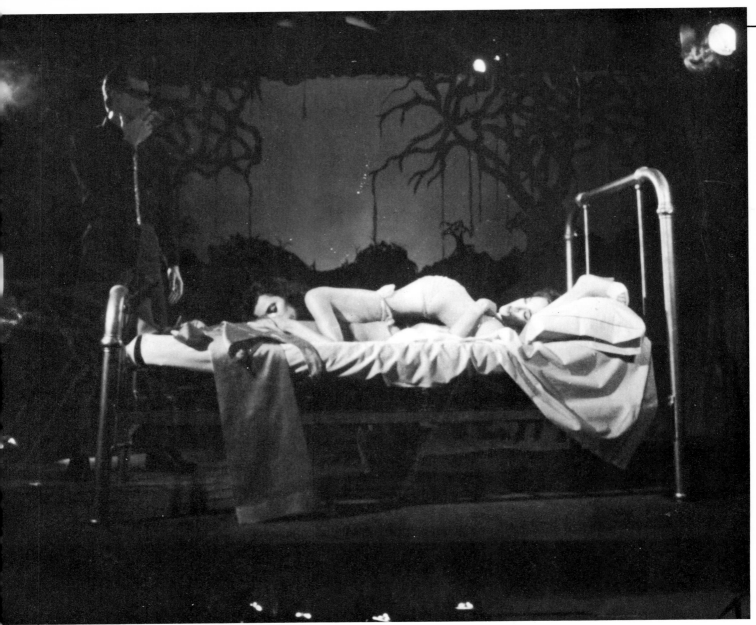

As sex superstar Johnny Rico waits his turn with Lana (on her back), Lana and Angel perform. They are the only sex performers in the film who seem to enjoy their work.

"Because so much of the film was shot with actual torch light . . . 'Dream' and cinematographer F. X. Pope gambled on using Fuji's newly developed 250 film, a more or less experimental film designed to capture darkness without fake illumination. (A year later it received a technical Oscar, prompting an indignant Pope to petition the Academy and claim some right to the honors. No luck.)"

The final reason the film is erotic despite the filmmakers' intentions is, as mentioned earlier, that they made us identify with the Cafe Flesh audience. So when virgin Angel (Marie Sharp) and Lana move out of the nightclub audience and onto the stage, from one arena to the other, they represent us leaving our seats in the theater, giving up our voyeurism, and joining the sexual performers on screen. It's particularly stimulating seeing Lana become a sexual performer at the end because for most of the film she has kept her clothes on—Snow proves she is an okay actress,

then surprises us by returning to her porno roots (she had appeared in one previous porno film). Similarly, the reason the sexual scenes in *I Am Curious (Yellow)* have such impact is that they come near the end, after we've spent much time with a clothed heroine (Lena Nyman) and gotten to know her well, other than in a sexual vein. I'm not sure why "Dream" allowed Angel ("Sex is great . . . I want to do it all the time") and Lana to show emotion and be so aroused while having sex, but because we identify with them, their attitude makes their sexual interludes, including one with each other, particularly exciting—I guess this relates to why it's supposedly more fun to go to Amateur Night at strip joints. But the filmmakers shouldn't think they failed: If watching the sex in *Cafe Flesh* is exciting but not satisfying (as some viewers have complained), then the film *does* succeed. The film confirms that when it comes to sex, voyeurism just can't replace participation.

Chilly Scenes of Winter

formerly titled *Head Over Heels**

1982   Color   United Artists Classics release of a Triple Play film
Director: Joan Micklin Silver
Producers: Mark Metcalf, Amy Robinson, and Griffin Dunne
Screenplay: Joan Micklin Silver
From the novel by Ann Beattie
Cinematography: Bobby Byrne
Music: Ken Lauber
Editor: Cynthia Scheider
Running Time: 93 minutes

Cast: John Heard (Charles Richardson), Mary Beth Hurt (Laura Conley), Peter Riegert (Sam), Gloria Grahame (mother), Kenneth McMillan (Pete), Nora Heflin (Betty), Jerry Hardin (Mr. Patterson), Tarah Nutter (Susan), Metcalf (Ox/Jim), Dunne (Mark), Allen Joseph (blind man), Alex Johnson (Elise), Beattie (waitress).

Synopsis: It has been a year since Laura left Charles and went back to her husband, Ox, and stepdaughter, Rebecca, but he thinks about her all the time, has imaginary conversations with her, and hopes she will come back. It doesn't help his loneliness that his unemployed best friend, Sam, who has moved in with him, sleeps with women in Charles's bed; his younger sister Susan has a new boyfriend, medical student Mark; and his boss, Mr. Patterson, wants him to help with his son's sexual problems. Rather than feeling sorry for his stepfather, Pete, whom he has never liked, for having to care for Charles's insane, suicidal mother, he envies him for having someone to take care of.

A report reader for Utah's Department of Development in Salt Lake City, Charles met Laura when she worked in the filing room. It was love at first sight. She was married, but had moved out of her house six weeks before. She didn't know if she did the right thing. On their first date Charles went to Laura's apartment, which had a lamp and mattress on the floor. He asked her to live with him. She refused. So he bought her a chair.

Laura did move in with Charles, in the house his grandmother left him. They were happy together, even when they didn't do anything. But she felt she didn't deserve to be happy after leaving a husband who had done nothing wrong and a young stepdaughter who loved and needed her. Charles thought Ox married Laura to have a live-in housekeeper and mother for Rebecca. Laura couldn't deny it. Laura couldn't understand why Charles liked her so much. She was more comfortable with Ox's indifference than with Charles's constant attention and flattery. She complained, "You have this exalted view of me and I hate it. If you think I'm that great then there must be something wrong with you." Her self-esteem was so low that she felt more comfortable choosing, as Charles said, "someone who loves you too little over someone who loves you too much." When Charles became too possessive, Laura returned to Ox and Rebecca. Charles never called her but became obsessed with winning her back. He watched her pick up Rebecca at school and often drove past her house, and he got friendly with flirtatious fellow worker Betty just to grill her about her friend Laura.

Charles calls up Laura and they make rendezvous plans. He is hopeful. She keeps the appointment but is too sick to stay. Time passes. Growing impatient, Charles and Sam drive to her house. She is stunned to see them there. They tell architect Ox they are interested in buying an A-frame from him. Charles and Laura sneak a hug in the kitchen. Charles blurts out to Ox that he loves Laura. They flee the ex-football player. Laura admires what he did.

Feeling guilty about being insensitive toward Betty, Charles invites her home for dinner. When she reveals Laura has again moved out on Ox, Charles demands her new address. Sam takes the insulted Betty home.

Charles visits Laura in her new apartment. He demands to know if she's coming back to him. Again he seems possessive. She says she needs time alone. He says he's already waited so long for her that he's going crazy. He realizes she can't make up her mind. He tells her good-bye. She closes the door behind him. In the time to come, Charles will learn to cope with the pain.

* *

**Head Over Heels* was released in 1979 by United Artists. It ran an additional four minutes at the end.

New York–based Double Play Productions is one of the contemporary cinema's most pleasant success stories. Consisting of two young creative producers, former actress Amy Robinson, the female lead in Martin Scorsese's *Mean Streets* (1973), and her DP partner, actor Griffin Dunne, this independent company has stayed afloat and prospered in the eighties while striving to make quality films with interesting characters and stories rather than impersonal mega-hits full of robots and special effects. Double Play and its predecessor, Triple Play, formed in 1977 by Robinson, Dunne, and Mark Metcalf, another struggling actor, have consistently made personally felt, efficiently produced, refreshingly offbeat movies: *Head Over Heels* (1979)/ *Chilly Scenes of Winter*, with Dunne and Metcalf in supporting roles, John Sayles's *Baby, It's You* (1983), with Rosanna Arquette playing a character based on Robinson in high school and college, Scorsese's nightmare comedy *After Hours* (1986), with Dunne starring, and Sidney Lumet's *Running on Empty* (1988). In each case, the producers selected projects to which they had emotional attachment, for they would spend an enormous amount of time and energy overseeing every aspect of production. Most neophyte producers make exploitation films to help them break into the business and, they claim, earn monies needed to make high-caliber films later—instead they usually make sequels to their exploitation films. To their credit, Robinson, Dunne, and Metcalf chanced debuting with the type of film they wanted to make all along.

Robinson fell in love with Ann Beattie's bittersweet first novel, *Chilly Scenes of Winter* (1976), and passed it along to Dunne and Metcalf, who agreed it would make an ideal first film. So they drove up to Boston, where Beattie was teaching—"It was like seeing three of my characters walk through the door," she later commented—and optioned the book for only $2000, versus $30,000 on completion of the picture. Beattie's only stipulations were that she appear in the picture (she plays a waitress) and be introduced to Dean Martin (she never was). In the cover story interview for the September 1985 issue of *American Film*, Robinson told Clarke Taylor:

> "[W]e didn't start out thinking, How can we break into Hollywood, but, rather, How can we make this low-budget movie, *Chilly Scenes of Winter*? We asked a lot of nuts-and-bolts questions. We had *some* connections to the business, especially on the creative side, and we used them to gain relatively easy access to the people at the studios. Also, when we first went out to Hollywood, it wasn't as though we were producers in from Tennessee, naive and empty-handed. We had a book by a rising literary star, Ann Beattie . . . We were in the right place at the right time . . . [W]e also had Joan Micklin Silver to direct at a time when there was interest in 'women's films.' "

Silver, an extremely talented, sadly neglected director-writer, had already made two impressive films, *Hester Street*

Charles and Laura meet for the first time in the office library and are immediately attracted.

(1975) and, a personal favorite, *Between the Lines* (1977), also with John Heard and also about survivors of the sixties. She, too, had loved Beattie's book and recognized its movie potential. While the producers, who were having difficulty raising money, were trying to find someone affordable to replace playwright Michael Weller (*Hair*) when he dropped out, Silver was tracking them down to offer her services as writer-director. With Silver involved, Claire Townsend, a creative executive at 20th Century-Fox, agreed to acquire the project. When Townsend moved to United Artists, she took it with her. UA financed the picture and released it in 1979 as *Head Over Heels,* having concluded that "chilly" and "winter" weren't good selling words. But the new title, ideal for an X-rated cheerleader movie or, as Beattie griped, a Fred Astaire musical, wasn't the least bit enticing—moreover, only word-of-mouth let Beattie fans know it was an adaptation of her novel. The movie might have disappeared into obscurity if not for a small devoted following, especially in Beattie's Boston.

United Artists quickly gave up on the picture (for instance, it was pulled out of New York in five weeks), but in 1982 its enterprising Classics division, which rescued another John Heard cult film, *Cutter's Way* (1982), and turned it into a minor hit, took over distribution, believing there was potentially a substantial audience for it. After all, it had received excellent reviews, it already had a cult, Beattie's fame was growing dramatically, and moviegoers

were becoming increasingly aware of leads John Heard, who had just starred in *Cat People* (1982), and Mary Beth Hurt, who had just starred in *The World According to Garp* (1982). The title of the book was restored and, at the filmmakers' suggestion, the four-minute-long "happy" ending of *Head Over Heels,* in which Charles returns home to find Laura waiting with his favorite dessert, was chopped off. Strategically distributed, properly publicized—its target audience was well-read moviegoers in their twenties and thirties—and carefully nurtured, *Chilly Scenes of Winter* did surprisingly strong business, eventually turning a profit.

Chilly Scenes of Winter is lovingly made, exceptionally written (the dialogue is terrific), and charmingly played by a talented ensemble: Heard and Hurt are wonderful (even if their characters are off-putting at times)—how could they not be offscreen sweethearts?—and Peter Riegert, the great Gloria Grahame (her final screen triumph), Kenneth McMillan, Nora Heflin, Jerry Hardin, Allen Joseph, Metcalf, and Dunne make strong impressions as the quirky characters who confuse the lives of the relatively sane Charles and Laura. (Charles's sister, Susan, played by Tarah Nutter, is the only practical, centered person in the picture.) It's a sophisticated *Love Story* (1970) that should elicit an emotional response from any of you (most everyone) who remember being childishly, obsessively, and head over heels in love and who remember doubling up in pain and sickness for a long time after the love of your life left without sufficient reason. You'll laugh at Charles's follies and the zany, disorganized world that he stumbles through (such a world is familiar to many of us). Yet the film, especially without the happy ending of *Head Over Heels* or the ambiguous ending of Beattie's novel (they reunite, but for how long?), is a sad-eyed, realistic look at how people can suffer the loss of everything important in their lives—the people they love, their romantic notions—yet still survive. In the sixties, the romantic notion of young people like Charles was to have a successful revolution; in the seventies, lonely Charles's new romantic notion is to rescue lovely Laura from her uncaring architect husband, Ox, and the unhappy home Ox has built and live happily ever after with her. Both romantic notions are crushed, yet Charles goes on (he takes deep breaths at the end), one of the sixties' lost generation that struggles through the irrelevant, nonsensical seventies.

Silver retains Beattie's sardonic humor without sacrificing her sense of melancholy, for the novel is foremost about *loss* and the undiminishing *pain* people suffer because of their loss. Beattie establishes that Charles has lost Laura; Charles and sister Susan have lost their natural father and are losing their mother to insanity; their mother, who mourns her first husband, is losing her mind; stepfather Pete is losing his wife; Laura has lost her husband and stepdaughter; Rebecca has lost her stepmother; Sam has lost his dog, his job, his apartment, and his knack for attracting women; Mr. Patterson's son has lost his chance to go to Harvard; Charles loses phone numbers, addresses, track of people; the young characters have lost the sixties (Charles is obviously aging because he "found his Frisbee in the closet a few weeks ago and didn't even give it a toss"). The punch-in-the-stomach pain that Charles suffers because he lost Laura is beautifully conveyed: He no longer has an "appetite" for life—"There is nothing in the entire

Once again, Charles's mother goes off the deep end.

store he wants to eat"; "He would have gone home and had water and cookies . . . Hydrox cookies (What happened to them? They used to be so good)"; *everything* reminds him of Laura; he can't stop fantasizing about getting her back; he repeatedly drives past her house; after a year he still hopes every phone call might be from her. He can't stop thinking about her, talking about her, even singing about her: "Laura, Laura, bo bora banana fana, fee fi, mo mora, Laura." He envies his mother for conveniently losing her mind ("I think one day she just decided to go nuts because that was easier")—he, too, would like to be anesthetized from hurt. Silver may not stress the *pain* Charles feels as much as Beattie does (he's always genial and seemingly even-tempered, rolling with the punches while *everyone* hits on him for favors), but she does deal equally with his obsessiveness, even adding a bit of obsessive lunacy: Charles builds a miniature of architect Ox's A-frame.

Silver's most significant change was to greatly expand the role of Laura, who, except for the brief cameo in which she drives to tell Charles she is too sick to keep their appointment, doesn't appear and reveal herself to us personally until the last sixth of Beattie's book. In fact, Charles's obsession for a figure from the distant past for five-sixths of the story—until Laura unexpectedly again breaks up with Ox—recalls the obsessive love Dana Andrews's detective has for Gene Tierney's presumably dead title character in *Laura* (1944). (Was Beattie thinking of that film?) By having Hurt's Laura appear in flashbacks that are interspersed throughout the film, we feel her presence in the *present,* as does Charles. Consequently, we don't equate his obsessive love with mental sickness, as we do Dana Andrews's necrophiliac (in general, characters in the movie aren't as pathetic as they are in Beattie's book). Because we see Laura with Charles, we understand how *she*—she's smart, funny, adorable—would have such a profound effect on *him*. We know why he misses their relationship so much. She really is enough to make him happy, to make up for all that is sad in his life.

Charles manages to keep a straight face as he shakes hands with his sister Susan's unhip boyfriend, Mark (played by the film's co-producer, Griffin Dunne).

So Charles can see Laura, he and Sam (right) *tell her husband Ox (played by co-producer Mark Metcalf) that they're interested in buying a house from him.*

These flashbacks also give us a chance to understand what's going through Laura's mind, an opportunity Beattie denies us. We become aware of Laura's dilemma: It's so unsatisfying and unrewarding spending her life with her husband (he doesn't make an appearance in the novel), who doesn't love her enough, yet it's equally hard to live with Charles, who loves her too much. We fully sympathize with Charles until a Silver flashback reveals he was so possessive of Laura that he even distrusted her visiting her gynecologist without him. Silver obviously saw hints of this irrational jealousy when Beattie has Charles accusingly question Laura about having dated a taxi driver (a bit also included in the movie). Silver develops another important theme that was only touched on in the book when Laura curiously asks Charles why he loves her so much. The reason Laura finds it easier to accept Ox's lack of interest in her than Charles's constant flattery and attention is that she has no self-esteem. She won't accept Charles's exalted view of her. She doesn't think a woman who would even consider leaving her husband (in the book, he tells her to leave) and stepdaughter to find personal happiness is worth anything; when Charles tells her she has an unfairly low opinion of herself, she objects: "I have a realistic opinion of myself. I'm an ordinary person—I can't live up to this thing that you have about me . . . In fact, I'm worse than an ordinary person since I left a perfectly decent man for no good reason." (This is also why Shirley Knight's pregnant housewife despises herself in 1969's *The Rain People.*) Laura states unequivocally: "I don't deserve to be happy." She equates happiness with living with Charles. She thinks she doesn't deserve Charles because he is a reward and she yearns for punishment. But as Pete tells Charles, "People should get what they want once in a while." Sadly, Laura only judges herself in context of the two men in her life, how they view her.

In Beattie's novel, when Laura gets a job she immediately becomes friendlier toward Charles and allows him to seduce her back into the relationship, as if a job gives her a secure identity that he can't wipe out no matter how stifling he becomes. In the movie, Laura has not found a job by the last scene—she establishes her identity by closing the door on Charles and committing herself to living alone and working things out on her own. Laura obviously needs time alone, so her final action makes sense. Nevertheless, I have mixed feelings about this ending. For one thing, having seen *Head Over Heels,* I can't help thinking that footage—happy footage—is missing. I feel the same when I see Don Siegel's version of *Invasion of the Body Snatchers* (1956), minus the optimistic studio-imposed ending. Silver filmed the original ending in an attempt to be faithful to Beattie, who did allow her lovers at least temporary reconciliation. But later Silver decided her ending was "too triumphant." Viewers no doubt respond better to the ending of *Chilly Scenes* because it more accurately reflects what happened to their own lost love affairs. However, in terms of these two characters, the original ending seems more logical. They would get back together, if only to break up a few more times. Charles and Laura are like the on-again, off-again couple Albert Brooks and Kathryn Harrold play in *Modern Romance* (1981). (Also, Charles's rude treatment of date Betty reminds one of Brooks's insensitivity toward date Jane Hallaren.)

Silver's script seems geared for Laura to achieve self-worth by learning to accept the rave reviews she gets from Charles. It's important for her to be around someone as encouraging as Charles. Of course, there is no one else like Charles. It makes sense that she didn't accept Charles's opinion on what is best for her simply because he was so insistent—but it would be acceptable if she reached the same conclusions (i.e., they needn't do anything in order to have a good time) during their time apart. Structurally, the new ending is also wrong. When Laura closes the door, it is the last we see of her. It's too abrupt a finale for the lead female character—and it gives us a bitter aftertaste toward both him and her—but I'm more disturbed that her action hands the film to Charles, making it his story. That would be fine—after all, the story in the book is Charles's alone—but Silver introduced the flashbacks and included one crucial scene in which Laura exists on screen outside of Charles's vision (she bakes cookies with Rebecca) for the specific purpose of making the story Laura's as well as his. Either the cookie-baking scene should also be eliminated so the film is only Charles's story or, to retain Laura's equal status, Silver should take us inside Laura's apartment to glimpse her behind that closed door (outside of Charles's vision again), reacting to what was the official conclusion of her past life. (Too bad the producers couldn't afford to shoot new footage for the re-release.)

Interestingly, Silver moved the setting of the story from New England to Salt Lake City. I'm sure she did this so location filming could take place close to Hollywood, but I think she also wanted to place Charles in a locale that epitomized the vacuous seventies. Here you would not so readily find the political, intellectual, or cultural stimuli (although even here there is a porno theater) or vital work (Charles's civil servant job in a bland high rise is *boring*) that we'd associate with a Boston. Without such benefits, Charles finds it no compensation to live in one of America's beautiful cities, because Silver places him only in

Charles ruins a potentially tender moment with unfounded jealousy.

unscenic sites, probably the only places martyristic Charles would wander. It's lucky that Charles and Laura have fun together even when they're doing nothing, because in Silver's Salt Lake City—where Betty can spend weeks planning party hors d'oeuvres—there's nothing to do. Charles has no reason to be living here after college, other than this is where he grew up. He is a representative of an unfocused generation that dwells on the sixties (they romanticize Woodstock—although he and Sam didn't go there, they could have) and still listens to music by Jimi and Janis (by no means are there as many musical references as in Beattie), but, with exceptions like Ox and like Susan's early-yuppie boyfriend Mark (amusingly played by Dunne), they don't think about meaningful jobs, making money, or their futures. They don't even take time to stock their refrigerators with anything but beer, or make their beds, clean up, or buy decent furniture. (Like Beattie, who lets readers know the look, "feel," and aroma of every location, Silver takes great care with indoor settings, making sure they suit the people in them.)

"What gives *Chilly Scenes* its considerable charm," wrote James Atlas in the *New York Times,* "is Mrs. Silver's willingness to devote her attention to the ordinary details of her characters' lives without excessively dramatizing them." The characters discuss problems as they drive around, have desultory conversations in kitchens, kill time in smoky bars, sit down for dinners (acting like adults since there are no parents around), argue in coffee shops, shop in supermarkets, cook (many scenes in this film revolve around food), spend time in bed, talk on the phone, shovel snow, listen to music, take kids to school, wile away eight hours a day at work. I love these scenes because they make the characters come alive—we know these people, and how they walk, dress, eat, and talk (we may even become nostalgic for our own chats in cars and coffee-shop arguments). Yet equally effective are scenes that are not of

the everyday variety: Charles's mother matter-of-factly informs her Thanksgiving guests, Charles and Sam, that she didn't cook anything; Charles's boss politely and awkwardly retreats from Charles's office after being told off; Charles looks directly at us and starts talking about Laura—in his state, he's probably imagining there's a camera there and he has an audience; Charles and Sam, pretending to be interested in buying an A-frame, pay a visit to Ox and Laura; with Ox only a few feet away in the next room, Charles and Laura hug tightly (it's the sexiest moment in the movie); Charles blurts out to Ox that he loves Laura, simultaneously stunning and impressing Laura; in one of the cinema's finest meet-cute scenes, Charles and Laura immediately recognize their mutual attraction and their desire to pursue a relationship, so they are willing to fight through the awkward customary flirtation lines; Charles takes Laura to her first porno film and though she complains it's disgusting she insists on staying to the end (a familiar scenario in the seventies); leaving the theater, Charles innocently compliments Laura, who has an inferiority complex, and this immediately sparks an argument (spats between lovers never make sense); Charles puts food in the backyard birdhouse, hoping he can bring them back in the dead of winter—just as he hopes to bring Laura back into his home. These scenes are only in the film. So is my favorite moment. Charles and Laura are dancing close when she expresses surprise ("You're kidding") that Sam is considered attractive by women. Seeing she prefers him to lady-killer Sam, Charles smiles with relief and pride and, with confirmation that she is unique among women, gives Laura a big hug. In the book, Charles is relieved "his best friend didn't love his girlfriend"—but this is much better. It is a sweet, tender moment between one of the cinema's most vulnerable heroes and one of its most fragile heroines. We feel the tremendous strength they get in each other's arms. If only they'd never let go.

Choose Me

1984 Color   Island Alive
Director: Alan Rudolph
Producers: Carolyn Pfeiffer and David Blocker
Screenplay: Alan Rudolph
Cinematography: Jan Keisser
Songs: Teddy Pendergrass
Editor: Mia Goldman
Running Time: 106 minutes

Cast: Genevieve Bujold (Nancy Love), Keith Carradine (Mickey DeLeon), Lesley Ann Warren (Eve), Patrick Bauchau (Zack Antoine), Rae Dawn Chong (Pearl Antoine), John Larroquette (Billy Ace), Edward Ruscha (Ralph Chomsky), Gaillard Sartain (Mueller), Robert Gould (Lou), John Considine (voice of Dr. Ernest Greene).

Synopsis: Dr. Nancy Love is a popular radio sex therapist. Because she refuses to talk about herself, her listeners don't realize she has no sex life of her own. Nor does she want one. Eve frequently calls for advice, using different names. An ex-streetwalker who bought a bar because it was already called "Eve's," she's been having an affair for three years with a rich, married tough guy named Zack. Also her bar aide Billy Ace keeps after her. She has seen so many relationships fail that she can't commit herself to a man, even though she would love marriage. Yet she can't resist men.

Mickey arrives at Eve's lounge. He loved the first Eve. Eve tells him that she shot herself over a man. (He may have already known this.) Eve and Mickey are immediately attracted to each other but she tries to resist him. At the bar, Mickey meets Pearl, who gives Eve a hard time for reasons Eve can't fathom. Pearl tells Mickey she's keeping an eye on Eve because she knows her husband, Zack, is having an affair with her. Mickey tells Pearl he never lies but that he is a pathological liar. He says he was married twice, escaped from a mental hospital, taught poetry at Yale, and was a prize-winning photographer. In time, he'll reveal he was a jet pilot and a spy in Germany and Russia.

Using the name "Ann," Nancy becomes Eve's roommate. She says she runs an answering service. Nancy doesn't know Eve is a frequent caller to Dr. Love and Eve doesn't realize "Ann" is Dr. Love. Now when she calls Dr. Love, she mentions Mickey, the new man in her life. She doesn't trust him but is attracted to him. She worries he is attracted to Pearl.

Mickey wins money from Zack playing cards. Zack tells him he doesn't want to see his face again. Mickey goes to Pearl's apartment. He takes pictures of her while she sleeps but they don't sleep together. Zack finds them together and threatens Mickey with a gun. He blackens Pearl's eye. Mickey flees to Eve's house. "Ann" is there. While he bathes, she looks at his scrapbook—he really was all those things he said he was. He seduces her. She turns down his proposal. Before she was on the verge of a breakdown; now she is sexually liberated. She turns him down. On the air, she now openly discusses sex, the thrill of giving in to your sexual impulses. She dresses sexually.

When Pearl shows up with a black eye and yells at her, Eve assumes Pearl was beaten by Mickey. In her car, she tries to push Mickey away but, as before, he draws her into his arms. Zack pulls him out and tries to beat him for sleeping with his wife. Hearing this, Eve is further convinced Mickey is unfaithful. She drives home. There "Ann" admits she slept with Mickey and wants to share him with her. This is the last straw.

Mickey arrives after Eve has left her house. So does Zack. Previously, Zack had called Eve and "Ann" had answered and given him excellent advice about his relationships. He wanted to speak to "Ann" again and is furious to see Mickey with her, too. They fight and Mickey flees with Zack's gun.

Mickey finds Eve on a roof. She threatens to shoot herself. But when he puts a gun to his head also, she runs into his arms. They make love. She will put her faith in him. They marry and go to Las Vegas for their honeymoon.

Eve contemplates suicide. Choose Me *is a comedy, but all the major characters suffer tremendous pain.*

EVE: *You're a lunatic.*
MICKEY: *That's why you chose me.*

I chose seeing *Choose Me*, one afternoon in 1984, over other first-run films playing in New York's east fifties, because, fortunately, the Baronet Theater ticket girl impulsively recommended it while I was warily gazing at lobby posters. "I don't know what it is," she said, "but there's something about it I really love." Since then I've come across a remarkable number of people who place it at the top of their list of recommended sleepers. Like the ticket girl, most are hesitant to explain their emotional response to the film, as if they assume such appraisals as "the acting is terrific," "the characters are likable and offbeat," "the story is full of surprises," "the movie has heart," and "the director seems to care" are too simple to properly convey its special appeal. But such remarks are not only accurate but appropriate for convincing others to see the picture, which is why it has had exceptional word-of-mouth. If you want to drive potential viewers away, synopsize the zany plot—it will sound like an Annette Funicello–Frankie Avalon beach movie, without the sand— or go into what is being said about modern romance. Just as the characters in *Choose Me* find that their relationships suffer when sexual spontaneity is supplanted by self-analysis, viewers will enjoy watching this film most if they reserve their analyses for another day and just go with their feelings.

The director (-writer) who "seems to care" is Alan Rudolph, a Hollywood maverick who began as Robert Altman's assistant director on *The Long Goodbye* (1973), *California Split* (1974), and *Nashville* (1975), co-wrote Altman's *Buffalo Bill and the Indians, or Sitting Bull's History Lesson* (1976), and has since created a cult canon of his own: Debut film *Welcome to L.A.* (1977) is still the picture most associated with his name; *Remember My Name* (1978), also produced by Altman, is his least known film; *Roadie* (1980) is his worst film, *Endangered Species* (1982) his most commercial/least personal, *Songwriter* (1984) his most forgettable, *Trouble in Mind* (1986) his weirdest, *Made in Heaven* (1987) his most muddled, *The Moderns* (1988) his most argued about, and *Choose Me* his best—how much warmer, funnier, more controlled, and more sincere it is than the similarly structured *Welcome to L.A.*! Initially, Rudolph's films were regarded as Altmanesque. I thought *Welcome to L.A.* was a (nasty) poor man's *Nashville*. His later works, including *Choose Me,* also have the ensemble acting, improvisation, intertwining story lines, off-the-wall humor, unexpected song insertions, satirical jabs, and constantly-on-the-make characters but now these elements are seen to be less characteristic of Altman than Rudolph, whose contribution to the style and content of *Nashville* was surely greater than we first realized.

One of the most interesting aspects of Rudolph's films is that while the characters are familiar (though quirky) they exist somewhere just to the edge of our familiar "real" world, perhaps in a parallel America. Rudolph titled his film *Welcome to L.A.* and then tried to disguise the fact that he filmed it in L.A. by using many nondescript indoor sets; *Choose Me* was also filmed in L.A. but the L.A. we see is not the L.A. we know; Rudolph went to Seattle to film *Trouble in Mind,* but set the picture in fictional Rain City. In the March 1986 issue of *American Film,* Rudolph told David Remsen, "I don't do realistic films. I don't even believe they exist. . . . By definition, movies are a lie on reality." Remsen described Rudolph's pattern for creating personal visions:

> Rudolph writes spare blueprint scripts that, in production, he nurtures into fully realized, self-contained celluloid worlds by spontaneously adding layers of humor, story, imagination, character, whimsy, and emotion. Especially emotion. . . . Character and mood are crucial; structured plot is much less important. In *Choose Me,* for instance, the lushly-hued atmosphere *is* the story. With *Trouble in Mind* (at $2.8 million, his first "big budget" independent film), Rudolph . . . attempted to create a straightforward plot. . . . But true to form, Rudolph claims he ha[d] "thrown away" the plot points so that the story emerges through the characters. Actors are the key to all of Rudolph's movies. "Sure, there has to be a concept first so that everyone has something to play with," he says, "but otherwise, it's actors, photography, music, editing, plot—in that order."

Rudolph was unhappy working for a studio, United Artists, when he made *Roadie* and *Endangered Species,* so he decided to return to the independent route for *Choose Me.* He wouldn't write the script until he knew how much financing could be raised. The eventual budget was just $850,000—$50,000 less than the cost of *Welcome to L.A.,* made in less expensive 1977. This meant that he had to

Eve is upset to hear her roommate Nancy confess that she slept with Mickey.

find actors willing to work at a fraction of their regular salaries in exchange for a share of possible profits, that cast and crew combined would number only 25 people (the average Hollywood film *crew* had 80 people), and that he had to hire technicians who'd work at low salaries to get positions a notch higher than they'd had on past films. Surprisingly, the picture made back its budget almost immediately. Released by Island Alive, it sold well to Australia, Canada, and the video market, earned $300,000 in 14 weeks at both a theater in Seattle and one in Los Angeles, and then added $100,000 in its first 4 weeks at New York City's Baronet, where I saw it and realized I'd never seen anything like it.

Rudolph's film is about our sad crazy-making society, where miserable, lonely people are so desperate to find the "perfect sex" and "true love" they've read and heard rumors about that they accept as gospel the radio rantings of pop sexologists like Genevieve Bujold's Dr. Nancy Love. Yet Rudolph tells his modern tale by drawing on two diverse forms from the past: classic farce and *film noir.* We'd probably think this film strictly a farce if the characters weren't so cynical and distressed (they constantly drink and smoke), if Teddy Pendergrass's moody songs weren't so haunting, and if Jan Keisser's photography and Steven Legler's art design—especially for the dream-world set outside Eve's lounge, which is bathed with red and blue light and has a street that reflects light, neon signs, and large round street lights that serve as full moons for lovers—weren't meant to remind us of forties and fifties *noir* films (even though those were made in black and white); furthermore, Pearl and Zack's wall is covered with posters of old movie melodramas.* Rudolph made sure we thought about *film noir* in relation to farce. Farce and

. . . .
*Posters of *All About Eve* (1950), *Lady in the Dark* (1944), *When Ladies Meet* (1941), and *Tales of Manhattan* (1942)—a film with a thread that connects diverse stories—comment on Rudolph's stories. When Mickey enters the apartment, he passes a poster for *Don't Bother to Knock* (1952). When Zack accuses him of sleeping with Pearl it's in front of a poster for *The Accused* (1948).

film noir are an odd combination since one tradition is, of course, comedic in nature, while the other is dark, pessimistic, dramatic. However, Rudolph points out there is a thematic connection between the two, in that both are about deception, distrust, entangled relationships, mistaken identity, and infidelity (bed hopping). I think he is showing how the forms intersect so he can then turn around and make us see the point where the two forms almost correspond yet, as we see in terms of this film, are completely different: In farce, there is *coincidence;* in *film noir,* there is *fate.* Coincidence certainly influences the lives of Rudolph's characters—that's how they all meet (or collide with) each other. It's fairly harmless. More worrisome is that at first Rudolph's characters seem willing to let fate dictate their futures—an indication that life has beaten them into passivity. However, they (specifically Eve, Mickey, and Nancy) will deliberately reject the fatalism that destroyed classic *noir* characters. They will make choices about their futures. Because they triumph the film becomes, ultimately, a happy-ending *comedy*—a farce that happens to have *noir* visuals and some, but not the most important, *noir* themes.

In *Choose Me,* the five major characters who make coincidental connections with each other—Lesley Ann Warren's Eve, Genevieve Bujold's Dr. Nancy Love, Keith Carradine's Mickey, Rae Dawn Chong's Pearl, and Patrick Bauchau's Zack Antoine, Pearl's husband—believe they can find happiness, which is what they seek, only in relationships. But they don't understand how sex, love, marriage, understanding, and communication relate to one another and what degree of importance each has in making a relationship successful. Their confusion is apparent in Pearl's question to Dr. Love: "Do you know what it is when you feel something for somebody and don't know what it is because if you knew what it was you wouldn't feel it anymore?" Only Yogi Berra could answer her.

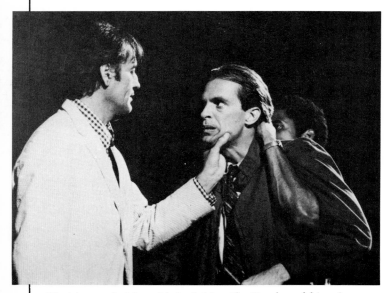

Having caught him with both his wife, Pearl, and his mistress, Eve, Zach attempts to beat up Mickey.

The characters are inextricably linked by more than the telephone lines they often use. Eve, who works on Adams (Adam's?) Street and lives on Garden Street, can't resist men and Mickey can't resist women—she should feel as guiltless as he does. Mickey and Nancy, whose daydreams overlap, are both *outsiders* who give others advice on love— yet Nancy has no idea what she's talking about and neither has had past success in their own love lives. Nancy has had no success with men and Eve has "had too much success," yet—like Pearl, who is nothing like either of them—they attract Zack and are attracted to Mickey (a human "mickey" who makes the female bartender and barfly woozy); as the only person around without sexual hang-ups, he is the ideal lover for Nancy. Mickey is a charming man who is occasionally violent, while Zack is a violent man who is occasionally charming, yet they are attracted to the same women, Eve, Nancy, and Pearl. Mickey and Pearl are both sexually uninhibited poets. Pearl would like to *be* Dr. Love.

These neurotic, schizophrenic characters all resort to deception. Eve pretends to be "Jane," "Diane," and "Karen" when she calls Dr. Love for advice; Pearl uses the name "Rita" when she calls Dr. Love; Nancy Love calls herself "Ann" when she moves in with Eve. Pearl won't let Eve know she is Zack's wife and won't let Zack know she's aware he's stepping out with Eve; Zack cheats on Pearl. Mickey made a profession of deception when he worked as a U.S. spy. He no longer lies (except when he tells Eve his gun was unloaded when he threatened to join her in suicide). But since he calls himself a "pathological liar," he must assume no one will believe him when he reveals his improbable history as a twice-married Yale poetry professor, prize-winning photographer, jet pilot, spy, and mental patient. These people put up so many false fronts that they are deceiving not only others, but themselves as well. Even Mickey will learn, from "Ann," that you don't know someone just because you slept with them—"What did we just do, become strangers?" he protests. (Earlier John Larroquette's bar-helper character Billy Ace was upset that after sleeping with Eve she acted like "we're *fucking* strangers.") What everyone discovers is that they're also strangers to themselves (Nancy speaks of Dr. Love in the third person) and must find or establish their own identities.

All these characters are victims of their pasts. They have been so brutalized by relationships that protecting themselves from further hurt has become their top priority. They want love but fear it is destructive rather than enriching. But self-defense also can be destructive (Mickey once killed in self-defense), and by insulating themselves within a wall of unhappy memories, people like Eve miss rare chances to attempt fulfilling relationships and achieve happiness. Eve, a former streetwalker, is on the verge of suicide because, after having witnessed firsthand many relationships and marriages shattered by wandering husbands, she can't commit herself to a man or the marriage she craves. Nancy Love had such unfulfilling sexual experiences in her distant past that she suppresses her strong sexual desires—on her show, she disassociates sex from love—to the point where she's cracking up. Pearl and Zack may break up because their marriage isn't as good as it was when they had sex all the time, before, she says, "we started talking and it stopped working."

Mickey—a Mr. Fixit, who will fix broken buses, broken soda machines, and broken people (Eve, Nancy, the breaking-up Antoines)—suffered the most in his past. He was captured by the KGB and brainwashed, twice was divorced, had the third woman he loved (the first Eve) commit suicide, and spent time in a mental hospital. In fact his pain when recalling his past is so great that, unlike the others, he refuses to also fret about a future or waste precious time talking and second-guessing his instinct to jump headlong into relationships with women. The greatest movie romantic since the Truffaut/Leaud–created Antoine Doinel, Mickey believes that if he wants to kiss a woman—his kisses are among the most sexual in movie history—this is proof he wants to marry her. He can't understand why the women he quickly falls in love with—"Ann" and Eve—distrust his instincts and their own and let opportunity escape. He knows that it's crazy to attempt a relationship in this modern world where talk is unproductive since you can't trust even the most honest person and there is no such thing as Truth; where people don't even know themselves; and where there are no experts on sex, love, or marriage (Nancy Love finally admits she is "a clown"). He knows you've got to be crazy to risk more pain to possibly find pleasure. But Mickey *is* a lunatic and, as Eve discovers, his lunacy is contagious. Under his influence she finally decides not to refer to catastrophic past relationships to help predict the outcome of her present relationship, especially since she's never been in love with anyone remotely like Mickey. She realizes: If you fall in love, you've got to *gamble* on this person who is available *now* or you'll never find happiness—you've got to chance getting burned again. That's why it's appropriate Eve and Mickey will honeymoon in Las Vegas.

Choose Me is a gamble that paid off. It's not a masterpiece and it won't become a classic, but it gives heart to moviegoers and filmmakers who are tired of the standard Hollywood product. It's a very good, extremely creative, winning picture that has numerous pleasures: clever, consistently witty dialogue; Legler's imaginative, thematically relevant set design; Pendergrass's songs; Keisser's stunning close-ups of smart, thinking female characters in emotional crisis; the way Rudolph takes five completely different people and weaves them in and out of each other's lives as if they were recklessly driven bumper cars; the scenes between Eve and "Ann" and Eve and Pearl, in which befuddled Eve can't believe two new wackos have entered her already chaotic life; Dr. Love's emotionless chatter on the radio; the scene in which Dr. Love and Eve unknowingly speak about the appeal of the same man (Mickey) in their radio/phone conversation—recalling "Ann" and Mickey's dining room scene in which Mickey segued from speaking about the appeal of Eve to speaking about the appeal of "Ann"; the way a third person often intrudes upon intimate scenes between two characters; the scene in which "Ann" looks through Mickey's belongings—Dr. Love is a snoop!—and we discover that he didn't fabricate those wild stories about himself; Mickey's seduction scenes; the way Mickey gets on Zack's nerves; the scene in which "Ann" tactlessly rambles on and on to the upset Eve about

Mickey and Nancy Love, after making love.

how helpful it was to have slept with Mickey; the way characters make us laugh in one scene and make us feel their anguish in the next; the touching climax in which Eve and Mickey choose not to kill themselves but make love on the roof instead; and the final shot of an uncertain but happy Eve as she rides with Mickey to Las Vegas. And I really like that Nancy never figures out that Eve is a frequent caller to Dr. Love, neither Eve nor Mickey figures out "Ann" is Dr. Love, Eve never figures out Pearl is Zack's wife, and neither Eve nor Pearl figures out Mickey told the truth about his past.

The characters are all worth rooting for, special enough to remember, and in their own ways sexually alluring. The cast is uniformly wonderful. Carradine, so unpleasant as a callous, goateed Lothario in *Welcome to L.A.*, plays another character who has the potential to give you the creeps—yet he manages to make Mickey very appealing. Bujold's comical performance as Dr. Love—she recalls loco Geraldine Chaplin in *Welcome to L.A.*, who hoped all phone calls were wrong numbers—is truly inspired; she takes her character in strange, unexpected directions. The delightfully spacey and energetic Chong, in her breakthrough role, adds spice to the film; the European Bauchau adds flavor. Best of all is Warren in a Susan Sarandon type of role. She is great. I think she deserved an Oscar for her performance. Or at the very least a Most Valuable Performer award for a jarring, funny/sad, deeply emotional portrayal that sets the tone for the entire picture.

Diva

1982 Color French les Films Galaxie–Greenwich Film Productions; released in the United States by United Artists Classics
Director: Jean-Jacques Beineix
Producer: Irene Silberman
Screenplay: Jean-Jacques Beineix and Jean Van Hamme
From the novel by Delacorta
Cinematography: Philippe Rousselot
Set Design: Hilton McConnico
Music: Vladimir Cosina
Editors: Marie-Josephe Yoyotte and Monique Prim
Running Time: 123 minutes

Cast: Frederic Andrei (Jules), Wilhelmenia Wiggins Fernandez (Cynthia Hawkins), Richard Bohringer (Gorodish), Thuy An Luu (Alba), Jacques Fabbri (Jean Saporta), Gerard Damon (the Spic), Dominique Pinon (Curé), Anny Romand (Paula), Chantal Deruaz (Nadia), Roland Bertin, Jean-Jacques Moreau, Patrick Floersheim.

Synopsis: Jules, a young Parisian postman, secretly tapes a concert by opera star Cynthia Hawkins, who refuses to record and prostitute her art. Jules wants the tape only for his own pleasure and wouldn't consider selling it. But he's observed by two Taiwanese who'd do anything to get the tape. Jules visits his idol backstage. He instinctively steals her gown. He goes to his loft, sits among wrecked autos and garbage cans, and listens to the prize of his tape collection.

The next morning, policewoman Paula waits at a cafe for prostitute Nadia, who has made a tape that reveals the identity of the leader of a drug and prostitution ring. Spotting pimp Spic and his henchman Curé, Nadia drops her tape into the pouch on Jules's moped. Jules doesn't see this, but helps her up when he knocks into her. Spic and Curé say they're police and order Jules to ride off. Curé kills Nadia with an ice pick.

Jules is attracted to a young Vietnamese girl named Alba whom he spots stealing classical records. She lives with Gorodish. A Zen freak, he sits in the bathtub or on the floor of his large, dark, empty loft, chain-smoking and dreaming ''of stopping the waves'' in a jigsaw puzzle on his floor.

Paula doesn't suspect that her boss, Saporta, is the gangster she's looking for. Nadia was his mistress. Paula realizes Nadia put the tape in a pouch. She searches for the moped owner. Saporta orders Spic and Curé to kill Jules and retrieve the tape. Meanwhile the Taiwanese break into Jules's loft, looking for the music tape. Jules thinks the police broke in and hides out with Alba and Gorodish.

Jules returns the gown to Cynthia. She feels close to him because of his genuine love of music.

The Taiwanese stake out Gorodish's loft. They contact him about Cynthia's tape. They also contact Cynthia's manager, saying that if she doesn't sign a record contract with them, they'll release the pirated tape. The manager can't persuade Cynthia to agree to the extortion.

In a wild chase, Jules eludes the police. He stays with a prostitute. He puts on a tape he finds in his pocket. It's Nadia's tape. He learns the prostitute is employed by Saporta. He flees with Spic and Curé on his tail. He is wounded but calls Gorodish, who rescues him. He and Alba take Jules to a distant lighthouse so he can recover. Gorodish listens to Nadia's tape. Alba is happy he will help Jules. Saporta meets with Gorodish at a warehouse. He places a bomb under the seat of Gorodish's Citroën. He buys a tape from Gorodish. The Taiwanese appear. They knock out Saporta and steal what they think is Cynthia's tape. They get in the Citroën and are blown up.

Jules is abducted by Spic and Curé and taken to his loft. They take Nadia's tape and place an altered tape that Saporta made into Jules's recorder. But Paula is there. She kills Curé before he can kill Jules, and wounds Spic. Saporta arrives. He kills Spic and is about to kill Paula and Jules when Gorodish turns out the lights. Saporta falls into an open elevator shaft. Gorodish slips away. Paula secures Nadia's tape.

Jules gives Cynthia his tape of her, and plays it for her. It's the first time she has heard herself. She is moved. They hug.

When French critics at Cannes unmercifully attacked Jean-Jacques Beineix's second feature, *Moon in the Gutter* (1983), he saw it as petty retribution. He claimed they were still furious that his debut film, *Diva*, had become a tremendous popular success and won prestigious awards despite their unfavorable reviews. They had been unwilling to accept his goofy romantic thriller, with its weird assortment of characters and relationships, bizarre decor, glittery camerawork (with jolting light patterns), and unusual variety of music, and accused him of pretentiously using ''style'' to cover up flimsy personalities and a preposterous story line. In an August 1983 interview with Dan Yakir in *Film Comment*, Beineix explained:

"There are French critics who thought that *Diva*'s success was stolen, because it didn't have their seal of approval. It was made against them, an attempt at a new kind of cinema, while they wanted to re-establish the 'old order.' They were angry because it was problematic for them, and it forced them to find different words and another way of looking at things. . . . If *Diva* became a hit, it was because the public supported it. The César for the film came a full one year after it had been working slowly, and the sudden recognition made a fire out of the embers."

Beineix was still griping about the French critics after the release of his third film, *Betty Blue* (1986). Again in *Film Comment* (February 1987), he told Marcia Pally:

"I'm still attacked by committees for the defense of the old regime who claim my work is empty, all surface images, and that I don't consider dramaturgy or the actors. But they are old-fashioned. They are like the academies of the 19th-century dealing with Impression. They think cinema should serve reality in a literal sense. They ask where the message is, but they don't see that the image is the message. They don't understand the theories of Toffler or McLuhan, which are not new. They don't see that we can use reality and give it another dimension in film. The image that begins with reality is open. We play with it."

Judging from the above quote, I imagine American critic David Denby of *New York* wrote the type of review of *Diva* that Beineix hoped to get in France:

The whole movie, with its alternatingly rapt and farcical unreality, is a good-hearted put-on, a mad combination of ritzy magazine graphics and intentionally cheap melodrama. . . . Silly? Only if you're totally indifferent to visual design and to the comedy of junk-movie archetypes bouncing off each other. . . . Everything has been heightened just enough to be funny. There must be plenty of moviegoers ready for the joke of a put-on raised to the level of art.

As in France, the American public was dazzled by *Diva*—it became a cult favorite and United Artists Classics' most

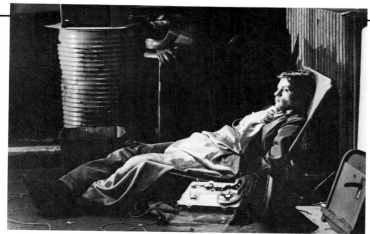

Jules lies in his loft, listening to his pirated tape of Cynthia Hawkins (right), *played by opera star Wilhelmenia Wiggins Fernandez.*

successful release. Unlike in France, American critics—with exceptions like Vincent Canby (who thought the film superficial) and Richard Corliss (who thought it had flair rather than style)—considered *Diva* a delightfully entertaining, highly original work and urged moviegoers to see it. While no one could deny that Beineix's work is self-consciously arty—he uses his frame like a pop art canvas—any adaptation of the wacky novel by Delacorta (Daniel Odier) warranted an audacious style.

The slim, fast-paced novel is the first in Delacorta's series involving roguish Serge Gorodish—a character indebted to Patricia Highsmith's Ripley—and his 13-year-old blonde, French ward/apprentice, Alba. They are an ideal couple: The one-time gangster has "age and experience" and she has "freshness, ambition, recklessness, intelligence, sensitivity, and a total lack of scruples." Alba is more sexually attracted to Gorodish than in the film, and is disappointed he wants to keep their relationship platonic until she turns 14. They don't live in as weird a space as the dark empty (except for a bathtub) loft that their film counterparts do, and there also is nothing remarkable about Jules's apartment. In the novel Gorodish is as obsessed by classical music as Jules. Delacorta's Gorodish always has an eye open for a money-making scheme and he convinces RCA messenger Jules (a postman in the movie) to allow him to sell his bootlegged tape of Cynthia Hawkins to the highest bidder. However, when he's impressed by Cynthia's dedication to her art—she'd rather buy the tape than be forced into signing a multi-million-dollar record deal—he returns the tape to Jules, who, in turn, returns it to Cynthia.

Besides the Gorodish-Jules conspiracy to sell the tape, there are other differences between the novel and movie. In most instances, I prefer Beineix's choices. Jean Saporta is not a corrupt policeman in the novel but a well-known gangster whose operation includes drugs and prostitution. This is essentially the Spic role in the movie, except that Saporta in the novel is more powerful: He has a corrupt cop under his thumb—a character named Boulanger, who is head of the vice squad—while in the film Spic is con-

trolled by a corrupt cop, Saporta. In both cases, Saporta is the top gangster. Spic and Curé do not exist in the book although Saporta does have a few innocuous hirelings running around. Years ago, Gorodish was Saporta's driver. Nadia is Saporta's mistress in the book, as in the film, but she isn't the one who drops the incriminating tape into Jules's moped satchel. Instead she gives it to her ex-boyfriend, Krantz, an honest detective—in the film, he's an informer—who, before Saporta kills him, passes it on to policewoman Paula. With Saporta on her trail, Paula drops it into the moped satchel—when she goes back to retrieve it, the moped is gone. Paula has a much bigger role in the novel: While Gorodish stands by in case things get too out of hand, Paula kills both Saporta and Boulanger. The pace of the novel is hectic, with quirky characters racing all around Paris (and the countryside) and sliding in and out of each other's story lines.

French critics attacked Beineix for his ridiculously elaborate action sequences, including the classic chase in which Jules rides his moped into the Metro station, but Delacorta included it and several other amusing, richly detailed cops-and-robbers scenes. He set the tone—Beineix only added to the excitement with spectacular visuals (he was in the speeding car that chased the moped). And still Delacorta took time to include moments when characters sing, listen to, purchase, steal, and talk about opera. This must have appealed to opera fanatic Beineix (whose attendance at a Jessye Norman concert in Bordeaux inspired his staging of Cynthia's opening recital, when she sings the aria from Catalani's *La Wally*). If the Marx Brothers seemed at home at the opera, then there was no reason Beineix couldn't use opera to anchor a sleazy, low-budget movie thriller involving drugs, murder, and prostitution. By drawing on opera to tell his story, contends Craig Brown of the *London Times,* Beineix gave his picture the resonance and substance that many French critics insist is lacking:

Comparisons [of the form of *Diva*] with the form of opera are fully justified: coincidences are unabashed and perpetual, comedy and drama are never separated and, most operatic of all, jokes, noises, and sequences crop up again and again and these repetitions are not—as some critics have yearningly suggested—symbols or metaphors or comments. They are there because they are funny or ingenious; they are repeated to make the film rhyme.

It is precisely Beineix's determination to mix diverse elements such as opera and a lowbrow crime drama that makes the film so outrageous and so entertaining. His actors come in all shapes and sizes and from various backgrounds. Beineix had difficulty tracking down majestic Wilhelmenia Wiggins Fernandez, whom he'd seen when Houston's Grand Opera Company had toured Europe performing *Porgy and Bess,* only to discover she was under contract to the director of the Paris Opera. He discovered captivating 14-year-old Thuy An Luu when she was roller skating at a Paris disco. His characters include a black American, a black French-African, an American Jew, a Vietnamese, two Taiwanese (Japanese in the book), a Spaniard, and a motley group of French. His oddball couples include Jules, a bland 18-year-old, white, French postman, and Cynthia, the taller, 30-ish black American star; Alba, a teenage, pleasure-seeking Vietnamese shoplifter, and Gorodish (played by charismatic Richard Bohringer), her 40-ish, white, Zen freak boyfriend; Spic, the tall, dark, and handsome Latin thug, and Curé, his short, blond, indented-faced, punk-garbed henchman (Dominique Pinon is a creepy screen villain); homicide chief Saporta and prostitute Nadia; and dedicated policewoman Paula and her on-the-make ("touch my thigh") male partner. Beineix under*scores* his odd couplings by mixing classical and contemporary music; impressionistic art (i.e., the lovely shots

of Jules, with white umbrella, and Cynthia on a quiet morning in a Paris street and in the park) and expressionistic, bathed-in-blue-light, Paris-at-night film imagery; "still lifes" (i.e., cinematographer Philippe Rousselot frames a bowl of fruit) in the style of Cézanne and Courbet and pop art, with its more contemporary still-life subjects (i.e., the fifties autos in the murals in Jules's loft); and the warm filmmaking of French humanists (from Renoir to Truffaut) and the impersonal high-tech contemporary filmmaking— distinguished by rapid editing, a mobile camera, chase scenes, characters being shot through opaque material or with colored light shining on them, and images being seen as reflections on glass, pools of water, and shiny metal. Surely Beineix set up so many contradictions for the sheer joy of it—it's fun to experiment—but I'd like to think it was done for thematic purpose as well. Perhaps Beineix is showing us that even in a world that is ugly—there's drug trafficking, prostitution, murder, theft, corruption— and full of lonely people (initially, Jules, Cynthia, Gorodish, Alba, Paula, and Nadia are withdrawn or isolated), and seemingly so impersonal—Beineix fills the screen with machines and gadgets (cars, mopeds, buses, the Metro, an escalator, a moving sidewalk, elevators, guns, stereos, tape machines)—love and music can still emerge triumphant.

In fact, what survivors Jules, Cynthia, Gorodish, and Alba have in common is a capacity to love people and love *good* music (the doomed Curé loses on both counts). Love and music are shown to be pure, purifying forces. The criminals are those people who prostitute love (sex-trade kingpin Saporta, top pimp Spic) or music (the Taiwanese record pirates, Cynthia's manager). In the minds of Delacorta and Beineix the businessmen who deal in record piracy are just as ruthless as down-and-dirty street criminals. It's inconceivable that Jules and Gorodish in the film would ever consider selling the bootlegged recording of Cynthia's concert—they don't want to make a profit off someone else's art because that would taint not the art but their appreciation of it. Zen freak Gorodish isn't at all materialistic. And Jules takes pride that while he has pirated tapes of famous singers he never attempts to sell them. He believes his thievery is more innocent than bored Alba's swiping of classical albums from the record store— but as the wise Gorodish points out, "there are no innocent pleasures." One can't steal another's music—her art, her soul—and remain pure for, as Cynthia protests, it is tantamount to rape. Interestingly, after Gorodish prevents the Taiwanese from taking Cynthia's recording and Jules returns the tape to Cynthia, neither has sex with the female they love—as they do in the book, after their "purification." Love is their achieved goal, not sex—sex lost its value earlier in the film, when Jules slept with the black prostitute (his surrogate for Cynthia). Because the French men come through for their foreign females, they can give and receive love from them—and that is enough reward.

It is by intention that the four major characters are not fully developed. They are each living outside life's mainstream and, as I stated earlier, are initially isolated, withdrawn, and lonely. Alba is just 14 so even though she is precocious and has surely had some amazing experiences, especially since Gorodish took her off the streets, she hasn't

Claiming to be a policeman, Curé chases Jules away from Nadia. Neither knows that the doomed Nadia has slipped the tape that incriminates homicide chief Saporta into Jules's postal pouch.

The young Jules and the younger Alba, both amateur thieves, would make the most logical couple in the film. But each is attracted to someone older.

had time to experience life to its fullest. Gorodish doesn't give her enough attention and since everyone else in her world is an adult, she feels alone. It doesn't help that she lives in a foreign country. Cynthia also lives away from her native country. She sings to strangers in concert halls, rehearses alone (until she lets Jules hear her), deals with vulturous record dealers, speaks to reporters who recognize talent but don't understand art. She travels with a manager who is hoping to sell her out. She can trust no one. Although she has fame, while the other three characters lead anonymous existences, she is probably the loneliest of all.

Jules is like an Antoine Doinel without personality (Frederic Andrei has the sweet face of Jean-Pierre Leaud, but none of the character). He is an observer of life, a *listener,* and, as a mailman, serves as a catalyst in other people's lives, but he is not a participant in life. He's harmless but adds nothing to the world. At the beginning of the film, his life is of no consequence, and if he were dead no one would notice. In fact, his loft is a monument to death and destruction, with murals of old Buicks and Chevys, wrecked autos and garbage cans (in Beineix's inverted reality, what should exist outdoors exists indoors), and tapes of concerts—ghosts from the past. Jules and

Gorodish are linked by their lofts.* Gorodish's enormous loft may be uncluttered but, dark and empty, it is as much of a tomb as Jules's. That it is devoid of possessions signifies he has broken from his past and past values and that the person he once was is "dead." He is desensitized to the world.

We are not told of Gorodish's past, as we are in the novel, and this makes him more mysterious and interesting. He becomes a myth figure, someone who undoubtedly

. . . .

*Hilton McConnico's striking set design is one of the reasons *Diva* received so much attention. Jules's pop art loft is an unforgettable set, but Gorodish's empty loft is equally daring. In the September 1983 issue of *The Movies,* the Memphis-born McConnico told Annette Insdorf: "The script said Gorodish's loft should be a very large black room with a bathtub. We looked for places but nothing was big enough. Finally when we went to the old Seita tobacco factory, we looked at this room and at each other, knowing it would be great for Gorodish. Then I started working on the color schemes: the walls are not black but charcoal gray, flat-finished, and the woodwork is black lacquer—to give it more friction and visual detail. Because finances were limited, I bought candy cellophane and covered the windows with blue. I also crushed the cellophane in the corners to look like cobwebs: you don't really notice it but you feel it in the light."

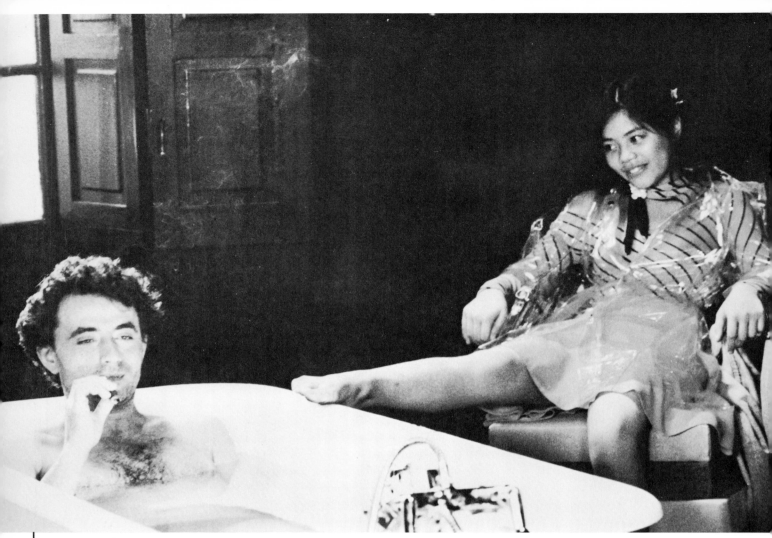

Jules's saviors: the eccentric Gorodish and Alba.

had so many dangerous adventures that he no longer craves excitement. We suspect he can outwit, outfight, and out-*anything* anyone he challenges—no one can intimidate him. He's the type of capable, fearless hero whom delicate young men like Jules would want as a protector. We imagine that Gorodish has a sixth sense for smelling trouble and the uncanny ability to make everything all right. He then disappears like the Lone Ranger without getting credit for his good deeds. He is Jules's godsend (or, as one critic asserted, his "fairy godmother")—a *deus ex machina* who suddenly appears anytime Jules is in trouble and rescues him. Because Gorodish must help Jules—initially because he is Alba's friend—he is required to physically leave his place of solitude and his repressive limbo state and again mingle with humanity. His own humanity comes through. When he commits himself to protect Jules, he reveals a sensitive side he has long kept hidden (perhaps since watching fellow soldiers slaughtered in Vietnam)—he finally can put a tender arm around Alba. He is also making a statement that life is important, and worth saving.

Jules's final act is noble and justifies Gorodish's action. By returning the tape to Cynthia, Jules rids himself of a symbol of the past . . . and of his own dismal past, when he'd sit alone, like an old man, cooped up in his dreary loft and listen to classical music. His gesture opens up a possible future for himself and Cynthia. And as Cynthia listens to herself for the first time, one suspects she may agree to make a record for her public—this would be a major, positive step toward ending her own isolation. She feels freedom. She can give herself to Jules on a personal level and to her devoted fans as well. Beineix is saying, I think, that if an artist—be it an opera star or filmmaker—happens to make money, it does not taint the art.

In the course of a good, interesting movie, characters should evolve. They do in *Diva*. The film is about how a singer's lovely voice and a series of strange circumstances cause Jules, Cynthia, and Alba and Gorodish to interact. The result is that all of them break out of their depressed past-obsessed states, reveal inner goodness (we already knew they were sensitive because of their love of good music), find love, and make commitments to the future. It's a cheery, sentimental theme that would seem out of place in typical low-budget crime thrillers. I think it's one of the reasons *Diva* is such a crowd pleaser.

Dr. Strangelove: Or, How I Learned to Stop Worrying and Love the Bomb

1964 British B&W Columbia
Director: Stanley Kubrick
Producer: Stanley Kubrick
Screenplay: Stanley Kubrick, Terry Southern, and Peter George
From the novel *Two Hours to Doom (Red Alert* in the United States) by Peter Bryant (Peter George)
Cinematography: Gilbert Taylor
Music: Laurie Johnson
Editor: Anthony Harvey
Running Time: 93 minutes
Cast: Peter Sellers (President Merkin Muffley/Dr. Strangelove/Group Captain Lionel Mandrake), George C. Scott (General Buck Turgidson), Sterling Hayden (General Jack D. Ripper), Keenan Wynn (Colonel Bat Guano), Slim Pickens (Major T. J. "King" Kong), Peter Bull (Ambassador Alexei de Sadesky), Tracy Reed (Miss Scott/"Miss Foreign Affairs"), James Earl Jones (Lieutenant Lothar Zogg).
Synopsis: General Jack D. Ripper, commander of the Burpleson Air Force Base, informs Lionel Mandrake, a British officer attached to his command, that the United States and Russia are at war. He tells Mandrake to shut down the base and cut off all communications to the ouside. He then contacts the 32 B-52 bombers of the 843rd Wing that are airborne, in the fail-safe position, two hours from Russia. He orders them to fly to Russia and drop nuclear bombs on specific targets. The *Leper Colony* is one plane to receive his orders. Major T. J. Kong assumes that America is under attack and is glad to do his patriotic duty.

Mandrake discovers that there is no war going on. He happily informs Ripper. Ripper refuses to call back the planes or reveal the three-letter recall code only he knows. He wants a full-scale nuclear war so that the Russians who are trying to "sap and impurify all our precious bodily fluids" will be wiped out. Mandrake realizes Ripper is crazy.

In the War Room, President Merkin Muffley is upset to learn from General Buck Turgidson that Ripper was able to launch the bombers without his authority. According to Plan R, Ripper had the power to *retaliate* after an initial attack by the Russians, so Ripper merely pretended there was a Russian attack. Turgidson suggests the United States carry out the attack Ripper started. Muffley is not amused. Turgidson is unhappy that Muffley invites Russian ambassador de Sadesky into the War Room. He provides the phone number of Premier Kissoff, who's on holiday with his mistress. Kissoff is furious when he learns what has happened. Muffley supplies the Russians with data about the planes, so that the Russians can shoot them down. Kissoff warns Muffley that if a bomb is dropped their doomsday machine, which isn't a rumor after all, will destroy the world. Muffley wants the recall code.

After a brutal battle soldiers break through Ripper's base forces. Ripper told them these attackers were Russians. Ripper kills himself. Mandrake figures out the code, but suspicious Bat Guano, the officer who took the base, makes it difficult for him to call the president. Mandrake uses a pay phone.

All the planes are recalled, except two that were shot down and the *Leper Colony*, which had its communications system knocked out by a Russian missile. It avoids radar by flying low, and it flies toward an alternate target—the Russians don't know where it is.

In the War Room, the crippled Dr. Strangelove, an ex-Nazi who now is the Director of Weapons Research and Development, tells Muffley that a doomsday machine is conceivable. He just doesn't understand why the Russians never informed the United States of this ultimate deterrent against nuclear attack. De Sadesky says it was going to be announced soon—Kissoff loves surprises.

Turgidson brags that American pilots can outfly Russian peons. That's why he expects the *Leper Colony* to complete its mission. He's right. But over its target, the bomb gets stuck. So Kong rides it out of the plane as if it were a rodeo bull. It explodes.

While his right arm does Nazi salutes and his right hand chokes him, Strangelove suggests that America's elite spend the next 100 years in mine shafts, where there will be 10 women for every man. He discovers he can walk. The world blows up.

Stanley Kubrick's "nightmare comedy" opened to great fanfare, critical reaction, and controversy in 1964. As viewers lined up at theaters showing the hit picture, it was debated in the newspapers, by critics, guest writers who were well versed on the nuclear issue, and readers in Letters-to-the-Editor columns. Politicians and military men wrote articles about it—some praised it, but most were offended that our leaders were portrayed as knaves and fools. Clare Boothe Luce attacked the film's anti-nuclear, pro-disarmament stance because she worried it would give America's European allies the impression it wouldn't risk nuclear war to help them. It was called anti-American by some. Others objected to nuclear war being treated so lightly—they preferred the somber tone of *On the Beach* (1959). But there were those who absolutely loved it. It was called "brilliant," "monumental," "the funniest film ever made." Robert Brustein, in the *New York Review of Books*, hailed it as "the most courageous movie ever made" and correctly identified it as "the first American movie to speak truly for our generation." Brustein:

> *Dr. Strangelove* is a work of comic anarchy, fashioned by a totally disaffected and disaffiliated imagination. . . . Kubrick has managed to explode the right-wing position without making a single left-wing affirmation: the odor of the Thirties, which clung even to the best work of Chaplin, Welles, and Huston, has finally been disinfected here. Disinfected, in fact, is the stink of all ideological thinking. For although *Dr. Strangelove* is about a political subject, its only politics is outrage against the malevolence of officialdom. Conservatives will find it subversive, liberals will find it irresponsible, utopians will find it bleak, humanitarians will find it inhuman—*Dr. Strangelove* is all these things. But it also releases, through comic poetry, those feelings of impotence and frustration that are consuming us all; and I can't think of anything more important for an imaginative work to do.

An obvious reason for the continuous popularity of *Dr. Strangelove* is that it has remained timely. In fact it seems even more relevant today than in 1964, a welcome alternative to *Red Dawn* (1984), *Rambo: First Blood Part II* (1985), and *Top Gun* (1986), box-office hits that irresponsibly cater to fans who fantasize about engaging in combat with the Russians. Not only do we worry as much about the Bomb as we did back then, but also, thanks to Watergate, numerous political blunders and corruption scandals, Three Mile Island and Chernobyl, and the Iran-Contra hearings, we have lost all faith in fail-safe systems and checks and balances, and aren't so sure that our military and political leaders are prepared to run even Camp Runamuck or lead the F-Troop. Today we have the queasy feeling that the individuals whose decisions determine our lives are petty, paranoid and irrational and that things are out of control. Indeed, who *is* in charge here? Maybe Jack D. Ripper seemed like an exaggeration in 1964—for who could imagine a renegade military officer conducting foreign policy behind the president's back—but doesn't he seem plausible now that we've met Ollie North and John Poindexter? *Dr. Strangelove* is still frighteningly funny because, as wild as the characters and events are, there is nothing in the picture that is beyond the realm of possibility. Perhaps we are laughing at ourselves for living in a world whose fate is in the hands of incompetents and buffoons. And perhaps the laughter is therapeutic for those of us who know we'll never be able to stop worrying about the Bomb.

Kubrick, Terry Southern, and Peter George adapted their biting screenplay from the 1958 British novel *Two Hours to Doom*—published as *Red Alert* in America in 1960—written by George, ex-RAF officer and British intelligence agent, using the pseudonym Peter Bryant. It's a serious book, with more than a passing resemblance to *Fail-Safe*, by Eugene Burdick and Harvey Wheeler.* Both novels are about a mistakenly initiated American mission to drop a nuclear bomb in Russia. Both feature a strong, liberal president who attempts to prevent nuclear war by aborting the mission, even providing the Russians with vital data so they can shoot down our planes, and, when one bomber gets through, offering to nuke an American city (Atlantic City in George's work) to compensate for a Russian city being destroyed. When Kubrick chose to make a film of George's book, he was determined to keep its serious tone. But, as he told *Newsday* critic Joseph Gelmis, his original concept went out the window and he decided to make his only comedy:

> "I started work on the screenplay with every intention of making the film a serious treatment of the problem of accidental nuclear war. As I kept trying to imagine the way in which things would really happen, ideas kept coming to me which I would discard because they were so ludicrous. I kept saying to myself: 'I can't do this. People will laugh.' But after a month or so I began to realize that all the things I was throwing out were the things which were most truthful. After all, what could be more absurd than the very idea of two mega-powers willing to wipe out all human life because of an accident. . . .
> "So it occurred to me that I was approaching the project in the wrong way. The only way to tell the story was as a black comedy or, better, a nightmare comedy, where the things you laugh at most are really the heart of the paradoxical postures that make a nuclear war possible. Most of the humor in *Strangelove* arises from the depiction of everyday human be-

havior in a nightmarish situation, like the Russian premier on the hot line who forgets the telephone number of his general staff headquarters and suggests the American President try Omsk information, or the reluctance of a U.S. officer to let a British officer smash open a Coca-Cola machine for change to phone the President about a crisis on the SAC base because of his conditioning about the sanctity of private property."

The film may be about American military and political posturing, but it is a wicked satire in the British tradition of *I'm All Right, Jack* (1960), a searing attack on management and labor, in which Peter Sellers plays a shifty union leader with a Hitler mustache. So even though Kubrick filmed *Dr. Strangelove* in England to accommodate Peter Sellers, I believe England should have been his first choice anyway. Kubrick credited Sellers for coming up with many of the film's funniest lines, though it's likely they were limited to those spoken by his three characters. Surely President Muffley, Lionel Mandrake, and Dr. Strangelove were Sellers's creations, completely, so one must wonder what these roles were like in early drafts of the script before Sellers joined the project. Kubrick said Terry Southern's contributions to the film were minimal, but it's likely he gave the film its "hip" American flavor. In his book on screenwriters, *Talking Pictures* (1974), Richard Corliss makes this conjecture:

> Southern is probably responsible for Major Kong, the bomber pilot who, upon realizing that his crew is heading for "Nuclear combat toe to toe with the Russkies," drawls that their sortie will result in promotions and personal citations for "ever' last one of ya, regardless of yer race, color or yer creed," and for Col. Bat Guano, who arrests a gallant British officer because "I think you're some kind of deviated prevert, and I think General Ripper found out about your preversion and that you were organizing some kind of mutiny of preverts." It's also likely that he contributed to Ripper's character the famous lines about allowing "the international Communist conspiracy to sap and impurify all our precious bodily fluids," and about women who "sense my power and they seek the life essence. I do not avoid women . . . but I—I do deny them my essence."

I assume George worked only on the early, serious drafts of the script, because the final screenplay not only altered the tone of the novel, but also altered George's characters, giving them different names and personalities, introduced new characters and plot devices, and injected familiar Kubrick themes that are antithetical to those advanced by George in the book. For starters, George's General Quinten became Jack D. Ripper. Quinten is a contemplative, fatally ill, deranged officer who believes that if America wins a limited nuclear war there will be permanent peace. Ripper, as played by Sterling Hayden, is a rip-snorting, paranoid, off-his-rocker officer who initiates nuclear war to wipe out the Commies who, he insists, introduced fluoridation to sap Americans' precious bodily fluids and are responsible for his own sexual inadequacy. Quinten's in-

---

*George insisted that Wheeler stole the plot of his 1958 book when he wrote the short story "Abraham '59," which was published in a small political quarterly, *Dissent*. But Wheeler claimed he had been unable to sell his story for two years and that its original title was "Abraham '57." When Max E. Youngstein's ECA unit planned an independent production of *Fail-Safe*, Columbia Pictures, the distributor of *Dr. Strangelove*, threatened a plagiarism suit against Wheeler and Burdick, the book's publisher, and ECA. All was resolved when Columbia took over financing and distribution of *Fail-Safe*, as well. There were reports that George received a financial settlement.

A publicity shot of Slim Pickens, who as Major Kong rides this nuclear warhead from his U.S. bomber to detonation on Russian soil.

telligent executive officer, Major Paul Howard, became Sellers's Lionel Mandrake, a veteran, stiff-upper-lipped British officer. General Keppler, a minor character who has a brief verbal altercation with the Russian ambassador in the novel, became George C. Scott's ignorant, hawkish, gung-ho, gum-chomping Pentagon-apologist General Buck Turgidson. The book's tall, sly Russian ambassador, Zorubin, became Peter Bull's plump, buffoonish Alexei de Sadesky. The dangerous, calculating Russian premier became the childish Dimitri Kissoff. The strong-willed, and nameless, president became the short, bald, well-meaning but ineffectual Merkin Muffley (meaning stupidity). Dedicated, patriotic young flight commander Captain Clint Brown became Slim Pickens's jingoistic, glory-hungry, middle-aged flight-commander cowboy, Major T. J. "King" Kong. Sonora Air Force Base became Burpleson Air Force Base, and the *Alabama Angel* bomber became the *Leper Colony*. The film introduced Sellers's Dr. Strangelove,

Keenan Wynn's Bat Guano, and the Russian doomsday device that will automatically destroy the world if America drops a nuclear bomb.

Whereas the novel ends optimistically, with the dropped bomb missing its target and nuclear war being averted in the present and future, Kubrick chose to have Strangelove stand up and announce to Muffley, "Mein Führer, I can walk!" and then, ironically, with Vera Lynn's World War I song "We'll Meet Again" on the sound track, have the doomsday device blow the world to smithereens.* It was the best possible ending for Kubrick's characters. In his view, playing power politics and making war are male games, extensions of the male politicians' and military officers' sex lives. These men don't stop thinking about sex just because a political-military crisis develops. So while fighting takes place all around him, Ripper reveals to Mandrake his bedroom problems; Turgidson first discusses the nuclear emergency over the phone while his bikini-clad mistress-secretary (played by Tracy Reed, daughter of British director Carol Reed) stands at his side, and he even receives her call when he is in the War Room— confirming the link between sex and war; Soviet premier Dimitri Kissoff is also with his mistress when he discusses the crisis with Muffley; just before the doomsday machine goes off, Strangelove interests those in the War Room in his mine-shaft proposal by enticing them with the prospect of having 10 beautiful, fertile women being allotted to every male survivor. The props and weapons are aggressive and phallic: the plane (in the opening, when it receives fuel from another plane, it is tantamount to intercourse), guns, missiles, Ripper's cigar, Strangelove's jutting arm, the dropped bomb that Kong clutches between his legs. These are sexually frustrated men—Dimitri and Turgidson have been called away from their lovers; the air force men on their suicide mission will never see or have women again; for different reasons, Ripper, Muffley, and Strangelove are incapable of sex. They have an increasing need for "sexual" release. The doomsday explosion is their mutual climax—the ultimate climax for military men and politicians because it is so destructive. George's novel does not have this sexual subtext.

Anyone who has seen *Paths of Glory* (1957) or *Full Metal Jacket* (1987) knows Kubrick regards military officers as insensitive, egotistical monsters and soldiers as their obedient sacrificial lambs. So his view of America's military would not have been in conflict with George's; in interviews George described American generals as "war-hungry psychopaths on the lunatic fringe." But Kubrick had no intention of being as polite to America's politicians as George was in his book; by no means would he make the president the hero he is in the book. Kubrick's point is: If America's military gets us into trouble, America's inept, confused politicians are incapable of getting us out of it. According to Kubrick, America's politicians wouldn't understand, much less be able to deal with, a nuclear crisis. In George's book, the secretaries of state and defense are

. . . .

*Kubrick filmed a long, high-priced custard-pie fight in the War Room, but fortunately he cut it because the slapstick didn't mesh with the satirical tone of the film.

Peter Sellers in his three roles: Left: British Group Captain Lionel Mandrake realizes that General Jack D. Ripper is dangerously insane. Below left: In the War Room, American president Merkin Muffley tries to calm Russian ambassador Alexei de Sadesky after informing him about the nuclear attack. Below: The German Dr. Strangelove tries to prevent his gloved right hand from strangling him.

in the War Room to advise the president and the chain of command is in position; it's significant that, at the beginning of the film, President Muffley is informed that the secretaries of defense and state *and* the vice-president are all out of the country. Muffley seems to have more sense than the others in the War Room, but at the end he, too, listens to Strangelove's maniacal mine-shaft proposal. He is helpless.

George's book reads like a Michael Crichton novel, with characters in various locations futilely trying to arrest a crisis situation before time runs out. However, it is the *film*'s themes that anticipate those found in Crichton's novels and films: Any "fool-proof" endeavor (i.e., scientific experiments, inventions) or system (i.e., Plan R) will fail because it was planned by imperfect man; any attempt to alleviate the problem will only make things worse (i.e., the Russian missile knocks out the *Leper Colony*'s communication system, preventing it from receiving the recall code); since man will be unable to rectify a terrible situation once things get out of hand, man can prevent catastrophes only by not allowing dangerous situations to

develop in the first place (i.e., disarm our nuclear arsenal). Crichton would agree with Kubrick that the creation of the Bomb is the root problem for all that goes wrong in George's story, but George believed the root problem is not the Bomb but foolish policy that allows lunatic American generals the capability to start a nuclear war without consulting the president. George didn't worry that both superpowers have nuclear bombs—he thought this was a necessary deterrent to prevent attacks by either side—and figured everything would be fine if only imperfect policy were corrected: So at the end of the novel, the president jettisons Plan R. Kubrick found George naive: Deterrents would work only if the superpowers acted in *rational* ways, but in our world, where all leaders' logic is suspect, there is no way to predict how any superpower will act in a given situation (i.e., the Russians keep secret their doomsday machine, the ultimate deterrent *if* it is known about). *Dr. Strangelove* argues that as long as the nuclear bombs exist and men know they exist, no amount of safeguards will prevent them from being deployed, by intention or accident.

Unlike George, but like Crichton, Kubrick shows a distrust of science (symbolized by the Bomb, embodied by the ex-Nazi Strangelove). To Kubrick, the Bomb represents a machine and the doomsday device represents a scientific creation, and in Kubrick films, as well as in Crichton's work, machines/"machines"—the HAL computer in *2001* (1968), the "killing-machine" marine who shoots his drill instructor in *Full Metal Jacket,* even the shot-up Coca-Cola machine that shoots liquid into Bat Guano's eye in *Dr. Strangelove*—turn on the men who created them. As well, scientific experiments—for example, the Ludovico treatment in *A Clockwork Orange* (1971)—go awry. Kubrick doesn't merely detest machines because of the danger that results when they break down, but also because the more we rely on them to solve our problems, the more we are relinquishing our humanity. This is a recurrent theme in Kubrick's works. Throughout his pessimistic films we find characters who have ceased being human: George MacReady's mad general in *Paths of Glory,* the emotionless space travelers in *2001* (when Keir Dullea's Bowman gets his emotions back and dismantles HAL, this is man's greatest triumph in Kubrick's films), Malcolm McDowell's "conditioned"-to-be-nonviolent Alex in *A Clockwork Orange,* Jack Nicholson's possessed madman in *The Shining* (1980), and the heartless drill instructor and his silent, robotized men in *Full Metal Jacket.* In *Dr. Strangelove,* as men rely on communication systems, planes, missiles, and bombs—none do what they are supposed to do—and, later, contemplate using a computer to determine the master race that will enter the mine shaft, we see humanity slipping away. Ripper has gone mad; nameless, faceless soldiers follow suicidal orders without question; nameless, faceless, speechless advisers sit around the president's Round Table without offering advice; Strangelove, who has paralyzed legs, an ugly wave of dead-looking hair, and a right "Heil-Hitler" arm that has a mind of its own, and who seems to be an extension of his wheelchair, is now, at best, part man, part machine; the superpowers have given up trying to talk to each other—the inability of people, especially Americans and Russians, to communicate is another common Kubrick theme—and instead build nuclear bombs to express what they are thinking. There are several references to "human beings" in the film, but it's appropriate that everyone in the film is a caricature because, as Turgidson admits to Muffley, "The human element seems to have failed us here."

Peter Sellers is so prominent in *Dr. Strangelove* that it's easy to forget the vital contributions of Hayden and Scott. With his booming voice and strong physical presence—Kubrick places this big man in a small room with low ceilings—Hayden is an extremely frightening, imposing figure. Look into Hayden's face and you'll know there's no way he'll listen to anyone. He's like a crazed version of the military eccentrics on TV's *The Avengers,* or a dictatorial Cub Scout leader, or the cab driver who speeds up when you ask him to slow down. With his array of stupid expressions, flaring eyebrows and sneaky yet twinkling eyes, and embarrassed, guilty voice, Scott is genuinely hilarious. The scene in which he tells Muffley what Ripper has done and that there is no way to recall the planes is one of the film's funniest bits. Like the true-blue

"American general," Scott's Turgidson never admits mistakes or acknowledges defeat (he's always upbeat), always tries to turn a strategic blunder into a military advantage, never shows weakness (when he falls down, he rolls to his feet and continues talking as if nothing happened), and always is wary of the Russians (he worries there will be a mine-shaft gap and the Russians will have an advantage when both powers emerge from the earth in 100 years). Ever the aggressor, he is the type who would tackle the Russian ambassador (Muffley admonishes them: "You can't fight here—this is the War Room!"). Kubrick often films both Ripper and Turgidson from below, as if they were heroic figures. He is actually mocking America's military, for these two loonies are the best it has to offer.

Many critics, especially in England, despised Peter Sellers because, they wrote, he was not a good comic actor, but simply a mimic. I'd venture that Sellers was an underrated physical comedian but there's no need for this argument, for even if he was simply a mimic, he was one of the best mimics to ever appear in movies. And in *Dr. Strangelove,* where, as Kubrick stated, "much of the impact hinged on the dialogue, mode of expression, and euphemisms employed," Sellers is marvelous. He plays Mandrake as a cross between Trevor Howard–David Niven RAF officers and a very subdued and subtle Terry-Thomas. He's very British: He'd never yell at his superior officer or at the telephone operator who won't put his call through to the president unless he puts in change. He never becomes overly excited: When Ripper informs him that a shooting war has begun, he replies with great understatement, "Oh, hell . . ." He is quite humble: He has a hard time admitting he was a P.O.W. and didn't reveal information despite extensive torture. And he tries to retain his sanity while the world goes crazy around him. When Ripper puts his arm around him, Mandrake acts with controlled anxiety, like we do when we discover that the fellow next to us on the bus is a weirdo. Mandrake, the one British character in the movie, is the only character with intelligence.

Sellers plays Muffley as a bland, fifties-style Stevenson Democrat. He has no hair, no regional accent, no strength, no initiative, no personality. No wonder, reasons Kubrick, he got elected. I love the way Muffley struggles to keep his temper when Turgidson informs him that Plan R, which the president didn't fully understand, made it possible for Ripper to launch a nuclear attack without presidential authorization, and when Turgidson suggests that the United States follow up the unauthorized attack with an authorized attack to catch the Russians "with their pants down" and destroy 90% of their nuclear capabilities while suffering only "modest and acceptable civilian casualties"—"no more than 10 to 20 million killed, tops, depending on the breaks." But Muffley's finest screen moment is his classic phone conversation with Kissoff, a Bob Newhart–like routine in which he talks in a wheedling tone, as if he were trying to convince a 5-year-old child to accept an emergency collect call:

> You know how we've always talked of the possibility of something going wrong with the bomb . . . The *bomb,* Dimitri . . . The *hydrogen* bomb. Well, now

General Buck Turgidson must alter his plans for the day when he's called to an emergency meeting in the War Room.

what happened is: One of our base commanders . . . he had a sort of . . . well, he went a little funny in the head. You know—just a little . . . funny. And he went and did a silly thing . . . Well, I'll tell you what he did. He ordered his planes . . . to attack your country . . . Well, let me finish, Dimitri. Let me finish, Dimitri . . . Well, listen, how do you think I feel about it? Can you imagine how I feel, Dimitri? Why do you think I'm calling you? Just to say hello? . . . Of course, I like to speak to you! Of course, I like to say hello! . . . Not now, but anytime. I'm just calling you to tell you something terrible has happened . . . It's a friendly call. Of course, it's a friendly call. Listen, if it wasn't friendly . . . you probably wouldn't have even got it.

Strangelove doesn't appear until late in the film and doesn't have enough screen time, but he has extraordinary impact. With that slimy fixed smile, thick German accent, dark glasses, double chin, gloved hand that gives Nazi salutes and tries to strangle him (no one acts as if this is unusual), and ugly misshapen hair (the worst since MacDonald Carey's in 1944's *Shadow of a Doubt*), his grotesque version of Wernher von Braun is one of the most horrific figures in movie history. He certainly fits the tradition of mad (often crippled) German scientists that dates back to the silent era. Considering the notorious careers of Nazi scientists who were recruited for the United States' rocket program after Germany's surrender in World War II, is there any doubt that even an amoral fiend like Strangelove would be acceptable as our Director of Weapons Research and Development? It's a chilling thought.

Sellers was also supposed to play Kong, but was replaced by Pickens when he hurt his foot. Some critics have complained that without Sellers in the Kong role, the film loses symmetry. But I think Sellers would have been better as Kong's co-pilot, a part that should have been rewritten so he'd be the one person in the plane who questioned the orders to bomb Russia. After all, Sellers's Mandrake and Muffley are the only voices of reason in their respective arenas, and the plane scenes could use such a character to create a little conflict. Of course, this character, the voice of reason, would be killed at the same time the plane's radio is knocked out by a Russian missile. This would have reinforced Kubrick's major point: This is not an Age of Reason.

A postscript. Peter George wrote one more novel: In *Commander I,* China starts World War III by destroying several major cities, but Russia and the United States blame each other. Then in 1966, the 41-year-old author, who was suffering from ulcers, killed himself with a shotgun.

Easy Rider

1969 Color Columbia
Director: Dennis Hopper
Executive Producer: Bert Schneider
Producer: Peter Fonda
Screenplay: Peter Fonda, Dennis Hopper, and Terry Southern
Cinematography: Laszlo Kovacs
Music Performed By: Steppenwolf, the Byrds, the Band, the Holy Modal Rounders, Fraternity of Man, the Jimi Hendrix Experience, Little Eva, the Electric Prunes, the Electric Flag, Roger McGuinn
Editor: Donn Cambern
Running Time: 94 minutes

Cast: Fonda (Wyatt), Hopper (Billy), Jack Nicholson (George Hanson), Luke Askew (stranger on highway), Karen Black (Karen), Toni Basil (Mary), Luana Anders (Lisa), Sabrina Scharf (Sarah), Robert Walker (Jack), Warren Finnerty (rancher), Sandy Wyeth (Joanne), Phil Spector (drug connection).

Synopsis: At the Mexico-California border, Wyatt and Billy serve as middlemen between Mexican cocaine dealers and a rich American connection. They make a lot of money on the deal. They buy fancy motorcycles, hide the rest of their money in their gas tanks, and begin a journey across the Southwest toward New Orleans for the Mardi Gras. When they are denied accommodations at motels because of the way they look, they realize they will have to camp out each night. They sit around the campfire and smoke grass.

There is some hospitality from strangers. A rancher allows Wyatt the use of his tools to fix his tire. He then invites them to dinner with his Indian wife and many children. Wyatt admires him for living off the land.

Wyatt and Billy give a ride to a long-haired stranger who's hitching across the desert. The stranger brings them to his commune, where about 20 young men and women and their children struggle to survive despite lack of food and water. The stranger tells them that about 30 people deserted the commune after a hard winter but the rest, all city people, are planting seeds to make sure a crop comes in. Billy thinks seeds won't grow in the soil, but Wyatt believes they will succeed. He admires them. While a mime troupe performs, Wyatt and Billy swim naked with Sarah and Lisa, two women from the commune. The stranger asks Wyatt to stay in the commune, but soon Wyatt and Billy are on the road again.

In a small southern town, Wyatt and Billy drive their motorcycles behind a parade and are arrested for parading without a license. They become friends with their cellmate, civil liberties lawyer George Hanson, who is sleeping off a drunk. George's father is an important man in town, so the police treat him and his new friends well. The three get out of jail. Wyatt invites George to come to New Orleans with them—George always wanted to go to an exclusive brothel there. When they camp out, George smokes marijuana for the first time.

Wyatt, Billy, and George enter a roadside diner and are taunted by a deputy and some local rednecks about the way they look. The three leave before there is trouble, although some teenage girls want rides on their motorcycles.

They camp in the woods. George tells Wyatt and Billy that the country has gone downhill. Now it has become dangerous for people who flaunt their freedom. As they sleep, men attack them with axe handles. George is killed.

Wyatt and Billy go to the New Orleans brothel. They invite prostitutes Karen and Mary outside to the Mardi Gras. They take LSD in a graveyard. Their "trips" are frightening, religious experiences.

Wyatt and Billy camp out. Billy says happily, "We've done it. We're rich, Wyatt. Yeah, man, yeah." But Wyatt responds despondently, "We blew it!" Billy doesn't know what Wyatt means.

Wyatt and Billy ride down a country road. Two rednecks in a truck drive alongside. They try to frighten Billy with a rifle. It goes off. Billy is shot in the stomach. Wyatt rides for help. The rednecks don't want witnesses. They turn around. They shoot Wyatt.

Each night, Wyatt (left) and Billy sit around a campfire, smoking marijuana and trying to have a sensible conversation.

Ten years after Jack Kerouac wrote *On the Road* (1957), at about the time Charles Kuralt delivered his first "On the Road" television segment, the road movie came of age. It was spawned by silent "chase" comedies, Westerns with drifter heroes, couple-on-the-lam classics like *You Only Live Once* (1937), *Dust Be My Destiny* (1939), *Detour* (1945), *They Live By Night* (1949), *Gun Crazy* (1949), the Humphrey Bogart trucker melodrama *they Drive By Night* (1940), seminal motorcycle-gang film *The Wild One* (1954), juvenile-delinquent pictures of the fifties, dragster films, and the Robert Mitchum moonshine-running cult favorite, *Thunder Road* (1958). The first new wave of road movies featured leather-jacketed bikers in confrontation with each other and the law (parents and school principals were not as prevalent in *these* youth films). For these young antisocial punks/misfits/outlaws/outcasts the *road* was the ideal place for them to exhibit, through speed and violence, their singular talents on their machines, flaunt their machismo, vent their frustrations, and express outrage toward the restrictive adult-run society. In these films, the road *belonged* to youth—that is why they were so popular with young viewers. In the late sixties and early seventies, another type of road movie emerged. *Easy Rider* (which bridged the two categories), *Then Came Bronson* (1969), *The Rain People* (1969), *Five Easy Pieces* (1970) (which becomes a road movie in the second half), *Wanda* (1971), *Vanishing Point* (1971), *Two-Lane Blacktop* (1971), *Deadhead Miles* (1972), and *Payday* (1973), etc., were geared for a more intellectual audience than the drive-in crowd that flocked to biker films—influenced by foreign films, they could play in art houses. Whereas mainstream reporters like Kuralt took to the road in search of characters and slice-of-life stories that, when strung together, comprise the crazy-quilt fabric that is America (Kerouac ventured into a more *subterranean* America), the directors of these films were interested in the alienated Americans who make odysseys not to discover the real America per se—although they will learn if happiness, peace, and freedom are as attainable as purported—but to find themselves. In these deeply personal, somewhat existential films, the open road serves as a metaphor for American lives, in a turbulent, confusing time, that are without direction or meaning.

During our era of restless middle-class youths and antsy yuppies, *Easy Rider* has become a legendary film, a celluloid symbol of freedom. It has been romanticized, as it was by young viewers who saw it, loved it, and missed the point back in 1969. It's again an American dream to just chuck it all and ride free and easy across our beautiful land as Wyatt and Billy do. In fact, this is on the minds of "trapped" characters in both Albert Brooks's yuppie comedy *Lost in America* (1985) and Tim Hunter's youth drama *River's Edge* (1987). However, they refuse to acknowledge/remember that Wyatt and Billy discover there is no real freedom in our cemetery-lined "land of the free" (their money frees them from responsibilities and, at one point, buys them out of jail, but it gets them no closer to freedom) and that learning this lesson costs them their lives at the hands of two Southern grotesques. One forgets that the "personal" films of the late sixties and early seventies were almost all pessimistic, and that *Easy Rider* was the biggest downer of them all. This film attempted to crush the optimism of a counterculture that believed it was changing things for the better, asserting it was living the lie. In an interview for *Rolling Stone,* Peter Fonda told Elizabeth Campbell:

> "[As Wyatt] I am representing everybody who feels that freedom can be bought, who feels that you can find freedom through other things, like riding motorcycles through the air or smoking grass. My movie is about the *lack* of freedom. My heroes are not right, they're wrong. The only thing I can end up doing is killing my character. I end up committing suicide; that's what I'm saying America is doing. People do go in and they think, 'Look at those terrible rednecks, they killed those two free souls, who needed to love, blah, blah, blah.' That's something we have to put up with. . . . 'Easy Rider' is a Southern term for a whore's old man, not a pimp, but the dude who lives with a chick. Because he's got the easy ride. Well, that's what's happened to America, man. Liberty's become a whore, and we're all taking the easy ride."

Easy Rider is so defeatist and so mocking of the sixties dropout-dreaming counterculture, its target audience, that I'm sure many of its devoted fans (those who took it seriously) eventually decided to forget about bumming around the country after graduation, switched their majors from liberal arts to business, and went on to become the yuppies of today. (Did Jerry Rubin like *Easy Rider*? How about the characters in 1983's *The Big Chill*?)

Easy Rider had tremendous impact upon release. I still remember the long lines outside theaters (the hairiest lines of all time?) and the emotional arguments it sparked among moviegoers and critics. As Bosley Crowther recalled in *Reruns* (1978), "Some thoughtful and well-respected critics took it as a devastating blast at the kind of hostility and intransigence felt toward contemporary free-wheeling youth by a bigoted middle-class society; others, less sympathetic, found it rambling and without specific point, distinguished only by the brief intrusion of Jack Nicholson in a secondary role." *Easy Rider* was a major personal triumph for Dennis Hopper, its director, costar, and co-writer, and Peter Fonda, its producer, costar, and co-writer. Initially they couldn't find backing for their $375,000 project since their only filmmaking experience had been directing the "LSD" sequences for the Roger Corman–directed, Jack Nicholson–scripted *The Trip* (1967). But Bert Schneider (of TV's *The Monkees*) became executive producer and got Columbia to distribute it. When it became a commercial blockbuster Hopper and Fonda became heroes to young moviegoers and temporary darlings of the industry—until Hopper flopped with *The Last Movie* (1971) and Fonda flopped with the much superior *The Hired Hand* (1971). Meanwhile there was a dramatic upheaval in Hollywood, and every studio started producing low-budget, vaguely leftist, "personal" films (including those other road movies I mentioned) geared for the college-age audience.

No film of the period better caught the fancy of young people in America. It's still hard to figure out why. (Of course, I've also never understood the immense appeal of 1971's *Billy Jack*.) We loved the great background music (including songs by the Byrds and the Band); admired Hopper for experimenting (often borrowing from Godard) with staging, camerawork, and editing; loaded our backpacks after seeing Laszlo Kovacs's brilliant photography of the stunning landscape of the Southwest (the visuals become uglier as Wyatt and Billy pass through the South and the film becomes more depressing); and were much taken with the funny, touching, star-making performance by Jack Nicholson as affable, alcoholic, southern ACLU lawyer George Hanson (a part written for Rip Torn)—grinning from ear to ear under his football helmet, smoking grass for the first time, talking nonsense about Venusians on Earth (acting "in an advisory capacity"), talking sense about America. But there was much that we objected to. For instance: Other than the scene-stealing Nicholson, no one bothers to *act.* When I first saw this film, the mannered Hopper got on my nerves more than Fonda, but now I detect humor in Hopper's performance ("Hey, man, we're not no travelin' bureau, man") and am more aware of how absolutely wretched Fonda is. Because he pretends Wyatt is *thinking* the entire picture (and all he comes up with is "We blew it!"?), he doesn't have to do anything . . . and he doesn't. If this isn't the cinema's definitive wooden acting performance, then he must have been Mark Frechette's inspiration for *Zabriskie Point* (1970). Fonda's not much of an actor to begin with so it didn't help that when Wyatt and Billy get stoned in the film, he and Hopper actually got stoned on camera rather than *act* as if they were stoned. It's as if someone shot novocaine into his face.

It's not easy spending time with reticent Wyatt and spacey Billy, even if they do have groovy motorcycles. They'd be

Although Billy rides alone, Wyatt shares his bike with Jack Nicholson's ACLU lawyer George Hanson (top), *who wants to go to a New Orleans brothel, a male hitchhiker* (above) *who is returning to his commune, and a female backpacker* (left), *in a scene cut from the final print.*

awful to travel with. Since they each have the depth of an inchworm, they're no joy to listen to. Almost every sentence includes the word "man" and reflects a grasp of Hippie Triteness '69: "The first thing—go and get us a groovy meal"; "I think I'm gonna crash"; "I'm just getting my thing together"; "It's not every man who can live off the land, you know"; "You do your own thing in your own time"; "Oh, I want to rap"; "I'm hip about time . . . but I gotta go"; "Dig me"; and Wyatt's "We blew it!"—it's the most significant thing either character says, but who knows (Billy doesn't) what Wyatt means by it. That they should have stayed in the commune? that they shouldn't have sold cocaine and used that tainted money to try to buy freedom? that they just ran out of marijuana? that they forgot their chess set? Wyatt and Billy are apolitical, inarticulate, sexist, overaged motorcycle bums. In 1969, we surely accepted their smoking marijuana—after all it was a symbol of sixties' rebellion, as unifying as an Indian peace pipe—but their selling cocaine, a scary drug in our eyes, set them apart from us. These former circus stunt drivers (originally, Hopper planned to show them performing at the beginning) had more in common with Hell's Angels than flower children, hippies, or yippies. It takes the much wiser George Hanson to explain to them why society is so hostile to them, and even then they don't understand.

Except for the inspired George, the other characters in the film are as insufferable as Wyatt and Billy. The females at the commune (Lisa, Sarah, Joanne), in the roadside cafe (teenagers) and in the New Orleans brothel (Karen Black's Karen and Toni Basil's Mary) are all stupid sex objects. They say such things as "I think he's beautiful," "So she gets all uptight and she breaks out some hash—and she won't give us any," and "Are you an Aquarius?" Even those who aren't on the sexual prowl are readily available for the men. The obnoxious, lamebrain male and female commune dwellers—dummies in the desert—are a sorry lot. I certainly remember people like Luke Askew's stranger, who refuses to name the city he came from because "all cities are alike" and who throws water directly on his jacket rather than washing his armpits. But Hopper, Fonda, and co-writer Terry Southern (added to give the film class) give no indication there were also more admirable, more socially involved members of the counterculture. Even many who dropped out and found alternative life-styles did so as their way of making a *political* statement.

In 1969, leftist critics and moviegoers compared *Easy Rider* unfavorably to *Medium Cool* (1969). Haskell Wexler's provocative, relevant film told apathetic and desensitized viewers it was time to become political activists, while all *Easy Rider* did was make us longhairs paranoid about traveling through the South. The script for *Easy Rider* is so infuriating because it seems that Hopper, Fonda, and Southern wanted it to be flimsy throughout so they wouldn't have to make strong political statements. I don't agree with Frederic Tuten, who wrote in the May 9, 1969, issue of *Film Society Review,* "Implicit in the politics of *Easy Rider* are the Chicago Convention, the civil rights struggles, the Berkeley People's Park conflict, the California grape boycott, Vietnam." I think there is a connection between Wyatt, Billy, and George being killed by Southern bigots and what happened to freedom riders during the civil rights movement, but I find little else political in the film. Except, perhaps, the ending. The film's brutal ending has long been a source of controversy. I think it is too abrupt, coming just when I expect the film to switch into high gear, but there is no denying its power. Critic Manny Farber didn't think much of the film but was impressed by the finale: "The finality and present-tense quality of the killings are remarkable: the beauty issues from

the quiet, the damp green countryside, and a spectacular last shot zooming up from a curving road and a burning cycle."

The deaths of Billy and Wyatt are so shocking that for a while we don't even bother to think of their thematic relevance, or if they have thematic relevance. As we grasp for a message, we wonder if Wyatt's "We blew it!" in the previous scene was actually Fonda, the film's producer, telling Hopper, the film's director, that they forgot to include a theme in their script. Hopper told Tom Burke of the *New York Times* (June 20, 1969):

> "Everybody seems confused about the end of the picture, and all I'm saying there is that we aren't very different from the two guys in the truck who shot us. That all of us, man, are herd-instincted animals, that we all need each other. And why can't the different herds mingle?
> "What I want to say with *Easy Rider* is: Don't be scared, go and try to change America, but if you're gonna wear a badge, whether it's long hair or black skin, learn to protect yourselves. Go in groups, but go. When people understand that they can't tramp on you, maybe they'll start accepting you. Accepting *all* herds."

I don't fully understand what Hopper, being sincere and idealistic, babbled to Burke, but I doubt if any viewer in the world will read into the end what Hopper thinks is there. (Nobody left the theater talking about how those ugly Southerners reminded them of Wyatt and Billy, about "accepting all herds," or about getting a group together to travel in the deep South.) Instead, I think the tragic ending confirms the message delivered earlier to Wyatt and Billy by George Hanson, just before his own death:

> What you represent to them is freedom . . . that's what it's all about, all right. But talking about it and being it—that's two different things. I mean, it's real hard to be free when you are bought and sold in the marketplace. 'Course don't ever tell anybody that they're not free, 'cause then they're gonna get real busy killin' and maimin' to prove to you that they are. Oh yeah—they're gonna talk to you, and talk to you, and talk to you about individual freedom, but they see a free individual, it's gonna scare them . . . It makes 'em dangerous.

The protagonists, wrote Richard Schickel in *Time,* "must collide with the casual, unthinking brutality of a nation that makes much of freedom, but will not tolerate radical expressions of it, and will, on occasion, mindlessly kill dreamers it does not understand." So *yes,* the ending does make a valid political statement. However, I'm not sure that satisfies me. I still don't like how this ending was intended to exploit our fears of traveling through small-town America (we already feared wandering far off campus and knew that entering a roadside diner was a chancy proposition), or how it played up to our sense of martyrdom.

Many people who see *Easy Rider* today consider it dated, but I don't think it was in tune with its time in 1969. In fact, what's most interesting about the film is that it was meant to be a throwback to the Western. Before Wyatt and Billy begin their journey, Wyatt tosses away his watch.

Even between takes, the "sheriff" doesn't seem to appreciate the scruffy motorcyclists.

We assume this act is meant to convey that our travelers have freed themselves from civilization's greatest restriction: time. Yet only a couple of scenes later, they discuss how they want to reach New Orleans in two weeks, in time for the Mardi Gras. If we figure this isn't just bad writing, then we must conclude that when Wyatt threw away the watch it didn't signify he and Billy were free of time restrictions but that they were embarking on a journey through land where there is no distinction between present time and past time. This idea is reinforced immediately by a second pretentious image: Wyatt fixes the tire on his motorcycle while a rancher shoes his horse. Throughout the film, there will be references to the past, particularly the Old West: Fonda's character is Wyatt, as in Wyatt Earp, whom his father, Henry Fonda, played in *My Darling Clementine* (1946); Hopper's character is Billy, as in Billy the Kid or Buffalo Bill, an earlier performer in a carnival (a Wild West Show); they travel through the Southwest, where the most famous Western heroes rode; there are shots of Monument Valley, background for numerous John Ford Westerns, including *My Darling Clementine;* Billy wears buckskin and has the long hair of Western buffalo hunters; Wyatt and Billy smoke marijuana, as Indians smoked peace pipes; stoned Billy jokes, "Out here in the wilderness, fighting Indians and cowboys on every side"; there are numerous cemeteries, including an Indian burial ground; the commune is like an Indian pueblo; there are still Indians in the Southwest and still lawmen who carry guns and wear badges and cowboy hats; strangers are still not trusted (hospitality/inhospitality is a key theme of many Westerns).

In Bosley Crowther's essay on *Easy Rider* in *Reruns,* he tried to draw a parallel between this Peter Fonda film and *The Grapes of Wrath* (1940), a Henry Fonda film. There is a connection between the two films: People travel across America in search of paradise, meet some hospitable people but for the most part are victims of injustice and bigotry—they are unwelcome strangers in their own land. However, I think there is more of a chance that *Easy Rider* was intended to be a modern-day variation on a Henry Fonda Western: William Wellman's *The Ox-Bow Incident* (1943), based on the novel by Walter Van Tilburg Clark. In that film, three strangers are unjustly accused of theft and are lynched by a mob prejudiced against outsiders. Like Wyatt and Billy in *Easy Rider,* they never comprehend what is happening to them, and that they are to be killed because of who they are rather than what they have supposedly done. Henry Fonda didn't play one of the victims, but was a drifter who recognizes bigotry at work and speaks on their behalf. As his character only delays their executions, he in a sense played the role Nicholson would have in *Easy Rider* (although Fonda does survive in his movie).

Over the years, there have been numerous announcements of a sequel in the works. The worst idea? In the June 1983 issue of *American Film,* Hopper spoke about *Biker's Heaven,* being written by Terry Southern and Michael O'Donoghue. Was Hopper kidding when he said the story "takes place one hundred years after a nuclear holocaust. This guy comes from outer space and brings Peter and me back to life to save America, which has been overrun by mutant bike gangs, black Nazis, and lesbian sadists." Armed with a magic "Don't Tread on Me" flag, they set out on a mission to find an honest man in the nuked-out United States and get him elected president. "You remember how we got kicked out of the restaurant? Well, this time, we go into a restaurant, and there are guys in there with leather and razor blades on their knuckles, and we knock out about fifteen of them." I wonder if Phil Spector would have made another appearance.

Rather than a sequel, particularly the just-mentioned sequel, I'd prefer Hopper reediting *Easy Rider* and reinserting all the footage he eliminated prior to release. I'd be curious to see the 220-minute version he originally assembled. I imagine it would give the picture some of the substance and the meaning it lacks in its present form. Of course, spending an additional 126 minutes with Billy, while he tries to formulate sentences, and Wyatt, while more of his brain cells die, won't necessarily make for an easier ride.

Faster, Pussycat! Kill! Kill!

also known as *Leather Girls*, *Mankillers*, and *Pussycat*

1966 B&W Russ Meyer & Associates
Director: Russ Meyer
Producers: Russ and Eve Meyer
Screenplay: Jack Moran
Cinematography: Walter Schenk
Musical Director: Igo Kantor
Song "Faster, Pussycat" performed by the Bostweeds
Editor: Russ Meyer
Running Time: 83 minutes

Cast: Tura Satana (Varla), Haji (Rosie), Lori Williams (Billie), Susan Bernard (Linda), Stuart Lancaster (the old man), Paul Trinka (Kirk), Dennis Busch (Vegetable), Ray Barlow (Tommy), Mickey Foxx (gas station attendant).

Synopsis: Varla, Rosie, and Billie, three buxom go-go dancers, race their sports cars in the desert. The tough Varla is the leader. Rosie is her lover and follows her orders without question. Billie always puts up a fuss, but she hangs out with the other two for kicks. Tommy, a young man from a car club, and his girlfriend, Linda, drive up to do some time trials. Varla challenges him to a race. She cheats and almost kills him, and then takes his stopwatch from Linda. She and Tommy have a brutal fight. His punches are no match for her karate chops. She breaks his back and kills him. The three women kidnap Linda. They gag and drug her. They decide to get out of the area.

A gas station attendant tells the women about a miserly old handicapped man, who lives with two sons, Kirk and the brawny, imbecilic Vegetable, on a nearby ranch. Varla is intrigued to learn that the old man received a huge settlement after a train accident and keeps his money hidden. The women go to the run-down ranch to search for the money. They devise a phony story to explain why Linda is tied up. They will tell the old man that Linda's boyfriend was killed in an accident, she flipped out, and her society parents hired the three women to bring their daughter back without publicity.

Kirk catches Varla peering in the window at his father and brother. She tells them that she and her friends thought the ranch was deserted and stopped to use the water tank. The old man is suspicious, but, being a lecher, he doesn't ask them to leave. He invites the women to lunch. He tells Vegetable that there is a lot of room in the desert in which to bury them.

Billie loves Vegetable's muscles. While she seduces him, she leaves Linda with the old man. The old man makes a play for Linda, who runs into the desert. She stops a truck, but it's Kirk. He doesn't believe Linda's story and returns her to the house. Varla slaps Linda many times. She warns Billie not to mess up again.

Everyone gathers for lunch. Rosie is upset to see Varla flirt with Kirk, hoping to get him to reveal where the money is hidden. Varla and Kirk go off to make love. Rosie can barely stand spying on them. When the drunk Billie passes out, Linda again runs into the desert. The old man and Vegetable give chase in the truck. The old man hopes to rape Linda—she reminds him of the young woman who caused his accident on the train. But Kirk and Varla drive up and prevent him from having his way. Kirk, who now realizes Varla is a wicked person, and Linda walk back through the desert.

Varla drives back to the house. She tells Rosie and Billie they must kill Linda and the three men so they can search for the money. When Billie refuses to go along with the plan, Varla kills her with Rosie's knife. Vegetable cries over Billie's body. Varla and Rosie run down the old man. The money falls out of his wheelchair. Varla orders Rosie to retrieve the knife. When Rosie asks Vegetable for the knife, he stabs her to death. Varla runs down Vegetable, but he is too strong to crush against a fence. She finds Kirk and Linda in the desert. She almost karate chops him to death. But Linda gets in the truck and runs her over. Linda and Kirk hug and drive off.

Remember when winos would approach us on the street and ask for a quarter for "a cup of coffee" or "a bowl of soup," and we'd walk past, resenting their attempt to con us into financing their next drink? (They loused things up for the needy who really wanted money for coffee or soup.) But the winos wised up and revised their come-on to "I'll give it to you straight, buddy, I gotta get myself a drink." And, grateful that they weren't lying about their intentions, we were willing for a time (until we realized this was a sneakier con) to subsidize their vice and give them our pocket change. The drunks chose to be "honest" about wanting money for liquor because they knew there would be a better payoff. Which brings me to Russ Meyer.

If Meyer were defensive about his sex-and-violence potboilers and his big-breasted heroines, viewers would mercilessly attack him and he'd be chased off college campuses rather than invited to Meyer tributes. But long ago Meyer realized he'd get a better payoff by admitting that he's a male chauvinist who's turned on by big-breasted women and makes exploitation films because he wants to make a lot of money. In our "tell-it-like-it-is" age, young people despise hypocrites and appreciate anyone who makes his motives clear and presents himself as he really is. Unfortunately, if we think someone "honest," we forgive him anything, which explains why we allow straight-from-the-hip politicians to get away with bad policy and why we allow Meyer to get away with offensive films. I don't think Meyer's films are important enough to get really angry about, but I find it annoying that he dupes viewers with his "honest" confession (remember Nixon's "Checkers speech"), which is calculated to blunt all attacks on himself and his work. In case his "honesty" ploy doesn't do the trick, Meyer has a safeguard. He correctly figured that because his films have "hip" tongue-in-cheek humor, "hip" young viewers would sense that his tongue is still in his cheek when he says his motives for making his films are purely mercenary. These young viewers exchange winks with Meyer, suggesting they know and Meyer knows that he is truly an artist, who has had success although he bucked the Hollywood establishment. As Meyer intended, young viewers think he is a kindred spirit and champion his films. He has become a cult hero on campuses. If a film society is in the red, it shows a Meyer film. It's upsetting that financially strapped college film societies no longer chance booking classic American films or those Bergman, Fellini, and Godard pictures that made us film fanatics in the sixties, but instead show Russ Meyer films. But it's no wonder: Last winter at the University of Michigan, a double feature of *Faster, Pussycat! Kill! Kill!* and *Beyond the Valley of the Dolls* (1970) earned five times as much as *Gentlemen Prefer Blondes* (1953) and *The Girl*

Three hot-blooded heroines ready for action. Left to right: Varla, Billie, and Rosie (also seen below, on her back).

Can't Help It (1956)! It's disheartening that young viewers are more attracted to Meyer than to Howard Hawks or Frank Tashlin, and that Tura Satana and Dolly Read (the star of *BVD*) can outdraw Marilyn Monroe and Jayne Mansfield, the actress who paved the way for Meyer's buxom beauties. I hope they don't prefer the Bostweeds to Little Richard.

I don't mean to insult college students who are Russ Meyer fans. After all, when I was a college student, I was an avid Meyer fan, too. Before there was a Meyer craze, I thought I'd discovered a great maverick filmmaker, an innovator, a man who was using exploitation films to showcase his off-the-wall sense of humor and not so he could laugh all the way to the bank. I laughed through *Cherry, Harry, and Raquel* (1969) twice! I joined the gang that went to a Meyer triple feature at the drive-in. I found his backwoods gothics, *Lorna* (1964), *Mud Honey* (1965), and

Vixen (1968), to be offbeat, amusing, and arousing. Back then, I wouldn't have disagreed with this assessment by Meyer's greatest devotee, director John Waters, in *Shock Value* (1981):

Russ Meyer is the Eisenstein of sex films. He is single-handedly responsible for more hard-ons in movie audiences than any other director, despite the fact that he has refused ever to make a hard-core feature. Married couples have flocked to his films for twenty years because they know Russ delivers and feel that the erotic images he is so famous for give them fodder for fantasies and actually add a little zing to their dull sex lives. Even without the credits, a Russ Meyer film is instantly recognizable—top notch production values, split-second editing, low-angle shots leering up at almost deformed, big-busted, domineering sex-starved heroines, and plot lines so ludicrous that all you can do is laugh along with the director. Russ Meyer makes films about sex and violence and you can tell he is proud of his work. . . . Russ Meyer has never made a bad film.

But Meyer has made bad, bad films. In 1970, I rushed to see his new film, his studio-financed, big-budget *Beyond the Valley of the Dolls.* That picture introduced many people to Meyer and became an instant cult favorite, but it disappointed many of us who thought his earlier films showed great promise. He only repeated his worst themes from his low-budget, independent films. Because of his mean-spirited send-up of *Valley of the Dolls* (1967), a film which was already a self-parody, we recognized that Meyer made campy films because he was incapable of making good serious films. This was confirmed by his follow-up *The Seven Minutes* (1971), dull trash. He couldn't trust himself with a serious scene or an actor who plays it straight. Rather than forging ahead, Meyer retreated to independently made exploitation films: the embarrassing *Blacksnake* (1972), about a woman who whips her slaves all picture long, and several films in the *Vixen* vein. It became increasingly clear that while Meyer was not without talent (he's best at action scenes), his talent was extremely limited. His style—with fast editing, weird camera angles, and absurd narration—no longer seemed innovative, but came across as a simply conceived style created by someone who was desperate for a style, any style. (However, I do acknowledge his effective, creative use of bright, cartoonish color in *Vixen* and later films.)

Because his films have broad, campy humor and exaggerated characters, Meyer got away with ugly, offensive material that would have infuriated viewers if his films were meant to be taken seriously. I'm not against all the female nudity and gory violence in Meyer's movies but I don't like when he merges the two and tries to sexually stimulate viewers with nude women being attacked, raped, or killed. It's not easy to laugh when Erica Gavin has a gun stuck in her mouth and her head blown off in *Beyond the Valley of the Dolls;* or when Meyer (an old-style moralist) groups a bisexual and two harmless lesbians with a murderous transvestite and a Nazi as the five "deviates" who must be killed in *Dolls* to set things right; or when he stages a tasteless S&M scene with a Hitler figure in *Up!* (1976); or when he stages a "humorous" gang rape in a bar in *Up!* I don't object to Meyer populating his films with vile characters—John Waters does the same thing to good effect—but it's evident that he includes creeps and "hicks" in his films just so he can also include objectionable dialogue. I like some of the performances by Meyer's women—Lorna Maitland in *Lorna,* Erica Gavin in *Vixen,* Tura Satana in *Faster, Pussycat!*—but I don't understand why Meyer actually thinks the women they play should be admired just because they are independent and sexually aggressive. Most are bubbleheads, nymphomaniacs, victims to be raped, or dangerously deranged. Because Meyer's films are supposed to be put-ons, he's never called to task, even though much of the offensive material, particularly in *Beyond the Valley of the Dolls* and his later films, is directed in a serious manner. But at some point every Meyer fan has to stop laughing.

When I became a Meyer fan in the late sixties, *Faster, Pussycat! Kill! Kill!* was not considered one of Meyer's important films. In fact, it was as obscure as *Motor Psycho* (1965) is today. The June 1967 issue of the adult magazine *Adam Film Quarterly* contained an on-location report on the film and essays on *Mud Honey* and *Motor Psycho,* but I never met anyone who saw the film. In Roger Ebert's long essay on Meyer in the January/February 1973 issue of *Film Comment,* he mentions *Pussycat* only in passing, which suggests he hadn't yet seen it. In fact, there really wasn't much curiosity about the film until John Waters let the world know that it was his all-time favorite film. Waters wrote in *Shock Value:*

> *Faster, Pussycat! Kill! Kill!* (Russ's tenth film) is, beyond a doubt, the best movie ever made. It is possibly better than any film that will be made in the future. I first saw the film in 1966 at a local drive-in after being attracted to the radio ad that blared "It will leave a taste of evil in your mouth!" At the time, I was totally unfamiliar with Russ Meyer's work, but after seeing *Faster, Pussycat! Kill! Kill!,* he became my lifelong idol. I went back to the drive-in every night of the run, even if I had to go alone. . . . I wrote Russ gushing fan letters, which he politely answered. I got a job as a film reviewer in a local underground paper for the sole purpose of raving about the film. If there is such a thing as a film being a bad influence on youth, here was the perfect example. Russ's nasty "pussycats" became a role model for all the characters in my productions—especially Divine. . . . For the past fifteen years I've driven hundreds of miles to catch the film whenever it's revived. I've rented the film and forced friends and members of my crews to watch it in hushed silence. When my own films started to catch on, I made sure to gush about *Faster, Pussycat!* in every interview.

I will never gush about *Faster, Pussycat! Kill! Kill!,* Meyer's wild, brilliantly titled film about three lethal women who'd probably kill anyone who called them pussycats. But I think it's the least objectionable of Meyer's films. It's so outrageous that it's funny and it only borders on being off-putting. Significantly, there are no rapes, just rape attempts, and even here Meyer doesn't resort to having his women's clothes ripped off. (I'm not objecting to there being rapes in movies—I just don't like how Meyer handles them.) So I can accept Meyer stuffing his four female leads—strippers Satana and Haji, Las Vegas showgirl Lori Williams, *Playboy* playmate Susan Bernard—into skimpy costumes and shooting them at every possible compromising angle so that their enormous chests seem to jump toward our eyes, even during those rare moments the juiced-up heroines are still. (What Meyer could have done with 3-D!) Their prominent breasts are almost always in mid-frame, and as often as not someone is making a reference to them. Meyer would have turned the "artistic" diving sequence in Leni Riefenstahl's *The Olympiad* (1936) into pornography. But in this film, in which the plot is so slim and the women so voluptuous, we can forgive Meyer for his indulgences. Even gratuitous nudity would be acceptable, as long as it's not linked to the violence. Considering Meyer directed the film, it's surprising there is no nudity and no link.

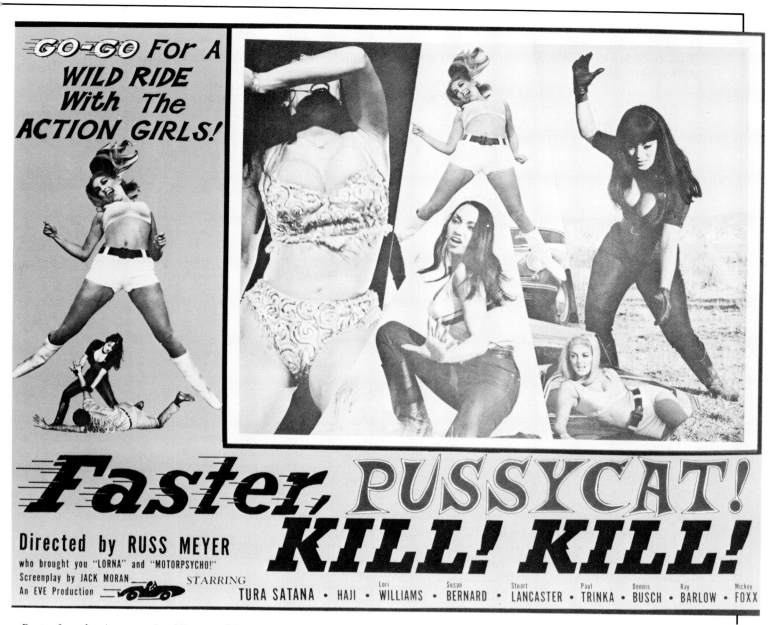

Poster for what is surpassing Vixen *and* Beyond the Valley of the Dolls *as Russ Meyer's most popular film.*

Because the campy humor isn't meant to cover up any offensive sex, violence, or morality, we can appreciate some quirky and amusing touches. I like that Tommy (Ray Barlow), Varla's first victim, appears wearing Bermuda shorts, and that girlfriend Linda emerges from the car in a bikini to ask if everyone is praising her figure (they aren't). It's very commendable, as Linda brags, that Tommy is champion of their car club and has earned the most safety points! But this certainly doesn't impress the three heroines. I think the race around the desert track is funny because it's impossible to tell what's happening and the music sounds like a distorted, sped-up, sax version of a couple of lines of "Jeepers, Creepers." I like the way Varla snatches Tommy's prized stopwatch from Linda, as if they were all in high school and she were a bully. I like the

way Varla constantly shouts, threatens people, laughs when she does something wrong, and thinks of becoming rich—it's easy to see that she served as model for Divine's amoral, narcissistic characters. I like that Rosie has an Italian accent—there's as much reason for Meyer to place an Italian in the California desert as there is for Chico Marx to have an Italian accent. And I like how Billie gets on Varla's nerves by constantly defying her, gets on Rosie's nerves by constantly dancing, and gets on our nerves by constantly using lines like "It's a gas" and "I'm hip." At times, she's more creative: "I'm not under contract to them and I've got a strong feeling option time is around the corner." All three women use swingin' lingo ("Break out the sauce"; "You're all shook up, aren't you, baby?"; "You really do have the hots for the long green") and double entendres ("Would you like to look under my hood?"; "My motor never breaks down"; "We don't like nothing soft"). Nobody in the film is capable of saying a straight line! For instance, when the men refer to Varla, they usually use an animal metaphor such as "she's more stallion than mare." Even the handicapped old man (Stu Lancaster, the only cast member with talent) gets into the act; speaking of the women, he says: "Fate threw us this package and all we've got to do is untie them pretty ribbons." But Varla gets the best lines. When the old man says pitifully, "I am tied to this chair for life," she retorts, "Better you should be nailed to it." At times, her lines seem written for Mae West: When Kirk grabs her as she peers through the window, she asks the ridiculous question, "What's the strong arm bit, or couldn't you tell I was a girl?"; when Kirk says he must have her, she responds that she "wants everything or as much as I can get. Right now, you're first on my list and I always start on top."

Perhaps John Waters's main contribution to film schol-

From behind, we watch the topless Billie shower. This is the closest the mysteriously conservative Meyer gets to nudity in this film.

arship was to track down Tura Satana, the striking part-Apache, part-Japanese karate expert who makes such an impression as the evil, dressed-in-tight-fitting-black Varla. A mother, she was working as a nurse and running a doctor's office in L.A., in 1981. She had also been in *Irma La Douce* (1963), *Who's Been Sleeping in My Bed?* (1963), *The Astro-Zombies* (1968), and *The Doll Squad* (1973). She had strong memories of working on *Faster, Pussycat!*, the film that has brought her lasting fame. She apparently got along with Haji and Lori Williams, but thought Susan Bernard was a stuck-up Hollywood brat ("I'd get so mad at her that I'd turn away and smash a railroad tie with a karate chop") and wasn't keen on her romantic scenes with Paul Trinka ("Those love scenes were real acting; the guy was a health-food nut and had bad breath!"). She told Waters: "When the film came out, everybody wanted to punch me. I got a lot of letters from guys who wanted me to beat the crap out of them."

Meyer told Waters that he meant *Faster, Pussycat!* to be a distaff version of his previous film, *Motor Psycho*, which is about three tough guys on a violence spree. Judging by the harsh treatment of the tiny bikini-clad Linda, one wonders if Meyer was also inspired by a desire to take the most famous and cheerful beach bunny, Gidget (who is much like Linda), and throw her into a violent gang picture, where she would be constantly abused. Or perhaps he wanted to show what would happen if three psychotic women visited the Ponderosa and wiped out the Cartwrights. *Faster, Pussycat!* certainly falls into the fast-paced and violent hot-rod/youth-gang genre created in the fifties, but if you made Varla, Rosie, and Billie men, turned Kirk into a pretty woman, and put all the characters on horses, then the picture could almost pass as a nonexistent third part of Monte Hellman's dusty, dirty, and violent existential Western trilogy, following *Ride the Whirlwind* (1965) and *The Shooting* (1966).

Say what you will about the film's bad acting, bad dialogue, and bad theme song, but the scenes of violence are quite startling. The deaths of Tommy (Varla breaks his back), Billie (Varla hurls a knife into her back), the old man (Rosie drives toward him and he rolls his wheelchair to meet her head-on), Rosie (Vegetable stabs her repeatedly), and Varla (Linda runs her over) are all boldly directed and have strong impact—like violent scenes in Sam Fuller and early Don Siegel films. All the action sequences have pizzazz and it's noteworthy that *women* are involved. This film came out before *The Avengers* came to America so it's particularly strange and thrilling to see Varla really go at it in hand-to-hand combat with Tommy and Kirk and, by using karate, gain the upper hand both times. My favorite moment in the film has no editing: During Varla's fight with Kirk, Meyer's camera points upward, toward the sky, from Varla's point of view. Kirk looks down at us. Suddenly his face falls out of the frame and is replaced by Varla's—now she is on top in their struggle, where she belongs. Stu Lancaster's character in *Mud Honey* stated: "Women is strange critters . . . sometimes they look small and weak, but sometimes they are anything but that . . . that's the first thing you've to learn about them." No matter how much learnin' about women Lancaster did, he never would have been prepared for Varla.

Vegetable terrorizes Linda.

*It's sex and sadism on the loose.
Left: Varla uses karate to get the
upper hand on Kirk. Below:
Only minutes before Varla had
seduced Kirk in a hayloft.*

Five Million Years to Earth

also known as *Quatermass and the Pit*

1968 Color British Hammer-Seven Arts, released in the United States by 20th Century-Fox
Director: Roy Ward Baker
Producer: Anthony Nelson Keys
Screenplay: Nigel Kneale
Cinematography: Arthur Grant
Music: Tristram Cary
Supervising Editor: James Needs
Running Time: 98 minutes

Cast: James Donald (Dr. Roney), Andrew Keir (Bernard Quatermass), Barbara Shelley (Barbara Judd), Julian Glover (Colonel Breen), Maurice Good (Sergeant Cleghorn), Duncan Lamont (Sladden), Peter Copley (Howell), Edwin Richfield (minister), Bryan Marshall (Captain Fuller), Grant Taylor (Sergeant Ellis), Robert Morris (Watson), James Culliford (Corporal Gibson).

Synopsis: Men doing expansion work at the underground station in the Hobb's End section of London uncover skeletons of ancient apes. Anthropologist Dr. Roney and his assistant Barbara Judd rush to the scene. Roney wonders why these ancient apes have such large skulls.

An assistant thinks she has found a pipe beneath the clay. Digging stops before it is unearthed because it may be an unexploded German bomb from World War II. Strangely, it has no magnetic hold, so it is not made of steel. Missile expert Colonel Breen is called in. He happens to be arguing with Professor Bernard Quatermass at the time, so Quatermass accompanies him. Now an intact ape skull is discovered. Quatermass realizes that since they were found next to the strange "missile" they should have been destroyed when it hit the earth—unless they arrived *with* the object. But they are five million years old!

Quatermass and Barbara learn that during the war there were strange occurrences in Hobb's End. There were bumps in the night, noises, ghost sightings . . . residents moved. The street used to be called Hob's Lane—Hob is a lay term for the devil. They investigate further and discover that there have been spooky happenings in the area dating back to Roman times—each time there was digging.

The object is uncovered. It is a large blue "missile." Although Quatermass objects, Breen orders electrician Sladden to drill into a sealed compartment. The special drill doesn't work. However, the wall disintegrates. Roney and Quatermass pull out a dead, locust-like creature that has horns and three legs. It looks like the demons in drawings all over the world. Quatermass theorizes they were Martians whose civilization was dying. Choosing to conquer earth by proxy, they abducted our ancient apes, altered their brains, and returned them to earth to breed with unaltered apes. These apes evolved, becoming men who retained the *evil* that the Martians had instilled into their simian ancestors. Quatermass worries that the "missile" has the power to reactivate the dormant evil and cause men to complete the Martian colonization. This is confirmed when Sladden is possessed and runs through the city. Until he finds safety in a church, there is much psychic activity and destruction. But Quatermass can't convince the government of the danger even when he shows, courtesy of Roney's unconscious-vision device, a televised vision of Barbara's/an apeman's thoughts: Five million years ago, locust-like creatures marched across Mars, killing and being killed.

Breen thinks it's all a German propaganda trick and invites the media to see the "missile." The "missile" glows. Breen burns up beside it. Buildings collapse, there is fire. Everyone rushes into the streets. Quatermass is possessed. Roney brings him to his senses before Quatermass kills him. Roney is one of the few who has no ancient evil in him. Others like him are killed by the evil, possessed mob. Quatermass knocks out the possessed Barbara. A great mass of energy appears in the sky—this glowing locust looks like the devil. Roney recalls that *iron* is the devil's enemy. He swings a huge metal crane into the energy form, grounding it. There is an enormous flash and fire. The "demon" is gone and earth is saved. But Roney is dead.

America's most rabid science fiction fans recognize *Five Million Years to Earth* as one of the genre's most intelligent, provocative entries of the last two decades and one of the best sf films ever produced in England. Yet its small budget, modest special effects, lack of name stars, and complicated, adult themes have prevented it from reaching sf dabblers or a large movie audience. It remains a sleeper in America and you're more likely to catch it on television, where it plays without fanfare, than in revival houses or on college campuses. But in Britain the picture is well known and much appreciated. In fact, *Quatermass and the Pit,* as it was originally titled, *The Quatermass Experiment* (1956), *Quatermass II* (1957), *Quatermass Conclusion* (1980), the similarly titled BBC-TV serials from which the first three films were adapted (the fourth film was made specifically for British television), and the title character, the indomitable Professor Bernard Quatermass, are as much a part of the pop culture as *Dr. Who.*

All three serials, as well as the three film adaptations, were scripted by Nigel Kneale, the first Britisher working in science fiction to deliberately incorporate horror elements (at a time horror films were coded "X"—for adults only—in Britain). What's most impressive about Kneale is that while he takes us out of the rational, scientific realm and off into fantastic directions (there are alien invasions and monsters; we learn—talk about culture shock—that we are descended from evil Martians), his work is consistently intelligent and never seems totally implausible, perhaps because it all makes sense to brainy scientist Quatermass. Kneale also has, writes British critic John Brosnan in his book *Future Tense* (1978), "an uncanny knack for combining contemporary sf themes with both mythology and traditional elements of the supernatural to produce stories that tend to bypass the forebrain and work directly on unconscious fears. 'It's the art of creating a state of unease,' says Kneale."

The popular Quatermass serials, each running six weeks, were broadcast in the fifties. In *The Quatermass Experiment,* which kept the nation in a state of unease in 1953, Reginald Tate's Quatermass realizes that the sole surviving astronaut of Britain's first manned space flight is transforming into an octopus-like alien creature. *Quatermass II* appeared two years later, with John Robinson assuming the title role following Tate's death. In this story, Quatermass discovers that aliens have infiltrated the British government and set up a mysterious base in preparation for a full-scale invasion.

Kneale quickly adapted his first two Quatermass serials into films for Hammer Studios. They were modest efforts directed by Val Guest, who'd later make the superb *The Day the Earth Caught Fire* (1962). American actor Brian Donlevy was brought to England to star in both films. That Hammer would then, for U.S. release, replace the titles, which were well known in England, with *The Creep-*

Quatermass (right), *Barbara, and Dr. Roney discuss the mysterious, newly discovered five-million-year-old ape skull.*

ing Unknown and *Enemy from Space,* respectively, is indicative that the studio believed the name Quatermass was far less a selling point to Americans, who hadn't seen the serials, than was an exploitation title coupled with a well-known, though past his prime, Hollywood actor in the lead role. Both pictures had fair success in America, as well as at home, and this led to an increased number of science fiction and horror films being made in England. Meanwhile, Kneale was busy writing a third *Quatermass* serial about a spaceship found in London amidst Roman ruins. John Brosnan quotes Kneale:

> "In the *Quatermass* serials, I always used what was going on at the time as a basis for the stories . . . in the late 1950s London was being rebuilt after the war and so a number of huge cavities were being dug . . . unexploded bombs were always being found and sometimes old Roman ruins would be exposed. And I thought—what if they found something else beyond that? What if they uncovered a spaceship? And this led to *Quatermass and the Pit.*"

The *Quatermass and the Pit* serial, with Andre Morrel as Quatermass, played on the BBC in 1958, *after* the movie versions of the first two serials had already made the rounds. Oddly, Hammer didn't ask Kneale to adapt it into a screenplay immediately, while interest in *Quatermass* was high; instead Hammer began its classic horror series with Peter Cushing and Christopher Lee and held off on *Quatermass and the Pit* for almost 10 years. By that time Hammer decided that casting a name actor in a lead role wasn't a prerequisite to having a financially successful sf or horror film, and that Quatermass shouldn't be played by an American (John Mills would take the role in *Quatermass Conclusion*). So little-known Scottish character actor An-

drew Keir was offered the plum part (and his joy must have lasted until he learned he was billed behind James Donald). Nevertheless, 20th Century-Fox changed the title to *Five Million Years to Earth* for American release because Americans still didn't relate the name "Quatermass" to science fiction.

Ironically, *Five Million Years to Earth,* far more intense and intellectually stimulating than its predecessors, was released in America in the same year as *2001: A Space Odyssey* (1968), the other major science fiction film to deal with the intriguing theme of "race memory." The blasphemous notion in *2001* is: Because our ape ancestors had contact with extraterrestrials who altered our evolution, we humans retain in our subconscious mind a concept of "God"—although we don't associate it with alien beings. The blasphemous notion in *Five Million Years to Earth* is: Because our ape ancestors had contact with evil extraterrestrials who altered our evolution, we humans retain in our subconscious mind a concept of "Devil"—although we don't associate it with alien beings. (Again, in 1972's Spanish-made cult film *Horror Express,* our "Devil" is an ancient astronaut.) Since *Five Million Years to Earth* was released prior to *2001* and had come from a 1958 television serial, it's tempting to say it beat Kubrick's more famous film to the punch with the "race memory" theme. But it's likely that among Kneale's sources for his serial and film were the original sources for *2001*; as John Brosnan notes, "The idea of the devil becoming implanted in the human racial memory as a result of contact with a horned alien species figured prominently in [*2001* scriptwriter Arthur C.] Clarke's 1953 novel *Childhood's End,* and the idea of an alien artifact being discovered underground was the subject of Clarke's 1950 short story *The Sentinel.*"

Brosnan points out that Kneale's decision to give his

Quatermass and Dr. Roney find an ancient locust-like Martian inside the missile. It will immediately disintegrate.

Martian insects three legs is a "nod" to H. G. Wells's Martians in his book *War of the Worlds*. I also believe Kneale was cognizant of George Pal's 1953 film production—or perversion—of Wells's classic. Kneale rejects that film's contention that men of science would work hand in hand with the government and military in dealing with alien beings. Independent thinker Quatermass is always at odds with know-it-all military men and government officials on how to approach a problem—he's usually the only one to realize there *is* a problem. In the *film* of Wells's work, God is responsible for halting the invaders (they die from germ contamination immediately after they destroy a church). In Kneale's story, a man who is possessed by evil (aliens) can find some comfort in a church (as does electrician Sladden), but it is man who halts the invasion and casts out the "devil." In Pal's *War of the Worlds,* scientist Gene Barry is impotent against the Martians. But in *Five Million Years to Earth,* James Donald's Dr. Roney ends the alien invasion by drawing on fundamental *scientific* law ("Mass into energy!"): By projecting a metal mass that is the iron crane into a "mass" of energy that is the incandescent horned demon in the sky, he grounds it and dissipates its energy.

Roney thrusts iron into the demon because he recalls iron is the devil's enemy. So before he applies *science* to the cause, he draws on his vast *knowledge*—anthropologist Roney is able to use his scientific knowledge only because he has knowledge of nonscientific subjects; in fact, he is learned in the supernatural, the area farthest from science. In film history, men and women of great intelligence,

knowledge, and scientific expertise have rarely been shown in sympathetic light; this is particularly true in sf and horror films, where such characters are typically antisocial megalomaniacs who evolve into crazed murderers or worse. So Kneale should be commended for writing a story in which we side with three scientists—Quatermass, Roney, and Barbara Judd (played by popular fantasy film vet Barbara Shelley)—and knowledge, intelligence, and independent thought are shown to be positive attributes.

The film has a political subtext, where knowledge and independent thought really come into play. The simple reason the script calls for Julian Glover's Colonel Breen to initially state the space vehicle might be an unexploded German bomb from World War II, and to later insist the ship and its unusual apemen and insect passengers were part of a German ploy to cause panic in London during World War II, is that Kneale wants to make us think of imperialistic Nazi Germany. When we see, on the unconscious-vision device, Barbara's visions of the locust-like Martians of five million years ago, they are marching en masse, recalling faceless, machine-like German soldiers on the move. We see, Quatermass points out, the ancient Martians "kill and being killed"; he could be describing the Nazis in Germany when he explains what took place on Mars: "Ritual slaughter to preserve a fixed society, to rid it of mutations." As the Nazis did in countries they conquered, the Martians wanted to rule earth by proxy. Most frightening and sickening to Kneale is that during World War II many people in occupied countries, including France, acted as if they were possessed by their evil "landlords," allowed the evil within themselves to surface, and, now essentially Nazis themselves, turned on their friends and neighbors—just as the Londoners in the film become evil under the Martian demon's influence and gang up on the few good people who remain defiant. Kneale raises the possibility that most of us have evil within us—even Quatermass!—ready to be unleashed if something as drastic as an occupation occurs. He worries that if England had been occupied by the Nazis, many people might not have acted differently from the French collaborators. He hopes that in such dire circumstances they wouldn't act like sheep, stop thinking for themselves, and fall into line. Quatermass is skeptical that the Martians can be defeated by applying a "too simple" scientific law, but Roney realizes that even the simplest act of defiance or independent thought may have tremendous results because those in control expect *no* resistance. He explains: "It's what they'd never allow for . . . that scrap of knowledge in minds that were free, that could use it." Roney is speaking of Martians, Kneale of fascists.

I do believe that, in this film, science, knowledge, and free thought are shown to be a more powerful weapon than religion. Yet it can be argued that Kneale intended his film to have religious significance. After all, the final confrontation is *literally* between good and evil. Dr. Roney, the rare man who did not evolve from the genetically altered apes, the rare man who was not influenced by the evil Martians, battles the "Devil" with the fate of mankind at stake. The pure man sacrifices his life on behalf of the tainted human beings on earth. This is, of course, the story of Christ.

Colonel Breen and his men examine the "missile" found at the underground station excavation site.

happens for most of the picture—remember, there are no live aliens for us to worry about. He manages to build suspense by using creepy music even when what's onscreen doesn't call for it (i.e., the opening shot of a policeman walking by Hobb's End Station); keeping background and secondary characters active, either working in the pit, where they might discover something at any moment, or gathering outside for information about what is happening in the pit; having Quatermass appear anxious at all times; and emphasizing the *mystery* elements of the story. There are few shocks, but the atmosphere is intense, as in a Jacques Tourneur horror film. In fact, the night scene in which the possessed Sladden runs through the empty streets and deserted cemetery while much psychic activity takes place recalls haunting nocturnal sequences in Tourneur's British horror film, *Night of the Demon/Curse of the Demon* (1958). Like Tourneur, Baker keeps us on edge, always thinking something is about to happen! As in Tourneur's film, nothing much really happens until the end, but the fascinating, terrifying clues the characters uncover keep us satisfied until the "monster" appears in the sky. The dramatic conclusion featuring the flaming horned demon (a Martian image that resembles our "Devil") and other impressive special effects rewards our patience: It is visually exciting and thought provoking. The climax leaves you stunned and worn out, just as Barbara and Quatermass are in the film's great last shot.

If we failed to make the Roney/Christ analogy until the end, it's because Kneale failed to sufficiently develop the character earlier. We were never made aware of Roney's goodness and purity (though I assume this is hinted when he's the only person who attempts to use the unconscious-vision device whose brain rejects thoughts of tainted ancient apes). In fact, it's easy to take Roney for granted, since he's so mild-mannered that the blustery, imposing Quatermass dwarfs him, and because the bearded Keir has more screen presence than Donald. But if you pay strict attention, you'll realize that Roney is much more important than Quatermass all along. Quatermass does some sleuthing, philosophizes, makes fascinating hypotheses, and argues with establishment figures, but he never gets anything he wants accomplished. Actually, the Quatermass character is superfluous. He could be eliminated because even his more significant lines and actions could easily be given to Roney and Barbara, whom, unfortunately, we know nothing about. Two strong characters are preferable to three skimpy characters, especially when it's so important to know what motivates these people. Of course, getting rid of Quatermass isn't the solution to improving a *Quatermass* picture . . . obviously Kneale should have provided more substance for him (including more telling lines like "I never had a career—only work"), the pivotal Roney, and Barbara, a character so underwritten that it could have been played by a 60-year-old actress without modification. The weak characters—covered up at times by fine acting—are Kneale's one failing and the only major problem with the film.

Five Million Years to Earth was directed by Roy Ward Baker, who is best known for directing episodes of *The Avengers* (including one in which Julian Glover played a colonel). He did an excellent job of overcoming a small budget that confined him to only a few sets (he compensated by cutting back and forth between characters in different locations) and limited him to only a few special effects. Baker's hardest test was to keep his audience interested and excited although nothing scary or catastrophic

As mobs run wild, and there is much destruction caused by psychic activity, Barbara becomes possessed, an evil agent of the glowing, locust-like mass of energy in the sky. While Roney battles the demon form, Quatermass runs toward Barbara to try to bring her to her senses.

Gentlemen Prefer Blondes

1953   Color   20th Century-Fox
Director: Howard Hawks
Producer: Sol C. Siegel
Screenplay: Charles Lederer
From the musical by Joseph Fields and Anita Loos, with music and lyrics by Jule Styne and Leo Robin
From the novel by Anita Loos
Cinematography: Harry J. Wild
Musical Director: Lionel Newman
New Songs: "When Love Goes Wrong" and "Anyone Here for Love," music and lyrics by Hoagy Carmichael and Harold Adamson
Choreography: Jack Cole
Editor: Hugh S. Fowler
Running Time: 91 minutes

Cast: Jane Russell (Dorothy Shaw), Marilyn Monroe (Lorelei Lee), Charles Coburn (Sir Francis "Piggy" Beekman), Elliott Reid (Ernie Malone), Tommy Noonan (Gus Esmond, Jr.), George Winslow (Henry Stofford III), Marcel Dario (magistrate), Taylor Holmes (Gus Esmond, Sr.), Norma Varden (Lady Beekman), Harry Carey, Jr. (Winslow), Ray Montgomery (Peters).

Synopsis: Intelligent brunette Dorothy Shaw and her best friend, dumb blonde Lorelei Lee, are showgirls from Little Rock. Both chase after men. But while Dorothy is attracted to good-looking but poor men, Lorelei wants to marry a millionaire. She loves money and diamonds. She is engaged to wealthy Gus Esmond, Jr., whom she has wrapped around her finger, but his father doesn't think she is good enough for him. Lorelei and Dorothy take a ship to France. Lorelei figures that if Gus truly wants to marry her, he'll come to her in Paris. Gus warns Lorelei that she must be faithful on the trip or his father will force a breakup.

Dorothy is excited that America's Olympic team is on board, but is disappointed they must go to sleep at nine. Lorelei tries to find a millionaire for Dorothy and arranges for Henry Stofford III to sit at their dinner table. She's overheard by Ernie Malone, a detective hired by Mr. Esmond, to keep an eye on Lorelei. He thinks she is trying to find a millionaire for herself. It turns out that Henry Stofford III is a little boy, but Dorothy doesn't mind because she's attracted to Malone, not knowing he's spying on her friend.

Lorelei carries on an innocent flirtation with elderly diamond-mine owner Sir Francis "Piggy" Beekman. She greatly admires Mrs. Beekman's diamond tiara. Dorothy is upset to spot Malone secretly taking photos of Piggy and Lorelei while they are in an innocent but suspicious pose. Knowing that Mr. Esmond will break off Lorelei's engagement to Gus if he sees such pictures, Dorothy and Lorelei plan to steal them back. They get Malone drunk and steal his pants, taking the photos. Dorothy breaks up with Malone, though he swears he loves her.

Piggy is grateful when Lorelei asks for nothing when she gives him the recovered photos without Mrs. Beekman seeing them. So he gives Lorelei his wife's diamond tiara. Malone records the conversation, which makes Lorelei come across as a golddigger. When he sends the tape to Mr. Esmond, the engagement is called off, and Dorothy and Lorelei become stranded in Paris without a line of credit. Moreover, Mrs. Beekman accuses Lorelei of stealing the tiara. Piggy denies knowledge of what happened to it and heads for Africa. Lorelei refuses to give it back.

Dorothy and Lorelei take jobs as performers. But Lorelei may go to jail unless she returns the tiara to Mrs. Beekman. She agrees to do it, but the tiara is missing. While Lorelei sings "Diamonds Are a Girl's Best Friend" and wins back Gus, who has arrived in Paris, Dorothy pretends to be Lorelei and stands trial in her stead. Meanwhile, Malone tracks down Piggy, who is trying to leave the country. He has the tiara. Malone brings him to court and the tiara is returned to Mrs. Beekman. Mr. Esmond sees the trial. Thinking Dorothy is Lorelei, he is happy when Gus introduces him to his fiancée . . . until he finds out that she is the *real* Lorelei. However, he is impressed by her honesty (she doesn't want to marry Gus for his money, but for his father's money) and intelligence—she says she is smart when she wants to be. Mr. Esmond agrees to let her marry his son.

At a double wedding, Dorothy marries Malone and Lorelei marries Gus. They are very happy.

*G*entlemen Prefer Blondes is one of the few cult movies that nobody has a quarrel with. First of all, it was directed by Howard Hawks, who is championed by film scholars and serious critics for his artistry and interesting themes (particularly in regard to male-female and male-male relationships); is a favorite of the mass audience because his films are so *entertaining*; and is hero to young philistine directors (like John Carpenter) who, looking for an excuse not to make small, personal "art" films, point to Hawks as an "artist" who made a lot of money from making commercial movies. And it stars Marilyn Monroe, to whom every self-respecting movie fan has a deep emotional attachment. In fact, the only controversy surrounding *Gentlemen Prefer Blondes* is over where it ranks among Monroe's films. Because it has such a lightweight story line and is directed in Hawks's deceptively simple style—the song-and-dance routines are so wonderful because they have no-frills choreography and camerawork—it has long been regarded inferior to Monroe's other famous films. But I think only Billy Wilder's *Some Like It Hot* (1959), with its hilarious madcap and bawdy humor, and its audacious sexual-identity theme, holds up better. While Monroe is equally dynamic and lovable in *How to Marry a Millionaire* (1953), *The Seven Year Itch* (1955), *Bus Stop* (1956), and *The Misfits* (1961), *Gentlemen Prefer Blondes* is far less flawed and far more entertaining (it is *consistently* enjoyable) than any of these pictures. Also it is the film that made Monroe a bona-fide star, first showcased her musical talents, and firmly established her screen persona. (Her image would remain intact but for one important change: She would become much more vulnerable.)

In 1949, when starlet Monroe's career was sputtering after a promising start—few noticed she'd done well in a large part in *Ladies in the Chorus* (1948)—she had a walk-on, actually a wiggle-on, past Groucho Marx in *Love Happy* (1949). (She got the part from Groucho after spending hours in front of the mirror practicing her soon-to-be-famous wiggle-walk.) Groucho was the first to recognize her unusual appeal. He called her a combination of three famous figures: vamp Theda Bara, who made victims of her male playthings and who represented dangerous sex; Mae West, who made aggressive female sexuality acceptable and who represented fun sex; and Little Bo Beep, the original blonde innocent. This contradictory image was reinforced in *Gentlemen Prefer Blondes*. As golddigger Lorelei Lee, Monroe is naughty and innocent at the same time—this is the secret to Monroe's sex appeal. Like Judy Holliday's Billie Dawn in *Born Yesterday* (1951), she is the stupidest of dumb blondes—to please men—yet is smart as a whip when she has to be. Like the women played by Monroe's idol Jean Harlow, she is thought by society to be amoral because she uses her body to get what she wants, yet she has a strict moral code and knows the difference between right and wrong (she doesn't consider her sexual conduct amoral)—that's why she's insulted to be accused of stealing the diamond tiara from a man, Charles Coburn's Sir Francis "Piggy" Beekman, when she could

Blond Lorelei Lee and brunette Dorothy Shaw, two little (show)girls from Little Rock, were played by a dynamic duo: Marilyn Monroe and Jane Russell, friends on- and offscreen.

so easily use sex to get him to give it to her (she'd consider this a *fair* trade).

What's interesting is that while we learn everything there is to know about Monroe's very open Lorelei Lee, this is the only important Monroe film in which virtually nothing of the actress is revealed—other than she had a great sense of humor (she's extremely funny as Lorelei) and loved to step out of herself on screen and sing and dance and play-act and act sexy (as when she sings an outrageously sensuous "Bye Bye, Baby" to Tommy Noonan). We don't sense the sensitivity, brittleness, confusion, fear, insecurity, guilt, hurt, sadness, isolation, and crushed romanticism that come across in her other roles. For once she is strong, resilient, confident, in control. She seems cheerful, giddy, and carefree, particularly in the escapist musical numbers like "Two Little Girls from Little Rock" and "Diamonds Are a Girl's Best Friend," the classic number that inspired Madonna's "Material Girl" video. Since Monroe wasn't all that happy while making the film, it is a remarkable performance.

Gentlemen Prefer Blondes began as a comic novel by Anita Loos. It was filmed in 1928 with Ruth Taylor and Alice White. It was also adapted into a play, and eventually it became a smash Broadway musical-comedy, written by Loos and Joseph Fields, scored by Jule Styne and Leo Robin, and starring Carol Channing as Lorelei Lee. Hollywood was interested in adapting the Broadway version and there were rumors that Channing would get the movie part—it's a horrible thought. Columbia wanted to buy the play rights for Judy Holliday, thinking Lorelei would be an ideal follow-up to her Oscar-winning Billie Dawn (a part Monroe auditioned for as a starlet). But Holliday didn't want to do it, ending Columbia's bidding war with 20th Century-Fox, which wanted the property for its resident queen, Betty Grable. Because her career was waning, Grable told studio chief Darryl F. Zanuck that she greatly desired to play Lorelei. So Zanuck announced that Grable would play the part. But he got second thoughts when he realized that Marilyn Monroe was the hottest property in town, voted Number 1 in the thea-

In films, Marilyn Monroe's characters were rarely courted by smart, mature, virile men. Lorelei is no exception. Left: Lorelei shows married Piggy one of the secret photos Ernie took of them. Below: Gus expresses love for Lorelei.

ter owners' Stars of Tomorrow poll. She had raised executive's eyebrows and temperatures with her sizzling-sexy performance—including a long, long walking scene—in the soon-to-be-released *Niagara* (1953); moreover, interest in Monroe skyrocketed nationwide when she readily admitted she was the most striking of the anonymous nude models in a celebrated "Golden Dreams" calendar, having posed on that red satin sheet for Tom Kelley in 1949, when she was in need of money. It did not go unnoticed that 20th's *Clash By Night* (1952) had become a hit, not because of stars Barbara Stanwyck and Robert Ryan, but because the calendar girl had a small part in it. Thousands of letters addressed to Monroe poured into the studio each week. *Life* would put her on the cover. So Zanuck changed his mind about Grable and gave the part of Lorelei Lee to Monroe. The deciding factor in his decision was that Grable would have cost about $150,000 to play Lorelei, while Monroe's contract would limit her to just $18,000. Monroe would demand and receive her own dressing room, but this wasn't compensation enough for her low salary, especially since top-billed Jane Russell, who was under contract to Howard Hughes, would get over $100,000 to play Lorelei's bosom buddy, Dorothy Shaw. And so a permanent rift developed between Monroe and Zanuck. It would widen when Zanuck refused to draw up a better

contract as she became a bigger star by making *How to Marry a Millionaire* and *The Seven Year Itch*, and then forced her to take roles she didn't want in *River of No Return* (1954) and *There's No Business Like Show Business* (1954). In 1955, Monroe would walk out on 20th and flee to New York to study at the Actors Studio; when she returned to Hollywood she formed her own production company. Zanuck's publicists would send out press releases downgrading her importance to the studio, and he'd sign Jayne Mansfield to be her successor. But Monroe was the hottest actress in the world and the 20th brass overruled Zanuck and brought Monroe back under her terms. (Zanuck wouldn't return to 20th until after Monroe's death in 1962.)

Even Zanuck admitted that Monroe's performance in *Gentlemen Prefer Blondes* was special. Monroe had revealed comedic flair in *All About Eve* (1950), as an empty-headed aspiring actress, and Hawks's *Monkey Business* (1952), as Charles Coburn's dumb-blonde secretary, who wasn't hired for her typing skills. But here, given more screen time, she revealed genuine comedic talent. She's a joy to watch, whether getting stuck in Malone's cabin porthole (a classic scene!), helping Dorothy pull off Malone's pants, or telling the ship's headwaiter that she'll eat meals in her room (meaning he must return the bribes of men who want to sit at her table) *unless* he seats her with the millionaire of her choice (who turns out to be the young boy, well played by George "Foghorn" Winslow). More surprising is Monroe's ease in the musical numbers, since at the time no one even knew if she could dance or carry a tune. In fact, when Zanuck saw the rushes he was so shocked that his sex symbol could actually sing that he had her perform for him to prove her voice wasn't being dubbed. Of course, Monroe's voice wasn't great, yet her song-and-dance performances are. There are moments in every number that give me chills, because I'm reminded of her extraordinary, underrated talents, and that she, as many people have commented, truly glowed in the dark, and truly made it seem that there was no screen separating her from us. She *was* the ultimate movie star.

It surely must have pleased Monroe that Anita Loos liked her performance in *Gentlemen Prefer Blondes*. After all, besides writing the source novel and Broadway musical, Loos had worked on several films with Jean Harlow, either providing the story or writing the script. Monroe identified with the top sex symbol of the thirties and wanted to play her in a film, until she read the script 20th offered her. Harlow, who *prefigured* Monroe, started the tradition of the non-virginal blonde. Her women, like Monroe's, were sexually uninhibited, funny, and wiser than they let on, could be counted on in a crisis, and had good hearts. The actresses were similar offscreen as well, playing sex goddesses for the press (i.e., both announced they slept in the nude, both made it clear they rarely wore underwear in public), yet wanting to be recognized more for their talents than their sex appeal. Both actresses died mysteriously at early ages, and, eerily, had Clark Gable as their last leading man—Monroe and Gable made *The Misfits* 34 years after Harlow and Gable teamed for *Saratoga* (1937), for which Loos provided the screenplay.

Loos often wrote about female camaraderie. For instance, her script for another Harlow-Gable film, *Hold Your Man* (1933), includes a sequence in which several female prisoners band together to help fellow inmate Harlow. Loos's adaptation of Clare Boothe's *The Women* (1937), with an all-star all-women cast, also deals with female friendship, as does *Blondie of the Follies* (1932), with Marion Davies and Billie Dove. Her versions of *Gentlemen Prefer Blondes* were, primarily, about the devoted friendship between flighty Lorelei Lee and sensible Dorothy Shaw. In addition to admiring Monroe, Loos was enthusiastic about Hawks's film adaptation because he and screenwriter Charles Lederer didn't drift away from her theme and make a film about Lorelei and Dorothy's relationships with the men in their lives, rather than with each other. That was the unfortunate tack taken in Monroe's follow-up film *How to Marry a Millionaire*—Monroe, Lauren Bacall, and Betty Grable may live together but their friendship, which is unconvincing, is secondary to their pursuit of men. This film is properly about the relationship between Lorelei and Dorothy. They are among the most loyal, protective, supportive female friends in movie history. They each regard their friendship as more important than their love lives. It may seem ridiculous to praise a film just because it presents women as friends, but think how few American films have had two good

female roles, much less two pretty women of the same age as friends. According to the great majority of male-written contemporary films, women don't have female friends. There aren't many films like *Julia* (1977), are there? So female friendship in films is not to be taken for granted.

It would seem that Hawks was an unlikely candidate to make a picture about the friendship of women. His other films were about the friendships between men: pilots, soldiers, race car drivers, cowboys . . . But unlike many male directors, Hawks liked the women he placed in his films. Lauren Bacall in *To Have and Have Not* (1944) and *The Big Sleep* (1946), Rosalind Russell in *His Girl Friday* (1940), Barbara Stanwyck in *Ball of Fire* (1941), and Angie Dickinson in *Rio Bravo* (1949), to name just a few of many, are extremely feminine yet have "masculine" attributes (they are loyal and brave, have senses of humor, are sexually aggressive, etc.) that make them perfect companions for the films' heroes. In fact, they are equals to the men in every way, which is why the men welcome them into their select circles. Hawks still has a male universe in *Gentlemen Prefer Blondes*, but while the women stay on a high plane, the caliber of men has dropped considerably. Even though they marry at the end of the film, Lorelei and Dorothy do not want to be welcomed into the male world. They remain outsiders. Their friendship is still solid, and that is all that is important. Hawks much prefers his blonde Lorelei and brunette Dorothy to the men who surround them. Hawks couldn't care less about Tommy Noonan's infantile Gus (a typically unsuitable Monroe movie mate) or Elliott Reid's deceptive Malone. That's why he squeezes them out of the frame in the last shot and ends the film as he began it, isolating on Lorelei and Dorothy. They smile because they have triumphed despite being stuck in the male-run world. Hawks and Lederer think that anything they had to do to succeed was fair play against the men making the rules. We even condone Lorelei's sneaky golddigging because all the males in her world are even more manipulative than she. It's only fair that Lorelei breaks the rules when the men with

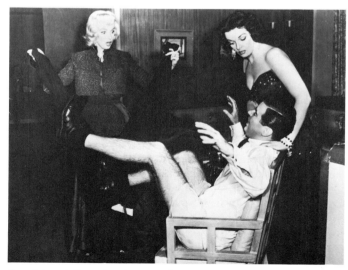

Lorelei and Dorothy do everything together. Here they pull off Ernie's pants to look for the photos.

As Lorelei, Monroe performs her most famous number: "Diamonds Are a Girl's Best Friend."

whom she plays are liars, deceivers, and male chauvinist Piggys. Suddenly philosophic, Lorelei puts things in perspective when she argues to Gus's father that men resent women (other than their daughters) for chasing men because they have money yet think it's fine that men chase women because they are pretty. It's a point dumb blondes might have made in countless films; Monroe's character should have made it in *How to Marry a Millionaire*.

The reason the friendship between Lorelei and Dorothy is so convincing is that Monroe and Russell became good friends while making the picture. When they were signed to costar, gossip columnists predicted a battle between "The Bosom" and "The Behind" (this wasn't long after Constance Cummings quipped that Monroe's "future is behind her"). But they got along from the start. It turned out they had much in common. Russell had preceded Monroe at L.A.'s Van Nuys High School, where she had been a classmate of and once acted with James Dougherty, Monroe's first husband. Russell was married to Bob Waterfield, former quarterback for the L.A. Rams, so she could advise Monroe on how to handle the courtship of baseball's Joe DiMaggio. Russell also knew what it was like to be a sex symbol. She had debuted in Hughes's infamous Western *The Outlaw* (1943), which was banned for three years because of minor sexual innuendo and major cleavage. She'd been subjected to wearing Hughes's specially designed bra, and by means of a pulley system having her breasts raised and lowered, according to her character's fluctuating passion. Although overlooked because of Monroe's presence, Russell is sensational in *Gentlemen Prefer Blondes*. She is the funny, sexually aggressive, confident female Jayne Mansfield should have played in her career. Russell's "Ain't There Anyone Here for Love?" number, with male athletes/dancers used as

decor, is a riot. Russell might have walked away with the picture but she willingly let Monroe, who played the blonde of the title, have the spotlight the younger actress so much desired. With sisterly affection, she'd tell Monroe how to play scenes when Monroe didn't understand what Hawks wanted from her; when Monroe was too frightened to emerge from her dressing room, Russell would escort her to the set; when Tommy Noonan complained Monroe "kissed like a vacuum cleaner," Russell comforted her. Hawks admitted that the film might never have been made if Russell hadn't befriended Monroe.

For this was the film on which Monroe became extremely difficult to work with, throwing temper tantrums, demanding numerous retakes (despite Hawks's desire to have spontaneity), and behaving like a frightened child. Monroe would be the biggest female star in the world by the end of the year, but those who saw her on the set couldn't tell she was a star at all. Hawks remembered her as a wallflower, with no sex appeal. He claimed no one even noticed her, although the crew would whistle at her double when she walked by. Of course, when she stepped before the cameras she suddenly became Marilyn Monroe, and she never looked more *alive* than in this film. I think *Gentlemen Prefer Blondes* is the easiest to watch of Monroe's major films because it is the only one that allowed her to slip completely out of the tough real world that would eventually destroy her and into a fantasy world— the most unreal world she'd ever enter in films—of songs and dances, many tight-fitting costumes, and diamonds. This is what she assumed all movies were like when she was a young girl looking for escape. Watching Monroe in *Gentlemen Prefer Blondes*, particularly during "Diamonds Are a Girl's Best Friend," you can tell how Cinderella felt at the ball.

Glen or Glenda?

also known as *I Led 2 Lives, I Changed My Sex, He or She?, Transvestite, Glenn or Glenda*

1952 B & W Screen Classics
Director: Edward D. Wood, Jr.
Producer: George Weiss
Screenplay: Edward D. Wood, Jr.
Cinematography: William C. Thompson
Music: Sandford H. Dickinson
Editor: "Bud" Schelling
Running Time: 67 minutes (although there are prints of 61 minutes and other durations in circulation)

Cast: Bela Lugosi (the Spirit), Lyle Talbot (inspector), Timothy Farrell (Dr. Alton), Daniel Davis (Glen/Glenda), Dolores Fuller (Barbara), "Tommy" Haines (Alan/Ann), Charles Crafts (Johnny), Connie Brooks (banker), Weiss.

Synopsis: The "Spirit" sits in his lab, among skulls and test tubes, and speaks of "startling things." The story must be told.

Transvestite Patrick/Patricia has committed suicide after having been arrested four times for wearing women's clothing in public. The inspector on the case visits psychiatrist Dr. Alton to learn more about transvestites. Dr. Alton tells him of the growing phenomenon. Many men wear women's clothing in private—probably even our mailman wears panties under his uniform. Society should be more tolerant because they aren't harming anyone. Dr. Alton tells the inspector of two case histories.

The "Spirit" says their stories must be told. He tells us to "Beware!" of a green dragon on our doorstep who likes to eat little boys and fat snails. He repeatedly speaks of "snips and snails and puppy dog tails."

Glen is engaged to Barbara. He is afraid to tell her that since he was young he has worn women's clothing and that now he is excited by Barbara's angora sweater. A transvestite friend warns him to tell Barbara before they are married because his own marriage ended when his wife came home early one day to find him in her clothes. During his "nightly visits to Morpheus, god of sleep," Glen has terrible nightmares—witnessed by the "Spirit"—in which Barbara rejects him for being a transvestite; the Devil (Glen's unloving father) attends their wedding.

Glen tells Barbara he wears women's clothing. She is shocked, but realizes she loves him too much to reject him because of this harmless problem. She proves her loyalty by handing him her angora sweater. Dr. Alton counsels them, telling them that eventually Glen may transfer the characteristics of the woman he created, Glenda, onto Barbara, and no longer have the need to be Glenda. If this doesn't happen, Barbara will still love and support Glen.

Like Glen, army veteran Alan often dresses up like a woman, Ann. Only Alan would like to be a woman. Dr. Alton explains that Alan is a pseudohermaphrodite: He has undeveloped female organs. After receiving therapy from Dr. Alton, Alan begins an endless series of hormone shots. Eventually, he has a sex-change operation. Ann is very happy.

Dr. Alton explains to the inspector that Glen and Alan were two different types of men who liked to dress like women. Their problems were solved in different ways: one through therapy and understanding, the other through an operation and understanding. Now, all that is left is for society to accept them.

A slightly out-of-focus shot of the Spirit fooling around in his laboratory. It's always enjoyable to see Bela Lugosi, but it's impossible to figure out what his role is in this film.

"Then one day it wasn't Halloween any longer."

There are so many *good*, poorly distributed films waiting for discovery that it's somewhat regrettable so much attention has been devoted in recent years to celebrating cinema's clinkers. Particularly annoying are the Medved-spawned "World's Worst Film Festivals" that are geared for smug-"hip" viewers (the equivalent of self-pleasing sports fans who do "the Wave") who will think a mediocre, average, or decent film is awful simply because the sponsors say it's awful, and respond accordingly. But, like anyone else who has spent a lifetime watching movies, I have a soft spot for a few of those many dreadful pictures I saw in the past, like *Meteor Monster* (1957), *Frankenstein's Daughter* (1958), *Incident in an Alley* (1962), *Eegah!* (1962), *Gunfighters at Casa Grande* (1965), and *Serpent Island* (1954), in which Sonny Tufts bares the ugliest (canal-marked) chest in movie history—but not the Henrietta Hesse vehicle *In Old Vienna, Yellowstone Cubs* (1963), *I Eat Your Skin* (1964), or *A Flea in Her Ear* (1968), with the inimitable Moustache. So in a sense I'm glad bad-movie devotees have stirred up interest in a whole slew of non-gems, including the works of the fascinating Edward D. Wood, Jr. Wood died of a heart attack in 1978—he had been an alcoholic, living in poverty and obscurity. But in the 1980s, his outrageously bad films have been resurrected and are enjoying tremendous popularity, and Wood is finally getting long overdue recognition as the least talented but most idiosyncratic director of his time. In the March/April 1987 issue of *Filmfax*, frequent Wood actor David Ward told Ted Okuda:

"[I]t's a shame [Wood] died before he became famous, because I think he'd be drinking it all in. He really wanted to leave his mark in the world of film, and I think he would have taken fame any way he could have gotten it. If it took a cult centering around bad movies to make him famous, he wouldn't have minded. . . .

"I've got to say this about Ed—his work may be far from great, or even good, but at least he made films. A lot of people out here [in Hollywood] have tried and tried to make movies, but have never been able to. He succeeded where many others have failed.

"And now his films are being shown everywhere. I know most people just watch these things to laugh at them, but they're paying good money to see them at revival theaters or to purchase them on video cassette. So whether they realize it or not, it's Eddie who's having the last laugh."

Wood's *Bride of the Monster* (1955), with friends Bela Lugosi and 300-pound Swedish wrestler Tor Johnson, its sequel *Night of the Ghouls* (1960), with Johnson, Duke Moore, Kenne Duncan (in a role intended for the dead Lugosi), and especially *Glen or Glenda?* and the legendary *Plan 9 from Outer Space* (1959), with Lugosi (whose untimely death meant Wood had to both hire a double and use Lugosi footage that was intended for another film), Vampira, Johnson, and Lyle Talbot, are essential viewing for lovers of bad films. They epitomize what *should* be shown at worst-film festivals. In fact, *Plan 9* is regarded as the "Worst Film of All Time"—at least it won an election conducted by Michael and Harry Medved for their book *The Golden Turkey Awards* (1980). If you check the movies highlighted in that book and that play in worst-film festivals then you'll see that what bad-movie fans consider the "worst movies ever made" are not really the worst movies, just the worst *watchable* movies. Certainly they aren't the most *evil*. Politically objectionable and/or racist pictures are not considered. Also ignored are porno films like *Male Chauvinist Pig*; atrocities like *Heat*, which juxtaposes Isabel Sarli sexcapades with horrifying footage of seals being clubbed to death; "shockumentaries" for which people were killed for the cameramen's benefit; government-financed health and propaganda films; the colorized *Maltese Falcon*; and blatantly distasteful exploitation films—their titles tell their stories—like *I Spit on Your Grave* (1977), *The Incredible Torture Show/The Bloodsucking Freaks* (1976), *Snuff* (1976), and *Ilsa: She-Wolf of the SS* (1974). And we also must reject those films that are *too* boring, like *The Clan of the Cave Bear* (1986). Like the too offensive films I've mentioned, it would drive people at worst-film festivals to the exits. Although they have wrongly become staples of such festivals, pictures need have more than a ridiculous premise (as does the 1938 all-midget musical Western *The Terror of Tiny Town*) or title/title song (as does 1980's *Attack of the Killer Tomatoes*) to be a true bad movie—banality/mediocrity just won't cut it.

Also movies that were meant to be bad in order to attract the camp-loving audience can't qualify—the hilarity must be unintentional: The beauty of a Wood film is that, while he realized his product was preposterous, he did the best he could considering he had no money or talent, and came up empty. These films aren't so bad they're good, as some fans contend—they just reach such an unbelievable level of ineptness and inanity that you've got to marvel at them. For a film to deserve to be lowered into the bad-movie pantheon, it must give viewers perverse pleasure. It should be fun to watch (at least once). Viewers should wonder how a film so bad could be made, revile yet revere the filmmaker for having the nerve to release such trash on the paying public, and sit through it to the bitter end. All films that play at worst-film festivals should be entertaining.

Wood's *Plan 9 from Outer Space* and *Glen or Glenda?* certainly deserve to be in the bad-film company of *Robot Monster* (1953), *They Saved Hitler's Brain* (1963), *The Creeping Terror* (1964), and Dwain Esper's mind-boggling *Maniac* (1934). But while they make it to the final round in my "Worst Film" contention—for which I use the guidelines laid down by more obsessive bad-movie fans—I don't think either should win. (I pick *Maniac*.) It's not that they're better made than the other films—they're not—but they have redeeming qualities. I actually received angry mail after suggesting in *Cult Movies* (1981) that *Plan 9* wasn't the worst film of all-time. I explained that Wood used his film as a forum for subversive politics that he couldn't have gotten away with in a better produced work; I wrote that Wood was more critical of America's government (which conceals much from the public) and military strategy (which calls for an arms buildup and nuclear proliferation) than any Hollywood-establishment director of the period dared be. In all honesty, I had tongue in cheek when I wrote of the thematic relevance of *Plan 9*—I reasoned that the director of such an abomination couldn't possibly be clear-headed enough to want to get a message across, let alone think of a message. But having since seen the even more delirious (try to figure out Lugosi's role) and daring *Glen or Glenda?*, I now believe what I wrote.

Wood's debut film is terribly made to be sure, yet it is one of the most audacious, most personal films in history. Wood dared tackle subjects, transvestism and transsexualism, that were movie taboos in 1952, even after Christine Jorgensen made headlines. And, to Wood's credit, he did it in a nonexploitive, nonsensationalistic way. The reason for this is that he wanted to calm rather than shock viewers: He presents transvestites as well-meaning, gentle men—this is a rare film where men sit at a table (like old-style soap opera women) and converse about their personal problems!—who need our sympathy because they are trying to solve identity problems that resulted from troubled childhoods. A transvestite himself, Wood was so committed to the picture's theme—society (and the police) should be tolerant of transvestites and understand them as human beings—that he opened himself to ridicule by playing Glen/Glenda and appearing on screen in drag.

In the part of the film dealing with "Tommy" Haines's Alan/Ann, Wood goes one step further: He gives support to transsexuals (this term is not used). He tries to make viewers understand that a sex-change operation is a healthy decision for men who feel they *are* women and want to be women in the physical sense, not just dress like them. He builds a case for Alan's character—he served this country well during World War II—makes us aware that Alan has both male and (hidden, undeveloped) female organs (Dr. Alton informs us he's a "pseudohermaphrodite"!), and makes us realize how much torture (hormone shots, operations) Alan is willing to bravely endure to become Ann,

An inexplicable scene from Glen's psychodrama-like nightmare.

the female he was meant to be all along. It was Wood's intent that we feel Ann made the correct and "natural" decision to undergo a sex change and that instead of feeling outraged or disgusted we should feel as happy as she does by the results. Wood truly believed his own character's philosophy: "We only have one life to live—if we throw that away, what do we have left?" Wood made this film when Hollywood filmmakers feared veering from the straight and narrow, so no matter how bad a director-writer-actor he was, you've got to admire his courage. I excerpt from Louis Black's program notes from *CinemaTexas*:

> The strength of *Glen or Glenda?*, and the source of its fascination, is the multi-layered juxtaposition of a number of elements including Wood's overall technical incompetence, the almost hallucinatory, often incomprehensible symbol-laden surrealism of certain of the sequences, the presence of Lugosi (with the contradictory responses he evokes as a recognizable star [and] a character in the film whose role and function is unclear) and, most importantly, the passion and conviction with which this narrative plea for the rights of transvestites is delivered. It is that intense, awkwardly inane sense of purpose, imbuing the whole film with an air of pathos and a thematic richness (no matter how confused it might be), that lifts *Glen or Glenda?* from the overloaded ranks of mundane, mishandled commercial film projects and injects it, with a hysterical sense of gravity, into the pantheon of the truly inspired, unrelentingly illogical, narratively inept or ignorant and thus uniquely innovative anti-masterpieces. *Glen or Glenda?* is so breathtakingly bad and yet so totally heartfelt that it is capable of a nonliterate visceral genius to which more carefully crafted films can only aspire.

Like other Wood films, *Glen or Glenda?* is distinguished by embarrassingly bad acting, dialogue, direction, cinematography, editing, music, cheap sets and, significantly, ugly costuming. As usual there are zany moments that are guaranteed to make you both laugh and cringe. Timothy Farrell's doctor asks Lyle Talbot's police inspector if he has come to see him "for business or pleasure?" (has any doctor ever asked this question?). In a phony scene, supposedly taking place in Africa, Wood shows us a plump black tribesman in a mask and several sexy tribeswomen dancing around him—it's meant to remind us that in primitive cultures, men rather than women pay attention to makeup and costumes. In the climax, Glen takes the angora sweater, not the virginity, of Barbara (played by Wood's wife, Dolores Fuller). Lugosi's grumpy "Spirit" sits in his skeleton-decorated lab babbling about "people—all going somewhere," and how "A new day *is* begun," interrupting the story to tell us that "the story must be told," warning us often to "Bevare of the green dragon who sits on your doorstep," and angrily reciting, "Oh, snips and snails and puppy dog tails!"

The scenes with Lugosi contribute to the film's structural problems and incoherence. Even without his mindless banter, there is enough confusion caused by flashbacks within flashbacks, the use of several narrators, stylistic changes throughout, nonsensical dialogue, and the inclusion of meaningless images (lightning, stampeding buffalo, cars on the highway) only because Wood had free use of these stock shots. What is Lugosi's Spirit doing in this film? (Is Glen's story none of his business?) I guess that the Spirit exists at the gateway between the conscious and unconscious world. That's why he can watch Glen's nightmarish visions in which he imagines what disasters will happen to him if he confesses to his fiancée that he is a transvestite. These scenes seem influenced as well by stag-party "smokers" (women strip, lie on a couch, and interact with each other, sometimes violently) and experimental films. They are like psychodramas in which the players (Glen, Barbara, Glen's father who is made up like the Devil, strangers) silently act out Glen's fears (at times there is pantomime against a black background)—in a rare understandable moment, Glenda can't lift a heavy branch off the prone Barbara, but Glen manages to do it. This sequence is full of symbols and symbolic action (*if* that bearded man who attacks the woman on the couch is Glen then some of it actually makes sense) and is quite surreal in nature. Wood is being extremely innovative here—he just falls on his face. Imagine the worst of Ken Russell, only done on the cheap. In his provocative article "Bad Movies" in the July/August 1981 issue of *Film Comment*, J. Hoberman wrote: "With their perverse, pioneering affection for the detritus of industrial civilization, the Surrealists were the first to cultivate an appreciation for bad movies . . . .The Surrealists courted disorientation: A film had a dreamlike latent content—and this could be precipitated by deranging or bypassing the manifest content of its storyline." Surely *Glen or Glenda?* would have been a masterpiece in the eyes of the Surrealists.

In an interview with Rudolph Grey for a book on Wood, George Weiss, who produced *Test Tube Babies* before trying to capitalize on the headline-making Christine Jorgensen sex-change story, claimed *Glen or Glenda?/I Led 2 Lives* was "an art picture. It was made for the art houses, not for Main Street." One would never guess this picture was intended for art houses, but there are times when it seems, incredibly, to have been modeled on those 16-mm civics films we used to see in elementary school. Except this film doesn't teach us to be good citizens by being understanding of immigrants/aliens (who aren't Communists), but to be tolerant of transvestites, who may need to wear women's clothing but don't cause society any harm. Wood's absurd script: "Give this man satin undies . . . and he can be a credit to his community and his government." Like most of those civics films, a policeman and a doctor (in this case a psychiatrist)—community standard-bearers—are present to discuss the major theme; there

are several shots of what could be Main Street in many towns; we see children in a schoolyard; we repeatedly see cars, full of people like you, me, and he/she, driving along the highway; and there is stock footage of our World War II army fighting for our free, democratic way of life. Also similar to civics films is that there are many stagy scenes in which two characters discuss the theme (with acting such as you'd find on *The Lone Ranger*) juxtaposed with staged, narrated sequences that are meant to drive a point across. For instance, Wood shows us how much easier it is for women to relax at home because they are allowed to wear less restrictive clothing; similarly, we see women in comfortable hats, and men who are forced to wear male hats that are so tight-fitting that they cause their owners to go bald. The shrewdly handled Alan/Ann sequence is much like those civics films in which we watch an immigrant move step-by-step toward becoming an American citizen. Alan goes step-by-step toward becoming an *accepted* American citizen—he speaks to a counselor, takes hormone injections, undergoes an operation, and finally, as Ann, like a newly naturalized citizen who must learn to act like Americans, begins to learn to act like a woman (i.e., there is a clip illustrating how a woman should brush her hair).

Viewers will find it impossible to believe the scene in which a man passes Ann on the street and makes eyes at her—because, quite frankly, she is quite bland looking. That's why it's amusing to read Weiss's explanation (in the Grey interview) for why his film failed:

> "[T]he criticism of *Glen or Glenda?* was, why did I use such ugly people? I tried to be authentic, which was wrong. These people were what they portrayed. . . . Then there was 'Tommy' Haines. I was criticized there. . . . Yet, Ed swore up and down that they were . . . transvestites. So, look, for the 10 or 20 or 30 dollars that they got paid, I wasn't going to say no."

In 1981, Paramount decided to cash in on the *Plan 9 from Outer Space*/Edward D. Wood, Jr., craze and give *Glenn or Glenda*, as the studio titled it, a major release. Paramount hoped it would become a cult phenomenon and, eventually, a midnight movie to rival *The Rocky Horror Picture Show* (1975). Two days before it was to make its April Fool's Day premiere at New York's Sutton Theatre, Paramount ran a large advertisement in the *New York Times*, in which it was compared to bold, unconventional, deeply personal classics, *Citizen Kane* (1941), *Napoleon* (1927), *Freaks* (1932), and *The Godfather* (1972). The following day, *New York* magazine called attention to the hoax. Then, on premiere day, Paramount withdrew the film and called off plans to give it a really big push. They cited, of all things, the assassination attempt on Ronald Reagan as the reason the film was withdrawn and the humorous campaign dropped. It's kind of a shame, because it would have been interesting to see what this film could have done with strong publicity. But I guess if Glen and Alan can change their sex, then Paramount can change its mind.

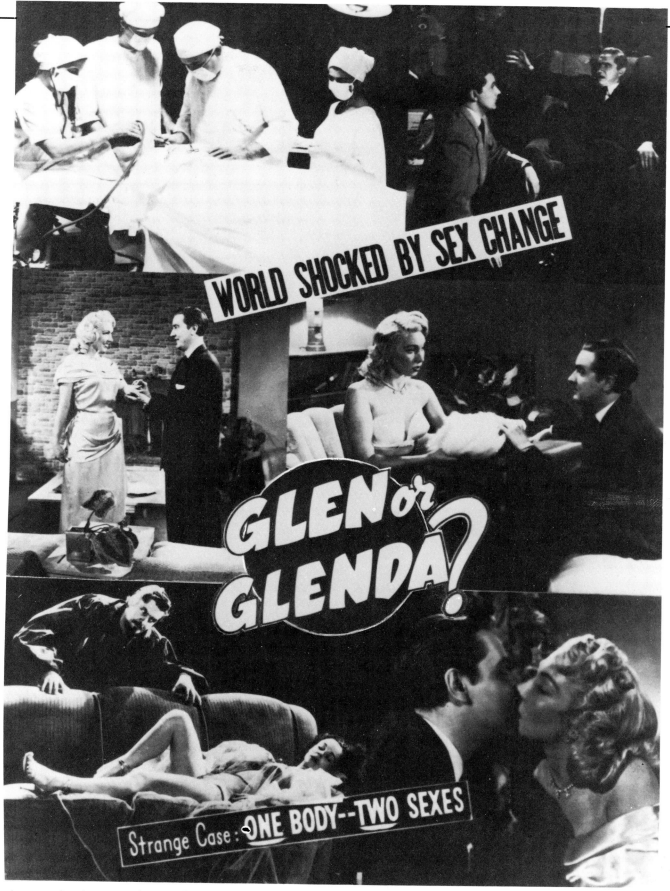

A poster showing unusual scenes from Glen or Glenda?, *including Alan's sex-change operation, Glen kneeling before the Spirit in his strange nightmare, Glen courting Barbara, Glen getting to wear her sweater, a bearded man (Glen?) dominating a woman in Glen's nightmare, and Glen and Barbara expressing their undying love for each other.*

The Gods Must Be Crazy

1980   Color   South African   C.A.T.
Director: Jamie Uys
Producer: Jamie Uys
Screenplay: Jamie Uys
Cinematography: Jamie Uys
Music: John Boshoff
Editor: Jamie Uys
Running Time: 109 minutes

Cast: Marius Weyers (Andrew Steyn), Sandra Prinsloo (Kate Thompson), N!xau (Xi), Louw Verwey (Sam Boca), Michael Thys (Mpudi), Nic de Jager (Jack Hind), Fanyana Sidumo and Joe Seakatsi (card players), Ken Gampa (president), Paddy O'Byrne (narrator).

Synopsis: Xi and his small nomadic Bushman band live in the deep Kalahari. They survive in the treacherous desert by hunting and using ingenious methods to collect water. These gentle people have no possessions, no money, no crime, no laws, no police, no judges, no rulers, no bosses. They are extremely happy. A pilot tosses an empty Coke bottle from his plane. The Bushmen think it's a gift from the gods; therefore it must be useful. They use it to make music, to do work, in play. But adults and children start fighting over it; it causes friction and even clunks a couple of them on the head. Wanting harmony to return, Xi sets out to find the edge of the world, so he can throw the bottle off and return it to the gods. He walks out of the desert.

Kate Thompson, who is white, decides she has had enough of the crazy-making crowded city. She accepts a teaching position in Botswana. Microbiologist Andrew Steyn, a white, agrees to pick her up at Mabula, although he becomes an idiot around women. His friend/assistant Mpudi, a light-skinned black, warns him that the jeep has no brakes and won't restart if the engine is turned off. After a difficult journey, Steyn picks up Kate. He is tongue-tied around the pretty schoolteacher. When the jeep stalls in the river, he carries her across . . . then knocks her into the water. They must make camp. Kate thinks he's weird and doesn't trust him because he keeps falling on her. Steyn accidentally pulls the jeep up a tree. Xi happens along. He tries to give the bottle to Steyn and Kate, whom he thinks are ugly and—noticing how they act—foolish for gods. They don't understand him. He walks away, disappointed in these gods. Mpudi tows Steyn and Kate toward town. Jack Hind, an egotistical local tour driver, gives Kate a ride, making Steyn jealous.

Xi kills a goat for food, not knowing it's part of a herd. He is arrested. Mpudi, who once lived with Bushmen, defends him but Xi is given a short prison term. Steyn gets him out of jail before he perishes by saying that he needs Xi to help him and Mpudi in their work.

Steyn's attempts to win over Kate go awry when he trips over words and any furniture that happens to be around. He wrecks her schoolroom. Jack courts her.

Having failed to assassinate a president of a northern state, black guerrillas led by light-skinned Sam Boca cross the border. They avoid arrest by abducting Kate and the children from her school. They walk toward the border, threatening to kill the hostages if anyone gets in their way. From a distance, Steyn, Xi, and Mpudi see the guerrillas and children. Xi dresses up as a female child and sneaks into their camp. He dips a pin into a drug Steyn gave him and puts Boca and several of his men to sleep. Kate and the children disarm them. But two guards who were off playing cards reappear and fire on them. They take cover. Kate doesn't see Steyn and Mpudi capture the guerrillas. Jack arrives and takes credit for the rescue.

Steyn tries one more time. He goes to Kate's classroom. He wrecks it, but she tells him he's sweet and gives him a kiss. He has won her heart.

Xi says farewell to his new friends. He walks until he stands on a cliff above the clouds. Thinking this is the edge of the world, he tosses the bottle away. He returns to his people.

After 30 years and 22 films, Jamie Uys, South Africa's top movie director, had his first major international success with this sweet, spirited, unabashedly silly bit of slapstick. It did great business all over the globe, becoming Japan's top-grosser in 1982 and France's in 1983, and a phenomenon in Sweden, West Africa, Canada, and America. It opened in the United States in 1983, but it did such poor business in test cities that its small distributor, Jensen-Farley, refused a promotion-free invitation to bring it to New York until a stronger title could be found. Six months later, the company went bankrupt. 20th Century-Fox Classics picked up distribution rights and booked it all over the country. At first, only the art-film crowd attended, but critic response and word-of-mouth were so favorable that eventually everyone from Junior to Grandma was flocking to the picture. It drew repeat viewers and played longer than six months in more than a dozen North American cities, including L.A., New York, Toronto, Miami, Phoenix, Sacramento, and Kansas City, where the manager of a suburban theater received poison-pen letters from his regular patrons because he held it over for 77 weeks.

Uys got the idea for *Gods* in the late sixties, when he met Bushmen while making a picture about animals in the Kalahari. Over the next 10 years, he often went back to visit them. Yet when it came time to cast Xi, the primitive Bushman who has his first contact with *civilized* men— the crazy gods—Uys didn't settle for someone he already knew. With his interpreter, Uys searched the Kalahari for three months before he found his man, N!xau—pronounced En-(click sound)-ow in Botswana—a Bushman who hadn't yet had his first contact with civilized men.

A few words about the Bushmen, or San. They are the last descendants of a yellow-skinned nomadic people who between 25,000 and 10,000 years ago, according to Laurens Van Der Post and Jane Taylor in *Testament to the Bushmen* (1984), lived all over southern Africa and, until between 4000 and 2000 years ago, were the sole inhabitants of the land. By the beginning of this century, those who had survived contact and violent collision with the black, Bantu-speaking tribes (including the Zulu) that migrated from the north and, beginning in the mid-1600s, the Dutch and British traders, miners, and settlers—and their offspring, the Afrikaners—were gone from the Cape colony, Natal, Basutoland, and the Orange Free State. "From then on," writes Taylor, "they were to be found only in an area so inhospitable that no one who did not have the knowledge of the Earth that the Bushman had could survive there—the Kalahari Desert."

But even here the Bushmen didn't find a safe haven. Over the years, an increasing number have left the Kalahari as survival has become more difficult. To a great extent, the wild animals that the Bushmen hunt, including the antelope, have been driven away by grazing cattle and goats owned by farmers of Ghanzi, to the west. Because

The Kalahari Bushmen try to understand the function of this peculiar object, an empty Coke bottle, which the gods dropped from the sky.

there is no rainfall for nine months of the year, no permanent standing water, and (because of the livestock) a steady decrease in edible and water-storing plants, many Bushmen have abandoned the nomadic life of their ancient ancestors for a sedentary existence near boreholes. Children have been sent to boarding schools in Botswana and Namibia and many adult Bushmen have deserted the desert entirely to take low-paying jobs for white and, more commonly, Bantu-speaking farmer patrons in Ghanzi or take construction jobs or join the Single Defence Force in Namibia. Of the 50,000 surviving Bushmen, only about 1000 remain nomadic hunter-gatherers and almost all of these are in the Central Kalahari Reserve in Botswana. It's nearly impossible to find primitive Bushmen who haven't had some contact with (and possibly been corrupted by) the outside world, who still have no sense of property or money, who are unaware of the indignities and discrimination suffered by Bushmen who left the desert and became menial workers for black and white bosses in Botswana and Namibia. Yet Uys discovered N!xau, whose small primitive hunter-gatherer band still followed the wild animals through secluded regions of the Kalahari, whose values had not been corrupted because he had never been out of the desert or mingled with the cash economy, and who believed there were only about 200 people in the entire world and that the missionary he'd once met was probably the only white man in existence.

N!xau agreed to play Xi, says Uys, because "he's a nice guy," and a Bushman would never think of turning down a request. According to Uys, nothing fazed him. Not meeting his second white man. Not being asked to *work*—he had no concept of the word's meaning. Not being photographed for the first time. Not appearing in a film—although he had never heard of movies, much less seen one. Not being asked to act—Bushmen act every night when they tell stories around the campfire. Not being paid wages—after he promptly let his paper money salary blow away (just as Xi does) because it had no value to him, Uys decided to set up a trust fund for him. Not even flying off in a plane for acting stints (for a total of 15 weeks over a 2-year period) and, after the film was a hit, to Japan, where he stayed in a hotel (he slept on the floor) and spoke to 100,000 adoring fans. N!xau's bemused, unimpressed first impression of civilization certainly comes across clearly when he plays Xi, a character who, like himself, is experiencing civilization for the first time. And because his reaction seems so honest, we must stop and, through his eyes, reflect upon our "superior" way of life.

We enjoy laughing at ourselves—our foibles, our rituals, our pretentious idiosyncrasies, our anxiety-causing obsession with money and power, our need to look busy while doing useless work, our world of sex, "violence, crime, laws, police, judges, rulers, and bosses"—*if* we're looking through the eyes of a likable, naive, nonarrogant, nonthreatening outsider. That explains much of the appeal of *Gods* as well as *Time After Time* (1979), in which Malcolm McDowell's H. G. Wells travels to modern-day San Francisco, and *"Crocodile" Dundee* (1986), in which Paul Hogan's Australian backwoodsman visits New York. I don't think the three films have ever been compared, but they have the same satirical premise: Amiable men, innocents, masters in their primitive worlds (Wells comes from the past, noble savages Xi and Dundee come—like Tarzan— from unchanging wildernesses), make Swiftian journeys through our hectic, chaotic world, are befuddled but not outraged by our people and customs, and eventually use their smarts to be triumphant here, too. Xi's such a genial, harmless fellow that we don't mind that he's not in awe of us "gods," that he lets the money we give him blow away, and, this should reassure our racist element, that he has no designs on our white women. As we ogle Kate in her bra and panties, Xi can barely hold back his laughter because she is "the ugliest person" he's seen in his life. The narrator reveals Xi's thoughts: "She was pale as something that had crawled out of a rotting log; her hair was quite gruesome, long and stringy and white as if she were very old; she was very big—you'd have to dig the whole day to find enough food to feed her." Is this the proper way to describe the leading lady?

I see *Gods* as a film about a man whose primitive world is in perfect *balance*, until civilization spreads its grasping hand, dropping a Coke bottle onto the untainted land of his people and causing it to become as topsy-turvy as our own world. A Coke bottle, explains Uys, "because it represents our plastic society." A Bible, a gun, a machine, a pack of seeds would have been equally destructive. Any change, even those we think are beneficial, ruins what is already perfect. This bottle is like a splinter that gets under healthy skin and causes infection. Xi is wise to take away the bottle that has made his world heavy with grief, and return it to the "gods" who unwisely created such a useless thing. With the bottle back where it came from (burying it was not enough), balance returns. Surely it's shortsighted of Uys to think the Bushman's life is idyllic ("they must be the most contented people in the world") just because there are those like N!xau who are happy, when it's well known that the traditional "wild" Bushmen are an endangered species. While watching the film, we don't worry about how sad the future will be for the Bushmen if they don't secure rights to water and land to develop themselves, free of incursion from Bantu-speaking tribes and their livestock. Instead we root hard for Xi to get rid of that cursed bottle so his people can again have a carefree life and we civilized people won't have ruined another paradise (which the Kalahari is in the eyes of these movie Bushmen).

It's easy to root for Xi because N!xau, with his Isiah Thomas smile, trusting eyes, and easy manner, is the most endearing of movie actors. Forget adorable Goldie Hawn— N!xau would be ideal for those star-studded Will Rogers Foundation fund-raising films that play in theaters every year. And he's a wonderfully adept physical comedian, which, combined with a knowing deadpan style, makes him the Bushman's answer to Buster Keaton. His slapstick highlights include Xi trying to throw the bottle back up to the heavens and having to duck when it comes back down (this is pure Keaton); pointing a stick, which is actually a gun, at its owner and, believing the man has suddenly become terrified by something standing behind him, joining him in running away; fleeing with Michael Thys's Mpudi from a lion; and standing on the hood while trying to steer a jeep that is going backward.

Tiny N!xau makes a delightful comedic partner of tall, white Marius Weyers, who plays Andrew Steyn, a character Uys played himself in his debut film in 1950. While N!xau (a hero in Japan) is a direct descendant of silent slapstick artists Keaton, Harold Lloyd, Harry Langdon, and the Keystone Kops, the top-billed Weyers (whom the French preferred) is linked more to Jacques Tati, whose tall, "civilized," silent Mr. Hulot would also wreck any peaceful setting he walked into. Through Hulot's character, we can observe how our weird, changing world operates—oddly, in this film, Xi, not Steyn, serves this function. Meanwhile, Steyn becomes the romantic stumblebum we all have been at least once in our lives—the "idiot" Uys says he was when he fell in love for the first time. Most people who don't like *Gods* have no patience for Steyn's slapstick scenes. They are particularly irritated by the sequence in which Steyn tries to drive his jeep, which has no brakes and can't be turned off, through a gate he must unlatch and open by hand—the jeep repeatedly rolls backward over the rocks he places behind its wheels, so he has to chase it down the long incline and try to hop in. The scene may seem overlong to today's viewers, but as David Denby pointed out in *New York*, it shows "Uys has mastered the solemnly methodical nature of physical comedy, the system of repetition and variation that gives slapstick a formal rhythm." I also laugh because I remember that night in 1970 when I stepped out of a borrowed car, watched in horror as it rolled down an incline toward a better parked car, and gave chase, diving in and hitting the brake with my hand. And when Steyn stalls in the high water while on his way to pick up Kate, I laugh because I remember being too late for my dream date in high school because I took a shortcut past the railroad tracks and wound up waiting for the longest train in history to pass by. I think the scene in which Steyn enters Kate's classroom, trips, and somehow gets his head under her dress is funny on its own—it anticipates the mud-puddle scene in *Romancing the Stone* (1984), in which Michael Douglas's face winds up in Kathleen Turner's crotch—but it has special significance in that Uys, a white South African, lets the black children laugh at his white hero. Steyn's final bit of slapstick, when he destroys Kate's outdoor classroom, may seem stupid but it's not much different from Woody Allen trying to impress blind date Jennifer Salt in *Play It Again, Sam* (1972) by holding up a "hip" record . . . only to have the album fly out of its cover and smash against the wall.

Among the picture's detractors are those who believe that it is racist. In America, it was picketed by the National Conference of Black Lawyers and other anti-apartheid groups. Some critics contended that while Uys believes he is no racist and, as Peter Davis wrote in *Cineaste* (Vol. XIV, No. 1, 1985), "[did] not deliberately set out to dehumanize blacks," his view of blacks was *colored* because

A couple destined for each other. Top: *On his way to pick up the newly arrived Kate, Andrew tries to keep his brake-less jeep from rolling down a hill . . . again.* Bottom: *Kate also experiences difficulties in the runaway jeep.*

Africans, that the film's ridicule and condescension goes unnoticed. . . .

Although we tend to hear of only the petty aspects of apartheid, its greatest manifestation is the manipulation of people within a finite space. For all its surface amiability, *Gods* is an expression of this aspect of apartheid. It often reveals this by inversion. Thus, while the landscape of *Gods* looks to me very much like South Africa, it is set in the mythical country of Botswana. Why do I call it mythical, when Botswana is an actual country? Because Uys' Botswana does not exist except in his imagination: features of the landscape, dress and custom are not to be found in the real Botswana. Uys's Botswana is instead a dream of a happy-go-lucky *bantustan*, those equally fictitious homelands that the South African government is creating all over South Africa, literally out of dust, for the dumping of black people.

All these people scurrying around the landscape of southern Africa, colliding in pratfalls, constitute a distorted microcosm of the clash of peoples and ideologies that is in reality deeply tragic. It is of no account what Uys *thought* he was doing in his film. What he has done, in fact (albeit a fact disguised by humor), is to create in *Gods* the never-never land that the architects of apartheid would have us believe in, where South Africa's intentions are for the good of everyone. In this land of make-believe, entire villages drop their work and turn out to sing a hymn of welcome to a white teacher—the relationship of black towards white is gratitude for the help being given, of white towards black, protective paternalism.

Davis's article is astute and I can't disagree with any point he makes. Certainly Uys feels protective paternalism toward the Bushmen, whom his narrator calls "the Little People of the Kalahari" in the *Nanook of the North*–like beginning, presents as playful, and describes as "pretty, dainty, small, and graceful." I believe Davis when he says Uys idealizes the life of the black in Botswana because, as I wrote earlier, he does the same with the life of Bushmen in the Kalahari; it's clear that Uys has no confidence in black-run governments or sympathy for the black (leftist) guerrillas who attempt to overthrow them*; and I wouldn't be surprised if the card-playing black characters are as offensive a stereotype in Africa as crap-shooting black characters are in America. However, I don't think

he is a white South African. I excerpt from Davis:

> Let me admit straightaway that I, too, found the film often funny (I also tend to like ethnic jokes). Inside and outside the gags, however, *The Gods Must Be Crazy* is saturated with the mindset of apartheid.
>
> The film's racism has been denied by most reviewers who see only the veneer of humor . . . The real reason for this myopia about *Gods*, I suspect, is that the Amos 'n' Andys who appear in it are Africans. If black Americans were being portrayed, the American audience would spot the insults and stereotyping at once. The myth of African backwardness and inferiority is so widely accepted, however, even by many

*It is a sneaky practice of contemporary filmmakers, particularly action directors and writers, to cast black actors as secondary but positive-image characters just so they can get away with other blacks playing negative stereotypes. For instance, if they're going to have a black pimp, a black drug dealer, and a black prostitute in their films, they counter these negative stereotypes with, say, a black cop, a black politician, and a black female judge. I think this attempt to establish a good-bad balance is hypocritical, not to mention deceptive. Still Uys might have helped avoid charges of racism if he had included a few more positive black characters to counter the stupid, murderous black guerrillas. There is one opportunity that he missed. He shrewdly had the guerrilla assassins kill the administrators of Agriculture, Public Works, and Education, the three cabinet members who might have done good service for the people. But I think Uys should have preceded the assassination scene with a short bit in which these three men tell the dictator their plans for reform—showing viewers that there are intelligent, caring, capable black officials waiting to accomplish excellent work if given the opportunity. Then, after they are killed, Uys might have had the dictator say he would have executed the three men himself if they weren't already dead.

Xi tosses the troublesome bottle off what he believes is the edge of the world.

this film is racist. Of course, it's just a feeling, perhaps my excuse for enjoying it so much. I just find it hard to call a film racist when viewers from all over the world have had such a positive reaction toward a black character and the black man who played him (especially since no one's opinion of apartheid is improved). And, considering the white population in this film, it seems absurd that the picture should be condemned for its demeaning portrayal of blacks. Remember: Our white hero wears red underpants, collects elephant dung, is chased by a warthog through the jungle while his pants are half down, pulls his jeep up a tree, is an "idiot" around Kate, is laughed at by black children. Our white heroine is squirted in the face by a black window washer who doesn't notice that the jeep window is missing, is knocked into the river by Steyn and becomes completely soaked, is trapped in a sticker bush while wearing bra and panties, has Steyn's head shoot under her dress while she tries to teach her class, and has her looks mocked by the black-skinned Xi. Jack, the other major white character, is a coward, a braggart, a jerk. The reverend has no personality. There are whites in the overcrowded city—a woman in curlers drives 20 feet to mail a letter and then returns home; people inch along the crowded highways; workers do impersonal jobs between food breaks and try to look busy. An unimpressive lot to be sure. Blacks in the film mock them; the white characters never have cause to mock the black characters. In my

opinion, the multiracial audience laughs with, not at, the good-guy black characters.

It would be hard to overlook the abundance of black buffoons in this film if the black children were also portrayed as buffoons; if the white characters weren't also buffoons and if the slapstick Keystone Kops nature of the film didn't require *all* civilized adult characters to act like buffoons; if the black Xi and Mpudi weren't the most sensible characters in the film; if whites and blacks in Kate's city office didn't work and eat together harmoniously; if Steyn didn't have such sincere, equal-terms friendships with Mpudi and Xi (neither calls him Bwana); and, most significant, if Uys didn't select N!xau precisely because he exhibits "this magic, this aristocracy, this self-pride." (Uys and N!xau, who was reported missing for a time, would reunite for *The Gods Must Be Crazy 2.*)

One more note: This movie can be enjoyed as much as a travelogue as an amusing narrative. Uys filmed in Panavision and it's a real pleasure to look at the landscape and the animals who inhabit it. I love the way Uys incorporates animals into his slapstick scenes, having a warthog chase Steyn, a lion chase Xi and Mpudi (a most appealing character), and, quite hilariously, a rhino charge out of the jungle and stamp out Steyn and Kate's campfire. And thankfully, Uys doesn't call on those overused simian jungle comedians for laughs—I guess he didn't want the baboons to show up his buffoons.

Imitation of Life

1959 Color Universal-International
Director: Douglas Sirk
Producer: Ross Hunter
Screenplay: Eleanore Griffin and Allan Scott
From the novel by Fannie Hurst
Cinematography: Russell Metty
Music: Frank Skinner
Editor: Milton Carruth
Running Time: 124 minutes

Cast: Lana Turner (Lora Meredith), John Gavin (Steve Archer), Juanita Moore (Annie Johnson), Sandra Dee (Susie Meredith, at 16), Susan Kohner (Sarah Jane Johnson, at 18), Dan O'Herlihy (David Edwards), Robert Alda (Allen Loomis), Karen Dicker (Sarah Jane Johnson, at 8), Terry Burnham (Susie Meredith, at 6), Troy Donahue (Frankie), Jack Weston (director), John Vivyan.

Synopsis: Lora Meredith, a widow with a 6-year-old daughter, Susie, has come to New York in hopes of becoming a famous actress. But she has found no work and lives in a cold-water flat. She loses Susie on the Coney Island beach but finds her safe with Annie Johnson, a black widow, and Annie's light-skinned 8-year-old daughter, Sarah Jane. Susie and Sarah Jane become quick friends, as do Lora and Annie. Annie has no place to live so she offers to become Lora's servant. Lora can't afford to pay her but allows Annie and the delighted Sarah Jane to move in. On the beach, she also meets Steve Archer, an aspiring photographer who takes a picture of the girls. He is attracted to Lora and courts her. Meanwhile Lora looks for jobs while Annie takes care of the kids, does the housework, and takes on menial jobs to help pay their rent. But Annie worries about Sarah Jane who tries to pass as white and is embarrassed about having a black mother.

Lora lies her way into the office of agent Allen Loomis. He realizes she is a fraud, but promises to make her a star if she'll do everything he tells her, no matter how low. She doesn't want to be cheapened and walks out on him. Steve tells her to hold on to her dreams. However, when he sells the photo of the girls and gets a job with a magazine, he asks Lora to marry him and give up acting. She accepts but changes her mind when Loomis gets her a job with famous director David Edwards. Steve and Lora break up.

When Lora tells Edwards what is wrong with her small scene, he is impressed and gives her the lead. She is a success. She becomes Edwards's lover. Over the next 10 years she becomes a great star by appearing in his Broadway plays. She, Annie, and the two girls move into a large, lovely house. But, surprisingly, she is unfulfilled. She breaks away from Edwards and stars in a working-class play. Steve comes to her celebration party afterward. Annie, Sarah Jane, and especially Susie are happy to see him. Lora hints to Steve that she would like to get back together with him, but her work obsession drives them apart. Susie is also becoming disenchanted with her mother for not spending time with her. She goes to Annie with her problems. When Lora goes abroad to be in a movie, Steve takes care of Susie, who falls in love with him. When Lora returns and it becomes evident to Susie that Steve loves Lora and they'll marry, she and her mother have a falling out.

Annie's health deteriorates as Sarah Jane draws away from her. Sarah Jane tries to pass as white. Her white boyfriend finds out she's black and beats her up and dumps her. She dances in a sleazy club until Annie informs the manager she's black. Sarah Jane tells Annie she doesn't want to see her again and flees town. Steve tracks her to Las Vegas, where she's working as a showgirl. Now extremely ill, Annie goes to see her. She promises to stay out of Sarah Jane's life, but tells her daughter to come to her or Lora if she ever needs help. Sarah Jane hugs her and is sad to see her go.

Lora is heartbroken when Annie dies. Just as Annie wanted, there is a glorious funeral, attended by thousands of mourners. A tearful, guilty Sarah Jane runs up to her coffin, admitting to everyone she is Annie's daughter. Sarah Jane rides off with Lora, Susie, and Steve.

The irony wasn't lost on producer Ross Hunter when he asked Lana Turner to star in a movie titled *Imitation of Life*, playing an ambitious actress who has a strained relationship with her troubled teenage daughter. The entire country knew that Turner had a troubled teenage daughter of her own, Cheryl, who, like Sandra Dee's Susie Meredith, spent most of her time at boarding schools (except when she'd run away). Fourteen-year-old Cheryl made national headlines the previous Good Friday when she killed her mother's gangster boyfriend, Johnny Stompanato, by stabbing him with a butcher knife. Turner backed Cheryl's claim that she'd only meant to frighten Stompanato when he physically threatened Turner, but had accidentally stabbed him when he menacingly approached her. Cheryl was acquitted of involuntary manslaughter, but the Hollywood press made mincemeat of Turner. Her career was in jeopardy before this scandal (MGM had dropped their former "Sweater Girl" after 18 years), and she now worried that it was irreparably damaged. So she was relieved to get Hunter's offer—she was happy to play any lead role, even one that called attention to, even exploited, her personal life. And curious moviegoers flocked to Turner's comeback film, perhaps hoping to get insight into the actress and her relationship with her daughter. *Imitation of Life* became Universal's biggest grosser of all time and Turner's biggest hit, reviving her career and, since she agreed to accept a share of the profits rather than take a high salary, ending her financial woes. Not surprisingly, Turner claimed the film was exacting to make and caused her to break down several times, yet afterward she spurned pictures with completely different themes, and jumped into Hunter's *Portrait in Black* (1960), in which her character's boyfriend (Anthony Quinn) is accidentally killed while menacingly approaching her troubled stepdaughter, again played by Dee.

Today, *Imitation of Life* is of less interest because of Turner than its director, Douglas Sirk, one of the major benefactors of *auteur* criticism in the late sixties and seventies. Sirk wasn't taken seriously in America until Andrew Sarris listed him in his "Far Side of Paradise" category of directors—his second-highest ranking—in his landmark book *The American Cinema* (1968). Claiming Sirk's bold style transcended his often ridiculous material, Sarris predicted, "Time, if nothing else, will vindicate Douglas Sirk." He was proved correct. In 1971, *Screen* devoted an entire issue to Sirk, and in winter 1977/1978, *Bright Lights* did the same. And when German director Rainer Werner Fassbinder announced, "Not any of us, not Godard or Fuller or me or anybody else, can touch Sirk," everyone took another look at his neglected career. As Detlef Sierk, he began making films in his native Germany in 1935 at age 35, after having spent a dozen years working in the theater as a writer and director. In America it's nearly impossible to see any of Sirk's German films, but according

A revealing shot that defines the relationships over the years of the four major female characters. Lora stands at a distance from her three housemates, looking down on Annie, paying little attention to Sarah Jane, and allowing her daughter, Susie, who doesn't seem happy, to find motherly comfort with Annie. Annie is the group's anchor, sitting in a chair—she's the symbol of the home—while the action moves around her. Sarah Jane stands alone, observing how the others relate to her and each other, and not knowing how she fits in. In the background is one of Sirk's familiar mirrors, reflecting an imitation of life.

to David Thomson's *A Biographical Dictionary of Film* (1975), they were preludes to his Hollywood melodramas and soap operas of the fifties:

> [T]hey immediately fell into the graphic fluency that distinguishes his later work. They also showed a rapid and uninhibited grasp of the principles of the melodramatic movie. In one sense they were studio concoctions: costume films, made with loving care for sets and clothes; studies of bourgeois society that employ the ponderous love stories to illuminate the lifelessness and hypocrisy within that class. Their abiding cinematic themes are music, sumptuous interiors that are always "drawn" by the camera rather than "shown," and anxious beautiful women. The meaning of the films is a subdued attack on society; like all melodrama, it knows that social decorum smothers love and lovers.

Sirk left Germany in 1937 and, after spending time in Switzerland and Holland, came to America and hooked up with various studios in the forties. His early American films made little initial impact, but today some come across as original and impressive: his debut film, *Hitler's Madman* (1943), *Summer Storm* (1944), *A Scandal in Paris* (1946), *Lured* (1947), *Sleep, My Love* (1948), and *Shockproof* (1949), which Sam Fuller co-scripted. Sirk went back to Germany in 1949, but returned to Hollywood the following year and began his extremely successful, decade-long collaboration with Universal-International, the least likely studio to employ the services of a true stylist. Sirk became Universal's top director, working 10 times with producer Ross Hunter, 10 times with photographer Russell Metty, 13 times with composer Frank Skinner, and 8 times with its top draw Rock Hudson before settling for Hudson's imperfect clone, John Gavin, who starred in Sirk's last films, *A Time to Love and a Time to Die* (1958) and *Imitation of Life*. Sirk made a few period pieces, but most of his films were about love, family, and the pursuit of happiness (which often meant *respectability*) in contemporary America. At the center of these pictures are a man and woman in love, but their affair is affected by children, in-laws, and society. The house (or other residence), usually the American security symbol, is just that in some Sirk films but in others it is a battle arena, which stands firm while relationships crumble within—the house is invariably Sirk's most important "prop" (character?).

His films of the early fifties were cheerful tributes to small-town America: *Weekend with Father* (1951), *No Room for the Groom* (1952), *Has Anybody Seen My Gal?* (1952), *Meet Me at the Fair* (1952), *Take Me to Town* (1953). His later films were more honest and personal, and revealed Sirk's growing disillusionment with his adopted country. They revealed his belief that there was a quake brewing beneath the happy American artifice. Because men and women have lost their most decent values striving after money, and weakening under the weight of ambition and social pressures, the "American Dream" has soured in *Magnificent Obsession* (1954), *All That Heaven Allows* (1956), *There's Always Tomorrow* (1956), *Written on the Wind* (1957), *Interlude* (1957), *The Tarnished Angels* (1958), and *Imitation of Life*, the last film Sirk made before permanently returning to Germany. Even those who survive in these films have caused those they love too much suffering and have endured too much pain themselves to feel completely content. Rarely is the lesson they have learned worth the terrible experiences they have had during the course of their films.

Among Sirk fanatics there is an ongoing argument over whether he made his melodramas with tongue in cheek or took them seriously. I'm among those who don't think his films have much "camp" appeal, but stand on their own as bold attempts by Sirk to improve on the assigned material, rather than mock, disregard, or subvert it. (I also don't think he looks down on his characters, no matter how foolish their actions.) When dealt a bad hand, he did the best he could. As he said himself: "You can't always conquer the material . . . but one of the foremost things of picturemaking, I think, is to bend your material to your style." All his major films have style to spare. It is simply better material that makes the two films he directed for producer Albert Zugsmith, *Written on the Wind*, from a Robert Wilder potboiler, and *The Tarnished Angels*, an adaptation of William Faulkner's *Pylon*, preferable in my opinion to his best films for Ross Hunter, *All That Heaven Allows* and the John Stahl remakes, *Magnificent Obsession* and *Imitation of Life*. The Zugsmith films are solid melodramas that appeal to the intellect as well as the eye, while Hunter's films are diluted-by-tears melodramas, manipulative soap operas that appeal primarily to the emotions. The Zugsmith films are excitingly unpredictable, with the characters seemingly existing on their own as if there were no cameras and no script, out of control, driven by destructive forces and passions. While not totally predictable, the Hunter films too closely follow soap opera conventions.

Imitation of Life is impeccably made, delightfully watchable, inconsistently acted Hollywood trash, with not one but two women who will sacrifice all for their children but aren't particularly good mothers (a soap tradition!), entangled relationships, an absurd story line, Ross Hunter gloss and glitter, fantasy lighting (Sirk and Metty experimented with color and texture), and stunning set design. Made in CinemaScope, it is Sirk's most sumptuous production, a feast for the eyes. Turner wears many Jean Louis gowns, furs, and Laykin et Cie jewels (provided by David Webb) that, as studio publicists pointed out, were worth an obscene amount of money. (Sirk must have enjoyed filling his frame with diamonds for the opening title sequence and then cutting directly to the Coney Island boardwalk and beach, which are crowded with the proletariat, for the beginning of his rags-to-riches, from-out-of-the-masses-to-being-a-star tale.) There are an inordinate number of sets: various stages and dressing rooms, city streets and alleys, nightclubs, offices, high-rise apartments, restaurants, schoolrooms, kitchens, living rooms, bedrooms. And nowhere is there a spot of dirt. Fittingly, only in confused Sarah Jane's room, where there are records on the floor, is there any disorder. And of course there is a large house—shared by the troubled Turner's Lora Meredith, Juanita Moore's Annie Johnson, Dee's Susie Meredith, and Susan Kohner's Sarah Jane Johnson—with a huge, dramatic staircase (one of Sirk's trademarks), books that come only in sets, and mirrors for his self-centered players ("shrunken souls with shiny faces," according to Sarris) to gaze into and see false, happy images of their real, unhappy selves: Sirk said, "I would have made the picture for the title, because it is all there—the mirror and the imitation . . ." The imagery is consistently striking (i.e., the sexy scene in which Sarah Jane and other showgirls do gyrations on the Las Vegas stage) but there

When Annie brings rain gear to Sarah Jane, the girl is embarrassed because now her teacher and classmates know that she is black.

The grown-up Sarah Jane passes for white while performing in a sleazy nightclub.

are two scenes (both with strong musical accompaniment) that stand out. The first takes place at night, on a deserted city street, and has Sarah Jane being slapped around by her white boyfriend, Frankie (played by Troy Donahue, who'd be Dee's lover in 1960's *A Summer Place*), who has learned she is black. Here, Sirk makes exceptional use of dramatic lighting, dramatic music, and reflections on glass and water. The second scene is Annie's tear-inducing "heavenly" funeral, with Mahalia Jackson wailing "Trouble in the World," horses pulling the hearse through the New York streets as bystanders look on respectfully, and Sirk occasionally filming the procession from inside an antique store to, I suspect, remind us of the past, when the five major characters first came together 10 long years ago.

Don't miss the opening scene, set at Coney Island in 1947, because it reveals almost everything essential about the five characters and establishes individual relationships that will not change much in the next 10 years. When Lora appears she is desperately trying to find 6-year-old Susie on the beach. We immediately see that she loves her daughter very much, but recognize that she doesn't keep too keen an eye on her. As will happen throughout her young life, when she's in trouble, Susie gravitates toward Annie when Mom isn't there. Annie is seated, the rock for the three restless females—Lora, Susie, and her daughter, Sarah Jane—to anchor to. She will be mother and friend to all three. Annie immediately expresses her desire to have a home for herself and Sarah Jane, and eventually she will come to symbolize the home—that's why Lora is so surprised years later to learn Annie has made so many

friends outside the house, and why it seems so draining and painful for Annie to leave the house to track down the teenage Sarah Jane. Like her mother, the 8-year-old Sarah Jane we see on the beach also wants to share Lora and Susie's home (then a cold-water flat), but whereas Annie expects to be a domestic, which she assumes is what a black woman must do if she is to live with whites—and Lora will irresponsibly allow this situation to develop— the light-skinned Sarah Jane hopes to be accepted into Lora's family, her *white* family. Gavin's Steve Archer is the outsider to this group of females, whom he adores and who adore him. Steve would like to be on the inside, husband to Lora and father to Susie. But Lora, who has too many other commitments to devote herself to Steve, makes him keep his distance. At times, Turner will again be the ice goddess she was in her early films. Interestingly, Susie never tries to play matchmaker between her lonely widowed mother and Steve—she already wants Steve for herself. If there is a healthy relationship at the beginning it's between Susie and Sarah Jane, but in the years to come the hopelessly naive Susie will be incapable of helping her friend resolve her problems of being a light-skinned black in a white man's world . . . and a white woman's house. Susie won't even notice that Sarah Jane doesn't feel she can go into the living room and join her, Steve, and Lora at the all-white post-play party.

Throughout the film, the five characters will try to get what they can't have, causing, as Michael McKegney wrote in *Screen*, "[Lora's] immaturity [to] turn to self-centered ambition, [Susie's] innocence to naiveté, [Annie's] self-sacrifice to masochism, and [Sarah Jane's] alienation to self-destructiveness.'' (Their frustration is heightened, no doubt, by their failure to have sexual fulfillment.) Steve wants Lora, but he resents her ambition because he isn't ambitious himself (he gives up becoming a museum-caliber photographer to become a successful commercial photographer and ad executive). Susie wants her mother to be at her side as she goes through difficult teendom; later she wants her mother to stay away so Steve can be her lover. Sarah Jane wants to be white and accepted into white society. (Whereas Susie craves her mother's love and attention, Sarah Jane rejects her mother's love and wants her not to interfere.) Annie wants Sarah Jane to lead the life she has set out for her. And Lora wants to find happiness through becoming a star, although it is stardom that destroys what would really bring her happiness (a close relationship with Susie and marriage to Steve). In all Sirk's films, life is terribly difficult and people like Lora must struggle and sacrifice much of their humanity and good values to get through it, but once they stop and look around at the world they've created for themselves, they'll be as sad as Lora after years of self-absorption. As in most Sirk films, selfish people like Turner—who is completely unaware of Susie's problems or Annie's outside life—must come to terms with the responsibility one has to others as well as to oneself.

There's a silly scene in *Imitation of Life* in which Lora and Annie agree that Lora's problems with Susie over Steve are *real*, as if Annie's with Sarah Jane are trivial.

But from our point of view, it's impossible to take Susie's crush seriously—after all, do we really expect Steve and Susie to wind up together? We can't really care about Lora's problems—they're mere conventions of the genre. So we focus on Annie and Sarah Jane, for their problems are not so common in the cinema. Unfortunately, the race issue is not well handled. Sarah Jane is made out to be thoroughly insensitive, when in fact her choice to pass for white has to do with her rejecting the demeaning black world that is presented to her. Even at home she has witnessed ''friends'' Lora and Annie taking on the roles of white mistress and black maid (Annie has even taught Sarah Jane to say ''Miss Lora''). When they lived in the tenement, while Lora went out looking for exciting work as a performer (a course Sarah Jane will take, emulating Lora), Annie stayed home and cared for the kids, answered the phone as if she were Lora's servant, and accepted menial work to lower the pair's rent. (In Stahl's 1934 film, Claudette Colbert and Louise Beavers became partners in an Aunt Jemima–like maple syrup company.) When, years later, Lora admonishes Sarah Jane for insinuating she's been treated demeaningly at home, Sarah Jane acquiesces that Lora and Susie have never shown any prejudice toward her. But the script should have had her attack Lora for treating Annie as her servant (no matter that Annie was paid enough to afford a fur coat, an expensive funeral, and Sarah Jane's college education).

Annie is made into Sarah Jane's whipping post, but it

Lora and the almost grown-up Susie, spending rare time together. So "perfect" is the set design that the books in the background come only in sets.

Lora and Steve at Annie's funeral.

might have been different if (even if this film was made in 1959) she had suggested to her daughter not to go to a black teachers college but to break down some racial barriers, be defiant, and improve the lot of her race rather than be satisfied with second-class status. Annie may be the nicest person in the world (which is why Sarah Jane can't stop loving her), but she isn't a very good role model, doesn't have any concept of her child's problems (any kid would be mortified by a parent who brought galoshes into the classroom), and makes no attempt to teach Sarah Jane pride in being black—all she can say is that being black is nothing to be ashamed of. Even in Fannie Hurst's 1933 source novel, the less educated black woman (called Delilah) tells her daughter to be proud to be black (because the Lord made her black). At very least, Sirk should have had Sarah Jane have second thoughts about her race just from seeing the large, integrated turnout at her mother's funeral. It's not enough that Sarah Jane admits her blackness by rushing to her mother's coffin (a moment for our tears). This act is, for some wrong reason, made to seem shameful when Lora pulls the crying girl away from the coffin so she won't make a public spectacle of herself. And when Lora, who has learned her motherly obligations, brings Sarah Jane into the car with her fiancé Steve and daughter Susie, Sarah Jane gets what she always wanted, to be part of an all-white family. So her identity problem

hasn't been resolved. (Sirk: "You don't believe the happy ending, and you're not really supposed to.") The best thing about Annie and Sarah Jane's scenes together is the moving performances by Moore (who's much less solemn as Jayne Mansfield's dancing maid in 1956's *The Girl Can't Help It*) and the white Kohner (legendary light-skinned black Fredi Washington, who related to the young girl's problems, played the part in the original). Turner has some strong moments, but Moore and Kohner, who both received Best Supporting Actress nominations, steal the film—Lora may cry up a storm, but Annie and Sarah Jane bring *us* to tears, as in the dramatic Las Vegas–farewell scene.

Interestingly, Moore deserved second billing but the studio placed her seventh (even behind supporting players Dan O'Herlihy and Robert Alda) with a diplomatic "presenting Juanita Moore as Annie Johnson" as if it were proudly singling her out rather than finding a way to list her below white actors—credits in newspapers always listed her seventh. So it's hard to trust the film. It makes you think that when Lora, Susie, and Steve are nice to Annie and Sarah Jane, act without prejudice, and mourn Annie's death, white audiences are expected, in a self-congratulatory gesture, to weep about the white characters' nobility, their refusal to act high-and-mighty toward people who have none of their advantages. An enlightened Sarah Jane would have really been angered by such condescension.

In a Lonely Place

1950 B&W Columbia release of a Santana production
Director: Nicholas Ray
Producer: Robert Lord
Screenplay: Andrew Salt
Adaptation by Edmund H. North
From the novel by Dorothy B. Hughes
Cinematography: Burnett Guffey
Music: George Antheil
Editor: Viola Lawrence
Running Time: 92 minutes

Cast: Humphrey Bogart (Dixon Steele), Gloria Grahame (Laurel Gray), Frank Lovejoy (Brub Nicolai), Carl Benton Reid (Captain Lochner), Art Smith (Mel Lippmann), Jeff Donnell (Sylvia Nicolai), Martha Stewart (Mildred Atkinson), Robert Warwick (Charlie Waterman), Morris Ankrum (Lloyd Barnes), Steven Geray (Paul), Alice Talton (Frances Randolph), Jack Reynolds (Henry Kesler), Ruth Warren (Effie), Ruth Gillette (Martha), Lewis Howard (Junior), Hadda Brooks (singer).

Synopsis: Since returning from the war, screenwriter Dixon Steele has been unable to write a hit. He drinks heavily, bad-mouths Hollywood for selling popcorn instead of striving for art, and continually gets into fights. It is rumored that he beat up his former girlfriend, Frances Randolph. His agent, Mel, gets him the chance to adapt a popular novel, if he won't try to change it to his tastes. He doesn't feel like reading such trash so when he learns that Mildred Atkinson, the hat-check girl at Paul's restaurant, has read the book, he invites her to his apartment to synopsize it for him. She breaks her date with boyfriend Henry Kesler. Afterward Dix sends her to a taxi stand. Early in the morning, police detective Brub Nicolai, who was under Dix's command during the war, wakes him. He escorts him to the police station where Captain Lochner informs Dix that Mildred was strangled and thrown from a moving vehicle. Because Dix shows no emotion, Lochner suspects he murdered Mildred. But aspiring actress Laurel Gray, a new neighbor in Dix's Patio Apartments complex, vouches she saw Mildred leave his apartment alone.

Dix is immediately attracted to Laurel, finding her the one female who isn't "coy or cute or corny." Laurel commits herself to Dix, against the advice of her confidante, Martha, a masseuse, who thinks Laurel should go back to the wealthy man she left. Under Laurel's influence, Dix stops drinking and starts writing.

At Lochner's insistence, Brub invites Dix to dinner. Dix demonstrates how he envisions Mildred's murder, having Brub and his wife, Sylvia, play the murderer and victim. Sylvia senses that Dix is a sick man. Brub just thinks he has a superior mind. Dix and Laurel are happy, yet both are anxious because of the ongoing investigation. Dix feels he is being hounded. He is infuriated when Sylvia lets slip that Lochner further questioned Laurel and Laurel didn't tell him. Losing his temper, he drives away from the beach at high speed. He has a slight collision and beats up the young driver of the other car. He would have hit him with a rock, but Laurel yells for him to stop. Having finally seen how violent Dix is, Laurel worries that he killed Mildred. This is what Lochner and Martha think. Dix says that Kesler is the logical suspect.

Laurel becomes so frightened of Dix that she agrees to his marriage proposal. Secretly she tries to arrange a flight to New York. Mel is upset that she is leaving Dix because she was his one hope for happiness. He takes Dix's finished script, thinking that if a studio bigwig likes it, the blow of Laurel leaving him will be diminished. Dix won't let Laurel out of his sight. They have a pre-wedding party at Paul's. He learns that Mel has taken his script behind his back. He slaps Mel. There is a phone call for Laurel. Dix jealously intercepts it—it's just from Martha. While Dix and Mel make up, the shaken Laurel returns to her apartment. Dix follows, missing a call from Brub to tell him that Kesler, who has attempted suicide, confessed to Mildred's murder.

Dix demands entrance to Laurel's apartment. He sees she isn't wearing his ring. He acts crazed. He picks up the ringing phone and learns she has made plans to go to New York. He starts to strangle her but stops when the phone rings again. It is Brub with the good news. But it's too late to save the relationship.

A publicity shot showing the intense Dix in his apartment while neighbor Laurel peers suspiciously through his window.

This dark, brooding melodrama is the sleeper among Humphrey Bogart's best films and is far superior to the other three pictures that his production company, Santana, made for Columbia: *Knock on Any Door* (1949), *Tokyo Joe* (1949), and *Sirocco* (1951). It is one of many films made during the Freud-fascinated forties and fifties that feature neurotic characters, and, as critic James W. Palmer pointed out, joined *Rebecca* (1941), *Suspicion* (1941), *Gaslight* (1944), *Spellbound* (1945), and *The Two Mrs. Carrolls* (1947), in which Bogart is a murderous artist, as films with "a plot centering on the [seemingly] homicidal lover or husband who is rightly or wrongly suspected of murder." Teamed with the always fascinating Gloria Grahame, Bogart gives a compelling performance as one of director Nicholas Ray's many decent men who can't control their violent tempers, who, as Colin McArthur observes, "carry within the seeds of their own destruction." As in *The Treasure of the Sierra Madre* (1949) and *The Caine Mutiny* (1954), Bogart plays a character whose cocky, tough demeanor—he's named *Steele*—covers insecurities and the roots of insanity. Palmer contends that "*In a Lonely Place* reveals Ray's [and Bogart's] preoccupation with outsiders and draws on Bogart's skill in portraying characters whose contrary personality in many ways mirrors Bogart's own Hollywood persona." Palmer:

Steele's belligerent stance toward Hollywood phonies, his spirited defense of friends, and his adherence to high professional standards are reflective of Bogart's own personality. More importantly, Steele's paradoxical character, at once sentimental and sadistic, playful and paranoid, gentle and combative, coincides with some of the contradictions in Bogart's personality.

Palmer figured Bogart would have enjoyed playing a role that "provided him with the opportunity to critique Hollywood on screen in a way that he had been doing for many years off screen," yet he also thought that "because Dix Steele oversteps the line of provocative needling with his nearly homicidal behavior, Bogart might have been discomfited by the role that otherwise mirrored so much of his own public stance toward Hollywood." Bogart disliked *In a Lonely Place*, and I think Palmer is correct in guessing the reason was that he worried viewers would think he was *exactly* like Dix just because they had many similarities.

In a Lonely Place takes an anti-Hollywood stance immediately, in the opening at Paul's, a sequence in which Ray uses the frame as a physical and verbal battlefield and zips cynical characters in and out of sight as if they were players in *All About Eve* (1950) or a Howard Hawks or Preston Sturges screwball comedy. Soon it's clear that Dix (like Ray and Bogart) has disrespect for a postwar movie industry that is more interested in selling popcorn than producing art; that is run by the crass, philistine sons (like Junior) of the pioneering studio heads; that has forgotten the old-time actors (like Dix's alcoholic friend, Charlie) who made their fathers successful; that caters to a silly, shallow audience (represented by Mildred Atkinson). Unlike Bogart, who was on the Committee for the First Amendment that went to Washington to show support for the soon-to-be-imprisoned Hollywood Ten, Dix does not voice disapproval of the political climate in town. There is no mention of the HUAC-instigated witchhunt, blacklisting, or paranoia that was affecting everyone in the film industry. Yet that is what this film is about. And this is why when Ray, Andrew Salt, and Edmund H. North reworked Dorothy B. Hughes's novel they turned her aspiring novelist (or so Dix claims) into a persecuted, paranoid veteran screenwriter—like eight of the Hollywood Ten (the other two were directors).

Ray, Salt (who wrote the scintillating, adult screenplay), and North (who did the adaptation) stick closely to Hughes's novel in some respects. For instance, the fiery relationship of Dix and Grahame's Laurel Gray (which many have equated to the recent, already-disintegrating marriage of Ray and Grahame) is quite similar, except that in Hughes's book, the two sleep together (the script seems to go out of its way to indicate they don't), Laurel also shows signs of jealousy, and Laurel (who isn't around for the book's finale) does manage to sneak out of town and away from Dix. Also Dix's relationship to Frank Lovejoy's Brub and Jeff Donnell's Sylvia is virtually the same, except that in the book Brub ultimately becomes convinced of Dix's guilt. But there are several major changes, all having to do with Dix's character. In the novel, he is newly arrived in Hollywood, an anonymous character having none of the acquaintances or fame of Bogart's screenwriter. He has no money of his own, and is somewhat of a leech, greedily accepting the Nicolais' dinner invitations, living on an allowance sent by an eccentric uncle, and using the apartment, clothes, and car of an acquaintance who, Dix insists, rushed off to Brazil. He has no talent whatsoever, as a writer (he lies that he's working on a detective novel) or anything else. While Bogart's Dix writes movies, the best Hughes's Dix can do is attend them obsessively. In the novel, Dix is not suspected of being a murderer until late in the story. The most significant change is that Dix *is* the murderer in the book.

In fact, Dix is a serial murderer in the novel, having committed sex murders in America and England. He mostly kills strangers, including Mildred Atkinson, but it turns out he also strangled the woman he loved in England, probably after she rejected him—the incident that caused his mind to snap. (That Hughes didn't give her a less irritating name than "Brucie" is just one of the reasons the book is inferior to the movie.) The novel explores the workings of the mind of a crazed individual, anticipating the many post–Kennedy-assassination books and movies that have examined what makes assassins, serial killers, and other violent sociopaths tick. We get a disturbing view of a paranoid loner, who resents those that have their lives together and, he suspects, look down on him, who feels he has the brains to outwit anyone—he enjoys matching wits with former army buddy Brub and other members of the police force—and who distrusts and hates women. He fears rejection (from Brucie, from Laurel) and becomes violently jealous. At the end of the novel, he is caught by police when he attempts to strangle Laurel, only to discover it's Sylvia acting as a decoy in a trap. I'm among those who hate when screenwriters reverse a novel's ending and have a character live instead of die, or be innocent of a crime instead of guilty. However, Ray and his writers didn't alter the book so they could give the picture a happy ending and please audiences. Their ending is much more depressing than having a homicidal maniac arrested—an innocent man has had his life ruined (Bogart pauses so Ray can place his "The End" title across Dix's back). They made the change to make the point that the paranoia felt by hounded screenwriters (and others) in Hollywood during this period was, unfairly, similar to that felt by hunted criminals. And that such paranoia could, understandably, cause those with violent tempers to do desperate acts that might wreck their lives.

Ray builds an atmosphere of paranoia quite simply. He does it by having his characters constantly gossip (usually about Dix) and spread rumors (i.e., that Dix beat up his former girlfriend Frances, although this seems unlikely from the seductive way she still acts toward him). He does it by repeatedly having phones ring so that his characters (and we) can wonder who's on the line. He has characters enter rooms to find others (i.e., Laurel) speaking on the phone—who are they talking to? In many scenes, Ray separates his characters with closed doors—there is much buzzing, knocking, and banging. When doors are locked or phones go unanswered, tension mounts. And characters spy on each other: Sylvia gazes at Dix as Brub escorts him to his car; Brub watches Dix through venetian blinds as he leaves the police station; Dix looks up through his window at Laurel on her balcony; Laurel tells Dix that

Dix's friends—Lloyd (holding him), Charlie (speaking to him), and Mel (at right)—calm him after a skirmish with Junior at Paul's. Junior (to Dix's left) and Paul (to Mel's right) stand in the background. ◄

As Brub looks on, Dix and Henry Kesler, the two chief murder suspects, shake hands. ▼

she watched him in his apartment through open venetian blinds; Mel peeks into Dix's apartment through his window. We look at characters through other characters' eyes.

For most of the picture, it is Dix's paranoia that mounts. Everyone, including Mel (who steals a look at Dix's unfinished script), is inquisitive about his life ("Stop snooping around," Laurel jokingly tells Mel). Everyone, including Laurel, keeps asking Dix questions, about the crime or about something trivial. Like a smart-alecky kid, he refuses to take the questions seriously (although they eat him up inside). Again, tension mounts as he refuses to answer even Laurel's nonthreatening "Where have you been?" ("None of your business") or "You really want to go [to a beach party]?" ("Be back in five minutes"). Because of his mature relationship with Laurel, the seemingly hopeless, uncaring Dix finally has a chance to get his life in order ("I lived a few weeks while she loved me"). He stops drinking, he has no more temper tantrums, he starts writing his script in earnest. He has the chance to become part of the Hollywood community. But it all falls apart once he is isolated by friends and police because he is the chief suspect in Mildred Atkinson's murder. Everyone talks about him behind his back or holds secret meetings about him. Conspiracies form: Brub and his superior, Captain Lochner; Brub and Sylvia; Lochner, Brub, and Laurel; Laurel and her perverse masseuse Martha (who informs her of Dix's rumored beating of Frances); Laurel and Sylvia; Laurel and Mel; Mel, the big-time producer, and Frances. As Dix learns that his best friend Brub, his loyal agent Mel, and his girlfriend Laurel have not been on the up-and-up with him (it's not even a question of them thinking him guilty of murder), he begins to feel like an outcast and, like the ultimate outcast, the Frankenstein monster, resorts to monstrous acts. (Ray doesn't condone Dix's attempt to strangle Laurel, but his point is that it needn't

have come to this.) As James W. Palmer writes, "By the time the murder is solved and the killer apprehended, all of the characters stand equally guilty of betraying the trust and loyalty that make love, friendship, and community possible. . . . The real crime that this film exposes is the undermining of human trust through the process of social exclusion." Are we, the viewers, being tested? Are we supposed to continue to trust Dix, despite the rumors, despite the violence we see him commit, despite the circumstantial evidence? I think so.

Although in his warped mind Dix can't see it, Brub and Mel actually don't waver in their loyalty toward him, and never seriously doubt his innocence. In fact, they try to help him all along, even if behind his back. Laurel is the one who deserts Dix. She loses faith in him. She begins to doubt his innocence, just as Vera Miles will come to doubt the innocence of husband Henry Fonda and suffer a nervous breakdown in Hitchcock's *The Wrong Man* (1957). Of course, we can't really blame Laurel for withdrawing from Dix by the end, not after the way he acts toward the young stranger on the highway, whom he beats up for calling him a "blind, knuckleheaded squirrel," toward Mel, whom he slaps, and toward her, whom he attempts to strangle. She can't stay with him after he proves that he is capable of murder, even if he didn't kill Mildred Atkinson. Interestingly, the film is structured so that in the last part of the film, once Dix's paranoia has driven him over the edge, the focus switches from Dix to Laurel, as she gets second thoughts about Dix's innocence. Their positions are reversed. Now she gets to experience some of the paranoia that drove Dix crazy! Now she realizes that he doesn't trust her, is suspicious of her motives, and is hiding facts from her. He keeps her constantly in sight ("He hasn't left me alone for a second"), intercepts her phone calls, and asks one question after another: "When did you get the pills?"/"Oh? When did you see your doctor?"/"Why didn't I know about it?" Under such pressure, Laurel can't sleep, can't get her thoughts together, and like Dix (who tells everyone, "You're lying!") can't determine what is the truth. She learns why Dix went crazy.

In most films in which a man is proved innocent at the end, it's clear that the man was incapable of the crime of which he was accused. *In a Lonely Place* is problematic because Dix proves that without psychiatric help he could eventually kill if in a jealous rage or if just one more person got on his back. Some critics contend the ending is reactionary because it justifies the police's hounding of Dix, in that it got him to reveal his true colors. (This would inadvertently also justify HUAC's hounding of suspected Communists in Hollywood.) But that's not the intention of the ending. It is meant to show that everyone is capable of violence (and insanity) if pushed too far. At the time Dix could have started leading a stable life, the police and those who turned against him made it impossible; if he hadn't been hounded, he would not have tried to strangle Laurel and most likely wouldn't have gotten into any more brawls.

Peter Biskind calls the film "conservative" in his book *Seeing Is Believing: How Hollywood Taught Us to Stop Worrying and Love the Fifties* (1983) because he thinks the end confirms the film's endorsement of "average" people. He writes:

> [Dix] is a violence-prone scriptwriter, and [Laurel], his girlfriend, complains, "He doesn't act like a normal person. Why can't he be like other people?" "Other people" in this case is [Dix's] old war buddy, [Brub,] a cop, and his wife. Wife says to [Brub], "I'm glad you're not a genius. [Dix] is a sick man." "No, he isn't," counters [Brub]. "There's nothing the matter with his mind except that he's superior." But in conservative films of the fifties, to be superior was to be sick, and the little lady has the last word: "I still like you the way you are—attractive and average." And at the end of the film, when [Dix] tries to strangle [Laurel], it turns out that she's right.

Dix is sick all right but not only because he *is* superior. He becomes sicker because he is persecuted for *acting* superior. This makes him suspicious. In no way does this film say it's preferable to be average. Brub and Mel, voices of reason, certainly admire Dix and value his friendship. They wouldn't want to change him. When Laurel wishes Dix were normal, Mel asks rhetorically, "Would you have liked him?" He then lectures: "You knew he was dynamite, he has to explode some times. . . . If you want him you've got to take it all—the bad with the good." Mel says he has no regrets for sticking by Dix through the hard times. Again, all Ray is saying is that anyone, be he "sick"/superior or normal, is capable of violence if pushed too far. Remember that under Dix's direction, average Brub lost his head and almost strangled Sylvia while acting out Mildred's murder. And remember that Henry Kesler, who *did* murder Mildred, was as average as you could get; as Mildred described him: "He's nice and substantial, the easygoing type. He lives with his folks and has a good job." Lochner's mistake is to assume that Kesler is innocent (Brub goes along with Dix's theory that he's guilty) because he acts emotionally when he learns of Mildred's death, as the average person would do, and to assume Dix is guilty because he shows no emotion. Of course, in the fifties, those who showed no emotion were equated with Communists and, in Hollywood, were candidates for blacklisting. Only later, when alone, does Dix send flowers to the Atkinson family, revealing his sympathy. Lochner didn't reason that since Dix was a platoon commander during the war he got into the habit of keeping his pain private when people he knew were killed. During the war, he probably sent many letters of sympathy home to families—and no doubt he did this without discussing it with anyone else. Does this film endorse the average person? No, it endorses superior people like Dix, even if they do tread an electrical high wire. Sure, they could commit murder, but chances are the average guy will do it first. Even Hughes agreed with this: In her novel, killer Dixon Steele described himself as "just an average young fellow."

Having just seen Dix have a violent temper tantrum, Laurel suddenly worries that he is the murderer, especially since he holds her in the same way the killer held Mildred Atkinson before strangling her.

It's a Mad Mad Mad Mad World

1963 Color United Artists
Director: Stanley Kramer
Producer: Stanley Kramer
Screenplay: William and Tania Rose
Cinematography: Ernest Laszlo
Music: Ernest Gold
Editors: Frederic Knudtson, Robert C. Jones, and Gene Fowler, Jr.
Running Time: 154/192 minutes

Cast: Spencer Tracy (T. G. Culpepper), Milton Berle (J. Russell Finch), Sid Caesar (Melville Crump), Mickey Rooney (Dingy Bell), Buddy Hackett (Benji Benjamin), Jonathan Winters (Lennie Pike), Ethel Merman (Mrs. Marcus), Edie Adams (Monica Crump), Dorothy Provine (Emmeline Finch), Terry-Thomas (Algernon Hawthorne), Phil Silvers (Otto Meyer), Dick Shawn (Sylvester Marcus), Jim Backus (Tyler Fitzgerald), Jimmy Durante (Smiler Grogan), William Demarest (chief of police), Peter Falk (cabbie), Eddie "Rochester" Anderson (cabbie), Andy Devine (sheriff), and all-star cast.

Synopsis: Smiler Grogan crashes in the desert. Four vehicles stop. They contain Monica and Melville Crump; weak-kneed J. Russell Finch, his sweet wife, Emmeline, and her constantly nagging mother, Mrs. Marcus; comics Dingy Bell and Benji Benjamin; and trucker Lennie Pike, who is transporting furniture. Before literally kicking the bucket Grogan reveals that 15 years ago he buried $350,000 in stolen money under "a big W" in Santa Rosita Beach State Park. When the eight travelers realize they are each too greedy to divide the money equitably, they decide the money belongs to whoever digs it up. They don't know that retiring police chief T. G. Culpepper, who has worked on the case for 15 years, is having them tailed.

The four drivers are reckless as they drive twisting desert roads. Pike's truck rams Russell's car, putting both out of commission. Russell convinces Pike to ride a girl's bike to the next town and hire a car. Then Russell, Emmeline, and Mrs. Marcus hitch a ride with smug Britisher Algernon Hawthorne, whom they offer 10% of the money. They speed past Pike.

Melville and Monica hire a rickety plane to speed up their journey. The trip terrifies them. Dingy and Benji charter a flight with alcoholic pilot Tyler Fitzgerald. He hands the controls to Benji and is knocked out. Incompetent air controllers try to talk the petrified Benji down. They crash safely.

Pike stops a car. He tells driver Otto Meyer about the money. Meyer drives off without him. Pike catches him at Irwin and Ray's garage and tries to kill him, but he's subdued by the owners, who think he's a homicidal maniac. Meyer flees. Pike escapes, steals a pickup, and destroys the garage.

When Russell insults Mrs. Marcus's crazy son Sylvester, she gets out of the car. Russell and Hawthorne turn her upside down to get the keys back. They drive off without Mrs. Marcus and Emmeline. Russell and Hawthorne get into a fist fight.

Meyer gives a lift to a hitchhiker off the main road. The man's son shows Meyer an "easy" way back. Meyer's car sinks in the river. He steals another car from its unsuspecting driver.

The Crumps land and go to a hardware store basement for a pick and shovel. They get locked in the basement. After many failed attempts, Melville blows a hole in the wall with dynamite. Like Dingy and Benji, they take a cab to the park. Both cabbies want in on the action.

Pike gives a ride to Mrs. Marcus and Emmeline. Mrs. Marcus calls Sylvester to tell him to rush to the park, which is near his home. Instead he comes in her direction and beats up Russell and Hawthorne for abusing his mother.

Everyone arrives at the park at the same time. They join forces and find the money in a suitcase under palm trees that cross in the form of a big W. But when they dig it up, Culpepper takes it from them. When they notice he's not headed for the police station, but is fleeing to Mexico, they give chase. The men catch him on the fire escape of an abandoned building. The suitcase opens and the money scatters among the spectators below. The fire escape crumbles and they all clutch a fireman's ladder, which sways under their great weight. They are all flung into the air. They all end up in the hospital, in bandages and casts. Yet when Mrs. Marcus slips on a banana peel, they all laugh.

It took producer-director Stanley Kramer three years from the time he bought William Rose's 10-page story outline and a then-astronomical $9.4 million to bring his all-star madcap comedy to the screen—in glorious color, 70 mm, and Cinerama. It was, Kramer still claims, the most difficult film he ever made. He even had to shoot in the Mohave Desert in the dead of summer, the only time his comedians could juggle their television and nightclub engagements. (The then-rare multiple-story-line structure meant the comics had to be available only when their scenes were being shot.) So Kramer had no intention of releasing his film without adequate fanfare. Throughout production, his publicists kept the press informed about happenings on the set—they even paraded three female extras in front of photographers after their legs had accidentally been grazed by bullets fired by a trigger-happy security guard during a fight. And between the time filming was completed and the picture was released to the public, in mid-November, rarely did a day go by without press releases to whet the public's appetite. Way back in May, chief publicist Al Horwits helped coordinate a Hollywood Friars Club "Mad Mad Mad Mad World" dinner to honor stars Milton Berle, Phil Silvers, and Buddy Hackett. There would be many more events to help publicize the film, including the importation of the international press to Hollywood in early November—flown in at a cost of $400,000 to Kramer and United Artists—to see the film, interview the stars, and be wined and dined. Meanwhile Kramer personally wrote an article about the making of his picture that appeared in newspapers, including the *New York Times*. Kramer wanted the public to believe that *It's a Mad Mad Mad Mad World* was unique—"a comedy to end all comedies"—and it helped that it would have its Hollywood premiere in the newly built Cinerama Theater on Sunset Boulevard and open in New York as the first picture in the refurbished New Warner Cinerama Theater on Broadway. On November 17, 1963, the day before it opened for the public in New York, there was a much-publicized, gala charity premiere benefit at the Cinerama Theater for the Kennedy Child Study Center in New York and the Joseph P. Kennedy Jr. Institute of Washington. In addition to the stars in attendance, most of President Kennedy's family was there, including his mother, sisters, brothers-in-law, sisters-in-law, and brothers Bobby and Ted. This would be the last happy gathering of the Kennedy clan for some time. John Kennedy would be assassinated in Dallas just five days later, an act that put a damper on *It's a Mad Mad Mad Mad World*'s opening week—although it would be a smash hit—and gave credence to the film's title.

Originally Kramer wanted to title his first comedy "Something a Little Less Serious" but it turned out a great

The eight travelers who know where the money is hidden—played by (left to right) *Edie Adams, Sid Caesar, Jonathan Winters, Dorothy Provine, Ethel Merman, Milton Berle, Mickey Rooney, and Buddy Hackett—can't agree how they should divide it.*

deal less serious than earlier films he had produced and directed, *The Defiant Ones* (1958), about black-white relations, *On the Beach* (1959), in which everyone on earth is wiped out by nuclear fallout, *Inherit the Wind* (1960), about the Scopes trial, and *Judgment at Nuremberg* (1961), in which German war criminals stand trial, and earlier films he had produced only, *Champion* (1949), *Home of the Brave* (1950), *The Men* (1951), *The Sniper* (1952), *High Noon* (1952), *The Wild One* (1954), and *The Caine Mutiny* (1954). It's no longer fashionable for serious critics to appreciate Kramer's successful "message" films, which have been termed "*uncontroversial* controversial films." But, except for the Edward Dmytryk–directed *The Sniper,* which is so confused that it comes across as reactionary, and Dmytryk's *The Caine Mutiny,* which is too afraid to offend the Navy, I admire his work. One can accuse Kramer of not going far enough on the issues (he never attacks specific targets), but he certainly went further than any other Hollywood directors during the "liberal" fifties in decrying injustice, bigotry, and nuclear proliferation. (It's not surprising that his films have long been popular in Russia.) His films may not be politically radical, but they were sincerely made (by one of the nicest men in Hollywood) and truthfully reflected his ideas and politics—which is more than can be said about other filmmakers of the era

who didn't even attempt to incorporate personal politics into their films.

Kramer's serious films always tell us, optimistically, that despite the prejudice, selfishness, and callousness on the part of some people in our troubled world, most people are good and humanistic, and that individuals have value. That's why I find it strange that Kramer's one comedy makes a mockery of humanity. The men and women who seek out the $350,000 in stolen money are stupid, loud, vulgar, mean, corrupt, shameless, and greedy (it's ironic that U.A. would make so much money from a film that shows how low people will go in pursuit of the buck). They are thoroughly repellent, the types you wouldn't mind being wiped out in *On the Beach.* In writing about the film, Pauline Kael quoted J. B. Priestley: "There is not a glimmer of affection for anybody or anything." Kramer may love his actors but he despises the "average Joes" they play—typical people riding down a highway. For a few minutes, we feel sympathy for Spencer Tracy's long-dedicated, poorly rewarded police captain, T. G. Culpepper, who wants the money to retire in Mexico, and for Dorothy Provine's long-suffering Emmeline Finch, who wants the money to escape her insufferable mother, Ethel Merman's Mrs. Marcus, and her ineffectual husband, Berle's J. Russell Finch, but they too end up acting like jerks (he's like a cowardly fox that has raided the henhouse; she wants the money to join a convent!). We miss a sympathetic character to root for, someone who has a noble purpose for acquiring the money (to save an orphanage? to buy groceries for the workers who were laid off after Jimmy Durante's Smiler Grogan robbed the tuna factory?), or who we know will regain his scruples once he finds the money. With such a person, the other schnooks could even be worse than they are. The only way Kramer could have gotten away with no good guys was to have given Jack Benny a lead role, instead of just a cameo (a highlight of the film). In movie and television history (with the possible exception of Dabney Coleman's Buffalo Bill TV character), the Benny character is the only one who has made egotism and avarice endearing. Wouldn't it have been wonderful to have watched Benny, who will do *anything* for a dime, match wits with Milton Berle, Phil Silvers, and Jonathan Winters for the money?

Kramer defended his evil world by saying, "Comedy is cruel; it is an attack on society." Perhaps he was referring to Chaplin's comedies, prominent among the many early slapstick comedies he wanted to remind viewers of. It's true that the classic slapstick comedies—of Chaplin, Keaton, Lloyd, Langdon, Laurel and Hardy, etc.—contained moments of cruelty and destruction. But such scenes were usually balanced by genuinely sweet or sentimental moments, and brief instances when our heroes (innocents) emerged triumphant in the cruel world. Those classics had heart. No one got hurt. When property was destroyed it was easy for us to take because it either belonged to our resilient heroes or, in the Laurel and Hardy films, to those bullies and buffoons who had already destroyed the heroes' property. Rarely did innocent bystanders have anything worse happen to them than get pies in their faces. It's one thing to watch Phil Silvers's Otto Meyer sink with *his* convertible into a deep stream—this is funny—but it's disturbing to watch Winters's Lennie Pike obliterate the garage owned by well-meaning Irwin and Ray, Sid Caesar and Edie Adams's Melville and Monica Crump destroy the hardware store basement, and passing cars being struck or forced off the road. I'm just thankful there's no scene with a car knocking over a poor street vendor's fruit stand— an obligatory bit in most contemporary comedies. I agree with Dwight MacDonald's 1965 assessment in *On Movies:*

> A comparison of the old silent comedies with *Mad World* is interesting. . . . They presented not people but abstractions from people whose physical catastrophes were no more distressing to the spectator than the pulverizations and the rebirths of animals in movie cartoons, since this is a magical world where nobody *really* gets hurt. But in Mr. Kramer's imitation, the old magical world has vanished: these comedians are flesh and blood and their sufferings are subject to the laws of the real world. The result is not amusing. An old man dying by the roadside after an automobile accident is not funny even if he is Jimmy Durante and even if we get many close-ups of his contorted face sweating with pain. A poor couple's pickup truck hurtling down the hillside out of control while the driver and his wife cling on desperately and their modest household goods spill out is not funny either, even if they are Negroes. A young married

couple trapped in the burning cellar of a hardware store is not funny even if a stack of cans of paint is about to catch fire and incinerate them and even if they are named Sid Caesar and Edie Adams.

I also agree with MacDonald that most of the stars are too old to be doing slapstick (even their stuntmen look too old). Watching the obviously ill Spencer Tracy (or his double) running up and down stairs and sliding down a high wire into a glass window makes me cringe. MacDonald: "There's something depressing about seeing Tracy, Durante, Berle, Ethel Merman and other aging, or aged, stars—Mickey Rooney has gone from adolescence to puffy middle age with no transition—so wrinkled and flabby, trying to cavort around like Keystone Kops; in the Sennett era, they who got slapsticked were younger."

It's odd that for a comedy meant to be a throwback to the slapstick era, Kramer would cast stand-up comics and television performers as his leads, rather than comics who specialized in physical comedy. Kramer claimed that his film was as universal as the silents because one could turn off the sound and still know what's going on. That's maybe the case, but if you leave on the sound, there's an awful— and I mean awful—lot of chatter. William Rose (who did a better job scripting the 1953 British car-race comedy *Genevieve*) and wife Tania Rose merely wrote three or four basic bits of dialogue and they are repeated throughout the picture in different locations. Worse, before anybody does anything, such as drive faster or from one place to another, Rose has them announce what they're going to do. This film is filled with superfluous dialogue. It's actually used to camouflage the uninspired sight gags. There are no visuals so spectacular that you are awestruck by the filmmakers' imaginations or technical proficiency. There is no rhythm to any of the slapstick bits, none of the

Spencer Tracy as T. G. Culpepper, his next to last film role, in the third of four films he'd make for Stanley Kramer.

intricate pacing, slightly escalating repetitiveness or build to a big-laugh payoff that distinguished the gags in slapstick classics. There's nothing more elaborate than the finale in which all the men swing high in the air on a firemen's ladder (here the stuntmen earned their money)—and, unfortunately, once they're up there, no one knows what to do with them.

In fact, the only scene in which the comedy seems to have been thought out carefully, where there is action and reaction, is the bumbling give-and-take scrap between Berle's Russell Finch and Terry-Thomas's Algernon Hawthorne. It's a down-and-dirty fight, with the two opponents almost taking turns in their attempts to harm each other (as Oliver Hardy did with his opponents) and, because they are such terrible fighters, harming themselves instead. I particularly like when Hawthorne is lying on his stomach and Russell attempts to kick sand in his face only to stub his toe on a hidden rock, when Russell hurls himself head-first at Hawthorne's stomach but misses and disappears over a cliff, and when the unsportsmanlike Hawthorne stomps on Russell's hands when he tries to pull himself back over the ledge. The best moment comes later, when the two desperate men each let loose with roundhouse punches and their fists collide. Other than when back-seat driver Mrs. Marcus needlessly shoves Hawthorne in the back so hard that he drives off the road, and the first time the runaway plane zooms within inches of the airport tower, there really are no funny visual moments. That's a shame, especially since many contemporary viewers, whom you can't convince to see silent films, assume this film represents slapstick comedies of the silent era.

It's a Mad Mad Mad Mad World is a disappointing, wrongly conceived film—although its many cultists would disagree—but it's by no means a total disaster. Despite all my own objections, I've sat through it several times over the years, in Cinerama and less interesting forms, and laughed pretty much during a couple of viewings. I can even enjoy Ethel Merman's screaming Mrs. Marcus. She was funnier when she married Ernest Borgnine, but she was a good sport to play such a character. Though I think the wrong types of comedians were cast, I'm glad, for posterity's sake, that so many great comics were brought together in one film. For instance, you'll treasure the two-shot at the beginning of the film of Berle and Caesar, the first comic stars of television. And it's fun seeing Phil Silvers do a variation on Sergeant Bilko. And Jonathan

In the funniest scene, J. Russell Finch (right) *and Algernon Hawthorne can no longer stand each other's company.*

Dingy and Benji in the high-flying slapstick finale.

Winters's he-man complaining about his mode of transportation: "But this is a girl's bike. This is for a little girl . . ." And I'm glad Kramer brought in Edie Adams, not only because she's a fine comedienne but also because she represents her late husband Ernie Kovacs, another of TV's comic innovators. Other performers—William Demarest, Paul Ford, Andy Devine et al.—make welcome appearances. Dorothy Provine was a strange choice for a wild comedy—she was best known for dancing the Charleston on TV's *The Roaring Twenties*—but she might have been funny if she had been allowed to do anything of consequence, because she is a funny heroine in Howard Morris's often-hilarious *Mad World* offshoot, *Who's Minding the Mint?* (1963), also with Milton Berle. Dick Shawn was a smart choice to play a totally whacked-out Sylvester Marcus, but after a few minutes Sylvester acts no more loony than anyone else. The only cast members I really object to are Buddy Hackett and Mickey Rooney, who should have been replaced by, if not Jack Benny, two much zanier performers. For countless years I've been hearing Hackett is hilarious in his uncensored Las Vegas comedy act. Well, I've never seen Hackett's Vegas act, and I've never seen him be hilarious. I've always liked Mickey Rooney, but though his name invariably makes moviegoers smile (as does Mickey Mouse), he has never been particularly funny. Comedy is not his strong suit. Weak on their own, there's no way Hackett and Rooney can be a funny comedy team. If you doubt this, then try to sit through *Everything's Ducky* (1961).

If this picture has a straight man—and it should have had several—it is Spencer Tracy. His performance is no more than adequate (there are times he is on and other times when he is shaky) but it doesn't matter: You'll feel tremendous warmth toward this great actor, knowing he was giving it his all despite failing health. In a 1967 issue of *Life,* Kramer wrote a lovely tribute to his recently departed friend. He recalled:

> During the filming of *Mad World* with all the comedians, I think Spencer Tracy was in poorer health than I [believed]: he had bad color and no stamina whatever. But then, even though this lack of energy showed, I think he had his best time ever during the making of a film. The comedians worshiped him. Never before or since has a king had a court full of jesters who strove only to entertain him so that his majesty might say, "That was funny," or just laugh or smile. Milton Berle, Jonathan Winters, Buddy Hackett, Phil Silvers, Mickey Rooney—even the silent Caesar—crowded about him and vied for his affection. They had it. And he talked about them to the very last; he loved them all.

It's a Mad Mad Mad Mad World now exists only in 35 mm and at 154 minutes. All the Cinerama prints were destroyed, but every few years a "Mad World Committee" headed by Eric Federing launches a campaign to have the film rereleased in 70 mm with the missing footage restored. According to Federing, the missing 38 minutes consist of a dance sequence featuring the voices of the Shirelles (but could this be the commercial jingle the Shirelles sing in the existing print?), media "news bulletins" about the race for the money, and 16 minutes of intermission music that is included on the sound track. I think the film is too long as it is, but certainly hope that the film's devoted cult following gets the opportunity to see the full picture. And while we're at it: How about bringing back Cinerama . . .

Liquid Sky

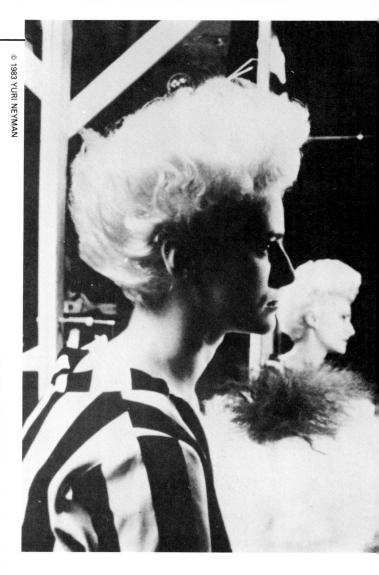

1983   Color   CineVista release of a Z-Films production
Director: Slava Tsukerman
Producer: Slava Tsukerman
Screenplay: Slava Tsukerman, Anne Carlisle, and Nina V. Kerova
Cinematography: Yuri Neyman
Special Effects: Yuri Neyman
Music: Slava Tsukerman, Brenda I. Hutchinson, and Clive Smith
Editor: Sharyn Leslie Ross
Running Time: 112 minutes

Cast: Carlisle (Margaret and Jimmy), Paula E. Sheppard (Adrian), Susan Doukas (Sylvia), Otto von Wernherr (Johann), Bob Brady (Owen), Elaine C. Grove (Katherine), Stanley Knap (Paul), Jack Adalist (Vincent), Lloyd Ziff (Lester), Sara Carlisle (Nellie), Kerova (designer).

Synopsis: A plate-sized alien saucer lands on the roof of a building on New York's Lower East Side, above the terrace and neon-lit penthouse of Margaret, a "hot" New Wave model. It's night so Margaret's at a downtown dance club, her blonde hair brushed straight up and her face painted in Kabuki style. Her weird, androgynous look makes her fit in with the New Wave–punk crowd. Gay male model Jimmy wants to buy heroin from Adrian, Margaret's mean lesbian lover, but he's broke and she doesn't give credit on drug deals. He resents Margaret having so much success, when he looks like her. He plans to be present at the photo shoot the next night at Margaret's apartment.

Promising her cocaine, a soap actor accompanies the perpetually dazed Margaret to her apartment. He shoves pills down her throat and beats and rapes her. This is witnessed by the alien in the saucer.

Johann, a German scientist, lands in New York. He uses a telescope on the Empire State Building and a homing device to track down the location of the alien ship on Margaret's roof.

Paul, a rich junkie, buys heroin from Adrian. He is attracted to Margaret. She is repulsed by him. She is annoyed when he asks her sexual preference. She says she doesn't think there is sexual differentiation. Both men and women treat her badly.

Johann tells Owen, an acting teacher, that aliens have been discovered in places where there are large amounts of heroin. They kill people who are having sexual orgasms because at that point the brain secretes a heroin-like substance. Owen isn't interested.

Johann doesn't know that Owen was Margaret's former teacher and lover. Owen visits Margaret. She resents that he wants her to dress and behave like a sweet housewife. She doesn't want to be anyone's pet or victim. "My cunt has teeth," she says.

Sylvia, a TV producer, is attracted to stranger Johann. She invites him into her apartment for a Chinese shrimp dinner. She lives across the street from Margaret, so he can keep watch on her apartment through his telescope.

Owen seduces Margaret. When he orgasms, the alien saps the heroin-like substance from his brain and kills him. Margaret doesn't know what happened. Sylvia and Johann watch Margaret and Adrian hide the body in a box. Sylvia doesn't believe that an alien was responsible.

Later Paul forces sex on Margaret. He is killed, too. Margaret is sure she has the power to kill anyone she has sex with. The pretentious camera crew arrives for the photo session and interview. Jimmy keeps insulting Margaret. While cameras flash she brings him to orgasm through fellatio. He disintegrates. Adrian makes love to Margaret to prove she wasn't responsible for Jimmy's disappearance. She also disintegrates. Margaret brings the soap star who raped her back to her apartment. She makes love to him. He disintegrates. Crazed, she steps onto the terrace, asking her imaginary "lover" to take her away. Johann enters and tells her about the aliens. She stabs him in the back. She climbs onto the roof to get close to the ship as it takes off. Sylvia and Kathy, Paul's wife, enter. They see Margaret above, in a stream of light from the ship. She vanishes.

Liquid Sky premiered in April 1983, exactly 10 years after Slava Tsukerman and his wife and collaborator Nina Kerova left Russia. The Moscow-born Tsukerman began directing films there in 1958. Having studied quantum mechanics, mathematics, and physics, he chose to make science-related documentaries and shorts (some animated) because they came under less government scrutiny than features. His best-known work, the fictional *Night of Decision* (1972), with themes he'd repeat in *Liquid Sky*, won an award at the Montreal Film Festival but, being about free will and determinism, was banned in the Soviet Union. In 1973, Tsukerman and Kerova, who'd married in 1968, were allowed to emigrate to Jerusalem. Tsukerman made documentaries for Israeli television, including the prize-winning *The Russians of Jerusalem*. But he wanted to make feature films and wrote a script about an American girl and Russian boy who fall in love in Israel. In 1976, he came to New York to secure financing. He found none, but he and Kerova decided to stay. He supported himself by writing for Russian-language newspapers; in his spare time he wrote scripts. For his screenplay *Sweet 16*, a science fiction feature for which he was promised financial backing, Tsukerman immersed himself in New York's decadent youth culture. Among those who auditioned for the film was Anne Carlisle, a student of painting at the School

Tsukerman said that he was the one who came up with the idea that a UFO "would find this [avant-garde] scene attractive." This undoubtedly stems from his own status in New York as an alien. "I had files on the decadence of New York, the drugs, everything. . . . I was interested in that all the time."

At the same time, however, the director wanted to make "an unrealistic film, not a documentary." "I wanted to show these people as educated, not just a bunch of weirdos. I wanted to show people living their lives as theatre about civilization."

[This] approach coincided with aspects of Carlisle's own life, which involved role-playing experimentation and artistic activities on the cutting edge of the cultural scene. Filming took on an aspect of living theatre for her, in that much of the pic was lensed in her apartment, which she felt the need to move out of after production was completed.

The picture's $500,000 budget was provided by Robert Field, a Pennsylvania real estate developer. After playing at the Montreal Film Festival and L.A.'s Filmex, it was picked up for distribution by CineVista, a small New York company. A bizarre blend of science fiction, social satire, and the underground-experimental film, *Liquid Sky* had all the elements to make it an ideal midnight movie: weird costumes, hair, and makeup; pulsating music (played on the Fairlight Computer Musical Instrument at New York's Public Access Synthesizer Studio); off-the-wall scenic design (Margaret's garish penthouse is lit by neon signs on the walls); special effects; a story involving sex and drugs; and a nonconformist lead character in the throes of an identity crisis. However, CineVista wisely chose to distribute it as a regular feature, and let it become a midnight movie later. It did poorly in its initial run in L.A. because its advertising was aimed at the youth music audience, but later advertising was directed toward older, more serious filmgoers and it became a modern commercial success in New York, Boston, and L.A., in a second run. It became the rare non–midnight movie to become an *instant* cult favorite. (Word-of-mouth was buoyed by the unusually quick release of the *Liquid Sky* video.) It immediately attracted a repeat audience, particularly at the Waverly in New York's Greenwich Village—ironically, its most devoted fans were from the specific New Wave–punk subculture that is mercilessly ridiculed in the picture.

Although the New Wave–punk scene is observed in the film by both alien astrophysicist Johann, a German, and the alien from outer space, and the film was directed by a Russian émigré who researched this scene, Tsukerman told Rickey that "I never thought for a second that it's a film seen through foreigners' eyes." While I doubt Tsukerman understood his film more than his befuddled viewers—the two films he likened it to were *Barry Lyndon* (1975) and *Raging Bull* (1980)!—what he told Rickey makes sense *if* what he wanted to do in his film was present a real subculture that is as alien to other Americans (even

of Visual Arts, an aspiring model (I believe), actress, and filmmaker (she'd made a 50-minute Super-8 film called *Fish*), and a member of the avant-garde club scene. Tsukerman told Carrie Rickey of the *Village Voice:*

> "When [Anne Carlisle] read the screenplay, she told me, 'It's the original new wave movie.' So I asked her, 'What is this *new wave?*' And the first time I went to a club and saw dancing like [robots], I thought, this would look great to an alien.
>
> "[Nina and I discovered that] new wave is a good mirror of American civilization; it's a performance, a compendium of culture. Instead of suppressing anything, new wavers exaggerate the conflicts of society, exposing the contradictions."

While Tsukerman waited for the money to begin shooting *Sweet 16,* Kerova and Carlisle worked on a separate script "about," Tsukerman told Rickey, "the crisis in relationships between the sexes." When *Sweet 16* fell through, Tsukerman didn't want to lose all the New Wave actors hanging around, so he took his ideas from his aborted film and teamed with the two women to write *Liquid Sky,* "incorporat[ing] their ideas about women's position and spen[ding] a lot of time arguing and educating each other." According to an interview in *Variety* (August 30, 1983):

Margaret and her lover-roommate Adrian stand on their patio. Behind them is the syringe-like Empire State Building.

those who live in or near New York's Lower East Side) as it would be to foreigners. The point Tsukerman (rather than Carlisle and Kerova) wanted to make is that New Wavers who use hard drugs and have sex without worrying about transmittable diseases are on a death trip. Characters court death: Adrian makes love to Owen's corpse; asked by his mother if he wants a ride uptown, Jimmy says ominously, "I'm going *down.*" These hedonists so want to achieve sensual euphoria (the film's title is junkie slang for heroin ecstasy) that they overlook the risks involved ("I don't want to think about tomorrow," states Adrian); they're smart people who have stopped thinking. It's as Owen tells Johann: "I don't think your punks need help from the outside to kill themselves." The alien only hastens their inevitable early deaths, killing both punks and those who prey on punks (whom they don't respect) for drugs and/or sex. That this alien absorbs a heroin-like substance that is created in the brain at the moment of orgasm is indication that Tsukerman believes (1) that sex is as destructive as shooting heroin ("Kill me, baby," Adrian tells Margaret as she forces her to have sex) and (2) that so much dangerous sex taking place proves supposedly smart people are thinking with their sexual organs rather than their brains.

The alien serves as avenging angel for Margaret, killing all those who sexually use and physically abuse her, and finally becomes her *deus ex machina,* rescuing and liberating her from her trapped, hopeless existence. We can deduce what happened to Margaret in her past. Years ago Margaret rebelled against her traditional upbringing and, asserting her independence, came to New York to make it as an actress and model. She mingled with those on the fringes of respectability, including artists and sixties' protesters (like Owen), and was disappointed to discover that even among these "enlightened" people, she was still expected to act in a certain way. She tells ex-lover and teacher Owen: "The way you want me to dress and behave is as sweet housewife, the slave of her husband's will." She left Owen and, still desperate for freedom, ventured into the more extreme New Wave–punk life-style. Then, without realizing it, she again was molded (or "taught," as she says contemptuously) to fit the norm. Not only did she become like everyone else in the scene—she took drugs, took a lesbian lover, featured an androgynous look, became a "mean bitch"—she actually became the symbol of the life-style, the model *Midnight Magazine* wanted on its cover. She became an Edie Sedgwick figure, bored and drugged out of her mind, surrounded by an uncaring, pretentious art crowd (including Kerova's insufferable designer), which she knows will drop her as soon as her star fades. What distinguishes Margaret from the vile people she associates with—Paula Sheppard's Adrian is as cruel and disgusting as the characters she played for John Waters; jealous Jimmy tries to bring Margaret down to his low level—is that she realizes that it all gone wrong. New Wavers may have fled the roles that society set up for them, but they have fallen into equally confining, impersonal roles; although they believe their every act is an expression of free will, they have fallen into traps as deep as those in the outside world. (Similarly, in *Night of Decision,* a scientist is told by his lookalike alter ego that it doesn't matter that he has freedom of choice because the results are predetermined.)

Margaret figures out that being *fashionable* is just as restrictive as being *traditional,* that being androgynous eradicates one's identity, that men at all levels of society want to demean and control women, and that women who hate women, as does Adrian, can be just as destructive to her as men who hate women. (I assume the last two themes were introduced by Carlisle and Kerova.) Even in her perpetual daze, she remembers her once-upon-a-time search for freedom and, becoming a worthy heroine, makes feeble attempts to finally achieve individuality (the reason annoyed Adrian calls her "an uptight WASP cunt from Connecticut"): She rejects heroin, she rejects men, she stops being a passive victim to men or women. The sadistic subculture almost destroyed her, so finally, with the help of the alien, she attempts to destroy it. Many viewers believe that Margaret is killed when she disappears in a wave of saucer light in the intentionally ambiguous finale (Rickey writes that "Margaret is the mirror of consumer culture whose only way out is to be consumed"), but, since the alien only kills those who have orgasms and Margaret hasn't had one the entire film, I hope she has simply been whisked away to an alternate universe where she can be herself yet automatically be different from all those around her—this is the ultimate freedom. But it's doubtful that Tsukerman would give Margaret an ending as optimistic as Steven Spielberg gave Richard Dreyfuss's dreamer in *Close Encounters of the Third Kind* (1977); Rickey writes:

> Of the film's denouement, which invokes a kind of amazing UFO grace, Tsukerman confides, "Oh, this cult of outer space. People love so much films about aliens because they believe the world is so terrible that they must have the illusion it's better out there. It's the same way with the American left, they have illusions that there are better countries. Me? I have no illusions. I have no disillusions." In *Liquid Sky,* too much freedom has a lot in common with no freedom at all.

Besides the interesting themes, there is much appealing in the film. Carlisle is superb. Yuri Neyman's cinematography and special effects are quite impressive. I particularly like the other-worldly shots of the New York skyline, with the Empire State Building spire looking like a giant syringe. Tsukerman's direction is imaginative and the Tsukerman-Carlisle-Kerova script is witty and, in the case of Margaret's final speech, poignant. The amusing scenes with Johann will delight all fans of sci-fi and horror movies. (What if Johann rather than Donald Pleasence's Dr. Loomis had tracked down Michael in 1978's *Halloween?*) He's a completely incompetent hero. Instead of going to author-

Margaret is treated with hostility at her photo session and interview.

ities with his tale of heroin-seeking alien murderers, he provides vital information only to Owen, who turns out to be a college acting teacher. He allows several deaths to occur in Margaret's penthouse because he's spending time with seductive "Do-you-have-a-laser-gun-in-your-pocket?" Sylvia (one of the film's funniest characters). He can't convince anyone he's telling the truth about the aliens: Owen brushes him off, thinking the tiny saucer is a child's toy; Sylvia wants Johann to stop his snooping, have shrimp with him, and make love; Adrian tells him to "Fuck off!"; Margaret stabs him in the back (as Jamie Lee Curtis's imperiled Laurie would have done if *he'*d run into the house at the end of *Halloween*). Both times this lunkhead warns someone about danger, he suddenly acts panicky, giving the impression he's crazy and doesn't know what he's talking about. Johann provides many laughs.

Although I think the film wears out long before the alien departs, I do enjoy *Liquid Sky.* But it's not that easy to recommend. For one thing, everyone who has sex in it is destroyed, a conservative story point for a film geared for the counterculture. Also, despite the abundance of humor, it's a mean film, with ugly characters, ugly language, and ugly images. In fact, one could argue that the filmmakers wouldn't have allowed Margaret a happy ending because they so brutalize her during the course of the picture. It becomes disturbing watching Margaret repeatedly slapped in the face by various men, even if Carlisle's also playing one of them, Jimmy.

I don't fully understand why Margaret and Jimmy are played by the same person (does alter ego Jimmy represent Margaret's sorry future if she doesn't leave the scene?), but Carlisle—the main reason to see *Liquid Sky*—is fascinating as both characters. They are each so believable, and so convincingly made up and attired, that it takes a while before new viewers realize that Carlisle is playing both parts. Carlisle obviously knows these characters well. Surely she identified with Margaret; probably she identified with aspects of Jimmy as well. I like the way she slowly reveals the inner strength of Margaret beneath the passive-female exterior and the vulnerability (his one redeeming feature) beneath Jimmy's tough-male exterior. This makes me think that if you put Margaret and Jimmy together, you get Anne Carlisle.

Martin

1978   Color   Libra release of a Laurel film
Director: George A. Romero
Producer: Richard P. Rubenstein
Screenplay: George A. Romero
Cinematography: Michael Gornick
Special Effects and Makeup: Tom Savini
Music: Donald Rubenstein
Editor: George A. Romero
Running Time: 95 minutes

Cast: John Amplas (Martin), Lincoln Maazel (Tata Cuda), Christine Forrest (Christina), Elyane Nadeau (Abby Santini), Savini (Arthur), Sarah Venable (housewife victim), Fran Middleton (train victim), Al Levitsky (Lewis), Romero (Father Howard), James Roy (deacon), J. Clifford Forrest, Jr. (Father Zulemas), Richard Rubenstein (housewife victim's husband), Gornick (voice of talk show host).

Synopsis: Martin, who looks about 20, takes a train from Indianapolis to New York. At night, he breaks into a sleeping car and injects a young woman with sodium pentothal. He tells her not to struggle or be upset because she won't feel pain. When she is asleep, he makes love to her and slits her wrist with a razor blade so he can drink her blood. She dies.

He is met in Pittsburgh by an elderly, hostile cousin, Tata Cuda. They take a train to Braddock, a dying industrial suburb. Despite Martin's denials, Cuda accuses Martin of being an 84-year-old vampire from the old country. He has taken Martin in because he's family, but says: "First I will save your soul. Then I will destroy you." Cuda puts garlic on the doors and holds up a cross when he fears Martin is attacking him—Martin eats the garlic and pulls away the cross, telling the frightened man "there is no magic." Cuda tells Martin that he can come and go but he will destroy him if he kills anyone in Braddock. He orders Martin to stay away from his granddaughter Christina, who lives in the house, but she befriends him. She is the only person Martin talks to. She thinks Cuda and others in the family have driven Martin to insanity. She hopes to leave Braddock with her boyfriend, Arthur, even though he treats her badly. She gets Martin a phone. He repeatedly calls a radio talk show and tells what it's like to be a vampire. He is known as the "Count" to all the listeners. The patronizing host thinks he's crazy.

Martin works in Cuda's grocery store. He delivers packages. One customer, Mrs. Santini, is taken with Martin. She's a friendly young woman who is depressed because her husband is unfaithful. Martin senses she wants to have sex with him. But, he tells the talk show host, he has never had sex with an awake woman.

Martin travels outside Braddock to find victims. He follows a pretty woman home. When her husband is away, he sneaks in and discovers her with her lover, Lewis. He jabs them both with sodium pentothal. He drags Lewis from the house, kills him, and drains his blood. He makes love to the young, drugged woman, but lets her live. In his (real or fantasy) past, he drained blood from a young woman in a mansion and was chased by people carrying torches.

Cuda brings home Father Zulemas to perform an exorcism. Martin remembers in his (real or fantasy) past others trying to perform an exorcism—he fled then; he flees now. He frightens Cuda by wearing a cape and putting false fangs into his mouth.

Martin agrees to have sex with Mrs. Santini. They become lovers and, as he tells the talk show host, he doesn't have the same desire to attack women. Christina becomes infuriated when Cuda tells Arthur that insanity runs in their family so he shouldn't consider having children with her. She leaves with Arthur. She promises to write Martin, but she won't.

Martin tells the talk show host he's getting "shaky." He attacks two bums and drinks one's blood. He narrowly escapes from the police. The police chase him and end up clashing with some young thugs. All are killed.

Martin finds Mrs. Santini dead in her bathtub. She slit her wrists with a razor blade. Cuda hears of her death and is sure Martin killed her. He drives a stake through Martin's heart.

One of the strangest cinema vampires, Martin doesn't use his eyes to put his victims into a trance before drinking their blood. Instead he uses an injection to dull their senses.

The three pioneering vampire movies, F. W. Murnau's *Nosferatu* (1922), Tod Browning's *Dracula* (starring Bela Lugosi), and Carl Dreyer's *Vampyr* (1932), had enormous, lasting impact but they left much to say on their subject. Decade after decade, filmmakers worldwide would explore and often diverge from the vampire lore set forth in these classics and in nineteenth-century vampire literature such as John Polidari's 1819 story "The Vampyre," J. Sheridan Le Fanu's 1871 lesbian vampire novella, *Carmilla*, and Bram Stoker's 1897 novel, *Dracula*. And moviegoers would never tire of vampire films because they dealt with such intriguing themes as eternal life and, in some cases, eternal torment, the battle between good (Christians) and evil, sexual conquest/seduction and submission, death as sexual climax, moral decay, power, possession, sacrifice, loneliness, guilt, survival, and bloodlust.

An inordinate number of vampire films developed cult followings: Lambert Hillyer's *Dracula's Daughter* (1936); Terence Fisher's *Horror of Dracula* (1958), the first of Hammer's 15-year series starring Christopher Lee as Dracula and Peter Cushing as Van Helsing; Roger Vadim's *Blood and Roses* (1960); Antonio Margheriti's *La Danza Macabre* (1963), with Barbara Steele; Mario Bava's *Planet of the Vampires* (1965); Curtis Harrington's *Queen of Blood* (1966); Roman Polanski's spooky spoof, *The Fearless Vampire Killers* (1967); *Count Yorga, Vampire* (1970); *Jonathan, Vampire Sterben Nicht* (1970), from Germany; *House of Dark Shadows* (1970), adapted from the cult television soap; *Vampyros Lesbos* (1970), by Spain's Jess Franco; Roy Ward Baker's *The Vampire Lovers* (1970), with Ingrid Pitt (who often played vampires), and its equally sexy sequel, *Lust for a Vampire* (1971); Stephanie Rothman's *The Velvet Vampire* (1971); Harry Kumel's *Daughters of Darkness* (1971); Dan Curtis's hit television movies *The Night Stalker* (1971) and *The Night Strangler* (1972), its sequel; *Vampire Circus* (1972); *Countess Dracula* (1972), with Pitt; John Hough's *Twins of Evil* (1972); Bob Clark's *Deathdream* (1972); *Blacula* (1972); *Ganja and Hess* (1973); *Andy Warhol's Dracula* (1974); *Grave of the Vampire* (1974); Brian Clemens's *Captain Kronos: Vampire Hunter* (1974); Tobe Hooper's TV movie, *Salem's Lot* (1979); the comedy *Love at First Bite* (1979); Werner Herzog's *Nosferatu, the Vampire* (1979); *Thirst* (1979), from Australia; *The Hunger* (1983); *Vamp* (1986), for which I may be a one-person cult; *Near Dark* (1987); and *The Lost Boys* (1987). And *Martin*. Like *Daughters of Darkness*, it is a vampire film that may have no vampire! In fact, George Romero's offbeat tale goes out of its way to indicate that vampire-suspect Martin is just a disturbed young man who believes he is a vampire and acts accordingly. It challenges the vampire legend at every turn and even mocks the portrayal of vampires in vampire movies: Martin is fangless, has average strength, wanders around in the daylight, bites into garlic, grabs crosses, attends a church ceremony, eats food, urinates, has orgasms. But still we wonder. It doesn't prove anything when he is killed by a stake through the heart: A human or vampire would perish.

If Martin is not a monster then Romero's story is even more frightening . . . because it is possible. Surely the disturbed, alienated Martin fits the personality profile of numerous sexual psychopaths in history. In fact, according to Paul R. Gagne's book on Romero, *The Zombies That Ate Pittsburgh* (1987), when Romero conceived the Martin character he was partly inspired by a Los Angeles serial slasher-murderer who drank the blood of his victims. At first, Romero "didn't know whether I wanted my character to be a vampire or just think he was a vampire." He came to a decision when he cast the role of Martin. He chose not to pick the middle-aged actor he had in mind when he wrote the early drafts of his screenplay but selected 27-year-old John Amplas, whom he'd seen at the Pittsburgh Playhouse, in *Philemon,* as a Christian disciple who is persecuted by the Romans. Romero obviously reasoned that a younger, less mature Martin—Amplas looks about 20—would be less able to withstand harassment by the likes of Lincoln Maazel's imposing Tata Cuda, less resistant to those who work on his mind (including other family members who previously insisted he was a vampire), and more afraid of adults and sex. Gagne quotes Romero: "I had to decide what Martin was so I wouldn't get tripped up with contradictions when we were shooting the film, so I decided that he was *not* a real vampire, and that was what John and I were working with. Understand, though, the film is open to other interpretations."

In their book *Midnight Movies* (1983), J. Hoberman and Jonathan Rosenbaum point out that *Martin* can be seen

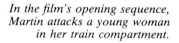

In the film's opening sequence, Martin attacks a young woman in her train compartment.

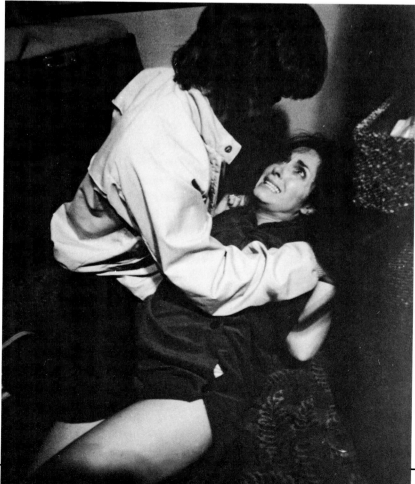

as a reworking of Gene Fowler, Jr.'s *I Was a Teenage Werewolf* (1957). In that film, high school student Michael Landon is constantly told by adults that he—a representative of all teenagers—is *bad,* just as Martin is constantly criticized by adults and reminded by Cuda and past family members that he is evil and "the family shame." Because of the negative reinforcement, Landon's teenager loses his head at times and becomes as violent as the adults expect him to be, giving into "animalistic"/inhuman impulses. Whereas adults have caused Martin to become someone so fiendish that he may as well be a vampire, Landon's teenager is literally turned into a monster by adults: Villain scientists inject him with a serum that gives him the appearance of a werewolf—interestingly, because of their instructions to him under hypnosis, it still takes a ringing sound to make him act as monstrously as these adults want him to. Vladimir Sokoloff's janitor, who speaks of werewolves in the Old World, is a benevolent version of Tata Cuda. *Martin* also recalls two Val Lewton classics. In *Cat People* (1942), Simone Simon's lonely young Serbian woman is either insane or intelligent enough to believe she is of a people who are cursed to be large, murderous cats if they dare make love—crazy or not, she soon kills as if she were a great cat. In Lewton's *Isle of the Dead* (1945), Ellen Drew's young Gypsy is so intimidated by superstitious Greek general Boris Karloff that she is almost convinced that she is a *vorvolaka* (a vampire-like creature) who is responsible for several deaths. I think *Martin* is equally linked to Brian De Palma's *Carrie* (1976), in which after years of being harangued by her religious fanatic mother,

Piper Laurie—who makes her feel wicked and shameful—and humiliated by her classmates, Sissy Spacek's troubled, lonely high school girl becomes the equivalent of a monster, unleashing her pent-up anger and (using telekinetic powers) committing mass murder.

We're inclined to feel as bad for Martin as we do for Carrie, because everyone treats him as subhuman, no one but *Christ*ina (perhaps because of her name) attempts to communicate with him, and Cuda gives him no chance to prove his innocence (he immediately warns Martin, "First I will save your soul, then I will destroy you"). We almost think it's admirable that Martin doesn't want to hurt the women he attacks and puts them to sleep with an injection. But at this stage in his life, he's really unsympathetic, like the Carrie in Stephen King's novel. He may not want to cause the women any pain—he begs them to stop struggling—but he chooses them to be his victims, attacks them when they're awake, rapes them when they're asleep and can't resist, opens their veins and drinks their blood, and leaves them dead. He has no sympathy for his victims. All he worries about (we can deduce from his calls to the radio talk show) is that people around him are crazy and that he will let his guard down and be caught. He is almost caught by police after slaying a derelict, and he feels no remorse that all the policemen and the young thugs he happens upon are killed during his escape. He acts sensitively to his lover, Mrs. Santini (Elyane Nadeau)—he even worries that he should have used a condom—but he admits being relieved when she dies. Cuda kills Martin for the wrong reasons but it's lucky for the world Cuda is crazy enough to do it—we should all want Martin dead. Someone who thinks he's a vampire and acts like a vampire is as bad as a vampire.

Martin marked George Romero's return to feature films after a five-year hiatus. He had burst onto the scene in 1968 with *Night of the Living Dead,* the low-budget, independently produced (by his Pittsburgh-based Latent Image), black-and-white exercise in terror that became a box-office blockbuster and one of the first and most successful midnight movies, and paved the way for the graphic horror cinema of the seventies and eighties. But the failure of his three subsequent films, *There's Always Vanilla* (1972), *Jack's Wife* (1973), and a *Living Dead* derivation, *The Crazies* (1973), caused Latent Image to go under. Romero quickly joined forces with producer Richard P. Rubenstein in the formation of Laurel Productions. Laurel stayed in the black by producing television sports documentaries, distributing foreign films, and publishing books. But Romero wanted to make movies. He and Rubenstein were able to get Pittsburgh businessmen Ron Rosen and Barney Guttman to put up $100,000 for a low-budget horror film. This wasn't enough to finance *Dawn of the Dead* (which eventually was made in 1979), but Romero and Rubenstein could afford to make *Martin* instead. It could be made on location in Braddock, an industrial suburb of Pittsburgh, and be shot in 16 mm, to be blown up to 35 mm. Originally it was intended that the entire film, not just the fantasy-like flashbacks, be in black and white. To keep to the small budget, Romero (doing a humorous turn as a priest who loves *The Exorcist*), Rubenstein (as a victim's husband), and Laurel cameraman Michael Gornick (as the

The religious Tata Cuda, who insists his nephew Martin is a vampire.

talk show host) would take small roles in the film. Friends and acquaintances filled out the semi-pro cast—Christine Forrest, who would play Martin's cousin Christina, would eventually marry Romero. Donald Rubenstein, the producer's brother, arranged the effective score. Tom Savini, whose work with Romero would catapult him to the top in the horror special effects makeup field and win him a cult of goreadorers, did double-duty work, playing Christina's inconsiderate boyfriend Arthur, and making all the bloody moments seem horrifyingly real.

Paul R. Gagne writes that Romero considers *Martin* his "most realized" picture, his "favorite" of his own films, and, "despite its failings," his "first real filmic success." *Martin* is a success, despite its minuscule budget and its faults. It has enough wit and sex to balance its shocking violence, if not its depressing tone. Amplas, Maazel, Nadeau, Sarah Venable (a Libra Films publicist who played Martin's housewife victim), and Romero come off best of the actors, but the entire picture is well cast—even the amateurs lend authenticity to the film. The choice of Braddock, Pennsylvania, as the film's major location was inspired. The Transylvania of the classic horror films is no more dying and decayed than this no-longer-thriving steel town: The mills have closed down, the church has burned down, shops have shut down; there are no new houses and no new cars; old cars fill automobile graveyards until they are crushed for scrap metal; married couples break apart, unmarried couples leave town in search of work and hope; the elderly carry on but there are few youngsters around; everything has a washed-out look.

The entire picture has style to burn, but Romero really shines during the two major attack sequences, in the tiny train compartment and in the large house. The second attack is a masterwork, not only by Martin (who uses amazing ingenuity) but by Romero, as well. It is, in fact, composed of several attacks by Martin on Venable's pretty housewife and her confused lover Lewis (Al Levitsky) and is set all over the house and in the yard. The housewife stays in the bedroom throughout, but Martin and the injured Lewis move from room to room, down corridors, in and out doors. At one point, the three characters are in different rooms, each holding a phone. The sequence begins with Martin breaking into the bedroom and surprising the naked couple on the bed. He is surprised and angry to see the housewife with a man, Lewis is jolted to see Martin because he assumes he's her husband, and she is terrified to see Martin because, as she tries to get across to Lewis, "I don't know him!" We understand how Lewis

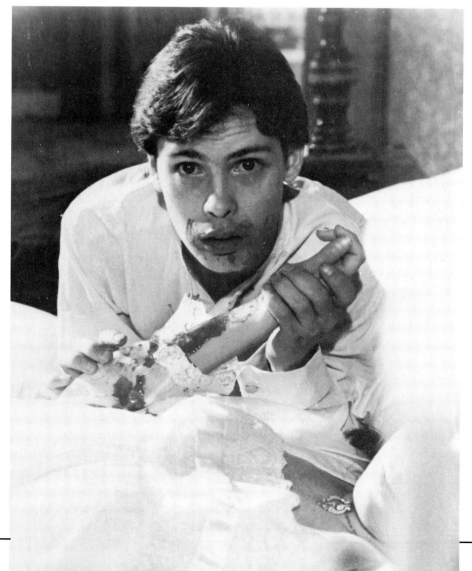

The younger Martin claims a victim in a sequence that is meant to be either a flashback or a fantasy.

A pretty housewife attempts to get away from Martin.

feels and how the housewife feels. Martin flies across the bed, jabs Lewis with the needle, and then quickly leaves the room, locking the door before the bigger Lewis attempts to grab him. It's the highlight of the film, a moment that is simultaneously amusing and chilling. But the rest of the sequence is not anti-climactic. (Am I correct in thinking Martin lets the housewife live?)

Most critics regard *Martin* as Romero's best film. However, I don't think it reaches the heights of *Night of the Living Dead*—even if that film no longer scares us. I wish the ending of *Martin* weren't so rushed and that there were another scene or two between the time Martin discovers Mrs. Santini's body floating in the bath and Cuda executes Martin. While I like the black-and-white sequences, I think Romero should have established that they are what Martin is thinking at the time. I think it's essential to establish that Martin considers these scenes his past, although we may conclude they are just his fantasies. If Martin isn't thinking these images at all then they are more misleading than they are enlightening. As mentioned, I think the attack in the train compartment is impressively shot, but it's an extremely unpleasant scene because it comes across as a prolonged rape. Romero was smart to have the pretty

woman (Fran Middleton) wear thick facial cream to deglamorize her, so viewers wouldn't be titillated and equate sex with rape, but the prop and make-up people weren't on the ball because the cream somehow vanishes early in the attack. It becomes increasingly upsetting as she becomes more terrified and helpless, as Martin strips the drugged woman, as he clutches her nude body, and as he slits open her wrist with a razor blade and drinks her blood, which results in his pleasure and her death. Romero should have turned out the lights.

Martin became a successful midnight movie in 1978, playing 11 months at New York's Waverly Theater. But it never received the attention of David Lynch's *Eraserhead* (1978), which was promoted more by Libra, their common distributor. Many viewers never realized it was directed by the man responsible for *Night of the Living Dead*. They stayed away, as did those who didn't realize it was a horror film—perhaps they feared it was a biography of Billy Martin or Martin Buber. Even today *Martin* remains relatively unknown, a restless sleeper (as are all vampires) that waits to be unearthed by horror fans looking not for buried coffins but buried, even less-than-full, treasures.

Miracle on 34th Street

1947 B&W 20th Century-Fox
Director: George Seaton
Producer: William Perlberg
Screenplay: George Seaton
From the story by Valentine Davies
Cinematography: Charles Clarke and Lloyd Ahern
Music: Cyril Mockridge
Editor: Robert Simpson
Running Time: 96 minutes

Cast: Maureen O'Hara (Doris Walker), John Payne (Fred Gailey), Edmund Gwenn (Kris Kringle), Natalie Wood (Susan Walker), Gene Lockhart (Judge Henry X. Harper), Jerome Cowan (District Attorney Thomas Mara), Porter Hall (Sawyer), Philip Tonge (Mr. Shellhammer), William Frawley (Charley), Alvin Greenman (Albert), James Seay (Dr. Pierce), Harry Antrim (R. H. Macy), Lela Bliss (Mrs. Shellhammer), Jack Albertson (postal worker), Thelma Ritter (pleased Macy's customer), Percy Helton (drunk Santa).

Synopsis: When her Santa Claus shows up drunk, Doris Walker of Macy's asks an elderly gentleman with long white whiskers to replace him in the Thanksgiving Day Parade. He then becomes Santa in Mr. Shellhammer's toy department. He sends parents to other stores, even Gimbel's, if Macy's doesn't have the best bargain on particular toys. Mothers compliment the store for "putting Christmas spirit over commercialism." Mr. Macy loves the new policy because it improves the store's image and, consequently, increases profits. Mr. Gimbel initiates the same policy in his store.

Doris, a divorcée, and her 7-year-old daughter, Susan, are befriended by their neighbor, promising lawyer Fred Gailey. He is disturbed by Doris's cynicism. She has taught Susan to believe only in reality and common sense. Susan doesn't believe in fairy tales, fantasies, or Santa Claus. Fred takes Susan to meet the new Macy's Santa. Susan is impressed by his real whiskers, his friendliness, and his ability to talk and sing with a little Dutch girl in her language. Doris asks him to tell her confused daughter that he's not really Santa. But he insists he is Kris Kringle. She worries that he's insane. Dr. Pierce, who runs the Long Island old-age home where Kris lives, assures her that he is harmless.

Kris and Susan become pals. He gets her to use her imagination. Hoping Kris will have the same influence on Doris, Fred invites him to share his apartment. Kris agrees because he considers Doris and Susan a test case. If he can't convince them to believe in him, then Christmas has lost its meaning. Susan confides in Kris that she wants a house like the one she has a picture of. If he can get it for her, she'll believe he's Santa. Kris pushes Fred to court Doris. They fall in love.

When the neurotic Mr. Sawyer, Macy's psychologist, depresses Albert, a kindly young Macy's worker, by attempting some amateur psychiatry, Kris bops him with his cane. Sawyer pretends to be badly hurt and insists that Kris be whisked to Bellevue. When Sawyer lies to Kris that Doris had agreed to send him to the asylum, Kris becomes so depressed he intentionally fails his sanity test and is committed. He learns the truth but can't get released. Fred defends Kris in a highly publicized trial. Worried about his career, Judge Henry X. Harper decides not to rule that there is no Santa Claus. Still he goes along with D.A. Thomas Mara that Fred must provide "authoritative" proof that Kris is Santa. All looks lost. Susan writes Kris a letter, using the courthouse address, saying she believes he is Santa. Doris adds that she believes him, too. Kris is cheered. A postal worker decides that the dead-letter office can get rid of thousands of letters addressed to Santa by sending them as well to Kris at the court. These letters are the needed proof, from an authoritative agency of the U.S. government, that Kris is *the* Santa Claus. Harper frees Kris. It's Christmas eve. Kris will be busy.

At a party the next day on Long Island, Susan doesn't get the present she wanted. She decides Kris isn't Santa. Doris, who now thinks like Fred, tells Susan to have faith even though it goes against common sense. Fred, Doris, and the sad Susan, who repeats, "I believe, I believe," drive home, using Kris's directions. Susan jumps out of the car when she sees the house from the picture. It's for sale. The confused Fred and Doris agree to buy it for Susan's sake. They will marry. They notice Kris's cane by the fireplace.

If a film discussion becomes too serious—for example, someone insists that the films of Jean-Marie Straub are "more obsessive" than those of Robert Bresson—mention *Miracle on 34th Street*, and watch tense faces soften, eyes water, and smiles form, as if these film combatants just had their childhood teddy bears returned. They may alibi that "*Miracle on 34th Street* is my child's favorite film" (how often I've heard this!) but in truth many of the toughest critics and most jaded film fanatics have a soft spot in their hearts for this picture they fell permanently in love with when they were youngsters themselves. Film history books ignore *Miracle on 34th Street* and many of us take it for granted (every year I'm surprised at its quality), but it's truly a wonderful film, for adults as well as children. And it's as vital to a happy Christmas season as *It's a Wonderful Life* (1946), *A Christmas Carol* (1951), and *The Bells of Saint Mary's* (1945), other yuletide treasures that have become cult favorites because of annual television broadcasts. (Though not on the high level of these films, 1942's *Holiday Inn*, 1954's *White Christmas*, and the 1983 sleeper *A Christmas Story* also have achieved cult status.) Is there anyone who can't use a *Miracle on 34th Street* fix every December 24th, when patience and money have run out buying overpriced presents in overcrowded stores, and it's impossible to recall the *meaning* of Christmas? I think not.

It's imperative to hear Edmund Gwenn's Kris Kringle rail against the commercialization of Christmas every year. And we mustn't miss these moments either: Kris telling the accessories store owner that Santa's reindeer in his window display are in wrong positions around the sled; Kris sending Thelma Ritter's shocked and pleased customer to a store that sells the fire engine her little boy wants; Kris cheering the little Dutch girl; the plastered Mrs. Shellhammer saying "Helloooo!" into the wrong end of the phone (twice!) and inviting Kris to stay in the spare room ("Why we'd love to have Santa Claus come and stay with us—I think it would be simply charming!"); competitors R. H. Macy and Bernard Gimbel shaking hands and, competing with each other, offering money and bargain rates to Kris so he can afford an X-ray machine for his friend Dr. Pierce; Kris teaching Natalie Wood's 7-year-old Susan how to use her imagination; Kris informing John Payne's Fred Gailey that he sleeps with his whiskers outside the covers; Kris picking bubble gum out of his beard after blowing too big a bubble; Kris bopping Porter Hall's twitching Mr. Sawyer on the head; the son and wife of Jerome Cowan's district attorney and the grandchildren and wife of Gene Lockhart's beautifully played Judge Henry X. Harper treating them with contempt for putting Santa Claus on trial; Harper saying "Overruled" and "Put them here on my desk"; Mr. Macy testifying under oath that he believes Kris is actually Santa Claus; Kris thanking the grateful Harper after the trial; Dr. Pierce walking unsteadily toward his new X-ray machine; Maureen O'Hara's Doris Walker, once a cynic ("You've got to be realistic and face facts"), refuting common sense ("There's got to be a way,

Brought by Fred to meet the new Macy's Santa, Susan is impressed that Kris's beard is real. Meanwhile a little boy in line grows impatient.

Albert, there's got to be!") and admitting to Susan, in front of Kris, that what she taught her was wrong ("You must believe in Mr. Kringle and keep right on doing it—you must have *faith* in him"); Susan racing around the dream house Kris promised her ("Mr. Kringle *is* Santa Claus!"); and Doris and Fred spotting Kris's cane by the empty house's fireplace.

This uplifting Christmas fable (titled *The Big Heart* in Great Britain), perhaps the only movie fantasy with no special effects, was scripted and directed by George Seaton, one-time radio "Lone Ranger" and one-time Marx Brothers writer. In his distinguished career, Seaton would be a three-time president of the Motion Picture Academy, president of the Screen Writers Guild, and vice-president of the Directors Guild; he would write and direct *The Country Girl* (1952), winning an Oscar for his screenplay adaptation of Clifford Odets's play, and the Ross Hunter blockbuster, *Airport* (1969), among many other film projects. But at the time, aside from *A Day at the Races* (1937), Seaton's only major previous credit was as screenwriter for the controversial religious drama *The Song of Bernadette* (1944). Oddly, one can find the roots of *Miracle on*

34th Street in Seaton's adaptation of Franz Werfil's novel. In *Miracle,* Gwenn's Kris Kringle firmly believes he is Santa Claus. Everyone in Kris's cynical world, but for innocent and impressionable children, either thinks he is lying or doubts his sanity (he is given Santa-ty tests, as the Marx Brothers would say). The highest (Supreme) court tries to condemn him for his beliefs, but ultimately the court legitimizes Kris, proclaiming him the one and only Santa, Saint Nicholas. In *Song,* Jennifer Jones's young French peasant girl, Bernadette Soubirous, firmly believes she had visions of the blessed virgin (in 1858). Everyone in her world, but for the ignorant peasants, either thinks she is lying or doubts her sanity (she is questioned by a psychiatrist). The Roman Catholic Church at first tries to discredit her, but ultimately legitimizes her, proclaiming her a saint. Both films are about *miracles*. Both films are about people who are out of the mainstream and have no power—a poor old man, a poor teenage girl—yet bravely stand by their astounding claims even though society threatens to punish them. And each film *preaches* that we must have faith instead of always relying on common sense. Having faith is tantamount to having "a suspension of disbelief" (a common fantasy and movie term) and is not only necessary if one is to believe in fantasies, fairy tales, legends, myths, and Santa Claus, but of course also is essential if one is to have religion. It would have been the logical step for Seaton to have followed *The Song of Bernadette* with a modern-day story in which society reacts to a man who claims to be Christ. But getting such a film off the ground would have been impossible—this was 30 years before *Oh, God!* (1977)—so Seaton settled for a safer protagonist, an old man who claims to be Santa Claus.

Valentine Davies first told Seaton of his idea for a Santa Claus story while they were vacationing on a Nevada ranch with their wives. Davies wanted his tale to be about the actual Santa Claus, but Seaton thought it would be better if it were about a man who only believes himself to be Santa Claus. (We'll never know who won out.) They spent 18 months working on Davies's original story and Seaton's screenplay adaptation. During this time, the competitive department stores were called Tracy's and Trimbell's. Armed with a 65-page treatment, Seaton went to New York and convinced Macy's and a more reluctant Gimbel's representative to allow their stores to be featured in the picture and even to agree to appearances by "Mr. Macy" and "Mr. Gimbel," even though they would not come across in a completely favorable light (their Christmas spirit rises only when their profits increase). As a result of the movie, Macy's would later hire a "do-gooder" named "Christine Kringle" who directed customers to bargains at other stores. The heads of the department store chains recognized the merits of the film much quicker than 20th's studio chief, Darryl F. Zanuck, who only gave his go-ahead to the project when Seaton and Davies agreed to later make *Chicken Every Sunday* (1949). Even when Zanuck saw the finished film, he didn't get behind it—20th released its Christmas film in June! Nevertheless, the picture caught the fancy of the public. The Catholic Church found the film "morally objectionable" (it gave it a "B" rating) because it presented a divorced woman in a favorable light, but the Academy liked it enough to give it a Best Picture nomination and award Oscars to both Davies and Seaton. There are a few minor script problems: Daniel D. Tompkins was not John Quincy Adams's vice-president, as Kris states, but James Monroe's; the scene with Kris and Fred at Bellevue is weakly written; it's stretching it to have Jerome Cowan's D.A. call the Post Office "authoritative"; and Kris and Susan should have a much stronger and emotional good-bye. But otherwise it is extremely well written and consistently clever.

When you think of *Miracle on 34th Street,* you think of the humor. The script provides the witty dialogue, offbeat situations, and funny characters, and, while O'Hara and Payne do a lot of double takes, it's played to comic perfection by a remarkable supporting cast. You also think of sweetness: Kris telling a little boy he'll get the fire engine he wants; Albert telling Kris why he likes to dress up as Santa and give presents to children; Kris teaching Susan how to mimic a monkey; Susan snuggling in her mother's lap, worrying about Kris and speaking fondly about him ("But I've got a feeling he *is* Santa Claus, mother—he's so nice and kind and jolly, he's not like anyone else"); Susan writing Kris a letter to cheer him up; etc. And, of course, you think of the sentimentality. If you're a repeat viewer, you probably get teary-eyed just anticipating Doris writing to Kris that she believes he is Santa, Dr. Pierce walking unsteadily toward his X-ray machine present, the joyous Susan racing through her dream house and clicking her heels ("There *is* a swing! There *is* a swing!"), and Santa thrilling that lonely little Dutch orphan by singing and conversing with her in her language (while the amazed Susan and the girl's tearful stepmother watch)—this is one of my all-time favorite sentimental movie scenes! Still, what makes *Miracle on 34th Street* so affecting is its hard edge.

Seaton's intelligent, skillfully plotted satire presents a warped America where altruistic people are considered out of their minds, where insecure neurotics like Sawyer have the power to send harmless old men to asylums, where department store Santas are supposed to manipulate children into wanting toys that their stores have overstocked, where everyone wants something. Seaton zeroes in on the bad side of the American character: People have become so ambitious in their careers, so power hungry, and so set on making money that they have suppressed their finer values. At no time is the good-versus-greedy battle within each person so evident as at Christmas. So it's a good thing Kris turns up when he does, when commercialism is rampant and people need him to put life into perspective. As Fred reasons when he comes to Kris's aid: "He needs me. And all the rest of us need him . . . [I]t's not just Kris that's on trial. It's everything he stands for. It's kindness and joy and love and all the other . . . lovely intangibles that are the only things that are worthwhile."

Kris makes his appearance during Christmas season, when people who should be in a *giving* mood are actually thinking more of themselves. Even nice people admit to their selfishness. Fred likes spending time with Susan but

Doris and Susan worry about Kris's chances at his Santa-sanity hearing. Their defenses down, they both feel that Kris may be Santa Claus after all.

At Kris's hearing before Judge Henry X. Harper, young witness Thomas Mara, Jr., reminds his father, the district attorney, that he was the one who told him that Santa Claus truly exists.

admits that he got to be friends with her so he could meet her mother; Albert admits that he enjoys playing Santa and giving kids presents because it makes *him* feel good. We don't condemn either, but unlike Kris, who expects no reward for his goodness and would do good even if it didn't make him feel good, they are not altruistic. What's most interesting about the script is that while everyone but Sawyer likes Kris, most actually use him for their personal gain. Doris hires Kris to replace the drunk Santa, not because she doesn't want to disappoint thousands of children (the reason Kris accepts her offer), but because she wants to do a good job as parade organizer. Shellhammer hires Kris to be the permanent Macy's Santa because "He's a born salesman. I can feel it." R. H. Macy goes along with Kris's policy of sending customers to different stores for bargains so that Macy's will "be known as the helpful store, the friendly store, the store with heart, the store that places public service ahead of profit and consequently we'll make more profits than ever before." Doris and Shellhammer don't fire Kris even though they worry he may be crazy ("maybe he's only a little crazy, like painters or composers or some of those men in Washington," Shellhammer rationalizes) because they don't want

to anger their boss, Mr. Macy, who gave them large bonuses for hiring Kris. This is also the reason Shellhammer offers to let Kris stay in his apartment. Fred's ulterior motive when asking Kris to stay in his apartment is that he thinks he will have a better chance of winning Doris with Kris around. Mr. Macy and Mr. Gimbel are certainly kind when they help Kris acquire an X-ray machine for Dr. Pierce but they are motivated most by their desire to have better public images than their competitors. (Susan asks Kris for an impossible present, but since she's not greedy and is, after all, a child, I won't list her, or other children, among those using Kris for personal gain.)

Mr. Macy testifies in court that he believes Santa is real—it is not a kindness to tell the truth under oath—but only after he worries that Macy's reputation will suffer if he says he thinks Kris is a fraud. Interestingly, those other people—four strangers—who help Kris "prove" he is Santa Claus are trying to make things better for themselves, rather than help Kris. Step 1: Charley, William Frawley's political boss, tells Judge Harper, "I don't care what you do with old whiskerpuss," yet he influences the judge to help Kris by explaining that if he rules there is no Santa Claus he'll damage the economy and infuriate the unions. Step 2: Up for reelection, Harper, in turn, decides that the court will "keep an open mind" about the existence of Santa Claus. Step 3: Not wanting to let his son believe he lied to him about Santa, D.A. Mara is forced to concede in an *official* capacity that Santa Claus exists. Step 4: The decision to send all the unaddressed Santa Claus mail to the court—the "proof" that Kris is *the* Santa Claus—is made by a low-level postal worker (Jack Albertson), who isn't concerned about Kris but with clearing the Post Office's dead-letter section ("Why should we be bothered with all that stuff"). Several wrongs (actions caused by selfish motives) have made a right: Everyone ends up feeling better and Kris is freed. It can be argued that Kris's presence caused people to inadvertently do good, that he directed negative energy into a positive result. I don't disagree. On the other hand, it can also be argued that Fred's motives for helping Kris are unselfish ("He needs me"), even though a court victory will help his career, he wants to impress Doris ("I take a little old man and legally prove to the world that he's Santa Claus"), and, as mentioned, he believes helping Kris will benefit everyone. I prefer to go along with Fred being unselfish. I see that as the film winds down, Fred, with his support of Kris (even though he is humoring him), Susan, with her cheer-up letter to Kris, and Doris, with her note to Kris that she believes him to be Santa (although she is skeptical until she spots the cane), all do great kindnesses toward Kris without expecting anything in return. This is Kris's triumph!

It's dismaying that Seaton thought Kris was just a man who thinks himself to be Santa Claus. Obviously he thought Kris is "proved" to be Santa only because of a one-in-a-million four-step series of odd occurrences, and that under the identical circumstances any old man with white whiskers who claims to be Santa would win the same favorable court ruling. But Seaton was wrong: Kris is the cause of all the odd occurrences; his Christmas spirit entered the people of New York; he initiated and directed the miracle on 34th Street. Kris is as responsible for the actions of the strangers who affected the court's benevolent ruling as he is for getting Mr. Macy and Mr. Gimbel to shake hands, getting Doris and Fred together, and finding the house for them to live in with Susan.

There is no doubt among *Miracle* fans that Kris Kringle is Santa Claus! We only wonder if that's not the real Santa playing Kris and using Edmund Gwenn's SAG card. In any case, when many of us think of Santa, we think of the Santa in this film. O'Hara (whom some people think too cold) and Payne (whom some people think unanimated) give fine, controlled performances. (If, say, a Jimmy Stewart had played Fred, then he would have dominated the proceedings and the film would have revolved around him rather than Kris.) And pretty, talented Natalie Wood captures hearts, as she would many times in her teen and adult years. Anyone would want Susan for Christmas. But it is, fittingly, Gwenn who steals the picture. With his convincing portrayal, he deservedly won an Oscar. "Never mind that his category was Supporting Actor and never mind that his role was the whole film," wrote *Miracle* fan, critic Harry Haun, in the New York *Daily News* (December 21, 1975), "Gwenn always looked on the award as a private victory for comedy performances." Haun quoted Seaton, who directed Gwenn in several more films before the actor's death in 1959:

> "He always contended that comedy performances were never adequately recognized, and he believed that to the end. Years went by and Teddy became ill. I'd see him two or three times a week. Then one day, I got a call that it was terminal, and I went to the hospital. When he opened his one good eye and recognized me, he sort of smiled, and I went to the bed. I said to him, 'Oh, Teddy, it must be awfully hard.' He smiled and said, 'Yes, but not as hard as playing comedy.' I walked away, and he died right then. That was the last thing he ever said."

The tearful finale: The ecstatic Susan informs the confused Doris and Fred that the vacant house they have entered is the one Kris promised her for Christmas.

Monsieur Verdoux

1947   B&W   United Artists
Director: Charles Chaplin
Producer: Charles Chaplin
Screenplay: Charles Chaplin
From an idea by Orson Welles

Cinematography: Curt Courant
  and Roland Totheroh
Music: Charles Chaplin
Editor: Willard Nico
Running Time: 123 minutes

Cast: Charles Chaplin (Henri Verdoux), Martha Raye (Annabella Bonheur), Isobel Elsom (Marie Grosnay), Marilyn Nash (the Girl), Robert Lewis (Monsieur Bottello), Mady Correl (Madame Verdoux), Allison Roddan (Peter Verdoux), Audrey Betz (Madame Bettello), Ada-May (Annette), Marjorie Bennett (maid), Helen High (Yvonne), Margaret Hoffman (Lydia Floray), Irving Bacon (Pierre Couvais), Edwin Mills (Jean Couvais), Almira Sessions (Lena Couvais), Bernard J. Nedell (prefect), Charles Evans (Detective Morrow), William Frawley (Jean La Salle), Fritz Leiber (priest), Barbara Slater (florist).

Synopsis: Henri Verdoux lies dead in his grave, marked 1880–1937. He is there because he engaged in "liquidating members of the opposite sex" as a business enterprise during the Depression, after he lost his job of 35 years in the bank.

It is now several years before. The Couvais family worries about Thelma Couvais's disappearance since she married a man named Varnay. "Who'd ever spend three months honeymooning with Thelma?" they ask. The police suspect a bluebeard has married and killed 12 women from different French cities for their money. Meanwhile, in the South of France, Verdoux, alias Varnay, has disposed of Thelma's body in an incinerator. He counts the murdered woman's money and calls the stock exchange to invest it. Widow Madame Grosnay comes to look at the house. She doesn't buy it because Varnay scares her off with his brazen advances.

Verdoux returns to Paris, where he owns a furniture store—a front. Told that he needs money in a hurry or he'll be wiped out, Verdoux hops a train and visits another of his wives, Lydia Floray, who thinks he's an engineer. He convinces her to withdraw her money and kills her.

Verdoux goes to his home in the country, where his real wife, who is an invalid, and son Peter live. He presents her with the deed to the house and garden. Although she is unaware of the murderous enterprise that supports her, she can see that he is under great stress. He explains that the times are desperate and many people are starving. She is glad he has a job.

Verdoux goes to Lyons to visit another wife, Annabella Bonheur. She thinks he's a ship captain and he assures her he thinks of her "even on the poop deck." He buys poison to kill her but the unexpected arrival of her maid ruins his plans.

Verdoux/Varnay starts sending daily flowers to Madame Grosnay to break down her resistance.

Verdoux learns of a painless poison from his chemist friend Morris. He picks up the Girl, a pretty, homeless young woman, and brings her back to his apartment over the furniture store. He plans to test his poison on her. But he changes his mind when he realizes she thinks life is beautiful and that she also took care of an invalid (he died). She is touched when he gives her money. He poisons the detective on his trail.

Verdoux/Bonheur tries to poison Annabella, but bottles get switched around. The maid puts the poison on her head, making her hair fall out. He puts peroxide into Annabella's wine, which he accidentally drinks. Next he takes her to a deserted lake and tries to drown her. But he falls in the water instead.

Madame Grosnay's resistance breaks down and she agrees to marry Verdoux/Varnay. But he must sneak out of the wedding ceremony when Annabella arrives as a guest.

Verdoux is wiped out when the market crashes. He stops killing women.

In 1937, the Girl, who is rich because a munitions manufacturer fell in love with her, takes the broke but still dapper Verdoux to a nightclub. He reveals his wife and son are dead. She wants to help him. Lena Couvais recognizes him. He could escape, but gives himself up to the police. In court he blames the war-hungry world powers for having encouraged his mass killing. He doesn't repent. He is executed.

Charles Chaplin's controversial "comedy of murders" was released when his popularity in America was in rapid decline. Although proven innocent by a blood test, he'd come across as the heavy in an ugly recent paternity trial instigated by Joan Barry, and he'd been branded a Communist or, at best, a "fellow traveler" by government officials, the American Legion, and the Hearst press. Chaplin considered *Monsieur Verdoux* the best film he ever made and, according to his *My Autobiography* (1964), expected it to make $12 million in the United States, but it received an alarmingly small number of bookings after the American Legion threatened to boycott theaters that showed it. Religious groups were already wary of the film because at one time the Breen Office considered banning it on moral grounds. Chaplin hoped it would open strongly in New York and that would spark such enthusiasm elsewhere that theater owners would have to play it. But harsh reviews in the *Daily News*, *Times*, and other New York papers curtailed attendance to such a degree that the Broadway Theater actually had to reduce ticket prices during the picture's six-week run to attract viewers. *Monsieur Verdoux* would flourish in Europe, but after only several months in American release, Chaplin withdrew his great film from distribution . . . for 17 years.

James Agee was one of the few American critics, and the most prominent, to champion *Monsieur Verdoux* in 1947. In addition to being an emotional defender of Chaplin's civil rights at a famous postpremiere press conference in which reporters ignored the film and subjected Chaplin to red-baiting, Agee wrote a glowing review in *Time* and a monumental three-part article in *The Nation*. He called *Monsieur Verdoux* "one of the best movies ever made" and added, "I love and revere the film as deeply as any I have seen" and "Chaplin's performance is the best piece of playing I have ever seen." The picture next played in the United States in 1964, when the political climate had changed, and most American critics wrote it was made 17 years ahead of its time and jumped on the Agee bandwagon. However, Dwight MacDonald of *Saturday Review*, one of the few critics who thought the film was as overpraised in rerelease as it had been underpraised in its initial release, attacked Agee for responding to "what's not on the screen but emotionally sensed": "For to call a badly flawed movie *great* because of its themes is like saying an orator is eloquent but inarticulate."

Monsieur Verdoux is flawed, but not badly. I like the pacing that MacDonald considered too slow and erratic, the repetition of images (train wheels spinning madly to indicate the furious pace Verdoux must keep to in order to keep his "business" going, and—eventually—that Verdoux is actually making no progress with his wild schemes; Verdoux running up and down stairs like characters in classical farces), and that Chaplin—who gives a *beautiful* performance—was willing to let the hilarious Martha "Big Mouth" Raye steal the scenes she plays with him. I also

Verdoux has a romantic effect on all women. Here the florist is overwhelmed with emotion as she overhears him say beautiful words to Madame Grosnay—she doesn't realize that she is his inspiration.
▶

Verdoux with "wife" Lydia Floray, the only woman we meet whom he kills during the course of the film. And her death is offscreen.
▼

Verdoux is reunited with the Girl, who is rich now that she has married a munitions manufacturer. She still is grateful that he helped her when she was destitute and depressed, and wants to help him now that he is that way. But it is too late.
▶

am impressed by the much-criticized casting, including unknown Marilyn Nash, who I think is ideal as the Girl. However, I do admit being a bit uncomfortable with how Chaplin allows Verdoux to be God to women, not only his potential victims, like the Girl, but also his invalid wife, who dies the moment he can't provide for her. I think the sudden deaths of Verdoux's wife and child are unbelievable—Verdoux may lose his savings, stocks, and property, the sanctuary for his family in the face of the Depression and the next war, but he is shrewd enough to immediately get enough money from any number of widows to keep his family going indefinitely. Which brings up this question: Why does Verdoux only kill women to make money, when it's obvious that he could easily make a fortune *swindling,* not murdering, both men and women? Is it just more convenient to do away with victims? Verdoux's attitude toward women is not sufficiently clear. He tells the Girl that he loves women but doesn't admire them because "Once a woman betrays a man, she despises him. In spite

of his goodness and position, she will give him up for someone inferior . . . if that someone is more physically attractive." This is Chaplin the scenarist showing his insecurity—considering the women Verdoux interacts with in this film, there is no reason he has this scornful view of women and acts as if he has been rejected or betrayed by them in his past. The Girl doesn't agree with his assessment because she is not like the women he describes. She replies, "How little you know about women." In this instance, Chaplin the martyr is hinting the Girl would marry the older Verdoux *if* he didn't assume she wanted no part of him and push her away, just as Claire Bloom's beautiful ballerina Terry would eagerly marry Chaplin's older Calvero in *Limelight* (1952) *if* he didn't assume she'd be happier with a younger man and withdraw from her life. So: *Monsieur Verdoux* is imperfect. But MacDonald's attack on Agee really has no basis. After all, aren't the most-loved films, including "cult movies," those pictures which viewers respond to with such emotion that they accept or even overlook their flaws? *Monsieur Verdoux* is more flawed—or better, has more problems—than *The Gold Rush* (1923), *The Circus* (1927), *City Lights* (1931), *Modern Times* (1936), and *The Great Dictator* (1940), but that's to be expected since it's a more complex film. In my opinion, it's the best of the marvelous lot.

The themes of *Monsieur Verdoux* are important, but I don't think it's a profound film—just an intelligent, provocative, audacious film—yet it contains many wonderful moments that have a profound emotional effect on me each time I see it. It's stunning how Chaplin balances hilarious comedy moments with deeply moving dramatic moments. Comedy highlights include the slapstick-sprinkled opening with the Couvais family, the type of loud, ugly, lazy, vulgar, gossipy in-laws W. C. Fields was stuck with in his films; the way Verdoux counts money or flips pages (like a lightning-quick card shuffler)—a reminder he was a bank teller for 35 years; for the benefit of the real estate man, Verdoux/Varnay pretending to be chasing a bee around the bedroom when he's actually chasing Madame Grosnay; all the scenes with Verdoux/Bonheur and Annabella, including the "American Tragedy" sequence in which he tries vainly to drown her in a deserted lake, the bit where he gets into a public slapathon with a swindler who sold Annabella a device that supposedly can change salt water into gasoline, and when he thinks he accidentally drank her poisoned wine; Verdoux/Varnay rushing into Madame Grosnay's Paris apartment and, forgetting what she looks like, embracing her maid and then, in another attempt, her friend; Verdoux/Varnay (Chaplin the acrobat) falling off the couch while proposing to Madame Grosnay but not spilling any tea from the cup he holds; Verdoux/Varnay spitting wine on the back of a man's head when he realizes Annabella is a guest at his wedding to Madame Grosnay; Verdoux looking away from his nightclub table just in time to see Almira Sessions's Lena Couvais spit up her drink.

Dramatic highlights include: Verdoux/Floray walking up the stairs and gazing at the moon before entering Lydia's bedroom to kill her; the moment Verdoux decides to take away the poisoned wine he intended for the Girl (Chaplin's music swells)—indication he is either playing God with her life or has allowed a touch of humanity to return; Verdoux expressing his love to Madame Grosnay over the flower shop phone with such passion that the florist (Barbara Slater resembles Marilyn Nash), who inspires his beautiful, poetic words, is overwhelmed; Verdoux's powerful lecture to the court; Verdoux telling the priest who visits his cell that only God can judge whether he has sinned and that he expects the Lord to have mercy on his soul because "after all it belongs to him"; about to be executed, Verdoux reconsidering and deciding to taste rum—one of the finer things in life—for the first time; and the last shot, in which Verdoux walks toward the gallows across a prison courtyard that is sunlit on one side and shadowy on the other, appropriate for a man who walked the fine line between good and evil.

In truth, if Chaplin had wanted to get back into America's good graces, he was imprudent making *Monsieur Verdoux.* It is obviously the work of a cynical man who feels disappointed that post–World War II governments are pursuing the identical money-and-munitions path toward war they followed after World War I and who has bitterness for being persecuted because of his politics, fame, and, if you listen to Verdoux, age. It is at once a plea for world peace/disarmament (which Communists of the period were calling for) and a scathing indictment of capitalism: Whether it's individual men or governments conducting *business* ("wars, conflicts—it's all business"), money made equates with murders committed. It dares call us hypocritical for being outraged that men commit individual murders when we extol genocide conducted by our warring nations ("Numbers sanctify," declares Verdoux); insinuate that we're as *guilty* as Verdoux and will join ("soon"!) the executed murderer in hell (or, if we're all *guiltless,* in heaven); blame governments like our own, which puts money into armaments while people are starving, for turning gentle men like Verdoux into murderers ("violence begets violence"); and infer that religion is incidental in what has become a vulgar, heartless world.

Chaplin chanced losing an overly serious segment of his audience when he lampooned Hitler and Nazis in his previous film, *The Great Dictator* (1940). But I would guess *Monsieur Verdoux* was an even scarier project for him. Comedians are by nature the most vulnerable of actors and the most desperate for approval. Today the majority of comics court the college-age audience, but in the past most comics chose personae that would appeal to children as well as adults. Their characters either acted like children or were the bumbling, daredevil, or clown types children would like to pal around with: Fatty Arbuckle, baby-faced Harry Langdon, stunt experts Buster Keaton and Harold Lloyd, Chaplin's Little Tramp, clownlike Harpo Marx, the "innocent" Lou Costello ("I'm a bad bad boy"), sweet dumbbells Laurel and Hardy, Jerry Lewis's "The Kid," Red Skelton's "Mean Widdle Kid" and "Freddie the Freeloader," Bert Lahr, Ed Wynn's "Perfect Fool," Jackie Gleason's "Poor Soul," etc. (W. C. Fields, Groucho Marx, Jack Benny, and Bob Hope were among the few who had adult personae.) Of course, comics—like cowboy heroes—knew it was risky to play villains and give their young fans a reason to rebel. So if a comic wanted to stretch and play a cad, he would cover himself by also playing the hero, as Chaplin did in *The Great Dictator,* where he played a kindly Jewish barber as well as dictator Adenoid Hynkel, and as Jerry Lewis did, in a Jekyll-and-Hyde sense, in *The Nutty Professor* (1962). But in *Monsieur Verdoux,* Chaplin had the nerve to play just one character—a Landu-based bluebeard whom no one, especially children, would fully embrace. Verdoux does exhibit tenderness, a love of beauty, a quick (though sardonic) wit, and other sympathetic qualities, and he kills only one person, a man, *on* screen, so we don't have reason enough to truly dislike him—especially with Chaplin playing him. And we can understand the reasons for his anger. But even as we laugh at Verdoux's zany attempts to make financial ends meet, we recognize that this once-sweet man has become a cold, calculating monster. It's hard to imagine Chaplin coming across as creepy, but Verdoux/Floray gives me chills before he murders Lydia. Verdoux may be the lead character, but we root for the Girl, Isobel Elsom's Madame Grosnay, and even Raye's Annabella (symbol of

Verdoux returns unexpectedly to rescue "wife" Annabella (Martha Raye's greatest film role) from a pair of swindlers.

indestructible vulgarity) to survive Verdoux's murder plots. Interestingly, Chaplin also recognizes their zest for life (which the shriveled, penurious Lydia doesn't have) and lets them live. Chaplin doesn't force us to like Verdoux and accept his murderous actions as being reasonable under the circumstances—as Stanley Kubrick does with Malcolm McDowell's Alex in *A Clockwork Orange* (1970). Indeed, Verdoux himself emerges from "a numbed confusion, a half dream world," and realizes that his murderous course cannot be *justified,* although it can be explained as the act of a society-created madman ("Despair is a narcotic—it blows life into indifference").

There is always a danger that audiences will think anything a lead character says reflects the personal philosophy of the director-scenarist, especially if the two people are one and the same. As far as I can tell, Verdoux the character expresses the philosophy of Chaplin only when he reveals his thoughts about women to the Girl and in those scenes set in 1937, when Verdoux speaks to us from his grave; to the Girl in the nightclub; to the people in the court; and to the men who visit his cell prior to his execution. In the 1937 scenes, his sanity has returned. In those scenes that take place during his murder spree, Verdoux gives a distorted, madman's version of Chaplin's philosophy. In the scene in which Verdoux brings the Girl to his room to poison her and they wind up exchanging views of the world, Chaplin does not want us to think Verdoux's emphatic words are correct, or reflect his own opinions. He has Verdoux tell her, "It's a ruthless world, and one must be ruthless to cope with it," only to have her counter, "It's a blundering world, and a very sad one, yet a little kindness can make it beautiful." Chaplin easily could have switched the order of these two evaluations and had Verdoux's pessimism emerge triumphant, but Chaplin wanted the Girl to express his own view, positive words for which even Verdoux has no retort ("You'd better go before your philosophy corrupts me," he says). We realize that the Girl, not Verdoux, is right. Verdoux, in fact, proves her point by generously giving her food, money, conversation and companionship, respect, and the little kindness necessary to make her sad world beautiful.

A case can be made that the Girl is Verdoux's alter ego. Both committed crimes to provide for the invalids they loved and protected like children, both pay attention to a stray cat, both think about death, the world, destiny. Both prostitute themselves, both marry for money. After the Girl tells him she has gone from rags to riches since a munitions dealer fell in love with her, Verdoux, rather than telling her to break away from the war profiteer, tells her that munitions is the business he should have gone

Lena Couvais recognizes Verdoux, who wants to be arrested.

into. But if Verdoux, who seems based in part on the mustachioed sharper Chaplin played in his first short, *Making a Living* (1914), has a true alter ego it is Chaplin's Little Tramp (a case can be made that the Girl, a world-battered but optimistic survivor—whom we first see as a prostitute/"tramp"—is also linked to the Little Tramp, another underdog). When we see the Little Tramp in films, we readily accept him as a universal character and, because we're so busy laughing, don't stop to consider how he got to be alone and destitute. But isn't it probable that, like the Everyman Verdoux, he was once a respected member of society who had misfortune and lost everything? We don't want to think about such things but perhaps he even had a wife and child who died after he could no longer support them. The Little Tramp is an eternal optimist who sees beauty (i.e., the "lights" in the city in 1931's *City Lights*) everywhere in his unfriendly world and maintains a sense of dignity despite his low station in life. Verdoux thinks only a man with "undaunted optimism" would hope

to make a living by murdering women, and he too finds beauty around him (flowers, young women)—but he is extremely negative about everything. Verdoux continues to act the gentleman, but he has stopped worrying about such things as self-respect and dignity.

The biggest difference between the two characters is that the Little Tramp makes no effort to return to society but stays on the outside as a human affront to the heartless rich who run the world, while Verdoux, who dreads being a penniless tramp, plays the financial "game" to reintroduce himself into the mainstream. Therein lies the lesson. The greatest tragedy of the film is that Verdoux the romantic who takes women's breaths away with words becomes a pragmatist and literally takes their breaths away with evil deeds. He embarks on a business enterprise befitting—"Business is a *ruthless* business"—the ruthless world he lives in, "liquidating members of the opposite sex." The Little Tramp ends up walking toward the sunset; Verdoux ends up walking toward the gallows.

The Naked Kiss

1964 B&W Allied Artists
Director: Samuel Fuller
Producer: Samuel Fuller
Screenplay: Samuel Fuller
Cinematography: Stanley Cortez
Music: Paul Dunlap
Editor: Jerome Thoms
Running Time: 93 minutes

Cast: Constance Towers (Kelly), Anthony Eisley (Griff), Michael Dante (Grant), Virginia Grey (Candy), Patsy Kelly (Mac), Betty Bronson (Miss Josephine), Marie Devereux (Buff), Karen Conrad (Dusty), Betty Robinson (Bunny), Christopher Barry (Peanuts), Monte Mansfield (Farlunde), Fletcher Fist (Barney), Edy Williams (Hatrack).

Synopsis: Kelly beats up her pimp Farlunde. He shaved her head for having organized his girls to walk out on him when he held back their money. She takes the $75 he owes her and leaves the city before his mob friends will pay her back. Two years later, after working in small towns, she gets off the bus in Grantville. She says she's a traveling saleslady, selling champagne, but Griff knows she's a prostitute. She can tell he's a cop. She spends the night with him—he gives her $20 for champagne—but he warns her not to work in respectable Grantville. He suggests she go to the neighboring town, and work for his friend Candy, as one of her bonbon girls.

But Kelly decides to remain in Grantville and go straight. She takes a room with the kindly, slightly daffy town spinster, Miss Josephine. She is hired by Mac to be a nurse's aide at the orthopedic children's hospital that was built by Griff's best friend, playboy Grant, the town's leading citizen and the great-great-grandson of the man who founded the town. She is firm but caring toward the handicapped children and they all fall in love with her. She also becomes good friends with Mac and two young nurses, Dusty and Buff, an orphan Griff brought back from the war. But Griff doesn't trust her and believes she is using the hospital as a front from which to peddle her body.

Kelly and Grant are immediately attracted to each other. They both love classical music and literature. However, when she kisses him, she senses something wrong. She shrugs it off. She falls in love and tells him she was a prostitute. He says he loves her and proposes. She accepts. Griff threatens to throw her out of town for duping his best friend. But she informs him that she told Grant about her past, although she didn't tell him of her night with Griff. Griff agrees to be best man.

Meanwhile Kelly gives pregnant Dusty $1000 to have her baby and get her life in order. When Buff takes a $25 advance from Candy to become a bonbon girl, Kelly talks her out of taking the wayward path and shaming herself and Griff. Kelly returns the money to Candy by stuffing it in her mouth.

Kelly drops in on Grant to show him her wedding gown. She catches Grant molesting a young girl. The girl leaves. Grant says he loves Kelly because she's as abnormal as he is. He promises her an exciting life together. She smashes him on the head with a phone and kills him. She is arrested for murder. The whole town disbelieves Grant was a child molester. Griff thinks she killed him when Grant tried to call off the wedding. She swears that Grant was a pervert—she could tell by his "naked kiss." But she can't remember what the little girl looked like. Griff brings in Farlunde and Candy to testify against her. They both swear she was trying to shake down Grant for money. Kelly says Candy only wants to get her back for getting Buff out of her grasp. But Buff is too embarrassed to back Kelly's story. Later Buff tells Griff the truth. Now Griff tries to help Kelly. Young girls are paraded past the jail. Kelly recognizes little Bunny. By being nice to Bunny, Kelly is able to get her to talk about "Uncle Grant" and their special secret game. Kelly is freed. The whole town forgives her. But she leaves town. She'll again be a traveling prostitute.

Sending someone to a Samuel Fuller melodrama with your ardent recommendation is a risky proposition at best. It's safer to go along so you can explain exactly *why* what they're seeing is so good, when their inclination is to think the opposite. As the French realized before the Americans, Fuller made some of the most original, powerful, and visually striking "B" pictures ever filmed, yet those unfamiliar with his work often regard it as camp and laugh at the sleazy stories, twisted characters, and visual flights of fancy. And they cringe at the dialogue, not only at the clichés and atrocious lines that invariably slip into Fuller's otherwise tough, frank screenplays, but also at the quotes Fuller has taken from famous poets and novelists and given to his characters. This is particularly true of Fuller's most highly regarded films, *Shock Corridor* (1962), about a reporter entering an asylum so he can solve a murder and become famous (only to have his plan backfire), and his finest melodrama, *The Naked Kiss*, about a prostitute entering society so she can become respectable (only to have her plan backfire).

It's not surprising that *The Naked Kiss* and *Shock Corridor* are usually linked by critics and twin-billed by repertory theater owners. (In *The Naked Kiss*, Fuller books *Shock Corridor* into the lone theater in Grantville . . . although it's too sordid to play in such a "respectable" town.) The two films have (if you stretch it) vaguely similar premises, star Constance Towers (she's the reporter's

Kelly thinks her fortunes have changed for the better when the rich, respected Grant falls in love with her. But in Sam Fuller films rich, respected men are usually scum.

stripper girlfriend in the earlier film), were financed by Leon Fromkess and Sam Firks, were photographed by Stanley Cortez, deal with lurid subject matter and perverse sex, and tread the fine line between trash and art. In both films, Fuller includes fantasy-dream sequences. In both, he incorporates some out-of-place personally photographed 16-mm travelogue-like footage. Both have absurd scenes only Fuller fanatics can accept; for example: the reporter being attacked by a horde of nymphomaniacs in *Shock Corridor;* Kelly and the handicapped kids (a good name for a singing group?) singing "Little Child" for Grant in *The Naked Kiss.* And both films have smashingly directed, unflinching shock scenes. There are few more startling sequences in Fuller's work than the opening in *The Naked Kiss,* in which the bald Kelly is already savagely beating up her pimp, and the exceptionally edited scene in which Kelly enters Grant's home and, while the "Little Child" tape plays hauntingly on Grant's machine, finds Grant molesting Bunny (who skips out), and kills him, her wedding veil covering his face.

Yet I think *The Naked Kiss* has fewer ties to *Shock Corridor* than to Fuller's previous film, *Underworld, U.S.A.* (1961). Although Fuller works on a more personal level in *The Naked Kiss,* and is more subtle and less violent, both films deal with corruption, of society and individuals. I see Towers's Kelly as sort of a combination of Cliff Robertson's ex-con, whose vengeful trail leads from a dark alley and concludes back in that alley (just as Kelly returns to being a prostitute), and his girlfriend, prostitute Dolores Dorn (as Cuddles), who wants to escape the gutter and become respectable. With their disreputable pasts these three characters would live on the street if they weren't taken into the homes of oddball spinsters (anticipating "town virgin" Miss Josephine, Robertson's surrogate mother collects dolls because she can't have kids). These women see their worth. Robertson and Dorn go out on a limb to show that their city's most respectable businessmen are mobsters and that the beloved philanthropist who makes available his swimming pool to underprivileged youngsters does so to recruit prostitutes and drug addicts; Kelly stands up to the police chief, Griff* (Anthony Eisley of TV's *Hawaiian Eye*), and exposes Michael Dante's Grant, whose "name is a synonym for charity," as a child molester. Kelly and the characters played by Robertson and Dorn, though shunned by society for being *impure,* inevitably cleanse society. Although good citizens wouldn't want them near their children, they alone are able to see that their unprotected children are in danger and attempt to help them. (When it comes to children, tough-guy Fuller is a sentimentalist.) As outsiders they have special insight into the rich, respectable men who run society and determine what happens to our children. They are well aware of their nasty, violent, often perverse sides. Having been victimized by these paragons of virtue, they don't trust them like the good citizens foolishly do.

• •

*"Griff" is Fuller's most frequently used character name. (Does anyone know why?) Reed Hadley plays John Griff in *The Baron of Arizona* (1950), George Wesley plays Griff in *Fixed Bayonets* (1951), Cameron Mitchell plays Griff in *House of Bamboo* (1955), and Barry Sullivan plays Griff Bonnell in *Forty Guns* (1957).

Kelly's ex-prostitute is a wild variation on Joan Crawford's ex–carnival girl in *Flamingo Road* (1949). In that film Crawford stays in a town she's passing through when deputy sheriff Zachary Scott (who anticipates Griff) gets her a waitress job, and later becomes romantically involved with powerful politician David Brian (who anticipates Grant, though he is politically rather than morally corrupt). Like the ex–carnival girl, Kelly attempts to prove herself *normal* by fitting into society. She rents a "pleasant" room in a nice section of Grantville, where houses have nice lawns, and girls jump rope on the sidewalk; she becomes a nurse's aide in Grantville's prestigious orthopedic hospital for handicapped children; and she agrees to marry Grant, scion of Grantville. She and Grant have conversations that normal, cultured people have: about Beethoven, Goethe, Byron, Baudelaire. They listen to "The Moonlight Sonata." They watch his home movies. Well, it's all too normal for Fuller's tastes: He shatters Kelly's dream (she does dream of happiness) by having her notice something wrong with Grant's kiss (his "naked kiss" is the sign of a pervert), then catch Grant molesting young Bunny, and then having Grant admit he wants her for his bride only because he thinks she is as "abnormal" as he is and can understand his perversion. All the time we watch the romance develop between Grant and Kelly, we wonder if Fuller knows how corny he is. But when Kelly discovers Grant with the little girl (is this the first film to deal with child molestation?), we realize that Fuller actually didn't want us to enjoy the Grant-Kelly romance (as we would a Cary Grant–Grace Kelly romance). Instead he wanted to irritate us with its corniness, and then shock us out of our complacency. In *The Director's Event* (1969), Fuller told interviewers Eric Sherman and Martin Rubin:

> "[W]hen I started the film as a shocker, the original impression I wanted was of a wonderful, almost dull, very, very ordinary love story: the poor girl from the wrong side of the tracks, the rich man who falls in love with her. Well, I hate those kinds of stories. So I knew I was going to have fun the minute she finds him molesting the child. . . . Suppose there's no child molesting scene. I wouldn't have made the story."

Kelly is revolted by Grant ("[Even] hookers," says Fuller, "who resent that they are resented by the country club set, would resent someone lower than they are"). In a daze, she kills her perverted fiancé by clubbing him with a telephone (also a weapon in 1944's *Detour,* 1968's *Midnight Cowboy,* and 1986's *The Stepfather*). When no one in town will believe she did them a service, she discovers that "normal" people are close-minded, accusatory, and hypocritical. She realizes that as long as one is not a pervert like Grant, it's preferable to be abnormal, an outcast from society. Deep down, she knew this all along because at various times she befriended outcasts: prostitutes (she organized a walkout on their crooked pimp), daffy "town virgin" Miss Josephine (twenties' star Betty Bronson, the title character in 1924's *Peter Pan*), spinster nurse Mac (thirties'/forties' comedienne Patsy Kelly), the handicapped children (she is awkward toward *normal* children), troubled foreign nurse Buff (Marie Devereux), and un-

As Candy (left) *looks on, Griff chats with one of her bonbon girls, Hatrack (played by Edy Williams), who got her job because of him.*

married, pregnant nurse Dusty (Karen Conrad). She makes a bold statement when she rejects the apologies of Grantville's populace who now put her on a pedestal ("they sure put up statues overnight"), and, refuting her attempt to be *normal,* voluntarily goes back to being a traveling prostitute. She accepts being an outcast. Fuller told Sherman and Rubin:

> "I [wrote] a scene where [Kelly] confronts the towns-people after they find out that she's innocent. First they were ready to lynch her, and now they want vindication. She tells them to go to hell. I didn't shoot the scene—no money. She calls them hypocrites, which is all right, *but* the important thing is that she realizes how happy she was in her profession. She says, in effect, 'What a thrill it is: when you get through laying any of those bastards, he pays you off and leaves. You don't have to listen to him or to his stories or to his lies, like I have to listen to your lies every day.' That's what I wanted. . . . I like . . . the idea of the girl going back to being a hooker. I just like it."

Fuller's violent, male-oriented films—war movies, Westerns, and melodramas with sensationalistic story lines that are fitting for tabloids—haven't seemed appropriate for feminist study. Nevertheless, with few exceptions, his women are a fascinating lot: They're intelligent, strong-willed, and gallant, and play a refreshingly nontraditional role in the screen action. It should be noted that Fuller looks at his women with admiration, and is sympathetic of their unenviable position in a male world. Of all Fuller's films, *The Naked Kiss* is the prime candidate for detailed feminist analysis. For one thing, other than the Barbara Stanwyck Western *Forty Guns* (1957), it's the only Fuller film with a woman in the lead role. And Kelly is strong, smart, self-reliant (she even buys her own wedding gown), and proud ("I never make change"). Being a hooker, she may not seem like a positive role model, but that's what she becomes, particularly to the other women in the film, because she refuses to play the victim. Like Fuller's male heroes, she faces up to her responsibilities (a major Fuller theme), she rights a wrong, she doesn't back down from a tough fight. She actively tries to make things better for her women friends (her fellow prostitutes in the city, the troubled Grantville nurses, and Miss Josephine, who needs assurance she's not batty) and the unfortunate, unprotected children of Grantville. Even though Kelly puts herself in danger, she stands up to Farlunde, who tries to exploit young women; Candy (forties' lead Virginia Grey), who tries to corrupt young women (it's fun watching her slap Candy and stick dirty money in her mouth); Grant, who tries to corrupt young girls; and Griff, who tries to

Left: *Because she is an out-cast herself, Kelly gets along splendidly with the handi-capped children at Grant's hospital.* Below: *But Kelly has trouble relating to "nor-mal" children like Bunny, the girl Grant molested.*

keep women like her in their place. Rather than compromise her integrity and make up with the citizens who condemned her for killing Grant, she leaves town and gives up her security. Whereas she once told Buff that prostitutes were "despicable failures as women"—a social and medical problem—she realizes that by willingly returning to prostitution she has triumphed over all the hypocrites. Society slapped her in the face and now she slaps it back.

Fuller's nicknamed roster of women is the female equivalent of one of his movie army platoons: Candy, Mac, Buff, Dusty, Rembrandt, Bunny, Angel Face, Marshmallow, Redhead, and Hatrack (a pre–Russ Meyer Edy Williams). I doubt that Fuller meant to be condescending when he gave his women such nicknames; more likely he was pointing out that they were regarded as objects in a man's world (even Candy, who must work across the town's border, is dependent on men). All women, even "town virgin" Miss Josephine, are thought of in sexual terms. The men who run things have no respect for women. Pimp Farlunde sells his prostitutes' bodies, cheats them of their money, shaves Kelly's head, and hopes to give false testimony to put her in prison. The bald lug at Candy's treats the bonbon girls like hunks of meat, grabbing any who cross his path. Civil leader Grant molests little girls and seeks a wife who is as low as he is. Police chief Griff picks up and sleeps with women who arrive in town and, though he tells young male punks to get out of town and never come back, sends the women (Kelly and Hatrack, to name

two) across the city line to work in Candy's brothel, where he can visit them. Griff may desire Kelly but he thinks of her in sexual terms ("[She's] enough to make a bulldog bust its chain"), constantly puts down her character (though he was willing to sleep with her), and refuses to believe she intends to go straight ("Your body is your only passport"). Griff will not trust Kelly or give her the benefit of a doubt. He won't look beyond her profession.

It is the women who come through: Miss Josephine lets stranger Kelly move into her house, saying, "Your reference is that face"; Mac hires Kelly "on the spot" to work at the hospital; Buff and Dusty come forward as Kelly's character witnesses, when everyone else in town (other than Mac and Miss Josephine) has turned on her. Kelly was friend, big sister, and/or daughter to these women, rewarding their faith in her, being there when they had no one else . . . and now they are there for her. At the end, these four loyal females stand together to bid Kelly farewell. It is a moment of strong solidarity of women, of outcasts. Kelly earlier told Buff that the "dread of everyone in my business is to end up alone," yet she now voluntarily goes off alone, showing these women that it's okay to be an outcast, that they can all make it on their own, too. As Kelly walks away, she plays with a baby, as she did when she arrived in town. This time the baby feels comfortable with her, no doubt because this time Kelly feels at ease with a "normal" child. She now knows she has nothing to be ashamed of.

Napoleon

also known as *Abel Gance's Napoleon*

1927 B&W (tinted) French Westi Société Générale des Films
Director: Abel Gance
Producers: Wladimir Wengeroff and Hugo Stinnes
Screenplay: Abel Gance
Cinematography: Jules Kruger, Léonce-Henry Burel, and Jean-Paul Mundwiller
Music: Arthur Honegger
Editors: Abel Gance, Marguerite Beaugé, and Henritte Pinson
Running Time: 220 minutes
Cast: Albert Dieudonné (Napoleon Bonaparte), Gina Manès (Josephine de Beauharnais), Vladimir Roudenko (Napoleon as boy), Alexandre Koubitzky (Danton), Antonin Artaud (Jean-Paul Marat), Edmond van Daele (Robespierre), Gance (Saint-Just), Nicolas Koline (Tristan Fleuri), Annabella (Violine Fleuri), Harry Krimer (Rouget de Lisle), Pierre Batcheff (General Lazare Hoche), Max Maxudian (Paul Barras), Chakatouny (Pozzo di Borgo), Marguerite Gance (Charlotte Corday), Jean d'Yd (La Bussière), Yvette Dieudonné (Elisa Bonaparte).

Synopsis: 1781. During a snowball fight between two armies of boys at the Brienne military school, 12-year-old Napoleon Bonaparte impresses his masters with his bravery, leadership, and tactical skills. But the defiant, serious Corsican lad is unpopular with his masters and bullying classmates. When two boys free his pet eagle, he fights with all the boys. He is tossed out into the cold. His eagle returns.

1790. At the Revolutionary Club des Cordeliers, Lieutenant Bonaparte thanks Rouget de Lisle for introducing "La Marseilles" to the people. Danton sings along with the emotional crowd, while Robespierre and Marat, the other "gods" of the Revolution, mock their fervor. Seeing hungry people, Bonaparte writes, "If we are not careful, the finest fruits of the Revolution will be lost." Napoleon spots attractive Josephine de Beauharnais on her way to see a palmist. The palmist tells her she will be a queen.

1792. France and England are at war. Captain Bonaparte and his sister Elisa return to Corsica for the first time in 12 years, to see their family. Bonaparte learns that nationalist leader Paoli wants to sell Corsica to England. He swears this will not happen. Pozzo di Borgo, Paoli's secretary and Corsica's attorney general, makes speeches against him and puts a price on his head. Stealing a French flag from Pozzo, Bonaparte flees troops on horseback. He sails away on a dinghy, using the flag as a sail. He survives a tempest. Meanwhile in Paris there's a "storm" at the Convention (the Revolutionary assembly), and the radical Jacobins of Robespierre, Danton, and Marat gain power over the moderate Girondists.

September 1793. Artillery captain Bonaparte joins the French army that besieges the port city of Toulon. He is appointed commander-in-chief of the artillery and allowed to proceed with his daring plan to oust English, Italian, and Spanish troops. During a storm, he leads his badly outnumbered troops to a decisive victory. He gains fame in France.

1794. Many people are arrested and executed by the Committee for Public Safety during the Reign of Terror. Marat is assassinated by Charlotte Corday. Robespierre consolidates his power by having Danton executed. Bonaparte is arrested for refusing to serve Robespierre. Josephine is also thrown into prison. Robespierre and Saint-Just are shouted down at the Convention and executed. Now Bonaparte and Josephine are freed.

Bonaparte has plans for France to invade Italy but can't get anyone in authority to carry them out. When Royalist forces attack the Convention, constitutionalist Paul Barras puts him in charge of the resistance. The insurgents are stopped.

Bonaparte falls in love with Josephine, Barras's mistress. Barras wants Josephine off his hands so he agrees to make Bonaparte commander-in-chief of the army in Italy if she'll marry Bonaparte. Bonaparte marries Josephine. Before going to Italy, he speaks to the ghosts of the Revolution. They tell him he is the leader of the Revolution.

1796. Bonaparte desperately misses Josephine when he goes to Italy. Bonaparte wins over his officers, who are scared of him. He boosts the morale of his tattered troops. He leads them through Italy to victory and glory.

Albert Dieudonné as Napoleon Bonaparte, about to lead his troops through Italy.

One of the major cultural events in America in 1981 was the screening of Kevin Brownlow's "reconstructed" version of Abel Gance's lost classic at Radio City Music Hall on January 23, 1981.* It was presented by Francis Ford Coppola, and his father, Carmine Coppola, who composed an original four-hour score and conducted a 60-piece orchestra. As they had been at Telluride in 1979 and in London on November 30, 1980, with Carl Davis conducting his score to a five-hour version, and as they would be at the Colosseum in Rome on September 11, 1981, and in other American and European cities, viewers were astonished. For many, especially those who had never seen a silent movie, it was a revelation; for both aspiring and veteran filmmakers it was a humbling experience; for film critics, film historians, and film fanatics, it was one case in which a film lived up to its legend . . . at least on a visual level. (Refusing to pay $20 for any movie, I waited

• •

*The 220-minute running time I have listed in the credits refers to the print that premiered in Paris on April 7, 1927. Kevin Brownlow lists 19 versions of the film, including ones he assembled, with the longest at over 5 hours; Gance's own version ran 7 hours. The version Images Film Archive distributes in the United States runs 235 minutes.

for *Napoleon* to go into general release, with Coppola's score on the soundtrack.) Everyone who took film history courses in college or read film history texts had heard of Abel Gance and *Napoleon* and accepted that he was a great pioneer filmmaker and his film was a tremendous achievement. We didn't stop to consider that our film professors, the textbook authors, and almost everyone else who championed Gance and *Napoleon* had never seen any of his films, not even shortened, bastardized versions of *Napoleon*. (At the time only 1936's *Un Grand Amour de Beethoven* was available, *if* you searched very hard.) The only valid source on Gance and his film was Brownlow, the British film historian and prize-winning filmmaker. My own curiosity was aroused by Brownlow's fine documentary *Abel Gance—The Charm of Dynamite* (1968)—which includes some of the most spectacular visuals in *Napoleon*—and his lengthy chapter on Gance in his classic book on the silent era, *The Parade's Gone By . . .* (1968), an essay other film historians borrowed from when they needed to write about Gance.

Abel Gance began in films in 1908 as a scriptwriter and 1909 as an actor.* In 1911, he formed his own production company, Le Film Français, and directed his first picture, *La Digue (ou Pour Sauver la Hollande)*. By 1918 he had made 20 films, including the early science fiction work *La Folie du Docteur Tube* (1915), and established himself as France's leading director, an innovator whose audacious storytelling techniques rivaled those of D. W. Griffith. Gance moved to a higher plane with his antiwar film *J'Accuse* (1919). As William M. Drew pointed out in *Take One* (July 1978), this was the "first European film to blend the documentary style with a fictional story.† . . . Equally astonishing in its technical innovations, *J'Accuse* contains use of a wildly-tracking camera, masking and superimposition of the image, and rapid cutting." Gance's second epic, *La Roue* (1922), filmed on location in Nice and the Alps, featured some flash-cutting sequences that would greatly influence Eisenstein when he developed his theories on montage.

Gance began preparing *Napoleon* in 1922, and began filming it in January 1925. He actually planned to make six films, covering Bonaparte's complete life. His initial effort would have three episodes: "The Youth of Napoleon," "Bonaparte and the Revolution," and "The Italian Campaign." The five remaining films would be *From Arcole to Marengo*, *From 18 Brumaire to Austerlitz*, *From Austerlitz to the Hundred Days*, *Waterloo*, and *Saint Helena*. But it soon became apparent that Gance would be fortunate to finish his first film. Gance had received initial financing from a Russian financier, a German coal magnate, and French financier Hugo Stinnes, but Stinnes died and other funds ran out. After six months, with a quarter of his film shot, Gance closed down production and tried

to raise money. He was able to get further backing when another Russian financier, Jacques Grinieff, helped form a production company, Société Générale des Films. So Gance could resume filming on both *Napoleon* and his documentary on the making of the film. But production shut down for good in August 1926, with the Italian sequence incomplete. Gance had spent more than 17,000 francs, utilized 150 sets (he shot on location where possible), and employed 40 stars, 200 technicians, and 6000 extras. Two extras were killed falling off horses and 42 were injured in a battle scene, star Albert Dieudonné almost drowned during the shooting in Corsica, and Gance (who played Saint-Just as well as directing) and his crew were badly burned when magnesium blew up during the Toulon battle sequence. Furthermore, Gance suffered a detached retina during his six months of editing the massive footage. In addition to the climactic Italian sequence, the "Double Tempete"—during which Gance cuts back and forth between Bonaparte adrift at sea during a storm and a "stormy" debate at the Convention (the Revolutionary assembly) in Paris—and the "Bals des Victimes" were filmed in Gance's breakthrough wide-screen triptych process, "Polyvision," which utilized three cameras on top of each other and, for screening, required three projectors and three screens. Gance intended all three sequences to be shown in Polyvision.

Napoleon received a standing ovation at its gala premiere at the Paris Opera on April 7, 1927. An edited

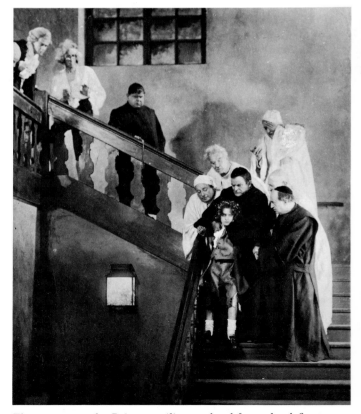

The masters at the Brienne military school force the defiant 12-year-old Bonaparte out into the cold after he tries to fight all the other boys.

---

*In addition to Brownlow's writings, I have referred to James Reid Paris's *The Great French Films* (1983) for background information.

†William Drew writes: "*J'Accuse* includes footage with real soldiers taken at the front by Gance during the close of the war. Eighty percent of the soldiers who portray the [ghosts of the] war-dead in the climax were killed in battle a few weeks after their appearance in this sequence."

Bonaparte swears to his family that Corsica will always be French.

version, it contained two triptychs and ran about 220 minutes. Gance's complete seven-hour version, without triptychs, was shown in two installments on successive nights. Four- and six-episode versions, without triptychs, were shown over a period of weeks. Abridged versions played in smaller theaters. The response was so enthusiastic that Gance expected Polyvision to revolutionize the silent cinema. Unfortunately, the release of *The Jazz Singer* (1927) later in the year doomed the silent cinema. Polyvision, a direct influence on Cinerama in 1952, was also doomed. When MGM bought the American rights to *Napoleon,* it released a 74-minute version without the triptychs which it feared would further change the art. (This version dealt primarily with the Napoleon and Josephine love story and ends during the Convention, with a close-up of George Washington.)

With the advent of sound, *Napoleon* disappeared forever. However, in 1935, Gance made *Napoleon Bonaparte,* using footage from his original film, and experimenting with stereophonic sound. Gance made films into the six-

ties, most notably *Lucrèce Borgia* (1935), *Beethoven,* a sound remake of *J'Accuse* (1937), and *Magirama* (1956), in which Gance again experimented with a three-screen process. (This was four years after Cinerama was first used.) In 1969, Gance was awarded a grant from Minister of the Arts André Malraux to prepare another film on Napoleon, to commemorate his bicentennial. Working with Claude Lelouch and Nelly Kaplin, Gance put together a documentary prologue, reedited sequences from earlier versions of his film, and shot new scenes with Dieudonné, who slimmed down for the role. *Bonaparte and the Revolution* (1971) would be the rare Gance film to be distributed in the United States, by Bob Harris's Images Film Archive of Rye, New York.

Kevin Brownlow's obsession with *Napoleon* began when he was a kid in the fifties. Already fascinated by silent movies, he sent away for two reels (containing the Marseillaise and Corsican sequences) of something titled *Napoleon Bonaparte and the French Revolution,* which was on 9.5 mm film. Any film fanatic will relate to his reaction:

"They changed my life." When older, Brownlow set out to reconstruct the lost film that he was desperate to see in its entirety. He got access to prints of various versions as well as all the negatives Gance used to begin *Bonaparte and the Revolution* from the Cinémathéque Français (with whom he had many fights). He contacted film archives all over the world, and bits and pieces trickled in. The British National Film Archive blew up prints to 35 mm. Images Film Archive secured rights from MGM and became the new American distributor. (Bob Harris would become very involved in the reconstruction.) By 1970, Brownlow had collected 5 hours and 58 minutes of film. Gance helped Brownlow put the existing footage in order and told him what was missing, consisting of more than two reels; he also informed Brownlow that in a moment of despair in 1952, he had destroyed the "Double Tempete" and "Bals des Victimes" triptychs. In 1973, Brownlow reconstructed the 18-minute Italian campaign triptych, and partially constructed versions played at the Pacific Archive in San Francisco and the AFI Theater in Washington. In 1979, outdoors in the bitter cold (so there could be no music), until 3 A.M., film enthusiasts were thrilled by the finished product that was unveiled at the Telluride Film Festival. This led to the silent-speed screening in London and the sound-speed 70-mm screening at Radio City Music Hall in New York. Gance, who died at 92, was able to experience the deserved worldwide appreciation that had eluded him for 50 years.

Certainly no other silent films, not even those of D. W. Griffith or the great Russian and German directors of the twenties, are as visually spectacular as Gance's *Napoleon*. It went beyond the boundaries of the medium. It will surprise many viewers that back in 1927 Gance was experimenting with split-screen photography, hand-held cameras, superimpositions (at times are 15 at once), rapid-fire editing, color tinting, close-ups, dollying, and

Paul Barras and his mistress Josephine, soon to be Bonaparte's wife.

wide screen. He strapped cameras and cameramen to horses; he attached one camera to a guillotine and placed another under water; he put a camera on a pendulum and swung it through the set. His intention was to make viewers feel part of the action. (Imagine how Gance would direct sports on television.) Each sequence will stun you with its technical brilliance and directorial bravura, the pageantry and poetry, its authentic re-creation of a time gone by, and the aggressive energy of all the interesting-looking actors and beautiful actresses Gance crowds into his frame. There are many scenes with extraordinary visuals: the snowball battle, the pillow fight, the emotional singing of the Marseillaise (remember this is a *silent* movie!), Bonaparte's horseback escape on Corsica, Bonaparte at sea during a tempest crosscut with the debate at the Convention (during which Gance puts the camera on a swing to simulate sea movements), the decadent victims' ball, etc. We see what would inspire France's Jean Cocteau, Jean Vigo, Carl Dreyer, Max Ophuls, and the New Wave directors. The triptych that gives the film a rousing conclusion is certainly a highlight, even if I don't think Gance succeeded in simultaneously showing on the three screens "the physical, the mental, and the emotional."

While the visuals are consistently impressive—the remarkable array of faces that fills the screen is as striking as the epic battles—there are problems in other areas. Granted that footage is still missing, but Gance was limited as a storyteller. For instance, his direction of the battle scenes is often confusing, so that they become dull even when looking marvelous. There are many times when I can't figure out what's happening, who the characters on the screen are, and what historical significance a scene has. Without checking your encyclopedia, can you figure out what's happening at the Convention during the Double Tempete scene? Here, as in many other scenes with historical significance, Gance doesn't bother to provide us with the facts we need. He was too intent on creating a visual metaphor that indicates the "storm" at the Convention matches the storm at sea Napoleon endures—it's a sensational visual sequence, but if any other director used this nonsubtle metaphor, he'd be mocked for being affected and obvious. There are holes. Gance has Bonaparte swear that Corsica will not be under British rule while he is alive, only to have Napoleon flee Corsica and leave it in English hands—there will be no mention of Corsica again, even though it would become part of France. Gance hammers home that Bonaparte is so in love with Josephine that he can't think of politics—when he looks at a globe he sees Josephine's face; when he kisses the globe, it's not Paris he's kissing but her lips—but then has him be late to their wedding because he is devising strategy for his Italian campaign. Gance presents Robespierre, Marat, and Saint-Just as perverse, self-serving men who have sold out the Revolution, yet when they come back as ghosts to confront Bonaparte, they are as noble as Danton, as patriotic as Napoleon, and completely dedicated to the objectives of the Revolution. There has been, with good reason, much criticism of this scene in which Gance makes the future emperor into the symbol of the Revolution, whose decision to conquer Europe and make it a "Universal Republic" meets with the approval of Danton,

In his element, Bonaparte initiates his daring plan to oust enemy troops from Toulon.

Robespierre, Marat, and Saint-Just. In an interview with Steven Kramer and James M. Welch in *Film Comment* (March/April 1974), Gance defended his point of view: "[Bonaparte] had real genius, both political and military, and truly republican ideas. He wanted to lead Europe towards a universal republic. He wrote that in his memoirs. Unfortunately, events forced him to make kingdoms in order to destroy all the feudalities of Europe. That was like replacing one casualty with another."

How different is Gance's Napoleon from the egocentric, personally ambitious bumbler—in battle and in bed—Sacha Guitry makes him out to be in his sardonic *Napoleon* (1955). Gance presents Napoleon as a figure of destiny who was always in the right place at the right time to help his troubled country. He is there when France needs an aggressive, fearless military leader to snatch victory from the jaws of defeat; when it needs someone to fight the English; when it needs someone to stand up to the leaders of the Reign of Terror who betrayed the Revolution; when it needs someone to stop the moral decay of the people; when it needs someone to put officers in line and to boost the morale of the starving, weary troops; and when it needs a visionary to see that France must expand its borders through military action (one reason people accused this film of being fascistic). Napoleon is a myth figure with powers given to him by the gods ("Napoleon had the vague feeling of a source of light growing within him"), a god who stands at the edge on a heavenly mountain peak, a Moses leading the French people to the promised land, and a force of nature, "made of granite heated in volcano," who thrives in storms, is constantly found "in the thick of *fire,* his element," and is equated with his eagle: When he reaches the mountaintop, the pinnacle of his success, he has an eagle's-eye view of the world. Too bad Napoleon doesn't come across as a human being (other than in scenes with Josephine). Albert Dieudonné, hailed by critics

worldwide, has tremendous presence—we can believe his steely glance would frighten men and mesmerize women—but I can never tell what his Napoleon is thinking or what is motivating him. He is without emotion, without fire. He is not the adult who should have developed from the fascinating youngster played by Roudenko, who was tortured by his isolation and loneliness, who had to withstand bullying (until it became too much), who tried to be stoic but couldn't hold back the tears. I don't even understand the nature of his love of France. Gance should have included scenes in which Napoleon explains himself to someone (Josephine?), or attempts a little self-analysis. Perhaps Gance could have quoted his memoirs more. Roy Armes writes:

> Central to Gance's conception was a very 19th-century romantic view of the artist. It has been well observed that just as *Un Grand Amour de Beethoven* depicts the artist as hero, *Napoleon* offers a view of the hero as artist. Though Gance himself played the role of Saint-Just, he identified himself as creator of the film with Napoleon as creator of a new France and master of the forces of history. Napoleon, the man of action, the politician and military genius, becomes largely a passive figure, a pensive visionary.

I hoped that the stir caused by the release of the reconstructed *Napoleon* would lead to renewed interest in the silent cinema and the rerelease of many silent classics that viewers would love. But there was so much hype surrounding Gance's film that viewers got the impression it was so much greater than other silent films that they would pale in comparison. Which is ridiculous. *Napoleon* may be the crowning achievement of the silent era, but it isn't the last word in silent films.

New York, New York

1977 Color United Artists
Director: Martin Scorsese
Producers: Irwin Winkler and Robert Chartoff
Screenplay: Earl Mac Rauch and Mardik Martin
Cinematography: Laszlo Kovacs
Production Design: Boris Leven
Original Songs by John Kander and Fred Ebb: "Theme from New York, New York," "There Goes the Ball Game," "But the World Goes Round," "Happy Endings"
Choreography: Ron Field
Supervising Editors: Irving Lerner and Marcia Lucas
Running Time: 137/153 minutes (rereleased in 1981 at 163 minutes)

Cast: Robert De Niro (Jimmy Doyle), Liza Minnelli (Francine Evans), Lionel Stander (Tony Harwell), Barry Primus (Paul Wilson), Mary Kay Place (Bernice), Georgie Auld (Frankie Harte), Dick Miller (Palm Club owner), Leonard Gaines (Artie Kirks), Clarence Clemons (Cecil Powell), Kathi McGinnis (Ellen Flannery), William Tole (Tommy Dorsey), Frank Sivera (Eddie Di Muzio), George Memmoli (Nicky), Diahnne Abbott (Harlem Club singer), Casey Kasem (DJ), Larry Kert (producer in movie).

Synopsis: On V-J Day, Jimmy Doyle joins the celebration at the Rainbow Room in New York. Like other ex-soldiers he tries to pick up women. He spots a woman sitting alone and makes a play for her. Francine Evans, a singer, is annoyed by his refusal to take no for an answer. It takes a very long time for her to get him to go away. Coincidentally, Francine's girlfriend Ellen has been picked up by Jimmy's army buddy Eddie. Eddie and Ellen borrow Jimmy's room for the night. When Francine goes the next morning to the hotel to find out what happened to her friend, she finds Jimmy in the lobby, being evicted for not paying his bill. Jimmy jumps into Francine's cab and insists she go with him to the Palm Club where he's auditioning as a tenor sax player. The Palm Club owner isn't interested until Francine sings along. He gives them both a job.

Jimmy and Francine smooch all the way back to their hotel. She promises to see him the next day, but she learns she is the new female singer with Frankie Harte's band. Her agent, Tony Harwell, informs Jimmy he has gone on tour. Jimmy quits his gig and goes after her. He tells her he loves her. Jimmy joins Harte's band. He's frustrated that Harte won't let him play his own, more progressive music. He tells Francine he's writing a song for her. He says he'll let her write the lyrics if she'll let him read her poetry. He's so touched that her poetry is about him that he drags her to the justice of the peace. She's annoyed that Jimmy doesn't bother to propose—so he gets down on his knees in the snow. She's won over.

Harte retires and gives the band to Jimmy. He has trouble getting bookings until Francine is made the star attraction. He resents that he must take a secondary position to her, and he gets annoyed when she tries to give band members instructions. Yet when she tells him she is pregnant and going to New York to have their baby, he becomes infuriated. With a new, inferior lead singer, Bernice Bennett, with whom he has an affair, the band hits hard times. Jimmy must give the band to his pianist, Paul Wilson. He joins Francine in New York. She isn't happy when he starts playing nights at the Harlem Club. She wants his attention. They argue. When they go to the Up Club to see Paul, Bernice, and their old band, Jimmy gets drunk and causes a scene.

Columbia Records producer Artie Kirks wants to sign Francine to a contract. Jimmy is jealous but doesn't interfere. However, they have a violent argument in the car. Jimmy admits he is furious about the baby. They strike at each other. She goes into labor. She has her baby in the hospital. He cries when she tells him she named the baby Jimmy. They say they love each other. They break up.

Years later, Francine is a big star of stage, screen, and records. Jimmy owns his own New York club, the Major Chord, and has the number-one song in the country, "New York, New York"—the instrumental he wrote for Francine. He sees Francine perform, and she sings the song with her own lyrics. He meets her at her backstage party and talks to their son. Afterward he calls her and she agrees to meet him. She changes her mind and returns to the party. He smiles and walks off alone.

M artin Scorsese tried a change of pace with this stylized, downbeat romance—with music—that is set in the big-band era. He didn't attempt to present the forties music scene as it really was but how it was depicted in Hollywood films of the forties and fifties. For his models he used the offbeat melodrama *Blues in the Night* (1941), about a traveling jazz band, as well as those glossy backstage musicals made at Warners and MGM, some starring Judy Garland. But he threw out the polished dialogue of those films in favor of naturalistic banter, figuring that the improvisation that characterizes his films with Robert De Niro seemed especially appropriate for a movie about *jazz* musicians, improvisers themselves. Interestingly, though his film takes place mostly in New York City, Scorsese made it obvious that the film was made on Hollywood sound stages and back lots: "That [is] a fantasy of New York up on the screen," he told Jonathan Kaplan in *Film Comment* (July/August 1977), "[s]o in the picture I tried to fuse whatever was a fantasy—the movies I grew up with as a kid—with the reality that I experienced myself." As Harry Kritzer would write in a 1986 issue of *Laser Works:* "It was as if a production designed for a Vincente Minnelli were suddenly taken over by the likes of John Cassavetes."

Scorsese took a chance with *New York, New York*, and his hot streak—*Mean Streets* (1973), *Alice Doesn't Live Here Anymore* (1974), *Taxi Driver* (1976)—came to a crashing halt. It died at the box office, even in New York, New York. Although a few of us detected numerous virtues in the film, and a cult immediately formed, most viewers—even devoted fans of Scorsese, De Niro, and/or Liza Minnelli—found it unappealing. Critics who should have known better unfairly panned it. Oddly, when it was rereleased in 1981, in its uncut 163-minute version, many of these critics overpraised it, reevaluating it as an ahead-of-its-time gem. And viewers followed their lead, loving the film the second time around. Why the complete reversal? Writing in *American Film* (December 1986) about videocassettes of restored films, Michael Barson explained why he changed his mind:

> The first time I saw Martin Scorsese's *New York, New York*, it seemed artificial and ponderous, with an awkward performance by Liza Minnelli as songbird Francine Evans and a somnambulant effort by Robert De Niro as jazz saxophonist Jimmy Doyle. . . . The pace was too slow, the scenes too long, the improvisation ineffective, and the ending anticlimactic. But after screening the uncut videocassette version—which contains the twelve minute musical number "Happy Endings" (also shown when the film was theatrically re-released)—I was blown away. Suddenly De Niro's performance seems touched with genius—the equal of anything he has ever done on film. Liza's uncanny impersonation of her mother, circa 1945, no longer seems faked. The rhythm of the scenes, the jazzy pace of the dialogue, the period sets and costumes and cars all now seem wonderfully authentic.

Francine sings to help Jimmy get a job at a club.

I disagree with Barson that the reinsertion of the lavish "Happy Endings" number is the reason he or other second-time viewers like the picture better. Even if we accept that a lengthy musical number can affect how we view the nonmusical aspects of a film, "Happy Endings" comes long after we've decided whether we like the performances, rhythm of the dialogue, pacing, characters, et al. In fact, it comes so late in the proceedings that it ruins the picture's momentum at a pivotal point, as it moves toward the finale. It is a show-stopper, in the worst sense of the term. Just when we expect the personal story to be resolved, the final scenes are overloaded with music, three numbers in a brief time span—"But the World Goes Round," "Happy Endings," and "Theme from New York, New York." We can accept the first and last numbers, but not an additional 12-minute number. Moreover, "Happy Endings" almost makes Minnelli's dynamic, spine-tingling "Theme from

New York, New York" anticlimactic. This is because it's so long, not because it's better. Despite all the hype, the elaborate "Happy Endings," in which movie actress Francine plays an usherette who meets a pioducer (Larry Kert) and then stars in several production numbers, is uninspired, sappy, and dull. The set design and costumes may be impressive (Minnelli's clothes match the walls), but the tune itself is trite, the choreography is unimaginative, the dancing is tame. It is by no means as much fun as the big movie production numbers it simultaneously sends up and pays tribute to, like Gene Kelly's "Broadway Rhythm" in *Singin' in the Rain* (1952) and Judy Garland's "Born in a Trunk" in *A Star Is Born* (1954). Moreover, whereas we could see Garland's Esther Blodgett as the actress in the "Born in a Trunk" movie scene, the actress who performs "Happy Endings" bears no relation to the Francine Evans we've seen the rest of the picture. True, some band singers went into movies, but at no time do we sense this is the course Francine will take. Anyway, *Singin' in the Rain* and *A Star Is Born* are about movies while this film is about music and shouldn't include such a long movie scene. I'd throw out "Happy Endings" again. The shorter version of the film is better.

My feeling is that viewers appreciate *New York, New York* more the second time around because they're better prepared for De Niro's Jimmy Doyle, who's not the romantic hero one usually finds in musicals. He is much like Gene Kelly's egocentric, self-serving entertainer in *For Me and My Gal* (1942), just as Minnelli's Francine will remind you of Garland's dumped-on singer in that film. But while Kelly's character reforms because of the love of his partner-wife (Garland), Jimmy remains a cad. Jimmy's so pushy, childish, manipulative, irresponsible, and domineering in the initial scenes that many first-time viewers are quickly repulsed by him, and wonder how Francine tolerates him for so long. He ruins the film for them, and they refuse to notice (or care) when he begins to reveal positive traits—especially since he continues to behave badly. However, second-time viewers know Jimmy's good qualities going into the film, and they realize that at film's end he will be alone in the world, a loser in love and in life. Because they know he is on a self-destructive path, they now can have sympathy for this man who can't control himself, who can't conform, who can't treat Francine the way she expects to be treated. Because they know Jimmy will be punished, it becomes easier to put up with his abrasive personality and callous, immature actions. And now that Jimmy doesn't make you want to exit the theater, it becomes easier to pay attention to the wonderful acting of De Niro, Minnelli, and supporting players Georgie Auld, Lionel Stander, and Leonard Gaines; the convincing sax playing of De Niro (Auld dubbed his music) and marvelous singing of Minnelli; the humorous improvisations; Boris Leven's stunning set design; Laszlo Kovacs's wide-screen cinematography; and what Scorsese is saying about his characters.

In 1977, Leonard Quart and Barbara Quart wrote in *Cineaste* (Vol. VIII, No. 2):

> There is a[n] . . . ambiguity about the film's attitude toward the male-female tensions and conflicts it portrays. It touches only lightly on the woman's ambition and drive for success, but it makes very clear the man's need for command and dominance. [Jimmy's] ego is fragile, and he displays both tyrannical rage and sullen vulnerability whenever his will is crossed and [Francine] wants to share in his decision-making, or whenever her success seems to be overshadowing his, [she] can only retreat to traditional female accommodation or tears.

They see Francine as a passive victim, who keeps the reins on her own life to boost Jimmy's ego, who hangs around just to be hurt. However, if you watch the film closely you'll see that it is Francine who determines the course of their professional and personal relationships. And it is Francine who constantly victimizes Jimmy and who ultimately destroys these relationships. He may do bad things, but she is the villain. She may be sweet and dewy-eyed and seem to be "perfect," but in truth she is unreliable and insensitive. She is kind enough to help Jimmy get a gig at the Palm Club. Yet despite her "I promise" to meet him the next day, and her knowledge that without her as his singer Jimmy will lose his new job, she runs off with Frankie Harte's band the next morning. Later, when Jimmy takes over the band, she and pianist friend Paul Wilson (Barry Primus) sit together reveling in reviews that state she is the best thing in the band . . . and then she has the gall to "innocently" suggest to Jimmy that they use some of the best quotes about the band—which are, of course, about her—for publicity. He may be irritated and jealous, but he agrees—he'll even put her name above his. We get mad at Jimmy for yelling at Francine when she "innocently" gives instructions to the band instead of deferring to her husband. But she's the one who's out of line; just because she has top billing doesn't give her the right to usurp Jimmy's power with *his* band. She's inconsiderate.

We get mad at Jimmy for yelling at Francine for becoming pregnant, and then for inconsiderately asking her to stick with the band until the baby comes although this may be precarious to her health. But Francine became pregnant without discussing it with Jimmy (yes, I know he should have been equally responsible), and then decides to go to New York for its delivery without considering that this may ruin her husband's budding career. Jimmy allows her to leave although he knows this means his band's days are numbered. She won't sing for Jimmy, yet when she arrives in New York she lets her agent Tony (Stander) talk her into singing on demos and commercials. When Jimmy comes to New York, we become angry that he would take a job playing nights at the Harlem Club instead of spending time with his pregnant wife. But Francine is

Jimmy shows his resentment toward Paul, who bought the band from him and brought it to New York.

Francine performs "Happy Endings" in a movie. This big production number was deleted when the picture was originally released.

not right to nag him about this and make him feel guilty; after all, if he hadn't lost his band because she came to New York, he'd be on the road during the remainder of her pregnancy, anyway. She doesn't understand that even though she is pregnant, he has to make a living playing his sax: "This is the most important thing to me besides you. . . . If I can't do this, then I'm not good for you and I'm not good for anybody." We get mad at Jimmy when he is jealous about Francine's success—she hasn't let her pregnancy get in the way of her own career—but she has accepted a record contract without bothering to discuss it with him or worry how it will affect him at a time when he's so down on his luck. She even comes to the club in which Jimmy works in order to finalize her own deal. Finally, years later, it is her choice not to return to Jimmy. She tells him at one point, "I just want you to be happy,"

but at no time does she make the effort to help him achieve happiness.

I do agree with Leonard Quart and Barbara Quart when they write "it is clearly [Jimmy] rather than [Francine] toward whom Scorsese is most sympathetic—as if being the romantic artist absolves [Jimmy] from 'bourgeois' responsibilities and decencies." Scorsese, De Niro, and Earl Mac Rauch (who began the script) and Mardik Martin (who took over) forgive Jimmy for being egotistical, for being temperamental, for putting down his fellow musicians, for being jealous of his wife's success, for being unfaithful, for smoking grass, for refusing to conform, and for not wanting a child, because this fits the profile of the typical insecure jazz musician. In their eyes, Jimmy is redeemed by his devotion to his music and his talent (he's an innovator who plays progressive jazz), his unqualified

Francine sings the title song, which deserved an Academy Award, but wasn't even nominated.

love for Francine, and his willingness to strip himself bare and humble himself in front of her: He never conceals his love for her, he kneels down in the snow to propose, he buys her a car full of flowers to apologize for creating a scene, he cries when she names their baby after him. (We're also supposed to like him better because he's friends with cool, *black* musicians.) Notice that all the film's tear-jerking moments are those in which Jimmy reveals his sensitivity.

It is by intention that Scorsese makes Jimmy so annoying at the beginning. Jimmy has difficulty showing his soft, vulnerable side, so it wouldn't make sense if he reveals this side right away. However, this creates a problem: We don't see why Francine is attracted to him. Is it simply because he overwhelms her? Moreover, since we don't fully understand him in these early scenes, we can't see why he is so quickly attracted to Francine, especially since she is only one of many women he tries to pick up in the Rainbow Room. Neither seems to be a prize. We need some indication that each discovers there is something special about the other. I think we need to see the exact moments they each fall in love. Both moments could quite easily take place in the Palm Club, when she first sees him

play his saxophone and he first sees her sing. It would make sense that they fall in love while watching each other perform: Both have trouble communicating verbally, but they reveal themselves through their art.

The screenplay is intentionally skimpy—or at least it seems slim after Scorsese trimmed the film from its 269-minute first cut. There is essentially no real, *quality* conversation between Jimmy and Francine, just rhythmic comic-duo patter that serves to complement their rhythmic musical numbers. They don't discuss their relationship or individual needs ("You don't understand," Jimmy insists), yet at one point she asks her uneducated husband if he knows the meaning of the theory of relativity. They have no families, no lifelong friends, no prewar pasts. They aren't *real* people and the world they travel in is stylized. The obviously fake forest, nonexistent subway (we hear it and see its shadow whizzing by), back-lit train, and prop snow, the red-orange sky backdrop, the studio streets, the marvelous decor, and the artificial light (in which a sailor and his lady dance a lovely *pas de deux*) make me believe Scorsese intended to create an expressionistic memory piece. Perhaps Francine, who doesn't realize her faults, is, in 1977, looking back on a time gone by.

The Night of the Hunter

1955 B&W United Artists
Director: Charles Laughton
Producer: Paul Gregory
Screenplay: James Agee
From the novel by Davis Grubb
Cinematography: Stanley Cortez
Music: Walter Schumann
Editor: Robert Golden
Running Time: 93 minutes

Cast: Robert Mitchum (Preacher Harry Powell), Billy Chapin (John Harper), Shelley Winters (Willa Harper), Lillian Gish (Rachel Cooper), Sally Jane Bruce (Pearl Harper), Evelyn Varden (Icey Spoon), Don Beddoe (Walt Spoon), Peter Graves (Ben Harper), James Gleason (Uncle Birdie), Gloria Castillo (Ruby), Mary Ellen Clemons (Clary), Cheryl Callaway (Mary).

Synopsis: Children find a murdered woman in a barn. Preacher Harry Powell drives away, having done what he believes is God's work. He talks to God constantly—he can't remember if this is the 6th or 12th widow he has married and murdered. He despises women because they arouse men's carnal instincts.

Nine-year-old John Harper and his 4-year-old sister, Pearl, play in their yard in Cresap's Landing, a small town on the Ohio River. Their father, Ben, drives up. He has killed for $10,000. He stashes the money in Pearl's doll and makes both kids swear not to tell anyone, even their mother, Willa, where it is. John is upset when the police knock down and handcuff his father.

Ben awaits hanging in the Moundsville penitentiary. His cellmate is Preacher, serving 30 days for auto theft. Preacher tries to cajole Ben into revealing where the missing money is so he can build a tabernacle. Ben recognizes Preacher is no man of God. He dies without revealing the secret.

Preacher arrives in Cresap's Landing. He tells Willa he was the preacher at the penitentiary. She's relieved when he says Ben told him he threw the money in the river. Preacher overwhelms Willa, Pearl, and the rest of the townspeople by quoting scriptures, belting out hymns, and delivering a sermon about good defeating evil. Only John distrusts and fears this strange man who has L-O-V-E and H-A-T-E tattooed on his fingers. Spurred on by busybody Icey Spoon and her ineffectual husband, Walt, her employees at the soda shop, Willa accepts Preacher's proposal. On their wedding night, Preacher admonishes her for expecting sex, ever. She hopes she will learn to be clean. Falling under his spell, she speaks of her sins at his revival meetings. She doesn't believe John when he tells her Preacher has been trying to get him to reveal where the money is hidden. But one night she overhears Preacher trying to force Pearl to reveal their secret. The broken woman is resigned to her death. Preacher stabs her with his switchblade. He tells the Spoons she ran off. Uncle Birdie discovers the body in her car at the bottom of the river, but is afraid to tell anyone lest he be blamed.

Preacher threatens the children. Pearl tells Preacher the money is in her doll to stop him from stabbing John. But the children escape with the doll, taking the skiff downriver. Preacher steals a horse and gives chase. The kids' journey is arduous. John knows that Preacher will never stop hunting them.

Found on the riverbank, John and Pearl are taken into the care of Rachel Cooper, a strong-willed 60-year-old Bible-storytelling widow. Three other orphans live with her: Ruby, Mary, and Clary. John comes to trust her, but he can't talk of his past.

Preacher arrives at the farm to claim his "flesh and blood." Rachel realizes he is no preacher and no father to the kids. She chases him away with a rifle. That night, Preacher lays siege to the house. Then he sneaks inside. Rachel shoots him. Wounded, he runs yelping into the barn. When the police arrest him, John is reminded of what happened to his father. Losing control, he repeatedly hits Preacher with the doll, and the money pours out.

Preacher is convicted of murder. Icey and Walt lead a mob that wants to lynch him. John and Pearl settle in with Rachel. She marvels at the way children abide and endure.

"Lord save little children! For each of them has his Preacher to hound him down the dark river of fear and tonguelessness and never-a-door. Each one is mute and alone because there is no word for a child's fear and no ear to heed it if there were a word and no one to understand it if it were heard. Lord save little children! They abide and they endure."

—Rachel, in Davis Grubb's novel
The Night of the Hunter

First-time viewers are invariably startled by how weird and how brilliant is Charles Laughton's movie adaptation of Davis Grubb's riveting best-seller. It is a fascinating, truly unique work, part gothic horror film, part religious parable, part child's nightmare, part fairy tale. It has a terrifying story line, uniformly outstanding and offbeat performances, including a chilling portrayal by Robert Mitchum as a psychotic phony preacher, striking cinematography by Orson Welles alumnus Stanley Cortez (who was behind the camera for the 1949 Laughton-starrer *The Man on the Eiffel Tower*), and excitingly unconventional direction by Laughton. In preparation for the film, Laughton studied the techniques of German expressionists and D. W. Griffith; from Griffith, he also took leading lady Lillian Gish and borrowed, from the Griffith-Gish and independent Gish classics, both a vision of a troubled bucolic America and the theme of innocents being cast adrift in a sinful world. His picture *looks* different from other films of the period—though Elia Kazan's *East of Eden* (1955), with its unusual camera angles, and Stanley Kubrick's *The Killing* (1956), with its multiplane staging (with props located between the characters and the camera), use similar ideas—and his characters are different. In 1955, critics complained the film was self-consciously arty and too vague because of all the symbols. (Actually, there are few major symbols other than Preacher's phallic stick knife, which opens when he's watching a stripper and when Ruby suggests something wicked, and the film's many apples, which represent sexual temptation and, according to critic Robin Wood, fertility and harvest.) The resulting box office was so dismal that the depressed Laughton quit working on his second film, an adaptation of *The Naked and the Dead,* and never dared direct another film. So he stands as one of the few directors—Leonard Kastle of *The Honeymoon Killers* (1970) is another—whose batting average for masterpieces is 1.000.

But let me go back to the early fifties, when Laughton found his movie career was sputtering. He joined forces with young, innovative producer Paul Gregory, and served as star and director of several enormously successful stage productions, including *Don Juan in Hell* and *The Caine Mutiny Court Martial.* Their plays were known for having minimal sets yet bold acting and direction, a combination Gregory and Laughton wanted to employ in their first screen collaboration, *The Night of the Hunter.* It's understandable why Gregory was attracted to Grubb's novel.

While Pearl sleeps, John's awake nightmare begins. A stranger, Preacher, stands outside in the darkness.

Another dramatic, expressionistic visual, conceived by director Charles Laughton and photographed by Stanley Cortez. Willa waits for her husband to kill her.

Like John and Pearl Harper, he was born in the Midwest (on a farm in Waukee, Iowa), experienced poverty and the misery of the Depression, and found he couldn't simply rely on adults for his welfare (which meant he worked at a very young age). Surely he saw a sorry parade of itinerant preachers warning potential sinners of God's wrath and passing the collection plate, if not as a youngster then when, as young impresario, he took plays into some 300 towns and villages on the long-neglected "Chautauqua circuit." Interestingly, when Gregory first approached Laughton in the late forties, it was to propose sending the actor around the country reading the Bible.

I guess Laughton was attracted to Grubb's story because it cried out for an unorthodox visual style, and because of Preacher. Laughton had loved playing villains who were ruthless, narrow-minded and obsessed, manipulative, believed in their omnipotence, and loved to hear themselves talk; men who became crazy from basking in their own glory. He didn't really care about the plight of John and Pearl Harper and so detested child actors Billy Chapin and Sally Jane Bruce that he had Mitchum direct them (they do an exceptional job). So it's remarkable that few films in history convey more heartfelt empathy toward helpless little children than *The Night of the Hunter*, and few have more insight into the cruel, dangerous, frightening world of young children, particularly orphans. For even when they are seemingly secure under their covers, they worry about being bitten by bedbugs and attacked by huge monsters that make shadows on their walls. And it doesn't take sleep to project unprotected kids like John and Pearl into a wilderness of fear and confusion. For such children—and this is the theme of the novel and film—nightmares continue even when they are awake.

In an essay printed in *On Film,* Robin Wood explained why he considers the movie, for all its apparent fidelity to the book's events, distinct from and decidedly superior to Grubb's novel:

> The difference is primarily of style and tone. That of the book is highly suspect, characterized by that gooey, pseudo-poetic self-indulgence that too often passes for "lyricism." The concept of nature plays a vital role in both book and film, but in the book this role is vitiated by Grubb's presentation. In his nature, frogs don't croak, they "chant their unending litany of love." . . . [Screenwriter James] Agee manages to trim away the fat of pretentious verbosity and the lush, sticky imagery of the novel. What he retains is the strongly planned structure of the fable which Grubb's language tends to obscure rather than illuminate. Where the book is self-indulgent and corrupt, the film is rigorous and pure. Here it is difficult to distinguish clearly Laughton's contribution from Agee's. In a sense "it's all in the script"—nearly. Laughton sets himself to realize Agee's intentions (the script abounds in striking cinematic ideas) with a humility surprising to those who know him only through his screen persona.
>
> Groupings and compositions, camera movements, even the difficult helicopter shots, are for the most part as demanded by Agee. Laughton's respect for Agee's intentions shows itself especially in his leaving stark and bare what almost any other director would have filled out and decorated.

Wood is too quick to discredit Grubb for the success of the film, give credit to Agee, and imply Laughton showed wisdom in adhering to Agee's story ideas rather than Grubb's and to Agee's cinematic ideas rather than the ones he formulated himself while directing theater (i.e., the spare sets) and studying classic films (perhaps the helicopter shots were inspired by the opening of Leni Reifenstahl's 1936 German documentary *Triumph of the Will?*). It has come to light in recent years, partly through the publication of Elsa Lanchester's autobiography, that Laughton paid Agee $30,000 for a script to assure studio interest, and then threw it out because it was much too long and wasn't faithful to Grubb's novel. The shooting script, which incorporates Laughton's cinematic ideas, and events and dialogue from the novel, was in fact written by Laughton. It has also been conjectured that Grubb collaborated on the script, but it's more likely his contribution was limited to providing Laughton with 119 pencil and ink drawings depicting how he saw each character or scene. Titles included: "Harper living room," "Cooper's house and farm," "(Preacher) Weren't you children afraid down there alone in the dark?," "Ruby watches lynching"—a scene not in the movie—"Rachel," "Preacher," "Ice cream parlor exterior," John's vest-eye view," "Exterior Miz Cunning-

At a Cresap's Landing picnic, Preacher impresses Willa and Icey Spoon (with back turned).

ham's second hand shop." Grubb eventually sent his drawings to a gallery with an explanatory letter. An excerpt:

> Laughton assured me with considerable passion that he intended the film to resemble as nearly my mental pictures in writing the book as was possible to achieve. . . . He was, like Von Stroheim, compulsive in this passion for verisimilitude. Long after I sold the screen rights to Laughton and Gregory for *The Night of the Hunter* and was well into my second novel I began to be subjected to a daily barrage of wires, phone calls from Hollywood and letters asking me for sketches, more sketches and yet more sketches of what this or the other scene looked like in my mind. So incessant was this interrogation that it kept me busy dividing my time between the new book, *A Dream of Kings,* and making drawings and sending them off air mail special to Laughton in Hollywood. He would even ask me to draw the expression on a character's face during certain scenes. I . . . can only declare, perhaps immodestly, that I was not only the author of the novel from which the screenplay was adapted, but was the actual scene designer as well.

I don't want to imply that Laughton made no changes from the novel, or that some changes (i.e., the wedding night scene) aren't improvements. However, I think the film's success is due to Laughton adhering to the tone of Grubb's novel, and not, as Wood suggests, deliberately seeking an alternate tone. Wood is correct in thinking Grubb preferred waxing poetic or piling on the imagery to making simple, direct statements. But, as Laughton understood, Grubb's style and tone were correct for the type of *story* he is telling. His story may be set in contemporary times, but place the words "Once upon a time" before it and you'll realize that he is writing one of those Tolkien-like fantasies that are set in a timeless, alternate universe, where there is, say, an ill wind to the east, pestilence and plague overtaking the land, an exodus of good people in the face of evil, and a journey/mission of survival undertaken by underdog heroes . . . with a seemingly invincible evil creature breathing down their necks. Grubb suggests that the Depression years, with all their religious hysteria, poverty, crime, lynchings, mobs, and wandering children, hark back to the Dark Ages, to biblical times, to mythical times. He transports Pearl, who's too young to realize what's happening, and John, whose trauma is so great that reality gives way to mental disorientation, into a nightmarish fantasy world: They may lose their lives just to keep a promise to their irresponsible father; their father is taken away, then he is dead; a mean stepfather with a knife moves in; their mother sides with him over her children; mother abandons them, then mother is dead; the stepfather wants to murder them; they must flee their home; children ostracize them because of what their father did; adults won't listen to them; their only adult friend (Birdie) becomes incapacitated when they are in grave danger; they can't trust the police (John calls them "blue men") because they beat and abducted their father; and God seems to be on the side of evil men like Preacher. It is, Grubb writes, "a world that hunted the children now," and like the baby Moses, they flee those who would kill children, and like Hansel and Gretel they wander into the wilderness and enter the house of a strange old lady (luckily, Rachel is no witch). Repeatedly, Grubb has his troubled characters sleep and have bad dreams to draw a parallel between their suddenly unreal world (Grubb's fantasy world) and any child's nightmare world; only when peace comes to them in their real lives can their nightmares stop.

Without a means to use Grubb's flowery prose or the time to include dream sequences, Laughton couldn't really draw the Depression America–fantasy world–child nightmares parallel that is advanced in the novel; he ends the film with Rachel's "they abide and they endure" speech rather than showing, as I'd prefer, John and Pearl going to sleep in Rachel's safe home and finally enjoying peaceful dreams. But he does the next best thing: He turns John and Pearl's story into a combination of a biblical tale and a Grimm fairy tale, and films it as if it were a nightmare. Laughton said: "It's really a nightmarish sort of Mother Goose tale we were telling. We tried to surround the children with creatures they might have observed, and that might have seemed part of a dream. It was, in a way, a dream for them."

In the opening Laughton immediately takes us out of reality. Harsh music is replaced by the sweet singing of children and the heads of Rachel and her five young wards appear in the sky, amidst the stars. She tells them to beware of false prophets (a Bible-story image), of wolves in sheep's clothing (a fairy-tale image). We realize what we are about to see is a *story,* a parable to illustrate her point—it might even be the nightmare John has that night after hearing Rachel's fretful words. An unreal world has been established and Laughton effectively keeps us there with his unusual visuals. He puts his camera in a helicopter and flies through the clouds to give us a bird's- or God's-eye view of the dusty landscape and the perspective is eerie: There are so many right angles that buildings and land boundaries look to have been drawn on a large canvas with aid of a straight ruler; houses and barns suddenly

have height, width, and depth, while parcels of land and waterways have become flat. Later Laughton situates his camera behind a character's head (Preacher in his car) or places a prop between the camera and a character's face, or covers the character with shadows; even indoors the camera is kept at a distance so we see characters in relation to the floors, walls, ceilings, and props. He uses an iris shot to zero in on John and Pearl peeking out their cellar window—and it is quite magical. The hauntingly beautiful shot of John and Pearl floating downriver in their skiff, with the starry sky and fertile far bank in the background and the fertile near bank in the foreground, is an image straight out of a Disney fairy-tale cartoon.

There is other surreal imagery: In a shadowy bedroom with walls that come to a point to make it resemble a chapel, Willa closes her eyes and waits for Preacher, Jehovah's messenger, to stab her to death; Preacher chases the kids into the river with arms outstretched, as if he were the Frankenstein monster; as the lynch mob rushes through the Moundsville streets at night the town takes on the look and feel of Babylon. Many settings are those a little child might pick to locate an adventure: a soda shop, a cellar, the front yard, the river, a boat, a barn, a picnic area. Laughton takes care to include all that is familiar to small towns—the wooden houses, soda shops, secondhand stores, grocery stores, billiard parlors, the bakery, the Bijou, river, boats, trains, picnics—but none of it looks familiar because of the startling ways Laughton and Cortez light the frame. In the day, it's either hazy or so bright that everything is washed out; at night there are dust, smoke, fog, and those spooky shadows (caused by stars or kerosene street lamps). Fairy-tale animals abound: bullfrogs, crickets, rabbits, birds, geese, owls, turtles, sheep, a spider in its web, and not only an actual fox but also a howling Preacher, who acts like a frightened fox caught raiding the henhouse when he zooms into the barn after Rachel shoots him.

If Rachel is as much Mother Goose (remember the old lady who lives in a shoe who has so many children . . .) as she is Mother Courage, then Preacher, a human wolf in sheep's clothing, is the classic deceitful fairy-tale villain who hides under boulders and behind trees in the forest and is ready to pounce on any innocent person who happens along. Like wolves and other sneaky villains in cartoons, including versions of and variations on old fairy tales, Preacher supplies the slapstick humor (only hinted at in the novel) that provides the necessary moments of relief from the truly gruesome proceedings: He tumbles out of his prison bed when Ben Harper punches him in the nose, he is hit square on the head with a hairbrush John throws at him, a shelf with heavy jars falls on his head, he trips in the dark on a jar on the cellar floor and does a pratfall, he has his fingers smashed in the door by John, he falls like Oliver Hardy into the river, his eyes open wide with terror when Rachel points her rifle at his rear and chases him from her property, he wails in pain after Rachel nips him with a shot and races at supersonic speed into the barn. His howling, his mock crying, even his creepy L-O-V-E versus H-A-T-E hand wrestling and his deep-voiced sermonizing have elements of absurd humor. Many fairy tales, from *Little Red Riding Hood* to *Snow*

Clutching a knife in fingers that are marked "L-O-V-E," Preacher threatens to stab John unless he reveals where the money is hidden.

White and the Seven Dwarfs, have sexual subtexts, and in this film, Preacher serves, of course, as the predatory lustful wolf (a figure in many funny Tex Avery cartoons) who waits for unsuspecting, innocent females to cross his path. He represents the manifestation of their subconscious—in other words, they desire sex. But unlike those other wolf figures, Preacher holds back his impulse to ravage women (after all, he believes he serves God) and instead punishes them for trying to arouse his libido and tempting him to sin—like crazy Anthony Perkins in *Crimes of Passion* (1984). He stabs them with his precious switchblade, obviously a sexual act. ("Don't touch my knife," he warns Pearl. "That makes me mad. Very, very mad.") Males (Ben, John, Birdie, even Walt) recognize his evil, but women, especially lonely widows, let their defenses down. Only Rachel doesn't fall for his sorry act. I assume this is because she's supposedly too old to be swayed by sexual longings; more acceptable is that her motherly instincts are stronger than her sexual instincts or that she is just too wise, too pure, and too strong for Preacher. Her attitude toward sex is enlightened, while Preacher's dates to the Dark Ages. She understands the sexual needs of females so she isn't disgusted, as Preacher would certainly

be, when young Ruby confesses that she's been sneaking around with the boys in town. By giving Ruby a brooch, Rachel shows she has no intention of suppressing Ruby's budding sexuality. She understands sex is natural and not something to be ashamed of—she would be horrified at Preacher's humiliating treatment of Willa on their wedding night, when he made her feel guilty and unclean for desiring sex. Rachel's concern, which she wants to express to Ruby, is that Preacher and the unfeeling boys in town can turn sex into something quite ugly and perverse.

The Night of the Hunter is a terrifying film, but every time I see it, I get all choked up about halfway through, anticipating Rachel coming to the aid of the two desperate children. How brave, unselfish, and caring she is—John and Pearl couldn't have found a better protector. She is the only one who recognizes their need for help, and the only one who has the inner strength and the faith to help them. In fact, if you think about it, she serves them as the priests serve the possessed child they don't even know in *The Exorcist* (1972), casting out the evil that threatens to destroy them. The strong-willed, God-loving woman proves too much for the strong-bodied heretic. I wish John's role wouldn't diminish so drastically toward the end of the

Publicity shot of Rachel and her brood. The troubled Ruby (left) and John eventually learn what a wise and wonderful woman she is.

film—Grubb includes John's cloudy impressions of the trial and its aftermath and ends with the children going to sleep on Christmas (a holiday for another endangered child)—but it's such a pleasure watching Rachel match wits and then do battle with Preacher. Especially since the two characters are played by Gish and Mitchum.

It's a triumphant return to the screen for Gish, perhaps the greatest film actress ever. She's still beautiful, still personifies goodness, and still exhibits tremendous power, grit, and determination. She's still a wonderfully natural actress and it is the humility and sincerity she projects as Rachel that perfectly counters the conceit and hamminess of Mitchum's Preacher. So this tiny actress manages to

hold her own with massive Mitchum—Rachel is never portrayed as underdog to Preacher—even though Mitchum was never more formidable, even as the sexual sadist in *Cape Fear* (1962). (Of course, Preacher is meant to be a pathetic coward.) When, in my favorite scene, Rachel, sitting with a gun, starts singing her version (with a reference to Jesus) of the hymn "Leaning on the Everlasting Arms" to soften the effect on her of the blasphemer's rendition—and for a moment they harmonize—you know that she can't be intimidated. She wins your heart and, if you're worrying about John and Pearl's welfare, your gratitude. Forget all those movie heroes: Gish's Rachel Cooper is the answer to every scared child's prayers.

Now, Voyager

1942 B&W Warner Bros.
Director: Irving Rapper
Producer: Hal B. Wallis
Screenplay: Casey Robinson
From the novel by Olive Higgins Prouty
Cinematography: Sol Polito
Music: Max Steiner
Editor: Warren Low
Montages: Don Siegel
Running Time: 117 minutes

Cast: Bette Davis (Charlotte Vale), Paul Henreid (Jerry Durrance), Claude Rains (Dr. Jaquith), Gladys Cooper (Mrs. Henry Windle Vale), Janis Wilson (Tina Durrance), Ilka Chase (Lisa Vale), Bonita Granville (June Vale), John Loder (Elliot Livingston), Lee Patrick (Deb McIntyre), Franklin Pangborn (Mr. Thompson), James Rennie (Frank McIntyre), Katherine Alexander (Miss Trask), Mary Wickes (Dora Pickford), Charles Drake (Leslie Trotter), David Clyde (William), Reed Hadley (Montie).

Synopsis: Lisa Vale is concerned about her sister-in-law Charlotte Vale, a young spinster who lives with her tyrannical mother in a lifeless Boston Back Bay mansion. She brings prominent psychiatrist Dr. Jaquith to meet Charlotte. The nervous, paranoid, plump Charlotte tells Jaquith that she once had an affair with a seaman, Leslie Trotter, on a voyage she took with her mother to Africa. But her mother broke off their engagement and has kept tight reins on her ever since. She knows that her mother never wanted her because she constantly browbeats her and makes her follow orders as if she were a servant. When Lisa's well-meaning daughter June teases Charlotte, she breaks down. This embarrasses the unsympathetic Mrs. Vale. She allows Jaquith to take Charlotte to his institute, Cascade. Charlotte loses a lot of weight, trims her eyebrows, and puts away her glasses. Instead of going home, she follows Jaquith's advice and takes a Caribbean cruise.

Charlotte is too self-conscious to emerge from her cabin for most of the trip, but when she does, everyone is impressed with her beauty. When the tourists go to shore, she shares a carriage with a handsome, unhappily married man named Jerry Durrance. She tells him about her breakdown and he is very understanding. He shows her a picture of his stern wife and depressed daughter, Tina—Charlotte recognizes that Tina was also an unwanted child.

Charlotte loses her inhibitions with Jerry, who calls her "Camille." And he is happy with her. When their tourist car crashes in the mountains, they spend a night together in a makeshift shelter. Soon after, they admit their love for each other. Their time together is joyous. But they say good-bye—he will return to his wife, and she to her mother.

Lisa and June are delighted at Charlotte's transformation. But mother wants her to return to being a dutiful daughter and servant-nurse. Charlotte almost gives in, but upon receiving camellias from Jerry, asserts her independence. From now on she and Mrs. Vale have an uneasy truce. Mrs. Vale is proud when Charlotte becomes engaged to wealthy Elliot Livingston. But when Charlotte meets Jerry at a party—because of her he has returned to being an architect—she realizes there is much lacking in her relationship with Elliot. She calls off the wedding. Mrs. Vale is furious at Charlotte. Charlotte tells her mother that she knows she was an unwanted child. Mrs. Vale dies of a heart attack. Charlotte blames herself.

On the verge of another breakdown, Charlotte goes to Cascade. She is surprised to find Tina there. No longer worried about herself, Charlotte takes Tina under her wing, without telling her she knows her father. The miserable girl blossoms into a happy child. She calls Charlotte "Camille." Charlotte takes her back to Boston to live with her. Jerry and Jaquith come to a party at the now-cheerful house. Jerry is thrilled with the transformation of his daughter and that Tina loves Charlotte. But he thinks he should take Tina home because it makes him uneasy how Charlotte sacrifices so much for her. Charlotte says she is rewarded. She needs Tina. Tina has become *their* daughter. Although his affair with Charlotte must end for the sake of Tina, he will visit *their* house often.

Now, Voyager will probably never lose its derogatory tag as the "quintessential old-style women's picture." And it shouldn't because it certainly is that. But what for so long has been regarded as no better than corny kitsch, bolstered only by a standout performance by Bette Davis, is today considered significant to women's film studies—as are some of the better "women's pictures" of the thirties and forties that have unusually strong and defiant female protagonists. Whereas in 1942 the New York *Daily News*'s critic Wanda Hale wrote it was "dull, heavy, and made with the deliberateness of a cat catching, torturing, and finally killing its mouse," in 1984 Jeanne Allen wrote, in her introduction to the shooting script, which is included in the University of Wisconsin/Warner Bros. Screenplay Series, that the picture offers "something rare and vital in American mass culture: the story of a woman's struggle to gain initiation into adulthood and a relative measure of independence." *Now, Voyager* definitely has a place in the classroom.

Nevertheless I think it's the rare film that's best enjoyed at home on television, where you can still take interest in its feminist themes but have the freedom to appreciate it more for being a schmaltzy romance and a classic Warner Bros. weepie. It's not a good choice for Mother's Day if your mother's anything like Gladys Cooper's Mrs. Vale. But it's ideal for late-night television viewing, especially when it's raining outside and you're huddled under your warm covers with the world's worst cold (with tissues handy) and can relate to all those characters suffering and getting better; or when, after overeating during your candlelit dinner, you and your honey are on the couch/floor *bundling* ("a New England custom that is reverenced and honored" according to Davis's Charlotte Vale) and can picture yourselves snuggling like Charlotte and Paul Henreid's Jerry in their makeshift shelter in the Brazilian mountains (actually that sounds a bit frightening), or on their Caribbean cruise, eating lunch with the sea in the background, standing on a balcony overlooking Rio (with Max Steiner's Oscar-winning theme in the background), and exchanging emotional good-bye kisses (there's nothing more romantic than farewells).

Just to be safe you'd better rent the video because most television stations chop out one-fourth of the 117 minutes in order to accommodate commercials in a 2-hour time slot. The flashback of the African-cruise sequence is often excised but for the final scene in which Gladys Cooper's Mrs. Vale and the captain catch proud Charlotte and seaman Leslie Trotter necking. This is unfortunate because this sequence reveals not only the romantic side of Charlotte (fueled by the novels she has hidden away) but also the nature of the tyrant-victim relationship of Mrs. Vale and her daughter. Also usually cut is the film's lone comedy sequence (complete with Franklin Pangborn), in which Charlotte is greeted by sister-in-law Lisa (Ilka Chase) and teenage niece June (Bonita Granville) after her Caribbean cruise, and stuns them with her beauty, confidence, and

Lisa introduces Dr. Jaquith to her mother-in-law, Mrs. Henry Windle Vale. He isn't intimidated.

popularity with the handsome men on board. And the next, more crucial sequence is often eliminated: Mrs. Vale immediately tries to push Charlotte back into her shell, but Charlotte, after being cheered by camellias from Jerry (he calls her "Camille"), insists on maintaining her independence (she will no longer be her mother's guest, unpaid servant, nurse, dutiful *child*), causing her shaken mother to fall down the stairs. Most TV versions cut from Charlotte saying farewell to Jerry in Brazil directly to Mrs. Vale sitting in bed with an "extremely painful" ankle.

Now, Voyager was adapted from the third novel of Olive Higgins Prouty's Vale-family trilogy. Published in 1941,

Dr. Jaquith tries to win the confidence of Charlotte, who is on the verge of a breakdown.

Prouty's lengthy book contains, as Jeanne Allen points out, themes suggested by the author's own life. Like Charlotte, Prouty came from a well-to-do Massachusetts family (her father was a professor); put off marriage for several years because of personal aspirations (establishing herself as a professional writer); felt considerable guilt about not adhering to social convention (by pursuing a professional career when she didn't need the money), especially after marriage to a rich husband (whose ego was the reason she didn't celebrate her fame or encourage publicity); donated much of her earnings to charity, just as Charlotte gives a portion of her inheritance to the Cascade institute; suffered a nervous breakdown (after the death of her fourth child), an act that was treated as a sign of weakness by her husband and social peers; spent time at a sanatorium, the Riggs Foundation in Stockbridge, Massachusetts, where Dr. Riggs gave her the advice and support that Charlotte receives from Claude Rains's Dr. Jaquith (who hands out "common sense when you want sympathy"); and achieved a degree of fulfilling independence (upon Riggs's suggestion, Prouty's husband agreed she should have her own "office" away from home, just as Mrs. Vale agrees with Jaquith to let Charlotte go to Cascade and then on an ocean voyage).

The book didn't receive favorable reviews or have very good sales, yet Warner Bros. snapped up rights because of the continuing popularity of Prouty's *Stella Dallas,* which had been made into a hit movie with Barbara Stanwyck in 1937 and was a ground-breaking radio soap opera, and *Lisa Vale,* the second part of the Vale saga. When it was reported that Warners would borrow Irene Dunne to star as Charlotte Vale, Bette Davis demanded the role from Jack Warner. Warner gave her the part, and assigned Casey Robinson—who had scripted Davis's *Dark Victory* (1939),

The Old Maid (1939), and *All This and Heaven Too* (1940)—the task of adapting Prouty's novel into a screenplay. Irving Rapper, the assistant director on two Davis films, *The Sisters* (1938) and *All This and Heaven Too,* was hired to direct. (Robinson would script and Rapper direct Davis's next film as well, *The Corn Is Green.*)

Giving one of her annual Oscar-nominated performances, Davis carries the film, evolving from repressed overaged child to generous mother, from neurotic to centered woman, from ugly duckling to lovely lady (those gorgeous Bette Davis eyes—once Charlotte's bushy brows are trimmed and glasses are removed—compensate for one of Davis's worst hairstyles). She was certainly correct in thinking she was right for Charlotte Vale. Notorious for standing up to the Warner Bros. brass, Davis understood how Charlotte feels to be crushed by a tyrannical mother who refuses to hear her words. And Davis knew how proud 20-year-old Charlotte is for having defied her mother by having an affair with lowly seaman Leslie Trotter (Charles Drake) right under her mother's snooping nose (I love how Charlotte triumphantly sashays away from her mother), and how relieved the transformed Charlotte is when she realizes she is "no longer afraid" to stand up to her mother. Davis knew how important it was for Charlotte to achieve independence and self-reliance. She could understand the peace Charlotte feels once she gains her hard-earned independence. And from her own "Lonely Life" she knew that independence meant making sacrifices that would make happiness impossible.

Without Davis, *Now, Voyager* would surely sink during Charlotte's first ocean cruise, long before young Janis Wilson, as the intolerably cloying Tina, drowns the film in a sea of tears. Davis's contribution is tremendous. Still we can pretty much discount her claim in her 1962 autobiography, *The Lonely Life,* that she extensively reworked Robinson's script so that it remained true to Prouty. Robinson's script was already quite faithful, even incorporating much of Prouty's succinct, witty dialogue intact. As Richard Corliss points out in *Talking Pictures* (1974), "Robinson pulled off a fantastic juggling act with elements that included mother hatred, adoptive-mother love, three nervous breakdowns, two ill-starred engagements, one adulterous affair, one platonic relationship, one huge, hostile family, and enough peripheral characters, each with his or her own idiosyncrasies, to dazzle Charles Dickens." Robinson's one major change was to not have Jerry also be recuperating from a nervous breakdown. Surely Robinson realized that it was considered inappropriate in Hollywood scripts for leading men to have breakdowns, especially during wartime. But he no doubt also realized his change would have a positive effect on how the audience perceives the story. There are already enough parallels in the lives of Charlotte and Jerry (who has a wife like Mrs. Vale and a daughter like Charlotte) to more than test a viewer's suspension of disbelief. More important, if we were also concerned about Jerry's mental state, we'd think it unforgivable of Charlotte to not only deny herself (physically) to him at the end but also take away his be-

A form of courtship: Jerry lights the now-lovely Charlotte's cigarette. When the romance intensifies, he will begin lighting her cigarettes while they are between his lips.

loved daughter. Jerry is already so much weaker than Charlotte at the conclusion that we feel bad for him when Charlotte admonishes him for thinking about taking Tina away (Davis always needs someone to yell at in a movie). By making Jerry a stable man, we can concentrate on Charlotte's recovery and growth and not worry about his feelings.

Robinson used many soap opera traditions, including *mother love, the search for happiness,* and a *nonending Back Street love affair* between an unhappily married man and a loyal unmarried woman. But, contrary to what many critics asserted in regard to Charlotte, his script is not about that soap opera staple, the self-sacrificing mother. Unlike Stanwyck's *Stella Dallas* and Davis's *Old Maid,* Charlotte does not sacrifice her happiness to benefit her "daughter"/Tina. The relationship she has with Tina is as mutually beneficial as her relationship with Tina's father, Jerry. As she tells Jaquith, Tina's need for her is only as great as is her own need to be needed. As she tells Jerry, she is more than rewarded for whatever she gives Tina: She gets a loving daughter; she forms a family with Jerry. Also, by being healthy enough to help Tina become healthy, she triumphs over the tyranny of both her own mother and Tina's. Charlotte has had her "sexual" flings, with Leslie and Jerry, and has even been engaged twice, to Leslie and Elliot (John Loder), so she now can devote herself to being a good mother, which she can't be if she and Jerry remain adulterers. Jerry understands that their relationship must be pure now that Tina has also become Charlotte's daughter. He also understands that they aren't sacrificing all that they have achieved together by discontinuing their romance. They only give up their romantic notion that it's reasonable to expect it all, to find complete happiness. That's the meaning of Charlotte's great, classic last line: "Oh, Jerry, don't let's ask for the moon! We have the stars!" (To some, it may look as if Charlotte's permanently pushing Jerry aside, but perhaps she's just putting him on hold—remember Jerry's wife hasn't been feeling too well. I don't agree with Davis who believed that since Charlotte outgrew Jerry she would be more attracted to Jaquith.)

Robinson's script is admirably constructed, with the emphasis on repetition. Almost everything happens twice, be it Charlotte being introduced to us with shots of her shoes ("before" and "after" her transformation), Charlotte taking two ocean voyages, Charlotte having two engagements, Jerry and Charlotte saying two tearful good-byes (at an airport—Henreid would have better luck in 1942's *Casablanca*—and a railway station), Charlotte going to Cascade two times, Charlotte recognizing that her unhappy childhood is being "rerun" by Tina. Characters constantly speak about others not on the screen, so that by the time we meet some of them (Charlotte, Tina), we know their problems. We learn that Charlotte and Tina have suffered for years, but Robinson compassionately doesn't let them suffer alone on screen. In fact, he places a protective character with them right from the beginning. Jaquith stands up for Charlotte against her mother in the opening sequence, telling her off to her face; Charlotte stands up for Tina against Miss Trask (Katherine Alexander). It's interesting that Miss Trask is used as a near-

villain in this scene in order for the parallel to be drawn, because except for the vile Mrs. Vale there's really no one who is mean in this film. In fact, the other people who populate Charlotte's world are the nicest, most considerate, and most helpful people you'll ever find in a Hollywood film. For instance, Jerry, who loves Charlotte deeply, wants her to find a husband who will make her happy. Even after being dumped by Charlotte, Elliot is not at all angry. Dora (Mary Wickes) is bubbly even after Mrs. Vale fires her as nurse. It's fitting that the film end with everyone having a great time at Charlotte's party. Another thing unusual about Robinson's characters is that they, including Mrs. Vale, are completely honest and open with one another. The relationship between Charlotte and Jerry is so special because from the start they hold no secrets from each other, exchange intimate confidences, and are completely straightforward. Even when Jerry asks Charlotte what his friend Deb (Lee Patrick) was talking to her about, Charlotte doesn't hesitate to tell him that Deb spoke of *his* private life. Charlotte is even willing to show Jerry a picture of herself when she was fat, ugly, and looked 20 years older. And Jerry takes no offense when Charlotte asks him if Tina was an unwanted child—he simply gives her a truthful answer. And that's the way it is with all characters in the film. Charlotte used to keep things from her mother (that she smoked, wore makeup, and had a collection of romance novels), but the new Charlotte speaks her mind—indeed her bluntness is what provokes Mrs. Vale's fatal heart attack.

There are a few minor problems with the screenplay. After seeing young Charlotte relish her naughty defiance of her mother on the African cruise, it's hard to accept that she would so easily slip back under her mother's thumb so as to be in the neurotic state Jaquith finds her. I find the scene in which Charlotte and Mrs. Vale discuss her engagement to Elliot misleading (perhaps we should blame Rapper or Cooper instead of Robinson). It hints at a developing friendship between mother and daughter, when such a friendship never materializes. (In fact, Charlotte won't grieve that her mother dies, just that she thinks herself responsible, and won't mention her mother after Tina enters her life.) For a moment, Mrs. Vale appears to soften, as if she were receiving unexpected enjoyment from (and freedom to be at ease with) her transformed daughter—like gruff Donald Crisp showing his tender side to Shirley Temple. Also, I don't understand how Jaquith can be so blind in his treatment of Tina, when he was so wise about how to handle Charlotte, who had identical problems. Finally, by the end of the film, why does Charlotte worry that Jaquith might take Tina away from her if she and Jerry are indiscreet? After all, if Jaquith takes Tina away, Jerry could just give her back. Tina's mother wouldn't care. (Anyway, I can't really understand very much of what Charlotte tells Jerry in this scene.)

But there is no need for things to make perfect sense in *Now, Voyager,* for Robinson writes it as a Cinderella-like fairy tale. There is fairy-tale logic: What are the chances that Charlotte would go off on a voyage and find handsome, gentle, understanding, too-good-to-be-true Jerry, who has a wife like her mother and a daughter like herself?

Taking on the role of "surrogate mother," Charlotte comforts the lonely, insecure Tina.

And what are the odds against Charlotte going to Cascade while Tina is there, and being given the opportunity to take care of the young girl as if she were her mother (or, better, fairy godmother)? That the characters don't live happily ever after is Robinson's (and Prouty's) concession to reality. After all, this is a fairy tale for *adults,* full of strange relationships that Freud would have worried about, and full of risqué material that the censors must have worried about. In this 1942 movie, Charlotte and married Jerry bed down for the night together in their makeshift shelter; adulterers are not punished; Charlotte tells Ja-

quith she "feels undressed" without her glasses and he says it's good for her to feel that way (prompting a subtle eye response from her); in the theater, Charlotte holds hands with fiancé Elliot on her left while secretly making rendezvous plans with Jerry on her right; and as they stare into each other's eyes, Jerry lights two cigarettes at once, one for him and the other for Charlotte. We realize this famous act has sexual connotations because when they didn't know each other well, Jerry gave cigarettes to Charlotte *before* he lit them. As they fall in love, he becomes bolder—perhaps he saw George Brent use this cigarette

Jerry and Charlotte look at each other with much love, but they don't let the now happy and pretty Tina know that they have had an illicit affair.

ploy with Ruth Chatterton in 1932's *The Rich Are Always with Us.* (Wouldn't it have ruined the film if Jerry lit everyone's cigarettes the same way?) As Richard Corliss comments, "If writing scripts like this was proof of Casey Robinson's craftsmanship, getting them past the Hays Office gives evidence of some kind of artistry."

Corliss also correctly contends that "The entire film is a tightrope walk above a tub of scalding bathos, but Davis, Robinson, and director Irving Rapper pull the act off with dignity." He writes: "In both script and performance, there are no waste motions, no false appeals to sympathy; yet no hesitation in tackling situations which, if poorly realized, might have evoked snickers instead and not tears."

(The only time I feel emotional is when Charlotte recognizes Tina and immediately goes to help her.) *Now, Voyager* had the potential to be embarrassingly bad, but it is instead embarrassing yet good. (Pauline Kael writes: "If it were better, it might not work at all.") It's like our nighttime soaps, like *Dallas,* junk elevated to art by talented individuals behind and in front of the cameras who should be working on something much better. *Now, Voyager* lucked out: Davis, Cooper, Rains, Henreid, the rest of the cast (except for Janis Wilson), underrated Rapper, Robinson, Steiner, cinematographer Sol Polito, and even makeup artist Perc Westmore gave this silly soap opera several touches of class.

Los Olvidados

also known as *The Young and the Damned*

1950 B&W Mexican Tepeyac release of an Ultramar film
Director: Luis Buñuel
Producer: Oscar Dancigers
Screenplay: Luis Buñuel and Luis Alcoriza
Cinematography: Gabriel Figueroa
Music: Gustavo Pittaluga
Editor: Carlos Savage
Running Time: 88 minutes

Cast: Estela Inda (Marta, Pedro's mother), Alfonso Mejia (Pedro), Roberto Cobo (Jaibo), Jesus Navarro (lost boy), Miguel Inclan (Don Carmelo, the blind man), Alma Delia Fuentes (Meche), Francisco Jambrina (farm school director), Efrain Arauz (Poxy), Javier Amezcua (Julian), Mario Ramirez (Julian's father), Jorge Perez ("Pelón"), Sergio Villareal.

Synopsis: Jaibo, a tough, orphaned teenager, escapes from a reformatory and returns to the Mexico City slums. He resumes command of a group of poor jobless boys, including Pedro, who is about 13. The products of broken homes, the illiterate boys spend their time smoking, drinking, and playing roughhouse games. Jaibo convinces the younger Pedro and Skinhead/Baldy to help him rob Don Carmelo, a miserly blind man who earns pennies by singing and playing instruments. Jaibo beats him and smashes his drum.

Pedro returns to the small home he shares with his young mother and three small siblings. He's hungry, but she won't feed him because he hasn't found a job. She has no affection for him, which hurts him badly. He grabs her food and runs away. Pedro befriends a scared boy, "Li'l Eyes," whose father abandoned him earlier in the day. They and Jaibo spend the night in the stable owned by the grandfather of gang member Poxy. Jaibo is attracted to Poxy's younger sister, Meche, but she rejects his advances.

Jaibo thinks he went to the reformatory because Julian, a teenager who works to support his family, squealed on him. Julian denies he squealed, but when his back is turned, Jaibo hits him with a heavy rock and beats him. Pedro pulls him off. Jaibo gives Pedro half of Julian's money and they flee before the boy comes to. Later the whole gang harasses and robs a legless man.

Li'l Eyes is taken into the home of the blind man, who makes him work for him and collect money while he performs.

It turns out Julian was killed by Jaibo's beating. Jaibo warns Pedro not to squeal. At night, Pedro slips into his bed. He dreams his mother hugs him and gives him a huge slab of raw meat, which Jaibo steals from him. In the dream he questions why his mother doesn't like him.

Pedro gets a job at the cutlery. He tells his mother he'll be good. Jaibo steals a knife at the cutlery. The owner thinks Pedro took it and sends police to Pedro's house. When Pedro sees the police, he thinks they've come about Julian. He runs away. Jaibo sleeps with Pedro's mother.

Pedro returns home. His mother takes him to the authorities, although he denies he took the knife. He is sent to a state-run farm for delinquents. An authority criticizes Pedro's mother for not loving her son. She comes to believe Pedro is innocent of the crime and that Jaibo was responsible. She no longer lets Jaibo into her house.

Pedro gets into a fight and angrily kills chickens at the farm school. But the kindly director makes him feel trusted by giving him 50 pesos with which to run an errand. Pedro intends to return to the school, but is waylaid by Jaibo, who steals his money. Pedro follows him to the slums and they fight in front of a large crowd. The stolen knife falls from Jaibo's pocket. Pedro yells that Jaibo killed Julian. Jaibo runs away. The blind man tells the police that Jaibo often hides in the ruins.

The blind man kicks out Li'l Eyes. Pedro goes to the stable to sleep. Jaibo is there. He beats Pedro to death. He runs to the ruins, where police gun him down. Meanwhile, Pedro's mother looks for her missing son. When Meche and her grandfather discover Pedro's body they worry authorities will think them responsible. They dump him in a pile of rubbish.

Publicity shot: Jaibo (with rock) and his younger cohorts Pedro (left) and Skinhead/Baldy beat and rob the blind Don Carmelo.

Luis Buñuel, the cinema's great subversive Surrealist, needed less than two hours to shake up the world with his first three films: *Un Chien Andalou* (1928), a 24-minute French short, co-directed by Salvador Dali, begins with a woman's eyeball being slit with a razor blade and then becomes more startling; *L'Age d'Or* (1930), a hysterically irreverent 60-minute feature, written with Dali, was banned in Paris after audiences rioted and threw smoke bombs at the screen and was banned in America until 1980—making Christ a sadistic libertine was only one thing viewers objected to; and *Les Hurdes/Land Without Bread* (1932), a 27-minute Spanish documentary, which wasn't as objective as its detached narration implied, was promptly banned in Spain because it was about a mountainous region where impoverished, ignorant people waste away from malnutrition and malaria while the flourishing local Catholic church solicits their donations. Buñuel would produce films in his native Spain between 1935 and 1937, but other than some documentaries commissioned by New York's Museum of Modern Art in 1938 and the U.S. Army in 1942, he wouldn't direct another film until 1947.

Buñuel ended his exile by signing a contract with Mexican producer Oscar Dancigers, with whom he'd team until the mid-fifties. Their first two collaborations—*Gran Casino* (1947), "a film with songs," and *El Gran Calavera* (1948), a comedy—were inconsequential, but their financial success let them make *Los Olvidados* (meaning "forgotten ones"). Dancigers suggested they make a film about the children in the slums of Mexico City. The idea excited Buñuel because he greatly admired Vittorio De Sica's neo-realist masterpiece, *Shoeshine* (1946), about two poor Italian boys whose friendship and lives are destroyed because of their cruel postwar environment. Before writing his script, with Luis Alcoriza, he explored the slums of Mexico City and researched the files of a local reformatory to come up with a film entirely based on real cases. Like the Italian neorealists, he worked with a minuscule budget (about $50,000), used nonprofessional actors, and often went with cinematographer Gabriel Figueroa out of the studio to film on location. "I tried to expose the wretched condition of the poor in real terms," declared Buñuel, "because I loathe the films that make the poor romantic and sweet." *Los Olvidados,* wrote J. Hoberman in the June 1983 issue of *American Film,*

> was very much the product of a "civilized" European sensibility. But Buñuel's anthropological detachment was complicated by his highly developed sense of disgust. Buñuel could not, in good conscience, subscribe to the sentimental naturalism with which the Mexican movie industry traditionally represented indigenous poverty. But neither could he use the barrios of Ciudad, Mexico in the service of another *Un Chien Andalou.* The solution was to treat the prevailing social conditions as a ready-made scandal. . . .
>
> Historically, *Los Olvidados*'s great originality is that it appears to be the first film to self-consciously depict the "natural" condition of the Third World. . . . What can be stated with more certainty, so far as an international film culture goes, *Los Olvi-*

dados puts the spectacle of underdevelopment on the map, while reproaching the prevailing Third World strategy of sentimentalizing the poor.

"This is not a documentary film," wrote Octavio Paz in 1951. "Even less is it a thesis, a piece of propaganda, or a morality fable. But while it doesn't preach—despite its admirable objectivity—neither is it correct to describe it as a film where purely superficial artistic values are paramount. The relentless passion with which Buñuel treats the theme recalls the great art of Spain."

No one knew what to expect when *Los Olvidados* "fell like a thunderbolt"—according to critic Raymond Durgnant in his book *Luis Buñuel* (1967)—on the Cannes Film Festival in 1951. Buñuel had resurfaced. "And," proclaimed France's most prominent critic, Andre Bazin, "the miracle took place: eighteen years and 5000 kilometers away, it is still the same, the inimitable Buñuel, a message which remains faithful to *L'Age d'Or* and *Los Hurdes,* a film which lashes the mind like a red hot iron and leaves one's conscience no opportunity for rest." Buñuel won the festival's prize for best director and was hailed, where once he had been assailed. Durgnant:

> In its location settings, in its serious study of juvenile delinquency, in its social protest, it continued the neo-realist tradition of *Shoeshine.* Indeed, it deepened it, with the introverted dimension of its dream-sequences. It was clearly a responsible film, but the violence of *Los Olvidados* was recognizably that of Buñuel's earlier films, and so, morally, seemed to re-

Pedro watches Jaibo (feigning an arm injury in order to hide a rock) challenge Julian.

Meche readies her knife as the blind man makes advances.

deem them. It indicated that Buñuel had been silent, true to himself, for twenty years. The image of the morbid Surrealist began to yield to that of the intransigent exile. Buñuel became a sympathetic figure.

Los Olvidados was distinctly the work of Buñuel, another "assault on the pieties of its audience" (as J. Hoberman described it), but this director whose earlier films were distinguished by surreal imagery was limited by Dancigers to only two surrealistic sequences. He wasn't allowed, for instance, to place 100 tuxedoed musicians high inside a building under construction, as incongruous background figures in a dramatic scene. Pedro's haunting, slow-motion nightmare, during which he hugs his mother, questions her for not loving him and not feeding him, and is offered a huge slab of quivering raw meat by her, only to have it snatched by Jaibo, is a stunning sequence ("perhaps the greatest of all movie dream sequences," suggests Pauline Kael), which is intriguing even to those who don't dabble in Freud. Jaibo's hallucination at the point of death of a mangy dog (superimposed on the screen) approaching his prone form is so unnerving that it's a relief when the badly injured Jaibo stops moving his head back and forth and dies. These are the only surreal moments in the movie, but at no time do we think the film *realistic* or *naturalistic,* even though we recognize it deals with real subject matter. Buñuel didn't have to resort to many obvious "alienation" devices (i.e., Pedro throws an egg that splatters on the camera lens) to let us know that he was moving away from the realistic-naturalistic narrative and offering, as J. Hoberman termed it, "neo*sur*realism." John Russell Taylor wrote in his book *Cinema Eye, Cinema Ear* (1964):

The film works quite acceptably on the level of a humane social document. (*Pitié pour eux,* it was called in France). . . . On another level, though, one can see it as not realistic at all . . . ; the nightmarish, hallucinatory quality of the film is quite disturbing.
  This result is achieved . . . by Buñuel's power to invest the most unexpected things with . . . the sort of imagist poetry which comes from an intense heightening of individual sense impressions, so that certain selected objects take on the quality of a fetish, an instrument of ritual significance in the reenactment of some private myth. So in *Los Olvidados,* it is with the cockerels which infest the action, heralding doom; with the dove whose soft body caresses the back of an invalid; the raw meat which sets the tone of the dream sequence; the terrible old blind man's [nail-studded walking] stick, the milk which the girl Meche pours over herself to make her skin beautiful. Nothing is ever allowed to be completely and merely what it appears, any more than the film as a whole.

There are other significant objects that can be added to Taylor's fetish catalogue: the cigarette and liquor bottles that the children pass between them to signify their toughness and attraction to vices, their unity, their early adulthood; knives, pipes, and sticks, the weapons with which the juveniles defend themselves and attack each other—significantly Jaibo has no chance against a policeman's gun; money, which buys food and, in Pedro's case, buys his mother's interest in him, and which Jaibo constantly steals, the miserly blind man fondles when alone, the farm director gives Pedro as a sign of trust, and Meche gives the Lost Boy as a sign of friendship; the string necklace with a dead man's tooth that the Lost Boy gives Meche to protect her; the blind man's musical instruments; Pedro's mother's broom, which becomes a weapon to kill an invading rooster; the flaming cutlery tools; the fancy brass beds that crowd the small houses; etc. And there are other animals: chickens, hens, donkeys, goats, and the stray dogs that represent the wild, hungry, and homeless boys of the slums. However, this film is not about objects and animals, but about children.

Los Olvidados won the International Critics' Prize at Cannes in 1951. It would, in fact, become a cult movie of critics (and true film connoisseurs). Moviegoers would recognize it as a great film, but not take it to heart as they would some of the Italian neorealist classics, like *Shoeshine, The Bicycle Thief* (1949), and *La Strada* (1954). Even those with unhappy endings had some humor, tenderness, sentimentality, and charm along the way; even the films of India's Satyajit Ray, in which hideous things happen to the impoverished lead characters, end with a glimmer of hope, a resurgence of the human spirit, a reaffirmation that human beings can survive horrible tragedies and suffering. But Buñuel gives his audience no such comfort. Pauline Kael:

> Luis Buñuel's ruthless—almost surgical—examination of how the poor prey on one another is the most horrifying of all films about juvenile crime. The one masterwork on this subject, it stands apart from the genre by its pitilessness, its controlled passion. . . . Buñuel doesn't treat his characters as ideas but as morally responsible human beings; there is little of the familiar American-movie cant that makes everyone responsible for juvenile crimes except the juveniles.

Buñuel's portrait of life in the Mexico City slums is rigidly unsentimental and pessimistic. In the Buñuelean slum, there is no virtue, no salvation, no state of grace. All inhabitants, even children, the handicapped, and mothers(!), are mean, indecent, selfish, corrupt, and violent. In the barrio, these indigent people are trapped— as surely as the rich would be trapped in that house in Buñuel's *The Exterminating Angel* (1962) and on that endless road in his *The Discreet Charm of the Bourgeoisie* (1972)—pushed together without privacy or protection from each other.* Men get drunk, fathers abandon their families, single mothers like Pedro's mother (whose husband either died or ran off five years before) have babies, crime and violence are everywhere (even the gentle Meche carries a knife). It is a breeding ground for juvenile delinquency. Unfeeling adults exploit children, forcing them to work for morsels of food or tiny or nonexistent wages

• •

*Manny Farber wrote in *Artforum* (Summer 1969) that Buñuel's "characters have suffered a nightmarish lack of privacy in all their domestic setups, with no refuge from gossip, prying eyes, nosiness. No secret can be cherished, no man or woman is allowed to singularize himself for long. The rancor and malice of the neighbors act to break down their resolves. All his population . . . bear the poor man's feeling of being prey for anyone who wants to harass him."

("You'll rest when you're dead!" a merry-go-round owner warns his two young assistants); parents give their children no affection, but a pederast offers Pedro money for sex, the blind man tries to seduce Meche with candy, Pedro's mother has an affair with teenager Jaibo. In turn, children—who look less frightening than Leo Gorcey, Huntz Hall, and the other Dead End Kids—brutalize and rob adults, including the blind man and a man without legs; Pedro steals food from his own mother. These children kill each other in fights, and police shoot them down as if they were rabid dogs. Jaibo is shot in the back and is left to die in rubble. Pedro's body is dumped into the garbage (by people—Meche and her grandfather—who didn't even dislike him). What a depressing, unforgettable image!

It's not surprising many viewers can't deal with the world Buñuel presents, especially since Buñuel's point is that there's nothing they or anyone else can do, short of revolution, to improve conditions. A well-meaning reformer like the state-run farm school director—a character liberal viewers will identify with—may reveal the inherent goodness in Pedro, but he is powerless to help the boy permanently. We expect a traditional, happy ending when Pedro obligingly runs the errand for this director who shows faith in him. Since Pedro's mother is finally showing concern for her child, we figure everything will turn out all right. But Buñuel won't allow it. As soon as Pedro reenters the city, Jaibo robs him. When Pedro returns to the slums, Jaibo kills him. Bazin:

> It is objectively much more serious that the [director's] experiment is made to fail from the outside and against Pedro's will, since in this way society is saddled with a double responsibility, that of having perverted Pedro and that of having compromised his salvation. It is all very well to build model farms where justice, work, and fraternity reign, but so long as the same society of injustice and pain remains outside, the evil—namely the objective cruelty of the world—remains.

Despite the opening-narration subtitles in the English language version ("the future contains the hope of guiding the children to a useful place in life"), Buñuel's film "eschews," as J. Hoberman contends, "reformist optimism. . . . *Los Olvidados*'s true heirs are those films like Hector Babenco's *Pixote* [1980, from Brazil] and Yilmaz Gurney's *Yol* [1982, from Turkey], that are less calls to revolution than populist representations of social conditions so atrocious that revolution seems to offer the sole solution." As long as slums continue to exist and there is poverty and hunger ("A full stomach improves people," asserts the farm school director), the Pedros, the Jaibos, and the noble Julians of the world are doomed. Pedro is younger and nicer than Jaibo but they are bound together because neither has a chance in life. In the slums, Darwinism doesn't apply: The strongest may prey on the weak, and even kill them, but they won't survive much longer. Most critics have pointed out the psychological link between Pedro and Jaibo, of how Jaibo represents the younger boy's darker side and his future (when his darker side will fully reveal itself). I think it should also be stressed that Pedro represents the older boy's more innocent past, be-

There is a mutual attraction between Jaibo and Marta, Pedro's mother, the two people who are ruining Pedro's life.

fore he committed serious crimes and when he also had a mother ("a saint"). This explains why Jaibo is drawn to Pedro and why he resents him so much.

The picture seems almost exclusively about the relationship between Pedro and Jaibo, but I think it is equally concerned with a third character, whom most critics ignore. The Lost Boy—nicknamed, according to different sources, either "Li'l Eyes" or "Big-Eyes"—is the outsider who enters the slums and, with those eyes of his, observes (as if he were an investigative reporter) the people who live there, including Pedro (whom he befriends), Jaibo (whom he antagonizes), the blind man (whom he moves in with and works for), Meche (whom he gets a crush on), and Meche's family. He gets special insight into these people and their miserable world. But he's like the reporter who does a story in an asylum and ends up mistakenly committed for life. He becomes another homeless, forgotten boy of the slums. The Lost Boy is a good boy, who voluntarily helps the blind man cross a street and challenges Jaibo for Meche's honor, but if his father doesn't return for him (and he won't), the Lost Boy will become, in turn, like Pedro, Jaibo, the vicious adults who work in

the slums and exploit children or Julian's drunken father, the blind man, and Meche's grandfather. Pedro and Julian lie dead at film's end, so it's too late to worry about them. Buñuel shifts our concern to the Lost Boy—*he* has a future. It's a good thing that Meche returns his lucky string necklace with the dead man's tooth because he will need protection.

Los Olvidados has so much power and beauty because you realize that Buñuel truly cares about his unfortunate youngsters who are stuck in the slums, and that he cries for them and would love to write them happy endings and more than random moments of contentment. You realize he controls his passion for the sake of truth and lets his children's lives run their tragic courses. He lets his children commit atrocious acts, not worrying that they may repulse viewers (and dissuade any of us from ever becoming foster parents to troubled children). Buñuel makes no moral judgments on his young characters—he doesn't like Pedro any more than Jaibo—and he invites us to share his view that, as Bazin writes, "These children are beautiful not because they do good or evil, but because they are children in crime and even death."

On Her Majesty's Secret Service

1969 Color British United Artists release of an Eon Productions film
Director: Peter Hunt
Producers: Albert R. Broccoli and Harry Saltzman
Screenplay: Richard Maibaum
From the novel by Ian Fleming
Cinematography: Michael Reed
Music: John Barry; songs performed by Louis Armstrong and Nina
Editor: John Glen
Running Time: 140 minutes

Cast: George Lazenby (James Bond), Diana Rigg (Tracy), Telly Savalas (Ernst Stavro Blofeld), Gabriele Ferzetti (Marc-Ange Draco), Ilse Steppat (Irma Bunt), Angela Scouler (Ruby), Lois Maxwell (Miss Moneypenny), Bernard Lee ("M"), Desmond Llewelyn ("Q"), Catherina von Schell (Nancy), George Baker (Sir Hilary Bray), Bernard Horsfall (Campbell), Yuri Borienko (Gruenther), Julie Ege (Scandinavian girl), Joanna Lumley (English girl), Anoushka Hempel (Australian girl), Mona Chung, Bessie Love.

Synopsis: James Bond, agent 007 of Her Majesty's Secret Service, has spent two frustrating years trying to locate the diabolical Ernst Stavro Blofeld, head of SPECTRE. In Portugal, he spots a beautiful stranger attempting suicide. After pulling her from the ocean, he fights off several men who try to kill him and abduct her. She drives away. But he sees her again that night playing baccarat at his hotel. Half-British, half-Corsican, she is the Countess Teresa di Vicenzo. When she loses she hasn't the money to cover her debt. Rather than let her be scandalized, Bond announces he and she are partners and pays her debt. Tracy feels obligated to Bond and offers herself to him. In the morning she is gone. Bond is abducted by several men and taken to the headquarters of Marc-Ange Draco, head of the crime syndicate Union Course. Draco is Tracy's father. He is worried about his daughter's depression and thinks she needs a man to love, someone like Bond, to whom she's obviously attracted. He tells Bond that if he will spend time with Tracy, he'll provide information that may help him find Blofeld. Tracy becomes angered at the arrangement and demands her father tell Bond the information he has—the name of Blofeld's lawyer in Switzerland—so Bond can back out. But Bond doesn't back out. He courts Tracy. She falls in love with him—she hopes he will love her someday.

Bond sneaks into the office of Blofeld's Swiss lawyer, Gumpold. He discovers that Blofeld has been trying to get Her Majesty's College of Arms and Heraldry to recognize him as a count, heir to the Bleuville title. Blofeld is in the Swiss Alps. Posing as genealogist Sir Hilary Bray, of the College of Arms, Bond travels to Switzerland, where he is met by Blofeld's personal secretary, Irma Bunt. By helicopter, they travel to Blofeld's isolated mountain fortress and institute, Piz Gloria, where Blofeld does allergy research. There are several beautiful female patients staying there. Bond takes two, Ruby and Nancy, for lovers. Each midnight, the girls go into a trance while Blofeld gives them instructions for when they return to civilization. They will carry disease bacteria, to be set free on the world when he instructs them from the institute. He will cause infertility in the world's plants and animals unless the United Nations gives him a pardon and recognizes him as a count.

Bond goes to Ruby's bed and finds ugly Irma there. Having made a slip to Blofeld that the real Bray wouldn't have made, Bond has been found out. Bond makes a daring escape on skis. Blofeld, Irma, and many men give chase. Bond is almost trapped at the carnival in Grindelwald, but Tracy turns up and drives him away. That night, Bond tells Tracy he loves her, and proposes marriage. Finally happy, she accepts. The chase resumes. Blofeld causes an avalanche. He abducts the unconscious Tracy. Bond, Draco, and Draco's armed men attack Piz Gloria in a fleet of helicopters. Tracy is rescued. The fortress is blown up. Bond chases and catches Blofeld as he speeds down a bobsled run. Blofeld is knocked out of the sled by a tree. Bond must keep going. Blofeld escapes with a broken neck.

Bond retires. He and Tracy marry. She thanks him for having a future. Blofeld and Irma speed by the honeymoon car and shoot Tracy. Bond weeps over his dead bride.

Ian Fleming began writing his best-selling James Bond novels in the early fifties, naming his sleuth after an ornithologist he admired, and loosely basing his cloak-and-dagger exploits on those of Merlin Minshall, a Special Operations agent with whom Fleming worked during World War II. In Fleming's still exciting adventures, Bond wore a bowler (as did Minshall), drove a Continental Bentley, and carried a Walther PPK. He was a refined gentleman and a superlative lover, but he was no gourmet, was vulnerable, and was often troubled, as in the eleventh book, *On Her Majesty's Secret Service* (1963), in which he contemplates resignation. Fleming's Bond hardly resembled Sean Connery, George Lazenby, Roger Moore, or Timothy Dalton: "A dark, clean-cut face with a three-inch scar showing whitely. The eyes were wide and level under straight, rather long black brows. The longish nose ran down to a short upper lip below which was a wide and finely drawn but cruel mouth." Numerous Bond movie and television projects fell through in the fifties, except for a live production of *Casino Royale*, starring Barry Nelson, on CBS's *Climax Mystery Theater* in 1954. Then, in 1961, producers Albert "Cubby" Broccoli and Harry Saltzman signed a deal with United Artists to turn out several Bond films, beginning with the modestly budgeted *Dr. No* (1963). So began the most successful and enduring movie series in history.

The surprising popularity in America of *Dr. No* and its follow-up, *From Russia with Love* (1963), the instant superstardom of Scottish Sean Connery, and the heightened interest in Fleming's Bond novels (due in part to President Kennedy being a fan) paved the way, it might be argued, for the British rock music invasion. For a time, Bond and the Beatles were a phenomenal one-two punch that made us believe Britain was where it was at, and hunger for anything (music, movies, miniskirts!) and anybody (Freddie and the Dreamers?) our one-time landlords would send our way. Movies would change along with rock, art, and society in the sixties, after Kennedy's assassination (even the New York Yankees dynasty crumbled), but the Bond films were a reassuring constant in the turbulent decade. We forgave them for being escapist rather than "relevant" because they were British, they had Connery, they were fun, and they were great date movies, for teens on up. Young people just didn't miss *Dr. No*—I still remember the long line of frozen people at a Trenton, New Jersey, theater—*From Russia with Love*; *Goldfinger* (1964), the first extravagant Bond film; a double feature of *Dr. No* and *From Russia with Love* (I recently discovered that the Princeton theater in which I saw this 007 duo no longer exists); *Thunderball* (1965); and *You Only Live Twice* (1967), the first disappointing Bond film.

What a terrific new hero was this debonair, virile Agent 007. He had the license to kill (we wanted to introduce him to our gym coaches); knew judo; was a well-educated gentleman with excellent taste in clothes, food, cars, and wine (a fine adult role model!); traveled to exotic locations

For this publicity shot, George Lazenby, the new James Bond, strikes the most familiar macho-hero pose.

around the world; met only beautiful women (whom he made love to even if they worked for the enemy); could take on the most terrifying villains; didn't panic when the fate of the world rested on his shoulders; had magnetic sex appeal and, not quite as important, a subtle sense of humor; and could prompt John Barry's famous theme song to play just by giving his name.

But James Bond would have been less than special if he hadn't been played by Sean Connery, who had charisma and dashing good looks and could act. Since our introduction to Connery and Bond came at the same time,* Connery and Bond were fused together in our minds.* We thought he was the only one who could play Bond— just as today we can't think of anyone but Clint Eastwood as Dirty Harry. So when Connery announced he was leaving the role that had made him famous—the first of three times he'd say "Never Again"—we were skeptical that Saltzman and Broccoli could find an acceptable successor for the upcoming *On Her Majesty's Secret Service*. Replacing Connery as Bond was much more jarring to us than replacing Roger Moore in 1987. According to the publicity of the time, there were 400 Bond candidates. From these, Saltzman, Broccoli, and director Peter Hunt (the editor on Connery's Bond films) narrowed it down to five finalists. On the strength of his audition in an action sequence, George Lazenby got the coveted role over John Richardson, who played opposite Raquel Welch in *One*

Because Lazenby was unknown around the world, beautiful Diana Rigg of the popular television series The Avengers *was brought in to play Tracy. Viewers could believe that Bond would give up every other woman in the world to marry her.*

....

*We hadn't noticed that since the mid-fifties, Connery had appeared in a number of films, most notably Walt Disney's *Darby O'Gill and the Little People* (1959), in which he had the lead, *Tarzan's Greatest Adventure* (1959), as a villain, and *The Longest Day* (1961).

Draco (behind Tracy) is relieved that his daughter has married Bond. But happiness will soon give way to tragedy.

Million Years B.C. (1966), Hans De Vries, Robert Campbell, and Anthony Rogers—who surely regretted losing their one golden opportunity to someone who would be handed stardom and blow it. In his late twenties, Lazenby was an Australian-born model who'd had success in Europe doing magazine and television ads and was best known as the "Big Fry" man.

The producers voiced confidence that Lazenby could replace Connery, yet privately they must have had grave doubts. Because of Lazenby's lack of experience and anonymity, they decided to break Bond tradition and hire a well-known actress for the female lead, selecting the popular Diana Rigg, who played Emma Peel on the British cult television series *The Avengers.* She was the best possible choice because she instantly provided the class, sex appeal, and acting skills Lazenby lacked—she also was an established *action* heroine whom most of us teenage boys had fallen for. That Lazenby wasn't featured on the film's poster—we see Bond from behind as he gazes at several sexy females—indicates that the filmmakers and United Artists weren't counting on the actor to sell their picture. (Also Lazenby may have been slighted because Hunt, Saltzman, and Broccoli intensely disliked him and didn't want to use him in future Bond films.) In his book *The James Bond Films* (1981), Steven Jay Rubin writes that it was originally intended that *On Her Majesty's Secret Service* begin with Bond undergoing plastic surgery and

emerging as Lazenby. Although this idea was scrapped it confirms that the filmmakers were equally afraid of introducing Lazenby as the new Bond and severing the link with Connery. The filmmakers wanted viewers to realize that while Connery was gone, this was a bona-fide James Bond film, not another of the many imitations. That's why Bernard Lee's "M" and Lois Maxwell's Miss Moneypenny, familiar figures to all who saw the Connery films, are presented early on; Lazenby's Bond makes a humorous reference to Connery's Bond in the teaser (when Tracy runs off, he comments, "This never happened to the other fellow"); in the opening titles, we see Connery's screen lovers Ursula Andress's Honey Ryder from *Dr. No* (still the most popular "Bond girl"), Daniela Bianchi's Tatiani Romanova from *From Russia with Love,* Honor Blackman's Pussy Galore from *Goldfinger,** Claudine Auger's Domino and Luciana Paluzzi's Fiona Volpe from *Thun-*

....
*Blackman preceded Diana Rigg on *The Avengers,* playing the leather-garbed Cathy Vale, but never received a similar degree of international recognition. Neither did Rigg's replacement, Linda Thorson, who played Tara King, or the female star of *The New Avengers,* Joanna Lumley, who, ironically, is one of Blofeld's patients in *On Her Majesty's Secret Service.* However, Rigg wasn't able to parlay her television fame into success as a cinema star, despite four fine starring efforts in *The Assassination Bureau* (1969), with Oliver Reed and Telly Savalas, this James Bond film, *The Hospital* (1971), and *Theatre of Blood* (1973).

derball, and Mie Hama's Kissy Suzuki from *You Only Live Twice;* when Lazenby's Bond clears out his office he comes across mementos of Connery's Bond's movie adventures and we hear John Barry themes from past films.

Ironically, while the filmmakers try to reinforce the connection between *On Her Majesty's Secret Service* and Connery's Bond films, screenwriter Richard Maibaum (who has written the majority of Bond films) intentionally moves out of the fantastic realm of the previous films and presents a fairly realistic spy thriller. There are no wild gimmicks, no treacherous females who try to murder Bond, no plot points that we absolutely can't believe. There is little glamour. While Bond does slip from one pretty woman to the next at Blofeld's institute—which is annoying since he's not being true to Tracy—this bed hopping, unlike Connery's dalliances, has thematic relevance. Having made love to these women, Bond knows what he will sacrifice when he asks Tracy to be his one and only, and, since we know what he is giving up, we grasp the depth of his love for Tracy. For once Bond has a legitimate love affair, one with meaning, loyalty, commitment. Molly Haskell wrote approvingly in the *Village Voice* (December 25, 1969):

> In a world, an industry, and particularly a genre which values the new and improved product above all, it is nothing short of miraculous to see a movie which dares to go backward, a technological artifact which has nobly deteriorated into a human being. I speak of the new and obsolete James Bond, played by a man named George Lazenby, who seems more comfortable in a wet tuxedo than a dry martini, more at ease as a donnish genealogist than reading (or playing) *Playboy,* and who actually dares to think that one woman who is his equal is better than a thousand part-time playmates.

Maibaum stuck fairly close to the novel, about the great tragedy in James Bond's life, and as a result, *On Her Majesty's Secret Service* is probably the most serious Bond film, with a suicidal heroine (in the book she lost her baby) and a frustrated protagonist who contemplates retirement after two years of failing to track down Blofeld and getting no appreciation from his boss, "M." It's the most cynical of the Bond films, with Bond turning not to the government but to a crime organization to save the world, with Bond unable to protect the woman he loves. And it certainly is the most tragic of the Bond films, with the true love of Bond's life, Rigg's Tracy, being killed when she finally has "a future." The film surely suffers because Lazenby hasn't Connery's polish as an actor, but I'm not sure I agree with those who insist that if Connery had played Bond it would definitely be the best of the entire Bond series. I'd love to see Connery opposite Diana Rigg (it's annoying when she makes love to Lazenby), but Connery's Bond, with his boundless humor and sense of fun and self-confidence, would be out of place in this picture. It actually works better with Lazenby because he is incapable of playing Bond as a bigger-than-life hero; for one thing he hasn't the looks—he comes across as no better than a bland, computer-generated Saturday-morning cartoon representation of Connery. Lazenby's Bond also hasn't the assurance of Connery's Bond and that is appropriate in the

crumbling, depressing world he finds himself. He seems vulnerable and jittery at all times. At the skating rink, he is actually *scared.* We worry about him not only when he is being chased by Blofeld's hired killers, but also when a short, unintimidating lawyer might return to his office and discover Bond inside. Connery's Bond cared about the women he met and loved, but he kept his distance because he wouldn't think of marrying and giving up future adventures and future affairs. We believe Lazenby's Bond would court Tracy, be touched by her love and loyalty, admire her intelligence and bravery, fall in love with her, give up his dangerous, globe-trotting profession and future love affairs to marry her, and be crushed by her death on their wedding day. Haskell:

> Indeed there is something downright Shavian if not Congrevian in this mating of true minds, who "dwindle" like Millament and Mirabell into marriage, and in the comedy-of-manners style of the film, which affectionately mocks the conventions it uses to disguise true feelings . . .
>
> The love between Bond and his Tracy begins as a payment and ends as a sacrament. After ostensibly getting rid of the bad guys, they are married. They drive off to a shocking, stunning ending. Their love, being too real, is killed by the conventions it defied. But they win the final victory by calling, unexpectedly, upon feeling. Some of the audience hissed, I was shattered. If you like your Bonds with happy endings, don't go.

On Her Majesty's Secret Service doesn't have Connery and it's impossible to ever fully adjust to Lazenby, but I think that it still might be the best Bond film, as many Bond cultists claim. At the very least, it ranks with *Goldfinger,* Connery's best film (though I think the underrated *From Russia with Love* may hold up better), and *The Spy Who Loved Me* (1977), Roger Moore's one top-flight Bond film. As mentioned, it offers Diana Rigg, and has an interesting love story and poignant ending. It also has a fine, power-hungry villain (Telly Savalas reprises the role cre-

Blofeld proposes to Tracy. She pretends interest.

The spectacular attack on Blofeld's mountain fortress.

ated by Donald Pleasence in *You Only Live Twice*), a suitable master crime (unleashing bacteria on the world), and a humorous subject involving egotistical Blofeld's determination to be declared Count de Bleuville. Moreover, it's probably the most exciting Bond film, mixing high (very high) adventure and Hitchcock suspense (the scene in the lawyer's office, Bond's hand-over-hand escape on the cable wire, the fight in the shed full of bells, the sharply edited fight on the speeding bobsled). From the moment Bond is captured by Blofeld and Irma Blunt, the picture moves into high gear. There is one beautifully edited (by future Bond director John Glen), elaborately directed, nerve-wracking scene after another. It's not surprising that the cable escape scene almost proved catastrophic to the stunt men. The thrilling ski chase down mountain slopes is lovely and amazing—stunt director George Leech and some Olympic skiers came up with some remarkable footage. Even some macabre humor—Blofeld men have bizarre deaths—manages to increase the excitement. The helicopter attack on the institute is like something out of *The Guns of Navarone* (1961). (Watching the way Tracy beats up a couple of male thugs during this sequence reminds us of how Rigg's Emma Peel used to put away villains on *The Avengers!*) And the Blofeld-Bond battle on the runaway bobsled almost makes watching the Winter Olympics superfluous. No Bond film has such sustained suspense.

On Her Majesty's Secret Service made a great deal of money and pleased most Bond fanatics (it's amazing how large the Bond cult is!), but Lazenby got little credit or praise and was never asked to star as Bond again. (His lone film success would be as a gay politician in Peter Bogdanovich's 1979 sleeper *Saint Jack*.) As the only Lazenby film, it is, naturally, the odd-picture-out in the Bond series. It's rarely screened in repertory houses and rarely written about in Bond overviews although it's the film that reveals an added dimension to the hero. And if it plays on television, it's usually a ridiculous, jumbled version, with Bond serving as narrator. As its many defenders attest, a film of its quality deserves much better.

One-Eyed Jacks

1961 Color Paramount release of a Pennebaker production
Director: Marlon Brando
Producer: Frank P. Rosenberg
Screenplay: Guy Trosper
From the novel *The Authentic Death of Hendry Jones* by Charles Neider
Cinematography: Charles Lang, Jr.
Music: Hugo Friedhofer
Editor: Archie Marshek
Running Time: 141 minutes

Cast: Brando (Rio), Karl Malden (Dad Longworth), Katy Jurado (Maria), Pina Pellicer (Louisa), Slim Pickens (Lon), Ben Johnson (Bob Emory), Sam Gilman (Harvey Johnson), Larry Duran (Modesto), Timothy Carey (Howard Tetley), Ray Teal (Barney), Hank Worden (Doc), Elisha Cook, Jr. (bank teller).

Synopsis: It is 1880. Young Rio, middle-aged Dad, and elderly Doc rob a bank in Mexico. The *rurales* track them to another town, where they are carousing with women. Doc is killed. Rio and Dad flee but are trapped on a mountain with only one horse. Dad rides off to get fresh mounts. He decides not to return to rescue his friend. Rio is arrested and spends five agonizing years in prison. When he escapes with his Spanish friend Modesto, he vows to find Dad and kill him.

Second-rate bank robbers Bob Emory and Harvey Johnson ask the legendary Rio and Modesto to help them rob a bank in Monterey, California. Rio agrees to lead them when he learns Dad is sheriff of Monterey. Rio rides to Dad's ranch outside of town. Dad is wary of him, but Rio insists that he bears no grudge after five years—he doesn't tell Dad he was in prison. Rio knows Dad is lying when he swears he was unable to buy horses and that he returned too late to help Rio. Dad invites Rio to supper, and introduces him to his Spanish wife, Maria, and his stepdaughter, Louisa. Louisa is attracted to Rio and asks him to stay for tomorrow's festival. He agrees when he learns that the bank will be closed until after the festival. Dad is relieved Rio is so friendly—but Rio still plans to kill him.

During the festival, while Dad, a popular man in Monterey, gets drunk, Rio and Louisa walk on the beach. He tells her he is a federal agent and must go to Oregon. He gives her a necklace, which, he lies, his dying mother gave him. She is touched. They make love. He confesses he lied. He regrets having conned her. She runs off. She tells Maria what happened but they don't tell Dad.

When bully Howard Tetley plays too rough with a saloon girl, Rio sticks up for her. Tetley tries to shoot him in the back, but Rio kills him. Dad, furious that Rio stayed out all night with Louisa, arrests him. In front of the whole town, he whips Rio and smashes his gun hand with his rifle.

For eight weeks, Rio recuperates in a fishing village. Bob and Harvey grow impatient waiting for him to give the go-ahead to the bank robbery. Louisa comes to the village to tell Rio she is pregnant. But she says nothing when Rio contends all that matters to him is killing Dad. After she rides back to Monterey, Rio decides that she is more important than killing Dad. He calls off the robbery. He plans to sneak into Monterey and run off with Louisa.

Bob and Harvey kill Modesto. They ride to Dad's ranch and tell him Rio is coming there to shoot it out. While Dad waits, they go to town and attempt to rob the bank. Bob kills the teller and a teenager in the bank, but is killed himself. Harvey flees—the townspeople assume Rio was behind the robbery and was probably the man who escaped. Dad and his posse arrest Rio when he rides toward town. Dad knows Rio had nothing to do with the robbery. He promises him a fair trial, and to personally hang him afterward. Maria and Dad argue viciously because he is willing to destroy their lives to cover up his act five years before.

Now Louisa tells Rio she is pregnant. He is delighted. She sneaks a gun to Rio. He beats up vicious guard Lon and escapes into the plaza. Dad fires on him. Rio kills Dad and then flees town. He tells Louisa that he'll return some night in the spring and that somehow they'll find a place to be together. He rides off.

Rio remains behind to fight the posse while Dad rides off, supposedly to get fresh mounts.

*H*eaven's Gate (1980) wasn't the first large-scale Western that—even if it had been a masterpiece—had no chance with audiences and critics because resentment had grown to mammoth proportions as filming went ridiculously over schedule and obscenely over budget and too many stories surfaced about the director being arrogant, self-indulgent, and obsessive—how dare anyone have artistic pretensions when making a Western. *One-Eyed Jacks*, Marlon Brando's lone effort as director, had a similar history. After almost four years of pre-production, filming, and post-production, it was released in the spring of 1961 to viewer indifference, and to biased criticism, as is evident in this excerpt from the critique in *Saturday Review:*

> If it weren't for [its] background, *One-Eyed Jacks* could be assessed as a sturdily competent job in a familiar vein and let go at that. But here we have another example of the unrest caused in Hollywood by the rebelliousness of its stars, a good many of them apparently unsatisfied with their enormous salaries and their opportunity to pick and choose their roles. A star isn't truly big these days unless he's the whole show. Some call it "asserting creative independence." At any rate, Brando, who has demonstrated that he can be a magnificent actor, has had it all his own way. He directed himself as he pleased, got the performances he wanted from his actors, and came up with a Western.

Producer Frank P. Rosenberg purchased the screen rights to Charles Neider's just-published novel *The Authentic Death of Hendry Jones,* back in the summer of 1957. Calder Willingham finished a first-draft screenplay in April and Rosenberg sent it to Brando. He thought it unlikely Brando would consider doing the picture—it was an adaptation of an unheralded novel and Rosenberg had no major films to his credit—but it was the policy of most Hollywood producers to give him first shot at all scripts. Fortunately,

Brando was searching for a film to be made by his new production company, Pennebaker (named for his mother), and, having had success in Elia Kazan's *Viva Zapata* (1952), he didn't mind playing another character who spoke Spanish, carried a gun, and rode a horse down Mexico way. In March 1961, Rosenberg wrote in the *New York Times:*

> It is generally accepted in Hollywood, as are other maxims equally unreliable, that waiting for Brando to read a script and give you even a negative answer will age a man faster than trying to explain to Premier Khrushchev why he can't go to Disneyland. Brando got this particular screen play on a Thursday evening. By the next Saturday it was all over but the negotiations.
> He was marvelously enthusiastic—so much so that I suggested cautiously that the script needed about six weeks of rewriting before it was ready for the cameras. He thought four weeks ought to handle it. Eight months later, we were still fixing the script.

By this time, Willingham had left, reportedly to fulfill another writing commitment—yet surely his shaky relationship with Brando contributed to his hasty departure. He was replaced by Guy Trosper, who had scripted Rosenberg's innocuous production *The Girl He Left Behind* (1956). Trosper did not work alone on what was then called "A Touch of Vermilion" (later it became "A Burst of Vermilion"). The long writing sessions at Brando's isolated Coldwater Canyon hilltop home also included Brando, Rosenberg, Rosenberg's assistant Carlo Fiore (Brando's longtime friend), and director Stanley Kubrick, who'd been engaged because Brando had admired *The Killing* (1956) and the Willingham-scripted *Paths of Glory* (1957). (Sam Peckinpah had been involved briefly before he had a falling out with Brando.) Rosenberg recalled their strange daily meetings:

> Each morning the sessions began equably enough. Everyone was calm and reasonable and in stocking feet—a requirement of the highly polished teakwood floors of Brando's Oriental modern house. Brando sat cross-legged on the floor within easy reach of a Chinese gong that had come with the house. When the discussion became too wildly emotional and nerves began to fray while some zealot was defending a story point as if it were a maiden in distress, Marlon would hold up the gong and strike it twice. This was the signal for everyone, including himself, to return to a neutral corner. Sometimes we took turns presiding over the gong, but Brando used it most. After all, it was his gong.

At Brando's urging, Rosenberg flew to Mexico City in early August to test 10 unknown young women at the Churubusco Studios for the role of Louisa. This resulted in the casting of Pina Pellicer, who had never been in a movie before and knew little English. Pellicer, a sensitive actress who would commit suicide several years later, arrived in Hollywood with, according to Rosenberg, "a strong feeling of guilt over having been selected over her older sister." Karl Malden, who had acted with Brando in the Broadway and 1954 movie versions of *A Streetcar Named Desire,* soon joined Pellicer on the payroll, with Brando's

assurance that shooting would start by September 15th. By November, Rosenberg recalled,

> Mr. Malden was making up his own legends and we were running up quite a bill. Money was going out at a rate rivaled only by the current tapping of United States gold reserves. Our skilled and expensive production staff was growing steadily. Construction had begun on the huge Monterey, California, set on the Paramount back lot where we were destined to spend many a freezing night. Charles Lang, Jr., was signed as camera man. Katy Jurado, Ben Johnson, Slim Pickens and others joined the cast. And the studio was becoming increasingly curious as to when somebody was going to say, "Action!"

The trouble was there was no longer a director on the film. The working relationship between Kubrick and Brando had been deteriorating by the day owing to a conflict over the basic concept of the story. Finally, Kubrick pulled out and took over the direction of *Spartacus* (1960). So Brando told Rosenberg that he wanted to assume director chores. Rosenberg worried that the production had become so big physically that even an experienced director would have difficulty keeping things under control, but he agreed to stand behind his star. Later he doubtlessly had second thoughts. Again I quote Rosenberg:

> [O]n Dec. 2, 1958, *One-Eyed Jacks* started shooting against the crashing surf of Monterey (the locale of Mr. Neider's novel) under the direction of Marlon Brando. Five days later I informed him that we were two weeks behind schedule—a mathematical incredibility that took its place among the legends but failed to impress Brando, who was now totally absorbed in getting the utmost quality on every inch of Technicolor film.
> He pondered each camera setup while 120 members of the company sprawled on the ground like battle-weary troops, or gazed at the seals playing in the swelling seas. Every line every actor read, as well as every button on every piece of wardrobe, got Brando's concentrated attention until he was completely satisfied. . . . Time and tide are costly in Hollywood, and Brando used both unstintingly in his efforts to get just what he wanted on the screen. He exposed more than 1,000,000 feet of film, thereby hanging up a new world's record. Of this we printed 250,000 feet. (For purposes of comparison, the average important motion picture uses about 150,000 feet of film.)

Shooting *One-Eyed Jacks* was expected to take six weeks. But this didn't take into account Brando's long improvisation sessions with his actors, his insistence that even background players understand "motivation" (a couple of times, he offered bonuses to the extras with the most convincing expressions), and his willingness to wait hours on end for sun and surf to be ideal. So filming dragged on for six months, finishing on June 2, 1959. And there was still an additional day, October 14, 1960, on which Brando filmed the new ending Paramount had insisted upon. Brando's print ran 4 hours and 42 minutes—the exact time it took the Mets to beat the Astros for the 1986 NL pennant in the longest play-off game in baseball history. But of

Dad has Lon prepare Rio for a public whipping.

course Paramount wouldn't agree to that length. So the picture was cut in half, and one entire subplot—an affair between Brando's Rio (in the book he's Hendry Jones, nicknamed "the Kid") and a Chinese girl in the fishing village—was eliminated entirely. While the whittling was under way, Brando starred in *The Fugitive Kind* (1960). Oddly, that film would be released almost a year before the premiere of *One-Eyed Jacks*.

The Authentic Death of Hendry Jones seems the least likely Western novel to be given epic movie treatment. Charles Neider's book is brief and spare, containing only two major sequences (told from several perspectives)—the Kid escapes from Dad Longworth's jail; the Kid, who is essentially unarmed, is killed one night by former friend Dad while trying to rekindle a romance with a young Mexican woman, Nakia. The middle part of the book, which links the two sequences, has the Kid and his gang fleeing to safety in Mexico but returning to Monterey so the Kid can see Nakia and possibly confront Dad. It hardly seems possible that it took so long to adapt such a simple novel. However, Arthur Penn's *The Left-Handed Gun* (1958), with Paul Newman as Billy the Kid, was released and it suspiciously contained, with slight variation, almost all of Neider's material, including his two major sequences and those scenes in which "the Kid" takes revenge on corrupt deputies who murdered someone close to him. Ironically, if Brando and Co. had faithfully adapted Neider's novel they'd have been accused of copying *The Left-Handed Gun!* So they knew they had to make changes. They devised a story on a much larger scale, made the relationships far more complex, and gave the lead character, Rio, redeeming qualities.

The novel begins with Hendry already dead and covers only the brief time between Hendry's stay in sheriff Dad Longworth's jail waiting to be lynched and the night Dad killed him. There are references to the time after Hendry's death, when his legend grew, and to his past when he rode with Dad, but there is no mention of Dad betraying Hendry, the act that is at the heart of *One-Eyed Jacks*. The

book is narrated by Doc, one of Hendry's three gang members. He admired Hendry but everything he relates about him makes us understand what a despicable character Hendry was—as we read, we realize Doc's admiration is no endorsement because Doc is despicable himself. In the movie, where we're supposed to sympathize with Rio, it would not have reflected well on him to have been friends with such a cruel man *after* his escape from a Sonora prison, when he's no longer under Dad's evil influence and is being redeemed through his relationship with Louisa. So Hank Worden's ruthless Doc is made partner of Rio *and* Dad during the bank robbery that opens the film, before Rio goes to prison. Doc is conveniently killed five minutes into the movie. And, after his prison escape, Rio is given a nice-guy friend, Modesto, whose loyalty tells us that Rio is worth something. In the novel, Modesto does not ride with Hendry's gang—instead he is Nakia's worshipful teenage brother. Bob Emory and Harvey French are the other members of Hendry's permanent gang; in the movie, Bob Emory and Harvey *Johnson* team with Rio and Modesto just to rob Monterey's bank. Bob is intensely disliked by the young gang leader in both the book and the film, but in the book he knows better than to anger Hendry or betray him. He neither sets up Hendry's arrest by telling Dad when Hendry will be riding into Monterey nor kills Modesto—Modesto is killed for no reason by bully deputy Lon (who kills no one in the film). Yet Hendry kills Bob for getting on his nerves—in the film, Bob is killed by a bank teller during a robbery.

The Dad in the novel pursues the Kid out of a sense of duty and not to cover up a past betrayal or because the Kid has slept with his daughter. In fact, Dad has no daughter, just two sons. Dad is nothing special in the novel, but he is, even in Doc's eyes, a decent man. The Kid's love interest, Nakia, is not angelic or as loyal as Pina Pellicer's Louisa: While the Kid is stuck in jail and waiting to be lynched, she marries a dying man for his money and sleeps with Doc. Yet she is still too good for Hendry Jones, who is scum. The novel's major theme is that outlaws like Hendry Jones (who is based on Billy the Kid), who were portrayed as heroes in Beadle and Adams dime novels and became legends, were actually swine. Hendry is a punk who kills men who haven't his skills with the gun just for the fun of it; he is killed accidentally by Dad when he foolishly walks into a cabin despite spotting Dad's deputies on the porch. It's hardly the stuff of legends. Hendry is a cold-hearted murderer, while Rio is a bank robber who commits no crimes after breaking out of the Sonora prison, and kills only in self-defense. Hendry is shallow, stupid, and unredeemable, while Rio, who was brought up by criminal Dad, is confused but intelligent, tough but basically a decent person, distant but desperate to let goodness (Louisa) into his life. Brando explained him this way:

> Our early-day heroes were not brave one hundred percent of the time nor were they good one hundred percent of the time. My part is that of a man who is intuitive and suspicious, proud and searching. He has a touch of the vain and a childish and disproportionate sense of virtue and manly ethics. He is lonely and generally distasteful of human contacts.

Although a Western, *One-Eyed Jacks,* like *The Left-Handed Gun,* fits into the troubled-youth films of the fifties and early sixties. Both films deal with fatherless young characters and their relationships with surrogate fathers, the kindly, ill-fated Mr. Tunstall in Penn's film, and Malden's corruptive Dad in Brando's film. Strangely, Neider didn't play up either a father-betrays-son theme (e.g., the father goes straight but leaves the boy to a life of crime) or a son-lets-down-father theme (e.g., the boy refuses to reform also), despite calling his characters Dad and Kid and revealing that they once were close. However, Brando and his scriptwriters did pick up on the names and try to establish an Oedipal conflict, with the father figure betraying the boy and the boy swearing revenge. When the prodigal son returns to Dad's home, Dad introduces him to his wife Maria and stepdaughter Louisa, not just calling them "my family" but "my *entire* family" to imply Rio's exclusion. By rejecting the bad Rio as his chosen child and adopting angelic Louisa ("I love her as though she were my own natural child"), he believes this automatically makes him respectable. But when Louisa does wrong in his eyes (becoming pregnant), he rejects her, too, feeling more betrayed by her than Rio does by him—this cad, who won't help any child in trouble, wasn't meant to be a father. In most juvenile delinquent films, the boy and girl fall in love despite *two* strict, unsupportive fathers. However, in this film, the boy and girl have the same *dad.* Regrettably, the film neglects the father-son relationship in the latter stages of the film in favor of the father-daughter relationship, and Dad begins to come across as no more than Rio's no longer tolerant older brother—which is essentially Pat Garrett's relationship to Billy Bonney in *The Left-Handed Gun.* If the scriptwriters wanted such a relationship then they shouldn't have kept the name "Dad" and they might have intimated he has incestuous feelings for Louisa so that Rio would become his sibling rival.

Dad was correct in assuming his association with Louisa would have a cleansing effect. When Dad pushes her away, he immediately returns to his true, reptilian nature. When Rio seduces Louisa he intends it to be a nasty payback to Dad and doesn't care if it shames her. But, as she tells Rio, she feels no shame—rather than the devil corrupting the virgin by impregnating her, she purifies him. Because of Louisa, Rio becomes a moral force. For an illegitimate baby to survive in Hollywood in 1961, and for Paramount to include its survival in the ending, it was necessary to convince us that the baby was conceived in true love and both the mother *and* father are *good.* Otherwise, the audience would think an unforgivable sin had been committed. (Anyway, I wonder how the Legion of Decency responded.) It's unusual having Louisa remain pregnant at film's end—it's certainly preferable to her being shot in the shootout and losing the baby, a standard Hollywood solution. In fact, the entire ending is atypical: Although Rio fights a fair fight with Dad, he kills him by shooting him in the *back;* the pregnant Louisa and the departing Rio make no hurried attempt to get married for the baby's sake; Rio flees without clearing himself of the bank robbery charge—since the revised script calls for him to live, one would expect him to be exonerated at a trial and then warmly welcomed into the community by the citizens of Monterey.

The fight between Rio and Dad is fair, but Rio is victorious because at one point he feigns being out of commission after Dad's bullet knocks the gun from his grasp—when Dad goes forward to kill his disarmed foe, Rio, with gun in hand, dives behind him and fires. This is the last act of deception in a film where everyone practices deceit. Brando the director begins the deceit parade in the first scene, when he opens with a close-up of Rio eating—we think he's having lunch, until the camera pulls back and reveals he's sitting in a bank, just relaxing while partners Dad and Doc are looting it. Soon Rio is seducing a proud Spanish woman with some well-worn words about how his dying mother gave him the ring he is now giving her. When Rio and Dad are trapped by *rurales,* Rio makes sure Dad is the one to ride for fresh mounts by rigging the selection process—Dad can't pick Rio's hand that has no hidden bullet because Rio placed a bullet in each hand. After five years in prison, Rio tells Dad that he holds no grudge against him—he also lies that he never went to prison. In turn, Dad tells Rio that he couldn't find fresh mounts five years before—he also lies that he went back to the moun-

Louisa visits Rio in jail so she can slip him a gun.

tain to rescue him but it was too late. Dad has told his wife and the citizens of Monterey that he once was a bank robber, but he won't let anyone know he betrayed Rio because that would reveal his true self. Dad prays before dinner, perhaps deceiving himself that God is listening to him. (During this meal, Rio thinks he's lying to Maria and Louisa when he says he has reformed, but now that Louisa has entered his life, that reforming process has actually begun.) While seducing Louisa, Rio lies that he works secretly for the government, that he's headed for Oregon, that he wants her to wait for him so they can marry, and that the necklace he offers her came from his dying mother. Louisa and Maria don't tell Dad that Louisa had sex with Rio. Later they will not tell him that Louisa is pregnant. When Louisa talks to Rio in the fishing village, she keeps secret that she is carrying his child. Dad acts chummy with Rio after he kills Howard Tetley in self-defense, but once out of the bar, he arrests him, whips him, and crushes his gun hand with a rifle butt. Bob and Harvey lie to Rio that they're riding away with Modesto. Prior to shooting it out with Modesto, Bob and Harvey sneakily remove the bullets from his gun. Bob may be telling the truth when he informs Dad that Rio is headed for his ranch, but he lies that Rio will be gunning for Dad—besides wanting to get Rio arrested, Bob wants Dad out of Monterey while he and Harvey rob the town bank. Dad plans to let Rio hang to satisfy himself, rather than telling the townspeople that Rio had nothing to do with the bank robbery. Louisa attempts to sneak a derringer past Lon. Rio is able to break jail because he bluffs Lon into thinking the derringer is loaded. And finally, Rio pulls a fast one during the shootout. Critic Dwight MacDonald was extremely displeased by all the deception, writing: "There is . . . a kind of psychological sadism: Everybody, including the hero, cheats and double-crosses; lies are as important a part of a he-man's equipment as his penis or his six-shooter." But I think deception should be the key ingredient in a film titled *One-Eyed Jacks*. It is essential to see beneath characters' facades, to see the other sides of faces. As Rio tells Dad, "I seen the other side of your face." Because of Rio, Maria and Louisa soon see the other side of Dad, as well. Also, fortunately, Louisa sees the other side of Rio's face and finds goodness.

One-Eyed Jacks is a solid adult Western, considering the extensive cuts and the father-son theme losing focus. Charles Lang's outdoor shots are lovely and memorable, particularly those with dust and dirt blowing across the plains (Sam Peckinpah would include such shots in his Westerns) and those with riders on the Monterey beach (an unusual image for a Western). There's not that much violence in the film, but it comes so unexpectedly and is so realistically brutal that it has stomach-churning power. There's no blood shed when the infuriated Rio hurls away the table in front of the shaking, too-terrified-to-speak Bob Emory, and challenges him to draw, but it's a great, unnerving scene—characters are on edge throughout the film, but here one (Rio) has the chance to explode. *One-Eyed Jacks* is a lot earthier and funnier than the average Western (perhaps due to Willingham). There are offbeat touches (a copy of the portrait *Mona Lisa* hanging behind the bar), sharp bits of dialogue, and some striking language: "Where

Brando steps out of character to work as director.

did you pick up the crow bait?"; "We don't hardly run into any studs like you anymore"; "I've had just about enough of you, jackass"; "You get up, you big tub of guts"; "Get up, you scum-sucking pig"; "You'll get a fair trial, and then I'm going to hang you—personally." (I also love the patronizing way Rio uses the name Bob every time he says anything to him.) Brando handles the large scenes quite well, although the final shootout between Rio and Dad is awkwardly staged and over too quickly. And he is sensitive and patient in the intimate scenes, allowing characters time to think before speaking and placing his camera on the person who is listening as often as it is on the one who is speaking. It's also effective when characters speak Spanish and we have to figure out what they're saying by studying their emotions.

The acting is fine down to the bit characters (Elisha Cook, Ray Teal, Timothy Carey), with villains Malden, Johnson, and Pickens coming off particularly well. Pellicer does an adequate job in her only film—it helps that her role has substance and that Brando takes her seriously. She seems average looking until Lang shoots her with her hair in disarray and blowing in the wind, with the beach in the background and the morning sun shining on her face—appropriately, at this moment Rio realizes he loves Louisa. In fact, the only actor who seems miscast is Brando. I can picture Elvis Presley as Rio without the film being harmed; at times, it's almost as if Brando were patterning his performance on Presley's rebel heroes (as well as those of James Dean). He is fine when tongue is in cheek and when violent, but at other times his method acting gets in the way—it gets annoying watching him roll his eyes and look off to contemplate the universe before delivering a simple line. Brando makes Rio seem too mannered and moody, as if Rio studied Stanislavsky in 1880. Brando also looks out of place. With his white moon face (emphasized by dark, buttoned shirts), high holster, and fancy bandanna, he's as imposing as a sagebrush version of Charlie Brown.

Over the Edge

1979   Color   Orion Pictures release through Warner Bros.
Director: Jonathan Kaplan
Producer: George Litto
Screenplay: Charlie Haas and Tim Hunter
Cinematography: Andrew Davis
Music: Sol Kaplan
Songs by: Cheap Trick, the Cars, Little Feat, Jimi Hendrix, Valerie Carter, the Ramones, Van Halen
Editor: Robert Berrère
Running Time: 95 minutes

Cast: Michael Kramer (Carl Willat), Pamela Ludwig (Cory), Matt Dillon (Richie White), Andy Romano (Fred Willat), Ellen Geer (Sandra Willat), Vincent Spano (Mark), Tom Fergus (Claude), Harry Northrup (Ed Doberman), Richard Jamison (Jerry Cole), Julia Pomeroy (Julia), Tiger Thompson (Johnny), Kim Kliner (Abby), Lane Smith (Roy Sloane), Eric Lalich (Tip), Jeff Fluery (young thug).

Synopsis: Vandalism, theft, and rowdyism by teenagers under 16 are an escalating problem in New Grenada, a planned white middle-class suburban community that was built in a barren desert. Life at home with neglectful parents is a drag. School, with teachers who constantly reprimand and lecture the kids, is equally boring. Except for the recreation center, which closes at 6 P.M., there is no entertainment. So the unsupervised, frustrated kids spend their time drinking, taking drugs, carousing, and committing crimes.

Fourteen-year-old Carl Willat is smart, is no troublemaker, has parents who love him. Yet he's very restless, and hangs out with wilder kids, including Richie White, who has had several run-ins with tyrannical cop Ed Doberman. Carl resents that his parents, like other adults in town, ignore how terrible this environment is for the young. His inattentive father, Fred, is preoccupied with his Cadillac business and luring Houston investors to New Grenada. Fred, Jerry Cole, and the other city planners decide to curtail plans for the drive-in and bowling alley the children want, to make room for industry.

Carl and Richie are arrested by Doberman, who is chasing after two boys who fired BBs at a police car. He doesn't think they're guilty but enjoys harassing them. Carl and Richie know the culprits were violent bully Mark and another young thug. But they won't squeal. At a party, Carl is upset to see Cory, the girl he desires, kissing Mark. Mark orders him not to squeal. He and his friend beat up and rob Carl.

Carl and Richie strike up a friendship with Cory and Abby, who have stolen a gun from a house. Carl and Cory become close.

The city planners order Doberman to close the rec center on the day Houston investors arrive. In order to do this he needs an excuse: He frisks Claude, a constantly stoned friend of Carl and Richie, and finds hash. The furious Carl boobytraps the car transporting the Houston visitors. Because of the rampant juvenile delinquency, they decide not to bring industry to New Grenada.

Pointing the unloaded gun, Richie scares Tip, a juvenile drug dealer, because he ratted on Claude. Later Doberman comes to arrest him. Richie and Carl flee. Doberman catches them. Richie points the unloaded gun. Doberman shoots and kills him. Carl hides out in the fields, where he has a friendly chat with Mark. That night he stays in an abandoned house with Cory.

The next night, the adults of New Grenada hold a meeting in the junior high school to discuss Richie's death and the problem with the youths. Fred becomes angry with Cole for worrying about declining property values instead of trying to help the troubled children. Rec center director Julia, the only adult who is popular with the kids, argues with Doberman. Meanwhile, Carl, Cory, Claude, Abby, Mark, and about 30 out-of-control children lock them in the cafetorium, vandalize the school, and set fire to the cars in the parking lot. Later, Doberman arrests Carl. But Mark shoots his car. It smashes into the rec center and explodes. Carl escapes but Doberman is killed.

Carl and a busload of kids, including Mark, are sent to a juvenile facility for a brief internment. Carl's parents hug him as he climbs aboard. He sees Cory and Claude wave. He smiles.

In early 1978, I was trying to round up filmmakers to write articles for a movie-star anthology I was compiling. A producer suggested I contact his friend Jonathan Kaplan. The name was familiar—I knew he was one of the new-breed directors who got a career push from Roger Corman—so I immediately called Kaplan and, without taking time to double-check his filmography, quickly rattled off those films of his I'd seen and enjoyed. I still hear him saying, "I didn't direct that . . . or that either. . . . No . . . that was someone else . . ." As it turned out, I hadn't seen any of Kaplan's films—the Corman-produced *Night Call Nurses* (1972) and *The Student Teachers* (1973), *The Slams* (1973), *Truck Turner* (1974), *Mister Billion* (1977)—except for *White Line Fever* (1975), but I'd forgotten he directed it and never brought it up during our embarrassing conversation. I relate this anecdote not to specify why Kaplan declined my invitation to write for my book, but to point out how much greater is Kaplan's reputation today, now that he has added *Over the Edge* and *Heart Like a Wheel* (1983) to his credits. While neither made the financial killings of Kaplan's earlier exploitation films, they received (over several years' time, in both cases) critical plaudits, developed strong underground reputations, and established Kaplan's identity in the industry—he has since been regarded as one of the most talented, if too-daring-to-be-bankable young Hollywood directors. With *Project X* (1987), he became a bit more mainstream.

Like *Heart Like a Wheel*, for which Bonnie Bedelia deservedly received an Oscar nomination playing world champion drag car racer Shirley "Cha-Cha" Muldowney, *Over the Edge* is based on a true story—a reason, I believe, it too was made with extreme care and conviction. Not that Kaplan didn't feel for those *Night Call Nurses* (*not* based on a true story), but he obviously felt an obligation to the characters in these two films to get it right. How easily another director could have turned either into standard exploitation fare. The incidents that take place in the film, in the planned community "New Grenada," actually took place in Foster City, California, which in 1974 had the highest rate of juvenile vandalism in the nation. As Kaplan told Seth Cagin of the *Soho News*, "It's about an absolutely documented real incident in which a bunch of suburban, upper-middle-class white kids revolted after a 14-year-old was killed by a cop. In real life the kids destroyed 150 cars, burned down a condominium complex, and knocked out their town's power supply. We couldn't afford to do all that for the movie, so we just had them commit acts of vandalism and destroy [a few] cars." There is one exaggeration in the film, however: Policeman Ed Doberman is killed when his car plows into the rec center and explodes—in real life, a cop was badly injured at a gas station.

Charlie Haas, who co-wrote the screenplay with Tim Hunter (who'd direct 1987's disturbing youth film *River's Edge*) first read about Foster City in a series of articles in the *San Francisco Examiner*. Haas, Hunter, and Kaplan

The young stars of Over the Edge. *Standing* (left to right): *Michael Kramer, Pamela Ludwig, Tom Fergus. Kneeling: Matt Dillon* (left) *and Vincent Spano.*

then visited the town. After talking with the kids for two weeks, and developing the simultaneous feelings of love for and fear of them that is so evident in *Over the Edge*, Kaplan decided he had to make a film about them and their stifling environment, a breeding ground for juvenile delinquents. Considering the nature of the script, it's not surprising that he had trouble finding a town that would let him shoot his film. Fortunately for him, Greeley, Colorado, had a school system that desperately needed money.

One of the reasons *Over the Edge* became a cult film is that after it received excellent reviews in such test markets as Chicago, Cincinnati, and Kansas City, it became almost impossible to see, sparking interest and word-of-mouth. It was initially set to be Orion Pictures' first film, but fan response in the test markets was so unenthusiastic—not surprising since it was promoted as a horror(!) film—that Warner Bros., the distributor, shelved it. Warners defended its decision with claims that no one would book a "gang picture" after the heavily publicized incidents of violence at theaters showing *The Warriors* (1979) and *Boulevard Nights* (1979). To make matters worse, there was no sale to network television because of the drug scenes. *Over the Edge* did not get an official premiere until De-

cember 1981, when the Warner Bros. Classics Division, which took over its distribution, opened it at New York's small but prestigious Public Theater. It received favorable critical response, even making Vincent Canby's Top Ten runners-up list for 1983 in the *New York Times*. But poor strategy involving theater bookings around the country as well as in New York (where it played in the artiest of art houses), shaky promotion that failed to play up the presence of budding teen star Matt Dillon or hype the explosive rock score featuring such luminaries as the Cars, the Ramones, and Van Halen, and the grimness of the subject matter kept it from achieving any degree of commercial success. Its audience would not grow until it turned up on cable more than a year later, began to play in repertory theaters, and became available on cassette (which is also how *Heart Like a Wheel* has found its audience). Still, for many potential admirers, this excellent, unusual picture remains virtually unknown.

Kaplan says that he originally sold Orion on his project by using the hook *Rebel Without a Cause 1978*. No youth film has such emotional impact on young people as Nicholas Ray's classic—with the exception, for some female viewers, of *Splendor in the Grass* (1961). Kaplan was too

Doberman arrests Carl and Richie for something they didn't do.

The kids in *Over the Edge* have parents who are equally neglectful, who never consider their children's needs yet expect them to be happy and trouble free. They refuse to deal with their children's problems because either they think them too trivial (Richie's "hip" mother shrugs off her son's arrest) or, like Carl's weak mother, they are afraid of starting an argument that might cause their children to pull farther away from them ("You weren't too hard on Carl, were you, dear?") or, like the parents of Vincent Spano's young thug Mark, they have completely given up on their children once they have gotten into trouble. Yet despite their chaotic, unstable home lives, these kids know what they're rebelling against, the *major* reason for their anxiety, frustration, and fury. And it's not their parents—although they are indirectly responsible for their misery. Their most extreme hatred is reserved for New Grenada itself, partly because of how it has changed their parents (effectively destroying their families). The parents lazily assume that their children are safe and happy in this all-white, upscale town, so they let their kids run free while they spend their own time thinking about money. As Lane Smith's visitor from Houston smugly comments: "It seems to me that you were in such a hopped-up hurry to get out of the city that you turned your kids into exactly what you're trying to get away from." I kind of wish Kaplan, Haas, and Hunter would have made Andy Romano and Ellen Geer's Fred and Sandra Willat "ideal" parents just to show that in New Grenada kids are doomed no matter what the home life. Jim Backus's hug of son James Dean at the end of *Rebel* signifies their relationship and, consequently, Dean's life should improve. On the other hand, Fred Willat's hug of son Carl at the end of *Over the Edge* is meaningless unless Fred and Sandra intend to take Carl and flee this corruptive town. In *Rebel,* Dean and Natalie Wood play house in a deserted mansion, pretending to be the ideal, loving, understanding parents Sal Mineo never had. In *Over the Edge,* Carl and Pamela Ludwig's Cory play house in a vacant townhouse. They sleep together as if they were husband and wife—but not as if they were mom and pop. There is no Sal Mineo child figure in the scene—perhaps these youngsters (and the filmmakers) realize that in New Grenada it's not fair to have children, no matter how loving and understanding you are.

New Grenada, a planned community of drab, yellowish, lookalike townhouses and condominiums, was built in the desert. There is more greenery in the science teacher's small "botany box" than in the entire town. It's desolate and barren and, with its deserted streets, vacant lots, and abandoned half-finished buildings, looks bombed out. The place needs character and more than a touch of pizzazz—ball fields, bowling alleys, a miniature golf course, movie houses—but the community planners want to bring in dreary industry instead. New Grenada was planned by adults for adults and run by adults. No wonder the kids, who are too young to drive elsewhere, are bored. They go out to the "fields" and walk through the high weeds just to feel they are breathing and in touch with nature, so it's quite evident—except to blind adults—they are restless for excitement and entertainment. There is absolutely nothing

smart to attempt to match it—I assume his fear of comparisons is a major reason he cast average-guy Michael Kramer as Carl Willat, the lead role, instead of giving the part to Matt Dillon, who instead received a supporting role, Richie White. (If Dillon—who is teen-idol handsome, has charisma, and convincingly plays teenagers who are frustrated by their inability to communicate verbally, especially with adults—had played Carl, everyone would have accused Kaplan of trying to create a new James Dean, a suicidal task.) But Kaplan, Haas, and Hunter (a Nicholas Ray fan) did take some plot points and themes of *Rebel* and update them to the present. Significantly, every time both films deal with the same subject, *Over the Edge* is more disheartening, indicating that it has gotten much worse for America's youth since 1955. Kaplan's brutally realistic film, a terrifying warning—with no resolution—about what is happening to America's best resource, makes *Rebel Without a Cause* seem optimistic.

The major problem shared by the teenagers in *Rebel,* a picture that contends parental neglect causes juvenile delinquency, is that they are unable to discuss all their minor being-a-teenager problems with their parents—that's why their natural confusion, frustrations, unhappiness, and minor problems get out of control. It's implied that if their home lives were stable and they were able to get the parental love, attention, and advice they crave, they would be able to handle most of their minor problems. But their home lives are in turmoil, and the atmosphere is too intense or chaotic for these kids ever to be rational enough to solve outside problems or figure out that the root reason they're unhappy and behaving so badly is parental neglect. Irrational, they don't really understand why (the cause) they're rebelling—which is why the frustrated Dean drops to his knees in the friendly policeman's office and repeatedly pounds his fists on the desk. But the cop (named Ray, as Nicholas Ray's surrogate) gives Dean badly needed fatherly advice and support, and we in the audience under-

positive they can do—no, they can't join a bowling league or even get jobs mowing lawns! So to relieve their boredom ("Stuffed peppers tonight—we don't want to miss that, do we Johnny?"), reveal their contempt for New Grenada, and surely a number of other psychological reasons they engage in casual thefts, break-ins, and vandalism; they beat up on each other; they risk physical injury (i.e., they play with guns); and sex, drugs, and alcohol become as integral to their lives as the rock music that drowns out the adult world. They realize they may get into bad trouble (Carl always sensed Richie would be killed), but they don't worry about the future since each dull day is endless. Activity of any kind is essential to the teenager's survival in New Grenada.

In *Rebel*, parents are solely to blame for their kids' problems—policemen like Ray sympathize with teens and teachers are neutral figures who have no influence on children (there aren't even any classroom scenes). In *Over the Edge*, all the adults of New Grenada, including parents, hostile teachers (who give trick tests and lecture on plants to kids who live in the desert), and the police (especially power-mad, child-hating Ed Doberman), are the enemy because what they want from New Grenada is exactly what the kids do not want. Carl and Cory resent their parents precisely because they have become less their parents than adults of New Grenada, whose goal is to make the community thrive financially while keeping the children under control. The adults of New Grenada admonish the kids, threaten them, lecture them, discipline them, deprive them of activities they enjoy, tell them what disappointments they are. There is no encouragement, praise, positive reinforcement, advice, or attempts at communication (all adults, not just parents, are guilty of this). The botany teacher nurtures his succulent plants, but he and the other adults who browbeat the children don't comprehend that the kids need to be nurtured as well. All the children learn from adults is materialism—the need to acquire things. The adults who don't bother to teach their children *values* instead worry that their properties' *resale values* will go down unless their children's delinquency is stopped. They are missing the point. And Carl is missing the point when he haughtily corrects his angry father, telling him Richie was just carrying a pocketknife, not a switchblade, and that Claude didn't have a full ounce of hash, as Doberman contends. Simply because his father got it wrong, Carl refuses to consider that Richie and Claude did wrong. Obviously, he has no system of values, no way to determine right and wrong. What do you expect considering that, in a conversation most kids have had with parents, his father says a disbelieving "Shit!" in response to what his son says, yet when Carl responds "Bullshit!" to his mother's foolish remark, his father becomes hysterical about Carl showing such disrespect. It's hard for Carl to get anything straight.

In *Rebel*, Dean is liked by all teenagers he comes into contact with, from neurotic weaklings like Mineo to troubled, father-neglected girls like Wood to cocky gang leader Corey Allen. This character links all teenagers—the film equates all teenagers, contending all are victims. In Kaplan's film, Carl wins over everyone, including the troubled, father-neglected Cory and Vincent Spano's tough thug,

As his wife, Sandra, looks on helplessly, Fred strikes their son, Carl, for talking back.

Mark. It is a reassuring moment when Mark shakes hands with Carl instead of beating him up for stealing away Cory (just as Dean won Wood's heart from Allen)—but it is a moment Kaplan dreads. He doesn't wish to equate all teenagers or link them together because of mutual victimization. He wants Carl, basically a decent boy, to stay away from Mark's lunatic, hardened-criminal element. It's a shame that circumstances unite them—and we see the horrible result of this alliance when all the kids of New Grenada lock up the adults in the cafetorium (a room whose very name tells you something about the type of school these kids attend), trash the school and parking lot, and cause the death of Doberman. *Over the Edge* is—along with *Rebel Without a Cause; The Blob* (1958); *Foxes* (1980); *The Outsiders* (1979), starring Matt Dillon; Tim Hunter's much better S. E. Hinton adaptation *Tex* (1980), also with Dillon; and *The Breakfast Club* (1985)—one of the few films that is completely in sympathy with teenagers. However, Kaplan admits, "I happen to believe these kids are potentially dangerous. A good demagogue comes along, and he's got his troops. And that scares the shit out of me." At one point, Richard Jamison's businessman Jerry Cole refers to the New Grenada teenagers as animals. At times, that's how Kaplan portrays them. They remind me of rats and other night creatures that come out when people are gone: They gather in the dark by the rec center, sitting on the ground or in little improvised hovels; in the party scene, their clutching bodies fill up the halls, the basement stairwell, and the basement of a house whose adult owners are away (it's like an underground tunnel system inhabited by rodents); they run out of the house en masse as the cops arrive, as rats or roaches would do if the lights went on; they vandalize the school and like scavengers destroy and steal from the cars in the parking lot. I was not surprised to learn that the original title of this film was "Mouse Packs."

Over the Edge is so powerful because Kaplan and his

The kids lock the parents and teachers inside the school and then go on a rampage. Top: The kids destroy the cars of the adults who are inside the school. Left: It becomes even more dangerous when Mark pulls out his rifle.

two writers completely avoided sentimentality (although there is sadness when we see human potential so callously wasted) and the clichés of the youth genre; they even stuck with a "melancholy ending to counter kids [in the audience] who thought the [earlier screen] violence looked like fun." Scenes are not just disturbing but truly haunting: the slow-motion sequence in which Carl is brutally beaten by Mark and his thug friend; Cory dancing while pointing a gun at Carl; Tom Fergus's constantly stoned Claude casually making drug purchases or guzzling hard liquor; Claude's mute younger brother Johnny (played by Tiger Thompson) staring at patterns on the television; in a rare tender moment, Carl and Cory walking through the fields like normal trouble-free teenagers, talking about how good family life was before they moved to New Grenada; Carl watching Cory walk into the sun*rise* and thinking how wonderful it could have been; the children-as-rat scenes.

If the picture has a flaw it is, oddly, that the professional actors who play the adults are much less convincing than the teenagers who, except for Spano, made their acting debuts in this film. What natural performers they are, and how deeply they understand their characters. These kids—especially Fergus's Claude and Spano's Mark—are all so real that it's hard to believe they aren't, God forbid, really residents of New Grenada. It would be so interesting to interview their characters today because it's hard to imagine anyone in New Grenada in his or her early twenties, particularly since the film implies that once these kids reach 16 there's a good chance they're prison bound. What if they went to therapy in lieu of jail and have repressed their troubled pasts? Then they're probably planning to seek good-paying jobs, buy drab houses, marry, and bear New Grenada's next generation of bored children. Talk about trouble in River City.

Psycho

1960   B&W   Paramount
Director: Alfred Hitchcock
Producer: Alfred Hitchcock
Screenplay: Joseph Stefano
From the novel by Robert Bloch
Cinematography: John L. Russell
Titles: Saul Bass
Music: Bernard Herrmann
Editor: George Tomasini
Running Time: 109 minutes

Cast: Anthony Perkins (Norman Bates), Janet Leigh (Marion Crane), Vera Miles (Lila Crane), John Gavin (Sam Loomis), Martin Balsam (Milton Arbogast), John McIntire (Sheriff Al Chambers), Lurene Tuttle (Mrs. Chambers), Simon Oakland (Dr. Richmond), Frank Albertson (Cassidy), Vaughn Taylor (George Lowery), John Anderson (car dealer), Mort Mills (policeman), Patricia Hitchcock (Caroline), Ted Knight (deputy), Virginia Gregg (voice of "Mother").

Synopsis: Marion Crane, a secretary at a Phoenix real estate office, is unhappy because her boyfriend, Sam Loomis, is too much in debt to marry her. So when her boss, Mr. Lowery, gives her $40,000 to deposit, she steals the money, packs her belongings, and drives toward Fairville, California, where Sam lives. Caught in a storm, Marion accidentally leaves the highway about 15 miles from Fairville. She takes refuge for the night in the otherwise vacant Bates Motel. Norman Bates, the friendly but strange young proprietor, tells Marion he rarely gets customers since the new highway was put in. Norman goes to his large house on the hill behind the motel to tell his mother that Marion will be coming for a snack. Marion overhears Norman's shrewish, domineering mother refuse to let Marion, whom she calls a slut, enter her house. So Marion instead snacks in Norman's office parlor, which is filled with birds that the lonely Norman has stuffed. Norman agrees with Marion that his mother is sick, but he won't institutionalize her. He says she is harmless, and that he will always care for her.

After seeing poor Norman in his "trap," Marion regains her senses and plans to return to Phoenix in the morning. Through a hole in the office wall, Norman watches her undress. Then he returns to his house. Marion showers. A tall figure with gray hair and in an old lady's dress enters the bathroom and stabs Marion repeatedly with a long knife, killing her. Norman is horrified to find the body. But he covers up his mother's crime. He puts Marion's body and belongings (he doesn't notice the stolen money) into her car, which he disposes of in a swamp.

Lila goes to Sam's hardware store in Fairville, hoping to find Marion. Sam is upset to learn of her disappearance and the stolen money. Milton Arbogast, an insurance investigator trying to recover the money, has followed Lila. Convinced Sam and Lila know nothing of Marion's crime, he goes to check all the hotels and motels in the area, including the Bates Motel. The nervous Norman lets slip that Marion was there. But he swears she drove off. Norman also lets slip he lives with his "sick mother." He refuses to let Arbogast meet her. Arbogast calls Sam and Lila, telling them he's going to sneak into the house to speak to Norman's mother. At the top of the stairs, a tall figure with gray hair and in an old lady's dress charges out of mother's bedroom and slashes Arbogast to death with a long knife.

Sheriff Chambers tells Sam and Lila that Norman's mother committed suicide 10 years before, after poisoning her lover. Confused, they check into the Bates Motel. While Sam keeps Norman occupied, Lila goes to the house to speak to his mother. Norman knocks out Sam and races into the house. Lila hides from him. She goes into the fruit cellar. She finds Mrs. Bates in a chair and spins her around. Mrs. Bates is a corpse. As Lila screams, a tall figure with gray hair and in an old lady's dress rushes into the fruit cellar, holding the long knife. It is Norman, in a wig and his mother's dress. Sam saves Lila.

Dr. Richmond informs Sam and Lila that 12-year-old Norman jealously poisoned his mother and her lover. He later dug up her corpse, and started wearing her clothes, conversing with her, and taking on her personality—killing women Norman was attracted to. Now in a cell, Norman no longer exists. He is Mother at all times.

I'm told that a small boy who stayed up to be scared by this masterpiece said afterwards: "I liked it, but it made me want to sleep in Mummy's bed." Let's hope his reaction wasn't typical.

—British critic Kenneth Tynan

Almost everyone who saw *Psycho* in 1960 remembers that terrifying experience as if it were yesterday, just as everyone remembers first hearing that President Kennedy had been shot. Today *Psycho* fans swap stories about how they closed their eyes during the film's violence (but not the sex) or literally ducked under their seats (I admit measuring the amount of room down there), or how it scared them out of several nights' sleep. Viewers really were afraid to take showers for a long time afterward (and I'm not alone in still occasionally thinking of *Psycho* when in a motel shower). I think that almost everyone who saw *Psycho* when it was released agrees that it is the scariest picture ever made. And it's a shame that most people, even adolescents, who see it for the first time today don't find it scary or sexy or innovative, but campy (it may be a black joke, but it's not camp). They don't feel the impact that we did when we first saw the film or experience the excitement. They don't realize how much more lurid and violent *Psycho* was than horror films of the past, and how unprepared everyone was for it. For instance, today's first-

Norman Bates stands by what has become one of the most famous houses in America. (It stands on the Universal Studios lot in Los Angeles.)

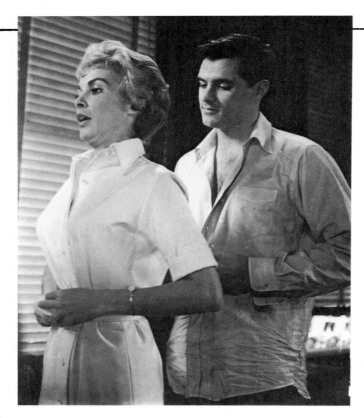

Top: *In the opening scene, Marion pulls away from Sam after making love to him in a sleazy hotel.* Bottom: *Marion is drawn toward Norman, who—according to critics who contended that Anthony Perkins and John Gavin resemble each other—may represent the sexually perverse side of Sam (the side Marion may secretly desire). However, this mirror-image publicity shot (in the scene itself, Norman carries a tray) confirms Hitchcock wanted us to recognize the link between Norman and Marion.*

time viewers already know that the major female character, Marion Crane (although played by star Janet Leigh), will be murdered only about 40 minutes into the film, and that the murderous "Mrs. Bates" is actually the dead woman's son Norman. But in 1960, we were completely shocked.

It wasn't the sex and violence alone that unnerved us, but—and this is what people usually forget—that we felt *guilty* about watching the sex and violence. Especially those of us who were youngsters. Today teenagers have seen their fill of gruesome movie murders and nudity, either in theaters (no one checks IDs) or at home, on cable or videos. They've been weaned on *Night of the Living Dead* (1968), guilt-causing *The Last House on the Left* (1972) and *The Texas Chain Saw Massacre* (1974), *Halloween* (1978), *Friday the 13th* (1980), *A Nightmare on Elm Street* (1985), Herschell Gordon Lewis gorefests, and innumerable gross-out sexploitation films—good and bad films for which *Psycho* paved the way. But remember, in 1960, in pre–rating-code days, the American cinema was tame. Parents could take their children to any movie without worry. That's why so many of us youngsters saw *Psycho*. And let me stress this: While watching the film, with all that exciting sex and horrific violence and the psychiatrist's endless revelations about the perverse relationship between Norman and his mother (we were happy to have this long scene, which today seems dull, to regain our composure), we knew it wasn't kiddie material—we knew we were getting away with seeing something meant for adults and we felt guilty about it.

Of course, our guilt made us enjoy the film more, but it also made us extremely nervous and vulnerable to be terrified. I believe that one reason we were so terrorized when Norman's mother comes into the bathroom and stabs Marion to death is that we related it to our own mother bursting through an unlocked door and ripping apart a dirty magazine she caught us with. (Hitchcock probably related Norman's mother in this scene to a mad censor who wanted to cut out all the nudity in his picture.) While staring at Marion nude in the shower, we youngsters (especially we boys) realized that the actress playing her really was nude for the cameraman and, even more titillating, that she posed for him so that *we* could see her nude. So the naked actress became our accomplice in a moment of naughtiness (like that little girl whom little boys play doctor with). To see Marion killed was so devastating because she was punished for what we were doing together, for what we were both guilty of. We felt guilt because she was killed (what an overreaction by Mrs. Bates!) and we weren't harmed (you can't die in your own nightmare). Perhaps this explained our whimpers or hiding-in-the-closet silence until the next scene.

Guilt *is* the key. Hitchcock decided to mercilessly manipulate all our emotions during *Psycho*—he wanted us to feel as if he were taking us through an amusement park "funhouse"—and I think the reason he was able to do this without resistance from his 1960 audience is that he constantly worked on our guilt. He doesn't just open the film inside the sleazy hotel room where Marion and Sam make love. Instead he makes us feel like voyeurs by beginning with his camera high in the sky, moving closer and closer to the hotel window, and then going inside into their sup-

The most famous and terrifying scene in motion picture history. "Mother" attacks the screaming Marion in the motel room shower. Top: Because the scene is strategically backlit, we can look directly into the murderer's face and see only shadows.

posed sanctuary, taking us inside to where we shouldn't be. We witness a scene that broke new sexual ground in 1960: Unmarried Marion and Sam are in bed (together!), handsome John Gavin with his shirt off and buxom Janet Leigh in just a half white slip and white bra (in those days, we never saw female characters in bras!). They will begin to dress but it doesn't become less exciting because we flies on the wall overhear them discuss their illicit relationship and how this hotel is the only place they can make love. Two scenes later, our guilt returns when we are taken into Marion's bedroom, and find her in a *black* (she committed a crime!) half slip and bra, preparing to run off with the stolen money.

Later we see Marion in her motel room as she starts to take off her bra and slip. Hitchcock won't let us watch her from within the room, but makes us peep at her through the hole Norman drilled in his office wall. So again he makes us into sexual voyeurs, even accomplices to pervert Norman (it's the first moment we identify with him directly). A few minutes later, Hitchcock lets us follow Marion into the bathroom, a most unusual setting for a movie scene! And for the first time in movie history, we see a toilet flushed, and what's more, it is flushed by a woman! And to cap this off, we get to watch major actress Leigh disrobe (we see her from the back and above the waist) at a time major stars didn't do nude scenes, and she doesn't even get privacy when she enters the shower because Hitchcock takes us inside with her. Such a moment was startling, though two earlier horror films, the Val Lewton–produced *The Seventh Victim* (1943) and Gerd Oswald's bizarre *Screaming Mimi* (1958), had shower scenes that (especially when combined) anticipated the one in *Psycho*. During both the more pleasant part of Marion's shower (when she tries to purify herself with soap and water) and the bloody (this too was new!) attack by Mother, we tried in 1960 to catch glimpses of Leigh's breasts (we didn't know that she used moleskin strategically and, though Leigh denies it, her double Marli Refro was filmed when the most explicit shots were required). The nudity came across, whether we actually saw it or not. (It took VCRs, with their freeze-frame and slow-motion capacity, to provide proof that viewers saw what they thought they saw 25 years before.)

Since there is no more nudity/seminudity in *Psycho* after Marion's death, Hitchcock couldn't just use sex to make us feel guilty about watching his film. Throughout, he makes us share the deep guilt of his characters. There's not a scene where someone doesn't feel guilt or paranoia; where someone doesn't lie or try to cover up a lie or crime, or isn't suspicious that the other person is lying; or where someone isn't someplace she or he shouldn't be. Start at the beginning. Marion is guilty over her secretive sexual encounters (during her lunch hours) with Sam in the cheap hotel ("This is the last time for this," she says prophetically). Obviously they use false names to register. Sam (who hangs his head when she leaves the room) is guilty he hasn't the money to marry her. In the next scene, we meet Marion's boss, Mr. Lowery (Vaughn Taylor), who secretly keeps a bottle of liquor in his desk. Marion lies to him that she's going to deposit the money he gives her. Soon after, she feels guilty for having stolen the money.

Her guilt/paranoia builds as Lowery spots her driving through town, the highway patrolman (Mort Mills) peers into her car window and asks questions, the car dealer (John Anderson) questions why she'd accept his first paltry offer on a trade-in. Moreover, she starts imagining the reactions of Sam and the people back in Phoenix over her theft.

Trying to cover her crime, Marion trades in her car, and uses a false name to register at the Bates Motel (Mary Samuels is also the name Meg Tilly's character, Sam and Lila's daughter, uses in 1983's *Psycho II*). She lies to Norman about where she's from. Norman feels ashamed (guilty) about his mother's uncivil response to having Marion visit his house. He feels shame that he can't defy Mother. Norman makes Marion feel guilty about having suggested he institutionalize his sick mother. He certainly feels guilt about liking Marion (if he weren't attracted to her, his puritanical mother wouldn't kill her). He has no business standing at a peephole and watching Marion undress, and this impotent man-child, who can't say the word "bathroom" to a woman, would certainly feel guilty about such a blatantly sexual act. Soon after, Norman covers up Mrs. Bates's murder of Marion. Lila (Vera Miles) suspiciously questions Sam about his involvement with Marion. Arbogast suspiciously questions both of them about their involvement. Norman acts guilty and paranoid when Arbogast suspiciously questions him. Arbogast goes into the Bates house, uninvited. Sam and Lila use false names to register at the Bates Motel. Sam makes Norman paranoid with his questioning. Lila walks through the various rooms of the Bates house—it doesn't seem such an unusual act, but how few times between Myrna Loy's Nora Charles and 1960 did a female movie character sneak alone into a house/apartment to snoop around? At the end, we learn from Simon Oakland's glib Dr. Richmond that in addition to covering up his mother's murders (which, actually, he committed while thinking he was Mrs. Bates), Norman has been covering up his own crimes for 10 years: He murdered his mother and her married lover, and he dug up and preserved her corpse. Because of our own uneasiness about sitting in the theater watching *Psycho* in 1960 we instantly identified with characters who ventured where they shouldn't be in the film (Marion on the highway with the stolen money; Norman at the peephole; Arbogast and Lila each sneaking into the Bates house) and related to all characters who felt guilty and paranoid about doing something wrong, even Norman. Indeed it is their guilt over the crimes they have committed and paranoia about being discovered that make us aware of the strong link between Leigh's Marion (Mary in the book) and Anthony Perkins's Norman.

In Robert Bloch's hair-raising pulp novel, based on the grisly real-life escapades of Wisconsin fiend Ed Gein (a murderer, grave robber, necrophiliac, and cannibal), we are introduced to Norman immediately (he's older and fatter and less easy to identify with than in the movie), and though we don't learn that Mother is dead until the end, throughout the book we are privy to his innermost thoughts. Joseph Stefano's script is quite faithful to Bloch, but we don't meet Norman for about 20 minutes, when Marion arrives at the motel. Yet the script, like the movie,

is not about Marion's theft but about our unraveling the identity of Norman Bates—which comes about because of Marion's crime. What's interesting about the script is that we learn about Norman long before we meet him, simply by observing Marion. There is good reason that when they finally meet, the guilt-ridden, paranoid Marion can readily identify with Norman, and learns from observing him that if she doesn't come to her senses, she is in danger of becoming too much like this neurotic, "trapped" young man (scramble the letters in her name and you get Nor-mai—like Norman, not quite Normal). As we watch Marion up until the time she meets Norman, we see how easy it is for a normal person to break a mundane life's routine and commit a crime, "not act herself," "go a little mad"— this is a familiar Hitchcock theme. And we see how one impulsive act can lead to other senseless acts, lying, escalating guilt and paranoia, and the submersion of one's real identity. From watching Marion (a typical boring "bourgeois woman," according to Hitchcock) go a bit balmy, we can deduce that an abnormal person like Norman would have much more extreme reactions to committing a crime, especially a more heinous crime than theft. Marion can put on the brakes to her building madness once she sees she is in danger of becoming like Norman (although she still doesn't realize how mad he is). However, Norman was already badly unstable when he killed his mother and her married lover, so he is too far gone to ever come to his senses.

In 1960, theaters wouldn't let you in if you missed the beginning of *Psycho* (a gimmick that attracted enormous crowds) and it's a good thing because the opening scene

in the hotel is vital. For one thing, it shows how dead parents can still destroy the happiness of their children. Sam can't marry Marion because he's burdened with his late father's debts. They can't make love at Marion's home because, as Sam jokes, they'd have to turn her dead mother's picture to the wall. Marion isn't the virgin she is in the novel (where she's linked to Norman by their mutual sexual repression), but she is uncomfortable with her sex life; she thinks it's not respectable—her mother, like Norman's, instilled in her a feeling that sex out of wedlock is wrong (of course, Norman's puritanical mother would never have let him marry). Marion doesn't complain that Sam pays alimony to his ex-wife, but she must be jealous that the money which could buy her happiness is going to another woman. Like Norman, who poisoned his mother when she turned her attentions from him to a male suitor, Marion is motivated to commit a crime because the person she loves is giving someone else (her rival) what she desperately needs.

In the next scene, in the office, we meet three people. Co-worker Caroline (Hitchcock's daughter Patricia returned to the screen) is married yet her mother still interferes in the relationship. Mr. Lowery is to Marion what Sheriff Chambers (John McIntire) is to Norman: Having known her for exactly 10 years, he would think her incapable of committing a crime. It's my hunch that the obnoxious, bragging, flirting, drunk client Mr. Cassidy (Frank Albertson) is meant to be the type of man who stole Mrs. Bates from Norman and convinced her to open a motel so they could make money. At any rate, Cassidy is a domineering father who uses his wealth to choreograph and control his daughter's life. How it must irritate Marion, who is over 30 and miserable because she and Sam don't have the money to marry, to learn that Cassidy is buying his 18-year-old daughter a house for a *wedding* present, and that he has made sure she has never had an unhappy day in her life. If Cassidy were a nice man who is using his life's savings to secure happiness for his unspoiled daughter, we would be infuriated when Marion steals his money. But since the $40,000 is this crude, rich man's pocket change ("I never carry more money than I can afford to lose"), we feel that Marion should steal it. We further identify with her when she does.

In her apartment, Marion looks at herself in her mirror (one of many mirrors in the film). Thus, the dual-personality theme is introduced. It's hard to believe that pretty girl in the mirror is a criminal, just as no one suspects that Anthony Perkins's friendly-looking and -acting Norman is a sexual psychopath. We notice on the wall a picture of Marion's parents, looking down on her as she commits her crime. The bathroom door is open so we also notice a shower. Along with Sam's earlier remark that placed a mother in context to sex, and the highway policeman's subsequent suggestion that Marion should stay in a motel ("just to be safe"), the shower gives us a good indication of what is in store for Marion once she meets Norman. The questions asked of Marion by the policeman and the car dealer put her on the spot, just as Norman will be when interrogated by Arbogast and then Sam. She is just as inept at answering questions, covering her guilt, and swaying their suspicions as Norman will be with his inquisitors. For me, the key early scene that tells us about Norman is when the paranoid Marion drives along and imagines conversations between people who discover her crime. We think Hitchcock is just using an interesting technique to present actual conversations before they happen, without having to cut back to Phoenix and the various characters. But at one point we hear Sam speaking to Marion when she arrives at his door in Fairville—this meeting will *never* take place. So in fact, Marion is hearing "voices" and fabricating conversations . . . as Norman surely does. However, at this point, she is stronger than Norman, and doesn't join in the conversations.

Marion and Norman finally meet. Norman comes down from the vertical "California gothic" house (the mother's womb), along the serpentine steps (the umbilical cord) to the long horizontal motel (which has phallic connotations, especially since this is where Norman commits his sex crimes). They face each other, two friendly people with secrets, false identities, guilt and paranoia, crimes in their pasts. As they talk about "personal traps" and "crazy acts," they understand each other. They were destined to meet exactly 10 years ago: when he poisoned his mother and she began work with the firm from which she'd steal $40,000. We understand how this woman named Crane came to this taxidermist, to her executioner. After committing her crime, she entered hell, Norman's permanent home, and he was waiting with (a) room enough for her. (There is no such thing as a purifying shower in hell.)

So by the time Marion is murdered, we have learned much about what drove Norman to committing his initial crime and what drove him deeper into madness. We understand irrational behavior. We will learn more about him during the rest of the film because we can relate what he does to what we saw Marion do, such as covering up a crime (when he tosses out the money, we recognize how absolutely meaningless was Marion's death), and lying when being subjected to questions. We also learn about him when Lila takes her audience-paralyzing tour of the Bates home. We're surprised by our transfer of identification from Mother's-victim Marion to Mother's-victim Norman—who's as sympathetic a victim of parental dominance as Perkins's institutionalized Jimmy Piersall in *Fear Strikes Out* (1957). It happens when Norman tries to sink her car in the swamp and for an instant it won't go down—we are relieved when it disappears completely. Our sympathies switch to other imperiled characters later on, but we never stop relating to Norman or sympathizing with him—that's why he is such an unusual villain and, today, a folk hero.

By no means do I want to give the impression that only those people who saw *Psycho* in 1960 could enjoy it. It is a great movie, with so much to appreciate: Perkins's astonishing, beautifully conceived performance, exhibiting Norman's gentleness, feeble wit, and pain . . . along with the deep-rooted madness (no actor ever got more into his character); lovely Leigh's very intelligent, controlled (even as Marion loses control), and daringly sexy performance; Stefano's witty yet diabolical script, which is full of many complex, chilling ideas; Bernard Herrmann's unforgettable violin/cello score that is so vital to the film's suspense; George Tomasini's remarkable editing, particularly in the 45-second shower sequence but flawless throughout; the art direction by Joseph Hutley and Robert Clatworthy (whose work on 1958's *Touch of Evil*—with Janet Leigh's character terrorized in a deserted motel—explains the similarly seedy look of the two films); the sliced-by-a-knife titles of Saul Bass (who claims he directed the shower sequence); and the striking black-and-white cinematography of John L. Russell (Hitchcock could only afford his TV cameraman). Russell moved his camera effectively, as when he twists into the shower drain with the blood and water and then twists out from Marion's eye (a great moment that, for some reason, is excised from this scene when it is replayed in *Psycho II*), and when he moves high into the rafters so we can't see Mother's face when she attacks Arbogast or when Norman carries her to the fruit cellar. He also gives us some beautifully composed static shots—the motel and house; a vertical phone booth between a car that juts out toward us and a hanging circular sign. Best of all, of course, is the direction of Hitchcock, who oversaw every aspect of his project (Stefano, who borrowed much from Bloch, and Herrmann had the most freedom).

Every director who makes suspense-horror films should study Hitchcock's work on *Psycho,* to see how he works his audience, to see how he keeps it off-balance. Never did Hitchcock pay more attention to the *time* element. We are repeatedly shocked because Hitchcock has violence occur *before* we expect it. When Marion showers, we see through the shower curtain that Mother has entered the bathroom—she doesn't sneak in but walks directly toward the shower without fear, and the attack quickly begins

Lila and Sam check into the Bates Motel.

(and, as mentioned, Marion is killed long before we expect it—had there ever been a lead female *murdered* in an American film?). When Arbogast walks up the stairs of the Bates house, we expect him to enter the room where we know Mrs. Bates is hiding behind the door, but instead "the old lady" charges out at him (accompanied by Herrmann's screechy violins), knife raised high, and starts stabbing him. I like the way Hitchcock "punctuates" his initial shocks to completely unnerve us: Each plunge of the knife into Marion's body (sexually repressed Norman's symbolic rape) is like an exclamation point (things move so quickly yet time stands still, as in the equally famous "Odessa Steps" sequence of Eisenstein's 1925 classic *Potemkin*), as are the violin screeches that accompany each slash; after Arbogast seems to walk backward down the stairs (a classic shot utilizing rear projection and a camera on a track), "the old lady" immediately jumps on top of him (how *quick* she is) and uses the knife to finish him off—period, period, period; when Lila turns Mother around and we are shocked because she is a corpse, Hitchcock adds punctuation by having Lila, like Marion earlier, give a rare Hitchcock scream and slap the bare light bulb with her hand so that there is an unsettling strobe effect (as in the attic murder in 1945's *The Picture of Dorian Gray*), and having another "Mother" (Norman with a crazed expression) storm in behind her. *Psycho*'s many classic scenes

and images (Mother in the bathroom with knife held high, backlit so we can't see her face; the crossed metal hands and the body-indented bed in Mother's bedroom; the almost subliminal shot of Mother's skeletal visage being superimposed over Norman's face; etc.) have been analyzed ad nauseam. But one image that is usually ignored sticks with me. It is of Mother fleeing the bathroom after having massacred Marion. With hindsight we can see the enormity of Norman's (sexual) identity problem: There is no reason for Mother to race out, because there is no one else around to catch her—unless she worries about Norman.

When *Psycho* was released most critics, perhaps perturbed because they weren't allowed to give away the plot or to attend special critics' screenings, attacked Hitchcock with the same viciousness with which Mrs. Bates attacks Marion. They tried to make him feel guilty about adapting Bloch's sordid novel, and for his unabashed treatment of sex and violence. (Paramount wasn't behind the project either, which may account for Hitchcock filming it on the Universal lot.) When it became Hitchcock's biggest hit, most critics changed their minds . . . and the film was soon rightfully regarded as a classic. It would take many years before it lost its notorious reputation (CBS wouldn't show it, even with nine minutes of deletions, in 1966). Yet, for those of us who vividly recall our first *Psycho* viewing, every time we see the picture its power is undiminished.

The Quiet Man

1952   Color   Republic release of an Argosy picture
Director: John Ford
Producers: John Ford and Merian C. Cooper
Screenplay: Frank S. Nugent
From the story "Green Rushes" by Maurice Walsh
Cinematography: Winton C. Hoch
Music: Victor Young
Editor: Jack Murray
Running Time: 129 minutes

Cast: John Wayne (Sean Thornton), Maureen O'Hara (Mary Kate Danahar), Barry Fitzgerald (Michaeleen Oge Flynn), Victor Mc-Laglen (Red Will Danahar), Ward Bond (Father Peter Lonergan), Mildred Natwick (Mrs. Sarah Tillane), Arthur Shields (Reverend Cyril Playfair), Eileen Crowe (Mrs. Elizabeth Playfair), Charles FitzSimmons (Forbes), Sean McClory (Owen Glynn), Jack Mac-Gowran (Feeney), Francis Ford (Dan Tobin), Ken Curtis (Dermot Fahy), James Lilburn (Father Paul), Mae Marsh (Father Paul's mother), Hank Worden (trainer), May Craig, Patrick Wayne, Antonia Wayne, Melinda Wayne, Michael Wayne, Pat O'Malley.

Synopsis: Sean Thornton arrives in Inisfree, which his late mother called "heaven." At first the townspeople are cool to the stranger, but they befriend him when they learn his parents and grandparents lived in Inisfree. Carriage driver Michaeleen Oge Flynn and old Dan Tobin even remember Sean when he was a child. Having left America, he wants to buy the small cottage he was born in. But the land belongs to the Widow Tillane and Red Will Danahar wants to add it to his property, so he can be a neighbor of the widow. Learning Will spoke about her in the pub, she spitefully sells the land and cottage to Sean. Bully Will becomes the sworn enemy of his new neighbor.

Sean falls in love with Will's beautiful, hot-tempered sister, Mary Kate, the moment he sees her in the meadow. She is immediately attracted to him as well and is excited to learn from matchmaker Michaeleen that Sean wants to court her. But Will refuses to let them marry. Sean is disappointed Mary Kate won't go against her brother's wishes—he doesn't understand the importance of tradition to her. He and Mary Kate are miserable.

Michaeleen, Father Lonergan, and the Reverend and Mrs. Playfair form a conspiracy. They tell Will that the Widow Tillane will marry him only if there is no other woman in his house. Wanting Mary Kate to move out, Will pays Michaeleen to serve as matchmaker between her and Sean. Mary Kate and Sean are expected to have a long courtship, according to Irish tradition, but neither can resist the other's advances. They get married.

Will's proposal to the Widow Tillane is rejected. He figures Sean was in on the deception and refuses to give up Mary Kate's dowry—her furniture and her money. Sean doesn't care since he has money of his own, and he can't understand why Mary Kate is so upset. She refuses to sleep with him until she has her dowry. She feels she is just his servant without it. He thinks she is greedy. Will gives Mary Kate the furniture but keeps her money. Mary Kate wants Sean to demand Will return it and to fight him if he refuses. But Sean won't fight, even though everyone thinks he's a coward. Only the Reverend Playfair knows Sean was once boxer Trooper Thorn, and that he killed a man in a prizefight and never wants to fight again for money. Playfair says he should fight for love.

Mary Kate talks with Father Lonergan, who is upset to learn she and Sean have been sleeping apart. That night she and Sean consummate their marriage. But in the morning, Mary Kate has fled—she loves Sean too much to see him embarrassed because he won't fight for her rights.

Sean drags Mary Kate from the train and five miles across the fields to Will. A crowd follows them. When Sean threatens to return Mary Kate, Will relents and gives him her money. Sean and Mary Kate throw it in a furnace. When Will swings at Sean, Sean knocks him down. The beaming, proud Mary Kate goes home to prepare supper. Meanwhile, Sean and Will brawl for hours, while everyone in town looks on and makes bets. Sean and Will come home drunk together—and Mary Kate serves dinner.

Will and the Widow Tillane begin their courtship. Sean and Mary Kate stop their farming this day, and rush into their happy home.

John Ford didn't like to talk about his work, but on occasion he admitted that of his 200-plus films, his favorites were *The Quiet Man* and *The Sun Shines Bright*, personal projects that were released back-to-back in 1952 and 1953, respectively. Both are much admired by Ford fanatics, but while *The Sun Shines Bright* is essentially unknown to the average moviegoer, *The Quiet Man* is perhaps Ford's most popular film. This leisurely paced, lovely-to-look-at, spiritedly acted romantic comedy-drama, which was filmed in Ireland, is also *the* cult movie of the American Irish who are nostalgic for their homeland (which they may know only from movies), a St. Patrick's Day television and revival house perennial, and, as critic David Thomson jests, "an entertainment for IRA club night."

In fact, we have been reminded of how dear the picture is to the American Irish by a tragic yet inspiring human interest story that has been in the news since July 1986. National headlines were made when Steven McDonald, a young New York police officer, was shot and paralyzed while trying to make an arrest in Central Park. When reporters flooded the hospital to find out more about McDonald, his pregnant wife Patti considered it significant to point out that her husband's favorite film is *The Quiet Man*, which he has seen countless times, and that he has tremendous passion for Maureen O'Hara. Always the trouper, O'Hara flew to New York and rushed to McDonald's bedside to give comfort and boost morale. Soon she was firmly established as a family member (of course, she would attend the baby's christening), and was actively involved with the couple as McDonald underwent extensive physical therapy in New York and Colorado.

It should be noted that not long after O'Hara's arrival in New York, she marched in a city parade, very much the stand-in for the fallen policeman. She later announced she wants to eventually be the first female Grand Marshal of the St. Patrick's Day Parade, reinforcing the connection between the holiday, the Irish, and *The Quiet Man*. The following St. Patrick's Day this link was called attention to again in an editorial about Reagan's Iran-Contra troubles in the *New York Post*. Dick Ryan, commentator on the Catholic Church, wrote:

> Now there have always been certain traditional options open to the Irishman when he has tasted misfortune or trudged into the dark night of his soul. He can, for instance, pour out a drink or three, cry a little, go out and belt someone, whine to the little lady, brood, or go off and write a poem. Or else he can go home and put a tape of *The Quiet Man* on his VCR and then sit back and watch how big John Wayne handled all his Irish demons.
>
> In the movie, of course, John, uh, Sean Thornton, did most of the above except write iambic pentameter. But then, setting up house with Maureen O'Hara [uh, Mary Kate Danahar Thornton] worked mightily for John as he drove out the doldrums and lived happily ever after.

The Quiet Man was adapted from Maurice Walsh's less complex short story "Green Rushes," which Ford purchased back in 1936, a year after he made his Oscar-winning Irish drama, The Informer. Ford wasn't able to get the project off the ground, but one wonders how seriously he tried, considering that if he'd made it then, it would have been filmed in black and white on a studio lot. In 1944, however, Ford did get serious and made handshake deals with John Wayne, Maureen O'Hara, Barry Fitzgerald, and Victor McLaglen to assure their participation in the film if he acquired financial backing. Each summer after that he went out on his boat, played Irish records, and dictated to O'Hara ideas and dialogue passages for The Quiet Man. But he could not interest studios in his film about Ireland—even though his 1941 Welsh film, How Green Was My Valley, starring O'Hara, won five Academy Awards, including Best Picture and Best Director. Perhaps they were scared off by Ford's insistence that he go on location to Ireland for the exteriors, whereas he had created the Welsh mining community on a 20th Century-Fox backlot. Finally Wayne took Frank Nugent's script to Herb Yates at Republic, a minor studio known primarily for churning out action films. Yates agreed to back the project if Ford, Wayne, and O'Hara (and McLaglen came along for the ride) would first make a Western for him. They gave Yates the uninspired cavalry film, Rio Grande (1950), and Yates gave them the go-ahead on The Quiet Man.

Ford, cast, and crew—90% of whom were Irish—soon traveled to Ireland to make the director's most personal film, one that would win him his fourth and last Best Director Oscar. Shooting, which began in June 1951 and lasted 10 weeks, took place in the village of Cong in County Mayo and in County Galway, from which Ford's parents had migrated to Maine before he was born. O'Hara got to act with her brothers Charles FitzSimmons and James Lilburn, both of Dublin's Abbey Theatre; brothers Barry Fitzgerald and Arthur Shields each had major roles; Wayne's children, Patrick, Toni, Melinda, and Michael, appeared in the race scene; Victor McLaglen's son Andrew served as assistant director; Ford's brother Francis played the amusing Dan Tobin, son Pat served as a second-unit director, and daughter Barbara was assistant editor. That Ford wanted this picture to be a "family affair" is indication of how close he was to the project.

After all, The Quiet Man represented dream fulfillment to Ford: By making this film, he got to visit the real Ireland of his ancestors, of which his mother often spoke; and through John Wayne's Sean Thornton (who learned of his birthplace from his mother), Ford (christened Sean O'Fienne) got to vicariously settle in the idealized Ireland of his daydreams and reject crass, materialistic America. The Ireland Ford presents has real elements, but it is not meant to be the real Ireland. Here everyone lives in harmony and Catholics, led by Ward Bond's Father Lonergan, pretend to be Protestants so that their friend, Arthur Shields's Reverend Playfair, won't have to move elsewhere. The rolling green meadows, blue skies, and quaint villages do exist and are as beautiful as we see them in the film, but at times it seems as if Ford and Winton C. Hoch (who won an Oscar for his gorgeous Technicolor cine-

Although they love each other dearly, Sean and Mary Kate don't get along nearly as well in the film as they do in this poster. But the poster isn't all that misleading: It conveys the joyful spirit of the film.

matography) are trying to capture the look of a fairy tale or one of Ford's daydreams about Ireland. Critic Manny Farber wrote that "a dense, gray atmosphere takes most of the hue and intensity out of the scenes and makes for a curious picture that takes place in daylight yet has some of the sunless, remembered look of a surrealist painting." Ford has been taken to task for presenting "stage Irish" characters rather than real Irishmen—Farber complained of "the dated mimickry of such stereotypes as the tippling village cabby, the thick-headed, bellicose squire, and the jovial village priest, who curses, jokes, and fishes from start to finish of the film"—but here too Ford intentionally veered away from authenticity because he wanted to show a romanticized, ideal Ireland, for the Ireland he dreamed about was populated by those "stage Irish" eccentrics he loved. Similarly he populated his Westerns with the types of men—stereotypes, perhaps—he wished had been in the real West.

Ford would have preferred an Ireland filled only with men who go to the pub (his father owned a saloon) with the same regularity as they work their farms or attend church, drink heartily (already thinking of their next drink),

As Michaeleen (second from left) *and Feeney* (second from right) *try halfheartedly to dissuade Sean and Will from becoming too physical on their first meeting, Father Lonergan* (center) *and the other pub regulars hope a fistfight is brewing.*

love a good fight, appreciate competition of all sorts, fish, brag, bet, argue, spread local gossip, curse *if* the priest is out of earshot, worry that they've sinned, love their beautiful land, form conspiracies (as do Fitzgerald's Michaeleen, Lonergan, and the Playfairs) and practice deception (even the Playfairs don't play fair), swap funny stories, quote Irish poets, burst into Irish ballads, shed a tear for Mother, toast fallen warriors ("Your grandfather died in Australia—in a penal colony," Lonergan reminds Sean, adding, "and your father—he was a good man, too"), and, like Michaeleen, "talk a little treason." And for Ford, the dream colleen of his romanticized Ireland was another likable stereotype: a beautiful, full-figured redhead who has a terrifying temper, the strength to stand up to formidable men, and a willingness to give body and soul— even if it means breaking tradition—to the man who captures her heart. O'Hara's Mary Kate is "a saint" in Sean's eyes (she probably reminds him of his mother, who was such a positive influence on him) and a vision ("Hey is that real?" he asks rhetorically when he first sees her. "She couldn't be!"), a force of nature (the weather always tells us her state of mind), and a symbol of the lovely Irish landscape (repeatedly Ford shows her in relation to the land). She is the Eve Sean finds in his version of paradise/Eden.

Ford often made films about men who seek salvation and/or search for paradise. This theme was dealt with in such Ford classics as *The Iron Horse* (1924); *The Informer; The Hurricane* (1937); *The Grapes of Wrath* (1940); *Three Godfathers* (1948), in which Wayne looks for New Jerusalem; *Wagon Master* (1950); *The Searchers* (1955), in which Wayne can't find peace on his return to Texas; and *The Man Who Shot Liberty Valance* (1962), in which Wayne helps "a garden grow in the wilderness." (In 1964's *Cheyenne Autumn,* however, the Indians are driven from paradise.) In *The Quiet Man,* Sean Thornton, who has killed a man in a prizefight, seeks salvation in Inisfree (often spelled Innisfree), which he expects to be "heaven" on earth. He finds that it is no "heaven"—as Mildred Natwick's Widow Tillane warned—but after he makes the effort to change things a bit, it does become paradise for him. The picture bears some resemblance to *Three Godfathers.* One-time killer Sean Thornton is redeemed because he refuses to fight again for money (personal gain) but does fight for love (making a personal sacrifice to save his marriage); proving himself a brave, worthy man, he is welcomed into the peaceful, religious Inisfree community—where the leader is Ward Bond's priest. In the earlier film, outlaw Wayne is redeemed because he is willing to sacrifice himself (and his freedom) in order to save a baby lost in the desert and, as a result, he is welcomed into the peaceful, religious community of Welcome, Arizona—

where the leader is Ward Bond's lawman. There definitely are parallels. But I see *The Quiet Man* more as a variation on *Angel and the Badman* (1947), a Wayne cult Western written and directed by James Edward Grant at Yates's Republic Studios. In that pacifist film (which Wayne produced!), the outlaw Wayne must refrain from violence to win Gail Russell and be accepted into her peaceful Mormon farming community; in this pacifist film, one-time killer Sean must fight one more time (against McLaglen's bully Will Danahar) to win Mary Kate and be accepted into her peaceful Catholic farming community. In each case, Wayne's character gives up the violent world he knew so he can live as a quiet, peaceful man in "paradise."

There is so much boisterous Fordian-style Irish humor, so much Irish blarney, so much singing and joviality, and so many quirky characters roaming about (Fitzgerald's portrayal is delightful) that one tends to overlook that just below the surface there is much seriousness, unhappiness, hurt, and guilt. Both Sean and Mary Kate are tormented in real ways and we feel for them. It is, in fact, how they resolve their serious problems that makes *The Quiet Man* such a thematically fascinating, "modern" picture. Sean is still tortured because he killed a man in the ring so he could win a purse. He rids himself of his "Trooper Thorn" ring name and tries to establish a new identity as he begins a new phase of his life in Inisfree. He hopes to regain his innocence by becoming the quiet peace-loving person, Sean

Thornton, that his gentle rose-growing mother wanted him to be. Yet Sean doesn't sense that Mary Kate might also feel the need to establish a *personal* identity when she enters a new phase of her life, as Sean's wife. Molly Haskell writes in *From Reverence to Rape* (1974):

> Behind a woman's defensive "game" there is the very real fear—a fear to which some directors seem more sympathetic than others—of losing herself in marriage, of losing her identity along with her name. The theme becomes the explicit subject of one of John Ford's loveliest (and from this point of view, most surprising) films, *The Quiet Man*.

Mary Kate hopes to attain her own identity, and make herself a worthy, *equal* marital partner to Sean, by entering their marriage with her dowry ("whenever I wed—what's my own goes with me"): her furniture ("The house may belong to my brother," she tells matchmaking Michaeleen, then proudly announces, "but what's in the parlor belongs to *me*") and her 350-pound savings. She fights for her identity, refusing to sleep with Sean until he gets Will to give them her belongings:

> I'll wear your ring, I'll cook, and I'll wash, and I'll keep the land. But that is all. Until I've got my dowry safe about me, I'm no married woman. I'm the servant I've always been, without anything of my own!

Matchmaker Michaeleen escorts Will when he calls on Mrs. Tillane (already in the company of Sean).

Publicity shot: The wedding ceremony is ruined when Will decides not to let Kate have her dowry. This causes friction between Mary Kate and Sean (who won't demand the dowry from Will).

Mary Kate is peeved that Sean won't fight Will for her dowry (she doesn't know he fears killing him), either for her sake or for his own, to disprove charges that he is a coward. "It is his refusal of his public role (his standing in the community) which prompts Mary Kate to refuse her private role," state Joseph McBride and Michael Wilmington in *John Ford* (1974). "Individual harmony is a condition of communal harmony." In her essay on the film in *On the Verge of Revolt* (1978), Brandon French writes:

> Mary Kate's battle for status in her marriage—not merely to have but to *be* something of her own—challenges the bases of conventional marriage, just as her behavior in general defies conventional femininity. She "wallops" men, stands up to her bearish brother, shows an aggressive interest in Sean, leads *him* in passion, and leaves him when he fails to respond to her deepest needs. Her break with tradition is epitomized at the end of the film when Mary Kate tosses away the stick which an old woman gave Sean to keep his wife in line. In doing so, Mary Kate rejects the notion of her husband's mastery, to which the older woman had obviously acquiesced. But at the same time, she rejects the opportunity to master *him*. Thus, John Ford rescues Mary Kate from the imprisoning myths of both the Good Woman Goddess and the Shrew, to which the film's reactionary symbologies would otherwise relegate her, and thereby creates out of the ashes of the past the image of a *new* woman.

And Ford creates out of the ashes of the past the image of a *new* man. Traditions must be broken. The marriage of Mary Kate and Sean survives because they each experience liberation. Even at the beginning of their relationship, this rose-planting man doesn't want to dominate Mary Kate or limit her to the traditional role of Irish wives. He expects her to also break tradition, which is why he is so disappointed when she won't marry him just because her brother won't give his consent; and he is thrilled that she is sexually aggressive (also breaking with tradition). French doesn't mention that Mary Kate isn't worried about Sean's reaction to her tossing away the stick because earlier in the film, after she stranded Sean in Castletown, she handed him a stick with which to beat her and *he* tossed it in the fireplace, without thinking twice. Furthermore, Sean doesn't force himself on Mary Kate sexually—as Rhett Butler does to that other O'Hara in *Gone With the Wind* (1939)—even though she thinks such drastic action is within an Irish husband's rights. He doesn't want to control or repress the independent-minded woman he fell in love with. When Mary Kate walks out on Sean it is not because he won't fulfill her needs, but because she loves him too much to live with him and remind everyone that he hasn't demanded her dowry from Will. She refuses to embarrass him—just as he refused to embarrass her by telling everyone they slept apart on their wedding night. Interestingly, by the time Mary Kate leaves Sean, she has slept with him, even though he has not come through for her. There is no more sexual blackmail (so later, when Mary Kate opens a blazing furnace and Sean tosses her money in, there is no embarrassing sexual connotation). Ford is telling us that Mary Kate's refusal to have sex is

Mary Kate shows her displeasure that Sean would rather grow roses than vegetables.

not the key issue; after they have sex, their basic problem remains. This is, we realize, a *mature* relationship. Mary Kate sleeps with Sean to show him she senses he has valid reasons for not fighting her brother, although she may not understand them. In turn, Sean then challenges Will for Mary Kate's sake, conceding that her reasons for wanting him to fight for her dowry are not trivial, foolish, or mercenary, although he doesn't think he understands them. (We sense that he begins to understand her need for her own identity when he gives her a carriage of her own—he may honk its horn at her as if she were his date back in America, but he lets her drive, which men in 1952 rarely let their dates do in America or Ireland.) The marriage of Mary Kate and Sean will succeed because they have learned that it is more important to have respect for and faith in one's spouse than to fully understand them.

Many people regard the lengthy brawl between Sean and Will (a fine comic villain), witnessed by everyone in Inisfree, as the film's highlight. (Ironically, the only person injured while making this film was O'Hara, who broke her wrist socking Wayne.) It is an amusing scene, much more fun than the unending brawl between Wayne and Lee Marvin in Ford's *Donovan's Reef* (1963). But I have more fondness for any of Sean and Mary Kate's amorous and rough-and-tumble scenes (including when he drags her across the fields to confront Will). They are one of the cinema's most romantic couples. Critics often speak of how couples create their own electricity on the screen—well, Sean and Mary Kate literally cause thunder and lightning when they kiss. They are the supreme matchup of Wayne and O'Hara, one of the cinema's most appealing,

most underrated, romantic teams. Handsome Wayne and beautiful O'Hara are wonderful together, exhibiting strength and, because their characters are in love, vulnerability and tenderness. I particularly like the sincere, respectful way Sean speaks to Mary Kate. She is flattered and surprised by how he approaches her (Wayne's characters are rarely condescending toward women), and this contributes to her falling for him. Ford was never known for "love scenes," but how incredibly erotic is the scene in which Sean finds Mary Kate, a virtual stranger, in his new cottage and immediately pulls her like a dancer into his arms and kisses her and, a moment later, has her daringly kiss him before fleeing; and the silent passage in the graveyard, in which they hold hands, race for shelter from the sudden thunderstorm (nature has reacted to her brazen decision to forgo traditional courtship and jump immediately into full-fledged romance), and then clutch each other (he drapes his jacket over her) and kiss twice (always the aggressor, she initiates the second kiss) as the rain soaks through his white shirt. No wonder Ford called *The Quiet Man* his "sexiest film" (although, as McBride and Wilmington point out, it is narrated by a celibate, Father Lonergan). There haven't been many sexier moments in film history than the final scene, when Mary Kate whispers into Sean's ear something so startling—and so pleasing—that he is taken aback . . . before smiling appreciatively (what a wife!) and quickly following her into their cottage. This is proof positive that "suggestive" sex in the cinema can be much more of a turn-on than explicit sex. What any of us—Irish and non-Irish alike—wouldn't give to know exactly what Mary Kate has suggested to the man she loves.

Ride the High Country

1962   Color   MGM
Director: Sam Peckinpah
Producer: Richard E. Lyons
Screenplay: N. B. Stone, Jr.
Cinematography: Lucien Ballard
Music: George Bassman
Editor: Frank Santillo
Running Time: 94 minutes

Cast: Randolph Scott (Gil Westrum), Joel McCrea (Steve Judd), Mariette Hartley (Elsa Knudsen), Ron Starr (Heck Longtree), James Drury (Billy Hammond), R. G. Armstrong (Joshua Knudsen), Edgar Buchanan (Judge Tolliver), L. Q. Jones (Sylvus Hammond), John Anderson (Elder Hammond), Warren Oates (Henry Hammond), John Davis Chandler (Jimmy Hammond), Jenie Jackson (Kate), Percy Helton (Luther Sampson), Byron Foulger (Abner Sampson), Carmen Phillips (saloon girl).

Synopsis: Twenty years ago Steve Judd and Gil Westrum tamed many towns in the West. But it's the early twentieth century, they have been forgotten, and these aging ex-lawmen have nothing—no money, no family, no prospects—to show for their contributions.

Judd rides into a thriving business community. He runs into Westrum, whom he hasn't seen for years. Westrum is running a crooked carnival shooting game and claiming to be the "Oregon Kid." He has taken a wild young man named Heck Longtree under his wing and is trying to make him as corrupt as himself. Hoping to get back his self-respect, Judd takes his first meaningful job in years. He is hired by town bankers to ride to Coarse Gold, and transport the miners' gold back to the bank. Because of frequent robberies on the mountain trail, he hires Westrum and Heck to accompany him. Westrum and Heck, who wants to kill Judd, secretly plot to steal the gold. On their journey, the cynical Westrum reminds Judd of how they were shafted by society, after sacrificing women and wealth to make the West safe for civilization. He hopes Judd will suggest taking the gold. But Judd remains honest.

The three men spend a night at the ranch of Joshua Knudsen, a Bible-quoting religious zealot who has kept his pretty, grown daughter Elsa a virtual prisoner so she'll have no contact with men. Heck and Elsa are immediately attracted to each other, but she doesn't like how forward he is with her. Angered, she says she's engaged to miner Billy Hammond, who is in Coarse Gold.

After her father slaps her for talking with Heck, Elsa runs away, joining the three men. When they arrive in the decadent Coarse Gold, Elsa and Billy decide to marry immediately—which makes Heck jealous and Billy's four lecherous brothers happy.

After a hellish wedding, the drunk Billy slaps Elsa and tries to force himself on her. Then his brothers try to rape her. Judd and Heck rescue her. Westrum forces the drunk Judge Tolliver to lie that he has no legal right to perform marriages in California. So Elsa rides away with Judd, Westrum, and Heck.

Heck has come to respect Judd, whom he once thought was just an old man, and doesn't want to rob him anymore. But he feels obligated to Westrum. Judd catches them stealing the gold and ties them up. He is infuriated with his friend for double-crossing him. In the mountains, the Hammonds catch up—they had beat up Tolliver and found out the ceremony was legal. They demand Elsa's return. Prior to a gun battle with the Hammonds, Judd frees Heck because he promises to remain his prisoner after protecting Elsa. Westrum is hurt when Judd won't free him. In the gun battle, Sylvus and Jimmy Hammond are killed. Billy, Elder, and Henry flee. Westrum escapes.

Judd, Heck, and Elsa arrive at the ranch. The Hammonds, who have killed Knudsen, wait in ambush. Judd and Heck are shot. Westrum rides to the rescue. He and Judd stand together, like old times. In a gunfight, the Hammonds are killed and Judd is fatally injured. Westrum promises Judd he will deliver the gold. Judd is touched when his friend expresses faith in him. Westrum and Heck and Elsa, who are in love, allow the proud Judd to die alone. He gazes at the mountains for the last time.

Sam Peckinpah's untimely death in 1984 hasn't stopped the fervent arguments over his controversial and influential body of work. It's still fun to debate the merits of his pictures; to perhaps champion the bawdy, lyrical sleeper *The Ballad of Cable Hogue* (1971) and his impressive, rarely screened debut film *The Deadly Companions* (1961), yet attack his wildly popular, ground-breaking films *The Wild Bunch* (1969) and *Straw Dogs* (1974), as well as the less significant *The Getaway* (1972), *Pat Garrett and Billy the Kid* (1973), and cult item *Bring Me the Head of Alfredo Garcia* (1974), or to rave about his cinematic artistry, his power, yet question his obsession—technically and thematically—for screen violence, his attitude toward women, his concept of "hero," and his theories on the nature of men (the male animal). Most of Peckinpah's films have devoted followings, but only *Ride the High Country* unites all factions, halts arguments, and brings outsiders into the Peckinpah fold. It is his one undisputed masterpiece and one of the greatest Westerns ever made.

Peckinpah's second film (he had directed TV Westerns, including his offbeat creation *The Westerner* and *The Rifleman*) was made on a modest budget by MGM, which had no faith in it until it won a prestigious award at the Venice Film Festival. It hasn't the scope of the expensive, expansive *The Wild Bunch*, but thanks to CinemaScope, cinematographer Lucien Ballard (who'd also photograph the later film), and some breathtaking scenery near California's Mammoth Lakes, it is equally beautiful. It has similar "epic"-though-past-their-prime characters, but I think here their camaraderie is better explored (I don't believe the members of the Wild Bunch have been riding together for years), and it remains tasteful—it correctly has been called "poetic" and "graceful"—despite adult themes and violent content, including fistfights, beatings, attempted rape, and seven major characters being killed. Best of all, it stars Joel McCrea (as Steve Judd) and Randolph Scott (as Gil Westrum). William Holden and Robert Ryan were equally fine actors but one didn't associate either with the Western. That's not important to *The Wild Bunch*, which is a protest-years' war movie in the guise of a Western, but *Ride the High Country* deals specifically with the changing (though not improving) American West at the turn of the century.

McCrea and Scott, veterans of three decades of screen shootouts and roundups, are icons of the reel West that we like to believe was the real West, like Tom Mix, W. S. Hart, Ken Maynard, Tim McCoy, Wild Bill Elliott, John Wayne, and Gary Cooper. As they ride tall in the

Right to left: *Gil, Steve, Heck, and Elsa ride the high country between Coarse Gold and the Knudsen ranch.*

saddle into the frame—immediately instilling an authenticity and physical dimension so necessary to the masculine genre—viewers assume their characters are (as in their previous films) brave, reliable, loyal, honest, resourceful, determined, fast-on-the-draw, capable of winning any barroom brawl, as rugged as the western landscape they love. Since a major theme of *Ride the High Country* is that the modern West (of the early twentieth century) shouldn't arrogantly discard the best of the old West (i.e., the conservative, Christian values embraced by Steve Judd), it's fitting that this modern Western put McCrea, age 57, and Scott, age 59, back in the saddle again, reminding us of how Western heroes should be played. Peckinpah (whose sentimental side has rarely been discussed) always gave last hurrahs, last chances to relive past glories, to men like Judd and Westrum whose contributions deserve tribute. This film does the same for actors McCrea and Scott, major contributors to the genre. No wonder they understand their characters so well! Because this picture capped their splendid individual careers—McCrea wouldn't make another film for eight years, Scott would retire permanently—it's indescribably satisfying watching them go out in a blaze of glory *together.**

. . . .

*The teaming of veterans Scott and McCrea for the film each intended to go out on recalls the 1942 "Roughriders" finale, *West of the Law.* That picture ends with Western idols Tim McCoy and Buck Jones (and sidekick Raymond Hatton) coaxing a young man to settle down with a girl on a ranch (anticipating the ending of *Ride the High Country*). They then say farewell to each other and ride off in different directions. Jones made only one more film, but he was a victim of the Coconut Grove fire before its release. McCoy quit the movies for politics and military service. He wouldn't return to motion pictures until 1956.

McCrea and Scott had similar backgrounds in film. Both began as extras in the late twenties. When McCrea won his first lead, in Cecil B. De Mille's *Dynamite* (1929), Scott was one of the actors he beat out for the role. Scott, a Virginian, was Gary Cooper's stuntman and voice coach on the 1929 Western classic *The Virginian*—McCrea, who often said he got roles Cooper rejected first, starred in the 1946 version. (Ironically, later in 1962 James Drury, villain Billy Hammond in *Ride the High Country,* would play the title role in *The Virginian* television series.) Scott got his big break starring in ten Zane Grey B Westerns churned out by Paramount in the thirties, and then, like McCrea, sought roles in other genres, in A films. He had a few good parts but didn't match the accomplishments of McCrea, who was a standout (and still underrated) leading man for such top directors as William Wyler, Alfred Hitchcock, George Stevens, and Preston Sturges.

After World War II, both actors appeared almost exclusively in Westerns. Most notably, between 1956 and 1960 Scott starred in seven fascinating character-study B Westerns directed by Budd Boetticher—all deservedly have achieved cult status. And McCrea played his one non-hero in Raoul Walsh's classic *Colorado Territory* in 1949, and appeared in three fine films directed by Jacques Tourneur—his pistol-packing rural parson in *Stars in My Crown* (1950), which he wrote in *Close-Ups* (1979) is "the film I am most proud of today," and his sharp-shooting judge in *Stranger on Horseback* (1955) may together be the basis of Steve Judd. The characters played by Scott and McCrea cleaned up Abilene, Sante Fe, Albuquerque, Fort Worth, Medicine Bend, Carson City, Wichita, and numerous other towns in the Wild West. It's amusing (an in-joke?) when Judd chastises Westrum (who bills himself as a one-time

If Elsa marries Billy Hammond, his unsavory brothers (clockwise) Sylvus (with jug), Elder, Henry, and Jimmy expect to have their way with her.

"Frontier Lawman") for fibbing they had tamed Dodge City and Wichita, thereby implying they had worked with Wyatt Earp, because Scott had played Earp in *Frontier Marshal* (1939) and McCrea had played him in Tourneur's *Wichita* (1955). Certainly one reason that the final shoot-out at the Knudsen ranch is so emotionally uplifting is that Peckinpah stages it like "the gunfight at the O.K. Corral" and, standing side by side, their heads high and their guns blazing, Judd and Westrum are like two Wyatt Earps—they have hit the big time!—and their foes, the barbarian Hammonds, come across like the Clantons, who were portrayed as barbarians in movies.

McCrea and Scott are so suited to their characters that it's surprising that the parts weren't written for them. In a 1978 interview with Patrick McGilligan for *Focus in Film,* McCrea recalled that Scott read N. B. Stone, Jr.'s script first. Then called *Guns in the Afternoon* (still the British title)—although "Guns in the Sunset" would have been more appropriate—it was given to Scott by Burt Kennedy, who had written four of the Boetticher-Scott Westerns. (One wonders if Kennedy intended to direct it.) Scott liked the script but, noting that he'd have to share star billing with another strong male lead, told producer Richard Lyons that he'd do it only with McCrea, who had officially retired. Lyons lunched with McCrea and asked him to play Gil Westrum because "he thought I was a little subtler than Randy, and so it would be a little more deceptive that I would double-cross him. But I said, 'No. I'm not going to destroy my image for one picture. My image is Steve Judd, not Gil Westrum. That's the guy who, through integrity, through his own honesty, he's gonna do it—the hell with how bad we were treated and how underpaid we were as marshals.' " McCrea was ready to politely bow out of the project if Scott wanted to play Judd. But over another lunch Scott said, " 'Well, I'll play either one, but

if I had my choice, I'd rather play [Westrum]. I've played the straight, honest guy so damn long that it would be more interesting.' "

So a deal was struck and the two multimillionaires (Scott was considered the richest actor in Hollywood) took the roles of two down-and-out former lawmen—has-beens and misfits in the Peckinpah tradition. Their performances and Peckinpah's direction are so natural, so deceptively simple, that *several* critics in 1962 insisted the picture has *no* message (they thought this was praise for a Western!). But be assured that it deals with numerous themes important to the Western genre and/or Peckinpah. And—this is no exaggeration—almost every action and line of dialogue has thematic relevance. *Ride the High Country* is, I believe, a parable, in which the corrupted Westrum, Ron Starr's novice sinner Heck Longtree, and Mariette Hartley's naive Elsa Knudsen learn by watching Judd the rewards of leading a moral, Christian life. Stone's script is actually very didactic. Yet the lines are so full of wit (there is much unexpected humor), warmth, and wisdom that you don't mind.

Many Westerns—King Vidor's *The Texas Rangers* (1936); Anthony Mann's *Winchester '73* (1950), *Bend of the River* (1952), and *Man of the West* (1958); Boetticher and Scott's *Comanche Station* (1960); Peckinpah's *The Wild Bunch* and *Pat Garrett and Billy the Kid,* to name a few—are about two men with common backgrounds (they hail from the same state, they had similar experiences in the Civil War, they are brothers, they rode together) who consciously decide to go in different (from a moral standpoint) directions. It's similar to *Angels with Dirty Faces* (1938), where a tenement boy grows up to be priest Pat O'Brien and his best chum becomes gangster James Cagney. Steve Judd and Gil Westrum were both upholders of the law; they were best friends and partners. However, like many movie Western heroes who helped tame the frontier only to discover civilization had no use for them, Judd and Westrum lost their jobs, their fame, their reason for rising each morning. They parted and went their respective ways.

As he drifted into obscurity, Judd did not sway from his moral road; rather than wasting precious time feeling contempt for a society that neglects his past contributions ("the only gratitude I expect is my paycheck—$20 worth"), he is concerned only with regaining his self-respect by taking respectable work and entering "my House justified." Sadly, Westrum has become corrupt. He is a liar, a cheat, a former lawman who is now willing to break the law for his own ends. When we first see him in his carnival booth, dressed in buckskin, with shoulder-length hair and a long, pointed beard, he resembles that other fallen angel, Lucifer. And he plays Mephistopheles to young Heck, leading him down an amoral path toward hell, with probably a few earlier stops in prison. "That boy you trained personally," Judd comments, "shows a substantial lack of good judgment." Westrum so resents society that he spends his life swindling citizens with a crooked shooting game (while Heck tricks men to ride their horses against his camel over a distance at which any camel is unbeatable), exaggerating his past exploits so he can get free booze in any saloon, and searching for get-rich schemes—like stealing the gold he, Judd, and Heck transport between Coarse

Steve keeps a gun on Elder while bride Elsa seeks his protection and groom Billy lies unconscious on the floor.

Gold and the town—before he gets any older. Trying to corrupt Judd so he'll want to go along with the theft, Westrum reminisces with his friend about opportunities lost in their distant pasts (Judd could have married a woman like Elsa, only Sara Truesdale left him because he wouldn't leave his lawman job); of past acquaintances no one else remembers, including a Mexican bootmaker, someone they once called "Old Man," and Doc, who—here Peckinpah laments forgotten heroes through Westrum—"gave thirty years of his life to make the West safe for decent people" yet had no one but Westrum at his funeral; of how they'd be justifiably rich if they were paid adequately ($1000 a pop) each time they were shot in the line of duty.

Westrum detests being old and complains about the trouble he now has riding, climbing, sleeping. He thinks having money will somewhat compensate for what he's enduring, but Judd will show him that what he really needs at his age is his dignity restored. Surely Westrum would gladly forfeit all the money in the world to just take away his friend's look of disappointment when Judd catches him

trying to steal the gold, the slap across the face Judd gives him (what a heart-wrenching moment!), and Judd's unwillingness to untie his hands so he can help fight the Hammonds in the mountains. Throughout the film, Judd is reminded that he is old, that he is considered an anachronism, that his past glory doesn't matter because "we're dealing with the present, not the past." Naturally, he becomes irritated when a uniformed cop tells him, "Old man, can't you see you're in the way?" And he's not thrilled that he must dodge automobiles (Peckinpah's oft-used symbol of the changing West), wear spectacles to read his contract, or cool his tired feet in a stream. But he takes it all in stride. He has much self-respect and realizes that no matter what society thinks, he can still make a vital contribution in the new West. Peckinpah and Stone provide him with a purpose: to replace Westrum as Heck's role model until Westrum reforms; to inspire Westrum into being the decent, honest, prideful Christian he once was; to be the kind, understanding father figure Elsa never had; to team with Westrum and wipe out some of the savagery (the Hammonds) that survives in the supposedly civilized West.

While Westrum teases Judd for having unyielding integrity, when he's alone with Heck, he always lavishes praise on his old friend, telling the cocky, skeptical boy (Westrum calls him boy, kid, or son), "Don't *ever* play him short," "You couldn't get close enough to Steve Judd to saddle his horse," and "It wouldn't take long for *Steve Judd* to find us." When he tells Heck, "You've got a lot to learn," it's likely he's thinking how much Heck could learn from Judd—good things. In his heart, Westrum wants Judd to be Heck's role model. And he puts his own defenses down, hoping (subconsciously) that Judd can influence him as well: He learns how much more important than money are pride, dignity, loyalty, work, the satisfaction of again fighting bad men with his best friend, and being redeemed in the eyes of this righteous man (in Peckinpah, noble final acts like Westrum's make up for past transgressions). Judd serves as moral inspiration for and the conscience of Westrum in the same way Pat O'Brien does for James Cagney in *Angels with Dirty Faces,* Humphrey Bogart does for Claude Rains in *Casablanca* (1942), and John Heard does for Jeff Bridges in *Cutter's Way* (1981).

Everyone in the film lives by a code of sorts: Those in town follow the *law;* in Coarse Gold, there is a *miner's court;* Judd signs a *contract* when accepting the job as gold transporter; Edgar Buchanan's Judge Tolliver may be a drunk but he remembers his *oath of office* when conducting the wedding of Elsa and Billy Hammond and delivers an eloquent speech; newlyweds are expected to adhere to *wedding vows;* Westrum has made (at least he thinks) a *pact with the devil;* Heck reluctantly agrees to rob Judd because he doesn't want to back out of his *bargain* with Westrum; the Hammond brothers, depraved as they are, are cognizant of their *"family honor,"* which is why they fight fairly at the end; Joshua Knudsen, who controls his daughter, is guided by his strict interpretation of the *Bible;* Judd won't sway from his religious-based *code of ethics.* The confused Elsa tells Judd, "My father says there's only right and wrong, good and evil, nothing in between. It isn't that simple, is it?" "No, it isn't," Judd reflects. "It should be, but it isn't." What Judd believes and Knudsen fails to understand is that no man can be a "perfect gentleman" (a term the Hammonds mock when Elsa applies it to Heck)—no one can achieve such standards, Knudsen's standards. All one can expect is that a person be *decent* (which isn't perfect); if, like Heck, he isn't decent now, he can, as Tolliver simply states, "change"—although Knudsen wouldn't think this possible. Even Judd admits he was as wild as Heck when he was a young man (of course, Judd identifies with Heck and thinks Heck's settling down on the ranch with Elsa will make up for his own missed opportunity with Sara Truesdale). Whereas Knudsen is puritanical, Judd has purity of purpose; whereas Elsa learns from her father to fear a wrathful God who speaks through his slapping hand, she learns by watching and listening to Judd that God is gentle and forgiving and speaks through the human heart.

Joshua Knudsen is such a stern, close-minded father (with incestuous tendencies) and religious zealot that it's hard to accept anything he says. Yet he is correct when he equates the civilized town we see at the film's beginning with Coarse Gold, the makeshift mining town that is, as he says, "a sinkhole of depravity, a place of shame and sin." There is a definite link between these towns, symbolized by the gold-transporting trail that joins them. In town, people may dress in suits and fine dresses, but decadence is as rampant as in Coarse Gold. There are drinking, brawls, gambling, crooked carnival games, and a girlie show (to which innocent young boys are attracted); people are obsessed with money; old-timers are treated like children; men like Heck paw women just as the depraved Hammonds do with the whores above. In fact, Heck's hellraising is quite similar to that of the Hammonds. Evidently, Peckinpah and Stone don't believe that "civilization," represented by business communities, is much of an improvement on the wild and woolly frontier and mining towns (like Coarse Gold) of the past. For Heck and Elsa to have a chance to live a *decent* life, they must live between the town and Coarse Gold, at the ranch in God's pure wilderness. (That's why the final fight is set there.)

Steve, Elsa, and Heck take cover from the Hammonds who are inside her farmhouse. Gil will ride to the rescue.

We must remember that Peckinpah built himself a cabin on Warren Oates's ranch, far away from civilization.

Ride the High Country boasts not only two wonderful lead performances (Scott was never funnier) by two stars of the genre, but also some fine work by newcomer Ron Starr (who didn't go on to stardom) and, even better, Mariette Hartley (her best performance). Hartley's smart, sensitive, sexually repressed yet gently rebellious Elsa is, along with Stella Stevens in *The Ballad of Cable Hogue,* the most sympathetic and interesting of Peckinpah's heroines. Elsa has the strength to have withstood years of her father's tyranny (which drove her mother away); to have questioned his interpretation of the scriptures rather than having been brainwashed by him; and to break away from both her father and her new husband Billy Hammond when they physically abuse her—although she realizes they may take physical retribution for her acts of defiance. And when she promises Heck she will wait for him if he goes to prison, she, in effect, shows she has wisdom enough to know that because she is out of her father's clutches and has no need to defy his word, she can gain control of those sexual urges that caused her to rush into marriage with a man she didn't love.

McCrea, Scott, Starr, and Hartley are supported by fine veteran character actors Edgar Buchanan (who played Old Man Clanton in the fine 1942 Wyatt Earp B film, *Tombstone, the Town Too Tough to Die*), R. G. Armstrong (a staple of movie and television Westerns), Percy Helton (an honest businessman here, but always crooked on TV Westerns), and the prolific Byron Foulger. The Hammond brothers, including Peckinpah regulars Warren Oates and L. Q. Jones, are well cast. It makes sense that the five actors look nothing alike because their characters probably had five different fathers. The Hammonds, whom Judd calls "red neck peckerwoods," are living proof that while time has passed in the West, the evolution from animal to civilized man has been retarded. They may shave and wash before the wedding to, as Elder Hammond states, "let the girl know she's marrying into a family of *men*," but Elder's less hypocritical when he jokes about Elsa having the "pick of the litter." When Sylvus is shot by Heck in the mountains, he dies, as Jim Kitses suggests in his book *Horizons West* (1969), "a lonely death in a barren, savage place: barbarous and meaningless, it is the death of a wolf."

The skirmish in the wind-swept mountains, which includes Sylvus's death, is one of several marvelous scenes in the film. There's also the tense dinner scene in which Judd quotes Proverbs, Knudsen counters with Isaiah, and Westrum, loving Elsa's cooking, "quotes" Appetite, Chapter 1. Even better is the tinted Felliniesque wedding-orgy scene in a brothel-bar, complete with a madam as bridesmaid, whores as flower girls, a drunk judge, and the boozing Hammond brothers ready to pounce on Elsa and the whores—it's every bride's worst nightmare. The final sequence is a classic. The injured Judd and Heck are trapped with Elsa in a ditch, while Billy, Elder, and Henry Hammond fire on them from the ranch house and barn. Westrum rides to the rescue, something he hasn't done in years, and joins Judd in the ditch. The smiling Judd ("Let's meet them head on, half way, just like always") and the

Western movie icons Randolph Scott and Joel McCrea, a marvelous team. When Heck gives Steve a sucker punch, Gil helps his friend up so he can teach the boy a lesson.

smiling Westrum ("My sentiments exactly") become partners again. The five men face each other. All are shot. The Hammonds die. Westrum assures the fatally injured Judd that he will deliver the gold "just like you would have." In lines John Wayne might have said to Dean Martin in *Rio Bravo* (1959), Judd responds, "Hell, I know that. I always did. You just forgot for a while, that's all." By Westrum's touched expression, you realize that Judd has restored his dignity—the most important thing for a Peckinpah hero.

Judd's death ("I want to go it alone" he tells Westrum) is one of the cinema's great endings, ranking up there with the final shots of such films as *Queen Christina* (1934), *The Roaring Twenties* (1939), *Citizen Kane* (1941), *Casablanca* (1942), *The Breaking Point* (1950), and *The 400 Blows* (1959). Ballard's camera is at ground level and is tilted upward. It is stationed behind the worn-out Judd, who is propped on his left arm and looks away from the camera, toward a distant black mountain set against the sky. It is a heavenly vision—and as he falls gently into the dirt toward us, we realize that Steve Judd, who is entering his House justified, will soon be riding even higher country.

The Road Warrior

also known as *Mad Max 2*

1981 Color Australian Warner Bros.
Director: George Miller
Producer: Byron Kennedy
Screenplay: Terry Hayes and George Miller, with Brian Hannant
Cinematography: Dean Semler
Costume Design: Norma Moriceau
Music: Brian May
Editors: David Stiven, with Tim Wellburn and Michael Balson
Running Time: 94 minutes

Cast: Mel Gibson (Max), Bruce Spence (the Gyro Captain), Mike Preston (Pappagallo), Max Phipps (the Toadie), Vernon Wells (Wez), Emil Minty (the Feral Kid), Kiell Nilsson (the Humungus), Virginia Hey (Warrior Woman), William Zappa (Zetta), Arce Whiteley (Gyro Captain's girlfriend), Steve J. Spears (Mechanic), Harold Baigent (narrator), Dog (dog).

Synopsis: The elderly narrator recalls the global war that turned the fuel-powered world of civilized steel cities into a vast, brutal wasteland where the survivors scavenged for fuel and food. He recalls Max, the road warrior, who lost his wife and baby in the aftermath of the war and, tortured by inner demons, wandered into the vast wasteland.

With his dog at his side, Max drove into the wasteland. He was chased by marauders, including the vicious Wez. He escaped and while the frustrated marauders looked on, took fuel from a crashed truck. When he returned to his camp, he was surprised by the Gyro Captain, a helicopter pilot, who threatened to shoot Max with his crossbow unless he got Max's fuel supply. The dog disarmed him. Before Max could cut his throat, the Gyro Captain said he knew of a huge fuel supply. The chained Gyro Captain took Max to a mountain overlooking a compound. The compound had been built around a fuel-pumping derrick. Wez and the other marauders, led by their masked leader, the Humungus, made camp outside the compound. They wanted the fuel. They tortured and killed several compound dwellers who tried to get past them. The Gyro Captain was upset to see a captive woman raped and murdered. Max offered to take an injured compound dweller back to the compound in exchange for fuel.

Max drove the man through the marauder camp and into the compound. But the man died and the compound dwellers, led by Pappagallo, would not honor his contract. None trusted Max but for the young, bladed-boomerang–throwing, mute Feral Kid. They disabled his car. Learning they wanted to escape to the "promised land" to the north and would need a truck to haul their huge tank of gas through enemy lines, Max offered to bring back the truck he took fuel from earlier in exchange for the fuel. When Max accomplished this feat with help from the Gyro Captain, the compound dwellers—including the Warrior Woman and the Mechanic—were grateful. But Max declined Pappagallo's invitation to drive the truck and come north with them. He feared attachments. He ordered the Feral Kid away from him.

Max was waylaid by the marauders. His dog was killed and he was left for dead. The Gyro Captain rescued him. Max agreed to drive the truck and haul the fuel. When he drove the tanker out of the compound—with the stowaway Feral Kid on board—all the marauders gave chase. This allowed most of the compound dwellers to sneak off in another direction. The Warrior Woman, the Mechanic, and another compound dweller were killed giving Max protection from atop the tanker. Pappagallo was killed while trying to pull the Feral Kid into his nearby car. The Gyro Captain, who provided Max with cover, was shot down but landed his helicopter safely. Many marauders were killed. Standing on the front bumper, Wez grabbed the Feral Kid. But the Humungus plowed head-on into the truck, crushing Wez, killing himself, and knocking over the vehicle. Max and the few remaining marauders discovered that Max had just been a decoy. He had carried sand in the tank, while the other compound dwellers had the fuel.

The Gyro Captain went north with the settlers, as their new leader. Eventually, the Feral Kid, who had been telling the story, became the chief of the Great Northern Tribe. He never saw Max again.

This is the second entry in George Miller's influential, thrill-a-second, futuristic trilogy—coming between *Mad Max* (1979) and *Mad Max Beyond Thunderdome* (1985), which George Ogilvie co-directed. *Mad Max* unexpectedly became Australia's most profitable picture upon release, raking in over $100 million on a mere $300,000 investment. The only country in which it didn't fare well was the United States. That's because three months after the enthusiastic AIP bought it for American distribution, the studio was taken over by the unenthusiastic Filmways. It needlessly had Americans re-voice then-unknown Mel Gibson and the other Australian actors, which made it seem like a dubbed spaghetti Western, and then dumped the picture into grindhouses. *Mad Max 2*, which was distributed worldwide by Warner Bros., surpassed the original's box office internationally; and as *The Road Warrior* in the United States, where Mel Gibson had since 1979 become quite popular, its fate was much better—unlike *Mad Max*, it detoured through resounding commercial success before achieving cult status.

I think the near-future post-apocalyptic alternate-world setting in the original is much more fascinating and frightening than the timeless wasteland in the second film (and in the third), simply because it's a vision one can relate to and appreciate other than on a subconscious level. Miller intentionally moved out of the realistic realm for the second film, using a narrator (the Feral Kid grown up) to emphasize "that this is *storytelling, fable, mythology*"—having a narrator from the distant future relate a story set in the near future throws time completely out of whack and makes the story fit even more snugly into a mythological framework. And though I don't like Max becoming a vigilante in *Mad Max* and think—as I wrote in *Cult Movies* (1981)—"it is less interesting as a story about *people* than as a marriage between a filmmaker's machines (his camera, his editing tools) and the motor-powered machines (cars, motorcycles) that he films," I still find that, overall, its characters and the relationships between them are more developed than in the sequel. However, I like both films equally, and understand why most moviegoers and critics consider *The Road Warrior* the better film. It isn't dubbed. Mel Gibson has even more screen presence than in *Mad Max;* his character has more shadings. Whereas *Mad Max* is a part-biker, part-horror, part-vengeance film, *The Road Warrior* attracted a broader audience because it seems to exist on a higher, classier, more cerebral plane—despite incorporating much material from those not-always-appreciated genres. And as mind blowing as the car stunts are in *Mad Max*, the $4 million sequel, which used 80 vehicles and employed 200 stunts, is even more spectacular.

What you watch with wide eyes makes your body shake. There is nonstop action and violence. There are furiously paced chases and terrifying crashes, which are shot close up by cameras that are inside speeding vehicles rather than

Max is momentarily the prisoner of the Gyro Captain, but he will soon reverse their positions. Eventually the two men will become friends.

on the side of the road. There are menacing, ritualistic, pageantry-obsessed characters. They wear leather, masks, and other weird medieval garb, and spiked, wildly colored punk haircuts; fire crossbows and flamethrowers; and race souped-up cycles and cars (chariots for these knights) across the mythical landscape. *"The Road Warrior,"* stated Andrew Sarris in the *Village Voice,* "is an honest-to-goodness movie-movie of such breathtaking velocity that it would spin hopelessly out of control if it did not have a charismatic hero at its core." "Never," declared Vincent Canby of the *New York Times,* "has a film's vision of the post-nuclear-holocaust world* seemed quite so desolate or so brutal, or so action-packed and sometimes funny as in . . . [this] extravagant film fantasy, which looks like a sadomasochistic comic book come to life." As *Time*'s Richard Corliss wrote, "Miller keeps the eye alert, the

mind agitated, the Saturday matinee spirit alive . . . , evoking emotion through technique." Corliss:

> . . . cars crash, somersault, explode, get squashed under the wheels of semis. Skinless bug-eyed corpses hurtle toward the screen. A mangy dog sups at a coyote carcass. A deadly boomerang shears off fingertips, creases a man's skull. That's entertainment? As a series of isolated incidents, no . . . But as garishly precise daubs in George Miller's apocalyptic fresco, they add up to exhilarating entertainment—and a textbook for sophisticated popular moviemaking.

Corliss was one of the few American critics to have gone out on a limb and recommended *Mad Max.* Like other critics, he found it easier to praise the sequel because it is thematically more palatable. In its final third, *Mad Max* becomes another bleak, if more imaginative and compelling, revenge film with a sociopath hero; ex-cop Max, quite mad, tracks down and brutally murders the gang members who killed his wife and baby; he loses his humanity in the process. As Sarris reasoned, "[The Road Warrior] is somewhat more satisfying as genre entertainment than *Mad Max* because its heroics are driven less by vengeance than a vision."

Miller told me in an interview for *Omni's ScreenFlights/ScreenFantasies* (1984) that he and partner Byron Kennedy, the late producer of the first two *Mad Max* films,

---

*Miller told me that the *Mad Max* films "fall into the category of post-apocalyptic storytelling—but they are not post-nuclear. When we discussed the kinds of events that might have led to this primitive world we depict, including the global war the narrator alludes to in the preface, the nuclear question was avoided entirely. That's because I firmly believe that a nuclear winter would at best leave a world of insects and grass. Even if we were to include human beings, they'd all have to be suffering enormous problems from radiation; perhaps they'd all be mutants. If we had wanted to accurately depict a post-nuclear future, we'd have made entirely different films."

*The Gyro Captain
and his new girlfriend.*

decided to make *Mad Max* for two reasons. First, they had a mutual "obsession for the pure kinetics of chase movies," from *Ben-Hur* (1960) to *Bullitt* (1968), from Buster Keaton and Harold Lloyd silent comedies to biker films such as *The Wild One* (1954) and those made by Roger Corman at AIP. Second, they were fascinated by Australia's car culture: In the sixties, deserted rural roads were used as much for sporting arenas as they were for transportation and there was a disproportionate number of highway casualties. (While an intern, medical school graduate Miller spent six months in a casualty ward—his exposure to road trauma was "a germinating influence on the *Mad Max* films.") Max's character was of minor concern in *Mad Max*. They were content to have him become another in the movies' long line of monstrous revenge killers because his vengeance story line would allow them to pursue their major interests. However, Miller and Kennedy decided to make *The Road Warrior* primarily to explore Max's character. This time they wouldn't be satisfied having a remorseless vigilante-killer as their lead. Such an objectionable character had appeal for the *Death Wish* (1972) audience but had no thematic interest to them. But they were intrigued by how such a character could evolve: becoming a myth-hero with universal appeal (Miller read Joseph Campbell's *The Hero with a Thousand Faces*); reluctantly interacting with and ultimately helping other lost, troubled people; regaining his humanity; and, because of heroics/good deeds, receiving redemption for those sins he committed in *Mad Max*. Miller told me:

"[When we made *Mad Max*], I don't think we thought very much in terms of heroes. . . . It was only a lot later, after we began to analyze Max's popularity in places as diverse as Japan, Switzerland, Australia, France, the United States, and South America, that I could see that *Mad Max* was a rather corrupted version of hero mythology. The film enjoyed success beyond the normal, exploitation car

films because we had unwittingly, unconsciously, been "servants" of the collective consciousness: *Mad Max* was in fact another story about a lone outlaw who wandered through a dark wasteland—similar stories had been told over and over again, across all space and time, with the hero being a Japanese samurai, or an American gunslinger, or a wandering Viking, etc.

"The truth is that I had a tough time making *Mad Max*. I was dissatisfied with the film and felt that we had been constrained by my inexperience and our small budget, and for a long time when I was cutting it, I honestly felt it was unreleasable. When the film succeeded financially, I thought it would give me the chance to go off and do something quieter. We didn't imagine that there would be a sequel. But the whole mythological question in regard to our hero made us want to do the first film *again*, to push that character a little further.

"*Mad Max* is a very dark film. We begin with an admittedly harsh world, but Max is a fairly normal man, working a day job as a highway cop, and having a wife and baby at home. . . . But the world catches up to him and his family is decimated; and he descends into his dark side. By the end of the film, mad, angry, crazy Max has become a full monster, the avenging demon. We leave him in the most pessimistic situation I'd like to leave any character. We must question whether he's redeemable. On the other hand, *The Road Warrior* starts with a pessimistic world and ends with there being the possibility of rebirth, no matter how dark the order of the day is. Max spends most of the film attempting to deny his humanity. Mel Gibson called his character a "closet human being" who doesn't want to be involved with other human beings because he believes an emotional investment will be too painful and also compromise his chances for survival. He can barely bring himself to have contact with his dog. But Mel Gibson has a quality of "goodness" to him, a "good core," and this comes out a fair bit in his character in *The Road Warrior*—so you know that Max is essentially ripe for change . . . you recognize he's ready to rekindle the spark of compassion within him. And that's best characterized by his friendship with the Gyro Captain and his regard for the boy, the Feral Kid. By the end of the film, he realizes—perhaps entirely unconsciously—that he can't live completely alone any longer, and that his life must have some greater purpose. He realizes that he has no choice but to drive the oil tanker for the people of the compound and be the one who is attacked by the marauders. It turns out that he was just a pawn of the collective, but even as a decoy he was responsible for these people gaining freedom and a new order emerging from the chaos. He begins to believe that, like all of us, he's part of the collective, like it or not. It's a much more optimistic outlook than we have in *Mad Max*."

It may seem contradictory that Miller attempts to establish Max as a universal myth-hero yet, at the same time, sets him on a journey to find his humanity and again become a mere human being. After all, most of the movie myth-heroes/superwarriors to whom Max can be compared—Clint Eastwood's "Man with No Name" in Sergio Leone's "Dollars" trilogy, Charles Bronson's "the Man" in *Once Upon a Time in the West* (1969), Eastwood's *Pale Rider* (1985), Toshiro Mifune's *Yojimbo* (1961), Sylvester Stallone's Rambo—realize, as we viewers do, that they will never be part of the human race again. That they are already "dead" is what makes them *and* Max (and even the lethally poisoned Edmund O'Brien in the 1949 melodrama *D.O.A.*) fearless and so formidable. They have nothing to lose. But it should be pointed out that Miller doesn't compare Max to any of the above figures, but to "a Ulysses or Sir Galahad, a hero with larger-than-life qualities and human limitations as well." Certainly Max is as laconic a superhero as Eastwood's Man with No Name, and just as efficient at killing off bad guys; Max, too, is left for dead by bad guys but has a Christ-like resurrection, and his humorous relationship with Bruce Spence's Gyro Captain definitely recalls Eastwood's with Eli Wallach in *The Good, the Bad, and the Ugly* (1967). But the road warrior differs from the Eastwood character in that he is emotional about his past (he slugs Pappagallo for downplaying the deaths of his wife and baby), is haunted by inner demons (Eastwood has no past, no guilt), and, in this second film, doesn't initiate fights—which Eastwood always does. So it's probably less appropriate to link Max with Eastwood's character than with Steve Reeves's *Hercules* (1960), the rare movie myth-hero who strives to be a human being (and mortal), and with Allan Ladd's *Shane* (1953), the rare movie myth-hero who displays admirable *human* traits.

Max has been compared to Shane, because he, too, is an outlaw who comes out of the blue to help a group of settlers/dreamers defeat villains that covet their property, and, while history moves forward, wanders off again into mythology. I also suggest Miller was influenced by two other Westerns. The premise of the film—a superwarrior and his amusing sidekick join an out-manned, ragtag outfit inside a compound/fort while enemy soldiers lay siege outside—is straight out of the Alamo segment of *Davy Crockett, King of the Wild Frontier* (1955); the scene in which Max drives the truck full throttle into the compound while the Gyro Captain flies above and the marauders are on

his heels is similar to the scene in *Davy Crockett* in which Fess Parker (as myth-hero Crockett), Buddy Ebsen, Hans Conreid, and Nick Cravat race through the Alamo gate just before Mexican horse soldiers catch up to them. I asked Miller about *Davy Crockett*—sure enough, he still remembers the excitement he felt as a kid when the picture came to Australia, and how essential it was to own a coonskin hat. *Hondo* (1953), with John Wayne playing Louis L'Amour's greatest hero, is also a probable influence on *The Road Warrior*. Wayne and his unpettable dog, Sam, race across the desert trying to flee hostile Indians, just as Max and his unfriendly dog try to flee a "tribe" of marauders in the desert. Sam is killed by an Indian spear—Max's companion is killed by a marauder's arrow. Whereas Max finds temporary safety in the compound, Wayne takes refuge at Geraldine Page's ranch, which, for the time being, the Indians will not attack. There is no counterpart for Page's character in *The Road Warrior*—soon after Virginia Hey's beautiful Warrior Woman says her first friendly words to handsome Max and he seems touched, Miller unpredictably kills her off in battle (this part was originally intended for an actor but was given unchanged to Hey). But Page's brave fatherless son (he'll fight adult Indians), played by Lee Aaker, who becomes attached to Wayne, anticipates Emil Minty's scene-stealing Feral Kid. The classic finale, in which Max drives the tanker (with the Feral Kid and the Warrior Woman on board) while the marauders give chase—the Indianapolis 500 if all drivers had weapons—can be compared to a similar scene in *Stagecoach* (1939), but it also recalls the final sequence in *Hondo*, in which bloodthirsty Indians chase Wayne, Page, and Aaker and their soldier-escorted wagon caravan across the desert. Incidentally, while many people have assumed Miller borrowed ideas from the 1975 cult favorite *A Boy and His Dog* (a post-apocalyptic world full of scavengers, a hero with a dog in the desert, a gang leader keeping his soldier on a leash), Miller didn't see it until after he had made *The Road Warrior*—he "was surprised by the similarities." However, Miller does give credit to *A Clockwork Orange* (1970), presumably for influencing Norma Moriceau's star-

The Warrior Woman and the other tribe members in the compound. To the right stands the solitary Feral Kid.

tling punk costuming, the slangy dialogue (more noticeable in *Mad Max*), and the ultra-violence.

In many Westerns and other action films, similar characters consciously choose opposite ways of life and become mortal enemies. The hero can understand the villain because he is much like him, except the bad guy has relinquished his morality; he can defeat the villain because he has the same capacity for violence, is as unscrupulous in battle, and has slightly more cunning. In *The Road Warrior* Vernon Wells's wildman Wez and mad Max have a bond they both recognize. Wez is the vile figure Max would be like if he completely relinquished his morality. They are each temporarily chained by the leaders of their respective camps, Mike Preston's Pappagallo and the fearsome Humungus, played by Swedish bodybuilder Kiell Nilsson. Pappagallo ("We haven't given up—we're still human beings!") admonishes Max for using the deaths of his wife and baby as an excuse to be "a scavenger, a maggot living off the corpse of the old world"; he asks: "Do you think you're the only one who suffered?" Similarly, the Humungus cools off scavenger-maggot Wez after his male lover is killed; he reminds him, "We've all lost someone we love." For a brief startling moment, the masked Humungus (what a great dirty wrestler he'd be!) has dignity and the grotesque Wez is as sympathetic as Max. Miller has reminded us that before normal society disintegrated because of a worldwide energy shortage—the *Mad Max* stories were triggered by the surprisingly violent Australian response to petrol rationing in the seventies—and many survivors let the reptilian side of their brains take over, the people who now inhabit the compound might have been friends with those marauders who now threaten them; Wez might have been a cop, like Max; the Humungus, who Miller thinks was a former military officer who suffered severe facial burns, might have served in the same outfit as his counterpart, Pappagallo. I asked Miller if viewers identified more with the good guys than the fancier dressed marauders. Miller:

> "I would hope, as a storyteller, that there is identification with both sides. I think a well-told story gives insights into all forces that interact in any conflict. I really think it's important. I find that in both *Mad Max* and *The Road Warrior,* the bad guys are more interesting than the good guys. On a pragmatic level, it's more fun for the actors and designers to be working with the marauder, bad-guy types than the good guys who, I'm afraid, can be rather boring. If I had a chance to do the films again, I think I'd give a bit more insight into both sides. Then hopefully, the audience would be able to see that those people with the broader knowledge, who are prepared for broader connections and want to stay alive and eventually move toward the organization of a new society, should be classified as 'good guys.' I think the 'bad guys' are designated 'bad' because basically they have chosen to limit their perspective. They are people who say, 'There's no hope, there's no chance for rebirth, so our goal is merely to survive, which we'll do by taking what's left.' And really that's all that differentiates them from the 'good guys.' Max is only marginally better than the Humungus [and Wez]; he is as committed as the marauders to survival at all costs, only he's hasn't the total amorality of the marauders."

Like *Mad Max, The Road Warrior* was attacked in many circles for having excessive violence. I could do without seeing the Feral Kid's boomerang slice off that old marauder's fingers, but I think the violence is functional rather than gratuitous. I disagree with Richard Corliss's claim (not meant to be criticism) that "our nerve endings [are soon] numbed by the movie's aimless carnage." Many people are killed, yet Miller doesn't allow us to become desensitized to death, especially single deaths; we're just as upset by the gallant death of the Warrior Woman in the last scene as we were by the murders of the raped compound woman and Max's dog earlier in the film. Interestingly, we sense the worth of the Gyro Captain (who Miller believes serves the most important function in the picture since he both provides humor and taps Max back toward his humanity) because we identify with his revulsion upon seeing the brutal rape-murder of the captured compound woman—he has seen countless murders but hasn't been desensitized either. Significantly, her murder and the dog's are two of many powerful incidents of violence that Miller implies, rather than shows. Miller:

> "I had censorship problems with the two films in certain countries because of the violence. And it was extremely difficult to make any cuts because, as you'd see if you looked at them frame by frame or sequence by sequence, there's not much violence on the screen. They appear to be more violent than they are. That was deliberate.
>
> "The question of how to use violence in films, or whether to use it at all, is very difficult to answer. I do know that there's an impulse in filmmakers and other storytellers to try and confront both violence and death and shed some light on each. Of course, there's a fine line between exploiting these subjects and examining them. And I'm not quite sure where the *Mad Max* films fall.
>
> "One thing that has helped me try to put everything into context is the notion that movies are really public dreams . . . that we share collectively in darkened theaters. And just like dreams have functions, *nightmares* help us confront our dark sides. The reasons we told these post-apocalyptic allegories, these warning fables, was to help us explore the darker, more unthinkable side of ourselves. These dress rehearsals for our own deaths help us experience that part of ourselves which we are unable to deal with in normal, conscious, everyday living. And I think that's the kind of impulse that gives rise to the violence in our storytelling. There's obviously a need for violence in stories, as it has always been present in them, whether we're talking about biblical stories or children's fairy tales."

The violence in *The Road Warrior* has thematic validity. The horrifying violence is what establishes it as one of the few post-apocalyptic pictures that doesn't suggest such a future is romantic. Even the majority of compound dwellers we care about are killed off. "This world is not meant to be inviting," says Miller. "It is brutal, scary, and forbidding." It's a world that has vast excitement and entertainment for us tourists who sit in our movie seats, but not even a madman like Max wants to live there—lucky for us he has no choice.

The great climactic chase. Top: The Humungus holds his chief warrior Wez in check until it's time for him to join the battle. Middle: Using a wild array of vehicles, the marauders chase the oil tanker. Below: Max pulls the Feral Kid to safety inside the speeding truck.

Seconds

1966   B&W   Paramount release of a Joel Productions presentation
Director: John Frankenheimer
Producer: Edward Lewis
Screenplay: Lewis John Carlino
From the novel by David Ely
Cinematography: James Wong Howe
Music: Jerry Goldsmith
Editors: Ferris Webster and David Newhouse
Running Time: 106 minutes

Cast: Rock Hudson (Antiochus "Tony" Wilson), Salome Jens (Nora Marcus), John Randolph (Arthur Hamilton), Will Geer (Old Man), Jeff Corey (Mr. Ruby), Richard Anderson (Dr. Innes), Murray Hamilton (Charlie Evans), Karl Swenson (Dr. Morris), Kheigh Dhiegh (Davalo), Frances Reid (Emily Hamilton).

Synopsis: Arthur Hamilton, a weary 50, is tired of his New York banking job and his empty marriage to Emily. While walking through Grand Central Terminal, he's handed an address by a stranger. That night, in his Scarsdale home, he receives a call from a man claiming to be his deceased college friend, Charlie. He asks Arthur, "What have you got now?" Arthur says, "I don't know." Arthur and Emily half-heartedly attempt to make love.

Arthur goes to the address and discovers the Company, a secret organization which, for a huge fee, will perform radical plastic surgery so a man can change his identity and be "reborn." Charlie, who has a new identity, suggested Arthur to the Company. Arthur is given tea and a sandwich and slips into a drugged hallucination. He sees himself attacking a young woman in a bed. He returns to consciousness. Mr. Ruby outlines the new life Arthur will have after the operation. He also describes Arthur's fabricated death: The Company's Cadaver Procurement Section will provide a body his size, carrying his identification, to be found in a hotel room fire. When Arthur balks at the operation, he's shown a film of his attack on the woman. Arthur is incensed at the blackmail attempt. The Old Man, the founder of the Company, gently asks Arthur, "There's nothing more, is there? Anything at all?" Having nothing to lose, he signs the Company's contract.

Through extensive plastic surgery and exercise, Arthur is transformed into the handsome, healthier, younger looking Antiochus "Tony" Wilson. Tony begins his new life as a painter in a southern California beach community. He has trouble adjusting and leads a solitary existence. One day on the beach he meets pretty Nora Marcus. Tony begins to open up to her. At a local wine festival, he enjoys himself for the first time. Tony throws a cocktail party to meet his new neighbors. He becomes drunk and talks of his past and the Company. He's shocked to discover that all the men at the party are also Seconds, and that Nora is a Company employee who was sent to ease his transition.

Posing as a college friend, the anguished Tony visits Emily. She matter-of-factly tells him that her husband was "dead a long time before they found him in that hotel fire." Defeated, numb, and with no place to turn, Tony returns to the Company. He wants to take on a new identity. But he won't refer another candidate because this may delay his own surgery. Tony meets Charlie, who also waits for his second chance at becoming a Second. Charlie is called to surgery . . . or so he thinks.

That night Tony is awakened by the Old Man, who laments about how the Company has grown so fast that the success rate with Seconds is very low. Tony insists he won't make the same mistakes in his third life because he'll make his own decisions. Suddenly orderlies strap him to a gurney. He's wheeled toward the operating room. He protests he hasn't had time to think through his next life. When he's read his last rites, he realizes that he is to be killed for the Procurement Section. He protests and struggles, but to no avail. He is gagged with a rubber hose. Heavily sedated, Tony's final thought/dream is of a man with a child perched on his shoulder and a dog at his side playing on a beach. Antiochus Wilson/Arthur Hamilton slips into unconsciousness, forever, to the sound of a cranial drill boring a hole into his brain.

Essay by Henry Blinder

Seconds had a troubled opening. It was soundly booed at the Cannes Film Festival, where it was America's official entry. Back home, it did receive some positive reviews (*Saturday Review*: "I haven't seen a better American film all year"), and dazzled many of us young cinema students, but it was an unqualified disaster at the box office. It would never be withdrawn from circulation like John Frankenheimer's other cult film, *The Manchurian Candidate* (1962)—which Frank Sinatra pulled until 1988 because of its political-assassination theme—but over the years it would rarely play on television or in repertory theaters. It, too, would not be released to the video market, or play on cable until 1988. No doubt *Seconds* would have drifted into obscurity long ago if not for its avid cult following, in America and around the world (Frankenheimer reports that members of the Royal Shakespeare Company are among those who attend an annual screening of his film in London). Because few movie fans have been able to track down *Seconds*, the raves by its devoted fans go uncontested and its reputation has continued to improve. Frankenheimer: "It's the only film I know that has gone from failure to classic—without ever being a success."*

There is no mystery about the reasons people stayed away from *Seconds* in droves in 1966. While it contained elements of the psychological horror film, the science fiction film (it's about the ultimate "nose job" of the future), and the search-for-one's-own-identity picture that proliferated in the sixties and early seventies, viewers couldn't slot it into any familiar genre. Also, as Frankenheimer observed in Jerry Oppenheimer and Jack Vitek's *Idol* (1986), "Those people who would go to see Rock Hudson movies didn't want to see this one." Most significant, *Seconds* is quite possibly the most depressing film ever made—it is a film of unrelieved despair. Lewis John Carlino, its screenwriter, admits it's "almost too painful to watch." He told me that he sat with a stockbroker friend at a screening of the film. Halfway through, his friend walked out, ashen-faced, sighing, "That's my life up there. I don't want to go to the movies to see that."

There is much to turn away from in *Seconds*. For those who are unhappy with their jobs, their love lives, their families, their family routines, their mortality, it hits the rawest of nerves. Although this may not have been intentional, it is also a hard slap in the new faces of those who have sought plastic surgery as a solution to emotional problems. In fact, almost everyone can identify with some depressing aspect of *Seconds*. Certainly we think of ourselves

*In addition to interviews I conducted in January 1988 with John Randolph, Lewis John Carlino, Jerry Goldsmith, and Edward Lewis, I have used quotes and incorporated background material on *Seconds* found in Jerry Oppenheimer and Jack Vitek's excellent book on Rock Hudson, *Idol* (1986).

A spooky poster incorporating a fish-eye lens shot of the strapped-down Tony being read his last rites.

when Rock Hudson's Tony Wilson hears Salome Jens's Nora Marcus give her impression of him: "What kind of a man is he? There's grace in the line and color, but it doesn't emerge pure. It pushes at the edge of something still tentative, unresolved—as if somewhere in the man there is still a key unturned." We're startled by Nora's insight. She not only described Tony, but us as well. For like Tony, we have an unturned key, an emptiness to our lives. Tony tells her what we're thinking: "That's quite an analysis." But in the next breath, Nora pulls the rug out from under us: "Not really. When you come to think of it—it sort of fits everybody, doesn't it?"

Indeed, Nora's analysis does fit *everybody*, not just Tony and ourselves. We feel foolish for thinking she'd made a great revelation about us, personally; it's as if we believed the messages we find in Chinese fortune cookies relate to us alone. In our haste to identify with what Nora said, we have been as shortsighted as John Randolph's Arthur Hamilton, Tony's original self. A part of everyone's life is unfulfilled—everyone has a "key unturned." This is the essence of the film. As Arthur proceeds with his "suicide"—he, in effect, *eliminates* himself from the living—he makes the fatal mistake of turning his key and becoming a Second, Tony, without having a dream of what he wants on the other side of the door. Nora's shrewd, offhand remark should serve as a warning to Tony that he had better quickly figure out his dream, what will bring Arthur/Tony fulfillment, or he will fail in this life, too. Unfortunately, Tony is so out of touch with his feelings and who he really is that her words don't register. True understanding comes too late, when he is awakened by

the Old Man (Will Geer), who founded and heads the Company (and wisely never had the operation himself!), just moments before he is taken away and murdered:

> OLD MAN: I sure hoped you'd make it, find your dream come true.
> TONY: I guess I never had a dream.
> OLD MAN: Maybe that's it. That sure might have been it.

What's truly sad is that Arthur/Tony does have a dream, which he comprehends only at the moment of death—the film's last shot of the man, child, and dog playing on the beach. His "Rosebud" is the close family relationships that he never really experienced, that he longs for now. If it's any consolation, we sense that if Arthur Hamilton, an unformed, incomplete person to begin with, had been granted a second chance as a Second as someone other than Tony, he still wouldn't have succeeded. The "unturned key" was too much a part of what was Arthur Hamilton. He was a failure in his first life, a failure in his second life, and would have been a failure in every other life. Perhaps only someone like Jimmy Stewart's popular George Bailey in *It's a Wonderful Life* (1946), who succeeds in his *first* life—although he mistakenly considers himself such a failure that he too would consider suicide—might make a successful Second.

Seconds is the living nightmare of a man who acts to fill his emptiness without having an idea of what to fill it with; he improves his physical appearance but can't enrich what is on the inside. The film is an unnerving roller-coaster ride into the heart of darkness. We begin by watching Arthur Hamilton figuratively commit suicide (shots of an actual nose job were incorporated into the gruesome operation scene); then we watch Tony Wilson travel a long, painful road to achieve one moment of clarity and hope; and finally we watch helplessly as his new dream of happiness is obliterated when he is a victim in one of the most harrowing murders ever filmed. This is not an easy movie to enjoy. But I think it's impossible to forget. For those of us who managed to sit through it, *Seconds* continues to haunt and disturb us.

David Ely's 1963 novel was inspired by a startling statistic: At the time, 80,000 middle-aged American men left their wives and children each year, never to return. Ely hypothesized that big business might want to capitalize on the legion of wealthy men who wanted to abandon their lives and families but didn't know how to go about it. In a way, Ely anticipated Ira Levin's *The Stepford Wives*. In both books, suburban men want to improve their imperfect lives: In Ely's work, the men pay a great deal of money to alter/replace themselves; in Levin's, the men pay a great deal of money to alter/replace their wives.

Ely's book was acquired by the production company of actor Kirk Douglas and producer Edward Lewis, the team that had already made five Douglas features in the sixties. Their previous film, *Seven Days in May* (1964), had been directed by John Frankenheimer, whom they now brought in to direct *Seconds*. According to John Randolph, Douglas bought the rights to *Seconds* so he could star in it, but bowed out because of prior commitments. Lewis told me differently. In any case, Lewis and Frankenheimer pressured Paramount to hire the only actor they felt was capable of portraying both Arthur Hamilton and Tony Wilson: Laurence Olivier. Olivier agreed to play the dual role, but Paramount turned him down because he wasn't a bankable movie star. Rock Hudson, who was most anxious to break out of romantic comedies and prove himself as a dramatic actor, wanted very much to do the film. Although Hudson wasn't ranked among the top ten actors at the box office for the first time since 1957, and the film would be a major stretch for him, Paramount was only too happy to agree to his playing the lead.

Lewis John Carlino, who'd written a series of one-act plays that received excellent notices and much attention in New York, took on his first screenwriting assignment, adapting Ely's novel. His screenplay is quite faithful to the book, but he introduced a few important characters and some of the film's most powerful scenes. Nora was added, providing Tony with a love interest. Carlino also came up with the wine festival scene, the only time in the picture Tony seems genuinely happy. Because this hopeful scene lifts Tony up, his fall is that much greater in the subsequent party scene, when he discovers that Nora works for the Company and all his male neighbors are Seconds. (Curiously, there are no *female* Seconds.)

Carlino has never been that happy with the completed film. He feels that his screenplay was about the importance of "connections"—to a family, to a past, to accomplishments—but Frankenheimer didn't include the scenes that got this theme across. For instance, he wrote a scene in which Tony, posing as Arthur Hamilton's friend, visits

Arthur's daughter in Denver. There he sees his new grandson for the first time. When his daughter discovers this "stranger" picking up her baby, she orders him from the house. This scene was thematically tied to a previous scene Carlino wrote, in which Tony meets a little girl on the beach and is reminded of his own daughter. The little girl's father calls her and they run off down the beach with their dog. As in the later scene, Tony is left alone, an outsider. In William Froug's book *The Screenwriter Looks at the Screenwriter* (1972), Carlino discussed the significance of the two scenes:

> It seemed to me that the way to do [*Seconds*] was to create sort of a modern Willy Loman. It was really the . . . Faustian thing of man trying to live a new life, and the . . . great tragedy is the sudden realization that what he's paid for his new life is his total alienation. There is no more continuity of existence for him . . . He is totally alone. That was [to be] the crux of the middle section of the film.

Unlike the Denver sequence, the beach scene was filmed, but Frankenheimer cut it from the film anyway, retaining only a few seconds as the last flash in Arthur/Tony's brain as the drill is boring it. When Carlino questioned leaving the abstract imagery at the end without including the full scene earlier, Frankenheimer told him it didn't need explanation: "Well, they'll get it. It's sort of a symbolic thing." Carlino feels the audience was deprived of seeing the complete circle of a man's frustrated life. I understand Carlino's point, but I don't think the final shot is too mysterious—coming right after Tony's talk about dreams with the Old Man, it clearly represents a dream realized too late. Also, I agree with Frankenheimer that the final shot works on a symbolic level. I find the imagery, without explanation, poignant and evocative. I doubt that it would have such impact if the two scenes Carlino wrote had been included.

What is perhaps the most powerful scene in the film is

not in the book. Ely begins his story with Arthur Hamilton going directly to the Company. Carlino restructured the opening so that we see Arthur's home life. We go home with Arthur to Scarsdale. That night, he and Emily start to make love, realize there is no passion, and simply stop. This painfully intimate, wordless scene is among the most graphic dramatizations of middle-age despair ever filmed. Randolph told me that before directing this scene, Frankenheimer told him to go home and "screw your wife all night" so that when it came time to shoot the next day with Frances Reid, all the passion would be gone. At the time, Frankenheimer was very interested in France's New Wave directors and worked to incorporate their style into this scene. He took all day, shooting from every conceivable angle. It has a unique, haunting look, due at least in part to the artistry of the legendary James Wong Howe.

Howe's distinctive black-and-white cinematography intensifies the grim mood of the film. His dark images, stark angles, cunning choices of lenses, and inventive camera movements create an unsettling atmosphere that conveys Arthur/Tony's disorientation and heightens his nightmare. Howe's contributions are a *major* reason the film has a cult. Interestingly, both Howe and Frankenheimer have gone on record as being unhappy with their collaboration, and have differed as to who is entitled to credit for intelligent decisions. For instance, Frankenheimer told *Millimeter*:

> "I found him terribly difficult to work with . . . The use of the 9.7 millimeter lens in *Seconds* was my idea by the way, and not his. I think he ended up hurting the movie. I just won't go along with all the mystique about James Wong Howe."

Howe told *Take One*:

> "I would say John needs a little help to hold him down a little; he tends to lose control. [For example, he uses a] hand-held camera when you don't need it.

I always ask 'Why?' He doesn't know. He just says, 'Give me a hand-held shot here, give me a zoom shot there.' . . . Now he didn't ask me for the fish-eye lens at the end of the picture. I said, 'Let's put the fish-eye on and see if it works.' He liked it and it worked. For the [Grand Central Terminal] . . . sequence, we put a camera with a wide lens on a wheeled suitcase carrier."

Oddly, John Randolph told me that Howe and Frankenheimer appeared to get along on the set: "They were like a couple of kids trying new ideas, experimenting with dollies, and attempting strange angles. In the scene where I attack the girl, they were flying me by wires and had the camera strapped to my shoulder."

Howe's visuals perfectly capture the sense of alienation Carlino wanted to get across. However, they also contribute to Frankenheimer's "Gothic" approach, to which Carlino strongly objected. Carlino told me he envisioned the film beginning with a naturalistic feel and then little by little descending into horror, rather than having the horror played up from the outset, with the frightening trip through Grand Central Terminal, and continuing all the way to the shocking murder at the end. He thought that the events that take place were horrifying on their own and didn't need any bizarre camerawork or spooky music. The tense, look-over-your-shoulder, oppressive quality that pervades the film is unquestionably a John Frankenheimer hallmark. (He has never made a comedy!) *Seconds* forms a kind of "paranoia" trilogy with his *The Manchurian Candidate* and *Seven Days in May*. Reinforcing Frankenheimer's scary vision are the terrifying Saul Bass title sequence, with the distorted, bandaged head, and Jerry Goldsmith's pounding, unsettling score. Goldsmith told me that using an organ was his idea. He felt that what the Company was doing was "a violation of the laws of nature" and he wanted to express that in musical terms. Although much less dramatic, Goldsmith's simple lament on the piano is surely one of the most melancholy passages ever written; it per-

*Tony finds
brief happiness
with Nora.*

fectly conveys the sadness and longings deep within Arthur/Tony.

Seconds is distinguished by the daringly innovative work of Frankenheimer, Carlino, Howe, Goldsmith, and editors Ferris Webster and David Newhouse, but the film's true power comes from the performances, especially by Hudson and Randolph. When offered the dual role, Hudson worried that he wouldn't be believable as Arthur Hamilton. So he settled for Tony, although he wouldn't make an appearance until about 45 minutes into the film. When the role was split, Frankenheimer got the opportunity to hire Randolph, who had been blacklisted for the past 15 years—Randolph was the last blacklisted actor to find work. (Frankenheimer also had enough pull to get Paramount to hire Will Geer and Jeff Corey, two other graduates

from the blacklist.) Not only did Frankenheimer admire Randolph's acting ability, but he also was informed by a plastic surgeon adviser that Randolph had a striking facial resemblance to Hudson and similar eyes. *Seconds* has an ensemble feel to it, undoubtedly because Frankenheimer, who directed live television in the fifties, had the principals rehearse for a week prior to filming—a rare practice at the time. Significantly, Randolph and Hudson worked closely together although they, of course, wouldn't act together. To create a single character, they studied each other's speech patterns and mannerisms. Randolph told me he later found out that Hudson watched his dailies. As difficult as the role was for him, Hudson could see the potential it held for his career. He saw it as his one chance to win an Academy Award. He even went so far as to test

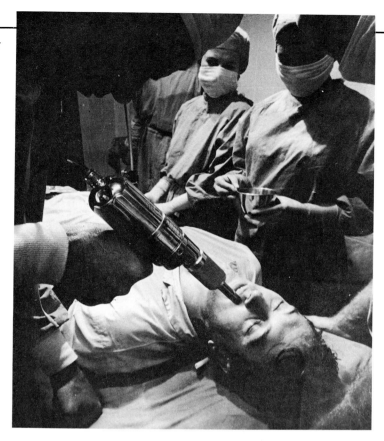

The chilling last second of
Tony Wilson/Arthur Hamilton.

for the Arthur Hamilton part *after* Randolph had filmed all of Arthur's scenes. This would have meant scrapping millions of dollars' worth of Randolph footage. If that had happened, says Randolph, "I would have blown up Hollywood." It's fortunate the idea was dropped because Randolph's performance is extraordinary, a blueprint of every middle-aged man who feels he has made the wrong choices in life. His tour de force is the seven-minute scene, without cuts, in which the Old Man coaxes Arthur into acknowledging the emptiness in his life and signing the contract to become "reborn." Frankenheimer cleared the set and let Randolph take all the time he needed before playing the emotional scene. It has an excruciating intimacy—it's almost too private to watch.

There is a profound sadness in Hudson's performance, which is so affecting that it clearly transcends acting. His homosexuality was an open secret in the industry at the time, but it was still extremely difficult for him to perpetuate the lie to his public. During the party scene, in which the drunk Tony makes a desperate plea for the right to his own identity, reality came crashing down on Hudson. Frankenheimer wanted Hudson drunk for the scene and got more than he bargained for. Hudson lost control and openly wept. In *Idol*, Salome Jens recalled:

"A lot of really traumatic feelings began to surface at that time. I'm sure it was because of what came up in the film and what he·was dealing with as an actor. I was aware that there was in him a great deal of pain. . . . There was a part of Rock that was very private, a part that was very sad, that he felt incomplete about. And when that thing came unloosed, he broke down completely—he could not stop. Whatever got released, it was an avalanche."

Hudson was also exceptional during the final sequence, when Tony is strapped to a gurney and wheeled to the operating room. Knowing that he is about to be killed, Tony is more alone than any man has ever been. Frankenheimer shot Hudson from above, using shock cuts to emphasize his struggle for survival. As in the party sequence, Hudson crosses the line between acting and reality. In shooting the scene, Hudson actually broke the heavy restraints. His screams of pain and desperation are agonizingly real. Here, again, the film becomes almost unbearable to watch. It's as if we're suffocating.

Reviewers were uncharitable to Hudson. However, he was extremely proud of his performance. With the possible exception of his portrayal of the embittered reporter in Douglas Sirk's *The Tarnished Angels* (1957), this was the closest he'd ever come to achieving true stature as an actor. A few years later, he'd give up movies for lightweight work in television. Salome Jens visited Hudson on the set of his hit seventies' series, *McMillan and Wife*. In *Idol*, Jens recalled:

"When he saw me, he gave this huge, wonderful hug—and I saw at that moment that there was a dream lost somewhere. There was something—I'm not trying to be romantic about this—something he had sold out. Something he had missed. A chance he had lost."

Another key unturned.

Sons of the Desert

1933 B&W MGM
Director: William A. Seiter
Producer: Hal Roach
Story: Frank Craven
Continuity: Byron Morgan
Cinematography: Kenneth Peach
Editor: Bert Jordan
Running Time: 69 minutes

Cast: Stan Laurel (Stan Laurel), Oliver Hardy (Oliver Hardy), Mae Busch (Lottie Hardy), Dorothy Christie (Betty Laurel), Charley Chase (Charley), Lucien Littlefield (Dr. Horace Meddick), John Elliott (Exalted Ruler), Billy Gilbert (voice of steamship official).

Synopsis: The Exalted Ruler of the California chapter of the Sons of the Desert fraternal organization tells the members that they must pledge to attend the annual convention in Chicago. Stan and Ollie make the pledge, but later Stan worries that his wife, Betty, won't let him go. Ollie tells his best friend and next-door neighbor that "every man should be the king in his own castle." However, when Ollie's wife, Lottie, learns he plans on going to Chicago, she puts her foot down. She insists that they vacation in the mountains. They have a tremendous argument, during which Lottie breaks several dishes over Ollie's head.

Ollie pretends to be terribly ill as the result of the fight with his wife. He sends Stan to get a doctor who will recommend to Lottie that Ollie travel by ship to Honolulu. Instead of going to Honolulu, he plans to sneak off to Chicago with Stan. Stan brings back a veterinarian, Dr. Meddick, who convinces Lottie that Ollie must go to Honolulu to avoid a nervous breakdown. She is afraid of sea travel, so she tells Stan to accompany Ollie. Forgetting the plan, Stan says he's going to Chicago because Betty said he could go. Ollie insists that if he's going to Honolulu then Stan's going with him.

Stan and Ollie go to Chicago. They march in the Sons of the Desert parade and then party at a nightclub. They meet raucous joker Charley, a delegate from Texas. Learning Stan and Ollie are from L.A., he is inspired to call his sister there, whom he hasn't seen since he went to reform school. He puts Ollie on the phone with her. After flirting for a while, Ollie realizes he's speaking to Lottie. Ollie hangs up before Lottie determines who it is.

Lottie and Betty are upset to learn the steamship returning from Honolulu was struck by a typhoon. The survivors will be returning the next day. While their wives wait at the steamship line, Stan and Ollie return, ready to tell of their carefree vacation in Hawaii. When they read newspaper headlines of the disaster, they try to flee. But the wives return. The boys hide in the attic. Trying to stay calm, the wives go to the movies. They see documentary footage of the Sons of the Desert convention. They see their husbands marching in the parade. They are furious. Lottie and Betty argue about which of their husbands will lie about what has happened.

During a rainstorm, Stan and Ollie, wearing nightclothes, try to sneak down the drainpipe so they can go to a hotel for the night. A policeman catches them and brings them to the front doors of their duplex. Confronted by their wives, Stan and Ollie lie about what happened, saying they got home after the typhoon knocked them overboard by ship-hiking. Stan is afraid to tell the truth because Ollie threatened to inform Betty he smoked a cigarette. But he breaks down and confesses.

Because he told the truth, Stan is treated like a king by Betty. She even lets him smoke a cigarette. Lottie bombards Ollie with all the crockery in her kitchen. Stan comes to the door and tells Ollie that honesty is the best policy. Ollie throws a pot and hits Stan on the head.

In his affectionate biography *Mr. Laurel and Mr. Hardy* (1968), John McCabe asserted that "Hardy without Laurel was like H_2 without the O." He's right. Laurel and Hardy were, as Ollie says in *Sons of the Desert*, like "two peas in a pod" (or, as dimwit Stanley figures, "two peas in a pot"). It's hard to believe that Stan Laurel, born in England in 1890, and Oliver Hardy, born two years later in Georgia, weren't born on the same day, in the same hospital, and that the chubby baby with the mustache didn't make room in his crib for his skinny, already lost and helpless friend, just as Ollie allows Stan into his narrow makeshift bed in *Sons of the Desert*. And so much do we identify Laurel and Hardy as a team that it's hard to believe that both actually pursued solo careers in show business long before they joined forces—it seems much more plausible that a slick producer found them at a bus station waiting for a Godot equivalent, offered them a contract only nincompoops would sign, and cast them in films as themselves. Yet in actuality, Hardy embarked on an active solo career as a movie comic in 1913, in *Outwitting Dad*, and Laurel, a former Music Hall performer, followed suit in 1917, with *Nuts in May*. That year he also appeared in *Lucky Dog*, in which Hardy had a minor role. Unlike Hardy, Laurel would also double as a gagman, and at one point wanted to give up performing entirely. Laurel and Hardy didn't again appear together until 1926, when they each joined Hal Roach's Comedy All-Stars for a series of shorts. In late 1927, Roach decided to give Laurel and Hardy their own series and soon had them churning out about one silent two-reeler a week—including the definitive pie-fight movie, *The Battle of the Century* (1928), and the hilarious traffic-jam and car-dismantling short, *Two Tars* (1928). They made the transition to sound in 1929, with *Unaccustomed As We Are*, and in the thirties began making features as well as shorts. Laurel and Hardy became favorites worldwide, known as Helan & Halvan in Norway, Gog und Cokke in Germany, Dick & Dof in Hungary, Stan es Pan in Poland, Flip i Flap in Roumania, O Bucha e O Estica in Portugal, Crik e Crok in Italy, Xonapoe & Azsnoe in Greece, El Tikhin & Ouel Roufain in Egypt, Hashamen ve Haraze in Palestine, and Siman ve Zaif in Turkey.

It was only as a team that Laurel and Hardy developed their familiar screen personalities. Typically, the aggressive Ollie—who thinks he's smarter than the numskull he is—tries to prove he is a big shot, often for Stan's benefit. Passive dimwit Stan, his one-man fan club, tags along, encouraging Ollie's foolish and dangerous ploys and sometimes trying to copy his antics. His presence assures Ollie's downfall and physical punishment: Stan often brags on Ollie's behalf, telling the biggest bullies what Ollie secretly

threatened to do to them; every time Stan ducks, Ollie gets it in the kisser; if Stan carries a heavy object it is bound to wind up on Ollie's foot. Ollie appreciates Stan because he's the only person foolish enough to believe his boasts and the only person devoted enough to stick with him after he is shown up for the coward and blowhard he is. In Ollie, Stan has found his ideal playmate. I see Laurel and Hardy as older versions of kids in Roach's Our Gang, essentially overgrown children (without parental supervision) who can't stay out of trouble. They can't avoid deep puddles, confrontations, or any object they might break, trip over, catch their clothes on, bang their heads against, squash their fingers in. They take childish delight in causing damage, but they never leave with the upper hand. If—with their ripped and muddied clothes, black eyes, and fibbing tongues—they had mothers to come home to, they'd spend most of their time standing in corners. Even in *Sons of the Desert*, where they play married men, they act like kids living with their mothers—Stan smokes when he's away from wife Betty; Ollie uses baby talk with his wife Lottie and, when afraid of her punishment for fibbing, adopts a babyish look and uses his fingers to draw

Top: *The husbands, Stan and Ollie.* Bottom: *The wives, Betty* (left) *and Lottie.*

invisible circles on the table. In his book, McCabe quotes David Robinson, writing in *Sight and Sound*:

> "[Stan is not] perhaps so much a fool as a child. (In *Be Big* [1930], his preparations for a day in Atlantic City consist of packing his toy yacht.) This child's innocence is a quality which Hardy shares with him, and which is, perhaps, the leading distinction of their comedy work. They are the most innocent of all clowns. . . . The motives which impel them have a childish logic; their jealousies and meannesses (they have been known to deceive each other) are mere babyishness. . . . In their films they are often given wives; but to them a wife is no more nor less than a kind of starchy, unyielding, unsympathetic governess, to be deceived (in simple things), outwitted and escaped for the afternoon. Stan and Ollie are, of course, always recaptured. Extra-marital interests are on the erotic level of taking an apple for the lady teacher."

McCabe adds:

> And this, if anything can be, is their form—innocence and blessed ignorance, out of tune with the sins and follies of the world. *This* is their artistic essence: no comedians in history were ever so innocent so funny, so endearing. . . . Their innocent ignorance makes them the epitome of all the Babes in all the Woods. The world is against them, and they care—but they do not mind. They are too eternally young to hold grudges, so they face the world with hope renewed daily, hourly. Their optimism is indestructible. Their ignorance is truly invincible because it is the angelic armor of perpetual childhood.

Laurel and Hardy were a team for 30 years. Yet their characters never grew up, and they never got any wiser. McCabe:

> In their earliest films, Ollie and Stan are simply dumbbells; sometime during the early thirties, slowly, complete and profound and delightful stupidity gained ascendancy. That this is character development in the usual meaning of the phrase is, of course, nonsense, but it is a deepening of characteristics that had only been suggested by the first films. It is not possible to tell when this point of utter vacuousness in mentality was reached. It was, in the main, a matter of accretion of stupidity gags until Stan and the gag-men started to think continually of his character as having not a mote of sense. The same process applied to Ollie. His dumbness, too, increased until it reached profound proportions. In contrast to Stan, his courtly facade gave him an appearance of rationality, and yet he was possibly more ignorant because he thought he was brighter.

Like the Little Rascals, Laurel and Hardy enjoyed a revival in the fifties and sixties when their shorts first played on television. (Two of the most famous hosts for L&H comedies were located in New York: Officer Joe Bolton and Chuck McCann.) In addition, they were among those highlighted in Robert Youngson's excellent, well-distributed silent comedy compilation films, *The Golden Age of Comedy* (1957), *When Comedy Was King* (1960),

and *Days of Thrills and Laughter* (1961). It's safe to say that children were most attracted to Laurel and Hardy during this time—especially since their comedies played on kiddie shows—and that they are the adults who most admire the team today. Unlike in Laurel and Hardy's prime, it is hard to find adults who became Laurel and Hardy fans as adults. There are several reasons for this. Since Laurel and Hardy were not championed by the intelligentsia of their era, as were the Marx Brothers, Buster Keaton, Harold Lloyd, and W.C. Fields and Charlie Chaplin—the only other silent comics to make the transition to talking pictures—it's generally assumed that their comedy wasn't "intellectually conceived." Few contemporary critics, other than Leonard Maltin, who hails L&H as the "greatest comedy team of all time," have accorded them the scholarly attention given those other classic comedians. Also, despite L&H's tremendous volume of work, they made very few films (shorts or features) in which their brilliance is evident. Few adults will have the patience to wade through their many mediocre and erratic films in search of their few gems. So it isn't easy to get adult viewers interested in Laurel and Hardy. But a good way to start is to point out that they are the inspiration for Ralph Kramden and Ed Norton on *The Honeymooners* (you can hook children by mentioning *The Flintstones*). Then make sure the first L&H films they see include classic shorts *The Battle of the Century*, *Two Tars*, *Big Business* (1929), and the Academy Award–winning *The Music Box* (1932), and features *Sons of the Desert*, *Way Out West* (1937), and *Block-Heads* (1938). Explain the team's special appeal: their distinctive voices and deliveries, their much-imitated walks, Ollie's tie-fiddling and Stan's head-scratching, mindless smile, and hysterical whimpering, their physical grace (even heavy Ollie is light on his feet), their innovative gags (among the few hilarious *destruction* gags in cinema history) that start small and escalate to catastrophic proportions (cars wrecked, houses destroyed, everyone on a city block engaged in a pie fight), their boundless enthusiasm, and their characters' unflinching camaraderie. Director John Landis wrote in *Close-Ups* (1978):

> "Most movie comedy teams are funny, but much of their humor is derived from their internal friction: They lash out at one another with verbal, and in some cases physical, abuse. But Laurel and Hardy have a special sweetness about them, a gentle politeness to each other, and it is that which makes them the equals of Chaplin in winning audience affection. . . .
>
> "Time and again anger, suspicion, greed, lust, and revenge come between them. Yet, no matter how violent the conflict, we remain secure that ultimately Laurel and Hardy will remain together, united in their struggle for survival in an often hostile world . . .
>
> "The magic of Laurel and Hardy is their love for each other. . . . [T]here is a loyalty that transcends all their trials. While it often seems that other comedy teams are together purely out of convenience, Stan and Ollie are an organic whole from the first frame of every picture. You never question their oneness. There is an intangible strength, something "thicker than water," in their relationship.

At the Chicago convention, Stan and Ollie watch Charley get into trouble with his paddle.

"The world of Laurel and Hardy is chaotic, and the boys are often forced to endure great hardship. What audiences appreciate—and what especially appealed to audiences during the Depression—is that they never waver from their optimistic nature. Laurel and Hardy are the best, the nice guys of the comic screen. And that is the secret of their lasting rapport with their audience."

March of the Wooden Soldiers/Babes in Toyland (1934) also has a cult following, but *Sons of the Desert* is Laurel and Hardy's most famous film, partly because its title is the name of the team's international fan club (formed in the mid-sixties by McCabe, McCann, Orson Bean, Al Kilgore, and John Municino). Also it's the L&H film that most served as model for *The Honeymooners* (remember the episode in which inseparable friends and neighbors Ralph and Norton travel to a Raccoons convention, and remember all Ralph's wild schemes and all the shows in which Ralph boasted about being "king in his own castle" only to be humbled later). *Sons of the Desert* doesn't compare to L&H's classic shorts and I don't think it matches either *Way Out West* or *Block-Heads*, yet despite uninspired direction by journeyman William A. Seiter and writing by Frank Craven and Byron Morgan, it is consistently funny, without the dead spots found in their other features.

Sons of the Desert was essentially a longer version of the L&H short *Their Purple Moment* (1928), in which Stan and Ollie slip away from their shrewish wives and have fun with a couple of floozies in a nightclub (before the wives show up). I think this film could have used a couple of floozies. Obnoxious conventioneer Charley (on the basis of his two-reelers, Charley Chase was getting more fan mail than any comedian in Hollywood at the time) is a fine character but just when it appears he'll have an integral part in the film (we suspect he'll turn up in L.A. and tell sister Lottie he met Ollie in Chicago), he disap-

pears. And suddenly the Chicago sequence is over without anything memorable happening. I can't buy it: It's impossible that Laurel and Hardy would go together to Chicago and not get into serious trouble—a couple of floozies could have done the trick. The team's features were often criticized for being no more than badly padded shorts, but there was no need for padding in *Sons of the Desert*—on the other hand there is much, including the Chicago sequence, that genuinely needs to be fleshed out. Oddly, the filmmakers shy away from any wild plot complications and any elaborate gags, and the result is that the film is too tame. For instance, they place Laurel and Hardy in a cramped attic with a rope, a box spring, a bare light bulb, a bicycle horn on the floor, a much too low ceiling, and an angry wife with a rifle downstairs—yet there are only a couple of toots and head bops and only once (when lightning strikes) does the hanging bed they share fall to the ground. Where is the repetition that distinguishes slapstick? Where is the buildup? Where is the wild climax? About the only gag sequence that escalates properly involves the iron tub full of scalding water. After Stan knocks poor Ollie into the hot water seat first, Lottie falls seat first into the water, somehow sitting down on the back of Stan's head as he leans forward, forcing him into the water face first, and holding him down while his feet kick helplessly. Now that's funny.

I don't like most of the scenes with the wives (they don't compare to the henpecking wives in W. C. Fields's movies), but those in which Stan exasperates Lottie (sneaking bites of her wax apples, butting into her conversations with Ollie, making her trip over the tub) are exceptions. Also funny, and endearing, is the scene in which Ollie and Stan return home, supposedly from Hawaii, ring their doorbells, and wait outside to greet their wives by singing "Honolulu Baby." This is the kind of zany musical interlude that lends charm to *Way Out West* and I wish there were more of these bits in this film. In the absence of classic comedy scenes, what I most enjoy about *Sons of*

The most loved comedy team of all time is in trouble again. Stan and Ollie find refuge from their wives' wrath.

the Desert is just watching Ollie and Stan move through life at their peculiar pace. When they arrive at the club meeting late, they don't walk down an aisle to get to two empty seats, but instead climb over everyone. Once seated, Stan—for no good reason—moves his chair closer to Ollie's, squeezing Ollie's fingers between the arms. At their duplex, they have trouble figuring out who lives where (Stan is more confused)—they ring the wrong doorbells, they get locked out of their respective apartments. Stan eats wax apples (without really enjoying them). Ollie is often victim of his wife's crockery-throwing temper tantrums. Throughout the film, when Ollie enters a door and turns to signal Stan to follow him inside, he finds that Stan has already entered and is standing in front of him. If a door is open, Stan will, of course, close it *before* attempting to leave. Usually, when Ollie (or Lottie) walks across a room, Stan will absentmindedly place some object on the ground so Ollie will trip over it when he returns. I'm surprised Laurel and Hardy don't do their familiar bit in which they keep putting on each other's hats and jackets. There is a distinct rhythm to their lives—everything takes longer than it should. They should constantly allot time for confusion and injuries. You know, it's a miracle they survive a single day. And that they do so with good cheer. We're glad that they haven't the brains to have learned their lesson (honesty is the best policy?) and will be involved in another foolhardy scheme the next day. Most important, their precious friendship has remained intact.

A Star Is Born

1954 Color Warner Bros. release of a Transcona Enterprises production
Director: George Cukor
Producer: Sidney Luft
Screenplay: Moss Hart
Based on a 1937 screenplay by Dorothy Parker, Alan Campbell, and Robert Carson
From a story by William A. Wellman and Robert Carson
Cinematography: Sam Leavitt

New Songs: music by Harold Arlen, lyrics by Ira Gershwin; "Born in a Trunk" by Leonard Gershe
Choreography: Richard Barstow
Editor: Folmar Blangsted
Editor of Restored Version: Craig Holt
Running Time: 135/154/181 minutes

Cast: Judy Garland (Esther Blodgett/Vicki Lester), James Mason (Norman Maine), Charles Bickford (Oliver Niles), Jack Carson (Matt Libby), Tom Noonan (Danny McGuire), Lucy Marlow (Lola Lavery), Amanda Blake (Susan Ettinger), James Brown (Glenn Williams), Dub Taylor (driver), Mae Marsh (party guest), Frank Ferguson (judge), Henry Kulky ("Cuddles"), Grady Sutton (Artie Carver), Percy Helton (William Gregory), Pat O'Malley.

Synopsis: Many Hollywood celebrities attend a gala show at the Shrine Auditorium. Oliver Niles, who runs his own studio, tells publicist Matt Libby to keep drunk star actor Norman Maine off the stage. But Norman knocks Libby down and wanders onto the stage while the Glenn Williams Orchestra performs. Vocalist Esther Blodgett incorporates him into the act so the audience doesn't realize he is drunk.

Later, the grateful and intrigued Norman tracks Esther to a small club where she is jamming. When he hears her sing "The Man Who Got Away," he realizes she is a great talent. He convinces her to quit the band and take a chance at living her dream to be a big star. He promises to get her a studio audition. Her friend Danny, the pianist, tells her Norman is just giving her a line.

Niles whisks Norman to a faraway location, so he loses contact with Esther before he can help her. She takes odd jobs to survive. When Norman hears her voice on a silly commercial, he tracks her down. He gets her a studio contract. Her name is changed to Vicki Lester. But no one pays attention to her, until Norman shrewdly figures a way for Niles to hear her sing. Niles casts her as the lead in a new musical. It is a hit. A star is born.

Esther agrees to marry Norman, hoping he will stop drinking. When they elope, this infuriates Libby, who despises Norman. Niles informs Norman that the studio is dropping him because his drinking has made him too great a risk. When he can't find work elsewhere, and his fame slips away, Norman starts drinking heavily. Eventually he ends up in a sanitorium. When Niles sees how distressed Esther is, he offers Norman a small part in a picture. This makes Norman even more upset. He pretends he has other offers.

When Norman gets out of the sanitorium, he hopes to stay sober. But at the racetrack, Libby insults him for living off his wife and they have an argument. Libby knocks him down. A gathering crowd assumes Norman is drunk. He gets up and orders a drink. Four days later, Esther and Niles learn he has been arrested for drunkenness, a car accident, and resisting arrest. When the judge threatens to sentence him, Esther promises to take care of her husband so there will be no more incidents. He is released into her custody.

While Esther and Niles think he sleeps, Norman overhears them. Esther loves Norman so much that she has decided to give up her career and go to Europe with him so he can recover. She feels she owes this to him for she believes he is responsible for the success she's had. She hopes they can both resume their acting careers abroad. But Niles tells her that Norman's talent disappeared years before. Norman is agonized by what he hears.

Norman tells Esther things will be better. Then he walks into the ocean and drowns. Esther goes into seclusion, intending to mourn forever. Danny insists she appear at a benefit at the Shrine Auditorium. He says that she is Norman's monument, that her love and success were the only good things in his life. If she kicks it away, it will be as if Norman never existed. Esther makes a surprise appearance at the Shrine. She introduces herself to a worldwide audience: "This is Mrs. Norman Maine."

James Mason and Judy Garland are Norman Maine and Esther Blodgett/Vicki Lester, who get strength from each other when the world is too cruel.

A star is *reborn*: That was the intention of Judy Garland's much-anticipated comeback film, her first screen appearance in four years. After she completed her last movie, *Summer Stock*, in 1950, she began work on *Royal Wedding* (1951), only to drop out because of health reasons. As had happened when she was unable to complete *Annie Get Your Gun* (1950), Garland was suspended by the MGM brass. They would no longer tolerate costly delays caused by Garland's tardiness, fluctuating weight, and health problems. Her unexpected suspension and increasing marital difficulties with Vincente Minnelli prompted a nervous breakdown and, reportedly, a suicide attempt. There were quick changes in her life: She filed for a divorce; she was dumped by MGM, her studio since she made her first feature, *Pigskin Parade* (1936), at age 14; and Sid Luft became her new agent. Luft, a minor producer-promoter, figured out how to keep her active and in the headlines at a time when she wasn't being offered movie roles. It was Luft who arranged Garland's triumphant singing engagements at London's Palladium and New York's Palace Theatre, reviving her career as a performer-entertainer and renewing studio interest in her. However, Luft, who married Garland in 1952, didn't want a studio to select her comeback film, so he convinced her to form her own production company, Transcona Enterprises. He would get

While Norman watches from the shadows, Esther sings "The Man That Got Away."

Warner Bros. to underwrite Garland's new film and provide studio space, let him serve as producer, and allow Garland to pick a mutually acceptable project.

In her MGM days, Garland had starred in a radio version of *A Star Is Born*, the David O. Selznick–William Wellman 1937 movie classic starring Janet Gaynor. Now, she thought that a musical version, with Esther Blodgett/Vicki Lester as a singer rather than an actress, would be an ideal comeback film for her. She knew that playing Esther would help her tarnished image. Esther would be the most mature character of Garland's career, a woman too sophisticated for Andy Hardy. Because Esther had a full set of emotions, Garland would get a chance to attempt some serious tear-shedding acting. As Esther, Garland could remind viewers of her own remarkable musical versatility, belting out an impassioned torch song, singing jazz or a pop tune, and performing a sensational song and dance. Through Esther, she'd be able to fully express what singing and performing meant to her. And, most significantly, as Esther, Garland would be able to present herself to the public—who regarded her as fragile and irresponsible—as a woman who is sturdy and responsible enough to care for a person, Norman Maine, with grave problems similar to those the public knew Garland had in real life. As Charles Affron points out in *The International Dictionary of Films and Filmmakers* (1984), "It is impossible

not to see the film's ultimate reflexivity in the way the figure of the unreliable star, the husband, is a surrogate for Garland herself. Each time [Esther Blodgett] 'bails out' Norman Maine and 'understands' his problems, it is Garland looking at Garland, not [at the actor]—Garland exposing her own fears and weaknesses through the male character."

British actor James Mason was cast as Norman Maine. If, in 1937, Gaynor could play a budding star even though her own movie career was on the wane and Fredric March could play the fading Norman Maine, even though his career was at its peak, then Garland figured no one would quarrel with her, a tarnished star, playing opposite Mason, who was peaking as an international star (in 1954, he also played the villainous Captain Nemo in Disney's big hit *20,000 Leagues Under the Sea*). George Cukor was signed to direct. And Moss Hart would write a screenplay based on, but more acidic than, the 1937 script by Dorothy Parker, Alan Campbell, and Robert Carson. (The improvisational feel to some scenes was due to the script being incomplete when shooting began.) Harold Arlen and Ira Gershwin would write new songs. The film would be in Technicolor and CinemaScope (a first for a musical), and utilize stereophonic sound. What was estimated to be a $2.5 million production ballooned into a $5 million extravaganza, employing 600 extras and requiring 106 sets and an enormous crew (10 of whom walked off during the many months of shooting). But the final result justified the additional expense and problems.

A Star Is Born and its stirring portrayals by Garland and Mason had tremendous emotional impact on both critics and those moviegoers who were fortunate enough to see it during its initial release in September 1954. For instance, the *New York Times*'s Bosley Crowther raved about the picture and, in a now-famous quote, stated that the "performances from Miss Garland and Mr. Mason make the heart flutter and bleed." Garland immediately became the favorite to win the Academy Award for Best Actress, and not only for sentimental reasons. However, by the time Oscars were handed out, neither Garland's performance nor the film was held in such high esteem. Because not long after the 181-minute *A Star Is Born* had its initial release, Warners—after announcing it was undertaking "a judicious tightening up" and "cutting minor dramatic scenes" so theaters could have more screenings per day and increase revenues—callously chopped out 27 minutes from all prints, including important narrative material and two Garland numbers. As Crowther then lamented, "Virtually every cut in the picture leaves a gaping and baffling hole, so that not only the emotional pattern but the very sense of the thing is lost." The cuts were especially devastating to Cukor, who was already upset because Warners had trimmed footage in order to accommodate the 18-minute "Born in a Trunk" number, which he hadn't directed and which he opposed because he felt it interrrupted the dramatic thrust of the narrative. Like Garland, he couldn't bear to watch the 154-minute version. But despite the protests of Cukor and many theater owners who wanted the option to book either the long or the short version, Warners took the original out of circulation entirely. This act simultaneously doomed the picture at the box office and damaged its Oscar chances. It didn't even receive a Best Picture nomination because, as Crowther predicted, come Oscar time, voters didn't know whether to judge the deserving original version or the much inferior shortened version. *A Star Is Born* turned out to be such a box-office disaster that a resentful Jack Warner wouldn't even take out ads to promote its Oscar nominees—and all, including Garland, lost. Hot actress Grace Kelly, who also played a suffering wife of an alcoholic has-been actor in *The Country Girl*, somehow beat out Garland. Perhaps some voters believed that Garland's role, which includes a scene in which Esther wins an Oscar, was more calculated to win its star an Oscar than was Kelly's, which had the beautiful actress wearing dowdy clothes and no makeup. But a sounder reason for Garland's defeat is that voters didn't realize the scope of her performance because, quite simply, they hadn't seen her full performance. The real shame is that without an Oscar or a hit movie to reestablish her as a viable movie star, Garland's comeback came to an abrupt halt. She wouldn't make another film for seven years.

To make matters worse, an even shorter version eventually slipped into circulation. In this 135-minute version, we don't see Norman Maine go to the Coconut Grove in search of Esther and ask the maître d' about other women who might be available. So we miss a view of Hollywood where stars are lechers and some people who work in restaurants are sexual procurers for the stars; we don't see that Norman's original intentions toward Esther were not honorable; and, without seeing Norman as a rake, we can't tell, later, exactly how much Norman's character improves under Esther's kind influence. Also cut is the beginning of the next scene, when Norman walks into the Down Beat Club and, sitting in the darkness, secretly watches Esther's emotional rendition of "The Man That Got Away"—a number filmed in one take. So we don't see exactly when Norman's attitude toward Esther changes and he, now sober, realizes that she is a great singer, whose talent gives him more ("little jolts of") pleasure and satisfaction than other women do (even in bed), and is too special to be another of his one-night stands. The final deletion I noticed is of Esther, Norman, Niles, and Libby filing out of the theater after Esther's wildly successful preview. We are deprived of Esther, shrugging off all the attention bestowed on her, running to Norman, kissing him, and sincerely saying, "Thank you." Here we really see the sweetness of Esther, her selflessness, her modesty, and her appreciation of Norman—at a time everyone else thinks him worthless. This, I fear, is the version that still turns up on television. So beware. (I don't know if there are still 35-mm prints in circulation.) It's interesting to note that, in 1967, after Warners announced a special screening of the full-length *A Star Is Born*, disappointed L.A. movie fans discovered that Warners was trying to pass off its 154-minute version as the full-length original, and the 135-minute version as the only shortened version.

Because the deleted footage from all prints was thought to have been destroyed six months after Warners ordered the film shortened in 1954, it was assumed that Cukor's musical, which critic David Thomson regards as "one of the greatest flawed movies ever made," would

Vicki and Norman tell Oliver (left) *and the unenthusiastic Matt that they plan to marry.*

never be seen again in its original form. The original *A Star Is Born* was given a "lost film" tag, and as a result, its legend grew and a cult formed. Having seen the complete version in 1954, Ron Haver, film archivist of the Los Angeles County Museum, was among those obsessed with the film. He became determined to find deleted footage that, he hoped, had somehow survived years in the Warners vaults. Using Cukor's shooting script and a complete mixed soundtrack that a young Warners editor discovered and Haver had restored, Haver was able to figure out exactly what footage was missing. Incredibly, through an exhaustive search of countless files and dusty film canisters, he managed to find most of the missing material—or at least alternate, discarded versions of missing scenes—including the two Garland songs. Based on his findings, Haver and Fay Kanin, of the American Film Institute, convinced Warners to spend $30,000–$50,000 for restoration of the film (using donated Eastman film stock). Publicity stills from Cukor's collection would be used creatively to fill in the gaps where original footage was missing. Sadly, Cukor died the night before he was to see the restored film at a special screening. The film premiered at Radio City Music Hall on July 7, 1983, and then was screened in Chicago, San Francisco, Los Angeles, and

Pleading for a job at the Oscar ceremonies, the drunk Norman accidentally slaps Vicki.

Dallas. The public reception was so strong and the critical reaction so laudatory that Warners reissued the film—the final great triumph for Ron Haver.*

The first restored scene comes prior to the sequence in which Norman goes to the Coconut Grove and the Down Beat Club. It's a short bit with Maine passed out on his bed while Libby (who is looking down on him, literally and figuratively) tells Norman's valet that the studio plans to abduct him in the morning and take him out to sea on location. So when we later hear Norman promise Esther a screen test the following morning, we know that, despite his sincerity, he won't be able to keep his promise. This scene prepares us for when Norman sincerely promises to try to stop drinking, but has no control over what happens to him. Also restored, early in the film, is a pivotal nine-minute sequence, coming right after Esther tells Danny she is quitting the band. It begins the following morning with a short scene in which Esther sees off the bus carrying Danny and the other band members—this scene, which, like all the restored scenes, has the original soundtrack, is composed of stills and an action shot of the bus departing (a shot that Haver found among stock footage from many Warners films). Obviously this scene is important because Esther literally watches her past and her security ride away. It shows that Esther has strength and confidence even without Norman. That's good because he, as we see in stills, is being whisked off to a movie location and she'll not get her promised audition—this is the first time the relationship of Norman and Esther is threatened because one of them must act in a movie while the other stays behind.

Esther's fortitude is reinforced in the next section of the restored sequence, a montage. Despite Norman disappearing and his promised screen test going up in smoke, and despite being forced to move to a run-down boarding house and work as a carhop in a hamburger joint after her money runs out, Esther's good spirits and her resolve to become a star are undiminished. During this section, Cukor cuts to Norman at sea on location, thinking about Esther and trying to locate her. We see that he makes a major effort to get her a screen test—it isn't as easy as it appears in the cut version—even doing some detective work before finding her on the roof of her boarding house (a scene depicted through the use of stills that, today, are quite haunting as they fill the large screen—Garland seems captured in time). This sequence of events not only provides the film with a bit of suspense (will Norman and Esther ever find each other? will Esther get her screen test?) but also shows us how deeply committed Norman is to Esther and to making sure she becomes a star. Doesn't it seem inconceivable that Warners would just cut out everything between Esther telling Danny she is quitting the band because Norman promised her a screen test and Esther's arrival at the studio?

The next restored moment has the nervously sick Esther climbing out of Norman's car on the way to her preview. It is, in a way, an intimate moment between the two. It

shows he can be caring when she's sick, just as she'll be when he's sick later in the film. And this moment is funny. He: "Are you all right?" She: "Fine. I wish I was dead." Also we get one of many ugly glimpses of L.A., with an oil derrick on one side of the street and a neon-lit Bar-B-Q restaurant on the other (no wonder she's sick). Another foolishly cut (and now restored) scene has Esther recording "Here's What I'm Here For" at the studio, talking to Norman on a staircase under an open mike (we don't hear them), and then listening with him and the studio hands to the playback of their conversation, which turns out to be his proposal, and Esther pointing out that he drinks too much. Then, since his proposal was heard by so many people, she doesn't want to turn him down—she accepts to the delight of the studio hands. It's an amusing scene showing the playful nature of Norman and Esther. It also shows that the studio hands who were hostile to Esther when she was a nobody have, now that she's a star, accepted her as family, and it marks the only time that movie people treat Norman kindly. The final major cut was of Esther's vaudeville-like production number, "Lose That Long Face"—one of many song and movie titles that comment on the relationship of Esther and Norman. The two parts of this number were meant to sandwich Esther's dressing-room confession to Niles about her misery from watching alcoholic Norman in misery, a scene that was retained in the 154-minute version. At the very least Warners should have kept the second, brief part in which the tearful Esther returns to the set and manages to put on her happy face when the music resumes. I believe this moment captures the essence of Judy Garland, who spent a lifetime singing away her tears.

The 181-minute A Star Is Born lives up to its reputation. It's a marvelous film with unforgettable portrayals by the two leads; entertaining musical numbers, including "Born in a Trunk" (whereas we are told Gaynor's Vicki Lester is a great actress, we are witness to the talent of Garland's Vicki Lester); and innovative direction by Cukor. He was known as a great director of women, and under his guidance, Garland the actress gives a truly warm, touching performance (despite having her usual problems on the set), and Garland the dynamic performer seems happy to have all the musical numbers to herself. But Cukor's direction of Mason is equally impressive. Cukor doesn't rely on Norman's words to express how he feels about Esther, but instead, in almost every scene, includes shots of the silent Norman as he looks at her. We see the smile, the admiring eyes, the glow of her goodness in his expression. (What a controlled actor Mason was!) Cukor obviously feels sympathy for Norman, and respect for him that even so-called friend Niles has lost—for it is Norman who detected greatness in Esther and sacrifices everything to assure her success and happiness. So Cukor directs Mason's Norman as a tragic character, not a pitiful one. And he grants him a most elegant suicide in the romantic surf—a poignant, gracefully directed scene. Cukor left the sentimentality for the finale in which Esther introduces herself, "This is Mrs. Norman Maine"—one of the cinema's greatest tear-jerker endings. Cukor was familiar with the story material in A Star Is Born. After all, he had directed the film that inspired the original A Star Is Born, the

....

*For Ron Haver's first-person account on the restoration of A Star Is Born, I refer you to American Film, July/August 1983.

Norman and Vicki are caught sneaking from the courthouse.

cynical *What Price Hollywood?* (1932), in which an actress (played by Constance Cummings) remains loyal to the alcoholic director (played by Lowell Sherman) who discovered her, almost wrecking her marriage to a former playboy (played by Neil Hamilton) in the process. However, Cukor had never directed a musical before, and had never made a film in color or CinemaScope. As always, Cukor came through. You'll appreciate his creative use of space, his swirling camera (particularly in long-take musical numbers), and his lighting: This was the first musical to use a dark, non-cheery color scheme. The next musical to use *film noir*ish lighting would be Martin Scorsese's *New York, New York* (1977), *A Star Is Born* variation starring Garland's daughter, Liza Minnelli. For his technical achievements, Cukor generously credited cinematographer Sam Leavitt, color consultant George Hoynington-Huene, choreographer Richard Barstow, and art director Gene Allen.

Credit for the film's success must also go to Moss Hart, who wrote the caustic yet compassionate you-and-me-against-the-world (Hollywood) script. What makes the film so special and so timely is how mutually supportive Esther and Norman are, especially at those times no one else has a hopeful word to say. Their initial excitement about and respect for each other never fade away. He gives her the confidence and encouragement ("Don't ever forget how good you are") she needs to give up her dead-end singing job and strive for the big time she's worthy of; when studio makeup men try to change her appearance, he assures her that her natural look is most appealing. He never feels spiteful of her success, even when feeling self-pity. She recognizes that her success is due to him ("He gave me a look at myself I never had before"), and won't turn her back on him when everyone else, including Niles (who fires him, as MGM dumped Garland), has deserted him ("I'm just giving back the gifts he gave me"). She says that none of her success has meaning without him, and her first thought upon winning the Oscar is "I wish Norman were here." He sacrifices his life so she won't give up her career and be destroyed by him. And at the Shrine, in the final scene, Esther identifies with Norman even after death, becoming his living monument. He was altruistic toward her (his lone rewards were her love, her success, and her singing to him privately), gladly spending his time supporting her and boosting her pride. We saw how he cringed when a mailman addressed him as "Mr. Lester," so we can imagine how proud he'd feel when Esther introduces herself to the world as "Mrs. Norman Maine." What a thoughtful, wonderful gesture. That's why few scenes in cinema history have such emotional impact.

The Stunt Man

1980   Color   20th Century-Fox release of a Melvin Simon Co. film
Director: Richard Rush
Producer: Richard Rush
Screenplay: Lawrence B. Marcus
From the novel by Paul Brodeur
Cinematography: Mario Tosi
Music: Dominic Frontiere
Song: "Bits and Pieces," lyrics by Norman Gimbel, sung by Dusty Springfield
Editors: Jack Hofstra and Caroline Ferriol
Running Time: 129 minutes

Cast: Peter O'Toole (Eli Cross), Steve Railsback (Cameron), Barbara Hershey (Nina Franklin), Allen Goorwitz/Allen Garfield (Sam), Alex Rocco (Jake), Sharon Farrell (Denise), Adam Roarke (Raymond Bailey), Philip Bruns (Ace), Chuck Bail (Chuck Barton), John B. Pearce (garage guard), Michael Railsback (Burt).

Cameron attempts a death-defying stunt.

Synopsis: Fugitive Cameron flees police. He tries to hitch a ride with a Dusenberg on a bridge, but the nervous driver kicks him out of the car. When the car spins around and speeds in his direction, Cameron thinks the driver wants to run him over. He throws a metal projectile. The car crashes through the railing and sinks. A helicopter hovers over the bridge. Inside is a pilot, a middle-aged man who stares at him, and a cameraman.

Cameron comes to the pier, where he joins a crowd watching a movie being filmed on the beach. It is a bloody battle, one that reminds him of his stay in Vietnam. When an "old lady" walking through the set plummets into the water, Cameron pulls her out. She takes off her makeup and he recognizes her as a young actress he's seen in commercials, Nina Franklin. She is the leading lady in Eli Cross's new film, playing the lover of an American fugitive behind German lines during World War I. Cameron meets Cross, who turns out to be the middle-aged man in the helicopter. Cross explains that the driver of the Dusenberg, Burt, had been performing a stunt for star Raymond Bailey, when Cameron accidentally caused his death. When Jake, the local policeman, threatens to shut down production because of Burt's death, Cross tells Jake that Burt isn't dead, that Cameron is Burt. Not wanting to be turned in to the police, Cameron agrees to pretend to be Burt, and to assume his role as stuntman. Chuck, the stunt director, teaches him stunts, but essentially Cameron learns on the job. Denise, the makeup girl, shaves off his beard and dyes his hair blond.

Cross is an autocratic director, whose major concern is to get his vision on screen, no matter whose feelings he hurts and whose life he puts in danger. Nina trusts him completely, but Cameron believes he isn't above letting him die in a stunt for the sake of his art. When Cross starts varying from Sam's script in scene after scene, Cameron begins to suspect that he has decided to kill off the American fugitive character when the Dusenberg goes off the bridge. Because he will be doubling for Bailey during the crash scene, he worries that Cross wants him to drown in the car so that the director can capture *real* death on film.

Cameron and Nina fall in love. But he is jealous of her relationship with Cross. They squabble. When Sam tells him that Nina and Cross haven't slept together for three years, Cameron returns to her and they make up. He tells her why he is a fugitive: He returned from the war to find that his partner in an ice cream parlor was now his fiancée's lover. He broke into the parlor. A cop entered and Cameron hit him over the head with a case of ice cream. The unconscious cop's nose got frostbite.

On the night prior to the final stunt, Cameron and Nina decide to run away. But Cross has posted guards. Cameron decides that instead of driving off the bridge during the stunt, he will just drive away to freedom. Nina hides in the Dusenberg's trunk.

The next morning, Cameron drives the Dusenberg at full speed across the bridge, intending to keep going. But an explosive has been rigged to the tire. The Dusenberg goes into the water. He climbs out safely. Cross did not set up his death after all. Nina is on the bridge with Cross—she says she was discovered in the trunk. She tells him how much she loves him. Cameron will work as Cross's top stuntman in his next film.

*T*he Stunt Man nearly didn't see the light of day, much less the darkness of theaters. In fact, it took nine years between the time the writing of the original screenplay began and the film had its official release. And it made it to the screen only because of the extraordinary persistence of its director (and uncredited co-writer) Richard Rush, who suffered a mild heart attack near the end of his long ordeal. In 1970, Columbia paid approximately $300,000 for the rights to Paul Brodeur's forthcoming existential novel, believing college audiences would flock to a picture about an alienated young man in confrontation with authority because it tapped into the counterculture's romantic notion of *escape* (in the novel, society dropout Cameron has gone AWOL from the army); it dealt tangentially (but no more) with the Vietnam War; it had the reliable reality-versus-illusion theme to appeal to those viewers who desired something cerebral; and it gave special insight into moviemaking, a topic that intrigued students of the era as much as politics. The studio offered the project to Rush, who directed three of the best exploitation films of the sixties: *Hell's Angels on Wheels* (1967), with Adam Roarke and Jack Nicholson (who was a candidate for Cross); my favorite Rush film, *Pysch-Out* (1967), with Roarke, Nicholson, Bruce Dern, and a very sexy Susan Strasberg in Haight-Ashbury; and *The Savage Seven* (1968), with Roarke and Robert Walker, Jr. Distinguished by frantic action, improvisation, and the mobile camera of Laszlo Kovacs, they earned Rush his first major studio picture, *Getting Straight* (1970), starring Elliott Gould as one of the few *real* counterculture characters in movies of the era. It was Columbia's top-grosser of 1970, prompting the studio to ask Rush to direct *The Stunt Man*. As Rush told *American Film* in 1981, he accepted the assignment because

> "[i]t had in it an irresistible metaphor for me. The idea of a fugitive hiding his identity by posing as a

stuntman* and falling under the dominance of a director seemed like a marvelous way to examine our universal panic and paranoia over controlling our own destinies. And it offered a chance to do it inside the structure of a big screen big action picture, which would be entertaining at the same time."

It took Rush and Lawrence Marcus, who wrote *Petulia* (1968)—another picture with a fragmented story line—nine months to complete a screenplay. By this time Columbia was heavily in debt and unwilling to make a picture that wasn't a guaranteed money-maker. So Rush, who had fallen in love with the project, bought the rights and shopped the screenplay elsewhere. Every Hollywood studio rejected it because, Rush believed, it had a mild antiwar theme, movies about making movies had a poor track record, and it didn't fit into any particular category. (There was no "life-is-a-movie" genre.) Interestingly, at the same time Rush also failed to find studio backing for another property he'd acquired, *One Flew Over the Cuckoo's Nest*. After two years, he gave up his option to that (and "the rest is history"). So the only film the much-in-demand director made over a seven-year period was the James Caan–Alan Arkin "buddy" picture, *Freebie and the Bean*, Warner Bros.'s top hit in 1974. Warners then said it would let Rush make *The Stunt Man* if he agreed to make it as a straight-line action story. This time Rush turned down the studio. To add insult to injury, about 30 days later the head of business affairs at Warners asked Rush if he'd mind if the studio used the title *The Stunt Man* for a film of its own. Rush:

> "I said, 'Hell, yes, I'd mind. I intend to make this movie.' He said, 'OK, OK.' Apparently, they had hired two guys to develop a straight-line action story. We went to arbitration on the title. I won, because ours was from a novel, and they had to call their film *Hooper* [1978]."

Finally, in 1977, supermarket kingpin Melvin Simon agreed to independently finance *The Stunt Man*. Shooting was completed in 1978, and editing in mid-1979. Several independent companies offered to distribute the film, but Rush realized the $6 million production budget could be recouped only if he convinced one of the major studios that had refused to produce his film to now handle distribution. Again he was turned down. (It didn't help that the film had no box-office stars and had an original running time of 150 minutes.) "They asked the same question: 'What is it? Is it a comedy? Is it a satire? Is it social commentary? Is it melodrama?' Of course, the answer was: 'Yes, it is all those things.' "

To prove his film was marketable, Rush previewed it in Seattle, in August 1979. It received more than 94% raves from the audience. Rush also allowed it to be reviewed:

"That's usually taboo [at sneak previews] because if you get bad reviews, you kill the picture's chances. But we were in enough trouble already, so it didn't matter. Things went extremely well: the reviews came out as though my mother had written them. We came back with these terrific results, but the industry said, 'That's not enough. Go do it some more.' "

Next the picture was previewed in Phoenix and Columbus, Ohio, to equally strong audience and critical reaction. And, sponsored by *Los Angeles Times* critic Charles Champlin, the film was entered in the Dallas Film Festival—local papers voted it the event's best picture. By this time a cult, partly based on word-of-mouth, was already developing. But Hollywood studios weren't convinced yet. So, still without a distributor, *The Stunt Man* began a test run at a Seattle theater. It broke records on opening night and did exceptional business thereafter. More impressive was a test run that began around Labor Day 1980 at the Avco in Westwood, near the UCLA campus. The film became the box-office champ of this highly competitive area. The following weekend, it opened in ten L.A. theaters and became box-office champ of the entire city. That same weekend, *The Stunt Man* won the *Grand Prix* at the Montreal Festival *and* 20th Century-Fox agreed to pick up the film for worldwide distribution, "which," said Rush, "made it one hell of a weekend after screwing around for nine years."

The Stunt Man did good business in some cities and college towns but didn't become the resounding commercial success Rush hoped it would be. Surely the film's subject matter no longer seemed novel after nine years: François Truffaut had made his paean to filmmaking, the very popular *Day for Night* (1973), and beginning with *Hooper*, there had been a proliferation of theatrical and television films about stuntmen. But certainly the major reason for the disappointing box office was that *The Stunt Man* was just too strange to appeal to all tastes. There have been few recent films that have so divided an audience.

Many viewers and critics were left cold, not understanding why it had become such a cause célèbre during its test runs. But others found it electrifying, one of the most daringly original American films in years. To show the degree of enthusiasm exhibited by its admirers, I offer this excerpt from critic William Arnold, then of the *Seattle Post Intelligencer*:

> There isn't a single frame of the movie that isn't a delight to the senses. The movie has everything: unforgettable performances (including perhaps [Peter] O'Toole's best screen performance ever), wonderfully bitchy dialogue, an irresistible score [by Dominic Frontiere], a fast and compulsive editing style, rousing action scenes and production values of epic proportions. It is also consistently funny, often hilarious. It is at once a comedy, an action adventure, a unique personal vision and a visually dazzling cinematic experience and, miraculously, it all comes together and works as an artistic unit.

Pauline Kael also championed the film in her *New Yorker* column:

*This recalls a real-life situation: Members of the French resistance hid out from the Gestapo by working as extras in crowd scenes for Marcel Carne's *Children of Paradise/Les Enfants du Paradis* (1945).

Working with material that could, with a few false steps, have turned into a tony reality-and-illusion puzzle, the director, Richard Rush, has kept it light-headed and funny—it's slapstick metaphysics. *The Stunt Man* is a virtuoso piece of moviemaking: a sustained feat of giddiness that is at the same time intense. Rush isn't afraid to hook you and keep hooking you. Despite the elaborateness of what he and his scenarist, Lawrence B. Marcus, were aiming at . . . Rush uses the pacing and the exhilarating, so-bright-it's-luminous visual style he developed on A.I.P. releases in the late sixties. . . . Rush is a kinetic-action director to the bone; visually, he has the boldness of a comic-strip artist, and maybe because *The Stunt Man* is about subjects close to him—paranoia and moviemaking, which may be the subjects closest to all dedicated moviemakers—there's a furious aliveness in this picture. The cinematographer, Mario Tosi, has brought back the airiness and energy of that early [Laszlo] Kovacs lighting. There's nothing delicate or subtle in this movie, but there's nothing fussy or dim in it, either. The music is the film's motor; it starts up with the va-room of Rush's motorcycle gangs.

Rush took so many years to get his personal vision across, and his work as director-writer is so imaginative and ambitious, that you have to root for his film. It deserves attention. That's why I'm glad it has a devoted following, even if I'm not part of it, and why I encourage everyone to read critics who like it and to see it, even though it's not a film I personally respond to. My reasons for not liking *The Stunt Man*, as opposed to *disliking* it, aren't at all deep. For instance, I think Steve Railsback (whom Elia Kazan recommended to Rush) is miscast. He's properly athletic and projects paranoia well, but he was better suited as homicidal-crazy Charles Manson in the TV movie *Helter Skelter* than as Cameron, who's supposed to be likable, sympathetic-crazy. Those eyes give me the creeps. To be fair to Railsback, he isn't all that's wrong with Cameron. The character is supposed to be a (paranoid) schizophrenic but, nevertheless, there should be more consistency to his responses. I can't figure out why Rush has Cameron smile at certain times and be upset at other times, when it seems just as logical for him to have reverse reactions each time. For no good reason, the reason Cameron is fleeing the law is kept secret from us. It's not just that we are disappointed when his secret is revealed (it's far less interesting than deserting the army) but the picture's confusing enough without the "Alice" who enters Eli Cross's mysterious movie "wonderland" being a mystery himself—unless we know Cameron better, we can't fully understand how he is being affected by his journey and the characters he meets.

Barbara Hershey also seems wrong as Nina. Hershey's a fine actress when she can really explore what her character is thinking—for instance, her thoughtful, impassioned performance in the otherwise silly *The Entity* (1983) deserved Oscar consideration—but there's no way to grasp Nina. Hershey's most effective when she's allowed to project her intelligence (even if her character is sexually promiscuous and/or naive) and she'd have been ideal as the Nina in the book, a tragic, vulnerable, exploited Marilyn Monroe figure making a sorry comeback in a B picture.

Richard Rush (kneeling) gives instructions to Peter O'Toole and Steve Railsback while filming a sequence that comes early in the film.

But as Rush and Marcus's unperceptive Nina, a fairy-tale/dream lover with the depth of Tinkerbell, Hershey actually gets on my nerves.

As for the film itself, I think it's surprisingly boring, considering all the action, oddball characters running around, impressive stunts, and sex. I like the bits when Chuck (nicely underplayed by stuntman Chuck Bail) teaches Cameron the rudiments of stunt work, but the elaborate stunt scenes actually slow down the film. And I think Rush was wrong to make them funny, like Keystone Kops routines, with Felliniesque circus music, rather than use them to build tension and increase Cameron's paranoia. Also I don't understand the point of having the stuntmen perform so Cross needs only one take to film their entire lengthy scenes, with action moving all about the Hotel del Coronado (the striking locale used in 1959's *Some Like It Hot*): Even if wildman Cross were the director, such scenes would be done piecemeal. Perhaps Rush wanted to heighten the film's surrealism.

While I much prefer the film to the even more cryptic book, it's unfortunate that Rush didn't retain Brodeur's most interesting themes: Stuntmen are similar to our soldiers in Vietnam; those men who give orders on the set (the film's Eli Cross is a combination of the novel's director, named Gottschalk, and an evil cinematographer) are as unconcerned about the welfare of stuntmen as officers are of their soldiers' welfare in the war. Brodeur also makes these points: One must be as crazy to be a stuntman as a soldier is to fight in a war; a stuntman is kept in the dark about the overall picture he is making, just as soldiers are unaware of the "big picture" of the war in which they are fighting; stuntmen and soldiers are willing to risk life and limb ("sacrifice" is a major theme of the novel) to follow orders; those in charge have no idea—nor do they care about—what stuntmen or soldiers must go through when they follow orders; stuntmen and Vietnam soldiers are expendable; nobody actually would do the foolish physical feats a stuntman does to please an audience . . . only a soldier would be required to do equivalent suicidal acts; in terms of the public that sees movies and watches news reports on TV, stuntmen and soldiers fighting and dying way off in Vietnam don't really exist; a person can lose his identity when he becomes a stunt double—as does Cameron (as in "Camera on")—as swiftly as if he joins the army. Rush does retain Brodeur's *illusion-or-reality?* theme. This is one of my least favorite themes because most films that use it—such as *Performance* (1970) and *Images* (1972)—turn out to be pretentious and incoherent. At least here it seems appropriate because *The Stunt Man* is about filmmaking, an art form that, paradoxically, uses illusions to create a sense of reality. The picture is full of replacements for the real thing: stuntmen, blanks, wigs, hair dye and makeup, a painting of the ocean (with the real ocean in the distance), the bird tattooed on Cameron's arm, false blood, mirror reflections, images on film, the friend who replaced Cameron as his fiancée's lover, the cop posing as a guard, actors playing parts, etc. It's no wonder that we can't figure out what's true and what is imagined, or tell where reality leaves off and illusion begins—especially since what we witness is subjective reality, from the paranoid Cameron's point of view. Whereas Brodeur drives you crazy with allusions to *reality* and *illusion* on almost every page—his Gottschalk's theory is that art, which repeats itself, is all that is real—Rush is more subtle and interesting. Unlike Brodeur he's not just telling us how difficult it is to distinguish illusion from reality (es-

pecially in the post-Watergate era) but that confusion, specifically paranoia, ruins our perception of reality. As William Arnold writes, Rush's theme is that "all of man's troubles stem from the fact that he is capable of grasping only incomplete and shifting fragments of truth, upon which he is forced to make value judgments." Rush:

> "In this [film] the game of 'Nothing is ever quite what it seems' shakes up our ritualistic views about violence and death. Maybe not only those. We're constantly inventing the truth. We're inventing ritualistic standards of good and evil, concepts of right and wrong, and we accept these as truths to live by. But a lot of these 'truths' are contradictory. . . . To the audience watching this film, seeing is believing. They take for granted that what they're seeing on the screen is 'the truth.' Then a moment later you add one more piece to the puzzle and they realize they're wrong. . . . We get only the information Cameron gets, and therefore we are prone to leaping to the same conclusion he leaps to."

Figuring out what is real and what Cameron imagines in his paranoid mind (i.e., is Cross trying to kill him?) is, I suppose, the challenge of the film. But I agree with *New York Times* critic Janet Maslin, who wrote, "[*The Stunt Man*'s] mysteries, though elaborate, remain largely uninviting." Anyway, nothing is cleared up at the end. The mystery just changes from an anxious "What is Cameron's secret?" to an irritating "What's going on?" There must be some degree of logic for us to have a chance to solve puzzles.

The major reason Rush's themes differ from Brodeur's is that so many years passed between the time the book was published and the film was released. One wonders what the original script was like, and how political it was, because in subsequent years Rush did nine rewrites to keep

Cameron finally tells Nina why he's on the lam as they playfully wrestle on top of open paint cans.

it timely. He told *American Film* how new themes evolved as the social climate changed:

> "The problem was that time was eroding our screenplay. The Vietnam War was receding into history. Our veteran was growing older. The plot was stretching the Scotch tape and string that were holding it together. Until I realized that what was happening to us could be used to solve the problem in the screenplay. That became the last rewrite.
>
> "If you recall the scene in the dining room, the writer [Allen Goorwitz/Garfield gives a wonderful performance as Sam, "Sancho Panza" to Eli Cross's Don Quixote] says to Eli Cross the director, 'Your problem is you always wanted to do this great big antiwar story and they wouldn't let you. Now they'll let you, but you haven't got a war. What you've got is egg on your face because Vietnam is long gone and your screenplay has lost its relevance.' And the director answers, 'Our story isn't about fighting wars; it's about fighting windmills. War isn't the disease; it's only one of the symptoms.' Then he goes on to say, 'Name the disease and maybe you've licked the screenplay.' Well, that put the whole thing in perspective I actually like much better. It was dealing less with the immediacy of a specific war, and instead starting to examine the nature of the panic that makes men fight wars and windmills. In terms of thematics, it was closer to where I wanted to go: What was the disease?"

Certainly the most interesting aspect of *The Stunt Man* is the relationship between insecure Cameron and the dominating, fire-breathing Cross, which isn't adequately explored in the novel. It is that between a son and father, a man and God. Cameron accepts Cross's protection and seeks his approval (he'll blindly try anything to win it). Yet because he also tries to establish his own identity (not an easy task for a stuntman or a fugitive using an alias)—within the confines of God's plan, Man desires to act and think independently—he risks making Cross cross. As Rush states: "We're insisting the gods are benevolent and hope they will be, and growing more paranoid every day in the fear they won't be." Cameron feels increasing paranoia toward his God, and begins to suspect that his role in His design is to be killed. Man is expendable. Cross won't tell Cameron differently—his subjects must have faith. There is a battle of wills and wits, with the equally stubborn Cameron and Cross testing each other. Cross tests Cameron to see if he'll go through with the final dangerous stunt despite thinking the director wants him dead; and Cameron tests Cross to see if he'll actually let him undertake a stunt that will kill him. When Cameron survives the final stunt, his faith is restored and the paranoia he has had since Vietnam disappears. Rush:

> "The unavoidability of our mortality makes us so scared and crazy that we'll do anything, we'll take wild risks, just to prove that we can tempt fate and survive. . . . Every time the stuntman goes up in one of those creaky World War I airplanes, he's literally flying in the face of destiny—and he survives. He reaffirms his power to exercise control over his life. But still, on some level, we don't have that power, not as long as the director is up there on that crane, or some greater force is working out a plan for us that we're not aware of."

When Eli pulls him into his rising helicopter, Cameron gets the message: Directors have the power of life and death over stuntmen.

And so Cross turns out to be no more a monster than the average God-like movie director. Truffaut in *Day for Night* may be a milder presence than O'Toole's Cross, but one shouldn't forget he's just as uncaring: He patiently sits with a star who is having a breakdown and feigns concern only because he wants to incorporate her exact words into his script. To get his personal vision on film, to create art, Cross will do everything required, from playing mind games with actors to risking the lives of stuntmen. Being a director, Rush can understand this—that's why he has an affinity with Eli Cross, making him a man with ideals and a social conscience, giving him the name he used himself when making exploitation films in the sixties, and giving the part to his favorite actor. O'Toole, who based his director on David Lean, eats up the scenery and the other actors, too, with a marvelously malevolent portrayal. Pauline Kael writes:

> It's great to see him playing a hellion. Using words like a cat's playthings, pouncing on them, teasing, and then showing his claws, he gives a peerless comic performance. It's apparent that Eli Cross has been conceived by Rush and Marcus as a protean figure— a man who has in him all the basic human attributes.

Kael thinks Cross is a combination of Sam Peckinpah ("[h]e's fierce-tempered and tough; he carries teeth-gnashing orneriness to an art form") and "Audrey Hepburn gamine—ethereal and fey." Imagine Raymond Massey's villain in *The Scarlet Pimpernel* (1934) directing a movie, and you've almost got O'Toole's Cross. Too bad so much screen time is spent on Cameron, because Cross— repeatedly descending from the sky, he's presented as a combination of Christ and Hitler in *Triumph of the Will* (1934)—is the real mystery figure. He's so full of contradictions, you can't figure him out—Kael asserts he "could be called almost anything and it wouldn't be wrong, and it wouldn't insult him"—but it's fun to try. O'Toole won the Best Actor Award from the National Society of Film Critics for his performance, and nobody would have complained if he'd also won his first Oscar since *Lawrence of Arabia* (1962). He is the main reason to see *The Stunt Man*.

The Terminator

1984 Color Orion release of a Hemdale production
Director: James Cameron
Producer: Gale Anne Hurd
Screenplay: James Cameron with Gale Anne Hurd
Cinematography: Adam Greenberg
Special "Terminator" Effects: Stan Winston
Stop-Motion Animation: Doug Beswick
Special Visual Effects: Fantasy II
Music: Brad Fiedel
Editor: Mark Goldblatt
Running Time: 107 minutes

Cast: Arnold Schwarzenegger (cyborg terminator), Michael Biehn (Kyle Reese), Linda Hamilton (Sarah Connor), Paul Winfield (Traxler), Lance Henrickson (Vukovich), Rick Rossovich (Matt), Bess Motta (Ginger), Dick Miller (gun salesman).

Synopsis: In the year 2029, the long war between machines and human guerrilla fighters continues.

Back in 1984, a large, sophisticated terminator cyborg, with human skin over its metallic frame, arrives in L.A. The machines have sent him from the future to kill Sarah Connor before she gives birth to John Connor, who will lead the guerrillas to victory. Kyle Reese arrives. John Connor sent him to save his mother. He hopes he can do it without weapons from the future—he couldn't take them through the time-displacement machine. Since the machine is broken, Reese knows he can't return to the future.

There are three Sarah Connors in the phone book. The Terminator brutally kills two of them and goes searching for the third, an unmarried young waitress. She is the one he is looking for.

When her date cancels, Sarah goes out alone, leaving roommate Ginger and her boyfriend, Matt, in the apartment. The Terminator breaks in and kills them.

Sarah panics when she learns of the two murdered Sarah Connors. Noticing she is being followed by Reese, she ducks into a disco. She calls home and says her whereabouts on the answering machine—not realizing the Terminator hears her. Then she calls Traxler, the policeman on the case. He tells her to wait there. The Terminator approaches and points his gun at her head. Reese stuns him with a hail of bullets. The Terminator shoots many bystanders but Reese and Sarah escape. There is a high-speed car chase. Reese tells Sarah that the Terminator won't stop until she is dead. He tells her about a computer-instigated nuclear holocaust ten years in the future, about the subsequent war between men and machines, and about her being mother to John Connor, savior of mankind. She is skeptical because she doesn't consider herself brave or capable.

They elude the Terminator, but are taken to the police station. A psychiatrist almost convinces Sarah that Reese is crazy. But then the Terminator drives into the police station and mows down all the officers, including Traxler. But Reese and Sarah escape again. They go to a motel. Sarah calls her mother, revealing where they are. The Terminator is on the line, using her mother's voice.

Reese shows Sarah how to make firebombs. He tells her that John Connor gave him her picture and told him about how important his mother was to him. Sarah Connor is a "legend" and Reese has loved her for a long time. She now loves him. They make love.

They flee the motel in a pickup just as the Terminator arrives. There is a high-speed chase, with the Terminator on a motorcycle. Both vehicles crash and Reese is badly injured. The Terminator tries to run them over with a tanker truck. Reese slips a firebomb into the tail pipe. There is an explosion and fire. The Terminator's skin burns off but, now all metal, it pursues them into a machinery-filled building. Reese sticks a firebomb into its frame. Reese is killed in the explosion. The Terminator's legs are blown off—it crawls after Sarah. She crushes it in a hydraulic press.

Months later, the pregnant Sarah drives into the desert, taping messages for her unborn son. She has accepted her role as "mother" to the revolution. A boy takes her picture. She buys it. It is the picture John Connor will give Reese.

A cyborg Terminator built like Arnold Stang would be a formidable opponent, but one that looks like former "Mr. Universe" Arnold Schwarzenegger (Stang's costar in 1970's Hercules Goes Bananas) *just isn't fair.*

If *Risky Business* gave the sex/youth film a much-needed dose of class in 1983, then *The Terminator* did the same for the science fiction film in 1984, proving talent, intelligence, and originality can make a positive difference in even the most formula-restricted genres. This modestly budgeted ($6.5 million) sci-fi thriller deservedly became a box-office (and later a video) smash, a cause célèbre of critics (even of the highbrow variety), and, as the *Village Voice* promised, "a bonanza for thinking cultists." Its wide crossover appeal was a surprise since not even hardcore sf fans expected much from a film that was directed by someone whose only credit was the undistinguished *Piranha II: The Spawning* (1981) and starred Arnold Schwarzenegger as a *robot* (actually a cyborg)—it seemed foolish to deny him *humanness* when the appeal of this former "Mr. Universe" was based on his having a better physique than all other *men* on earth.

But it's easy to see why *The Terminator* became a sensation. The direction of James Cameron, a Roger Corman alumnus, is assured, immensely imaginative, and often dazzling. The script by Cameron and producer Gale Anne Hurd, his soon-to-be wife, not only is loaded with wit, clever touches, and jolts by the second but also injects bright, interesting ideas into the tired time-traveler-tries-to-alter-history premise. The *noir*ish cinematography by Adam Greenberg, rapid-fire editing by Mark Goldblatt (a movie buddy of mine in the sixties at the University of

Wisconsin), and special effects work by Stan Winston (who created the terrifying full-scale mechanical "Terminator"), Doug Beswick (who created the two-foot-tall stop-motion "Terminator" puppet model), and Pete Kleinow of Gene Warren, Jr.'s Fantasy II (who animated Beswick's puppet model) are genuinely impressive. And the casting couldn't have been better, with the likable Linda Hamilton, a spunky, unintimidating actress who is sexiest in jeans and sneakers, as the heroine (three years before starring in the cult TV series *Beauty and the Beast*), one-time villain Michael Biehn as the hero, and always-the-hero Schwarzenegger as the villain. As the cyborg Terminator, Schwarzenegger, who rejected the Kyle Reese role, unexpectedly became a villain for the ages, a nightmare incarnate. Like Yul Brynner's evil cowboy robot in *Westworld* (1973), the Terminator is without fear, without feelings (it kills in broad daylight, in plain view; instead of getting frustrated when its quarry escapes, it relentlessly resumes the hunt), is nearly indestructible, and, unlike Brynner, is so big and muscular that it could destroy everyone in its path even if it were human. This top-of-the-line Terminator even has been programmed with a perverse sense of humor—it must actually get a kick out of telling the desk sergeant it is Sarah Connor's friend!—which is part of the reason Schwarzenegger seems to enjoy playing the part. As a robot, Schwarzenegger was allowed to be funnier and more violent than in his hero roles—and his fans loved it.

When released, critics rated *The Terminator* the most exciting science fiction film since *The Road Warrior* (1981). Comparisons to George Miller's cult favorite make sense because it, too, has bone-crushing violence, spectacular action sequences, riveting car chases (in which not one fruit or vegetable stand is destroyed), unrelenting suspense, abundant black humor, and a bleak vision of a post-apocalyptic future (although Miller's film doesn't present a post-*nuclear* future). Both films have bizarre time frames: *The Road Warrior* takes place in the near future and is narrated by someone in the more distant future; *The Terminator* is set in the present, but the memories of Biehn's time-traveler Kyle Reese are not of the past but of the future (we have flash*forwards* rather than flashbacks), and he unnerves Hamilton's Sarah Connor by speaking of what she'll do in the future while using the past tense. Cameron doesn't move his camera as much as Miller, but he also keeps things from dragging by having his characters in constant motion—walking, running, riding mopeds or motorcycles, or driving small cars, large cars (a Cadillac at one point), pickup trucks, tanker trucks, an ambulance, a jeep. Here, too, there is a marriage between the filmmaker's gadgets and the gadgets/machines (especially vehicles) that dominate the screen. Like Miller, Cameron keeps tension high by smartly complementing his dramatic visuals with jarring sounds: engines revving, tires screeching, cars crashing, metal smashing into concrete, explosions, glass shattering, guns firing, sirens blaring, music blasting (in the Tech Noir disco), dogs barking, objects being crushed, people screaming, And like *The Road Warrior*, *The Terminator* has shocking death scenes (the disco and police station massacres are strikingly staged) and is punctuated by pain; unlike the cyborg, the *humans* feel the effects of being shot, stabbed, and injured repeatedly (even when Sarah and Reese make love, pain mixes with pleasure) and after a while we share their agony. I suppose the pain motif is the film's worst aspect, for it appeals to the soldier-of-fortune crowd, those viewers who con-

The Terminator tracks down Sarah Connor. It's unnerving that the Terminator is so much bigger and stronger than Sarah but still uses a weapon against her.

sider the Terminator their (fascist) hero, enjoy the gunplay and carnage, and like to crush beer cans on their heads.

Both films venture into myth and into religion, offering a Christ figure (they suffer for man's sins; they are resurrected from a "dead" state; they save humanity) who becomes a rebel leader. Sarah represents the Virgin Mary—she will give birth to John Connor (a Jesus Christ figure we only hear about), who will become savior of the people on earth. Reese represents the messenger angel Gabriel who told the Virgin Mary she would become pregnant. Reese tells Sarah she will give birth, but he isn't through after the Annunciation: He goes further, impregnating Sarah himself. Appropriately, it is not a *mortal* man who is the father of John Connor—roommate Ginger tells Sarah jokingly that they are "better than mortal man deserves"—since Reese has not been born yet in 1984, the father is someone who does not actually exist, who isn't mortal, although he helps determine man's destiny.

It can be argued that *The Terminator* is another Reagan-era anti-abortion film in which a single woman wisely decides to have her baby rather than *terminate* her pregnancy. After all, the Terminator has been sent from the future to commit a "retroactive abortion"—killing Sarah before John Connor is born—and we root against the success of his mission. But I believe Cameron and Hurd think of Sarah as an independent, leftist woman of the sixties and seventies, an era when unmarried women who gave birth to and raised their children stood in defiance of the pro-nuclear-family political right. That the screenwriters don't see Sarah on the side of Moral Majority forces is obvious: They don't consider her unworthy of being the mother of humanity's savior just because she isn't a virgin when she has sex with Reese. And they don't consider the Terminator an agent of contemporary pro-choice groups, but, as Lillian Necakov pointed out in the Spring 1987 issue of *CineAction*, "the embodiment of macho and a male-dominated world, and in a sense an extreme right-wing world, since the Terminator is associated with a stormtrooper through his boots," paramilitary outfit, "[Austrian] accent, and the fact that we are told there are death camps in the future run by Terminators." Sarah's decision to bear John Connor, the result of her only sexual experience with Reese, is the final step in her political evolution from waitress-servant (who is unaware of her strength or potential) to committed revolutionary, and from the frightened, eyes-closed-when-there-is-danger woman whom Reese has to pull to safety from the Terminator to the brave, determined woman who pulls Reese to safety. Sarah giving birth to John Connor is a political as well as a personal act; she has decided to give birth to a future revolution that is necessitated by anti-humanity policies undertaken in her own time, our time—the Reagan years.

That Cameron and Hurd have Reese, the father, be the virgin rather than Sarah, the Virgin Mary mother figure, is indicative that they wanted to break away from sexual stereotyping. Necakov writes:

> It is refreshing, in the '80s, to find a film in which women are allowed power and control, and, above all, are not subordinated by the male. At the same time the woman is not sexually objectified, and she is

allowed to transcend genre role expectations. From the very first time we see Sarah, we are aware of her strength and independence. . . . [T]hat Sarah drives a moped seems significant: it immediately sets her apart, while at the same time paralleling her with the only other motorcyclist in the film—the Terminator, until the end the most powerful character in the film.

> Sarah and Reese's camaraderie also plays an important role. In the motel scene, Sarah helps Reese make bombs. She is also left with the gun when Reese goes out to get supplies. She is allowed possession of the symbolic phallus. . . . When [they] make love, it is Sarah who initiates it. And during their lovemaking, Sarah is the one who is on top [most of the time]—in the "dominant" position. . . .

> Perhaps the point at which Sarah is allowed the ultimate transgression of her position as a woman is near the end of the film when she destroys the Terminator, the symbol of ultimate masculinity and power. . . . The fact that Sarah is the one who destroys it makes the transference of power to Sarah even more subversive. . . . Although there are other moments in the film when Sarah helps Reese fight the Terminator . . . it is only at the end, after Reese's death, when she is completely on her own, that we see Sarah as a strong, independent woman who is responsible for her own survival.

Reese, played by the slight-of-build, weak-voiced Biehn, bucks the trend of eighties' macho heroes. He makes an interesting adversary to Schwarzenegger's huge Terminator, because he is obviously *human*. We admire his bravery and identify with his underdog status; yet refreshingly we aren't in awe of him because he isn't as formidable as a Sylvester Stallone, Chuck Norris, or Arnold Schwarze-

Kyle and Sarah hide out in a motel. Here they consummate their love.

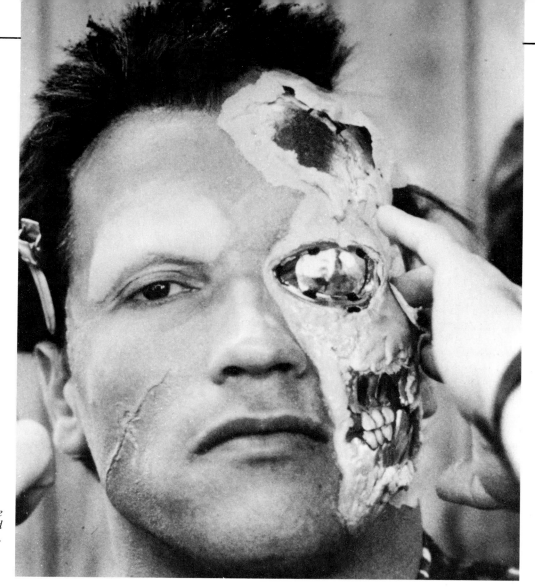

The Terminator examines the damage done to his face and eye.

negger superhero. The relationship between Reese and Sarah is special because he respects her from the beginning—he learned about her from John Connor—so she doesn't have to prove herself to gain equal status. Unlike many male heroes, he isn't so initially protective that he keeps the female in a helpless mode, unable to prove to him or herself that she can come through in a crisis. Reese encourages Sarah to attempt brave acts (she has no choice), not asking, "Are you up to driving 100 miles per hour from the passenger seat while being shot at?" before telling her to take the wheel while he returns the Terminator's gunfire, and not asking, "Will you feel safe from the Terminator if I leave you alone with a small gun?" before he leaves the motel to get essential supplies. In the future he learned that women have courage and can fight—and he admires them for such qualities. He is not so weak that he fears Sarah, the woman he loves, will reach a point where she realizes she can get along without him. In fact, that is what Reese wants to happen. Cameron: "For me, the important theme . . . within the film is strictly human and personal. It's the idea that the main character is forced into a situation of having to take responsibility for her own fate and her own survival. [So] I stripped away one by one

the people who could help her." Cameron could also have been describing his next film, *Aliens* (1985), in which Sigourney Weaver's Ripley has to go one-on-one with a seemingly indestructible adversary after the entire platoon that accompanies her is wiped out.

Because Cameron got co-screenwriter credit with Sylvester Stallone for *Rambo: First Blood Part II* (1985), with its racism and orgiastic violence, he has had to ward off accusations that he is a reactionary. But Cameron only wrote four drafts before Stallone altered it to his liking ("the action is mine, the politics is Stallone's," Cameron told Aljean Harmetz), and *The Terminator* and *Aliens* are progressive films that extol human virtues. Ripley is too *alive* and cherishes life too much to have been called a "female Rambo," as many critics carelessly did. Sarah, too, is supposed to inspire us; as Cameron told Thomas McKelvey Carter in *Starlog* (December 1984), "None of us may think much about [the effect] our actions as individuals might have on the future, but those actions do have consequences."

Thematically, *The Terminator*, Cameron's "romantic nightmare," is left-of-center: Its hero and heroine are revolutionaries; its women and men are equal; it has anti-

Minus its skinlike outer layer, the metallic Terminator stalks Sarah.

nuclear bias. It also takes an anti-technology stance. The villain of the piece is the ultimate machine of the future, constructed when machines and weapons are identical, by machines (including computers) programmed to systematically exterminate the human race (they even have death camps). How could such a future happen? Cameron has Reese speak of powerful computers which, circa 1994, united against humanity and caused a nuclear holocaust, and bombards us with images of contemporary machines to emphasize our growing dependency on technology: a garbage truck, a coin-operated telescope, cars, traffic lights, parking meters, an escalator, a moped, a time clock, sophisticated guns, telephones, televisions, a crane, a tractor, a radio, a headset, an answering machine, microphones, a TV camera, an electric clock, strobe lights, a disco's music system, a refrigerator, a police intercom, a beeper, a video recorder, a generator, a pickup truck, a Coke machine, a motorcycle, neon signs, an oil truck, a computer, a hydraulic press, an ambulance, a jeep, gas tanks, a tape recorder. It is poetic justice that the Terminator is destroyed by another machine, the hydraulic press that Sarah turns on. And it's an extremely exciting moment. But thematically it's wrong: It justifies our dependence on machines in grave situations when Reese's earlier words about the renegade computers told us such dependency is suicidal. A human being should destroy the Terminator to confirm the triumph of man/woman over machine; so it might have been better if Cameron had left one firebomb Sarah made in her possession for the final confrontation.

Like all stories dealing with characters who travel into the past to alter history, *The Terminator* leaves a few loose ends (which don't take away from our enjoyment of the picture). Sarah Connor may survive and John Connor will be born, but won't the deaths of all the other 1984 victims of the Terminator affect the future? For instance, what if roommate Ginger would have been the mother of Reese? That could really cause problems. Also, now that Sarah has become political, should she spend the next 10 years trying to prevent the computer-instigated nuclear holocaust of 1994 or should she devote all her time to preparing her son for the later war between man and machine? Remember that Reese told Sarah that he fought beside John Connor in a *possible* future. That future would most likely be much better if Sarah made sure computers are not given control over our nuclear arsenals. However, if there were no nuclear holocaust, there would be no war, and John Connor would have no reason to send Reese back to 1984 . . . which means Reese would live past 2029, he and Sarah would never meet, and John Connor would not be born . . . and Sarah would not become politicized and attempt to make sure computers are not given control over our nuclear arsenals. So what should Sarah do?

I guess it's a moot point since it's likely Sarah will be kept busy protecting her growing child and herself from other terminators that will arrive from the future. Sequels can be turned out with machine-like precision until 2029. No wonder Schwarzenegger's Terminator seems to be congratulating himself on his choice of "immortal" words when (in the picture's funniest moment) he warns the desk sergeant, "I'll be back . . ."

That Hamilton Woman

also known as *Lady Hamilton*

1941   B&W   United Artists
Director: Alexander Korda
Producer: Alexander Korda
Screenplay: Walter Reisch and R. C. Sheriff
Cinematography: Rudolph Maté
Art Director: Vincent Korda
Music: Miklos Rozsa
Editor: William Hornbeck
Running Time: 124 minutes

Cast: Vivien Leigh (Emma, Lady Hamilton), Laurence Olivier (Lord Horatio Nelson), Alan Mowbray (Sir William Hamilton), Sara Allgood (Mrs. Cadogen-Lyon), Gladys Cooper (Lady Nelson), Henry Wilcoxson (Captain Hardy), Heather Angel (Mary Smith), Halliwell Hobbes (Reverend Nelson), Gilbert Emery (Lord Spencer), Miles Mander (Lord Keith), Louis Alberni (king of Naples), Norma Drury (queen of Naples).

Synopsis: A middle-aged woman, looking disheveled and worn out, is thrown into Calais prison for stealing a wine bottle. She tells her skeptical young female cellmate that she is Emma, the Lady Hamilton. In 1785, at age 20, she came with her mother, Mrs. Cadogen-Lyon, to the art- and statue-filled palatial home of Sir William Hamilton, the middle-aged British ambassador to Naples. A flirtatious, frivolous young woman, she thought she would be joined by her lover, Charles Greville, Hamilton's young nephew. But Greville sent her to be mistress to Hamilton, who admired her beauty, so Hamilton would pay his debts. Rather then return to England and again be a shop girl, artist's model, and worse, she stayed with Hamilton. She learned French, Italian, singing, and music. They eventually married and she became an expert hostess and the confidante of the queen. Her mother thought it wrong that Hamilton never slept with his young bride.

In 1793, the British fleet arrived in Naples. Horatio Nelson, a renowned naval hero, asked Hamilton to ask the king for troops. This would take time, so Emma got the troops by going directly to the queen, "the real king of Naples." Nelson was impressed. When Nelson departed, Emma asked Hamilton to explain world affairs to her. He explained that England's fleet has repeatedly fought dictators bent on taking over the world.

Nelson returned in five years, having lost his right eye and arm in battle. The fleet desperately needed provisions to battle Napoleon's fleet in Egypt. Emma secured the provisions from the king. After he defeated Napoleon's navy, Nelson returned to Naples and Emma rather than England and his wife. When he collapsed, Emma took care of him. Their love for each other grew. But since they were both married, he left. When there was a revolution in Naples, Nelson sailed back and rescued the king, queen, Hamilton, and Emma. Rumors spread that the married Nelson returned solely for Emma's benefit. Hamilton warned Emma to leave Nelson alone or his career would be ruined.

But when Nelson returned to England, Emma, her mother, and Hamilton went with him. Nelson gave a speech in the House of Lords, stating that England must keep a wary eye on Napoleon, in case he rose again. Nelson prepared to leave with Lady Nelson to avoid scandal, but he ran to Emma's side when she fainted. Humiliated, Lady Nelson left Nelson but refused to divorce him. Hamilton died penniless after his art collection was lost at sea. Emma made no attempt to get his house because she thought she'd be "rich" enough with Nelson's baby. But after her daughter's birth she had tremendous debts. Nelson said he'd take care of her. He retired and they moved to the country. Emma was very happy, but then Captain Hardy asked her to convince Nelson to return to service because Napoleon had mounted a powerful navy. She told Hardy no, but realized that Nelson was the only person who could save England. She told Nelson that she told Hardy he would come to his country's aid. She knew she would never see him again.

Nelson's brilliant strategy led to a decisive English victory at the Battle of Trafalgar. But he was fatally injured. Before dying, he worried what would happen to Emma.

Her young cellmate asks Emma, "And then? What happened after?" Emma replies, "There is no *then*. There is no *after*."

Vivien Leigh and Laurence Olivier had been the romantic leads in two other Alexander Korda films prior to *That Hamilton Woman*, the historical drama *Fire Below England* (1936) and *21 Days* (1938), as lovers who spend three weeks together before he stands trial for murder. However, since these were minor British movies, made before either actor was well known outside England, they received little international attention. Korda believed offscreen lovers Leigh and Olivier (who'd get divorced and marry in 1940) could be as exciting a romantic team onscreen as they were off, but initially Leigh made less of an impression when teamed with Olivier than when romancing Conrad Veidt in Korda's spy-romance *Dark Journey* (1937) and Robert Taylor in her first American-made film, *A Yank at Oxford* (1938), and Olivier caught Hollywood's eye not with Leigh but with Merle Oberon (soon to be Mrs. Korda) in *The Divorce of Lady X* (1938). In 1939, Leigh, playing Scarlett O'Hara opposite Clark Gable's Rhett Butler in *Gone With the Wind*, and Olivier, playing Heathcliff opposite Oberon's Cathy in *Wuthering Heights*, independently established themselves as the cinema's greatest lovers. Their lofty positions were reinforced in 1940, when Leigh, at her most breathtakingly beautiful, costarred with Robert Taylor in the classic tearjerker *Waterloo Bridge*, and Olivier won the hearts of Greer Garson in *Pride and Prejudice* and Joan Fontaine in Alfred Hitchcock's *Rebecca*. So the stage was set for Korda to reunite Leigh and Olivier onscreen, in *That Hamilton Woman*, a faithful telling of the illicit love affair between Lady Emma Hamilton and Lord Horatio Nelson, England's greatest naval hero.*

With its romance and its call to war, *That Hamilton Woman* was a big hit in 1941, in America, in England, and even in the Soviet Union, where it was a rare non-Soviet film to receive general distribution. Unfortunately, today most American moviegoers, even devotees of *Gone With the Wind* and *Wuthering Heights*, are indifferent to it—most have never even seen it. They wrongly assume that viewing it is anticlimactic after having sighed and cried through the two earlier, more famous films, and that it was made so quickly (without a complete script) and on such a low budget (i.e., we recognize that miniatures were used for the British fleet) because Korda was less interested in quality than cashing in on the popularity of Leigh and Olivier. In fact, *That Hamilton Woman* is truly one of the greatest, most elegant, most mature romance movies. Leigh and Olivier play their scenes with such convic-

· ·

*The film pretty much follows the chronology found in the history books. However, there are some points where the books differ from one another. For instance, according to some, it was Lady Nelson who fainted, at the *theater* (not outside the House of Lords), when she saw how much attention Nelson paid to Emma. And according to Flora Fraser's *Emma, Lady Hamilton* (1987), Emma was not the beauty George Romney painted when she returned with Nelson to England, but was so fat that she could hide her pregnancy.

tion and passion (the burning volcano in the background conveys their sexual longings) that they make their previous screen romances seem almost artificial, mere preludes ("semifinal" love matches?) to the real thing. I never tire of watching Leigh and Olivier together, and admiring their talents, grace, physical beauty, and sex appeal (no matter that Olivier's Nelson loses an eye and an arm), and trying to detect their feelings for each other when they made this film. So I see the film repeatedly. Still, my devotion doesn't compare to that of critic Andrew Sarris, whose love for the film is legendary. By 1970, as he wrote in the *Village Voice*, Sarris had already seen the film 83 times—not including television viewings! His obsession began way back in 1945, when he was 17, yet, like all of us who find it frustrating to plead a case for our favorite movies, he still had difficulty pinpointing the reasons the film held so much fascination for him:

> What then was the extraordinary appeal of *That Hamilton Woman* to me? It's a rather sketchy rendering by any standards, and Olivier spends most of the movie with a patch over one eye and an otherwise ravaged countenance. The Battle of Trafalgar is boring as those things go, but as is often the case with a movie by Alexander Korda, a certain care, a certain charm, even a modicum of wit creeps into the pageantry and the passion. It's nice the way Alan Mowbray says of Vivien's loose-fitting Emma that the pattern of her youth has been "lower and lower, and up and up." Anything spoken with a British accent seemed just that much wiser in those days.
>
> One of Miklos Rozsa's lushly imperial scores cannot be underestimated as one of the factors in making me see *That Hamilton Woman* so many times. Favorite movies so often coincide with favorite scores. And to this day I can hum the score to *That Hamilton Woman* upon request. The contrived flashback structure of the story also contributed to the cyclical quality of the film so that it seemed eternally renewed. . . .
>
> [Then there is] the enchantment of that magical moment when Olivier's Nelson says to Leigh's Emma, "People don't believe that there can be friendship between a man and a woman," and Vivien Leigh smiles with twinkling complicity: "Do you?" and Olivier slowly smiles back, very awkwardly creasing his cheeks, as he acknowledges for all time the precious privilege of being admitted to the arms of a beautiful woman with a marvelously grown-up sense of humor. . . . I am sure that Nelson and Lady Hamilton have stolen my love by cleverly concealing their vulgar, reactionary personalities behind the facades of Laurence Olivier and Vivien Leigh. . . .

That Hamilton Woman's most celebrated fan was Winston Churchill, England's wartime prime minister. When it was released, he announced that *That Hamilton Woman* was his all-time favorite movie. We could commend him for his excellent taste and suggest that he had potential to be as astute a critic as Sarris, but it's likely he'd have endorsed this film even if it were much inferior. That's because Churchill had a personal investment in it (the reason Korda was reluctant to use his words of praise to promote the film). Indeed, Churchill asked his friend Korda to make a film about England's past that would include propaganda

material relating to England's present; gave Korda the idea of making this picture about England's greatest naval hero, Horatio Nelson; and, it is suspected, personally wrote Nelson's speech to the House of Lords in which he warns, "You can't make peace with dictators, you have to destroy them."

Korda filmed *That Hamilton Woman* in Hollywood. When the outbreak of war in Europe had made it difficult to make movies in England, he had relocated to the United States to complete *The Thief of Bagdad* (1940). Churchill had encouraged the move and, according to nephew Michael Korda's *Charmed Lives* (1979), asked Korda "to set up his offices in New York and Hollywood, and to link them to a world-wide motion picture corporation. These offices would exist for their own sake as a moneymaking enterprise of Alex Korda's, but they would also serve as 'cover' for British agents working in what was then neutral America. American isolationists had made it difficult for British intelligence operatives to work freely in the United States, but a movie company offered unparalleled opportunities for concealing intelligence work, and Alex could even himself act as courier. What could be more natural for a film mogul than to travel, and who would think twice about eccentric hiring practices?" Korda was depressed that back in England, his departure was regarded as cowardice and defeatism in the face of Nazi aggression, and he hoped that both *That Hamilton Woman*, with its pro-British propaganda, and his intelligence activity, when made public, would allow him to return home in triumph.

By the time Korda finished *That Hamilton Woman*, several American-made films had already been released or were in production that were intended to convince the public that the United States should join the war against Germany. These films included *Confessions of a Nazi Spy* (1939), Errol Flynn's propaganda-filled swashbuckler *The Sea Hawk* (1940), Chaplin's *The Great Dictator* (1940), *The Mortal Storm* (1940), *Escape to Glory* (1940), *Four Sons* (1940), Alfred Hitchcock's first non-British film, *Foreign Correspondent* (1940), *World Premiere* (1941), *Underground* (1941), Fritz Lang's *Man Hunt* (1941), *All Through the Night* (1942), *Mrs. Miniver* (1942), Ernst Lubitsch's *To Be or Not to Be* (1942), and *Casablanca* (1942). Such films incensed proponents of isolationism, including the America First Committee, which charged that the studios were intentionally making pro-war films, and Senator Gerald Nye, who vowed that the Foreign Relations Committee would look very carefully at the work of "British agents" in the movie business. "These efforts," writes Michael Korda, "were supported very effectively by the German consul in Los Angeles, and the German ambassador in Washington, who tactfully suggested that the American movie industry had been infiltrated by Jewish money and British agents, and was being turned into a propaganda instrument designed to drag innocent Americans into the war." Korda had wisely structured the film so that Emma, rather than Nelson, would be the central character, so that the emphasis would be on their affair and the film's political statements would seem less obvious. Yet he realized that *That Hamilton Woman*, with its British flag waving (literally speaking), Nelson's denouncement of Hitler-like dictators, and Emma's silly geopolitical lesson from Sir

The most famous couple of the English cinema and theater was perfectly cast as English history's most famous couple. Left: *The gorgeous Vivien Leigh as Lady Emma Hamilton.* Above: *The gloriously handsome Laurence Olivier as Lord Horatio Nelson.*

William, during which she learns that the British navy has kept the seas free for centuries, was an easy target for the isolationists looking for films that clearly advocated America's joining the war effort. Korda was understandably apprehensive when he was subpoenaed to appear before the Foreign Relations Committee. He, according to Michael Korda, "to his great discomfort, became aware that he was about to be made the scapegoat for Hollywood, and that he might well be deported as a foreign agent." However, Korda never appeared at the hearings set for December 12, 1941, because five days before that the Japanese attacked Pearl Harbor, and America entered the war.

As it turned out, Korda had more trouble with the Hays Office over morals than he did with the American Senate over political content. Chief censor Joseph Breen refused to give the completed film a Production Code seal of approval, on the grounds that it condoned adultery. Korda argued that his intention wasn't to defend or condemn adultery, but simply to present historical facts, but Breen insisted that Korda voice disapproval. So Korda reluc-

tantly filmed a scene in which Nelson confesses that he knows his affair with Emma is wrong. However, he excised the scene once the picture was released. Remaining is the emotional hallway scene, in England, in which Emma tells Nelson that they should part: "Because [our relationship] is wrong, it cannot bring happiness." Significantly, her words are later disproved when the widowed Emma and the still-married Nelson find happiness together on their country estate. It is precisely because neither Nelson nor Emma regrets the decision to continue their affair despite what it will do to their social standing—they wouldn't do anything differently—that the film is so daring. Korda may not have intended to condone adultery in general, but he certainly approved in the specific cases of Nelson and Lady Hamilton, Olivier and Leigh, and (Korda, Leigh, and Olivier were definitely thinking of them) King Edward and Wallis Simpson. (Leigh related to Mrs. Simpson, who received her divorce but then learned Edward wouldn't be allowed to marry her.) These were three affairs of the heart that Britishers took special pride in.

Certainly a major reason for the appeal of *That Ham-*

Sir William Hamilton doesn't mind that his marriage to Emma is platonic because he regards her as just another lovely part of his art-statue collection.

ilton Woman is that we sense Leigh and Olivier are acting out their own affair under the guise of playing Emma and Nelson. No doubt Korda drew on the parallels between the two affairs—after all, when he made *21 Days*, he took pleasure in having Leigh and Olivier's lovers running off together, because in real life he helped Leigh and Olivier sneak off for trysts in the country. Supposedly, Korda agreed to make a film about Nelson and Emma because he thought it would help Olivier and Leigh get through a difficult time in their relationship, when there were jealousies over career success—they'd play parts with equal status—and they were trying to recover from an embarrassing engagement on Broadway in *Romeo and Juliet*. Perhaps he hoped the film would serve them as a form of psychodrama, that, playing illicit lovers, they'd be reminded of their own happier times. Surely Leigh could relate to a young woman marrying someone much older and then falling madly in love with a married man, closer to her in age. In 1932, when she was 19, she married 31-year-old Herbert Leigh—later she fell for the married Olivier, only 6 years older than she. She thought Olivier as

great an actor as Emma thought Nelson a naval officer. When you read how Anne Edwards, in her best-seller *Vivien Leigh* (1977), describes the budding relationship of Leigh and Olivier circa 1936, you realize she could just as easily be describing the early relationship of Emma and Nelson, who found her refreshingly different from his strained, serious wife, Lady Nelson (effectively played by Gladys Cooper*):

> After the fourteen weeks it had taken to shoot *Fire Over England*, Olivier and Vivien had become dependent upon each other. He had never before met a woman quite like her. She was the extreme opposite of [his wife] Jill [Esmond], who was cool and calm at all times, dispassionate, a good friend more than a

．．．

*It is to the credit of Korda, screenwriters Walter Reisch and R. C. Sheriff, and Cooper herself that Lady Nelson doesn't come across as an outright villain. When the distressed Lady Nelson turns her back to the camera and puts her arms on the mantle, you feel as much sympathy for her as you ever do for Nelson and Emma.

Below: *Emma visits Nelson on his ship.* Right: *Nelson enters Emma's domain.*

lover. Vivien was exciting, unpredictable. She had a great sense of humor, was daring, intensely passionate, and at the same time thoughtful, loving, and considerate. She made him feel he was her entire world, that she lived for him. Yet she was the most intelligent woman he had personally known, far brighter by his own admission and better-read than he. And he was certain she was one of the most beautiful women in the world.

Watching Leigh and Olivier play Emma and Nelson, you sense their love and appreciation for each other. It's hard not feeling emotional when Nelson dictates a letter to a deeply moved Emma, telling Lady Nelson that "Lady Hamilton is one of the very best women in the world, and an honor to her sex"; when Emma changes from happy-go-lucky to serious—as she does throughout the film—when she comes on board Nelson's ship and discovers that he lost an eye and arm in battle (her sorrowful expression may be due in part to Leigh being seasick from the rocking boat); when, in an intimate moment at an inn table, she guesses his calm expression denotes "Nelson allowing himself to be just a little bit happy" and he reveals it denotes "Nelson in love"; when she runs onto the Naples balcony to say good-bye to Nelson and, while that volcano spouts in the background, they kiss passionately and Nelson says, "I know that I must not come back . . . and I know nothing in this world can keep me away"; when, again on the balcony, as 1800 arrives, Emma adds Nelson's name to a list of people who determined eighteenth-century history, and Nelson kisses her, saying, "Now I've kissed you through two centuries"; when the gallant Nelson's first words upon being told he's dying are "Poor Emma—what will become of her?"; and when Emma pulls her shades and faints upon learning of Nelson's death. We see how fulfilling true love is, and how painful it can be.

Of course, the scandalous affair between Emma and Nelson has few equals in romantic annals, and Leigh and Olivier do it justice. Olivier is rigid as usual (it makes sense as Nelson), but extremely dashing; Leigh (this is her best performance) is radiant, alive, aware, available. Like Scarlett O'Hara, Leigh's Emma is brainy, witty, flirtatious when need be, serious when she wants to be, able to handle any situation or impress any person, beautiful, optimistic, talented (she dances, she does mimicry like Shirley Temple's young characters), helpful, caring, passionate, loyal. I love the way she sweeps into a room; I want to know what she's thinking those many times she looks off into the horizon. We males feel envious of Nelson because he has found the "perfect date."

Alexander Korda's best film is less a glorification of Nelson than a tribute to the bravery, intelligence, and resourcefulness of women. Indeed, it seems to say that where there's a great man, a great woman is running interference for him—and Emma is given much credit for Nelson's successes in battle. As Emma tells Nelson, "Has it ever occurred to you that women can sometimes be of more help then men?" I think Korda was playing up to American women, whom he wanted to send their men into war against the Nazis. He wanted them to relate to Emma, who begins as a manipulative, self-obsessed, self-impressed young woman concerned only with bettering her own lot in life, but ends up giving up the man she loves (who loves her greatly but loves his country even more) and her happiness for the sake of the world. In world affairs, as in romances, one must be willing to make monumental sacrifices.

The Thief of Bagdad

1940 Color British United Artists release of a London Film Production
Directors: Ludwig Berger, Michael Powell, Tim Whelan and (uncredited) Zoltan Korda, Alexander Korda, and William Cameron Menzies
Producer: Alexander Korda
Associate Producers: Zoltan Korda and William Cameron Menzies
Screenplay and dialogue: Miles Malleson
Scenario: Lajos Biro
Cinematography: George Perinal
Special Photographic Effects: Lawrence Butler
Art Director: Vincent Korda
Music: Miklos Rozsa
Supervising Editor: William Hornbeck
Editor: Charles Crichton
Running Time: 106 minutes

Cast: Conrad Veidt (Jaffar), Sabu (Abu), John Justin (Ahmad), June Duprez (princess), Rex Ingram (djinni), Miles Malleson (sultan), Morton Selten (king), Mary Morris (Halima).

Synopsis: A blind man with a scruffy dog begs for alms in ancient Bagdad. Jaffar, the king, tells his slave girl Halima to bring him to a rich merchant's house, for there lies the princess in an eternal sleep. The blind man tells the harem girls about the recent past, when he was King Ahmad, Jaffar was his Grand Vizier, and the dog was the teenage boy Abu, a thief.

Ahmad wanted to get to know his subjects, to give them happiness. Jaffar wanted to conquer the Earth through fear. Jaffar advised Ahmad to mingle with his people incognito. Ahmad heard a man's prophecy that a young boy, "the lowest of the low," would save the people from the tyrant Jaffar. Jaffar arrested Ahmad and usurped his throne. On the eve of Ahmad's execution, Abu was arrested and thrown into the same cell. Abu stole the guard's key and he and his new friend escaped to Basra.

Ahmad saw the princess, the sultan of Basra's daughter, ride by on an elephant. He fell in love. With Abu's help, he sneaked into her palace and romanced her. She joined him in swearing everlasting love. But the sultan promised her as bride to Jaffar, who gave him a mechanical horse—a new toy for his precious collection. The princess fled to her sister's, but was captured by slave traders and sold to the rich merchant. Ahmad and Abu were arrested. Jaffar put a spell on them, making Ahmad sightless and turning Abu into a dog, that would be lifted only when he held the princess in his arms. The grieving princess went into a deep sleep.

The princess is revived by Jaffar. She goes to see a doctor on a ship, hoping he can cure Ahmad. But it is Jaffar's ship. She is kidnapped. She lets Jaffar hold her, knowing that will free Ahmad and Abu from their spell. They return to Basra. Jaffar kills the sultan when he wants to call off the wedding.

Ahmad and Abu are separated when Jaffar causes a storm at sea. On shore, Abu frees a huge djinni from a bottle. The djinni wants to kill him but Abu tricks him back into the bottle. He frees him again after he agrees to grant Abu three wishes. The djinni flies him halfway across the world, to the Temple of Dawn. Abu kills a giant spider and secures the All-Seeing Eye. He sees that Ahmad searches the mountains for him and has the djinni bring him to his friend. Ahmad gazes into the Eye and sees that Jaffar has tricked the princess into smelling the Blue Rose of Forgetfulness. The djinni grants Abu's wish that Ahmad go to Basra. Jaffar has almost convinced the princess that she loves him and has never loved another. But before they kiss, Ahmad appears and she remembers everything. After a brutal fight, Ahmad is taken prisoner. Jaffar says he will execute Ahmad and the princess in the morning.

The djinni leaves Abu alone in the desert. Abu angrily throws down the Eye. He spins and spins and ends up in the Land of Legend. He is to be the successor to the kindly old king. He takes the king's flying carpet and Arrow of Justice and rides to Bagdad. He prevents the execution. The oppressed people see him and, remembering the prophecy, rebel. Jaffar attempts to flee on the magic horse, but Abu's aim is true. Ahmad takes the princess for his queen. When he announces Abu will go to school, the boy flies off on his carpet, looking for fun and adventure.

The British movie industry's greatest fantasy film. With its truly *special* special effects and its enchanting vision of a mythical world that exists only through storytelling, *The Thief of Bagdad* was, along with *King Kong* (1933), one of its influences, the major source of inspiration for F/X master Ray Harryhausen when he worked on *The 7th Voyage of Sinbad* (1958). And these three films, plus *The Wizard of Oz* (1939), another of *Thief*'s influences, were directly responsible for countless youngsters becoming fans of the fantasy film genre, and for some of them becoming, when they got older, filmmakers who specialize in fantasies full of special effects.

The last hurrah for the Korda brothers team, producer-director Alexander, director Zoltan, and art director Vincent, *The Thief of Bagdad* had its genesis, I suppose, in Persia, 23 centuries ago. As legend has it, the shrewd Scheherazade kept her bored husband, Schariar, the sultan of Samarkand, from executing her by entertaining him with a new story each night for 1001 consecutive nights. For her much-needed material, she relied on anonymous Oriental folk tales that had found their way into ancient Persia, the Arab-speaking countries, and probably India. Her "Arabian Nights" tales of Sinbad the Sailor, Ali Baba, Aladdin, and others would pass down through the ages, becoming increasingly Muslim in spirit. The first European edition of *Thousand and One Nights* was Antoine Galland's liberal French translation in the early eighteenth century. Subsequent French, German, and nineteenth-century English translations would borrow from Galland.

The Arabian Nights tales were ideal for movie adaptation, and during the silent era, two classics emerged. In Germany, Lotte Reiniger, with special effects help from Walter Ruttmann, made the 65-minute silhouette cutout film *The Adventures of Prince Achmed* (1926). It predated Disney's *Snow White and the Seven Dwarfs* (1937) by 11 years, making it the first animated feature. However, Alexander Korda certainly was more influenced by Raoul Walsh's American-made, live-action epic *The Thief of Bagdad* (1924), starring an extremely athletic and charismatic Douglas Fairbanks. In fact, when it came time to do his own version of the story, Korda imported William Cameron Menzies, who did the still-wondrous special effects on the Fairbanks film, to be an associate producer.

Korda, the most important filmmaker in England at the time, supposedly decided to remake *The Thief of Bagdad*—which was to be the first in a series of "super productions"—to prove England could make a fantasy film on par with America's forthcoming *The Wizard of Oz*, to promote optimism at a time the world feared Nazi aggression would lead to war, to properly showcase the design talents of Vincent Korda and the cinematography of George Perinal, and to provide a strong vehicle for his major contract players Conrad Veidt and Sabu. The teenager from Mysore had made an impressive debut in *The Elephant Boy* (1937), which had been produced by Korda and codirected by brother Zoltan and Robert Flaherty. Korda knew the silent *Thief of Bagdad* was regarded as a classic

Jaffar's messenger Halima speaks to the blind Ahmad, who clutches Abu, now a dog.

seaport, 25 full-sized ships and a fleet of junks, sampans, and fishing boats were constructed; hundreds of workers built the sultan's magnificent open-air palace (which seems suspended in the heavens), the minarets of ancient Persia, and the mosques. Korda's writers—including Miles Malleson (who plays the sultan), Lajos Biro, and (uncredited) Sir Robert Vansittart, chief diplomatic adviser to the British government—incorporated props that would call attention to color, such as the "Blue Rose of Forgetfulness." In addition, the other directors who were soon busy on the project—little-known Michael Powell, Veidt's director on the recently completed *The Spy in Black* (1939), Tim Whelan, Menzies, Zoltan Korda, and even Alexander Korda—made sure to emphasize color: Viewers remember the bright clear colors, the blue skies and seas, Jaffar's black galleon with its blood-red sails, Jaffar's blue eyes, the multicolored diaphanous silk gowns of the harem girls, Jaffar's white outfit and black cape, the red All-Seeing Eye, the white flying horse, the white-bearded wise men, and the dark-skinned Abu, djinni, and guards of Jaffar. Through it all, for over nine months, Korda somehow kept Berger in the dark, away from the great outdoor Denham sets, waiting to begin his assignment. In *A Life in the Movies: An Autobiography* (1987), Powell recalled that when Korda sent him to Cornwall with Sabu and a crew, Korda told Berger they were going to do mere second-unit work—in actuality, it was prime material. Because shooting was going on in several locations simultaneously, under different directors (none having a finished script),

and that moviegoers who remembered Fairbanks wouldn't accept another adult actor as the thief (one wonders if he considered Errol Flynn). So he decided that his version would be completely different from the original film—although it too would borrow from various Arabian Nights tales—and that Sabu would play the title role, even though this meant youngsters would be the only ones to identify with him. Originally Korda hoped Jon Hall and Vivien Leigh would play Ahmad and the princess. However, Hall, who'd star in popular Hollywood-made Arabian Nights films in the forties, rejected his offer and Leigh (who probably didn't seriously consider playing the innocuous princess) rushed off to America and her destiny. So Korda settled for stage actor John Justin, kind of a pitifully poor man's Douglas Fairbanks, Jr., without his humor, and contract player June Duprez.

Korda did get his first choice of director, German exile Ludwig Berger, but he soon regretted it. He hired Berger because of his well-known version of *Cinderella* (1926), a stylized black-and-white fantasy film. Berger rewarded Korda's faith by filming some excellent, stylized test scenes with Sabu and Veidt. But by this time, Korda had changed his concept of the film. He was thrilled by Vincent's designs and began to imagine how spectacular his film would be in Technicolor—such a picture would make memories of the color-tinted Fairbanks version quickly fade. But Berger was adamant about making a small-scale, stylized film in black and white. His attitude didn't stop Korda from proceeding with his project as he wanted. He brought Natalie Kalmus, the head of Technicolor, onto the project. Previously Technicolor had prohibited trick photography, but Korda directed his special effects team of Lawrence Butler and assistants Tom Howard and Johnny Mills to consult with Kalmus and figure out how they could include the necessary rear-projection process shots, double exposures, miniatures, and matte shots. Meanwhile Korda told Vincent to alter his early designs, to draw everything in color and on epic scale. He would move the production from the confining Denham Studio sound stages and build enormous outdoor sets. For the scenes of Basra and its

As the evil Jaffar looks on hopefully, the princess smells the Blue Rose of Forgetfulness.

In the most memorable sequence, the giant djinni lifts Abu.

some technical people never received proper credit. For instance, according to Powell, Osmond Borradaile did a significant amount of principal photography, yet Perinal received sole cinematography credit.

That *The Thief of Bagdad* was completed at all is remarkable, because on September 2, 1939, the day after Germany invaded Poland, Korda shut down production. His entire staff began work on *The Lion Has Wings* (1939), a propaganda film about the RAF and England's preparation for war. Powell directed and it starred Merle Oberon, Korda's wife from 1939 to 1945, Ralph Richardson, and Duprez. Away from Korda, Powell then quickly filmed *Contraband* (1940), with Conrad Veidt, and went on to become England's top director in the forties (usually collaborating with Emeric Pressburger), turning out such classics as *49th Parallel* (1941), *The Life and Death of Colonel Blimp* (1943), *A Matter of Life and Death* (1946), *Black Narcissus* (1947), with Sabu in a key role, and, of course, *The Red Shoes* (1948). When filming resumed on *The Thief of Bagdad*, Powell was too busy to return. Anyway, Korda shifted the entire production to Hollywood, where he would remain. (He'd next produce and direct 1941's *That Hamilton Woman*.) Those scenes with Sabu's Abu and Rex Ingram's flying djinni were filmed by Zoltan Korda in Arizona's Grand Canyon and Painted Desert instead of Africa, as planned. Somehow the film was completed in time for a Christmas 1940 release in both Great Britain and the United States.

It's easy to understand why children (in England, America, and Russia)—who weren't born when Fairbanks played the thief—loved this film. It contains most everything a young fantasy fan desires: a handsome prince; a beautiful, fetchingly clad princess; a clever, independent, optimistic, law-breaking, school-avoiding teenage hero; a diabolical dressed-in-black villain; a flying carpet; an "alive" six-armed mechanical woman (which anticipates Ray Harryhausen creations); a giant genie in a tiny bottle; slave girls; an enormous spider; a dog that was originally a boy; a toy horse that can fly; fantasy lands; a spacious palace (the light used to accommodate the color film was enough to illuminate a small city); action (though not enough) and adventure; colorful sets, costumes, and scenery; special effects. But I assume the critics who were so generous to the film judged it mostly on its appeal to kids. You can forgive its flaws, but it's impossible to deny their existence. And while you can get pulled into the magical world on the screen—Perinal (who was regarded as a wizard with lighting), Vincent Korda, and Lawrence Butler deserved their Academy Awards—you'll likely have the dissatisfied sensation that the adult filmmakers were detached from the fantasy world they created, "where everything is possible when seen through the eyes of youth." In *Charmed Lives* (1979), Michael Korda, son of Vincent Korda, wrote tellingly:

> *The Thief of Bagdad* . . . had received the attentions of three [credited] directors, on both sides of the Atlantic, with the inevitable result that the footage was somewhat hard to fit together into a coherent whole. Alex's passion for size had been amply gratified, but the actors were dwarfed by the sets and the special effects, and the film was curiously lacking in warmth. He himself felt it was a "showman's film," but it suffered from much the same defect as a three-ring circus: there was too much going on, and a great deal of it was simply flashy spectacle for its own sake. *The Thief of Bagdad* represents what he thought the pub-

Abu gives instructions to the djinni that will help Ahmad escape the mountains and rescue the princess.

lic liked, not what he liked himself, and in truth, he was bored by it and quite happy to leave to Zoli the task of completing the final version.

Korda's film opens clumsily with flashback scenes narrated by the blind Ahmad, as he sits in Bagdad with a dog by his side. The picture barely recovers from this awkward beginning, which (1) complicates a simple story by confusing us about *time* and (2) infers that John Justin's Ahmad and not Sabu's Abu (a dog when we first see him) is the film's main character and our hero. Credit the filmmakers for trying to get across that we are watching a *story*, as if told in the time of Scheherazade, but a narrator over a linear story line would have worked much better. If the film had opened where the flashback begins, with shots of the human Abu running through Bagdad and coming upon Ahmad speaking with Jaffar, then we would realize immediately that the boy is our hero, the character whose adventure this is, the person we're supposed to identify with. As is, we identify with Ahmad because he is the main character in the flashback; because he, and not Abu, fits into the sleeping princess's life—he, and not Abu, can save this sleeping beauty with a kiss. Because Ahmad is such a boring character—as a king, he was like a lazy "playboy" who never did anything worthwhile, and not a wise, benevolent ruler—we feel disappointed following *his* drippy, lovesick exploits. Only the scene in which Ahmad meets and romances the princess has any flair—it is like a ballet without dancing. But we want *adventure*, not romance between two superficial characters, and Abu alone provides it.

About halfway through the picture, the always-smiling Justin and the lovely but dour Duprez (who'd do better in 1945 in *And Then There Were None*) sort of fade out. That's good because it allows the top-billed Veidt and Sabu to dominate the screen. They make splendid adversaries and provide humor—"Strange how an unpleasant child can be a decent dog," Jaffar comments, before ordering the decent dog thrown into the ocean. The pace really picks up once Abu meets Rex Ingram's intimidating, laughing, thunder-voiced giant djinni. It's unusual watching a long sequence in a British production that features characters played by a dark-skinned Indian boy and an American black man. It's also the highlight of the film. In fact, the adventures to which the djinni takes Abu are far less interesting than the journeys themselves, with the scared boy clinging to the giant's hair as he soars through the air, heading for—the djinni delivers his lines with gusto!—"the highest peak of the highest mountain," where sits the head of the Goddess of Light, "supported by seven pillars, and the seven pillars are set on the shoulders of a djinni whose strength is beyond thought, and the djinni stands on an eagle and the eagle on a bull and the bull on a fish and the fish swims in the sea of eternity." Clearly delivered in booming voice by Ingram, an American actor who played "de Lawd" in *The Green Pastures* (1936), these ridiculous lines are like poetry. They make us anxious about what Abu will come across in the Temple of Dawn, where he will try to retrieve the All-Seeing Eye. The set is fascinating, but the natives who guard the Goddess of Light aren't very threatening (couldn't they throw a few spears at Abu?), and composer Miklos Rozsa (whose work on the film is erratic) ruins the fight between Abu and the giant spider with adventure music more appropriate for a swashbuckling scene than this potentially frightening sequence.

Also disappointing is the climax of the final action scene, in which Jaffar tries to escape on the mechanical white horse, but is shot down by Abu's Arrow of Justice. Jaffar had stood his ground against Abu and Ahmad before, and he still is capable of casting powerful spells, so why does he flee so quickly? And couldn't he at least abscond with the princess to make things more exciting? Sure, the princess would have fallen from the horse, too, but if Abu and Ahmad were riding the magic carpet when the arrow was shot, then there could have been a thrilling midair rescue. It's the logical sequence of events.

Potentially, the most interesting character in the film is Jaffar. There is a sympathetic side to him that is not really explored. He does have a good side—he is capable of loving the princess as much as Ahmad does. At times (i.e., when he speaks through curtains), he reminds me of Anton Walbrook's impresario Boris Lermontov in Powell's *The Red Shoes*, whose coldness masks his love for Moira Shearer's ballet star, Vicky Page. In some ways, his role is similar to that of the tortured Beast in Cocteau's fantasy *Beauty and the Beast* (1946), who has an old man send his beautiful daughter to him, but—though he won't harm her or force himself on her—can't make her love him as he loves her and forget the handsome man outside his castle. Here, too, a king crumbles in the face of beauty. Only Korda doesn't want Jaffar to reveal he has the inner beauty of Cocteau's Beast. Jaffar is evil personified, a Hitler figure, a dictator who rules through fear, a bully who reveals his cowardice and—in this context his last act makes sense—will run away if anyone fights back.

It's hard to tell if, in 1940, *The Thief of Bagdad* had propaganda value, other than just putting audiences in cheery moods. But the filmmakers did try to develop a politically relevant subtext. Not only did they make an analogy between Jaffar (played by a German expatriate) and Hitler, but they also presented us with a world of masters and slaves to remind us that the joy of freedom ("Freedom!" screams the djinni) is without equal. The most interesting aspect of the film is its cry to battle (for revolution?). In this film, the frightened and oppressed turn the tables on their oppressors; people, including Ahmad and the princess, experience freedom for the first time; the powerless take over, the powerful are vanquished; the "lowest of the low" becomes king. Leaders give orders, cast spells, threaten others with slavery and death. But their unfortunate subjects are never defeated. Our young boy outsmarts the djinni who wants to kill him and makes the giant his slave. Jaffar blinds Ahmad so he'll have access to the princess, but his plan backfires because, as he tells his captive, he himself is "cursed because I can see only you." Jaffar tells the princess to be his bride and "obey your destiny" but he finds himself offering to be her slave and immediately following her orders to return to Basra. The princess's heart beats so strongly with love for Ahmad that even Jaffar's spell isn't strong enough to put her under

Jaffar uses the princess as a shield when Abu and Ahmad lead an insurrection from aboard a magic carpet.

his thumb; her tears are enough to move her sultan-father's heart and get him to withdraw his demand that she marry Jaffar. The appearance of the young boy in the sky, the savior they'd heard about through lifetimes of misery, causes Jaffar's subjects to rise in rebellion, battle his soldiers, and overthrow the tyrant. The message is clear: Those dictators on top now are bound to topple (like Jaffar tumbling from his horse), if the people remember the price of free-dom and rise as one. Early in the film, when Ahmad tells Abu he has never known freedom, Abu contends that he, the thief of Bagdad, has had nothing but freedom. In the film's last shot, as Abu rides his magic carpet away— "look[ing] for fun and adventure, *at last!*"—we realize that only now, with Jaffar dead and order to the world established, can Abu, or anyone else, have freedom, much less enjoy it.

The Thing

also known as *The Thing from Another World*

1951   B&W   RKO

Director: Christian Nyby
Producer: Howard Hawks
Screenplay: Charles Lederer
From the story "Who Goes
   There?" by John W. Camp-
   bell, Jr.

Cinematography: Russell Har-
   lan
Music: Dimitri Tiomkin
Editor: Roland Gross
Running Time: 81/87 minutes

Cast: Margaret Sheridan (Nikki), Kenneth Tobey (Captain Patrick Hendry), Robert Cornthwaite (Dr. Arthur Carrington), Douglas Spencer (Ned "Scotty" Scott), James Young (Lieutenant Eddie Dykes), Dewey Martin (Bob, the crew chief), Robert Nichols (Lieutenant MacPherson*), William Self (Corporal Barnes), Eduard Franz (Dr. Stern), Jon Dierkes (Dr. Chapman), Sally Creighton (Mrs. Chapman), Paul Frees (Dr. Maurice Vorrhees), George Fenneman (Dr. Redding), David McManon (General Fogerty), Norbert Schiller (Dr. Laurenz), James Arness ("the Thing").

Synopsis: Air force captain Pat Hendry is ordered by General Fogerty to fly to a North Pole research station. Nobel Prize winner Dr. Carrington and other scientists have reported a crash in their vicinity. A Russian plane? Pat, co-pilot Eddy, navigator MacPherson, crew chief Bob, Corporal Barnes, and Scotty, a reporter, make the trip. Pat feels fortunate to see Nikki, who works as secretary to Carrington. He liked her immediately when they met in San Francisco, but he'd been too forward with her. A good sport, she's interested when he suggests they begin over.

Fifty miles from the research center, the soldiers and scientists discover a large flying saucer beneath the ice. They detonate a thermite bomb to free it, but it blows up. They find a hideous eight-foot alien embedded in the ice. They cut out the chunk of ice and take it back to the research station. Carrington and his followers insist they defrost and study the alien. But Pat says they must get permission from General Fogerty. Also Scotty must get Fogerty's approval before filing his "Man from Mars" story. Carrington and Scotty are angry.

While Nikki and Pat get better acquainted, Barnes sits with the ice block in the storeroom. He covers it with an electric blanket. The ice melts. Barnes fires at the defrosted alien. Unharmed, it jumps out the window. It kills two sled dogs, but has its arm ripped off. Carrington examines the arm and discovers the Thing has no arterial structure, no nerve tissue. It is no animal, but a vegetable, an intellectual carrot that can reproduce asexually, through seeds. Carrington marvels that it has no emotions and no heart, that it is "our superior in every way."

Carrington and his backers find a dead, bloodless sled dog in the greenhouse. They know the Thing will return and set up guard without telling Pat. They fear Pat will order it killed, and its secrets will be lost. The Thing returns and kills two scientists, draining their blood. Its arm has grown back. Pat and his men lock it behind the greenhouse door, and Pat is almost killed in the process. Pat orders Carrington confined to his lab. There Carrington, who's too tired to think straight, harvests the seeds from the severed arm. The plants grow at an alarming rate. Nikki realizes Carrington is no longer rational. She tells Pat of his experiment. Pat orders the plants burned.

The men can't figure out how to fight the alien, who isn't affected by cold or bullets. Since it's a vegetable, Nikki suggests cooking it. When it bursts into a room, the men set it on fire. The Thing dives outside into the snow. They know it will be back. The Thing turns off the heat in the research station, forcing everyone into the generator room. Pat agrees with a suggestion by Dr. Redding and Bob that they trap the Thing in an electrical force field. However, when the Thing approaches, Carrington turns off the generator. He runs to the alien and tries to communicate. The alien knocks him aside, breaking his collarbone. It attacks the others, but is caught in an electrical fly trap. It is cooked until it disappears.

Nikki decides she and Pat should marry. While they discuss this, Scotty finally transmits his report. He tells the world of the brave men who won a battle for the human race. He warns everyone to "Keep watching the skies!"

• •

*Listed in the credits as Lieutenant "Ken Erickson."

In British critic John Brosnan's excellent book *Future Tense: The Cinema of Science Fiction* (1978), he contends that "serious sf fans tend to regard [*The Thing*] with disapproval and consider it a typically Hollywood treatment of an sf masterpiece." I find this statement startling, completely contradicting my own experience. In America, at least, *The Thing* is the only science fiction film that *every* serious sf fan—including today's sf filmmakers—loves and agrees is a masterpiece, the first masterpiece of the fifties sci-fi cycle. In fact, to qualify as a true fan of the genre, one must see this film many times. Moreover, it's the rare sf film that has won approval from critics and moviegoers who usually look down on the genre. Because of its monster, violence, use of shadows and darkness, spooky music (by Dimitri Tiomkin), suspense, and shocks (i.e., the marvelous jump-out-of-your-seat moment Pat warily opens a door in order to search the greenhouse, only to find the huge Thing standing right at the entrance), it has appeal for horror movie fans (who aren't necessarily sf fans). And because of the military characters and their military conduct, the military hardware (the plane, radios, guns, bombs, outfits), and the military strategy employed to subdue the monster, the film has appeal for war-movie fans—like *Aliens* (1986), it can be seen as a war movie posing as a sci-fi film. Also it has perverse appeal for those of us who wonder what the result could be if we defrosted and served those five-year-old vegetables in the freezer.

The Thing may be about a thawed killer carrot on the rampage, but it has class. (This is no *Attack of the Killer Tomatoes!*) This is to be expected since it was produced by Howard Hawks, the major reason non-sf fans seek it out. Christian Nyby is listed as director, but after years of denials Hawks conceded not long before his death in 1977 that he directed most of the film himself but offered his former editor this screen credit so he could get a union credential. Certainly the picture bears the distinct Hawks signature: It has an unobtrusive waist-level camera; long takes; a frame that serves as a verbal and physical battleground; characters whizzing in and out of that frame; snappy, rapid-fire, overlapping dialogue (it becomes quicker to build tension); improvisation; humor in the midst of turmoil; characters finding refuge from a hostile outdoor environment inside their vehicles (in this case Pat's airplane) and an indoor "headquarters" (in this case, the research station); a male universe where men respect each other's talents, knowledge, and rank; men learning to work harmoniously under pressure, with each—professionals all—contributing his singular expertise to get the difficult task done; action heroes (Hawks always liked flyers); a strong, brave leader (Kenneth Tobey's Captain Patrick Hendry) who can outthink any enemy but is easily outmaneuvered by a beguiling woman; and an attractive female (Margaret Sheridan's Nikki) who is quite feminine, yet has passed the test and is allowed to pal around with the men. Nikki types and takes dictation, makes and serves coffee, knows how to cook carrots of all sizes and origins ("Boil it, stew it, bake it, fry it!''), wears a tantalizingly tight sweater, and wants to marry, settle down, and have kids, but the men are more impressed by her fortitude and intelligence (she figures out how to oppose the Thing), her ability to drink Hendry under the table, and her ability to keep her wit and wits during a crisis. The men, who give each other nicknames (Scotty, Mac) derived from their last names, show she's one of them by giving her a male Nikki-name derived from her last name, Nicholson. (We never know her real first name.) Pat further shows his respect for Nikki by letting her remain with the men in the room that the Thing is about to break into, and gives her the important assignment of turning out the lights at a strategic time.

Nikki is a prize, and Pat determines that his life won't be complete, or much fun, without her.

In the first science fiction films of the fifties, George Pal's seminal *Destination Moon* (1950) and *Rocketship X-M* (1950), viewers thrilled to space exploration and, in the latter film, the discovery of an alien race. *The Thing* was excitingly different in that the alien came here, to Earth; yet because it is set in the frozen Arctic (some outdoor filming took place in Montana, some indoor photography took place in an L.A. meat-packing plant's refrigerator), we still feel as if we're exploring alien territory. It was released in April 1951, the peak year for flying saucer hysteria, just eight months into the Korean War. To be

Before he became a television institution as Matt Dillon on Gunsmoke, *James Arness left his mark on the science fiction cinema as the title character in* The Thing. *He is never shown as clearly as he is in this publicity shot.*

The scientists and air force men figure out the size of the alien ship beneath the ice.

germane, Hawks and screenwriter Charles Lederer (with an assist from Ben Hecht) devised a story that mocked the UFO paranoia (a killer carrot from space?) and simultaneously, on a deeper level, keyed on America's post–World War II paranoia about invading Communists. They immediately make it clear that there is a correlation between outer space aliens and Communists: Soon after Pat states, "The Russians are all over the Pole, like flies," Scotty starts referring to the Thing as "the Man from Mars," the *Red* Planet. Ironically, the novella from which their *timely* script was loosely adapted, the award-winning *Who Goes There?*, was written by John W. Campbell, Jr. (as Don A. Stuart) back in 1938, long before the UFO phenomenon and Cold War that are integral to the film. From Campbell, they took only the alien-crashes-on-earth premise, the sense of paranoia, and the frozen setting, an ideal environment for a Cold War polemic. But the fact they switched the locale from the South Pole to the North Pole was indication that the film and novella would be poles apart. The most drastic and peculiar changes made by Hawks and Lederer had to do with the look and properties of the alien. Their Thing may resemble humans more than Campbell's, but it is vegetable rather than animal. Carrington and the other scientists are astonished that it can reproduce asexually, through spores/seeds, but this trait is less impressive than what Campbell's Thing is capable of doing. It's somewhat surprising Lederer didn't also give his Thing the ability to transform into the exact replicas of its victims . . . minus the emotions, because Americans

in 1951 certainly would have drawn a parallel between a dehumanizing monster and the brainwashing Communists that were in the news. Such an alien definitely would have made it more obvious that the film was dealing with the Cold War. Initially Hawks intended his monster to at least look like Campbell's, a grotesque, tentacled creature with three red eyes, blue hair like worms, and a sucker-shaped mouth, but he abandoned that idea. Some thought was given to making it a spidery creature, but Hawks finally decided to hire tall James Arness (his stunt double was Tom Steele), put him in Frankenstein makeup, and dim the lights—for the scene in which the cooking Thing shrinks, tiny Billy Curtis replaced Arness. (John Carpenter's 1982 remake was faithful to Campbell's story and monster concept, and included spectacular transformation scenes. Unfortunately, Carpenter wasn't interested in a political message, the characters were too shallow for us to be upset when they were dehumanized, and we were more afraid of the filmmakers—with their vicious streaks and large special effects budget—than the monster.)

In Hawks's films, the action hero manages to perform his duties/tasks admirably even though he is distracted by unfamiliar feelings of love for the beautiful woman who has recently entered his life. To him, love and war are equally dangerous. In this picture a parallel is drawn between the Cold War and the Battle of the Sexes. At first, while the alien monster is on ice, or—to be more precise—*in* a block of ice, Nikki gives Pat the cold shoulder. Nikki and Pat show signs of "breaking the ice," and starting

The worried Nikki looks at Dr. Carrington, while the rest of the scientists study the thriving plants he has harvested from the seeds of the alien's severed arm.

their relationship from scratch, at about the time the Thing starts to thaw out. In a strangely kinky romantic scene, Nikki, in tight sweater, has Pat at her mercy, sitting in a chair with his hands tied behind his back. This sequence was cut from the reissue prints that play on cable television, although it provides Sheridan with enough screen time to justify her top billing and is a vital cog in the Cold War/Battle of the Sexes connection. For just when Pat reveals that his hands aren't really bound and that he can grab Nikki if he chooses, we see that the Thing has been freed from his ice prison and can attack the humans if it chooses. From this point on, Nikki and Pat are on a blazing path toward marriage and the Cold War literally heats up. There is fire—flames cover the mattress Pat hands Nikki (conveying his desire to go to bed with her, and her acceptance)—and electricity (like that which flows between the soon-to-be lovers). Nikki recognizes she can't be without Pat and delivers a line charged with sexual innuendo: "If I start burning up again, who's going to put out the fire?" It's important to note that Nikki and Pat don't make love during the course of the film. With the Thing on the loose, and mankind in jeopardy, they have no time. With the "hot war" raging, Nikki and Pat must put their love affair on the back burner. Hawks and Lederer are saying—and this is one of the three major themes of the picture—that if we are invaded, then love, freedom of the press (Scotty angrily points to the Constitution in his vain attempt to convince Pat to let him report the discovery of the alien), and the pursuit of scientific knowledge may have to be put on hold in the national interest, while the military does its job.

This is the first science fiction film to have scientists and the military in conflict over how to deal with aliens. In general, scientists want to communicate with aliens in order to benefit mankind, while the military wants to destroy them in order to save mankind. We immediately distrust Robert Cornthwaite's Dr. Arthur Carrington, as we do most geniuses in horror and science fiction. Because he wears an insidious goatee and a Russian fur hat and fur-

lined coat and speaks scientific mumbo-jumbo ("Speak English," Scotty pleads), we recognize his "foreignness"—as well as that of his most devoted follower, Dr. Maurice Vorrhees. We worry that he has drifted into the Communist camp because of how he beholds the alien. He reveres its ability to reproduce asexually, "without pain or pleasure," and envies it for having "no emotions and no heart." These traits, which we were taught in school to associate with Communists, are the reason he considers the alien "our superior in every way." (Notice how Pat Hendry, who's as patriotic as Patrick Henry, takes his men off to the side so they don't have to listen to Carrington's cockeyed, antihuman views.) Carrington doesn't only talk, he takes action—actually facilitating a full-scale invasion by harvesting its seeds (he has some botany box). The evidence is stacked against Carrington and we'd probably convict him of being a traitor. However, I don't think Hawks and Lederer view him as traitor, or even a villain—that's why the men are happy Scotty reports Carrington was one of the heroes in the battle with the alien.

At one point, Scotty tells Carrington, "If you were for sale I could get a million bucks for you from any foreign government." Well, the point is that Carrington will not sell himself to any foreign government, including the Soviet Union. He doesn't want to deal with politics, or with the military. His alliance is with mankind and he doesn't choose sides: "There are no enemies in science, just phenomena to study." Hawks and Lederer actually admire Carrington's purity of purpose. It's just that during the tense Cold War, science should be geared for national, not universal, interests. Scientists like Carrington are so devoted to helping mankind that they become blind—Carrington can't think clearly because he doesn't sleep—to genuine threats against mankind. Because they work independently from their country's military, their achievements may actually be in conflict with the interests of the military. They may inadvertently be helping the enemy, mankind's enemy, as does Carrington. This is why Hawks

In Howard Hawks films, characters work in groups. Here, everyone but Carrington figures out how to dispose of the Thing. Standing, left to right: Dr. Chapman, Scotty, Carrington, Nikki, and Pat, who takes a back seat to those who are more expert. Kneeling, left to right: Eddie, Bob, and Dr. Redding.

The Thing is set on fire during an attack.

and Lederer believe that in troubled times, scientists should defer to the military. Which isn't to say science and scientists have no place in a military operation. This picture is not anti-science, as Vivian Carol Sobchack contends in her book *The Limits of Infinity: The American Science Fiction Film* (1980). Carrington and his extremists are balanced by reasonable men of science, Dr. Chapman, Professor Wilson, and Dr. Redding (played by Groucho Marx's TV announcer, George Fenneman), men whose advice Pat seeks out and adheres to. Pat understands nothing about science: When Redding explains how the locale of the saucer was deduced, Pat shrugs, "You lost me"; he has no ability to grasp Carrington and Dr. Stern's lecture on intelligent plant life on Earth; when scientist Redding and science expert Bob, Dewey Martin's ingenious crew chief, start laying out and explaining the electrical trap for the Thing, the baffled Pat can only say, "I don't get you . . . What are you talking about? . . . What do you mean fly trap? . . . We'd better get out of the way." But he has faith in science, as all men who fly planes must have, and incorporates it into the military game plan. He uses thermite bombs to try to free the saucer that is encased in the ice—although the only thing he knows about them is that they explode—and agrees to let Redding and Bob hook up the electrical trap that confuses him. The Thing is destroyed because of Science, because the scientists willingly join forces with the military. Military strategy coupled with scientific application is a powerful combination—this is the film's second major theme.

The third major theme is that America's armed forces can turn back any type of invasion. Our army can defeat any enemy. The soldiers we see are extremely efficient, quick thinking, well disciplined, confident, graceful under pressure, brave (they always volunteer for dangerous assignments), and talented. They know the S.O.P. (standard operating procedure), they know how to take orders—they actually anticipate orders—and, though respectful of superiors, they are not shy about offering sound advice to them. What makes Pat such a good leader is that he realizes that his men are more expert than he in their par-

ticular areas and is not embarrassed to take their advice or let them proceed with some action without first fully explaining it to him. His crew functions so well because there is a division of labor, with everyone playing an equal part. He trusts and respects his men. There is a running gag in the film: know-it-all Bob gives sound advice to Pat, Pat agrees to do what Bob suggests, and Bob tells Pat, "I think you're right, sir." Pat doesn't care about credit (he answers Bob, "I think *you* are"), just that the job is done correctly. Being an air force captain, he's wise enough to know he needs all the help he can get in a ground action. Because Pat doesn't pull rank on his men, because he treats them like friends, because he works side by side with them (taking guard duty, doing menial labor), and because he uses their input to help formulate his decisions, his men will follow his orders without question. And a great percentage of Pat's dialogue consists of orders. For instance, when at the saucer site, he says, "Bob, clear the slide off and bring it over here. Eddie, get the ship warmed up and be ready to get out of here in a hurry." When the Thing is about to burst into the room, he tells Eddie, "If it comes in you wet it down," tells MacPherson, "And you, Mac—touch it off and don't miss," tells Bob and Barnes, "You two be ready in case it needs more," and tells Nikki, "Come here. Get in the corner. And hold this in front of you. Turn off those lights." Pat gives so many orders during the course of the film that he admits to Nikki, "I've given all the orders I want to give for the rest of my life." "If I thought that were true," she jokes, "I'd ask you to marry me." But when he immediately starts giving more orders, she jokes again, "Sorry, *General*, I've changed my mind—it's all off." Everyone gives Pat advice, but he knows that only he, as leader, can give the orders. None of his men questions this, and he accepts his responsibility. That's why everything runs so smoothly, and why in the final battle the Thing is killed without our side suffering any casualties. *The Thing* is a tribute to our armed forces. Even as we "Keep watching the skies!" as "war correspondent" Scotty exhorts us to do, we can feel secure because these fine men are ready, willing, and able.

Touch of Evil

1958 B&W Universal
Director: Orson Welles
Producer: Albert Zugsmith
Screenplay: Orson Welles
From the novel *Badge of Evil* by Whit Masterson
Cinematography: Russell Metty
Music: Henry Mancini
Editors: Virgil M. Vogel and Aaron Stell
Running Time: 93/108 minutes

Cast: Charlton Heston (Ramon Miguel "Mike" Vargas), Janet Leigh (Susan Vargas), Welles (Hank Quinlan), Joseph Calleia (Pete Menzies), Akim Tamiroff ("Uncle Joe" Grandi), Marlene Dietrich (Tanya), Joanna Moore (Marcia Linneker), Ray Collins (Adair), Dennis Weaver (the night man), Mort Mills (Schwartz), Victor Millan (Manolo Sanchez), Valentin de Vargas (Pancho), Lalo Rios (Risto), Joi Lansing (blonde), Joseph Cotten (doctor), Mercedes McCambridge (gang member), Zsa Zsa Gabor (strip joint owner).

Synopsis: In a Mexican border town, someone places a dynamite bomb in the trunk of Rudy Linneker's car. As the American big shot and his blonde mistress drive past the customs gate, they are killed. Celebrity cop Hank Quinlan arrives on the scene and, with his idolizing partner, Pete Menzies, begins the investigation. He resents that Mike Vargas, a Mexican narcotics agent who witnessed the explosion, plans to observe his work. But the crime was, technically speaking, committed on both sides of the border. Vargas postpones going to Mexico City with his new bride, Susie, an American.

When Susie is alone on the street, she is approached by a young Mexican thug, whom she dubs "Pancho." He takes her to Papa Grandi, who runs the town's vice now that Vargas has put his brother in jail. In a threatening tone, he tells her that Vargas had better not build a case against his brother.

Quinlan crosses into Mexico for the first time in years. He visits Tanya, a prostitute he once knew well. She notices he has gotten fat eating candy. He has been eating it since he quit drinking.

One of Grandi's young thugs, part of the huge Grandi family, attempts to throw acid in Vargas's face. Vargas wants to send Susie ahead to Mexico City, where he'll go for the Grandi drug trial. She decides to go to an American motel, so she can get some sleep. She doesn't know the Miradora is run by Grandi.

Quinlan's bum leg tells him that Linneker's murderer is Sanchez, a Mexican shoe clerk who wanted to marry Marcia Linneker, the dead man's daughter. Quinlan understands why Linneker wouldn't want a Mexican for a son-in-law. Menzies discovers dynamite in a shoe box in Sanchez's bathroom. Vargas realizes Quinlan planted it because he had seen that the shoe box was empty before Quinlan went into the bathroom. He threatens to expose Quinlan to authorities. Quinlan starts to drink again. He tells Menzies about his wife, who was murdered 30 years ago—he knew who the killer was but couldn't arrest him because there was no evidence.

Vargas looks up Quinlan's cases in the Hall of Records. He shows Menzies that Quinlan repeatedly planted evidence for Menzies to discover. No matter that he only framed guilty men.

Quinlan agrees to Grandi's plan to discredit Vargas. At the Mirador, the youth gang drugs the terrified Susie. They bring her unconscious to Grandi's hotel and make it seem as if she has shot up heroin. Quinlan strangles Grandi and leaves his body near Susie, so she will be accused of the crime.

Vargas beats up Pancho and other gang members while looking for Susie. He is upset to learn she has been arrested for drug addiction and murder. But Menzies knows she is not guilty. He shows Vargas Quinlan's cane—he found it by Grandi. Menzies now believes that Quinlan is in the habit of framing people.

Menzies wears a microphone that is rigged to Vargas's recorder. He gets Quinlan to confess. But Quinlan figures out what's going on. He shoots Menzies with Vargas's gun. He tells Vargas he'll be blamed. Before he can shoot Vargas in "self-defense" and destroy the incriminating tape, Quinlan is killed by the dying Menzies. Vargas and Susie drive away.

Orson Welles the screenwriter turned out the sleaziest story imaginable—with seedy characters and locations, drugs, sex, corruption, murder, racism, etc. Welles the director emphasized the lurid elements yet shot it like an artist, employing some of the most audacious visual strokes of his career. The result? *Touch of Evil* is a masterpiece. It is not as significant as *Citizen Kane* (1941), which taught other directors how to tell a story through film (cinematography, editing, sound, framing, lighting, etc.) and taught viewers how to watch and listen to a film to get the complete story (i.e., "Rosebud"), but it has imagery that is as startling as anything in *Kane*, and identical themes, and is even more entertaining. In fact, it challenges *The Lady from Shanghai* (1949) as the most enjoyable of Welles's films. Andrew Sarris wrote in the *Village Voice* that *Touch of Evil*'s cult "is partly hardcore Wellesian, partly auteurist, partly *film noir*ist," but it surely has a broader base that includes those who recognize and greatly appreciate the film's technical virtuosity and thematic complexities yet know nothing about film aesthetics, film theory, or Welles's other films and recurrent themes. Throughout, even lowbrow viewers are reminded that this film didn't just happen, but is the result of its director making unconventional choices on every shot. Indeed much pleasure comes from watching Welles *choose* the correct ways to place actors within the frame, light a scene, move the camera, incorporate sound or music, and have his characters interact.

A major reason that the film is so delightful is that it is obvious Welles had fun making it. After all, he got to play one of the screen's most slovenly villains—to play Quinlan, who looks like something the cat refused to drag in, he wore a putty nose and makeup that aged him 20 years,

Quinlan shows Vargas the evidence. But Vargas knows there was no dynamite in this shoe box a few minutes before.

handpicked the messy outfit, and, though he was heavy himself, used additional padding to show what eating too much candy can do. He got to cast friends Marlene Dietrich as a raven-haired prostitute (a Mexican or a gypsy?), Zsa Zsa Gabor as a strip joint owner, and, in uncredited parts, Joseph Cotten as a doctor and Mercedes McCambridge as a lesbian gang member. He got to experiment with sound, music (supplied by Henry Mancini), space (there is much deep-focus photography), and editing. He got to attempt some bizarre camera angles, employing wide-angle lenses—at times he had Russell Metty shoot fat Quinlan from below as he walks forward, giving us the impression he is toppling off the edge of the world. And he got to film some extremely complicated one-shot sequences. The one-take opening, during which Metty panned, lifted, boomed, and lowered his camera to follow the action—including the placement of dynamite in a car trunk, the car being driven across the border, and Vargas and his new bride Susie being introduced—begins a few blocks on the Mexican side of the border and ends on the American side. It is an astonishing shot, and is justifiably famous. In his excellent study *Orson Welles* (1972), Joseph McBride writes of the necessity of doing this sequence in one uninterrupted shot:

> If Welles had cut back and forth from the couple [Vargas and Susie] to the car, he would have implied either a parallelism or a contrast. Instead he suspends any kind of moral statement until the couple kiss— and he cuts to the car exploding. An image for the violent disruption of their relationship, clearly, but, even more strongly, a linkage of actions which implies a cause-and-effect relationship. In some unknown way, Welles is saying, something about this couple contains the seeds of violence and murder.

This scene also stands in contrast to what happens next: When all the players gather at the crime site, Welles rapidly cuts back and forth between them, setting up the loyalty the Americans feel for Quinlan and indicating the budding friction between Quinlan and the outsider Vargas.

Almost as impressive as the opening is the scene in which Quinlan grills Sanchez, Vargas knocks over the shoe box, and action takes place all over Sanchez's small apartment. Unlike the opening, where Metty had all of outdoors to move his camera, this one-take sequence takes place in a very small space to illustrate that Sanchez is feeling *trapped* (it's appropriate that it's referred to as the "shoe box" scene). In an interview with James Delson for *Take One* (July/August 1971), Charlton Heston recalled that Welles devised this scene not only for impact but also to get Universal's spies off his back:

> "[It] was the first day's work on the picture. And Orson deceived the studio [by scheduling] the scene for three days of shooting. . . . He, in fact, had rehearsed the scene in his home with the actors over a Sunday or two. He proceeded to lay out the scene in terms of *one* shot with a crab dolly, that encompassed all the eight or nine performers who had lines in the scene. The action ranged through two rooms, a closet and a bathroom, and . . . 13 pages of dialogue. It was quite a complex shot, with doors having to be opened, walls having to be pulled aside—very intricate markings, inserts of the shoebox, and things like that.

> "When you're shooting, the production office is informed when the camera turns over the first time. . . . And of course [Orson delayed] turning on the camera. . . . Lunch went by, and the uneasy little groups of executives began to huddle about in the shadows, not quite willing to approach Orson but increasingly convinced that they were on the brink of disaster. . . . Finally, at about 4:30, we turned the camera on. And of course it was tricky. We did . . . seven or eight takes. Finally, we got a print, just before six o'clock. And Orson said, 'OK, that's a print. Wrap.' He said, 'We're two days ahead of schedule. We go to the other set tomorrow.'

> "Everybody thought it was marvelous. Of course, he never did that again, you see, but they always thought he might. . . . They never gave him any trouble again after that. They thought, 'My God, he did three days' work in one day.' "

Welles would have trouble with Universal after he finished his picture—the studio denied him final cut and assigned Harry Keller to direct insert scenes.* But while he was making the film (that is, *after* a great deal of his script was thrown out), Welles enjoyed his artistic freedom. He felt as he did when he first came to Hollywood and RKO gave him free rein on *Citizen Kane* and the film medium became his "electric train." *Touch of Evil* did, in fact, mark his return to Hollywood filmmaking. Because of his reputation as an irresponsible director who went over budget, didn't listen to studio brass, and walked out on films before they were edited to a studio's liking, Welles had been unable to get a Hollywood studio to let him direct since *The Lady from Shanghai*. He must have had great satisfaction playing a character whose good reputation gave him the freedom to do anything he wanted, and writing and directing a film that warns us not to judge men by their reputations. Heston claims that he got Welles the director assignment. According to his interview with Delson, when Heston heard that Welles was to play the heavy in the picture, he suggested to studio execs that they ask Welles to direct as well. But in his adulatory essay on Welles in *Close-Ups* (1977), producer Albert Zugsmith took credit for choosing Welles as director. Having just produced *Man in the Shadow* (1957), with Welles as the villain, Zugsmith

> . . . found Welles wanting to try his hand at taking one of Universal's story properties and making a film in the Orson Welles manner. Since my experience with Orson on our first film had turned out well, I kept an eye out for something suitable to his vast talents as a director, writer, and actor. Eventually the book *Badge of Evil* was assigned to me. A first-draft screenplay had already been written, so Orson took that and the book to read. When he developed a satisfactory approach to rewriting the script, I got Universal to give us the go-ahead.

It's interesting that Zugsmith should point out that Welles read Whit Masterson's novel, because Welles denied this

*Until 1976, it was thought that only the studio's 93-minute print existed. But a 108-minute print was discovered by UCLA film archivist Bob Epstein. The longer version does contain Harry Keller's inserts but it is supposedly much closer to Welles's version. This longer version is available on video, but the short version still plays on television and in many repertory theaters.

to critics. While there are great differences between the inspired screenplay (what dialogue!) and the dull, mundane novel, I assume that at the very least, Welles—or the unnamed writer of the original script—read the novel just to see how much he could twist around. Also, it should be stressed that some themes in Masterson's book are recurrent themes in Welles's work.

Welles wisely switched the major setting from Masterson's unspecified city in southern California to a Tijuana-like Mexican border town (although filming took place in Venice, California). He immediately creates a tantalizingly sordid atmosphere that is sadly lacking in the book. He takes us into a surreal, nightmarish world of rowdy bars, strip clubs, and flea-bag hotels; of strippers, soldiers, and youth-gang members; of crowded main strips that intersect with empty, creepy *film noir*ish back roads and alleys. Here one gets the sense that there are no police, except those on the take, and vice laws are being broken behind every closed door. There's little logic to this world: Here it makes sense that Vargas would turn his back on a blind shop owner so she won't know what he's saying on the phone. Or that Susie could be accused of strangling to death thick-necked Grandi with her stocking. It's Mexico, but it's a strange Mexico, populated by characters who could be played by Marlene Dietrich and Akim Tamiroff, and where 40-year-old Mercedes McCambridge could turn up playing a youth-gang member, a deviant with a leather jacket and butch haircut. By shifting his action back and forth across the border, Welles uses this environment metaphorically, to call attention to the divisions between Mexicans and Americans; past and present/future; frontier towns (like those this town recalls) and civilization; law and anarchy; the powerful and the unprotected; the real and the reputation (of Mexico as well as Quinlan). Welles worked on the script for *Man in the Shadow*, about the abuse of Mexican migrant workers, and here he sides with the young Mexican Vargas over the aging American Quinlan; narcotics agent Vargas is nowhere near the detective Quinlan is, but, with his strong morality and sense of justice (not to mention his attention to personal appearance), he's certainly the better role model. This is one reason *Touch of Evil* is unique among American films.

The decision to make Vargas a Mexican was Welles's. Interestingly, in the novel, the Vargas equivalent, assistant district attorney Mitch Holt, is American, as is Quinlan. It's his wife, Connie, who is Mexican. Whereas Janet Leigh's American-born Susie, despite Vargas's protests, flees to America to be comfortable (she should have known better), Connie, at Mitch's urging, goes to Mexico for safety. In the novel, Connie returns to the U.S. and goes directly to California's Frontier Hotel, where she is given a shot of sodium pentothal and set up as a "marijuana addict"—not a murderess. Before winding up in Grandi's Mexican hotel in the movie, Leigh's sexy Susie (Welles was one of the few directors to emphasize her large chest) becomes the lone and quite vulnerable guest at a motel where Dennis Weaver's "night man" is an infantile sex degenerate. It's a sequence that prefigures Leigh's visit to the Bates Motel in *Psycho* (1960). In the novel, there is no neurotic "night man" (Welles described him as a "Shakespearean lunatic")—in the novel Quinlan says the night man's

If his career and reputation are to be saved, Quinlan realizes he must lower himself and deal with Grandi.

"[you've] got another think coming" line. Also: In the novel, there's no Tanya (the one character who truly understands Welles's Quinlan), no recognizable gang members, and no real Grandi figure.

By making Vargas and Susie newlyweds—Mitch and Connie have been married for several years—Welles manages to create tensions that are not in the book. We realize that Vargas hasn't had the time to prove himself to Susie, as a husband and protector, or to get her to see the worth of his native country. More important, his marrying an American beauty is an affront to Quinlan, not only because Quinlan is a racist but also because Quinlan is reminded that his own marriage ended 30 years ago with his wife's murder, the time his decline began. He sees that their future has begun, while his own future, as Tanya points out, "is all used up."

Oddly, the book's Quinlan, though heavyset, is the counterpart for the film's Menzies (played by Joseph Calleia). He's a bad detective but good cop, who idolizes his equally famous and shrewder older partner, McCoy (the film has no character with this name), and unwittingly helps him frame suspects for crimes. Unlike in the movie, those framed aren't always guilty, including the young man (Shayon, the book's equivalent of Sanchez) whom McCoy sets up for Rudy Linneker's murder. McCoy is the brains of the operation, Quinlan the brawn. It is Quinlan who, hurt that he has been duped for so many years, teams with Holt, wears a microphone, and attempts to get McCoy's confession on tape. Before killing himself, McCoy shoots Quinlan.

In the book, Holt, not Quinlan or McCoy, is the major character. He not only exposes McCoy but also finds the real murderer. The film, however, is about Quinlan. Heston:

"I would say the only major error that Orson made [while making] the film was his conviction to conceal something: the fact that his part was the best part in the film, as he had re-written the script. In fact, it was evident anyway—I knew it. *Touch of Evil* is about the decline and fall of Captain Quinlan. My part is a kind of witness to this."

If Welles's Quinlan is the major character in the film, then Masterson's Quinlan (the Menzies counterpart) is the hero of the book. As Holt says, "Once I got started on this thing, I didn't have a choice but to follow through to the end. But Quinlan did have a choice, a terrible problem of loyalties. That's the standard to judge by."

Welles wasn't interested in playing heroes like Vargas or Menzies (his hero in *The Lady from Shanghai* even denies he's a hero—indication of Welles's discomfort), and so repeatedly opted for villains. Not ordinary villains, but villains with admirable qualities. After all, classic tragedies are about potentially great men who stopped acting nobly on their paths to the thrones of their particular worlds. "The weakness of the strong," wrote François Truffaut, "is the subject that all of Orson Welles's films have in common. The fragile giants who are at the center of his cruel fables discover as the film unfolds its 'ribbon of dreams,' that we can preserve nothing; not youth, not power, not love, and that life keeps tearing us apart." In Welles, ambition destroys great men, and men are—significantly, this also is the theme of Masterson's book, from which I now quote—"victims of their own reputations." In Welles, men are ruthless as they make their way to the top, and then abuse their power to maintain their lofty positions and keep their false reputations intact. *They* want to be heroes. But, as the disappointed Menzies knows, real heroes must have pure pasts. It's interesting that Vargas investigates Quinlan's *past* to find out who Quinlan is *now* (Holt also searches the Hall of Records)—this search for a great man's past, and the subsequent discovery of consistent moral corruption (the reason he was able to make it to the top in the first place), was also essential to *Citizen Kane* and *Mr. Arkadin* (1955). At a particular time in their lives all these potentially great men foolishly relinquished their morality (and their chance for "greatness") and began their public climbs. "Quinlan [used] official power for personal and corrupt purposes," writes Joseph McBride, "like Kane and his newspapers and Arkadin and his financial empire." Quinlan's *cane* links him to Kane; it is the symbol of Quinlan's lost morality, just as the sled "Rosebud" is the symbol of Kane's lost innocence. He uses the cane because he took a bullet intended for Menzies; he leaves it behind in the hotel room, by Grandi's corpse, as a subconscious gesture to reveal his guilt to Menzies. We feel sympathy for Quinlan as we do other Welles villains, like Charles Foster Kane, his title characters in *Macbeth* (1948) and *Othello* (1955), and Harry Lime in Carol Reed's *The Third Man* (1949), of which, because of its setting and intertwining themes of loyalty and betrayal, *Touch of Evil* constantly reminds me (pretend there's zither music and you may agree). This is because, like these other men, Quinlan feels betrayed by the one man he loves and trusts and whose adoration he thrives on. McBride quotes Welles: "Quinlan is the God of Menzies. And, because Menzies worships him, the real theme of the scenario is treason, the terrible impulsion that Menzies has to betray his friend."

Quinlan is reunited with Tanya, the only person who understands him.

A publicity shot of Charlton Heston and Janet Leigh, who play Mike and Susan Vargas. It captures the sleazy nature of this art film.

Menzies acts toward Quinlan as Joseph Cotten's "moral" characters act toward Welles's characters, supposedly his friends, in *Citizen Kane* and *The Third Man*.

We further sympathize with Quinlan because we recognize that his crimes against criminals are the result of his wife's murderer getting away scot-free because of lack of evidence—we notice that even super-moral Vargas resorts to two-fisted justice for the sake of his wife. Also, unlike McCoy in the book, Quinlan never frames anyone who is not guilty, including Sanchez. His motives are pure, if not his actions. In our current reactionary age of *Dirty Harry* (1971) and *Death Wish* (1974), moviegoers would surely think the liberal, by-the-book Vargas is naive and impotent, and hail Quinlan as the type of no-nonsense lawman we need to battle the bad guys on their own terms; they would cast the liberal Welles (if he were still alive) as Vargas and the conservative Heston as Quinlan, and make Quinlan the hero. But Welles would never have played Quinlan as a hero. He understood the reason for Quinlan's sins, but wouldn't forgive him for committing them. He said, as quoted in Georges Sadoul's *Dictionary of Films* (1965), "I firmly believe that in the modern world, we have to choose between the morality of the law and the morality of basic justice. That is to say, between lynching someone and letting him go free. I prefer to let a murderer go free than to let the police arrest him by mistake."

Heston makes a sturdy, if stiff, protagonist, and Leigh is likable, as usual, and, as *Variety* attested, "as sexy as all get-out" despite having a broken arm during filming and wearing a cast (it was cut off for the motel scene and replaced afterward). Also memorable are Tamiroff (his bad guy is funnier than he is frightening), Calleia (who gives a lovely performance), and Dietrich, delivering the film's best lines in her famous ironic tone: "You're a mess, honey," she tells Quinlan, "you'd better lay off those candy bars"; "He was some kind of man," she says of the dead Quinlan; asked by Schwartz if she liked Quinlan, she responds, "The cop did. The one who killed him. He loved him." But Welles dominates the frame, just as Quinlan dominates his domain. The way he throws his weight around, his body serves to balance the frame, much as Sydney Greenstreet's used to do. At his worst, when he didn't care about a project, Welles the actor could have been replaced by Harvey Korman without noticeable differences. But at his best, as in *Touch of Evil*, he was a prodigious actor and remarkable presence. He is on the screen only a few minutes in *The Third Man*, yet when you think back on that film you could swear he has equal screen time with Joseph Cotten. And when watching *Touch of Evil*, even when Quinlan's not in a scene, you think about him constantly. Watching Welles play Quinlan, I am reminded of a tribute written by François Truffaut in 1975, when Welles received the American Film Institute's Life Achievement Award. I excerpt:

> His physical and intellectual precociousness, his port-liness, his stature and the depth of his voice have imposed upon Orson Welles parts of men older than he. Since the inception of his career, he has played kings and men of power, tyrants or monsters, in short, abusive characters.
>
> As he himself is a poet, a humanist, a liberal and

an artist primarily conscious of sound (he is the most musical filmmaker) one can see that this good and non-violent man was caught in a contradiction between his own personal feelings and those he has to portray. . . .

He has resolved the contradiction by becoming a moralistic director, always showing the angel within the beast, the heart in the monster, the secret of the tyrant. This has led him to invent an acting style revealing the fragility behind power, the sensitivity behind strength. The character created by Welles walks toward the camera but never straight on toward the lens. He must step sideways like a crab, cross the set diagonally with his eyes directed backstage. Orson Welles hardly ever looks into his partner's eyes—or just long enough to exchange glances. His eyes rest on a point above his opponent's head, for the Welles hero, who in reality is almost always a Shakespearean hero, can only have dialogue with the clouds.

While Pete Menzies coaxes Quinlan into talking about his framing of Sanchez, Vargas secretly records their conversation.

Walkabout

One of the film's many beautiful images: the young aborigine, on his walkabout, seen in relation to his lovely, mysterious environment.

1971 Color Australian 20th Century-Fox release of a Raab-Litvinoff film
Director: Nicolas Roeg
Executive Producer: Max L. Raab
Producer: Si Litvinoff
Screenplay: Edward Bond
From the novel by James Vance Marshall
Cinematography: Nicolas Roeg
Music: John Barry
Editors: Anthony Gibbs and Alan Patillo
Running Time: 95 minutes; some prints run 100 minutes

Cast: Jenny Agutter (girl), Lucien John (her brother), David Gumpilil/Gulpilil (aborigine), John Meillon (father), Peter Carver (no hoper), John Illingsworth (husband).

Synopsis: A 14-year-old English girl and her 6-year-old brother live with their parents in an apartment complex in Sydney, Australia. Their father drives them into the desert for a picnic. He tries to shoot the boy, then commits suicide. The girl doesn't want her brother to know their father is dead, so she leads him in the other direction, saying their father will meet them later. They lose their way in the desert. When all looks lost, they find a quandong tree by a small pool of water. They quench their thirst and hunger. But when they wake up, all the fruit has been eaten by birds and the water has dried up.

A teenage aborigine boy, who is on a walkabout—he must prove his manhood by surviving alone in the desert—happens along. The girl becomes annoyed that he doesn't understand her English, but the boy communicates with him through grunts and sign language. The aborigine uses a long reed to draw water from the mud. He leads them toward civilization.

On their journey, the girl and the aborigine don't communicate verbally. But the boy and the aborigine have no trouble understanding each other. They become close.

It is not an unhappy time. The boys hunt, the girl swims nude in a jungle pool, the three camp and play together. The girl becomes increasingly relaxed near the almost naked aborigine. At one point, she hangs from a tree limb, allowing him to see her in her underwear.

At last, the aborigine brings them to a deserted farmhouse. Suddenly she is again reserved around the aborigine, who doesn't understand why she has reverted to her past ways. He is annoyed when she demands he fetch water. When he sees her without her blouse, she backs away. She becomes very nervous and worries about his intentions.

The aborigine takes the boy to a nearby road. Then he lies in an animal graveyard and paints a skeleton on his body. He returns to the house and dances naked for the girl. He makes offerings to her. She does not respond. He dances into the night, getting wearier and wearier.

In the morning the boy and girl find the aborigine dead in a tree. Neither shows surprise or sadness. They go to the road that the aborigine pointed out and walk to a miner's ghost town. The girl admits to the boy that their father is dead. She can't explain why. There is only one person at the miners' camp—the batty man is not intrigued by their sudden appearance and just tells them not to touch anything.

Years later, the girl is a young woman. She lives in the same apartment complex. Her young husband comes home and tells her that he has gotten a promotion at work (at another worker's expense) and that he'll be making more money. As he hugs her, she thinks back to the pool where she swam. She is a girl again and sits naked with the aborigine and her 6-year-old brother on a large boulder in the middle of the water. They look happy.

Before turning to directing, Nicolas Roeg was the celebrated cinematographer of such films as Roger Corman's *Masque of the Red Death* (1964), François Truffaut's *Fahrenheit 451* (1967), John Schlesinger's *Far from the Madding Crowd* (1967), and Richard Lester's *A Funny Thing Happened on the Way to the Forum* (1966) and *Petulia* (1968), which used the fragmentary narrative style that would later characterize his own films. For his directorial debut, Roeg wanted to make *Walkabout*, based on James Vance Marshall's popular novel about a white girl and her younger brother who, while lost in the Australian outback, meet an aborigine boy who leads them to safety. In the Winter 1973/1974 issue of *Sight and Sound*, Roeg told Penelope Houston and Tom Milne why he was attracted to the book:

> "It wasn't the visual side of the book at all. It was that here were two people—two people in effect, since the little boy acts as a chorus to the aborigine and the girl—who by this curious moment of fate were at a point where they could have been in love with each other. They had everything to offer each other, but they couldn't communicate and went zooming to their own destinies, through the odd placement of identity, the identity other people had put on them."

Roeg interested National General in distributing an adaptation of the book, and convinced fellow Englishman, playwright Edward Bond (who had never been to Australia, much less the outback), to write it. After scouting locations for eight weeks, Roeg returned to find that in lieu of a script Bond had written 14 pages of handwritten notes. "They were *exactly* what I wanted. I never wanted it to be anything but a play; I wanted it to be like *Our Town*, but with Australia as the setting. But while we were talking, I was thinking: I've got to present this as a first draft to National General . . . fourteen sheets of airmail paper!" Eventually Bond wrote a 63-page script—"an extraordinary piece: it had no scenic detail, nothing—it was a play." But National General rejected it and the project collapsed. Roeg went on to co-direct, with David Cammell, the controversial *Performance* (1970). It, too, was about a character entering a strange environment, a collision of opposites (cultures), and, as a result, self-realization. (Roeg would deal with similar themes in 1974's *Don't Look Now,* 1980's *Bad Timing/A Sensual Obsession*, 1985's *Insignificance*, and *Eureka*, finished in 1981 but not released until 1985.)

Meanwhile Bond's script made the rounds. Eventually Si Litvinoff and Max Raab decided to produce it, and *Walkabout* became Roeg's first film as *solo* director. Shooting began in Sydney in August 1969. Soon after, Roeg, his crew, and young stars—lovely 16-year-old actress Jenny Agutter (this was her breakthrough role), Roeg's 7-year-old son Lucien John (he had never acted but was a natural), and 16/17-year-old aborigine David Gulpilil (Gumpilil in the credits), who had traveled performing ceremonial dances, but had never made a movie—ventured into the most remote reaches of the outback. Looking for disparate locations (he didn't want the journey in the film to actually be possible), Roeg crisscrossed 14,000 miles of outback, filming such awesome locales as the Flinders mountain range, the red desert surrounding Alice Springs, and areas never traveled by white people. In fact, Gulpilil, whose family had left the bush for a government station when he was young, had never been to the desert—he became so disoriented and despondent that everyone had to move elsewhere.

I usually have no patience with pictures that are heavy on symbolism and light on words, take time to establish mood but intentionally keep the characters from communicating those feelings/thoughts that are influencing their actions, and are so loaded with *technique* that we lose track of the story and spend all our energy trying to, perhaps, determine a time frame and/or distinguish between reality and illusion (a tricky task since the director is probably implying there is no difference). After all, it's much easier to enjoy a film when you understand it! Yet I never tire of seeing *Walkabout*. It is an amazingly beautiful, unique, spellbinding picture; an erotic, eerie, ethereal work which, like other Roeg films, those of Peter Weir, and David Lynch's *Eraserhead* (1978), is fascinating because it contains enough familiar material (including lead characters) to be coherent (at least on one level) yet also contains intriguing mysteries we can ponder but never solve. (I even can appreciate that the characters don't express themselves because the film is very much about their inability to communicate.) *Walkabout* is as "deep," profound, and complex as the individual viewer cares to make it, for each time you come up with an interpretation, several unanswerable (unless Roeg sits there with you) questions arise. It is, first, both a simple love story, a *Romeo and Juliet–*like tragedy about a boy and girl from different worlds/ cultures, and a marvelously photographed glimpse at a haunting, extraordinary setting few people have seen. I can enjoy the film on this elementary level, as have count-

less children and the teachers who have shown it to them. (Both *Parents* magazine and *Seventeen* recommended it to children despite the full-frontal nudity, sexual subtext, and brutal scenes of animals being killed that temporarily got the picture an R rating.) But it's always a worthwhile challenge to attempt to discover the puzzle pieces in a Roeg film and figure out his deeper themes—with Roeg, there's no shame if you come up short. One interesting way to approach this film is to compare it to the book because there are several significant instances where Roeg and Bond deliberately moved away from Marshall.

Marshall's novel opens with the girl, called Mary, and her brother, Peter, stranded in the outback; we learn that they are white children from Barbados, West Indies. Roeg begins his film with a wordless sequence in Sydney, so he can get several of his own ideas across. Agutter's unnamed girl practices *harmony* in music class. Yes, this English girl has become one with her Australian classmates but, as her uniform suggests, at the expense of her individuality and identity; and it's sadly ironic that by attending an all-white girls' school she has learned nothing about "harmony" among diverse peoples. Her unnamed younger brother (an intelligent performance by young John) is much less acclimated to his new environment: He is an unhappy English boy in Australia, looking miserable on the crowded streets, wearing his boys' school uniform, listening to the droning bells—this life is too restrictive and unhealthy for any young boy (he should be in a natural setting, like the outback). Their father, played by John Meillon, has also found it hard in this new environment—business pressures and failures have taken their toll and he has become suicidal. The girl has already been conditioned to act in the proper, civil manner of all Australian schoolgirls, but through the unhappy father and his uncomfortable son Roeg establishes the difficulty people have adapting to any different culture—even one that is quite similar to their own—because they must try to develop a new identity for themselves. We can sense how much more difficult it would be for these people to adapt to a stranger environment

The boy easily communicates with the aborigine, but the girl makes no attempt.

The aborigine boy leads the girl and her brother through the wilderness.

than Sydney (like the outback) and to mingle with a totally alien people (like the aborigines). Roeg is preparing us for how the girl and boy will react once they are cast into the outback and meet Gulpilil's aborigine. Obviously the girl, who has accepted a repressive life, will suffer greater culture shock than her brother.

In the Sydney sequence, there are two revealing images. Roeg shows the girl and boy swimming in the chlorine-colored water in the pool of their sterile apartment complex—behind them is the sea; Roeg focuses on a brick wall and then pans to reveal the wilderness behind it. Roeg is showing us the startling proximity between the timeless natural world and our modern, less beautiful man-built world. We are reminded that cities were constructed in what was once a wilderness, that we came from the wilderness and, in a Jungian collective-unconsciousness sense, retain memories of an ancient past when we were all primitive people. In *Walkabout*, as in other Roeg films, the past and present exist simultaneously—they overlap (later the boy will see a camel caravan from some past time pass through the desert; the aborigine will suddenly reexperience watching white hunters slaughter animals). And there is a collision of cultures (Roeg's favorite theme)—Roeg is amazed by how many diverse peoples live on our tiny planet without mingling—in which seemingly opposite people (i.e., a white English girl and an aborigine) attract each other and have the potential (unfulfilled here) to unite/merge. Roeg believes that privileged white children of the city should get along with primitive aborigines of the outback despite their radically different cultures and backgrounds—after all, their common ancient ancestry

means that they have common traits, that they are brothers and sisters.

In another sequence not in Marshall's book, the father drives his children into the desert, supposedly for a picnic. As the girl leans over to pick up the picnic basket, the camera sneaks a peek under her short uniform skirt—our first indication that she is blossoming sexually from a girl to a woman and, perhaps, that her father's attitude toward her is becoming unhealthy. As he studies his work papers, his mind turns to mush and he attempts to shoot his son—perhaps to put him out of the misery both feel. Then babbling as most civilized men do about having "no time to waste"—although time is meaningless in this desert that is overrun with prehistoric gila monsters, horny toads, snakes, land crabs, ants, etc.—he douses himself with gasoline and shoots himself. He dies in flames. A Roeg concept: In nature everything that is harmful (an agent of death) also is beneficial. Here fire causes a death, but later it will provide warmth and nourishment for the children. Similarly, the hot sun that scorches their bodies, parches their throats, and threatens to kill them as they march into the desert will provide them with light, knowledge, warmth, and nourishment (without the sun there would be no food). In this world, barren trees will suddenly bear fruit; water can be drawn from the sand. That which means death one instant means life the next . . . and vice versa.

The children wander through the outback, while Roeg presents what is truly some of the most gorgeous nature photography in movie history, of reptiles, mammals, birds, mountain ranges, cloud formations, the sun, the moon, the desert sands, etc. We are transported back in time

through Roeg's startling images and John Barry's sometimes epic, sometimes surreal score (some passages are
played on the traditional aborigine instrument, the did-
geridoo; the score includes Stockhausen's "Hymnen"). The
children carry a radio, which the children in the book don't
have, and it is their link to zany, mundane civilization—
Roeg is surely amazed that people can walk through this
primitive, timeless world, yet be so close to civilization
that they clearly hear urban radio stations. After nearly
dying of thirst in the desert, they find an oasis, with water
and a rare quandong tree (Roeg located one of only 14 in
Australia) that provides fruit and shade. This is an Eden,
complete with—if we believe our eyes—long, sex-symbol
snakes that slither down the tree as the girl dreams, sig-
nifying that as she sleeps there is a sexual awakening.
Agutter told me in a 1981 interview:

> Changes to me personally come across in my perfor-
> mances. They affect my choices on how to play a
> role. But when I made *Walkabout* I really was a
> schoolgirl, like the girl I played. At 16 I had only a
> limited view of the world and only that to draw on.
> Later I would lose my innocence and not be able to
> play such a role. Roeg was right in casting me when I
> was on the verge.

*Publicity shot of two young stars who would have interesting
movie careers ahead of them: Jenny Agutter and David Gulpilil (who'd appear in such films as* The Last Wave, The
Chant of Jimmie Blacksmith, *and* "Crocodile" Dundee).
*The sexual feelings between the girl and the aborigine are
conveyed in an erotically photographed scene in which they
play in a tree and smooth human and tree limbs seem to
intermingle.*

By this point the film story has caught up with the novel's. But in Marshall's work, the children are stranded in
the wilderness after a plane crash—there is no mention
of parents or a suicidal father. And—this is connected—
in the book, Mary is 13 and Peter 8, while Roeg's girl is
about 14 and her brother is about 6. It becomes apparent
why Roeg made these changes (along with taking away
the names of the children to make them universal characters, archetypes). The girl in the book acts like big sister;
in the film she assumes a motherly role, even using a
mother's voice and intonations, making sure her brother
is clean, nourished, unafraid, and civilized-looking in case
anybody happens along (he thinks this is absurd). When
the boy spots the aborigine, as he walks toward the lost
white children across distant desert dunes (one of several
biblical images in the film), he automatically says, "Dad!"
He's mistaken in thinking the aborigine is his natural father,
which he discovers when the teenager comes closer, but
in terms of this film, he was correct in thinking his "dad,"
and his mother-sister's potential mate, is approaching. In
the book, the girl becomes jealous of the male, brotherly
bond that forms between her brother and the aborigine—
as a girl, a sister, she is left out. In the film, there is no
need for such jealousy. Because the boy is so much younger
than the girl and the aborigine he, in essence, becomes
their son. Whereas the girl continues to act like a mother,
the aborigine fills the father void, holding the boy's hand,
listening patiently to his chatter, and teaching the boy to
hunt, paint his body, and survive in the rugged wilderness.
When they camp by a climbing tree, and the three of them
play together like father, mother (she is uninhibited for
once), and child (who likes to be tickled), they have the
family picnic the girl and boy expected with their father.
The three of them are a potential family—she's the age
of aborigine girls who are married with children—if only
this "mother" and "father" would consummate their relationship. Subconsciously (at least in her case), they are
sexually attracted to each other: Roeg conveys this in the
scene they play in the tree by caressing, with his camera,
their lithe bodies, their skin, and their arms and legs, and
juxtaposing these sensual images with equally erotic shots
of the human-limb-like branches and the vagina-like
branches-to-trunk intersection of the tree. But he's too
much of a gentleman to force himself on her and she's too
repressed and confused to understand her emerging sexual
feelings. She becomes frightened, pulls back, and refuses
to attempt communication with the aborigine—her chatty
brother has no such reservations. Her brother seems to
recognize she has changed: When, in a very sensual
scene, she bathes nude in a jungle pool (the first of
Agutter's many nude movie swims), he watches from
a distance rather than joining her as he did in their Sydney pool.

In the movie, once the aborigine comes into their lives,
the girl and boy no longer have to worry about survival.
The main point of interest is whether the girl will acknowledge her sexual attraction to the boy; the journey
could become as much a "rite of passage" for the girl as
it is for this aborigine who is on a walkabout to prove his
manhood. (If he errs in his conduct it is that he forgets
courtship and sex are part of the stage in an aborigine

The aborigine has painted himself in order to dance for the girl.

boy's life that comes *after*, not during, a walkabout.) Sexual tension heightens. She seems ready for sexual contact when she takes her purifying swim, but when they reach the deserted farmhouse and she remembers her "superior" roots, she automatically treats him as a (black) servant. She sends him to fetch water—since the first thing she ever asked him for was water, it's obvious she hasn't changed. Unfortunately, she has not allowed her instincts to supersede her conditioning; she denies herself self-realization, womanhood, and the experience of "brotherhood." Roeg: "The girl came nearly to the point where she could have changed, but then in one moment, when she sees [the farmhouse], she slipped all the way back, tumbled back into the mould." Water. It's the only word she will say in the aborigine's language and it's the only word he will say in hers (although there are indications that he might secretly understand English). In the wilderness, water was the source of life, but in those scenes set in civilization it is a disruptive force: The water in the pool keeps the children from enjoying nature, the sprinklers at the deserted mining camp keep the kids off the grass, the word "water"—said in a condescending manner—finally insults the boy and breaks his heart. He will paint a skeleton on his body and perform a long mating dance (I don't believe it's a dance of death or farewell, as it would be if it were in Marshall's book). She refuses to understand he is courting her. Feeling rejected, he, like her father—who also was destroyed by contact with civilization—commits suicide. She barely reacts (though she unconsciously brushes ants from his bare chest) when she finds him hanging from a tree, just as her father was "buried" in a tree by the aborigines who came upon his body. Perhaps these men are "being returned to the womb" (remember how Roeg symbolically used the branches-to-trunk connection in the earlier scene). Throughout, trees have symbolized life, birth, and hope—now they become symbols of death.

Backtrack to the book. The boy and girl are not safe once the aborigine takes them under his wing. Survival, not sex, is the issue. The aborigine's main concern is defying death (which is what one does on a walkabout), not

having sex with the girl. She never gets over his nakedness—it is an affront to her values—and, for no reason, is terrified that he has sexual designs on her. In a passage that corresponds to the film scene in which the bare-chested girl fearfully runs through the farmhouse to avoid his eyes, he walks toward the nude girl as she swims, misreads the terror in her eyes, and thinks she sees death hovering over him. He wills himself to die. As life leaves his body, all barriers break down between them and she rests his head in her lap. "And in that moment of truth," Marshall writes, "all her inbred fears and inhibitions were sponged away, and she saw that the world which she had thought was split in two was one." Interestingly, after the aborigine dies in the book, the girl and boy still must reach civilization on their own. They use the survival tactics taught them by the aborigine to get them to safety—they have his spirit inside them and the girl, who had earlier tried to coax the aborigine into wearing her panties to cover his nakedness, ends up stark naked yet completely at ease.

This ending differs from the ending of the film, in which the girl and boy dress back up in their uniforms and blindly return to civilization. They have—or at least the girl has—failed to recognize how much better the wilderness is than the civilization they left behind, heard about constantly on their radio, and come upon at the end. The deserted farmhouse and the miners' ghost town—watched over by a batty man who says, "Don't touch anything!"—are places where civilization equates with shattered dreams, rules, order, fences, private property.

Only years later, when the girl has married a ruthlessly ambitious young businessman and lives in the same apartment complex she did as a teenager, will she think back on the most important event of her youth and realize what happened and what she gave up. She thinks of herself, the aborigine, and her brother—a family that should have been—sitting naked on a boulder in the middle of the pool in which she once swam. This isn't a memory but a wish. Paradise wasn't lost because the girl, the boy, and the aborigine never had it—the shame is that it was there for the taking if the girl had wanted it *then*.

The Wanderers

1979   Color   Orion release through Warner Bros.
Director: Philip Kaufman
Producer: Martin Ransohoff
Screenplay: Rose Kaufman and Philip Kaufman
From the novel by Richard Price
Cinematography: Michael Chapman
Editors: Ronald Roose and Stuart H. Pappe
Running Time: 113 minutes

Cast: Ken Wahl (Richie), John Friedrich (Joey), Karen Allen (Nina), Toni Kalem (Despie Galasso), Alan Rosenberg (Turkey), Jim Youngs (Buddy), Tony Ganios (Perry), Linda Manz (Peewee), William Andrews (Emilio), Erland van Lidth de Jeude (Terror), Dolph Sweet (Chubby Galasso), Michael Wright (Clinton), Burtt Harris (marine recruiter), Val Avery (Mr. Sharp), Dion Albanese (Teddy Wong), Price (bowling bankroller).

Synopsis: It is the Bronx, 1963. Richie, the head of the Wanderers, an Italian youth gang, finally gets girlfriend Despie to go all the way. Meanwhile his best friend, Joey, is trying to convince fellow Wanderer Turkey (who has shaved his head) not to attempt joining the rough Fordham Baldies. When Joey, who is small but brave, insults the Baldies, he and Turkey must run for their lives. Richie and Buddy come when they hear their whistle, see the Baldies, and join them in flight. A muscular stranger, Perry, appears and beats up several Baldies and makes huge gang leader Terror back down. Joey learns that Perry has moved into his building. They become friends. Both have problems at home: Joey is scared of his macho father, Emilio; Perry's mother is an alcoholic.

When Richie's teacher, Mr. Sharp, tries to teach "brotherhood," he increases friction between the Wanderers and the black Del-Bombers. Richie and Clinton, the head of the Del-Bombers, agree to rumble. The Wanderers have no luck recruiting other gangs, including the Wongs, who all know jujitsu. But there will be no rumble. Bowling club owners Chubby Galasso, Despie's father, and his equally tough brothers wager some black businessmen on the outcome of a football game between the two gangs. The teenagers have no choice but to change their form of combat.

Richie, Joey, Buddy, and Perry stand on the sidewalk, "accidentally" bumping into girls so they can grab their breasts. Richie runs into a pretty, non-Italian girl named Nina. She is annoyed but attracted to him. Richie introduces her to Joey—although he's attracted to her. When she drives off, they follow in Perry's car. They get lost and find themselves surrounded by the Ducky Boys, a violent gang of short, young Irishmen. They barely escape. Sneaking home late that night, Joey discovers Emilio has been having sex with Perry's mother.

Nina is Joey's date at a party at Despie's. While everyone makes out downstairs, Richie and Joey play strip poker with Nina and Despie. They cheat. Despie becomes furious that Richie is attracted to Nina and runs out crying. Richie and Nina go to her car and make love. Hoping to get in good with the Baldies, who were so drunk they just accidentally enlisted in the marines, Turkey comes to the party and draws the Wanderers outside to be beaten up by the Baldies. But the Baldies drive off. Perry beats up Turkey. Joey and Despie find Richie with Nina in the car. They are furious. Nina drives away. Turkey wanders into Ducky Boy territory. They chase him—he falls to his death.

On the day Kennedy is killed, Richie and Despie make up. She informs him she's pregnant. When Chubby insists they marry, Richie is too afraid to refuse. He'll join the family business.

The Del-Bombers are humiliating the Wanderers at football, until Richie, who had been ostracized by the gang, joins in. He and Joey make up: "Wanderers forever." But the Ducky Boys charge the field. There is a battle royal. The battered Wanderers, Del-Bombers, Wongs, and Emilio chase the Ducky Boys away. The crazed Emilio slugs his son. A bachelor party is held for Richie. Clinton, Teddy Wong, and Peewee, of the Baldies' Ladies Auxiliary, are welcome guests. Richie is heartened when everyone sings "The Wanderer." Joey and Perry drive off to California.

Richard Price was in his early twenties when he wrote his critically acclaimed first book, a highly original, wickedly comic, sentimental but hard-centered recollection of an Italian youth gang who lived in his Bronx housing project circa 1963. His story was essentially fiction but the Wanderers, the Del-Bombers, the Fordham Baldies (who had their heyday in the late forties), and even the creepy Ducky Boys were real, as was the wild football game. So was the early-sixties atmosphere he vividly re-created. Although he was Jewish, didn't run with a gang, and went to a school (Bronx High School of Science) other than the one (DeWitt Clinton) the Wanderers (and other street gangs) attended, Price knew and idolized his young Italian neighbors. And when he wrote his book, he created a character with whom he identified, the Italian Richie (Ken Wahl in the film), "your basic all-around kid, leader of the Wanderers maybe, but scared shitless about half the time."

Director-screenwriter Philip Kaufman had been in a gang back in the fifties in Chicago and, as he told critic Michael Goodwin in *American Film* (November 1983), "had been wanting to do a gang movie for years—the urban experience, the darker side of teenagers growing up." He had directed a film about the most famous gang of all time, the Cole Younger–Jesse James Gang, but *The Great Northfield, Minnesota Raid* (1972) is, of course, a nineteenth-century Western. His *The White Dawn* (1974), about the "polarization" between stranded whites and their Eskimo hosts, *Invasion of the Body Snatchers* (1978), in which humans are threatened by aliens, and his later *The Right Stuff* (1983), about how our pioneer astronauts united in the face of government exploitation, aren't "gang pictures" but contain "bonding" themes central to that genre. Clearly he has always been interested in the actions of groups/gangs of underdogs, as well as the distinct personalities who comprise such tight-knit units but manage to retain their individuality. So it's easy to see why he was attracted to Price's story. Many critics who loved the book would later accuse Kaufman of doing the novel a disservice. For instance, Janet Maslin of the *New York Times* contended that the film "loots rather than adapts [Price]." But Price would disagree: "I love that picture. It's not my book, and I don't care. The spirit is right, and the way Phil Kaufman directed it showed me another way of looking at my own book."

Since studios and producers usually adapt books with mass appeal, few cult novels are turned into movies and almost none of those become cult movies. *One Flew Over the Cuckoo's Nest* (1973) was an exception, and it was—as United Artists and producers Saul Zaentz and Michael Douglas hoped—a commercial success and multiple Academy Award winner before it became a cult favorite. Another exception was *The Unbearable Lightness of Being* (1988), which Philip Kaufman adapted from Milan Kundera's novel. Orion Pictures wouldn't have proceeded with Kaufman's film (co-written with wife Rose Kaufman) of

Left to right: *Wanderers Buddy, Richie, Joey, and Perry stand around watching all the girls go by.*

Price's novel if Orion hadn't expected it to be a tremendous hit, especially since it was riding the crest of the gang-picture wave. Cult status could come later, after it had commercial success. But *The Wanderers* had the misfortune to be released after violence at theaters showing *The Warriors* (1979) and *Boulevard Nights* (1979) made theater owners afraid to book gang pictures and patrons reluctant to attend them. So without a market, instant cult status was the best it could achieve. And that's a shame. Since *The Wanderers* is about gangs it was pigeonholed as nothing more than a "gang picture" when in fact it touches on the universal experiences of the average American teenager. It might easily have been promoted as an *American Graffiti* with slick pompadours and teased hairdos, tight sweaters and push-up bras, and gold-on-maroon satin jackets. It deals not only with gang rivalries, but with growing up, loyalty, brotherhood, macho fathers, clumsy sex, and how music reflects the rebellious spirit of youth. And its appeal is based less on violence than early-sixties nostalgia for friends, foes, make-out parties, romance, copping feels, great rock 'n' roll, bowling, football, school, hairstyles,

clothes, and a time (according to the *movie*) that was more innocent than the Vietnam years ahead.

The end of the innocent age is reflected by the death of a Wanderer, Turkey (Alan Rosenberg); the assassination of Kennedy, the first Catholic president; the recruitment of the Fordham Baldies into the marines; high school graduation; sexual initiation; Wanderer Richie marrying Despie (Toni Kalem), becoming a father, joining the Galasso family business, and settling down in Despie's parents' basement; key Wanderers Joey (John Friedrich) and Perry (Tony Ganios) fleeing home and neighborhood and driving off to California; and rising young folk singer Bob Dylan confirming that "The Times They Are a-Changin'." It ends as it should, sadly but without complete defeat: Richie still belts out Dion's "The Wanderer" although it's not the most fitting song for his bachelor party. But unfortunately we don't know what the end of this troubled but secure era and the beginning of a new era will mean to the individual Wanderers. While we have seen glimpses of Richie, Joey, Buddy (Jim Youngs), and Perry throughout the movie that made us care about and like them, we never really got beneath the surfaces of any of them. For example, we have no idea what Richie's home life is like. We recognize them—and Despie—but as *types* rather than people. Turkey was the only Wanderer who worried that being in the gang was a dead-end proposition . . . and he proved to be right. Janet Maslin:

> The beauty of Mr. Price's novel was its economy and thoroughness in locating the Wanderers' exact place in the world. Without venturing outside a very circumscribed environment [the 10-block radius of the intersection of the Grand Concourse and Fordham Road], Mr. Price was able to suggest what these characters would aspire to once their adolescences ended, what alternatives they believed life could offer and what sorts of possibilities they were not even able to imagine. The movie, on the other hand, has a lot of trouble figuring out where the Wanderers stand.

Kaufman was at a disadvantage in that he was forced to make the handsome, romantic Richie the lead character, when Joey is much more compelling. If the film had concentrated on Joey, and his feelings about the Wanderers, his troubles with girls, his violent streak, his unhappy home life, his hatred and fear of his father, and his ambitions (he is an aspiring artist) it would come across as the American equivalent of the British sixties-youth-gang-film-with-rock-music, *Quadrophenia* (1979), in which Phil Daniels plays a similar, though more high-strung, obsessive character.

Surely the film would have benefited from a scene or two in which Richie and Joey, or Joey and Perry, open up to each other, so we can get more insight into their fears, their goals, their dreams. There is room for such quiet moments, because there are superfluous scenes that should have been discarded. For instance, it's a terrific moment when Nina (Karen Allen), who is not in the book, goes into Folk City and hears the young Dylan, but it doesn't belong in this movie about Italian youth gangs. Movie audiences, who will relate to Nina, will be jolted by this scene, but Dylan has nothing to do with Richie (who stands *outside* looking in), not in 1963 or in his future. (Anyway, how does Richie turn a Bronx corner and find himself on 3rd Street in Greenwich Village?) There are other scenes (some taken from the book) that don't work. I like the classroom scene in which the liberal Mr. Sharp (Val Avery) attempts to be Glenn Ford in *The Blackboard*

Richie and Joey are terrorized by Terror (right) *and the other Fordham Baldies. Peewee* (left) *roots on her bald buddies.*

A nightmarish scene begins when the bald Turkey foolishly propositions a Ducky Boy outside a church.

Jungle (1955) and teach "brotherhood" to his class, only to have tensions increase between the Italians and blacks. But the animosity shown between Richie and Clinton (Michael Wright) is as unconvincing as the new-found friendship they display at the final bachelor party. The football game, although based on a real event, comes off as an awkwardly filmed cliché, not as funny as the Marx Brothers' football romp in *Horse Feathers* (1932), not as raucous as the game in *M*A*S*H* (1970), and not even as off-the-wall as the all-female strip-football contest in the cable-cult film *H.O.T.S.* (1979). It's scary when the Ducky Boys attack the field, and I'm thankful the contest is over, but the sight of the short Irish lads battling youths in football uniforms is quite ludicrous, like Indians fighting knights in shining armor. (Audiences do cheer, however, when the Wongs join the good guys.)

Many critics detested the earlier, equally surreal scenes with the Ducky Boys because they are filmed as if part of a horror film, with mist, shadows, wild camera angles, scarred faces, and eerie music. I find them among the best moments in the film, and quite appropriate. They properly convey the terror every gang member must have felt back then when he found himself stranded in strange, hostile territory—anyone who emerged from the shadows took on monstrous proportions. The Ducky Boys are the stuff

of legends, memory, nightmares. They deliver the violence that the Fordham Baldies and all the other gangs only threaten in the film. Price says he has firsthand knowledge of the Ducky Boys. If so, he'll have scary sensations for the rest of his life. And the Ducky Boys scenes will stick with viewers for years. Even so, I am aware that these scenes contribute to the inconsistency of tone that is the film's major problem. There are no smooth transitions between comedic and dramatic (even brutal) moments in *The Wanderers*. Of course, Price and Kaufman would argue that there were no smooth transitions between funny and terrible events in the lives of the Wanderers; moreover, things that were tragic then may seem funny with hindsight. But the film comes across as a series of disjointed vignettes. If there is a common theme it is that no matter how imposing one person is, there is someone out there who can intimidate him. And no matter how tough a kid is, adults have the power.

I have gotten the impression that most people who love *The Wanderers* not only forgive its flaws but actually like the film better because it's so erratic and unpolished. There is much to appreciate that, its cultists believe, more than compensates for the picture's shortcomings. For instance, *The Wanderers* has tremendous energy, due in part to a terrific rock score. The songs by Dion, Frankie Valli and

Richie and Joey can't believe their "luck" when Despie (left) and Nina play their crooked game of strip poker.

three lesser Seasons, and many non-Italian singers are used effectively to create excitement and provide humor: A highlight is watching the strutting Baldies congregate on a corner while the Four Seasons' "Walk Like a Man" blasts on the sound track. The film's high energy level is also a result of the lively young performers. Former Chicago gas pumper Ken Wahl gives a charismatic, star-making performance, which didn't make him big box-office (he'd end up starring in TV's *Wiseguy*). John Friedrich, Toni Kalem, Alan Rosenberg, Linda Manz—fresh from Terrence Malick's *Days of Heaven* (1978) to play Peewee— enormous Erland van Lidth de Jeude (as Terror, head of the Baldies), and pretty, naughty-eyed Karen Allen stand out.

At times *The Wanderers* flirts with greatness. As memorable as the Ducky Boys scenes is the strip poker game played by Richie, Joey, Despie, and the already sexually liberated Nina (she reads *Lady Chatterley's Lover*). The boys openly cheat and the girls go along with the "seduction," betting and losing, with a smile, one piece of clothing at a time. All anxiously wait for what will happen next. It's a wonderfully funny scene, and extremely titillating for both male and, I believe, female viewers. This game will eventually lead to Richie and Despie splitting up, Richie and Joey fighting and ending their longtime friendship, and four shaken characters going their separate ways, but it will make viewers wish they could go back to their youths for just a hand or two, to experience either what they missed or what was a highlight of their lives. Surely Richie and Nina, the benefactors of the game (they have sex afterward), wouldn't give back this experience in order to prevent the pain it causes. Since you endure so many terrible times as a youth, you need a few exciting events for the memory bank. Such experiences will make you want to relive your youth years later. It's safer to just see *The Wanderers*.

Where the Boys Are

1960 Color MGM
Director: Henry Levin
Producer: Joe Pasternak
Screenplay: George Wells
From the novel by Glendon Swarthout
Cinematography: Robert Bronner
Music: George Stoll
Original Dialectic Jazz: Pete Rugolo
Title Song: performed by Connie Francis; lyrics by Howard
Greenfield, music by Neil Sedaka
Editor: Fredric Steinkamp
Running Time: 99 minutes

Cast: Dolores Hart (Merrit Andrews), George Hamilton (Ryder
Smith), Yvette Mimieux (Melanie Coleman), Paula Prentiss (Tuggle Carpenter), Jim Hutton (TV Thompson), Francis (Angie), Barbara Nichols (Lola), Frank Gorshin (Basil), Chill Wills (police
captain), Roy Harrity (Franklin), John Brennan (Dill), Vito Scotti
(maître d'), Percy Helton (motel operator), Jack Krushchen
(counter man).

Synopsis: Merrit has a high IQ, but her grades are down at Kenmore
U. She tells the dean that, like 98% of America's coeds, she is overly
concerned about sex. She argues with her gray-haired Courtship
and Marriage professor, telling her it's too late to warn today's
coeds about random dating and premature emotional involvement.
What they need to know is if a girl should "play house" before
marriage. Her opinion is "yes." This impresses her friend Melanie
but the professor is stunned. It will be determined after spring break
if Merrit is to be expelled.

Merrit, Melanie, Tuggle, and Angie leave the frozen Midwest and
drive to Fort Lauderdale, Florida, where 20,000 students have migrated for their spring break. The girlfriends hope to meet boys.
They share a room in a motel—every night other girls who can't
afford high rates move in and sleep on the floor. Tuggle becomes
involved with TV Thompson, a zany Michigan State student whom
the girls picked up on the road. All he can talk about is sex. When
Tuggle tells him she's "a good girl," he drops her. But he can't stay
away from her. He continues to talk about sex, but she's only interested in matrimony, a subject he ignores.

Merrit worries about Melanie because after only one date, she
falls for Dill, who lies and says he's from Yale. When Dill leaves
town, Melanie dates his roommate Franklin and falls deeply in love
with him. Melanie remembers what Merrit said in class.

Merrit is picked up on the beach by Ryder Smith, a rich senior
from Brown. He takes her to his rich grandfather's beach house and
on his boat. She tells him that she has done a lot of dating. But
when he compliments her on her romantic talents she is offended
because she doesn't want to be thought of as promiscuous. He
wants to sleep with her, saying sex is just as routine as shaking
hands. He echoes what she told her professor: People should get
"acquainted" before marriage. But she's not sure anymore.

Hockey player Angie has trouble finding a date until she meets
Basil, a kooky jazz bassist. She impresses him with her singing.
Angie and Basil, Tuggle and TV, and Merrit and Ryder go to a
nightclub. TV becomes infatuated with Lola, a sexy exotic swimmer,
and jumps into her tank. Soon everyone jumps in. They spend a
little time at the police station.

When TV and Lola start playing around on the beach, Tuggle
walks out on him. In tears, she goes back to the apartment. Melanie
calls from a motel. Franklin didn't keep their date, but sent Dill
instead. He forced himself on her. Tuggle finds Merrit and Ryder
on the beach. Merrit admitted to Ryder that she is a virgin and was
scared of going all the way with him. But after he insisted he loved
her, she agreed to have sex with him. Instead they drive with Tuggle
to find Melanie. They almost hit the stunned girl as she walks along
the highway. She is sideswiped by another car, but Ryder pulls her
to safety. They take her to the hospital. Merrit is angry at all men
and pushes Ryder away. TV arrives. He tells Tuggle he's been faithful. They hug.

Angie, Basil, Tuggle, and TV drive north. Merrit will stay with
Melanie until she's able to go home. She meets Ryder on the beach.
They express their love for each other. During the next year, she
will visit him at Brown. They will get to know each other.

The best of the beach movies was released a year after
Sandra Dee played *Gidget* and went with Troy Don-
ahue to *A Summer Place* and three years before Annette
Funicello and Frankie Avalon had their first *Beach Party*.
It was adapted from the third novel by Glendon Swarthout. In his second novel, *They Came from Cordura*,
Swarthout stranded six men and one woman in the desert.
For his follow-up, he again situated the action in the sand
but reduced the ratio of men to women to 4 to 1—of the
20,000 students who flocked to Fort Lauderdale for Spring
Break circa 1960, 16,000 were male. If Swarthout's book
had been about four boys who went south it wouldn't have
had much appeal. What readers, and ultimately moviegoers, wanted to know was what kind of young women
willingly travel to such an environment, to where the horny
boys are? Certainly they couldn't be virginal or virtuous,
or intelligent. Or could they?

The 1958 novel takes the form of a book written by
Merrit, detailing her odd adventures over Spring Break in
Fort Lauderdale, including boy juggling, hotel pool-hopping,
wild partying, and an aborted boat trip to Cuba to join
the revolution. Merrit, a small-town girl who attends a
large Midwestern college, not only philosophizes about
sex and the single girl student, but also covers such "crucial
topics as The Influence of Walt Disney on Religion, Large
Families, Education, Virginity, The High IQ, Faith, The
Luck of Henry Thoreau, Stimulation, How Society Makes
It Tough for Kids, Love, Etc." Today, it's a bit uncomfortable reading Merrit's thoughts on intimate topics since
the words given this representative of American coeds
were actually written by a man. (At least, when watching
films we have the naive belief that if an actress really
objected to dialogue written for her character by a male
screenwriter, she could demand a rewrite.) But, in truth,
you can't be too outraged: The book's story line is so
chaotic that it's hard to figure out exactly what Merrit's
opinions are on any subject and whether Swarthout respects those opinions (and her character) or mocks them
for getting her into so much trouble.

If you have only seen the movie, in which Dolores Hart's
Merrit has never gone all the way with a boy although she
has dated frequently and advocates premarital sex, then
you'll be surprised that Merrit in the novel is no virgin,
even at the beginning. In fact, at the U., Merrit had aggressively sought the right man to deflower her. How far
should a girl go? To Fort Lauderdale. And now in Fort
Lauderdale, she happily sleeps with all three men who ask
her. Her attitude toward sex is as casual as that expressed
by George Hamilton's Ryder Smith in the movie, when
he tries to smooth-talk Merrit into his bed ("Sex is no
longer a matter of morals"); for instance, she says of virginity: "In my opinion it's ridiculous and picky of society
to turn it into an institution. The whole deal is simply not
monumental." In the movie, Merrit and Ivy Leaguer Ryder
become a couple, while one classmate-friend, Paula Prentiss's Tuggle Carpenter, hooks up with Jim Hutton's wacky
Michigan State student TV Thompson, and another, Con-

Publicity shot of the four female leads. Left to right: *the seated Paula Prentiss, Dolores Hart, Yvette Mimieux, and Connie Francis.*

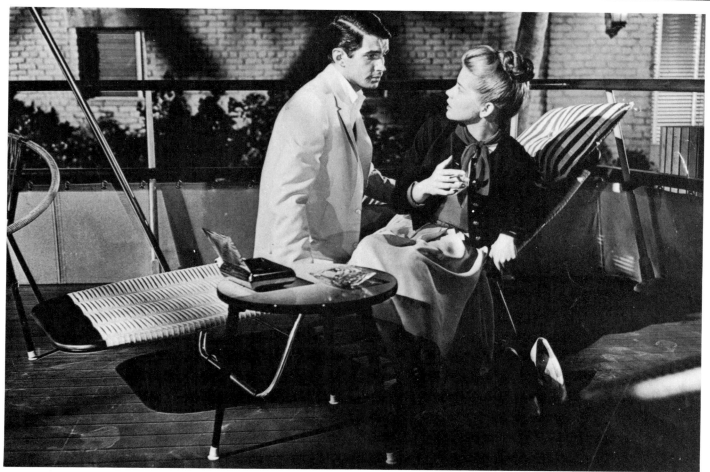

Merrit and Ryder argue about sex.

nie Francis's Angie, latches onto Frank Gorshin's weird jazz bassist Basil. None of these couples has sex. It's much different in the novel: Barbara Tuggle—the *only* girl who accompanies Merrit from college—runs off with some fellow named Quent (who's not in the film), and Merrit has Ryder, TV, and Basil all to herself—and she sleeps with all three. She anticipates the heroine of Spike Lee's 1986 comedy hit *She's Gotta Have It*. For the movie, screenwriter George Wells took those escapades Merrit had in the novel and divided them among Merrit, Tuggle, and Angie, merely eliminating the scenes in which Merrit consummated relationships with Ryder, TV, and Basil. The Merrit in the novel is *not* the Merrit in the film. In fact, Merrit's physical description of herself in the book sounds much more like Prentiss's statuesque Tuggle than Hart's diminutive Merrit: "I am five-nine in heels and I weigh in at one thirty six. My statistics are 37–28–38. I wear an eight and a half B shoe. I may not be feminine but I am damn ample." Tuggle has a less important role in the novel, and there is no Angie at all, just a "motherly" minor character named Miriam, roommate to Susy. Susy, a sucker for Ivy Leaguers who becomes promiscuous in the Florida heat and attempts suicide after being used by several Yalies (*real* Yalies in the book), including one named Dilworth, is half the inspiration for Yvette Mimieux's fallen

Melanie. The other inspiration is, once again, Merrit. Melanie will quit Kenmore U. and go home after her ordeal—being raped by Dill, hit by a car, and disgraced, rather than pregnancy, is Hollywood's punishment for her promiscuity. On the other hand, in the novel, the promiscuous Merrit—here's another surprise—does wind up pregnant (she doesn't know which of her three lovers is responsible) and will drop out of school, go home to have her baby, and then resume her education at a smaller college. Interestingly, unlike Melanie in the film, she doesn't become hysterical—she won't force marriage on Ryder, TV, or Basil, since she doesn't love any of them and none would be a responsible father. And she feels no disgrace, at least on the surface. She doesn't think her pregnancy is a punishment. (I doubt if Swarthout is punishing her, just warning intelligent young women like her to use their brains when it comes to sex.) She writes her father: "Your daughter and her high IQ made a few mistakes down here, I went sort of morally berserk for three or four days due to my youth and Florida and inexperience and smalltown background, etc., some spastic, promiscuous things I never did before and never will again, I swear." Only at the end of the book does the tone switch from humorous to serious, and as we remember the romantic course taken by Merrit we wish we hadn't been amused—she seems in control, but who knows how upset she is. I think of the Whoopi Goldberg monologue in which a bubbly teenager recalls her silly, laughter-causing path to seriousness: pregnancy and a mutilating self-induced abortion.

Swarthout's Merrit assumes that regardless of society's dictates the majority of American coeds will willingly engage in premarital sex. Therefore, *whether a single girl should give up her virginity* is not even an issue in *her* book, but it is an important issue in *Swarthout*'s book. And it is the major issue of the movie adaptation. Hart's Merrit stuns her graying female professor by stating that she's behind the times to warn coeds about random dating and immediate emotional involvement—coeds already experience both every Friday night—and that it's time to tell them it's practical that "a girl should play house before marriage." Having a 138 IQ, a few points higher than the novel's Merrit, the movie Merrit isn't so quick to jump into premarital sex just because she advocates it—she is smart enough to realize, subconsciously at least, that in *her* case premarital sex must be reserved for relationships founded on true, old-fashioned love. The picture ends quietly on the beach with Merrit and Ryder's sexual flame seemingly extinguished under a wave of love and mutual respect, but listen to their words. Merrit agrees to travel several times over the next year from the Midwest to visit Ryder at Brown and looks forward to their getting to know each other better—we recall that "getting better acquainted" was the term Ryder used euphemistically for premarital sex ("more marriages go on the rocks simply because people aren't better acquainted") when trying to coax Merrit to sleep with him on the boat. So finally on the beach, she is essentially agreeing to a long commitment and marriage *if* their sex works out. (I'm sure many viewers will interpret this scene differently.) This is pretty strong stuff for a film considered campy because of its outmoded attitude toward sex. The film is dated in many ways, but it's surprisingly more advanced than other films of its period in regard to sex; like *A Summer Place* and *Splendor in the Grass* (1961), it was the rare youth film about *sex* (the main reason it has a cult), the dialogue about *sex* is frank, it's clear that Merrit, Melanie, and Angie come to where the boys are for *sex*. Today, you have to cringe when Tuggle reveals her top priority is marriage: "Girls like me weren't built to be educated. We were made to have children. That's my ambition—to be a walking, talking baby factory. Legal, of course." But idealistic Merrit, after wisely taking her time to decide if she'll give her virginity to Ryder, doesn't let us down, doesn't betray her belief in premarital sex when the circumstances are correct. Indeed, for today's confused coeds, I think she is a good role model.

I don't want to give the impression that *Where the Boys Are* should be taken all that seriously. After all, any picture about the students who migrate to Spring Break in Fort Lauderdale is bound to be somewhat stupid and junky, even if it cost a lofty $2 million in 1960 (courtesy of Joe Pasternak), was made on location, and was filmed in CinemaScope; in addition, don't forget, this picture actually has George "Mr. Tan" Hamilton striding across the beach—an image that never fails to delight camp-movie addicts. But I do think it is above being enjoyed only on a camp level. There is much to appreciate. It's fun getting a look at the fabled Fort Lauderdale without actually having to go there. Director Henry Levin doesn't get so involved in the various romances that he forgets about the setting; he conveys the madness by repeatedly crowding his frame with revelers. He also makes the most of quirky bit characters. George Wells's script may be about sophomores but it never becomes sophomoric like most college sex comedies; it is surprisingly intelligent, contains unexpected insights into the coed condition, smoothly blends serious moments into the comedic framework, strives for the offbeat, and features a lot of clever dialogue. I like the dialogue in and the direction of the boat scene in which Merrit and Ryder sit an inch apart but don't see eye-to-eye about sex; there's a funnier, equally memorable scene in which Tuggle and TV lie by the pool:

> TV (smooching TUGGLE): Are you a *good* girl, Tuggle?*
> TUGGLE: Please, I don't want to disillusion you or disappoint you.
> TV: No, no, no, no. I won't be disillusioned or disappointed. Are you a *good* girl, Tuggle?
> TUGGLE (reluctantly): Ummhmm.
> TV (disillusioned and disappointed): Oh . . .
> TUGGLE (leaving): I knew it.

Wells and Levin, both over 50, acknowledge that young people can act impulsively, make mistakes, and at times even be jerks, yet they are very supportive of them. They portray their young heroes and heroines as caring, smart, and, ultimately, responsible. They admire their spunk, determination, and ability to wade through enormous problems. They draw a distinction between genuine cads like fake Yalies Dill and Franklin and most harmless young men who think it's their role to be on the make. Once Ryder ("Experience—that's what separates the girls from the Girl Scouts") and TV ("In the final analysis—everything comes down to sex") learn that young women have more important things (love, communication, support) to offer them than their virginities, they drop their seductive acts and reveal their sensitive sides. What's unique is that Ryder, TV, and Basil are attracted to women specifically because they are their equals, intellectually (Merrit may have an IQ 2 points lower than Ryder's but she wins their verbal sparring contests), physically (Tuggle is first attracted to TV because he also is tall and has big feet), and talent-wise (Angie wins Basil by singing). They are not intimidated by the women's strong personalities; in fact, Ryder says admiringly, "You're a pretty strong girl, Merrit." The men realize they aren't strong enough to carry a relationship on their own shoulders—they need women of equal strength if the partnership is going to survive.

It's unusual to find a youth picture in which men show such respect for the women they're attracted to, and it's equally rare to find a film of any kind made prior to or after the women's movement began in which young women are so supportive of each other. They aren't rivals over

. . . .
*This scene recalls *A Summer Place*, in which young Sandra Dee worries that if she has sex she will no longer be a "good girl."

Merrit and Tuggle tend to Melanie. These young women don't go where the boys are if they need each other's help.

individual men, nor are they jealous when a friend finds love when they can't even get a date. They root for each other because one's success is a triumph for all young women in the throes of sexual confusion. Most important, these women are there for each other. Merrit helps Melanie talk through her problems. She even asks the sad Melanie to accompany her and Ryder on a boat trip, even though Melanie's presence will ruin her own romantic plans. When Melanie gets into bad trouble, Tuggle and Merrit (and Ryder and TV) forget their own problems and plans and rush to her aid. Just because these young women fall in love with men doesn't mean they must desert their girlfriends. The women whom Wells and Levin give us are gems: They are strong, intelligent, funny, sexually aggressive, and unselfish. That the director and screenwriter wanted their camaraderie to come through is obvious: Rather than making Merrit the "star" of the Kenmore foursome, they provide almost equal screen time to Tuggle, Melanie, and Angie—in fact, Melanie's story line is the most compelling of all—and cast Yvette Mimieux, the most beautiful of the four actresses, as Melanie rather than as Merrit. Surely Dolores Hart was not one to worry that a prettier actress had been cast in another part. Perhaps these particular actresses were chosen because they were secure enough with their own screen presences not to attempt stealing scenes from each other. They complement each other beautifully.

Surely it is the fine cast, composed of performers who never reached the Hollywood heights they deserved, that puts *Where the Boys Are* over the top. They are several classes above the usual performers in youth films—check out *Where the Boys Are '84*. The amusing Prentiss and

Hutton make a wonderful duo (I'd like to have seen them paired in another film, or a TV comedy series). Lovely Mimieux proves she should have been a top sex symbol of the sixties (she might have been if Levin had wanted Melanie to be a bitch, rather than a vulnerable victim). Francis, in her movie debut, is engagingly spunky—and I've always liked the way she sings the title song. Hamilton is surprisingly inoffensive. Barbara Nichols does a hilarious turn as Lola, an erotic swimmer and floozy ("I think that's a stinking shame," she says sympathetically). Gorshin, as nearsighted bassist Basil, and Chill Wills, as Fort Lauderdale's police captain (who declares "war on higher education"), are funny in their movie debuts. Best of all is Dolores Hart, one of the most likable and talented young actresses of the period. She didn't achieve everlasting fame because Hart was more interested in heaven than stardom. In 1963 she became a cloistered nun. That's why it's strange watching Hart as Merrit, telling the dean she has sexual longings and her professor that she believes in premarital sex. This contributes to the film's mystique.

Dolores Hicks was born in Chicago in 1939 (some sources say 1938). By 1942, her parents were divorced and she was living with her grandparents. She attended a Catholic grammar school and at age 11 decided on her own to convert to Catholicism. Because her grandfather was a projectionist, she saw many free films in her youth, sparking her interest in movies and theater. As she said years later, "I prayed every night about becoming an actress." In elementary school, she played Joan of Arc in a play. Her first stage role at her high school in the San Fernando Valley (her mother had re-wed and settled there) was the lead in *Joan of Lorraine*. She briefly attended Marymount

The police captain listens to various explanations for why (left to right) *Lola, TV, Tuggle, Merrit, Ryder, Angie, and Basil were arrested.*

College as a theater major—naturally, her major triumph was as the lead in *Joan of Lorraine*. A male friend sent her picture and a descriptive letter to Hal Wallis; Wallis interviewed her and signed her to a seven-year movie contract. With her well-scrubbed good looks, intelligence, sincere delivery, and genuine talent, she made a good impression opposite Elvis Presley in her debut film *Loving You* (1957) and was even better in *King Creole* (1958), teaching Elvis morality. Between the Presley films, she had the second female role in George Cukor's *Wild Is the Wind* (1957). In 1959, before she turned 20, she played on Broadway, earning excellent reviews in *The Pleasure of Her Company*. She then returned to films, making *Lonelyhearts* (1959) with Montgomery Clift, *Where the Boys Are*, and a series of obscure films: *Francis of Assisi* (1961), playing her one screen nun, *Sail a Crooked Ship* (1962), *Lisa* (1962), and Henry Levin's *Come Fly with Me* (1963), playing "my first witchy part. I even had to learn how to smoke and it took me three months to get out of the habit." During Hart's brief period of stardom, she was often the subject of fan magazine articles. She wrote a long article in *Movieland and TV Time* to refute gossip about her printed in other magazines. She claimed she never said, "I want to be sexy," and that she was not seriously involved with any actor she'd been linked to. She was more interested in talking about her faith than men. She mentioned a religious retreat she'd gone to in high school, and a priest there who convinced her marriage was not to be

taken lightly—this caused her to break up with her boyfriend. Louella Parsons wrote: "Somehow I have a strange feeling that Dolores is a lonely girl. Despite the philosophic tone of her conversation I get the impression that she is going through a period of mental and emotional growing pains and that she does not yet know exactly who she is."

Everyone wanted to know when she was going to get married, especially after she called off her engagement to an L.A. businessman. She responded tellingly: "I'm happy and everyone else is trying to make me unhappy [by pushing me to get married] just because everyone else is saddled with a horrible man. [When I get married] it's going to be for all time. I believe marriage should be a total commitment. It should take precedence over everything else in a woman's life." At age 24, Dolores Hart, saying she found God in the movie business, entered the Regina Laudis Monastery in Bethlehem, Connecticut. At age 31, Sister Judith, as she was now called, became a full-fledged member of the Benedictine order in a rite called the Solemn Consecration of the Virgin, which, as she wrote in a press release, "is expressive of woman's greatest liberation." She sealed her pledge to spend the rest of her life in the cloistered monastery, praising God, studying scriptures, working in the fields, observing total silence but for 40 minutes a day (I don't know if this time limit changed through the years), and never having contact with the public. She had permanently withdrawn from where the boys are.

Appendix
Cult Movies Vol. 1 contains:

Aguirre, the Wrath of God

All About Eve

Andy Warhol's Bad

Badlands

Beauty and the Beast

Bedtime for Bonzo

Behind the Green Door

Beyond the Valley of the Dolls

Billy Jack

Black Sunday

The Brood

Burn!

Caged Heat

Casablanca

Citizen Kane

The Conqueror Worm

Dance, Girl, Dance

Deep End

Detour

Duck Soup

El Topo

Emmanuelle

Enter the Dragon

Eraserhead

Fantasia

Forbidden Planet

Force of Evil

42nd Street

Freaks

The Girl Can't Help It

Greetings

Gun Crazy

Halloween

A Hard Day's Night

The Harder They Come

Harold and Maude

The Honeymoon Killers

House of Wax

I Married a Monster from Outer Space

I Walked with a Zombie

Invasion of the Body Snatchers

It's a Gift

It's a Wonderful Life

Jason and the Argonauts

Johnny Guitar

The Killing

King Kong

King of Hearts

Kiss Me, Deadly

La Cage aux Folles

Land of the Pharaohs

Laura

The Little Shop of Horrors

Lola Montès

The Long Goodbye

Mad Max

The Maltese Falcon

Man of the West

Night of the Living Dead

The Nutty Professor

Once upon a Time in the West

Out of the Past

Outrageous!

Pandora's Box

Peeping Tom

Performance

Petulia

Pink Flamingos

Plan 9 from Outer Space

Pretty Poison

The Producers

The Rain People

Rebel Without a Cause

The Red Shoes

Reefer Madness

Rio Bravo

Rock 'n' Roll High School

The Rocky Horror Picture Show

The Scarlet Empress

The Searchers

Shock Corridor

The Shooting

Singin' in the Rain

Sunset Boulevard

Sylvia Scarlett

The Tall T

Targets

Tarzan and His Mate

The Texas Chain Saw Massacre

Top Hat

Trash

Two for the Road

Two-Lane Blacktop

2001: A Space Odyssey

Up in Smoke

Vertigo

The Warriors

Where's Poppa?

The Wild Bunch

The Wizard of Oz

Cult Movies Vol. 2 contains:

Altered States

The American Friend

Barbarella

Basket Case

Beat the Devil

Bedazzled

The Big Heat

Blood Feast

Blood Money

A Boy and His Dog

Breathless

The Bride of Frankenstein

Children of Paradise

A Clockwork Orange

Cutter's Way

Dark Star

Daughters of Darkness

The First Nudie Musical

Godzilla, King of the Monsters

The Great Texas Dynamite Chase

High School Confidential

His Girl Friday

Last Tango in Paris

The Man Who Fell to Earth

Marnie

Massacre at Central High

Mommie Dearest

Monty Python and the Holy Grail

Morgan!

Ms. 45

My Darling Clementine

Night of the Demon

Nightmare Alley

The Parallax View

Phantom of the Paradise

Picnic at Hanging Rock

Pretty Baby

Quadrophenia

Salt of the Earth

The Seventh Seal

Some Like It Hot

Sullivan's Travels

Taxi Driver

To Be or Not to Be

Vanishing Point

White Heat

The Wicker Man

Willy Wonka and the Chocolate Factory

Wuthering Heights

Zardoz

About the Author

Danny Peary is a film and television critic, sportswriter, and scriptwriter. He has a B.A. in history from the University of Wisconsin and an M.A. in cinema from the University of Southern California. His previous books are *Guide for the Film Fanatic, Close-Ups: The Movie Star Book* (editor), *The American Animated Cartoon: A Critical Anthology* (co-editor with Gerald Peary), *Cult Movies, Cult Movies 2,* and *Omni's ScreenFlights/ScreenFantasies: The Future According to the Science Fiction Cinema* (editor). He lives in New York City with his wife, Suzanne, and daughter, Zoë.